perfume

Richard Stamelman

perfume

Joy, Obsession, Scandal, Sin

A Cultural History of Fragrance from 1750 to the Present

Principal photography by Michael Freeman

A DAVID LARKIN BOOK

RIZZOLI NEW YORK

First published in the United States of America in 2006
by Rizzoli International Publications, Inc.
300 Park Avenue South
New York, NY 10010
www.rizzoliusa.com

© 2006 Richard Stamelman

2006 2007 2008 2009 / 10 9 8 7 6 5 4 3 2 1

ISBN-13: 978-0-8478-2832-6
ISBN-10: 0-8478-2832-8

Library of Congress Cataloging-in-Publication Data

Stamelman, Richard Howard.
  Perfume : Joy, Obsession, Scandal, Sin : a cultural history of fragrance from
1750 to the present / Richard Stamelman ; principal photography by Michael
Freeman.
    p. cm.
  "A David Larkin Book."
  Includes bibliographical references and index.
  ISBN-13: 978-0-8478-2832-6
  ISBN-10: 0-8478-2832-8
  1. Perfumes--Social aspects. 2. Perfumes--History. 3. Perfumes
industry--History. I. Title.
  GT2340.S73 2006
  391.6'3--dc22
                                    2006021526

DESIGN: DAVID LARKIN

Printed in China

For Kate—

Ô parfum, chargé de nonchaloir!
Extase!

—Charles Baudelaire

Contents

Abbreviations

Barillé / Laroze	Elisabeth Barillé et Catherine Laroze, *Le Livre du parfum* (Paris: Flammarion, 1995).
Calvino	Italo Calvino, "The Name, The Nose" in *Under the Jaguar Sun,* trans. William Weaver (San Diego: Harcourt Brace Jovanovich, 1988).
Delbourg-Delphis	Marylène Delbourg-Delphis, *Le Sillage des élégantes. Un siècle d'histoire des parfums* (Paris: Jean-Claude Lattès, 1983).
Faure	Paul Faure, *Parfums et aromates de l'Antiquité* (Paris: Fayard, 1987).
Girard	Sylvie Girard, *Le Livre du parfum* (Paris: Messidor, 1986).
H&R	*H & R Fragrance Guide / Duftatlas / Atlas Olfactif. Fragrances on the International Market,* 3rd rev. and updated edition (Hamburg: Glöss, 1995).
HB	*Harper's Bazaar,* New York.
Irvine	Susan Irvine, *Perfume. The Creation and Allure of Classic Fragrances* (London: Aurum, 1995).
Lefkowith, *Art*	Christie Mayer Lefkowith, *The Art of Perfume. Discovering and Collecting Perfume Bottles* (London: Thames and Hudson, 1994).
L'Officiel	*L'Officiel de la Couture et de la Mode de Paris,* Paris.
Le Guérer	Annick Le Guérer, *Les Pouvoirs de l'odeur* (Paris: Editions François Bourin, 1988).
NYT	*New York Times*
Parfumerie française	*La Parfumerie française et l'art dans la présentation* (Paris: La Revue des marques de la Parfumerie et de la Savonnerie, April 1925).
Pillivuyt, *Flacons*	Ghislaine Pillivuyt, *Les Flacons de la séduction. L'Art du parfum au XVIIIe siècle* (Lausanne: La Bibliothèque des Arts, 1985).
Pillivuyt, *Histoire*	Ghislaine Pillivuyt, *Histoire du parfum. De l'Egypte au XIXe siècle. Collection de la parfumerie Fragonard* (Paris: Denoël, 1988).
Süskind	Patrick Süskind, *Perfume. The Story of a Murderer,* trans. John E. Woods (New York: Alfred A. Knopf / Washington Square Press, 1986).
3000 ans	*3000 ans de la parfumerie. Parfums, Savons, Fards et Cosmétiques, de l'Antiquité à nos jours,* exhibition catalogue (Grasse: Musée d'Art et d'Histoire, 1980)
V-NY	*Vogue,* New York.
V-P	*Vogue,* Paris.

Acknowledgments

A PERFUME, while initially the concept of one person's imagination, cannot come to completion without the participation of many different noses, hands, eyes, and minds. Changes to the original idea for the scent and its harmony of notes are suggested by many individuals drawn in one way or the other into a lengthy process of collective development: the team of perfumers who refine the olfactory concept; the growers and suppliers who cultivate or locate the primary floral, animal, and synthetic materials; the designers who conceive the shape of the bottle and its packaging; the chemists who manufacture the fragrance; the conceptualists who find the name for the scent and define the visual, musical, and textual aspects of its advertising; and the list goes on.

In a similar manner, the original concept for this book has been cultivated, distilled, condensed, and refined over more than a decade through encounters with different individuals whose suggestions and corrections have been of inestimable value. I should like to acknowledge my profound gratitude to those friends, acquaintances, colleagues, scholars, and specialists, whose assistance, counsel, and instruction have helped turn the concept of *Perfume: Joy, Obsession, Scandal, Sin; A Cultural History of Fragrance from 1750 to the Present* into a reality.

First and foremost, I should like to thank the perfumer Jacques Polge, Director of the Chanel Perfume Laboratories in Neuilly sur Seine, France for his wise counsel, invaluable help, and loyal friendship over the years. In his work and life, the profound affinity between poetry and perfume, so intensely and sensitively felt by the great nineteenth-century French poets, has its modern incarnation. Without his insights into the poetics of perfume creation—an expertise he was unstintingly and patiently willing to share with me—and without his enthusiastic assistance, wonderful kindness, and gracious hospitality (not the least of which was the use of his magnificent library) over the years, *Perfume* could not have been written. I am also grateful to his administrative assistant at Parfums Chanel, Virginie Roussel, for her indefatigable energy and lightning-quick efficiency in solving problems, getting information, and opening doors to contacts that would have otherwise remained closed. As Curator of the Chanel and Bourjois Perfume Archives, Patrick Doucet could not have been more generous with his time, energy, and patience, even at the busiest of moments, in hunting for and locating historical materials and realia concerning Chanel and Bourjois perfumes. For the hundreds of photocopies and scanned images of hard-to-find sources he made for me over many years, for his good humor, his resourcefulness and his friendship, as well as for his discovery of a nearly impossible-to-find work of poetry by Count Robert de Montesquiou, which

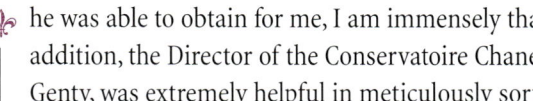 he was able to obtain for me, I am immensely thankful. In addition, the Director of the Conservatoire Chanel, Marika Genty, was extremely helpful in meticulously sorting out the details that made it possible for me to reproduce a number of Chanel and Bourjois advertisments and images.

I would also like to say a word of thanks to the perfumer Jean-Paul Guerlain who was willing to take time from his busy schedule to meet with me and answer my questions and to Elisabeth Sirot, Director of Public and Press Relations at Guerlain, for the invaluable press releases, advertising brochures, and other documents and images concerning Guerlain perfumes which she generously gave me. In Paris as well, Marcel Cohen once again revealed the depths of his warm friendship by introducing me to the art of Françoise Quardon and by obtaining slides of her intriguing work connected to *Echt Kölnisch Wasser No. 4711*. I am grateful as well to Françoise Quardon for explaining at length her extraordinary work and for allowing me to reproduce her stunning *Hommage à Milena*. Other French friends and acquaintances gave advice and encouragement during the years the book was being researched and written: in particular, Nasser and Isabelle Assar, Yves and Lucy Bonnefoy, Didier and Claire Cahen, Marie-Claire and Maurice Dumas, Jacqueline Chenieux-Gendron and François Gendron, Viviane et Jacky Crasson, Catherine Dana, Claude and Hélène Garache, Colette Guedj, Etienne-Alain Hubert, Hélène Jacquest, Daniel et Cécile Lançon, Bernard Pathé, Denis Polge and Rose Deren, Olivier Polge, Alain Madeleine-Perdrillat, Cécile Matton, James Rentschler, and Fabienne Reymondet. I wish also to thank the Société Française des Parfumeurs and its former president Francis Thibaudeau for inviting me to lecture at one of its Paris meetings, thus giving me the opportunity to test my ideas before a group of experts, and in addition for making me an honorary member of the society. Finally, I should like to thank the staff at the Librairie Tschann on the Boulevard du Montparnasse for efficiently locating the many books on perfume that I needed for my research.

Innumerable friends, colleagues, and students in England and the United States were unstintingly helpful in sharing with me their experiences of perfume and in offering advice about the book from its beginnings to its present form: above all, Harry Beskind, Walter Brown, Roger Cardinal, Rhonda Garelick, Gerard Gasarian, Jim Gold, Mary Jean and Ronald Green, Judith Greenberg, Lynn Higgins, Berel Lang, Reed Lowrie, Carol Ockman, Jorge Pedraza, Antony Penrose, M. J. Prest, Isabel Roche, Mary Russell, Michael Sheringham, Rebecca W. Stamelman, Jane and Rob Sunshine, Virginia Swain, Cheryl Tano, John Umlauf, Hayden White, Emma Wilson, and Patricia Zohn. Special thanks are owed as well to Mary Bryden, Katharine Conley, Jacqueline Chenieux-Gendron, Jim Drobnick, Marie-Claire Dumas, Rhonda Garelick, Susannah Heschel, Leah Hewitt, Stephen Nichols, Gerald Prince, and Michael Sheringham for inviting me either to give lectures or papers at their universities and at conferences or for publishing early versions of some of the book's material. I also thank the editors of the journals *Pleine Marge* and *Sites* as well as Berg Publishers for allowing these versions to see the light of day and for granting me permission to reprint them here.

At Dartmouth College and Williams College the technical expertise of certain individuals was invaluable. Without Susan Bibeau, Manager of Humanities Computing at Dartmouth, my computers would have never recovered so quickly from operating glitches and viruses. At Dartmouth as well, Otmar Foelsche, Director, and Thomas Garbelotti, Senior Analyst, of Humanities Resources helped print out different versions and various drafts. Were it not for the acquisition and interlibrary loan departments of the Baker (Dartmouth) and Sawyer (Williams) libraries, in particular the dogged efforts of Patricia Carter at Dartmouth and Alison O'Grady at Williams, many arcane works on perfumery would never have come my way. At Williams, Renée De Candia, departmental secretary at the Center for Foreign Languages, helped me in different ways to coordinate teaching and research activities. Another colleague at Williams I should like to thank is the former Dean of the Faculty, Thomas Kohut, who made it financially possible for me to obtain permissions to reproduce certain works. I am grateful to him and to Williams College for their support. To the inspiring Williams students enrolled in the various French and comparative literature courses I have taught for many years, I want to express a grateful word. In particular, I should like to thank those undergraduates in "The Fashioning of Fashion" (a course taught in 1998, 2000, and 2003) as well as those students in my poetry, modernism, and Venice courses not only for their enthusiastic participation, but for their penetrating and challenging questions and observations.

Released time for research and writing is always a blessing. For the months of sabbatical and leave which enabled me to write *Perfume,* I should like to thank first the John Simon Guggenheim Memorial Foundation for the award of a year's fellowship and second the trustees of Williams College for the approval of sabbatical time. Moreover, I thank the Department of French and Italian at Dartmouth College for allowing me to serve on a regular basis as a visiting scholar.

A word of thanks must be offered as well to all those individuals at American, English, and French museums, libraries, and collections; at perfume companies; at law firms; at photo archives; and at art agencies who diligently corresponded with me regarding permissions and who ultimately sent me some of the illustrations printed in this book. In Paris, Thierry Devynck, curator of *affiches,* and Sylvie Pitoiset, head of the Fonds Iconographique, of the Bibliothèque Forney were particularly helpful in providing visual materials related to perfume advertisements and labels as were Bénédicte Corbier and Marie-Hélène Gourmelon of the Fédération des Industries de la Parfumerie who supplied me with brochures and catalogues. In Upperville, Virginia, Mrs. Rachel Lambert Mellon, founder, and Tony Willis, head librarian, of the extraordinary Oak Spring Garden Library, were exceedingly gracious and overwhelmingly hospitable in allowing me to look at their marvelous collection of early nineteenth-century perfume labels. In addition, Cristin O'Keefe Aptowicz of Artists Rights Society, Merry Armata of the Sterling and Francine Clark Art Institute, Gretha Arwas and Victor Arwas of the Victor Arwas Gallery in London, Jennifer Belt and Ryan Jensen of Art Resource, Nathalie Clemence and Augustin de Montalivet of Nina Ricci (Puig Prestige Beauté), Cris Criswell and Conrad M. Rippy of Levine Plotkin & Menin, Ian Falconer and Tonia F. Barringer of Falconer Exhibits, Holly Frisbee of the Philadelphia Museum of Art, Anthony Penrose and Arabella Hayes of the Lee Miller Archives, Caitlain LeDonne and Brooke Sansosti of the Carnegie Museum of Art, Frederik Leen of the Musées Royaux des Beaux-Arts de Belgique, Ellen S. Mazzer of the Norman Rockwell Museum, Julien Messemackers of the Intertalent Agency (Paris), Jennifer Palmer and Jessica Marx of Art + Commerce, Martine Smadja of Lancôme (L'Oréal), Norma Stevens of the Richard Avedon Foundation, William Wyer of Ursus Books in New York, and several others whom I wish I had the space to name were immensely generous with advice, help, and permissions concerning the illustrations reproduced in the book Finally, for the weekly respite from writing and research, provided in the form of good food and cheer at a Vermont Inn, I thank Sally and Tim Wilson.

In Grasse, the world's capital of perfume, the following individuals went out of their way to teach me about perfume, to provide me with images of perfume, or to make available for my perusal indispensable works on the subject. Marie-Christine Grasse, Chief Curator of the Museums of the City of Grasse, and her staff at the Musée International de la Parfumerie, one of the great perfume archives in the world, were gracious to a fault in allowing me to consult the museum's vast holdings, both textual and visual, at a time the building was closed for a two-year renovation. In particular, I should like to say "merci" to Nathalie Darra for helping with permissions, to Sylvie Delcombel for showing me the museum's extensive library, to Carlo Barbiero for scanning and reproducing several important images, and to Claudine Chiocci for sharing with me her impressive knowledge concerning the history of perfume bottles. A "thank you" is also in order to Jean-François Vieille, co-owner of SOTRAFLOR (Society for the Transformation of Floral Products) near Grasse for having given me an afternoon of his time so that I could watch the picking of jasmine, the weighing of the harvest, and the beginning of the extraction process, which would ultimately lead to the production of *essence concrète* and *essence absolue.* As he guided me from field to factory and demonstrated in careful detail the different stages of jasmine extraction, he was a patient and astute teacher. And so was Joseph Mul, who gave me a fascinating mini-lecture on the botany and care of the species of jasmine plant native to Grasse, which he delivered with great gusto and humor in an October field fragrant with jasmine and rain. I shall not easily forget his passionate declaration, as his extended arms took in the field before him, that when a man gives a woman a bottle of perfume, it is "tout un champ de jasmin" he is really giving her.

To Stefanie Spray Jandl, Associate Curator of the Williams College Museum of Art, I am indebted for her enthusiastic encouragement and for her introduction to Marc Jaffe, a gifted editor who has generously and faithfully served as my agent and become a valued friend. It is to Marc that I also owe many thanks for his having, in turn, introduced me to David Larkin who brought *Perfume* to his publishing colleagues at Rizzoli. David's dedication, persistence, and consummate skills as a gifted designer and editor of art books have given *Perfume* its extraordinary beauty and elegance. To both Marc and David I cannot express sufficiently my deep gratitude.

At Rizzoli, my editor, Tricia Levi, was an extremely careful and wise reader whose suggestions, corrections, and meticulous attention to detail have made *Perfume* a better organized and clearer book. For their confidence in me and in my study of perfume, I thank Rizzoli's publisher, Charles Miers, and its managing editor, Ellen Nidy. For their work in publicizing *Perfume* I am grateful to Pam Sommers, publicity director of Rizzoli, and her assistant, Meg Nolan. Finally, some of the photographs included in this book owe their considerable beauty to the talent of the photographer Michael Freeman. I am fortunate to have had his assistance.

Over the years, my family has accepted with indulgence and without complaint the various colognes I have tried, the bothersome questions I have posed, and the long-winded discourses on my research to which I have subjected them. To my daughter, Emily; my son-in-law, Steve; my son Jeremy; my daughter-in-law, Maggie; and my young granddaughters, Julia and Eliza, I express my heartfelt thanks for their forbearance and their love. To my sister, Jane Sunshine, I am indebted for her reports on the latest perfumes to come on the market, her fieldwork at the perfume stands of various Manhattan department stores, and her archiving of relevant articles from different magazines. Finally, to my wife, Katharine Conley, words are not enough to express my love for her encouragement, support, and advice during the researching and writing of *Perfume;* only a fragrant scent could say it all. For if perfumers have a muse, as some do, who inspires the perfume they create, and if I were a perfumer, then she would be the muse behind my creation. I thank her not only for wearing *Anick Goutal, Gardénia Passion, Rive Gauche, Le Dix, Calèche, Jardin de Bagatelles, Must II, Allure, Coco Mademoiselle, Chance, Pur Poison,* and *Prada* over the years I have known her, but for bringing fragrance into my life and enveloping me in the scent of happiness.

NOTE:

Perfume: Joy, Obsession, Scandal, Sin is a detailed study of a subject—the cultural representation of perfume—that has not received the scholarly inquiry it has long merited. Although there are several books on the history of perfume, on the classic fragrances of the twentieth century, on flacon design, on the history of odors and hygiene, and on the science of perfumery—and to all of these works I am most indebted—none to date has looked at the subject in a panoramic and synthetic manner that locates in perfume the expression of a society and the spirit of a given historical time and place. The nineteenth-century perfumer Eugène Rimmel said it more succinctly than anyone when he remarked that "the history of perfume is, in some manner, that of civilization," a sentiment echoed by the contemporary perfumer Serge Lutens: "A perfume, when it is truly a perfume, adheres to a culture.... It becomes our shadow."

Another perfumer, Edmond Roudnitska, one of the great inventors and theoreticians of perfume in the twentieth century, once remarked that "about perfumes the greatest number of inaccuracies have been written." In all likelihood, he was thinking of the considerable difficulty facing anyone who tries in a precise manner to capture the insubstantial, imprecise reality of perfume. I hope that such inaccuracies as Roudnitska identifies have not found their way into *Perfume*. If errors there be—whether of commission or omission—they are mine, and I take full responsibility for them.

Regarding the translations: I have tried wherever possible to use translations of foreign works (mostly French) already published in English. In some instances, I have slightly modified these translations to bring their meaning closer to the originals. All other translations from the French are my own.

Norwich, Vermont, April 2006

The Scented Imagination: Perfume in Everyday Life

Chapter 1

Every history has its parallel, "imaginary"
history, but it is the hardest thing to capture.
— *Guy Thuillier*

It remains a decisive truth of history —
a truth the historian ignores at his peril and
to his loss — that much of the past has
taken place underground, silently, eloquently.
— *Peter Gay*

The history of perfume is, in some manner,
that of civilization.
— *Eugène Rimmel*

The Radiance of Perfume

IT IS A PRIVATE, domestic, banal moment of quiet pleasure and dreamy intimacy (fig. 1). Stepping from the tub, a woman stands in the bathroom of her apartment on the rue Lepic in Paris's eighteenth arrondissement. Proudly, confidently, even aggressively she faces the light streaming through the gossamer curtains of the window. Pushing forward to greet it, the woman welcomes the light, for she knows herself to be its equal, if not its rival. Head raised, one hand enveloping a bottle of perfume, the other slowly, absentmindedly, rubbing scent on to her body, the woman loses herself in reverie. The language of her naked body, its pose and poise, expresses the pleasure of this intimate, self-indulgent moment. Moving assertively outward to offer itself to the light flooding in through the window, standing tall to meet the shimmering challenge of the day which has enflamed the room—head lifted proudly upward, shoulders thrown boldly back, breast tautly raised, back gracefully arced, all weight shifted to the left leg while the right knee remains ever so slightly bent and the feet lie peacefully cushioned in dark purple slippers—the woman's body performs a dramatic spectacle of invitation and resistance. It also articulates and then resolves a conflict between flesh and spirit and sense and *es-sence*, for the woman's presence results as much from sensual corporeality as from spiritual light. Not only has she stepped out of the tub and into the light, she has transported herself from one world—the drab, monochromatic, material section of the bathroom with its ponderous, shapeless, utilitarian objects of containment (tub, washbasin, pitcher, mirror)—to another world, dazzling, radiant, and full of unlimited possibility. Once the drabness of ordinary life has been sponged away and left behind in the grayish water of the tub, the body is prepared for a rite of sublimation, the divinization that perfume offers. As the dazzle of light spiritualizes the room, so the intoxicating aroma of perfume sublimates the woman's body, turning flesh into vapor and skin into air. One need only compare the glowing, dappled, luminous carnation of the woman's perfumed body, enveloped by light, to the tiny, white, statuesque image enclosed in the mirror, to perceive the difference between the banal and the sublime, the one giving birth to the other in the most routine of everyday activities: namely, bathing.

Making Perfume Visual

The candid forthrightness of the body of his lover, Marthe de Méligny (she would become his wife in 1925) which Pierre Bonnard gives to this painting of 1908—alternately called *The Bathroom* (*Le Cabinet de toilette*), *Nude Against the Light* (*Nu à contre-jour*), and possibly *Eau de Cologne*, when first exhibited in 1909—expresses a delight in the powerful presence of a body whose sensuality is as luminous as light itself. Yet, despite the radiance that envelops her, the woman's flesh has a dense physicality and an opacity that resist the sunlight. The mass of her body is impervious to the rays that seem easily to penetrate and dominate the other material objects and fabrics in the room: the curtains, the wallpaper, and the sofa slipcover, all reduced to an overheated and luminous transparence of white, yellow, and pink hues. Between the transparent, piercing, overwhelming light, which sets fire to everything it touches, and the resistant physicality of the woman's body, enlivened by the intruding waves of the light's warmth, but too empowered to give up its autonomous, self-absorbed sensuality, one object, ever so tentatively held out to the light, mediates the encounter. The bottle of perfume, which Marthe, a frequent subject of Bonnard's bathing paintings, nonchalantly holds in her right hand, is the all-important barrier and go-between, positioned at that point of confrontation where body and light touch as they dramatically push and pull against each other. The bottle is filled with a liquid as yellow as the wallpaper and as golden as the glowing radiance advancing from behind the window curtains.

The perfume in its vessel is yet another form of light within the painting. For what is perfume, generally speaking, if not a golden or amber liquid, a bottled light: what Shakespeare called in his Fifth Sonnet "a liquid prisoner pent in walls of glass"? But it is a prisoner that, once liberated, unleashes an explosive radiance which, as it expands into the air, fills space with fragrant vapors (and molecules) moving in ways akin to the shifting rays of trembling light and the shimmering waves of rising heat which emanate throughout Bonnard's room. Here, the life-affirming explosion of light—the flamelike contours it adopts as it passes through curtains vibrating with an almost animate radiance—becomes the representation of scent itself. Light translates fragrance, reveals the mechanics of its expansion, gives form to its vaporous emanations, and makes visible its invisible presence. As paradoxical as it may seem, odor is reinterpreted as sight. Seen but not smelled, perfume becomes visual; it is expressed and represented through the medium of light. Like wind, whose reality is perceived through the effects it leaves in its wake—bending tree limbs, blowing snow, scudding clouds—perfume, in order to be seen, must first undergo a transformation, a change of state; it must become shimmering, liquid light. The ordinary, banal event of bathing and perfuming, always a moment of intense intimacy, becomes in Bonnard's gifted hands a spectacle, if not an epiphany, of light and scent.[1]

The wavering, airy radiance created by the interplay of light and fabric—the flamelike arabesques of the white curtain, the pink-red swirls of the sofa, and the yellow-green patches of the wallpaper—reproduce the wavelike after-effect of perfume, what the French call "sillage" (wake). The vaporous effects of the light capture the invisible, yet in its own way luminous, aroma emanating from the bottle and from the woman's body, as if perfume had become radiance and perfumed flesh a source of light. The painting presents a spectacle of light, which is also a mise-en-scène, a theatricalization, of scent. This spectacle, moreover, is an epiphany not only of light but of eros (love); perfume eroticizes the body. It occasions a performance of self-display whereby the body, asserting its physical and sensual presence, makes a scene of its own privacy, turning intimacy into drama, theater. The narcissism of the *toilette* and of the act of perfuming the wrists, elbows, neck, and cleavage, not only makes the body sensually perceptible to smell by transforming flesh into aroma; it broadcasts the body far and wide, projecting it and making public its intimacy; it "outs" the body, so to speak, in a controlled and measured manner.

Perfume speaks the body; it *is* the body but in a different form. It enables the body to change its presence in the world, modify its signature, and redefine its identity. To choose a perfume is to assert one's body, or more precisely to choose a certain way of being that body. As early even as the sixth century, a woman's beauty, according to the Kama Sutra, was determined not by her physical appearance but by her odor. Through a language of airborne shouts and whispers, the spectacle of perfume, like that of haute couture, boldly publicizes and yet quietly evokes the sensuous reality of skin and flesh, now accessible, perceptible, breathable, but not visible, through the expansiveness of scent. The private body moves onto the stage and into the spotlight of the world; and there, as in the theater, the revelation of what is intimate and personal is seen as both real and imaginary. The smell of the woman's body is revealed and hidden at the same time, because the experience of intimacy, even when perfume embodies and publicizes it, and the protocols and rituals a woman follows when dressing, are constructed. Intimacy is first and foremost the fashioning of intimacy, and perfume plays an essential role in its fabrication, in what the poet Baudelaire called "the lofty spiritual significance of the *toilette*."[2]

In *Le Cabinet de Toilette,* Bonnard accomplishes the representation of what, in visual terms, is unrepresentable. His visualizing of scent comes into conflict with the reality of representation: how does one figure, or imagine, or give the sensation of an odor so that one may see it? What image, what color, what visible form, or what scene captures the essence of a perfume? This is a question of interest to poets as well. Charles Baudelaire, Stéphane Mallarmé, and the French symbolists in the nineteenth century wondered what combination of image, word, name, sound, rhythm, music, and metaphor might describe and re-create a sensation of olfactory delight, a spiritual experience of bliss and ecstatic oneness far beyond the sensual world which had initiated it. Perfume manufacturers and advertisers in our own day have similar problems: How can one evoke in a name, a slogan, an image, and the design of a bottle the conceptual idea and the imaginary theme or narrative behind a perfume whose fragrance is usually experienced only after the image or the name has become public? Perfume, of course, has its own structure, architecture, music, and terminology; it is composed of orchestrated accords like musical notes and complex harmonies, called "head" or "top," "heart" or "middle," "soul" or "base" notes. It possesses its own unique system of classification, which organizes fragrance into basic concepts according to their floral, oriental, chypre, and fern qualities and then divides them yet again into subfields distinguishable by their green, fruity, fresh, sweet, ambery, spicy, aldehydic, animalic, citrusy, woody, or leathery attributes (*H& R*, 8, 11).

Perfume Representation

Obviously, to be perceived as an odor, perfume is in no need of translation into another medium or language, especially for those people whose sense of smell is as keenly and artistically developed as visual and poetic faculties are in other gifted people. But having such a keen sense of smell is rare in human beings today because the ability to perceive odors has progressively declined over the ages, ever since hominid quadrupeds began to stand and move on two feet and ever since humans decided to cocoon themselves within deodorized and sanitized environments. Moreover, the hostility toward smell as reflected in the writings of idealist philosophers from Plato and Aristotle to Kant, Schopenhauer, Hegel, and Simmel—all of whom associated smell with a certain degree of animalism and baseness—and the elevation of vision as the queen of the senses, the sensual faculty par excellence for thought and intelligence, have had a deleterious effect on odor and perfume.[3] To see or envision the theme or concept of a fragrance has become essential to perfume representation, as writers, artists, musicians, designers, and advertisers have attempted to describe, narrate, paint, sing, and, in general, imagine the sensuality, or exoticism, or intoxication of a fragrance. Moreover, the language of perfume designation is notable for its ambiguity and subjectivity, if not for its incomprehensibility, to all but a few experts. How, for example, does a non-specialist distinguish between a green floral and its cousin, an aldehydic floral scent, or tell the difference between a fresh, or a woody, or a floral-animalic-chypre fragrance? And how does one find the exact words to describe the difference between these aromas?

A good part of the problem can be traced to a question of vocabulary, to the absence of exact words to describe smell (and even taste, for that matter). We talk about odors, whiffs, scents, perfumes, fragrances, aromas, emanations, incenses, bouquets, vapors, breaths, exhalations, effluvia, effulgence, stenches, and miasmas; but beyond these words, which have come down to us from antiquity, the signifying power of language is limited.[4] Moreover, one of the "discontents" of civilization, as Freud discovered, is that we must be taught disgust; infants are

"Initial A." Incense in the Synagogue. Illustration by E. Bourdelin from Eugène Rimmel, *The Book of Perfumes* (London: Chapman and Hall, 1867).

In the effort to envelop and preserve the ephemera of scent, modes of painterly and linguistic description will always embrace more absence than presence; they will consistently lose more than they will capture. A scent always dissipates, leaving in its wake no more than a faint echo, a lingering trace. Perfume is a "here" en route to a "there," a today floating away in the direction of a yesterday, a possession paradoxically coinciding with an imminent loss. Created from blossoms and petals which have surrendered their floral odors, and their "lives," perfume is, when all is said and done, a concentrate of loss, the distilled spirit of now-dead roses, macerated jasmine blossoms, or steam-withered lavender: "an essence of absence."[7] The drama of perfume tells a tale of loss; it is a fable about the impermanence of life, a story of something gained and something taken away. And the attempt by poets, painters, musicians, dancers, glassmakers, and designers to transpose this drama of presence and absence into artistic forms and media other than those perceptually linked to smell stumbles against the same obstacle: the insubstantiality and impermanence of the subject—perfume—always too volatile, fleeting, and vaporous to be possessed or captured by metaphor, color, and musical or choreographic form.

Rubbed into the skin, a perfume blends with the odor molecules of the body; the combined fragrances of flesh and scent then vaporize into the atmosphere. Through the medium of perfume the body becomes an airborne essence, a vapor, even though this transformation lasts for only a short time before evaporating. Perfume is a language; through it the body gains expression and the spirit and soul of the body (its desires, needs, feelings) are roused from muteness to speech. The skin is the surface, the page, onto which this language is "imprinted" or impressed for a

unaware of the difference between "good" and "bad" odors. In general, therefore, the descriptive language of smell lacks complexity and richness; often, our use of terms to designate odors is overwhelmingly impressionistic; the realities to which these terms refer remain vague, if not unknown. How can one imagine, let alone re-experience, some of the scents mentioned in the Bible: the balm of Gilead, or the erotic perfumes the lover in the *Song of Songs* wears, or the odor of sanctity emanating from Saint Theresa of Ávila, celebrated for her four different scents of saintliness, about which we can only know what an ancient text tells us? How can one begin to re-experience the perfumes with which Cleopatra, arriving at Tarsus in 41 B.C., made Antony and the winds "love-sick," according to both Shakespeare in *Antony and Cleopatra* (II, ii, 199) and Plutarch in his *Life of Antony* (26, 1–4). It would be nearly impossible to re-create the "strange invisible perfume"— the intermingling fragrances of *kyphi,* an ancient, mythical form of Egyptian incense, arising from her hands and of *aegyptium,* a blend of almond oil, honey, cinnamon, orange blossoms, and henna, emanating from her feet—that arises from Cleopatra's barge, like the majestic sounds of a trumpet declaring her imminent arrival (*Antony and Cleopatra,* II, ii, 216–218).[5] Similarly, what formula can help recompose the scent Marie-Antoinette wore that night in June 1791 when she was arrested in Varennes, or the smell of the exiled Napoleon dousing himself with an imitation eau de cologne on the island of Saint Helena? People long to recapture the smell of the past, and yet rarely does this smell completely restore that past in its immemorial intimacy. Regarding our olfactory history, the word, as the historian Paul Faure writes, is "incapable of supplying anything more than an approximation."[6]

Cleopatra's boat—its stern made of gold, its sails colored royal purple, its silver oars moving in harmony with the sounds of flutes, pan pipes, and cithers, its wake leaving the river's banks fragrant with marvelous odors, as Plutarch describes the event in his *Lives*—sails up the river Cydnus to a meeting with Antony. "Cleopatra on the Cydnus." Illustration by W. Thomas from Eugène Rimmel, *The Book of Perfumes* (London: Chapman and Hall, 1867).

Fig. 2 In the democratic spaces of today's department stores and malls no generation or class is excluded from the seductive appeal of a perfume's "sinful" powers, as Ian Falconer humorously shows in *A Whiff of Sin*.

short time before scent transforms the body into an altogether different, less substantial, more ethereal, and invisible incarnation of being.[8] Perfume compresses the body's senses of sight, touch, and hearing into one super-sense: smell. Having written its different mixture of notes and accords on the skin, perfume then writes the perfumed body on air, into air, as air. It takes the body out of itself (beyond its visible, palpable, audible, physical self) and transports it into an immaterial dimension where the body, now cloud and mist, continues to "speak," but, like any translation, through a differently nuanced syntax, vocabulary, and sonority. Written on the wind, the body, insofar as it is perfume, transcends the limits of space. It reveals, as one French writer has remarked, "an entire garden in the fold of an elbow."[9]

Perfume in Everyday Life

When perfume is mentioned, when a scent is inhaled, or when fragrance is advertised, a host of images, scenes, dramas, and fantasies pop into mind. Here is a smell, which produces the most intensely visual (and culturally determined) of responses; we see the perfume in some instances as an image before we even perceive it as an odor. In Western culture, perfume evokes dreams of luxury and elegance, longings for romantic love, fantasies of self-transformation, and desires for liberation and transgression. For example, leaning over a counter in which several different sizes of perfume bottles are displayed, a middle-aged matron tells the salesperson helping her that she is looking for "something that will make me smell thinner." Another matron, a bit dowdier and more unfashionably attired, is approached by a smartly dressed saleswoman, perfume atomizer in hand, who asks this unlikely client if she would like to try "Whore of Babylon." A third, an elegant dowager-type, is given little choice, as the artist and illustrator Ian Falconer imagines her. As she debates with herself which pair of gloves to purchase, her head is suddenly enveloped in a perfumed mist arising from the hand of a tall, slender, mini-skirted young saleswoman who has suddenly materialized holding an atomizer, its fiery red label boldly advertising a new fragrance called "SIN" (fig. 2).

Despite the humorous aspect of such representations (all cartoons from the *New Yorker*[10]), none of the events portrayed is anything more than an exaggerated and comic version of a scenario played out thousands of times a day in a consumerist society that discovers its arenas of play, pleasure, and spectacle in the department store, the boutique, and the mall. These three somewhat ironic representations of perfume suggest an image of fragrance and an attitude toward scent that are culturally determined and collectively enacted. Like the cure we believe a pill can give, perfume is seen as a magical potion, an alluring lure, a dream in a bottle, an enchanting "prisoner pent in walls of glass." If the miracle of prolonged life occasioned by distillation can transform the elusive scent of flowers into what is literally and scientifically called an "essence" or a "spirit," then the promise of other powerful wonders lies within the vessel's crystal walls. One need only read perfume labels or listen to their names in order to know that love, passion, envy, sin, magic, mystery, exoticism, elegance, glamour, spontaneity, zest, youth, excitement, happiness, dream, joy, rapture, intoxication, paradise, peace, eternity, innocence, tenderness, fragility, insouciance, languor, boldness, excess, folly, nudity, femininity, masculinity, sexuality, Paris—even, as the cartoons suggest, thinness and sinfulness—are a mere drop away. Yet, there are some experiences perfume, as culturally defined, cannot offer and that one would never want the genie in the bottle to make appear. These experiences—of dowdiness, prudishness, gracelessness, unhappiness, depression, aging, illness, and death—are precisely what perfume seeks to mask.[11] As perfume surrounds a body with a fragrant aura and as its notes and chords fuse together in a harmonious, aromatic whole, so the idea of perfume is enveloped by—and its image blended with—the literary, musical, sensory, psychological, religious, and symbolic associations which, since the time of the pharaohs, have attached themselves to the experience of fragrance, creating what can be called an "image-system," or what some theoreticians call an "imaginary." This image system of scent is a culturally constructed and unconsciously pervasive repertory of images, beliefs, practices, and associations; it is always present, burning under the surface of everyday reality like, according to the French critic Roland Barthes, "an incompletely extinguished peat fire."[12] Perfume has been the provocative inspiration and metaphor for so many similar realities and experiences occurring in the social and cultural worlds of daily life—for the elusive intensity of erotic desire, for the waxing and waning of memory, for the transience of life, for the mysterious spirituality of being, for the intoxicating, and thus dangerous, sensuality of the body, for the control of the feminine—that it has played a powerfully formative, although often invisible, role in the definition and expression of cultural values for many centuries, particularly from the end of the eighteenth century to the beginning of the third millennium.

The "image system" that forms the scented imagination is a mode of perception, a mind-set created from a nexus of poetic, philosophical, and psychological meanings, from a system of culturally coded images, and from a network of personal and collective fantasies that all swirl around the perception of perfume, itself a sensory experience determined by both conscious and unconscious, poetic and psychoanalytic, private and consumerist desires. This is because fragrance, whether perceived in a room of people or evoked by the words of a poem, whether suggested in the photograph of a couple embracing or in the painting of a woman stepping out of her bath, whether called into being through an exotic and provocative name or through the graceful contours of a crystal bottle, passes by necessity, as it moves toward consciousness, through other media: through skin and air, membranes and synapses, images and texts, light and glass. In this movement through other spheres and states, perfume calls into being a complex system of representations and an intricate network of personal and cultural associations. It creates an image system, which the culture of fashion sustains in the form of costly scents, luxuriously designed flasks, richly poetic names, and erotically charged symbols. The art and artistry of perfume, the chemistry and psychology of fragrance, and the fetishized desire for objects of conspicuous consumption enable the scented imagination to operate at different levels and within different arenas of cultural production, in what the German philosopher Walter Benjamin, writing about fashion in general, called "the dream consciousness of the collective [that] awakes … in advertising."[13]

Perfume Attributes and Qualities

From the "sweet loving" which myrrh, frankincense, and cinnamon celebrate in the *Song of Songs* to the dream of a rapturous, blissful, living scent, capable of stealing and preserving the essence of a beloved woman in Patrick Süskind's 1985 novel, *Perfume: The Story of a Murderer;* from Shakespeare's description of the sails of Cleopatra's barge, "so perfumed that / The winds were love-sick" (*Antony and Cleopatra*, II, ii, 198–99) to the synesthetic claims of a recently marketed scent (*Anick Goutal)* that "Perfume is the music of my dreams"; from the violet, lemon, hyacinth, iris, heather, yarrow, and gentian fragrances, producing feelings of gloom, vexation, anxiety, and self-loathing that a spurned mistress, bent on revenge, applies assiduously to her faithless lover's body in the fictional *The Pillow Boy of Lady Onogoro* to the promise of expansive intensity suggested in the slogan for a recent scent (*Hanae Mori*), "A drop of perfume … an ocean of love," perfume has been envisioned as many, contradictory things. First, it is a language, with its own special grammar, lexicon, and syntax. Second, it is a sign and trace of a presence now gone or of a past lost to oblivion yet still subject to recall and recovery. Third, it is an expression of the body's silence and the skin's muteness, raised to expressiveness through the expansion, volatility, and airiness of scent. Fourth, it is an identity and an otherness, capturing the essence of the other whose secret being it expresses. Fifth, it is a memory, recalling the traces of lost persons, places, and events. Sixth, it is a name, by which the fragrance becomes a narrative or a scene—of desire, of fantasy, of erotic longing—adding further to the endless construction within culture of the collective imaginary. Seventh, it is a seductive deceit or subterfuge, tricking an unsuspecting lover into betrayal, confession, and his or her undoing.

Eighth, it is an artful mask, momentarily hiding the persistent presence of decay, decomposition, and death which underlie organic existence. Ninth, it is a kind of music, composed of floral and animal fragrances whose top, middle, and base notes create subtly orchestrated harmonies. Tenth, it is a substance lying between matter and spirit, earth and air, and, given the literally indescribable reality of smells, beyond the signifying hooks of language and writing. Eleventh, it is an instrument of sexual control, disciplining the female body through the transformation of natural odors into more aesthetically pleasing, more socially acceptable, and thus less "menacing" scents—a denaturalization with unforeseen erotic and social consequences. Finally, it is a commodity produced by a system of collective desires and cultural representations articulated through the careful manipulation of image, design, text, display, and advertising.

In the chapters that follow, these diverse attributes and qualities, which give life to the scented imagination, will be examined primarily insofar as they have, during the past 250 years, produced poetically and culturally determined representations of experiences—at once odorous and visual—in literature, painting, music, opera, theater, interior design, decorative and poster art, perfumery, glass-making, fashion, advertising, the architecture of world's fair exhibitions, and the design of Parisian department stores. If there is history in this book, it is not the history of perfume but that of the representations of perfume: a history, that is, of the constellation of images associated with the experience of perfume. This image system is part of the worldview of a culture; it taps into, and at the same time fashions and revises, the belief system and the repertoire of images which a culture stores and keeps ready for immediate use. The social strategies, the forms of perception, and the symbolic systems associated with the sense of smell participate in the formation from age to age of a scented imagination in which the real and sensory experience of perfume is inextricably linked to the public's general awareness of what is real and sensory in the world.

The Overly Scented World

Bending to the wishes of individuals suffering from allergies or more serious forms of "multiple chemical sensitivity" disorder, as it is called, the citizens of Halifax, Nova Scotia, in the late 1990s, turned designated areas of their city into "fragrance-free zones." Employees of businesses located in these zones were forbidden to wear perfume, cologne, after-shave lotions, hairsprays, and other heavily scented beauty products. Yet, even in our increasingly deodorized society we are still inundated by odors and scents, both pleasant and disagreeable. We buy aromatherapy products to relax our frazzled nerves. We allow into our kitchens, bathrooms, and homes a cacophony of fragrances that issue from paper tissues, room deodorizers, detergents, shampoos, bath oils, cat litter, and so on. Aromas once reserved for perfumes and body oils now fill our home spaces with smells of coral, mint, tea, lavender, patchouli, verbena, bamboo, or a tropical rain forest. Jasmine-scented mattress pads, lavender-infused rugs, and even Nokia cell phones with coffee-scented faceplates are on the market. In the magazines we peruse, a stew of competing odors reaches our noses from microencapsulated scent strips, while our children enjoy turning the pages of scratch-and-sniff books. One day, digitized scents communicated from computer to computer will be common. With an odor-enabled system and a printerlike device capable of mixing and dissipating scents—such computer-generated scent delivery systems like iSmell and FirstSENX have been developed by DigiScent, AromaJet, and TriSenx—one could send love letters enveloped in jasmine or lavender fragrances. Scented fantasies of love are easily realized now that Proctor & Gamble has developed "Scentstories," a CD-like player that spins scented wax disks designed to inspire reveries around such themes as "wandering barefoot on the shore" and "exploring a mountain trail."[14]

Beyond the home, public spaces (not, of course, in Halifax!) are becoming increasingly perfumed. After many complaints about the smells of sulfur and body odor in the Paris subway system, the French transit authority commissioned a scent, appropriately named *Madeleine*, from Quest International, a large fragrance company, to be mixed bimonthly into the wax used to clean station platforms. Quite possibly, *Madeleine* might not have worked in the New York subway, for the simple reason that "tastes" in scents often reveal different national preferences; the odor of cleanliness for the French is associated, for example, with lavender, for Americans and Germans with pine, and for inhabitants of Asia with rose.[15] Yet, the New York Transit Authority was not, in principle, excluded from the realm of scents. In 2003, a New York perfume company, Bond No. 9, launched a collection of sixteen perfumes (it now offers twenty-five scents), dedicated to "making scents of New York," to "bottling the creative energy and spirit of the city," and to marking "every New York neighborhood with a scent of its own." Each bottle displayed the image of a New York City subway token, and each carried the name of a well-known area of the Big Apple—"Broadway Nite," "Chelsea Flowers," "Nuits de Noho," "New Haarlem," "Nouveau Bowery," "Little Italy," "Chinatown"—or alluded to a uniquely Manhattan state-of-mind; "Hot Always" and "New York Fling" are two such examples.[16]

With one spritz from a can or with a cartridge dropped into the interior air vent (of the 2005 Citroën C4), the inside of our automobiles can have that generic "new-car smell" or some other aroma. Yet, some scents are vehicle-specific, capturing the "essence" of a particular luxury car. Cadillac, for example, has engineered a fragrance, named "Nuance," which it rubs into the leather seats of its vehicles. For a lot less money, however, we can envelop ourselves in the aura of a Jaguar, Ferrari, or Corvette. Such colognes (to be applied to one's skin and not to the automobile's interior) must, according to the chief executive of Ferrari North America, "inspire the same emotions as the car—speed, adrenaline pumping ... I'm not selling cars; I'm selling a dream." If Parfums Jaguar, Ferrari's competitor on the highway and in the bathroom, is any bellwether—its sales for 1998 approached $2 million—then the dream is indeed being sold, and bought. This is a dream that can reach super-sized proportions when notes of cardamom, peppercorn, tonka bean, and leather combine in the scent *Hummer* to appeal to the "rugged, adventurous, 100 percent man" who wants an "olfactive sensation [that] imparts a healthy brawn in a veneer of sophistication." The same masculine type is targeted by the cologne *Legendary Harley-Davidson*, which an advertisement in a Portuguese edition of *Cosmopolitan* touts as a scent both "fresh and strong, sensual and hot ... a breath of freedom."[17]

If one has the means to acquire these automobiles, then one should not blink twice when purchasing what are advertised as the "World's Most Expensive Perfumes." Clive Christian's fragrance *1872,* costing $595 for an ounce and a half bottle with a 24-carat gold-plated and sterling silver neck, his *No. 1* at $1,820 (the bottle is inlaid with a diamond), and his *Imperial Majesty* (in a limited edition of 10 Baccarat crystal, 18-karat-gold flacons, studded with a 5-carat diamond) costing $225,000 are indeed the most costly perfumes available today. Should it be three-quarters of the world's surface that we want contained in a bottle, then Coty, the celebrated cosmetics and perfume company, has, in collaboration with the Club Méditerrané, created the relaxing smell of a seaside vacation, called *My Ocean*. Yet, for those who hate to relax, preferring instead the athletic, on-the-move life, Adidas, the sneaker manufacturer, has created *Adrenaline*, whose slogan, "Unleash it," is accompanied by a crescendo of active, one-syllable words, like "surge, rush, fierce, thrill."[18] For the more urban types who seek the edgy energy of the city, Calvin Klein's *CK One* offers a collector's-edition bottle decorated with looming black figures and roughly drawn letters designed by the New York City graffiti artist Futura and other internationally known urban artists. Graffiti is not the only form of writing that perfume has appropriated. Parfums Carven introduced its scent *Ma Griffe* ("My Signature," "My Sign") in 1946, while forty-two years later Bic, the French pen manufacturer, marketed a scent in small glass bottles whose portability matched that of the company's ubiquitous ballpoint pens. Encouraged to take the small vials wherever they went, women were called on to literally "Put Paris in your pocket."[19]

Tastes in perfume and cologne are eclectic, sometimes refined, sometimes vulgar, but almost always determined by the icons, desires, and image systems generated by a consumer culture. People buy scents named for or produced by celebrities, past and present—*Luciano Pavarotti, Jordan by Michael, Glow by Jennifer Lopez, Manifesto by Isabella Rossellini* ("A Celebration of What You Are"),

Uninhibited (from Cher), *Curious* and *Fantasy* (from Britney Spears), *Donald Trump: The Fragrance, Misha* (from Mikhail Baryshnikov, advertised as "classic but a little crazy"), *Pavlova* ("The Woman. The Legend. The Fragrance")—hoping that some of their operatic, athletic, acting, musical, entrepreneurial, and choreographic talents will rub off.[20] Numbers grab our attention and not only celebrated ones like Chanel's *No. 5* or *No. 19.* There are numbered fragrances like Perry Ellis's *360°;* Yves Saint Laurent's *M7,* an allusion to the British secret service; Van Cleef & Arpels's *First* ("every woman deserves to be first"); Calvin Klein's unisex *CK One;* and Carolina Herrera's appropriation of Manhattan's classic area code: *212.* Even a mere letter will suffice, as in *L, eau de parfum,* released in February 2006 as a tie-in fragrance for a cable television drama called "The L Word," about a group of lesbian friends living in Los Angeles. Sometimes, however, adults seek more than trademark perfumes and colognes. They feel the need to purchase hypoallergenic prestige scents for their children and domestic pets, like *Oh My Dog!* ("The first perfume created for the most sensitive noses") and *Oh My Cat?* both produced by Dog Generation. *Oh My Dog!* is "a fresh clean unisex scent, which evokes the smell of a puppy . . . a puppy with notes of rosewood, mint, freesia, iris, vanilla, and sandalwood," while *Oh My Cat?* blends mandarin, bergamot, and olive leaves with sandalwood, musk, and vanilla notes. Pet owners are instructed not to spray the toilet water directly on the fur of their animals.[21]

Scent Associations

In addition to fragrances for animals, there are animal scents for humans. Musk from the deer of that name, ambergris from whales, castoreum from beavers, and civet from a large Ethiopian cat have been essential ingredients in expensive perfumes for centuries. (Civet has been called the most evil smelling of the four animal scents.) One does not, of course, wish to smell like these animals. An exception may be the frog. During the 1994 Christmas season, Bloomingdale's in Manhattan did a booming business selling *Amphibia.* Inspired by Jim Henson's Kermit the Frog, it was a scent jazzed up with fruity, green, spicy top notes, a heart note of lily-of-the-valley, gardenia, and raspberry, and a base note of pimiento berry, tonka bean, musk,

"Civet Cat (*Viverra civetta*)." Illustration from Eugène Rimmel, *The Book of Perfumes* (London: Chapman and Hall, 1867).

vanilla, and moss.[22] Scenting animals may be arguable, but there would be universal agreement about the redundancy of masking the clean odor of a baby or toddler with fragrances like *Burberry's Baby Touch, Tartine et Chocolat, Baby Babar, Petit Ange, La Rose du Petit Prince*, and *Petit Guerlain*, or about even encouraging expectant mothers, suffering from morning sickness and the temporary loss of smell that can accompany pregnancy, to wear *En Attendant* (Expecting), created by the French company Fragrance Forward; yet, these scents sell well.[23] If we choose not to scent the skin of our children, we can involve them in perfume play. "Parfumaster" is a French game of detection in which players are asked to smell and then identify a host of odors as distinct as rubber and chocolate.

Like the alluring aromas of the kitchen, many of which bring back memories of childhood, perfumes have recently been designed to smell as good as food. In the 1990s perfume design began to move away from heavy, sensual, animal scents and to favor the sweeter, more "gourmand" notes of what the perfumer Jean-Claude Ellena has called "croque-moi" perfumery (from the French word "to munch"). Thierry Mugler's *Angel,* a sensuous oriental with chocolate, caramel, and cotton candy accords; Origins's *Ginger Intense,* spiced with ginger and jasmine; Escada's *Ibiza Hippie,* with a fruit cocktail of lychee, pear, blackberry, and wild cranberries offset with water hyacinth and blue freesia; Bulgari's *Omnia,* a full tray of sweet and spicy delicacies like mandarin, ginger, cardamom, black pepper, saffron, masala tea, and white chocolate; and Cacharel's *Gloria,* dominated by an amaretto scent somewhere "between bitter almonds and candied cherries" topped with hibiscus, vanilla, rose, and ambergris notes, all sound more like mouthwatering desserts than perfumes. With its line of seven "Sweet" scents, one of which carries the name *Sticky Cake* (almonds, pistachios, and honey blended with iris), Comme des Garçons does not even try to hide the connection between fragrance and sugar. One American fragrance brand is even called *Candies* and another, a Donna Karan perfume, invites women to "*Be Delicious,*" to "take a bite out of life." Yet, for those who prefer to be reminded not of their favorite meal or bonbon, but of their favorite cocktail, especially if their friends have made them a "designated driver" for an evening's outing, there is *Infusion,* made by Bombay Sapphire, the gin company, and based not on actual gin but on the ten botanical elements (juniper, lemon, coriander, etc.) which compose Bombay's eighteenth-century recipe. The perfumer Suzanne Lang has mixed the perfume cocktail which she has conceived according to a somewhat different recipe: a blend of pineapple, coconut, vanilla, fig, and ginger notes combine to create a sweet and sour fragrance called *Pineapple Martini.* Sometimes, moreover, we seek in a bottle the smell (and pastoral experience) of the great outdoors. Barbour, the British clothing manufacturer known for its wax-coated hunting jacket, has satisfied this longing with a bucolic perfume smelling like "a stubble field in

July, a bluebell wood in May—or a wet Labrador all year round." The great outdoors has also inspired another cutting-edge scent, an eau de cologne evocative of "a crisp, clear blue-sky day somewhere in the Swiss Alps." Borrowing the tried-and-true motto of the Boy Scouts, *Swiss Army, Eau de toilette*, advertises itself under the banner "Be Prepared."[24]

Perfume and Politics

In the rough-and-tumble world and smoke-filled back-rooms of politics, perfume has a place, even if it is most often only metaphorical. During the election campaign for prime minister, when asked what he thought about a poll showing that his Labor party might win more seats in the Knesset, Shimon Peres, the Israeli politician and Nobel Peace Prize laureate, was quoted in the *New York Times* as saying: "polls are like perfume . . . Nice to smell, dangerous to swallow." Yet, for the surrealist poet Joyce Mansour, politics and perfume are mutually exclusive terms, so contradictory in fact that they can perhaps only coexist in a surrealist image: "He stood before me," she writes of a character in a story from the 1970s, "as useless as a politician in a *parfumerie*." At the conclusion of a suit for libel in 1987 brought by Jeffrey Archer, the millionaire British novelist, against a tabloid that had accused him of having sex with a prostitute, the judge, who was quite taken with Mrs. Archer's persuasive testimony about the faithful marriage she and her husband enjoyed, instructed the jury in the following stirring words: "Remember Mrs. Archer in the witness box. Your vision of her probably will never disappear. Has she elegance? Has she fragrance? Would she have, without the strain of this trial, radiance?" To the obviously smitten judge at least, Mrs. Archer possessed an aura of beauty, grace, and loyalty, an air of moral dignity, which the word "fragrance" nicely captures. If perfume moves through the political arena and the courtroom, then it can even permeate a society under threat from international terrorism. As one would expect in a globalized world dominated by pan-cultural consumerism, a culture where fame quickly becomes gain, the marketing of Osama Bin Laden T-shirts in Indonesia and of boxes of Bin Laden sweets in Afghanistan was only equaled by the bottles of "Usama [*sic*] Bin Laden" cologne spray hawked on the streets of Lahore, Pakistan, and by the creation of the floral perfume, *Yeslam* ("a profound yet gentle message in a bottle for all who long for inner peace"), inspired by the formula of *Air de Paris* (1920s), which the terrorist's half brother, Yeslam Bin Ladin [*sic*], has been developing.[25]

Of course, scent mixed with politics and perfume combined with litigiousness often leave a disagreeable odor. The largest cosmetic firm in the world, the French multinational company, L'Oréal, which today owns Helena Rubinstein, Cacharel, Ralph Lauren, Giorgio Armani, and Lanvin, was accused of harboring Nazi collaborators and avid anti-Semites during the German Occupation of Paris, and more recently, in the 1980s, of surreptitiously participating in the Arab League's boycott of Israel. A case with fewer geopolitical and moral ramifications and fewer embarrassing consequences was the breach-of-contract suit filed by the Revelations Perfume and Cosmetics company, a small Pennsylvania manufacturer of a low-end fragrance called *Truth,* created in 1999, against Calvin Klein Cosmetics (owned by the conglomerate Unilever) over the latter's *Truth Calvin Klein* scent, which was first marketed in 2000. Revelations's claim that Calvin Klein had trespassed on its market is not an unusual occurrence in an industry where companies copyright the names of future, often never-to-be-created scents and where the resulting trademark disputes, copyright infringements, and accusations of industrial counterfeiting often have to be settled in a court of law. Yves Saint Laurent had his legal troubles as well with the powerful and well-organized French champagne industry which had little appreciation for his 1993 fragrance *Champagne*, advertised as "the perfume of success." Wine growers and distributors vociferously opposed his sacrilegious appropriation of a sacred name which, to their way of thinking, could have only one possible meaning in French history. Saint Laurent lost the suit and renamed his fragrance *Yvresse*, a pun on his first name and an appellation that still suggests, albeit to a more subtle degree, champagne's sparkling, fizzy personality. One of the more interesting conflicts between law and perfume was played out in a suit brought by the popular radio host of a Detroit country music station who was sickened by a colleague's use of Lancôme's *Trésor*. Fired from her position in 2001 after filing a complaint, the radio personality sued Infinity Broadcasting, her employer, in U.S. District Court, contending that exposure to *Trésor* had caused her to lose her voice, to miss work, to depend heavily on medication, and to feel "an electric shock quell through my entire body"; her doctor warned that extended exposure to the fragrance could end in her death. After eight days of deliberation, the jury of all women handed down a verdict awarding the plaintiff $7 million in punitive damages, $2 million for mental anguish and emotional distress, and $1.6 million for past and future compensation, a decision that will probably be reduced on appeal.[26]

Capturing Scent

Perfumers currently have more than 400 natural smells and almost double that number of synthetic odors from which to work. A database called "Parôm" has inventoried more than 1,500 aromatic molecules and hopes eventually to contain a complete inventory of the 25,000 odors identified on Earth. Yet, the search for new ingredients and new ways to disseminate these fragrant substances in everyday life never ends. Givaudan-Roure, one of the world's largest fragrance companies (the creator of Yves Saint Laurent's

Opium, Nina Ricci's *L'Air du Temps*, and Calvin Klein's *Obsession*, among other celebrated perfumes) has its own teams of scent trekkers and trappers, biochemists, tropical biologists, and fragrance chemists looking for new smells in and under the rain forest canopies of Latin America, the Amazon, and equatorial Africa. These abundant but almost unknown fragrances, from flowers, leaves, tree bark, mushrooms, even beetles, may eventually find their way into food, perfumes, and pharmaceutical products. Through a technology of scent capture known as "headspace analysis," originally developed in the 1970s, the odor molecules

Fig. 3 Floral odor molecules from rose petals are captured inside a glass globe and then analyzed by computer in this headspace experiment conducted near Plascassier, Grasse.

floating in the air (the "headspace") around a petal or leaf, or any object for that matter, are sucked into an airtight glass globe which has been hermetically placed over the object (figs. 3, 4). The scent molecules are made to pass through a charcoal or silica filter where they become stuck. A sample of the captured molecules is then drawn into a vial and later subjected to gas chromatography and mass spectrometry which separate the molecules into their constituent elements while determining their proportional quantities; in this way, the molecules can, potentially speaking, be synthetically replicated. The molecular structure of the scent, along with a description of its reaction with other molecules and its "hedonics" (the pleasant moods it produces), are then stored in a computer database.[27]

Even the centuries-old dream of capturing the fragrance of skin has not gone unheeded. Despite Montaigne's assertion, borrowed from Plautus, that "the most perfect smell for a woman is to smell of nothing," many are the lovers, poets, perfumers, and scientists who have attempted to discover and describe what the title of a postwar Italian film called the "scent of a woman." Using headspace analysis, Braja Mookherjee, a scientist for International Flavors & Fragrances, an American scent company, and his team have isolated the "body scent of a beautiful girl," as he calls it.[28] This essence of female beauty was derived by analyzing the odors of four fair-skinned women, two of whom were virgins and two "mature" women. They were asked to avoid spicy or odorous foods (onions, garlic, and asparagus) for several days, to bathe with scentless soap, and to refrain from any physical activity that might make them sweat. The epidermal area of investigation—according to Dr. Mookherjee, "the purest zone of the female body"—was identified as the surface of the lower stomach right below the navel; it was here that the glass globe, used in headscape analysis to trap aromas, was placed. Spectrometric examination of the captured scent molecules revealed that one half were identical to the aroma of the lotus flower and the other half similar to the smell of the cotton blossom—in other words, the odor of fresh linen dried in the sun. The scent of a woman thus resembled a blend of lotus and linen.

Perfume and the Plague: The Scent of Epidemics

From ancient times—its earliest appearance in Europe was in Athens in 430 B.C.—to the nineteenth century, bubonic plague, the "Black Death," which killed as much as three-quarters of the population of Asia and Europe in a twenty-year period during the fourteenth century, was thought of primarily as an odor: a noxious smell passing from person to person and house to house, and which only certain prescribed counterodors could defeat. In keeping with the notion that to fight fire one uses fire, fourteenth-century doctors advised the populace to disinfect their homes with strong natural scents and to carry handkerchiefs or sponges soaked in vinegar, especially when going out in the streets. They also counseled their wealthier and more aristocratic patients to wear around the neck, waist, or finger ornate, bejeweled scent boxes in gold or silver containing rare and costly substances like musk or ambergris, the aromas of which were believed to offer protection against the pestilential air. Certain odorous substances, like incense, myrrh, violet, mint, lemon balm, as well as a concoction of sandalwood, camphor, storax, and roses called a "pomme de cedre" (cedar apple), were considered antidotes to the disease and were frequently inhaled (Le Guérer, 295, 127, 130).

Doctors in the sixteenth century had an arsenal of aromatic remedies like cinnamon, rose, civet, orange

Fig. 4 Measuring fragrance dispersion from jasmine petals.

blossom, and musk. To a few physicians, however, these ingredients were hardly strong enough. Does one "tame the force of a lion with that of a lamb" or neutralize the power of "arsenic with that of candied sugar?" one doctor asked in 1617. Of course not, he concluded, because only malodorous and violent odors like those of gunpowder, arsenic, quicklime, turpentine, ammonia, and even animal excrement could battle the stench of plague. While such powerful substances as these were used primarily to disinfect the homes of deceased victims, less corrosive and more aromatic scents were employed to protect healthy adults and decontaminate the everyday objects (linen, fabric, letters) that they had touched. To the bodies of persons of more delicate constitution, like babies and pregnant women,

even more gentle aromas were applied. In treating an infected patient, doctors wore scented gloves, open at the fingertips so as to allow them to take the patient's pulse; they also perfumed their patients' clothing; washed their faces and hands with scented lotions; dabbed their temples, lips and nostrils with perfumed balms; and put scents in their mouths (Le Guérer, 136, 141, 146, 148).

During later epidemics, especially in the seventeenth century, the fumigation of an infected house was generally entrusted to professional perfumers who, after sealing all windows and doors, moved from room to room with a hot pan from which a slowly melting aromatic substance gave off thick plumes of scented smoke. During the plague wars, the perfumer-fumigator had an ally in the plague-doctor, whose protective uniform has to be one of the most outlandish and inefficient costumes ever invented (fig. 5). In all likelihood, it was a "virtual" costume, never actually worn at the time—although the mask does figure in Venice's annual Carnival—since many doctors found it offensive to the dignity of their profession. Designed by Charles Delorme, a court physician, during the 1619 epidemic, the costume, which covered the body from head to foot, was made of black morocco leather; later, a leather mask with glass, gogglelike eyes and topped with a flat hat

Fig. 5 During the plague epidemics that struck Europe, few people would enter a contaminated residence with the exception of fumigators or "parfumeurs" (the word entered the French language in 1528) and plague doctors (shown in this engraving by Fürst from 1656) whose leather clothing and scent-filled mask did little, unfortunately, to ward off the disease.

was added. Protruding grotesquely from the mask was a long ducklike bill, its interior filled with aromatic substances designed to filter and perfume the air which the physician inhaled.[29]

Perceptions of Scent in Culture

What, one may ask, do these complex procedures for warding off plague, for disinfecting interior spaces and household objects, and for protecting physicians behind the "armor" of a sinister leather costume reveal about the ways scent in seventeenth-century French culture was viewed, conceived, used, and, above all, imagined? What set of ideas, beliefs, attitudes, desires, hopes, worries, fears, truths, misconceptions, and moral codes, predominantly unspoken and unconscious, surrounded the theories about (and the use of) perfume during the plague years or, for that matter, during any given period in the history of a society? What different kinds of image systems did perfume express, articulate, and communicate and how did different social groups feel, perceive, and appreciate the sensations inspired by those systems?

Clearly, the use of scent during Europe's many plague epidemics expressed, albeit covertly, an attitude toward disease (it was an airborne odor), toward smell (it could kill but also, at the same time, restore life), toward the body (the science of plants and the knowledge of their essences could neutralize the body's fetid exhalations), toward the city (it was a place of dangerous, corrosive stenches), and toward death (the spirituality of perfume could mask the odors of decomposition). In certain respects, death can be considered the "base note," so to speak, of all perfume base notes. Perfume expresses a desire for sublime beauty, pleasure, and delight, all the more potent and intense for floating on a layer of death and for having been launched from the body (the cadaver-to-be, so to speak) whose future degradation it is the express duty of perfume to disguise. The cluster of images, feelings, and desires traditionally associated with scent intersected with the notions and practices that constituted other cultural image systems: systems associated with the body and the senses; with hygiene, science, and medicine; with pathology and death; with spirituality and religion; and with, of course, everyday life. How men and women nourished, clothed, scented, exposed, purged, protected, and controlled their bodies; how they exchanged and communicated information about them; and how they looked upon their own sensuality—either privileging the higher "social" senses (sight and hearing) as identified with the intellectual worldview of the upper classes or debasing the lower "animal" senses (smell and touch) associated with peasants and workers—are indispensable, as Alain Corbin writes, for understanding the "social cleavages" and the social practices that run like an underground stream through culture. Embedded in the sensory practice and behavior of social groups, a particular attitude and ideology are hidden: "Within perfume bottles and around the lips," the philosopher Michel Serres writes apropos of smell and taste, "there lies an entire culture."[30]

The nineteenth-century perfumer, Eugène Rimmel, casts his net wider in declaiming that beyond the mere culture of perfume "there is a *civilization* of perfumes." The "frontier between the perceived and the unperceived" and "the norms which decree what is spoken and what is left unspoken" in a culture (or civilization for that matter), writes Corbin—for example, the determination of modesty, the definition of obscenity, the understanding of transgression, the recognition of what is considered shocking, the protocols of flirtation and seduction, the practice of sexual intercourse—have their own history which subtly, silently, and unconsciously merges with the history of a sense like smell and that of a sensual substance like perfume. The routine rituals, habits, and compulsions of everyday life—those mechanical, automatic gestures clouded over by the impervious fog of repetitiveness—

have a history which, often left unrecorded, is consequently lost. "The banal is frequently silent," Corbin observes. This is because the ordinary would have automatically become *extra-ordinary* had it not been considered insignificant and ephemeral, had it not been quickly forgotten or, as was often the case, had it been consciously perceived in the first place. When all is said and done, the essential aspect of banal daily experience is, as the historian Guy Thuillier reminds us, its vast muteness.[31]

Yet, such silent banality has its own stirring eloquence; it speaks volumes about the formation of what Corbin calls "the social imagination" and about the nature of the perfumed imagination as well, which the banal everydayness of life covertly articulates and represents. "The experience of life reveals that what is not spoken, what is not written, what is ineffable, is often more important than what is spoken or written: in particular, desire, pleasure, suffering, sadness, inner thoughts, and dreams," Thuillier writes. Thus, a drop of perfume is much more than a mere drop of perfume. In addition to the pleasure and evocativeness of its fragrance, it bears witness to a complicated nexus of social practices, moral attitudes, sensual desires, physical impulses, instinctive gestures, interpretative acts, and codes of sensory behavior. An entire world—"a field of actions, operations, gazes, and desires," Yves Pelicier notes—arises and takes wing on the aromatic cloud of scent. Within the spiritual essence of scent lies the spirit of its time. The "language" of fragrant perfume gives voice to the language of a culture, for it is an inescapable truth, as Thuillier remarks, that "facts of everyday life are social facts laden with meaning." In every historical era, the fragments of a sensory worldview and the actual forms by which it is put into practice are left behind. These remnants constitute what Corbin calls a "sensory archeology," which must be pieced together to construct an "idea" of the ways a particular society, class, and culture sensed (and lived) its everyday world and the daily ways it used materials and designed artifacts in order to experience these sensations.[32]

Ascending and expanding into the atmosphere of this culture, the emotional and subjective associations which perfume expresses penetrate and mix with a host of other socio-cultural phenomena. Perfume determines and is determined by social attitudes toward odors (the kinds of smells deemed pleasant or repugnant), or by social norms regarding the spoken and the unspoken (silence about smells was most often the rule), or by the social conventions dictating perfume fashion (in the eighteenth and nineteenth centuries scents were applied to fabric—linen, handkerchiefs, dresses, and the like—but never to the skin). Standards of smell, for example, changed considerably among the upper and middle classes from the late eighteenth century onward; after 1750 the fashion for the natural effaced the heavy, intoxicating, animal-based odors which had been favored. Strategies of deodorization began to proliferate. To the eighteenth-century bourgeois perfume was an agent of dissipation and immorality. Did it not just disappear into thin air, thus revealing the extent to which it represented a preference for pleasure over work and for waste over the solid accumulation of capital? Turning up its collective nose at odors that earlier periods had willingly tolerated, the nineteenth century encouraged new attitudes and comportments toward perfume, bathing, and codes of public health; it also poetically glorified smell, according to Corbin, as "the privileged instrument of recollection." The modesty and prudishness of the mid-nineteenth century, moreover, dictated that women of good taste and good standing wear only simple floral scents; those fragrant with heavy animal-based ("animalic," as they are called) or jasmine fragrances were marked as belonging to the marginal world of prostitutes and courtesans. Consequently, the preference for floral over animal scents constituted a system of signs which offered social and moral instruction in the protocols of amorous conduct and sensory behavior sanctioned by nineteenth-century culture: in particular, the rules or manners of courtship or flirtatiousness deemed appropriate or inappropriate in various social encounters between men and women. The cultural associations evoked by perfume were closely tied to those images of femininity sanctioned or rejected by society, to those protocols determining the presentation and representation of the female body, to those conventions regarding dress and hygiene, and to those canons of fashion dictating the "right" or "wrong" way to stylishly clothe or expose the body. Moreover, perfume reflected (and still reflects today) the ideas women had or were compelled to have about their bodies, their sexuality, and their power or lack of power within society.[33] The representation of perfume in literature, art, music, advertising, and design through the nineteenth and twentieth centuries mirrors, as we shall see, the social and cultural transformations in the daily lives of women, the evolution in the power relations between the sexes, and the changes in the ideology and imagery of femininity.

The image system associated with perfume is saturated with desire; the representations, expressions, and modes of implementation, which project this system into the real world of everyday experience, are infused with longing and fantasy. The presence of desire is not in itself essential to the existence of perfume's unique image system. What is important is that this desire remain unfulfilled, that longing keep the fires of desire permanently enflamed, and that the satisfaction of desire be no more than a passing lull in a storm of passionate need. The image system unconsciously evoked by perfume exists because desire perpetually remains desire. Otherwise, it would cease to be what in truth it is: namely, an imaginary cluster of images, the very illusion of which creates its reality. "The value of an image," the French philosopher Gaston Bachelard writes, "is measured by the extent of its *imaginary* aura." Perfume has "infinite resonances," he observes, because scents "bind memories to desires, an enormous

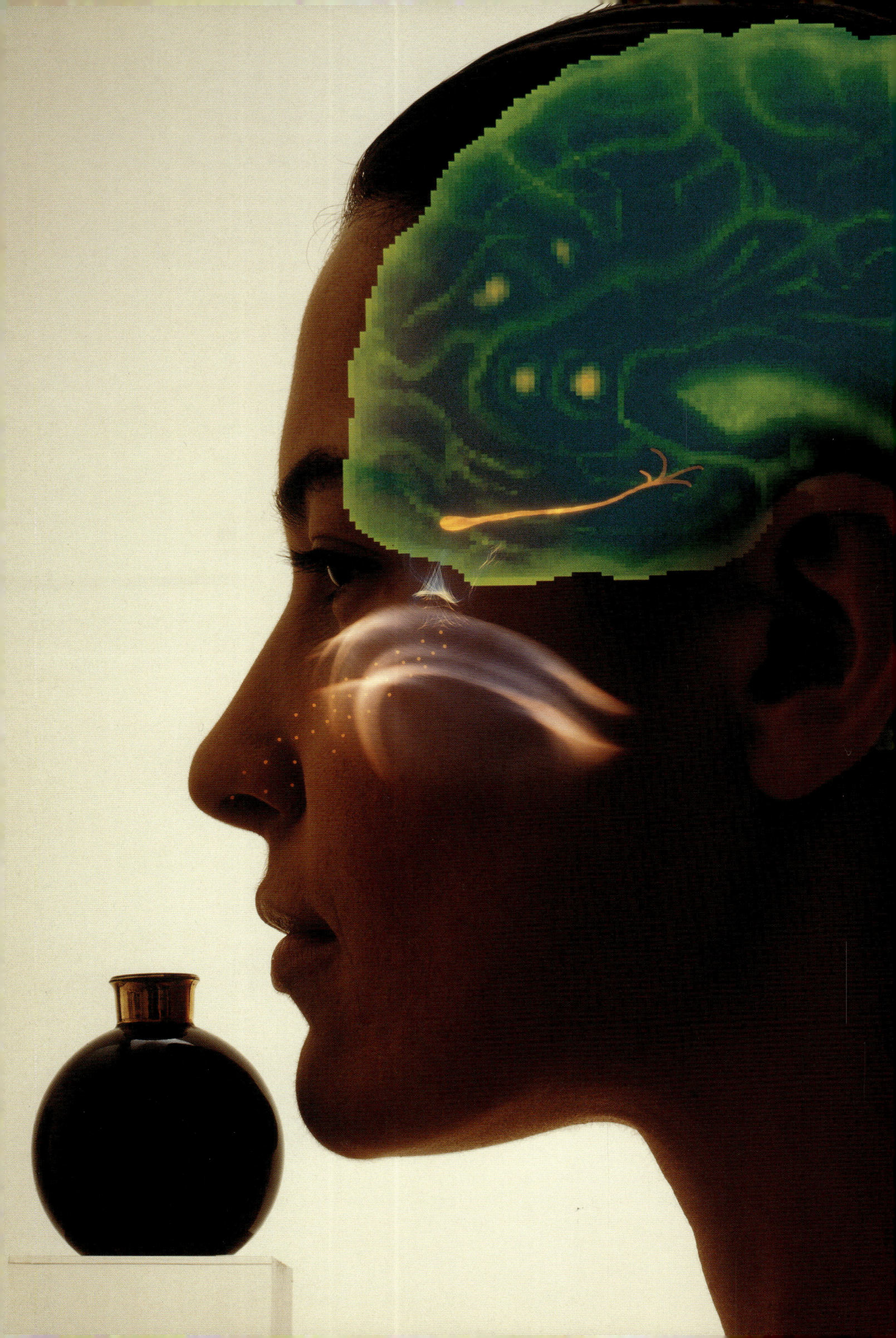

past to an immense and unformulated future."[34] By means of its various representations, the scented imagination performs a drama of unsatisfied desire, all the more ephemeral and volatile for the aura of irreversible loss that ultimately envelops it.

Experiencing Perfume: The Mechanics of Smell

If, as Italo Calvino writes in his short story on perfume, "Everything is first perceived by the nose, everything is within the nose, the world is the nose" (p. 71), then odor, smell, perfume, fragrance, aroma, and bouquet are primal experiences. Physiologically, they animate a world and initiate an experience, which is physical and spiritual, sensory and mental, affective and mnemonic. The mechanics of smell present a dramatic, highly complex, and still imperfectly understood network of rapid movements, connections, transmissions, bursts, firings, and charges, as the following simplified scientific description reveals. Moving swiftly through the nasal passages where they are warmed and moistened, odor molecules stimulate tiny hairlike cilia at the ends of millions of sensory nerve cells embedded in the mucus layer, known as the nasal epithelium, lining the nasal cavities. The epithelium of each nostril contains about 30,000 olfactory sensory neurons per square millimeter and between three to five million sensory cells—the sheepdog, by way of comparison, has 220 million olfactory cells. These sensory cells are the only nerve cells in the body with a capacity for regeneration, which occurs every four to eight weeks. Once they touch the olfactory cilia, the aqueous odor molecules become lodged in microscopic cavities on the surface of each cilium, a process of binding determined by the similarity, the precise "fit," between the chemical constitution of the cavity and that of the molecule. The identification or recognition, if it can be called that, of various odor molecules is thus determined chemically.[35]

Once lodged in its appropriate hollow, the odor molecule stimulates the receptor neuron connected to the cilium which is now its home. This initiates the firing of a pattern of electrical charges which travel along the axons connecting the olfactory sensory neurons in the epithelium to the olfactory bulbs (fig. 6). Located behind the bridge of the nose, the olfactory bulbs are protuberances of the brain extending into the warm air of the nasal cavity. The neuronal charges speeding along the axons pass through two synapses; no other sense (neither vision, nor touch, nor audition) involves as few connections. No larger than a dime in size, each olfactory bulb assimilates and processes the olfactory messages at certain locations or "switch boxes," called glomeruli, where the signals are interpreted according to the similarity of the odorant receptors they express. For example, the multiple odor molecules emitted by a rose are separated on the glomeruli (according to the research of Linda Buck and Richard Axel whose study of olfactory circuitry earned them the Nobel Prize in medicine for 2004) into distinct, spatially separate bits of information; this information is then relayed to the olfactory cortex, which analyzes it and then associates it with other kinds of information. (The olfactory cortex, for example, can distinguish the odor of burning leaves from that of burning tires, the smell of a predator from that of a mate.) From here the electrical signals travel directly to the brain along the pathway of the olfactory nerve which extends from the bulbs to the limbic system of the paleo-cortex, the older brain, involved with memory and emotion. Contact with the limbus region is direct. Olfactory messages, unlike signals from the other sensory organs, which must first pass through the switching station known as the dorsal thalamus, reach the paleocortex with a speed that accounts for the lightning rapidity of odor-triggered memories. Upon reaching the limbus, certain odors provoke it to activate the hypothalamus and pituitary gland, setting in motion the production of hormones, a process that affects the autonomic nervous system and regulates the body's sexual, gustatory, metabolic, respiratory, and thermal functions. Through the limbic system, olfactory information also reaches the neo-cortex, the part of the brain involved with the higher functions of intellect, language, and conscious thought. The olfactory messages are here further refined and integrated with information coming from the other senses. Although it is still not known how the brain ultimately interprets the signals sent to it by the olfactory receptors, it is clear, nonetheless, that this interacting circuitry of stimuli, signals, discharges, electrochemical pulses, and codes causes an intense experience to surge into being. Touched by the outside air, the receptor neurons in the cilia and the olfactory bulbs permit the brain to have direct, physical contact with the world.[36]

Only where the senses operate and sensations arise can experience be said to begin. The term "experience" is, the French sociologist, Michel Maffesoli, writes, "an open-sesame linked . . . to the *primacy of the senses.*" This is because the experience of perfume depends upon the reality of a sensual and hedonistic system of powerfully imagined or remembered experiences. Odors, as the narrator of Patrick Süskind's novel *Perfume: The Story of a Murderer* observes, have a "power of persuasion stronger than that of words, appearances, emotions, or will. The persuasive power of an odor cannot be fended off, it enters into us like breath into our lungs, it fills us up, imbues us totally. There is no remedy for it" (p. 98). Perfume appropriates what is imaginary to heighten what is sensual, and it controls the sensual to intensify the imaginary. The experience of the scented imagination is, as Maffesoli would admit, not a sum of individual situations, but "an accumulation of collective facts, most of the time unconscious, which mark the boundaries of life in society."[37]

Opposite:
Fig. 6 To reach the brain's center of memory and emotion (the paleocortex), odor molecules stimulate the sensory cells lining the nasal passages, activating them to send electrical charges to the olfactory bulbs. After processing the information, the olfactory bulbs relay the neuronal signals along the olfactory nerve to the brain's limbic system, which controls memory and feeling.

Perfume and the Representation of History and Culture

Style, goes the cliché, makes the man, but it also makes the culture. "Dress (*la toilette*) is the expression of society," Honoré de Balzac remarked in 1830. The erudite or elegant man, he observed, who seeks in every epoch to study "the clothes of a people would write the most vivid and nationally true history." Seventy years later, Octave Uzanne, an expert on French beauty and fashion, offered a similar observation. Dress, he said, is the most eloquent and vocal of styles because it expresses the essence of mankind, of "man with his political opinions, of man with the text of his existence"; as for woman, her dress, he continued, is "the visible paraphrase of her psychic state." Insofar as it is a phenomenon inseparable from dress and fashion and is a social reality essential to culture and civilization, perfume eloquently expresses the psychological needs, social values, and symbolic associations of its age. Testimony to this fact comes from several different quarters. The twentieth-century writer Colette strongly asserted that "perfume must represent the melodic theme, the clear, direct expression, of the trends and tastes of our epoch." Alain Corbin observes that "to exclude the sense of smell from the history of sensory perceptions simply because of the infatuation with the prestige of sight and hearing" not only risks marginalizing the profoundly eloquent interior life—the dreams, fantasies, and desires—of a large group of individuals in any given historical age; it also rejects the idea that "the history of the mignonette, lily, and rose is just as informative as the history of coal." For the Russian-born French perfumer Constantin Weriguine the ubiquitous presence of the ambient culture intensifies the conception of a scent: "Whatever ingredients the perfumer has at his disposal, his creative sense will be tightly bound to the breath of his era and the site of his work. For this reason, French perfumes breathe Paris."[38]

Although at a given moment in time perfume may offer a representation of a culture, is this representation representative? Despite the intensity with which perfume captures and expresses the hidden spirit of an age and despite the complex interrelated system of tastes, beliefs, values, and practices invisibly coalescing around the reality of scent, can perfume provide an accurate and meaningful historical reflection of the ordinary customs of a past society? Such questions abound. Given the confused immediateness of everyday life in which so many trends, styles, and ideas in a present moment of time connect and then disconnect randomly and impulsively, given the ephemeral, evasive, and subjective quality of odors, given the fundamental ineffability and "untranslatability" of scents into visual, auditory, and semantic forms, given the connection between perfume and what is fundamentally imaginary (desire, fantasy, dream), and given, finally, that perfume's image system remains mute, unconscious, and unknown to those who, blindly attracted to it, would be hard-pressed to articulate its allure—is perfume a faithful and accurate representation of culture, especially the culture of fifty or 150 years ago? Is there a seamless link between the use of perfume in daily life and its representation in literary, artistic, and cultural forms of expression? Does literature, for example, offer proof of certain social practices? Corbin is not certain. Poetry, as well as fiction, he explains, is "a source for the history of image systems . . . But it does not confirm certain practices," if only for the reason that the writer may have embroidered what he or she had witnessed. Yet, literary descriptions of the material objects and social practices of everyday life do have the kind of gravitas or authenticity associated with the telling detail or the repeated gesture; they are not merely ghosts or hallucinations. However, Corbin is right to counsel caution here; the hunt for the missing link between an actual cultural practice and its literary or historical representation must be conducted meticulously, if only because, as the protagonist of a novel by the Portuguese writer José Saramago remarks, "history was real life at the time when it could not yet be called history." An everyday activity or social ritual described in a novel needs to be confirmed, if possible, by other, primarily historical, sources of cultural evidence. "A lot of life," observes the historian Eugen Weber, "is about things so trivial that we do not bother to record them— only sometimes to note their absence, as with manners. But the *petite histoire* [that of daily life] is made of details, and it can surely help to make vaster and more important processes clear."[39]

The history of the images and attitudes, which invisibly, covertly, even odorlessly permeate the air of the everyday past—for example, the unspoken habits and practices associated with eating, dressing, lovemaking, sleeping, the consciousness of time, the awareness of silence, and other aspects of material culture—is, indeed, often beyond representation. Such an "archeology of the everyday" is arbitrary, fragmented, porous, and marginal; there is no there there. It is a history of what in ordinary life has no history. For the historian this can be disorienting because the history of the everyday, writes Thuillier, has "no numbers, no guaranteed sense of an evolution, no precise dates, no global explanations"; one has no choice but "blindly to feel one's way, avoiding traps, and putting faith in one's intuition." This is a history at the margins of the historical, at the frontier separating the remembered from the forgotten, the memorable from the trivial. It draws up from the deep and dark well of the past "the unspoken, the unseen, the unknown . . . the unreported, the insignificant, [and] the unsaid." It seeks to make the implicit explicit and the tacit obvious; it labors to give voice to what is mute, to endow with narrative coherence what has never before been shaped by language or made meaningful through narration. This kind of history offers a chronicle of the private intimacies of the everyday: the cares and worries (about family, food, shelter, fatigue, the body), the desires and pleasures (offered by money, sex, clothes, childhood), the experiences of fate (as determined by illness, suffering, war, death), and the transformations brought about by technological innovations (like water, electricity, the telephone, and the automobile). Ultimately, however, this is an imaginary history because it attempts to encircle what cannot be embraced, to give narrative form to what has never been narrated, and to represent the unseizable and "invisible everyday" ("l'invisible quotiden").[40]

Scents and Senses of the Past

A diligent and concentrated effort, Thuillier argues, must be made to historicize what is beyond history, to imagine what is imaginary in culture. Certain historical realities generate their own particular image systems, and in this unconscious proliferation of beliefs and practices a temporal coherence or continuity can be identified. Indeed, perfume can give a representative representation of the past. It has its own history, which coincides, sometimes centrally, other times tangentially, with the history of the culture which it mirrors and in which it participates just as activities like sleeping, dreaming, touching, or walking reflect the mental attitudes and social behavior of a culture. Perfume was part, moreover, of the lives of certain social classes and groups which used it according to their own conventions, practices, and modes of appreciation. The visual perception of the world—the way forms in space were viewed—also has a history all its own, the narrative of which is grounded not so much in a sequence of events as in a covert network of attitudes and beliefs: the favoring of certain geographical scenes or landscapes at different historical moments; the preference for certain colors, lines, or shapes (the straight, the curved, the vertical, the circular, the arabesque) in the everyday life of the 1920s as opposed to the 1860s; and the retraining and disciplining of the gaze through new inventions (the camera, the microscope, the telescope), new sources of light (electricity), a new concern for eye care, a new perception of speed (the train, the airplane), new cultural images (advertising, cinema, TV), or new ways of living (the eight-hour workday, the greater availability of leisure time, and so on).[41]

Questions about the historical reliability of the representation of the cultural past as expressed by systems of images and beliefs relate to the art of perfumery as well, although the difficulties encountered here are less historical than aesthetic. How does the perfumer re-present the natural fragrance of rose or jasmine; how can he or she capture the essence of its vapor in an altogether different (namely, liquid) form? It goes without saying that chemical means exist for duplicating such a fragrance and that processes of extraction can, in certain instances, be used to appropriate the flower's inherent scent. In this case, the fragrance of rose or jasmine is not as much a representation of the flower as its emanation captured and preserved in another form and medium although, as is true of any kind of conversion, something is always lost (and gained) in translation; the liquid perfume does not smell precisely the way the flower in its natural environment does.

Of course, the perfumer does more than just replicate or capture already existing aromas. The idea or image or silhouette of a scent, which suddenly appears as a precise odor in the perfumer's olfactory imagination, in the same way that a chord of notes might resound in a musician's ear or a harmony of colors might come alive in the painter's optical unconscious, demands to be transformed into reality. Similarly, the musician may give voice to the chord by noting it on a score and then playing it on a piano to verify the harmony; the painter may express a sensation of colors by dabbing paint on a canvas and then shaping the juxtaposed colors into forms and lines. The perfumer may give body to the concept of a scent, to the "idea" that comes to him or her as an odor, by mentally and sensuously imagining new blends of primary ingredients, some never before combined in a similar manner, which the perfumer, thanks to his or her vast olfactory memory, knowledge of raw materials, and artistic intuition, suspects will blend harmoniously with one another. In each case, the composer, the artist, and the perfumer proceed—by means of trial and error and the impulsive, yet knowledgeable juxtapositions of notes, colors, and odors—from an initial sound, an embryonic vision, a remembered smell to the creation of new combinations and configurations. An act of mental composition no less auditory, visual, or olfactory for having taken place in the mind initiates creation. The work of art, therefore, will be much more than the re-presentation of the original idea, for the latter has been extended, corrected, shaped, and even sometimes discarded, as the musician, painter, and perfumer work at giving it form and reality.

Basic Elements of Perfume Creation

First and foremost, the creation of a scent takes place in the mind. Yet this "concept" is paradoxically "neither an idea, nor an image, but a smell," as the perfumer Jacques Polge, director of the Chanel perfume laboratories since 1979 and the creator of Égoïste, Allure, Coco Mademoiselle, and Chance, among other scents, has observed. Or more precisely, it is "an idea that has a form, has an odor": the odor of "lightness or freedom," for example.[42] The process may take off from a smell the perfumer remembers from the past, or from the stored memory of primary perfume ingredients (jasmine, rose, tuberose, etc.), or the accords the perfumer tends to prefer and has already used in the past, or from a family of related, hallmark scents associated with the signature style of a particular perfume house

Jean-Paul Guerlain, creator of Guerlain's *Chant d'Arômes*, *Habit Rouge*, *Samsara*, and other scents; Chartres, France.

(such as Guerlain's perfumes from the 1880s to the 1920s with their oriental-ambery or floral-sweet blend of natural, synthetic, and animal ingredients), or from a note belonging to a great classic scent of the past, or from a striking new fragrance of the present, both of which express in different ways the fashion of their times. As in all art, imitation is the highest form of flattery, and the preference in a given historical period for a particular style of scent, whether light or heavy, ephemeral or tenacious, innocent or erotic, may determine the scent-idea that comes into the perfumer's mind as might also the historical influence of certain perfumes: for example, the different reinterpretations given over the years to the composition of Coty's *Émeraude* (1921), which inspired Estée Lauder's *Youth Dew* more than thirty years later.

A perfume is always an expression of its time; it is, according to Polge, nothing less than fashion become poetry: "la poésie de la mode." A perfumer must therefore take into consideration the fashion of the historical moment from which his or her perfume comes into being: the ways it confirms or resists the reigning style or the ways it attempts to establish its distinctiveness (its "signature") among the scents of the time. The perfumer may decide, for example, to present the sensual or sexual constituents of a fragrance differently, using new combinations of wood and spice notes or new accords of musk. A so-called "classic" perfume is even more distinctive because it has the gift of speaking, as it were, both to its own historical time and to the future. However, the perfumer cannot help but create a perfume which, despite its link to the past, will always express the present and the continually evolving idea of femininity inherent to this present. Like a painter

whose vision of the landscape, although influenced by Monet, moves in accord with her or his own idiosyncratic way of seeing and interpreting the world, the perfumer only borrows from the styles of the past so as to give these styles an unexpected and innovative turn. Perfume depends "on a culture," Polge remarks. "To come up with something new in perfume creation, you have to be aware of what already exists."[43]

A particular association of images and feelings is present as well in the perfumer's mind as he or she conceives and combines odors. This is a constellation of concepts and smells arising from the other odors he or she knows intimately: those she or he has favored in the creation of earlier perfumes; those belonging to the evolving history of modern perfumery; and those emanating from childhood, from a landscape, from memory, or from the presence of a loved one. As the trial-and-error composition of a scent progresses within the perfumer's mind, he or she may wish from time to time to test the idea by impregnating thin strips of white blotter paper, called "keys" ("*touches*" in French), with the fragrance under study. Or he or she may apply the scent directly to the skin so as to sense how the fragrance is evolving, verify its structure and harmony, and, if need be, modify the titration of its ingredients. These "essais" represent a trying-out of the olfactory idea. The perfumer, as Jean-Paul Guerlain describes the creative process, "turns around and around and even inside the scent. My dreams come to me as a succession of olfactory visions. A perfume does not impose itself; it must translate a precise emotion. After much groping in the dark the perfume begins to resemble the image which I had forged abstractly in my mind."[44]

Flowers with and without Odors

Among the many different kinds of odors available to the perfumer are scents that are emanations, not representations or interpretations, of flowers; these scents come from a flower's natural oils which have been removed, filtered, and purified through what in some instances are centuries-old processes of expression, maceration, distillation, volatilization, cooling, and evaporation. The flower's petals produce a scented oil, the oil hardens into a solid, called a *concrete*, and the concrete, washed with solvents, becomes a liquid, called an *absolute*, the purest essence of the flower. (Of course, small constitutional and olfactory differences, caused by trace residues of solvents, even of the purest and highest quality, will occur between the aroma of the most carefully produced absolute and that of the flower in its natural habitat.) Thanks to advances in chemistry, today there are many more potential natural ingredients for a perfumer to use. While only six jasmine compounds were known before 1940, there are now over 200, and the number continues to grow. The discoveries of chemists have been vitally important to the development of modern-day fragrances. Working to uncover "new" odorous elements in sometimes ordinary natural phenomena—odors that have never been perceived in isolation before but have always been present—the chemist replicates with precision the newly discovered scent molecules, resynthesizing them so that they emit the same odor as they do in nature. This is a technique of re-creation, of duplication; it does not involve the invention of a "synthetic" or unreal substitute. The term "synthetic product," Polge observes, is unfortunate because "people hear 'synthesis' and they immediately think 'synthetic,'" which is not the same thing. "Products made directly from flowers, like rose essence and rose absolute," he continues,

> have always existed, created either through extraction or distillation; these are rose components with which we have been acquainted for a long time. But there are also molecules of fairly recent discovery, one-thousandths of the smell of a rose [what are called, for example, *damascones*]: the nearly metallic, even fruity side of the flower which chemists have succeeded in giving us.[45]

The perfumer also has at her or his disposal odors based on flowers whose fragrances cannot be captured or directly removed from their petals or blooms. Lily-of-the-valley, lilac, freesia, honeysuckle, gardenia, and orchid cannot, by distillation or other forms of conversion and extraction, be successfully and aesthetically converted into a perfume essence. Sometimes, the heat of the extractive processes; the chemical reactions triggered by the addition of solvents like ethyl alcohol, benzene, and petroleum ether; the inherent fragility of the flower; or the rapid volatility of its scent weaken, degrade, even destroy the odor, making capture difficult if not impossible. Sometimes, the odors, once captured, are so disappointing that perfumers decide that such efforts do not reward the intense labor and high cost required. Yet, these recalcitrant natural scents do figure into perfume composition either because they have been replicated synthetically (a kind of chemical clone) or because they can be approximated through a combination of other scents. Gardenia, as found in Chanel's *Gardénia* (1925) or Anick Goutal's *Gardénia Passion* (1990), is not the scent of the natural flower, which cannot be successfully extracted. Yet descriptions of these perfumes promise that the heavy, intoxicating, sensual aroma of the flower is very much present, as indeed it is, although this is achieved by other than purely natural means. While Anick Goutal's fragrance is characterized as "a heady harmony of pure gardenia," Chanel's *Gardénia* is described as "burst[ing] with the unforgettable essence of the finest French garden" and, in an advertisement from 1935–1939, as a product of "the south of France where grow the most fragile, exquisite and lyrically fragrant of gardenias. To Chanel belongs the secret of reproducing their perfume, flower-fresh."[46]

Jacques Polge, creator of Chanel perfumes (*Égoïste, Allure, Chance*); Neuilly sur Seine.

Besides the fragrances that are direct emanations of flowers (those captured and purified floral essences) and those synthetisized scents which duplicate and replace natural scents, modern perfumery also employs fragrances of flowers that, curiously, have no fragrance whatsoever. The arum lily, poppy, tulip, peony, fern, primrose, and lotus are all odorless;[47] yet their names are often included in the descriptions of perfume creations. What, one may ask, does an odorless flower add to the composition of a perfume? Clearly, it cannot be fragrance, since the flower does not have any. Rather, the flower brings to the perfume a reality more insubstantial and otherworldly than scent itself. It contributes the spirituality, symbolism, and poetry of the word evoking it or the image enveloping it. It lends to the perfume composition those imaginary qualities, dreamlike associations, and cultural identifications which are inseparably attached to its history, name, and use in different societies. This constellation of images and ideas is yet another "ingredient" in the perfume's composition, either born at the time the original concept comes into being or, more likely, added after the fact and after the act of creation, when the naming, advertising, and labeling of the scent take precedence. Once the perfumer has given the fragrance its final form, other players enter the scene, whose task it is to commercialize the perfume by describing it in words and images that will distinguish it from other scents past and present. The so-called "presence" of the fundamentally odorless lotus blossom works, for example, more evocatively as a name than as a floral scent; it gives the perfume with which it is blended a Buddhist resonance, an air of tranquility and spiritual well-being coming from the symbolism of the flower itself. Similarly, the primrose adds no odorous note to a scent but in alluding to spring expands the evocatively poetic aura of the perfume. The arum, on the other hand, may contribute to the fragrance it composes nothing more than an aesthetic image of a beautiful flower or the poetic beauty of the syllables forming its name. Finally, the fern, which is odorless, provokes images and memories of dank, mossy, shadowy forests.

Strange as it may seem, odorless flowers can indeed come to have a "scent" when they are combined not with a perfume but with its idea, description, and text; naming is paramount, as are advertising and packaging. "Today," the perfumer Jean-Claude Ellena notes, "we are into a perfumery of concepts where the image is more important than the scent. Perfumers only want to illustrate an idea, a ❧ lifestyle." This is a truth self-consciously testified to by *Viktor & Rolf, le parfum* (1996), an elegantly, even artistically, presented perfume bottle containing a "fragrance" that has no scent and that, with a postmodernist panache and irony characteristic of the two Dutch conceptualist fashion designers (Viktor Hörsting and Rolf Snoeren), turns this novelty to creative and economic advantage.[48] It is the image and the concept, not the scent, which compose this perfume, turning it into a playful game in which what is absent (a true perfume smell) is also present (in the form of a conventional perfume bottle and name). In fact, the absence of perfume is precisely what the perfume sells. Disappearance becomes a commodity, an object of consumerist desire, like consumption itself endlessly trying to embrace what disappears into thin air: the always

Fig. 7 Girl decanting perfumes, fresco, first-century A.D. In first-century Rome, according to the naturalist Pliny, the Elder, the most expensive and luxurious scents were a Balm of Judea and different varieties of cinnamon. Romans used perfumes immoderately, scenting their horses and dogs as well as their military banners. The emperor Nero had more than a year's supply of incense burned at the funeral of his wife, Poppaea.

unfulfilling, yet sought-after object whose reality is short-lived because what is desired is not really the object but the inexhaustible idea that endless desire signifies.

Having faced the difficulties inherent to the duplication, replication, and representation of scents, the perfumer (and the consumer) must confront one final dilemma. How can one interpret or imagine, let alone smell and perceive, a scent that is purely imaginary, a fantasy fragrance with no source or origin in nature and with no referent other than its name or the text describing it: a perfume, that is to say, so conceptual as to be virtual, so imaginary that it must exist first as language, as word? Kenzo's fragrance called *Flower* (2000) is composed of the scent of "poppy springing miraculously from asphalt," a bizarre juxtaposition of the floral and the urban. The concept-perfume *Comme des Garçons 3*, created by the Japanese couturier Rei Kawakubo, contains an ingredient called "volcano flower." The absence of a real scent to replicate and of an actual botanical reality to represent calls into question the role of figuration in perfume design. The image of the volcano flower is visual not olfactory, metaphoric not realistic, poetic not literal. Its abstractness demands that first and foremost it be perceived in the mind's eye, conceptualized as an image of bursting, boiling red-hot magma paradoxically combining with that of a flower's cool freshness. Where indeed, one may ask, does this flower grow? Not, surely, in the sterile ash or the rock-hardened lava at the lip of an active volcano where the temperature alone would incinerate it. The ingredient could, comments Mark Buxton, the scent's creator, "have just as easily been called moon flower or black flower … because the idea was to keep away from a figurative composition and to translate the original and minimalist world of Rei Kawakubo's fashion." An abstract, even deconstructionist, fashion style is matched by an equally conceptual and fictional perfume. "We let ourselves be carried away by the image," Buxton continues, "asking ourselves what indeed would a volcano flower smell like. Not fruit, not wood, not iodine … By elimination the idea of an accord based on rose oxide (metallic in odor), greenness, tar, balsams, and spices slowly imposed itself." Thus, a series of free associations around the paradox of a mineral, inorganic flower (possibly volcanic, possibly lunar) led to the concept-scent Buxton created: a "presence in abstraction," as Giorgio Armani once called perfume.[49] Of an equally symbolic, imaginary, and above all visual nature as the volcano flower are the odors of the "coral flower" and "the flower of mother-of-pearl" conceived by the perfumer Michel Almeirac for Rochas's *Aquawoman* (2002). Where in nature could one experience these non-existent fragrances? Certainly not underwater where inhaling would bring instant death.

It is hard to be too critical of these contemporary inventors of fictional scents like *Aquawoman* (or its masculine sequel *Aquaman*), because their creations are not any more imaginary, conceptual, or faith-based than the four different odors of sanctity Saint Theresa of Ávila's body was said to emit. Of primary importance here is not the smell but the vision—of the refreshing zest, saltiness, and opalescence of the sea, of the purity and holiness of the saint—that the odor is charged with calling into being, even though the visual evocation of the ocean will in due course cause the sea's salty smell to rise into consciousness. The goal is not to call to mind scents but images and their myriad associations, in the hope that the poetic resonance of a name like "coral flower"—with its evocation of the splendor of reefs and the magnificence of marine life, even that of the mermaid rechristened as "aquawoman"—will give birth to a new fragrance, one existing solely in and through the medium of language. Naming coincides here with creation, and perfume, as a result, is sometimes more a poem than an aroma, more a word than a fragrance, more a concept than a sensation, and more a creation of advertising than a sensual experience of smell.

Fragrance in Art

Seeing, touching, tasting, hearing, and smelling an odor represent a fusion of the senses and an overlapping of perceptions that French poets like Baudelaire, Rimbaud, and the symbolists attempted to initiate. Yearning for a "mystic blend of senses mine, / Fused in one perfect harmony! / Her voice, a fragrant perfume fine; / Her breath, the sweetest melody" ("Tout Entière"), Baudelaire dreams of a scent that will literally sing to his soul and of perfumes "fresh and cool, like babies' skin, / Mellow as oboes, green as meadows" ("Correspondences"). Rimbaud, who hears vowels as colors—"e" is white, "o" is blue—sees perfumes as "black" ("Le Bateau ivre") or "red" ("Métropolitan"). Describing the telling sign of a secret tryst betrayed by the lingering traces of a vocal scent, the sixteenth-century poet John Donne calls to the bar "a loud perfume, which at my entrance cryed."[50] Determined to represent the physical experience of perfume, these poets, as well as other artists, painters, and musicians, use sound, word, sight, color, and touch—sensory phenomena that trigger their artistic response to the world—to reveal what it means, imaginatively speaking, to hear a scent, to see its color, to taste its flavor, and to touch its body.

Fragrance in Painting, Photography, and Still Life

The celebration of light and intimacy in an instant trembling with the possibility of timelessness, as Bonnard's *Le Cabinet de Toilette* represents it, transforms scent, as we have seen, into a shimmering radiance. Fragrance and the sensations of warmth and well-being it occasions are given color, form, and spatiality. The invisible floating whirls and arabesques of perfume are perceived through the medium of light. Despite Bonnard's sensually luminous figuration—it is one of the few paintings to evoke the effects of perfume—and despite Baudelaire's efforts to dream of perfumes emanating from sights, sounds, and tastes, the visualizing of olfactory sensations reveals, more often than not, the limits of representation. Many are the images that realistically portray a woman in the act of applying perfume or cosmetics to her body. A fresco in the Villa Farnesina (an outstanding example of early-sixteenth-century Italian Renaissance architecture) shows a first-century Roman woman pouring perfume into a vial (fig. 7, see page 36).[51] In the late nineteenth century the French artist Georges Seurat in *Jeune femme qui se poudre* (1888–1890) uses a pointillist style to create a vibrant portrait of his mistress at her dressing table, powder puff in hand, looking at her face in a mirror in front of which stand two perfume bottles. A more ritualistic and orientalist figuration is John Singer Sargent's *Fumée d'ambre gris* (Smoke of Ambergris) from 1880 (fig. 9). The painting shows the intense concentration, composure, and inwardness of a woman completely enrobed in white, her head enveloped by the canopy of a shawl extended like a sail to trap the fragrant smoke arising from an incense burner at her feet. The grace, with which the woman holds out the shawl to the rising incense, and the pure whiteness of her robe and of the marble walls around her, as well as of the smoke floating upward from the silver perfume burner, have an elegant purity which captures the sacred spirituality of perfume. Similarly ritualistic, although more blatantly excessive and hyperbolic in its overwrought representation of the rapture of scent, is an oil painting by the English artist and illustrator Vera Willoughby, one of a series of steamy scenes of harem life she painted in the 1920s. In the work, called *The Perfume of Ecstasy* (fig. 10), thick serpentine coils of spiraling incense have so intoxicated a half-naked woman kneeling before the statue of a demonic god that she throws her head back and elevates her breasts with her hands in a trancelike gesture of ecstatic possession and self-surrender. Under the influence of fragrant incense, the woman becomes, like perfume itself, an offering to the gods. Willoughby's depiction reveals the outward, physical manifestations of perfume possession. While the woman in Sargent's painting reveals the dignity, composure, and introversion associated with prayer and meditation—she is as spiritually folded in on herself as she is physically enfolded by her white gown and shawl—Willoughby's woman, under the spell and enchantment of scent, has lost all self-control; she is possessed.[52]

Aesthetic and iconic images of perfume are evident in other forms of visual representation as well. A still life by the painter Maria Izquierdo, a work called *El Gato Sabio* (1943), places together a cat, several kinds of fruit, a pipe, a head, an opened book, and a perfume bottle while the photographer Lee Miller in *Scent Bottles* from 1933 (fig. 11) captures a formalist art deco image of a staggered row of identical, rectilinear perfume bottles, each labeled with the name of a common fragrance: "woodscent," "lavender" "violet," and "verbena." Since the glass bottles sit on a mirror, reflecting and complicating their skyscraper verticality, the sleek, clean lines and geometrical purity of their forms give them a classical and minimalist beauty; an ordinary, everyday object is transformed into an extraordinary, formal work of art. Another collection of objects, a mixed-media still life from 1991 by Louise Bourgeois, entitled *Cell II* (fig. 12), is an enigmatic, autobiographical work juxtaposing the "bat-wing" perfume bottles of Guerlain's *Shalimar* (1925), arranged in three tiers according to size, with the marble sculpture of two clasped hands; as in Miller's photograph, the objects, displayed on a glass-top table, have a reflective depth. Perfume in *Cell II* is an autobiographical symbol of bereavement and consolation, the sign of a lost beloved. It represents the scent of the past incorporated into the air of the present, for the sense of smell, Bourgeois remarks, has "the great power of evocation and healing"; in 1932, it enabled her to confront as a young twenty-year-old woman, the death of her mother. Mourning, like an empty bottle of perfume, never, it seems, loses the trace of its scent.[53]

Not surprisingly, fragrance has often been represented in painting through images of flowers. In *Allegory of the Senses: Smell* (Prado, Madrid) from the early seventeenth century, Jan Brueghel de Velours and Peter Paul Rubens create a representation of different species of odorous flowers and animals. Yet, such allusions to smell have ultimately a metaphorical, symbolic, and allegorical function which converts odor into non-olfactory, visual

Fig. 8 A man of all scents. *The Perfumer's Costume*, after N. de Larmessin, engraving, late seventeenth century.

Fig. 9 The spiritual, if not religious, power of scent gives rise to thoughts of a higher deity, enfolding the priestess in the aroma of sanctity as captured in John Singer Sargent's oil on canvas, *Fumée d'ambre gris* (*Smoke of Ambergris*), 1880.

Fig. 10 This represen-
tation of perfume,
entitled *The Perfume
of Ecstasy* (oil,
c. 1920) is by the
early-twentieth-
century English artist
Vera Willoughby.
She is known for
the illustrations
she contributed to
translations of Greek
love poems and for a
series of paintings
depicting harem life
and as seen here the
erotic, rapturous, and
trance-inducing
properties of scent.

Fig. 11 A sleek, streamlined order and a uniform, geometric simplicity give to Lee Miller's photograph, *Scent Bottles,* 1933, an art deco coolness and purity. Miller, an American living in the Paris of the twenties, had been introduced to photography by another American expatriate, Man Ray.

surrogates, a mediation, of course, that suppresses smell and privileges sight. The profoundly sensual experience of perfume, realistically and graphically interpreted by Willoughby in *The Perfume of Ecstasy*, and symbolically recast in a visual medium by Brueghel and Rubens, is given a more inwardly turned, emotional, and sensual treatment by the abstract expressionist painter Jackson Pollock. In one of his last works (fig. 13), Pollock, "possessed" by the perfume not of ecstasy but of art, appears to associate the volcanic release of energy and creativity at the moment of artistic composition with the phenomenon of permeation which propels scent in and through the air. In the random whirlwind of colors and the frenzied turns and counter-turns of thick ribbons of paint, Pollock offers an abstract interpretation of the swirling, spiraling, intersecting, and diffusing movement of perfume. In this painting, which has and does not have a title—it is called *Untitled (Scent)*—from 1953–1955, Pollock covers the entire canvas with massing and dispersing "clouds" of paint to create an "all-over" effect suggestive of the "all-over" sensation of perme-ation and perfusion which perfume, once launched into the air, sets in motion.[54] More realistic in style is *The Perfume-Seller* by Pietro Longhi, the eighteenth-century Italian painter, whose representation of a group of elegantly attired masked Carnival revelers (the man and woman at

the center wear black Venetian tricorn hats, black capes, and white dominoes) are accosted by a poorly dressed woman carrying a basket of perfumes (fig. 14).

Similarly realistic, although much more consciously satiric, is the imaginary portrait of a late seventeenth-century perfumer whose body and dress are composed of the tools of his trade. Entitled *The Perfumer's Costume* (Musée international de la parfumerie, Grasse), an engrav-ing after N. de Larmessin (fig. 8, see page 38), the portrait was created as part of a series of representations in which the characteristic and distinctive objects of a given vocation

An old-fashioned perfume "organ," as it is called, displaying rows of bottles containing different aromatic ingredients; twentieth century.

41

Fig. 12 Clasped hands and rows of Guerlain's bat-wing *Shalimar* bottles of different sizes, carefully arranged on a mirrored surface, in *Cell II* (detail), a mixed media work of 1991 by Louise Bourgeois (American, b. France, 1911), symbolically figure the loss of childhood and the death of a beloved mother.

Fig. 13 The turning whirl of colors captures the spiraling movement of perfume. Jackson Pollock, *Untitled (Scent)*, c. 1953–1955, oil and enamel on canvas.

Fig. 14 The canals of Venice, entryway into Europe for silk, spice, and perfume products of all kinds from the East, were lined with warehouses odorous of aromatic gums, resins, balms, and primary ingredients like musk, civet, myrrh, and incense. Perfume vendors moved from quarter to quarter during the city's great season of Carnival, as represented here in Pietro Longhi's *The Perfume-Seller*, 1757, oil on canvas.

were used to compose the anatomy and dress of the artisan or craftsman in question. The work shows a perfumer whose head is adorned with an inverted incense burner from which clouds of smoke arise and whose shoulders take the form of open scented fans, while in one hand he holds little balls of soap and in the other a swatch of scented leather (traditionally called "peaux d'Espagne").

His upper torso is covered by a chest of shelves each labeled with the names of the different scented products it displays: on the first shelf are flasks containing "essences of all kinds"; on the second, jars of "pomades from Rome and Florence"; on the next, small round oval soaps ("Savon de Naples"); and on the last, bottles filled with different varieties of scented waters ("Eaux de Senteurs de Mille Fleurs,"

"Eaux de la Reyne d'Hongrie," "Eaux de Fleurs d'Orange"). Still other specialized products are attached to the skirt of his costume: little packages labeled "tobacco," "cedar," "malt," and "rouge d'Espagne"; scented gloves; a sponge; a large vessel containing perfumed lozenges for the mouth; pastilles for burning; scented wax from Spain; and, finally, bottles of myrtle water and angel water and packets of Cyprus and other powders.

Perfume is no stranger either to the homespun American humor of an illustrator like Norman Rockwell (fig. 15). One of his more celebrated works carries a title as far from the elegant world of perfume as one could imagine. Appearing as the cover to *The Saturday Evening Post* for June 2, 1951, "Two Plumbers," represents two Laurel-and-Hardyesque figures (one thin, the other portly), in work clothes and caps, standing in front of a dressing table in a bedroom whose pink floral wallpaper, curtains, and flounces leave no doubt about the femininity of its occupant. One plumber carries a tool box, several monkey wrenches, a blowtorch, and a toilet plunger. A broad smile of surprise and pleasure illuminates his face as he receives a full blast of perfume from the small fragile atomizer that his colleague, a cigar butt in his pursed lips and an unlit match behind one ear, delicately holds in his large, thick hands. Exploiting the contrast between vulgarity and refinement, work and luxury, necessity and excess, and of course masculinity and femininity, Rockwell's humor does not appear kindly disposed toward perfume or even women, for that matter.

Representations of scent provide different images of perfume—as an enhancement of feminine beauty (Seurat), as a ritualized communication with the divine and the irrational (Sargent and Willoughby), as a commodity for sale (Longhi and Larmessin), as a sign of gender and class difference (Rockwell), as a metaphor for artistic creation (Pollock)—and different images of the perfume bottle—as an aesthetic form (Lee Miller) and as a symbol of maternity (Louise Bourgeois). What they do not represent in a visual way, with the possible exception of Willoughby's, Pollock's, and, to a lesser extent, Sargent's paintings, is the intense, affective experience of perfume itself: namely, the subjective sensation and feeling that come from inhaling a scent.

Fragrance and Music

The art form closest to perfume, and the one that provides perfume with its distinctive vocabulary, is music. Creators of scent, for example, are called "composers"; their compositions are constructed from aromatic ingredients, odorous forms, and scent molecules called "notes," "chords," "tones," and "accords," which are then combined into "themes" and "leitmotifs." The thin strips of blotter paper perfumers smell to evaluate a perfume's composition are referred to as "keys"; and, finally, the perfumer's worktable, a curved desk holding in graduated order row upon row of bottles of primary ingredients, was, at least from the latter half of the nineteenth century to the early years of the twentieth, appropriately named a "perfume organ" and sometimes a "harmonium" (see page 41). Perfume composition shares with music, moreover, the same ineffability and the same resistance to linguistic modes of reproduction; at least, some nineteenth-century poets thought so. The way sound disperses and disappears into the air is not unlike the permeation and evaporation of perfume; both are sustained by elusive and ephemeral realities. The purpose of music, writes the contemporary English novelist Ian McEwan, in a description that could apply to perfume as well, is "to create this pleasure at once so sensual and abstract, to translate into vibrating air this non-language whose meanings were forever just beyond reach, suspended tantalizingly at a point where emotion and intellect fused."[55]

The intentions of scent are no different from those of music as McEwan conceives them, except that where emotion and intellect join in music, feeling and memory touch in perfume. Yet, despite these similarities, representations of perfume in music have been as rare as they have been in the plastic arts. The hesitant choreography of invisible clouds or mists of perfume floating slowly into the air, the ghostly insubstantiality of a scent left behind, and the wavering presence of a trace signaling an absence correspond to the impressionism of a composer like Debussy. In fact, one of the pieces from the first book of his *Preludes for Piano* (1910), entitled "Les sons et les parfums tournent dans l'air du soir" ("Sounds and perfumes turn in the evening air") musically evokes a fusion of sound and scent. In our own time, popular songs, like Madonna's "Candy Perfume Girl" in her 1998 album *Ray of Light* (where perfumed flesh is a "magic poison," "a fever steam," a "candy" to be desired and devoured), or the Cape Verdean singer Cesaria Evora's love song "Miss Perfumado" (*Miss Perfumado,* 1992), have alluded to scent. Possibly the most striking and original musical composition during the second half of the twentieth century to evoke the elegance and sensuality of perfume is Duke Ellington's and Billy Strayhorn's long work, *Perfume Suite,* created in 1944.

Ellington's and Strayhorn's elegantly swaying sometimes velvety, sometimes jumpy and violent, melodies evoke the gamut of feelings, the psychological riffs, and the run of high and low moods that perfume inspires in the person who smells it. In his spoken remarks introducing the *Suite,* Ellington explains that he and Strayhorn "attempt not to describe the various labels we find on commercial perfumes as much as trying to capture the character a woman seems to take on wearing perfume." Presenting "love, pure love, the under-the-balcony type serenade," as Ellington puts it, the first of the composition's four movements expresses an elegant sophistication, a mellow

The Saturday Evening
POST
June 2, 1951 – 15¢

A MISSOURI MAILMAN LOOKS AT BRITAIN
Link Kilby's Story of How Socialism Looked to Him

CHEYENNE

smoothness or suavity (a word as suited to scent as to music), and a sense of warm, sensual loveliness that contrast sharply with the second movement where the whine of a muted trumpet gives the music a disquieting edginess, if not a strange nervousness. With the third movement, sprightly and upbeat, the piece regains a feeling of simple innocence and well-being before asserting in the fourth and final part a brashness and a pride (in one's self, one's body, one's scent) which a shrill trumpet—along with the smooth, flowing harmonies of the other brass instruments set against it—evokes. In *Perfume Suite* Ellington and Strayhorn present the music of perfume as a feeling and a mood. They articulate the way perfume gets inside the woman who wears it and speaks intimately to her; they capture an inner vision of perfume, a psychology in other words. The idea of the piece, Ellington explained, was to show

> what perfume does to or for the woman who is wearing it, and each part portrayed the mood a woman gets into—or would like to get into–when wearing a certain type of perfume. Thus, *Under the Balcony Serenade* [first movement] pictured a woman who feels, on wearing this perfume, that she is the better half of Romeo and Juliet. *Strange Feeling* [second movement] has to do with the mental violence that comes with intentions, either to do or to be. *Dancers in Love* [third movement] is naïveté, a stomp for beginners, where it is very difficult for the boy partner to determine what kind of perfume she is wearing, because they are dancing at such a great distance. This is not important to her, because she just wants to dance! The last [movement] is *Coloratura*, and here the attitude is that of a prima donna who feels she is always making an entrance.[56]

Fragrance and Architecture

Another art form not usually linked to scent, although there are compelling reasons why it should be, is architecture. Perfume, like architecture, exists in space, in the physical world. And like architecture it appears as a vertical construction built on a base (the soul note) from which arise middle and top sections (the heart and head notes), except that where the stone or steel structure is designed to last for decades, the structured lifespan of the perfume can only be measured in seconds, minutes, and hours. Once they take on architectural form, the three "floors" of the perfume undergo rapid change; the top and middle layers collapse leaving the more "permanent" base. Moreover, the physical and material reality of architecture, like perfume, has a distinctive spiritual dimension. Architects "insist on this physical, material approach to architecture . . . it is the only way to arrive at the immaterial or the spiritual," Jacques Herzog (who with his partner Pierre de Meuron

designed London's Tate Modern museum) observes. The architectural and spatial configuration of perfume appeals to Herzog who dreams of one day designing a fragrance (juice, bottle, and packaging). A contemporary architect who has in fact realized Herzog's dream is Richard Meier (the creator of the Getty Museum) whose spare architectural principles are reflected in a minimalist white perfume bottle with the look of a sleek skyscraper, which he designed in 1985 for Hugo Boss's *No. 1*, a fragrance for men.[57] Perfume and architecture are arts, then, built on a human scale; they conform to the body. They humanize, even personalize, space. They give surfaces character and identity, layering them, albeit briefly in the case of perfume, with feelings of pleasure, both physical and aesthetic, and with fantasies of intimacy, warmth, and well-being. Occupying the rooms they permeate, scents give these spaces the character of a decor, filling them with memories and decorating them with a kind of furniture of the past. Perfume, it would appear, is not only architecture, it is also interior design.

The Art of the Bottle and the Body

The bottles incorporated into Lee Miller's photograph (*Scent Bottles*) and Louise Bourgeois's mixed media construction (*Cell II*), the one formalist and geometric, the other symbolic and enigmatic, represent the perfume bottle as a visual object whose connection to the sensual experience of scent is secondary to the overall conceptual meaning of Miller's and Bourgeois's works of art. Miller is attracted more to the aesthetic form of the bottle than to its association with perfume; Bourgeois is taken more with the autobiographical (and symbolic) quality of the *Shalimar* bottle as a reference to her mother and a sign of femininity than with its reality as a popular and classic oriental fragrance conceived by Raymond Guerlain in 1925. In both instances, perfume comes across as subordinate to an artistic vision determined to use it for other ends. One bottle, however, that does indeed have the visual shape of a perfume bottle and at the same time expresses the sensual reality of perfume—a perfume flask that embodies and represents nothing short of the sensation of perfume, a bottle at once the signifier and the signified of perfume—is in reality no bottle at all. It is a *calligramme*, a poem about perfume written in the shape of a perfume bottle by Charles-François Panard (1674–1765) (fig. 16).[58]

"How my / flask / does seem good to me!" the opening lines, cast in the shape of the perfume bottle's stopper and lip, passionately announce. "Without it / boredom / tracks me, / hurts me," the next lines, those of the bottle's neck, declare. In the twelfth line, at the point where the bottle's neck descends to meet its waist and the poem begins to flare horizontally outward—here the two-syllable lines of the neck begin to expand incrementally to lines of four, six, eight, ten, and twelve syllables, a poetic protrusion in

```
                    Que mon
                    Flacon
                 Me semble bon!
                   Sans lui
                   L'ennui
                   Me nuit,
                   Me suit.
                   Je sens
                   Mes sens
                  Mourants,
                   Pesants.
                Quand je la tiens,
              Dieux! que je suis bien!
             Que son aspect est agréable!
          Que je fais cas de ses divins présents!
       C'est de son sein fécond, c'est de ses heureux flancs
        Que  coule  ce  nectar  si  doux,  si  délectable,
        Qui rend tous les esprits, tous les cœurs satisfaits.
        Cher objet de mes vœux, tu fais toute ma gloire.
        Tant que mon cœur vivra, de tes charmants bienfaits
        Il    saura    conserver    la    fidèle    mémoire.
        Ma muse à te louer se consacre à jamais,
        Tantôt dans un caveau, tantôt sous une treille,
        Ma lyre, de ma voix accompagnant le son,
         Répétera cent fois cette aimable chanson :
         'Règne sans fin, ma charmante bouteille;
          Règne   sans   cesse,   mon   flacon.
```

Fig. 16   When poem, perfume, and bottle become one with love. Charles-François Panard, *Calligramme*, seventeenth to eighteenth century.

harmony with the swelling of the bottle's visual shape and, as we shall see, with the beloved's body—Panard writes: "When I hold her, / My God! I do feel good." It is at this crucial line, the place where the poem becomes ample, both visually and semantically, that the poem's very subject, the bottle (the masculine "*le* flacon"), is transformed into a direct-object pronoun that has suddenly and surprisingly become feminine: "je *la* tiens"; the poet no longer holds *it*, the bottle, but *her*, the beloved. The form of the calligrammatic flask expands as does its meaning; the bottle is still a bottle, of course, but it is also the body of an adored woman. Whatever the poet says about the bottle applies to the woman; whatever he says about the woman applies to the bottle. She is the new vessel for the perfume. From both flask and body "flows the sweetest and most delightful nectar, / Giving fulfillment to every spirit, every heart." Both body and bottle bestow "divine presents," "lovely gifts," and "glory"; each in its own right is "the precious object of my desires." As the poem winds down to its conclusion and the bottle's form narrows to its base (composed of lines of decreasing numbers of syllables), the poet fervently addresses the double subject of his adoration: "Reign without end, my lovely bottle; / Reign without cease, my flacon."

In this shapely poem what are the aspects of the scented imagination that are poetically and graphically illustrated? The poem-as-bottle appears as a vessel in which the essence (the liquid scent and the spirit) of song, perfume, and the beloved coexist. Perfume is shown to possess the power of life. It keeps boredom at bay, invigorating the poet's tired senses, and overwhelming him with intoxicating feelings of happiness, warmth, and satisfaction. Invading his inner being, perfume penetrates his

heart and leaves there a lasting and "faithful memory." Scent not only deepens his love; it inspires poetry, another vessel for fragrant love. The poem will have the insistence of scent—the "muse" of poetic inspiration henceforth "dedicates herself to never-ending praise" of the beloved—and the persistence of scent—the poet's song will repeat itself "a hundred times" over. This is the tenacious evocativeness of perfume from which are born life, love, memory, poetry, and song, all compressed into a small, delicate bottle (filled with words and with scent) which shall, as the poem's last lines assert, "reign." Perfume gains immortal life when scent becomes word, a transformation central to the idea of the scented imagination, as Shakespeare also recognized when in the fifth of his *Sonnets* he wrote, "But flowers distill'd, though they with winter meet, / Leese but their show; their substance still lives sweet."

The Poetry of Perfume

Many are the images of perfume that constitute the scented imagination. First, there is the sweetness of perfume, the balm that dissipates worldly cares and lightens body and spirit. "Give me an ounce of civet; good apothecary, sweeten my imagination. There's money for thee," commands Shakespeare's Lear (*King Lear*, IV, vi, 132–34). But perfume, even at its most intense and tenacious, cannot maintain illusion forever; it has its limits in masking pain, covering guilt, and chasing away the demons of sin and crime: "Here's the smell of blood still; all the perfumes of Arabia will not sweeten this little hand," Lady Macbeth laments (*Macbeth*, V, i, 56–58). Second, there is the ambiguity, the bipolarity, of perfume; it can "sweeten" reality but not for all time. It has an intense, dazzling presence in which flickers the shadow of imminent absence. Fragrance may dominate the air, but through this joyful expansion only dissipation and loss ultimately come into being. Lodged at the heart of scent is indelible death: a death overcome—the perfume survives the withered petals of its birth—and a death overcoming—the perfume disappears into a tomb of air. "These lacquered leaves / where the light paddles / And the big blooms / buzzing among them," writes the contemporary American poet Richard Wilbur, "Have kept their counsel, / conveying nothing / Of their mortal message, / unless one should measure / The depth and dumbness / of death's kingdom / By the pure power / of this perfume."[59] To a poetic mind, sensitive to the sensual and existential details, so often overlooked, of daily existence, perfume is a symbol of the vibrant here-and-now of life in which stirs the forthcoming thereness of death.

A third aspect of the scented imagination, at least as poets have attempted to express it, centers on scent as the remembrance of things fragrant, as the trace of a lost past recaptured in the intensity of the present. Here perfume reveals its power of permeation. Odor and memory expand to fill the air; the present is overlaid with the fragrant immediacy of an insistent past. "And there grows in the mind," the poet William Carlos Williams observes, "a scent, it may be, of locust blossoms / whose perfume is itself a wind moving / to lead the mind away." Perfume is both centripetal—it is the concentrated essence of a flower "pent in walls of glass"—and centrifugal—the very act of its self-expression requires its self-depletion as it floats away in the air. Perfume is a "here" that soon becomes a "there." First confined to a bottle, then liberated to make its mark on the air, and finally to become no more than a trace of its former self, perfume is a substance continually in transit. It signifies passage, a moving away. It seems always to point to what is elsewhere: the otherness of some lost time and place. "A bottle of perfume has leaked and made awful brown stains," the young narrator of Elizabeth Bishop's poetic short story, "In the Village," remarks, as she helps her aunt and grandmother to unpack her mother's valise; the mother has returned after a very long, troubling absence. "Oh, marvelous scent, from somewhere else! It doesn't smell like that here; but there, somewhere, it does, still," the young girl whispers to herself. "The world of sad brown perfume"—to the child a world of primal loss and abandonment—is a place of sad leaks and awful stains. But those ugly vestiges of fragrance evoke another world, a "somewhere else," a "there," in which the sweetness and delight of perfume and of a mother's closeness, which once existed, "still" do indeed exist. Perfume is a vestige whose aura is hope. Even when it soils, yellows, and darkens the present, even when it becomes an indelible spot on the fabric of a life, an irremovable sign of loss, it still gives off the odor of a once beautiful and fragrant past: "And the smell, the wonderful smell of the dark-brown stains. Is it roses?" the child asks herself, as if in identifying the odor and speaking its name (the beginning of poetry) she will master the loss.[60]

The Betrayal of Perfume: John Donne

One literary work that is a cornucopia of images and ideas associated with the imaginary of perfume is John Donne's dramatic love poem "The Perfume," the fourth of the *Elegies* he composed between 1593 and 1596. Like Panard in his calligram, Donne takes perfume as a metaphor for the beloved woman and her body; but he goes further than Panard will a century later. Perfume is a physical reality along with the body that the two lovers share, and this exchange of caresses and scent sets in motion a drama of betrayal. Rather than simply experiencing perfume as a sublimation of the woman's femininity—the skin's breath surrounding the body like an aura—and then adoring and celebrating it, the poet sees perfume as a symbol for the beloved and a metaphor for his erotic relationship with her, a surrogate he can much more easily and safely criticize than the flesh-and-blood woman it encompasses. The fervent indictment he raises against the treachery of perfume, so blatantly a betrayal of his love, carries an accusation of the woman who wears it; both are untrustworthy. Migrating to the skin of the lover with whom the beloved has just slept, her perfume gives them both away. While the girl's suspicious parents can detect no signs of the couple's erotic activities—no strange colors on her face, no new rings or "armelets," no telltale indications of "the sinnes of . . . youths ranke lustinesse," no evidence that "thou'art swolne"—and while the girl's siblings tell no tales and the spying servant the father has hired "could never witnesse any touch or kisse," love nevertheless makes itself known, not through the hard evidence of sight, but through the testimony of smell (*Elegies*, 7–9). "But Oh, too common ill, I brought with mee / That, which betray'd mee to mine enemie: / A loud perfume, which at my entrance cryed / Even at thy fathers nose, so wee were spied," complains the lover. Smelling produces sight and knowledge. Perfume turns visual, vocal, even verbal. It unveils, it tells, it speaks. It replaces the senses of sight and sound which have been discreet, for they have given nothing away; in fact, the poet has mastery over them, as he sneaks quietly into the beloved's bedchamber: "I taught my silkes, their whistling to forbeare, / Even my opprest shoes, dumbe and speechlesse were." However, an all-too-loquacious perfume has unsuspectingly revealed more than it might have ever intended: "Onely, thou bitter sweet, whom I had laid / Next mee, mee traiterously hast betraid, / And unsuspected hast invisibly / At once fled unto him, and staid with mee." Herein lies, perhaps, the lover's strongest accusation: namely, that the scent worn by the woman for him and him alone has incestuously traveled (via the lover's body and clothing) to the father's nose. Through the medium of smell the father comes to discover the young man who will usurp his power, steal the capital (the "hope of his goods") which his daughter represents, and thus challenge his patriarchy.

Addressing the perfume, once friend but now enemy, while at the same time under his breath, addressing the woman as a carnal body which the perfume seductively envelops, the poet, with angry sarcasm, exclaims: "Base excrement of earth, which dost confound / Sense, from distinguishing the sicke from sound." Perfume knows how to betray because its origins are in the bowels of the earth, in the decomposing matter of flowers, in death itself. A substance disguising the baseness of its source behind a veil of spirituality and sublimity, perfume depends for its power of intoxication on tactics of illusion and confusion through which the good hides the bad, the sound the sick, the maiden the whore. When a lover breathes a scent of sublime delightfulness, he has no idea that what enters him and his life is the stench of disease and death. Behind the purity of perfume and the beauty of the beloved who wears it, lies subterfuge. Perfume is a form of prostitution where love is no more than an act, feeling no more than a pretence, beauty no more than an untrustworthy scent covering  deceitfulness, and allure no more than death's lure: "By thee the seely [i.e. silly] Amorous sucks his death / By drawing in a leprous harlots breath." Moreover, perfume is exaggeration and excess; it troubles the natural order of things, changing nobles into dandies, men into women, and reality into hyperbole and excess: "Though you be much lov'd in the Princes hall, / There, things that seeme, exceed substantiall." And so, in the end, the poet curses what he had once adored: "You'are loathsome all . . . / . . . / If you were good, your good doth soone decay."

Disabused of his illusions regarding perfume, the poet becomes more savvy and practical as the poem ends. Ceasing the vituperative attack against perfume, he now seems to embrace scent as the only possible solution to his dilemma. Having first been lured to the woman by perfume and having then been betrayed to the father by the same perfume, the poet now imagines taking control of this powerful substance, using its magic to hasten the father's death and allow himself and the beloved to remain together. The poem ends with the expression of a desire whose fulfillment must remain, given the final questions which are raised, uncertain: "All my perfumes, I give most willingly / To'embalme thy fathers corse [corpse]; What? Will hee die?" At first dishonest and then treacherous, perfume now becomes downright patricidal. The indicting scents, which had placed the lovers in a compromising position, will now become their preferred weapon against the father's authority. The tables are turned. Perfume becomes an ally in an imaginary fantasy in which the poet dreams that the scent which had enveloped the beloved and then betrayed his love will attach itself finally to the father's embalmed body; it will facilitate the patriarch's undoing. The perfume, which the father had merely inhaled earlier in the poem, will now take control of the paternal body. Where perfume had once betrayed the lovers, it now promises their triumph.

Fragrantly, it shrouds the patriarchal corpse, ritualistically dispatching it, at least in the poet's imagination, to its grave. Curiously, the image of perfume in the poem migrates from the woman to her lover, then from the lover to the father, and finally from the father to his corpse: a conjoining of love and death (Eros and Thanatos) which is a fundamental reality of the scented imagination.

The image of perfume in Donne's elegy has many features and aspects that in future centuries would continue to be expressed and represented in poetry, fiction, painting, glass design, advertising, and the collective imagination of European culture in general. Perfume in Donne's poem signifies love and sexual union; it embodies illusion, treachery, betrayal, and subterfuge; it is base, materialist, and even excremental; it is a medium of communication; and, finally, it is both a reality and the mere semblance of a reality, a substance without substance. Perfume is fundamentally ambivalent: bitter and sweet, bad and good, sick and sound, invisible and visible, apparent and real, deceitful and true, ephemeral and enduring. Moreover, perfume as imagined in the poem moves in fundamentally contradictory ways, following centripetal and centrifugal trajectories. Perfume enters and departs. It is inhaled and exhaled, contained and expressed, absorbed and released, concentrated and dissipated; it is here and there. Donne's conception of perfume calls into question the primacy of vision and audition; one does not need to see or hear in order to understand. The olfactory sensations perfume provokes impart knowledge: of oneself, of the other, of the world. Scent creates its own kind of "sight" and "sound," having a demonstrative truth equal to that generated by instances of seeing, hearing, and speaking. Perfume is loud, it cries, and it lets itself be spied; it is neither "dumbe" nor "speechlesse." An indelible trace, a damning presence, a permanent sign, an irremovable stain, an incontestable piece of evidence, it stays—and it betrays.

The Empire of Perfume:

Scent in Nineteenth-Century French Culture

Chapter 2

*The nineteenth century . . . is the set of noises
that invades our dreams, and
which we interpret on awaking.*
—Walter Benjamin

*Fashion is the most immeasurable change
experienced by social man;
it casts its weight on all of life.*
—Honoré de Balzac

IN OUR AGE of sanitized cities and deodorized residences is it possible to imagine—not intellectually but physically and sensually—the aggressive smells of a Paris street at the beginning of the nineteenth century? Can one sense the odor of mud and standing water, of sweating horses galloping by, of rotting fish, stinking meat, and putrid fowl offered for sale, of fetid sewage stagnating between thoroughfare and walkway, of cadavers decomposing in the Cimetière des Innocents? Or from a more aristocratic vantage point, can the historian—the expert in the history of smells—recreate the "image" of the scents floating in the air of an imperial ball? Can one re-experience the collective aroma produced by elegant women rapidly waving their perfumed fans, by fragrances emanating from scented leather gloves and wigs, by the eau de cologne arising from Napoleon's profusely scented hair, or the overwhelming aura of musk and civet issuing from his wife, the empress Josephine? Perfume dies, as we know, and with it, eventually, the society it has scented. As ephemeral as fragrance are the subjective sensations, mental associations, and cultural customs that govern its everyday use. More than a personal or even an intimate practice, the use of perfume is fundamentally a social phenomenon.

Although the processes of smell have undergone no change whatsoever—the olfactory bulbs have remained the initial locus for the capture of odors since human ancestors began to roam the land in prehistoric times—the culturally determined perception and psychology of smell have, and these changes, at least since the late 1700s, have been radical. What defines sweet or repellent odors, light or heavy scents, and socially acceptable or morally suspect aromas is not a question of the natural processes of smell or perception, but of the social codes and interpretations surrounding them: in other words, what a culture—and different social classes within that culture—consciously and unconsciously decides to accept and reject, desire and forbid. Smells define and are defined by an image system formed and tempered by society. This system is disseminated often in highly unconscious ways by the practices and gestures of everyday life: for example, how the bourgeois gentleman of 1840 washes himself in the morning before venturing into the world; how the fashionably bourgeois woman selects the clothes she will need to wear at different moments of the day (for a promenade in the Bois de Boulogne, for a visit to a department store, for afternoon tea, for a ball); what anxieties about self-display, social rivalry, and the dictates of the social code go through her mind as she constructs her appearance; how she goes about performing the intricate, secret rituals of dressing herself; and, finally, how her understanding of the body's functions, her awareness of personal hygiene, and her concerns about the effects of water, soap, powders, and cosmetics have been determined by the habitual, often unconscious, decisions she makes every day. These are the perceptions, sensations, and gestures that define the idea and practice of the image system: in this instance, that of the body as it intersects with proto-cols of dress, odor, and perfume in everyday life.[1] The body is a theater, its visible spaces dependent upon what goes on in unseen wings, its stage made all the more bright by a surrounding darkness, its spectacle of gestures enhanced by more private desires, and its sequence of movements directed by realities as much cultural as personal.

What then was the "everyday" experience of perfume in the nineteenth century and how was it linked to the body, to dress, and to realities of cleanliness, appearance, and social status? In order to think about the nineteenth century in terms of the "everyday," first and foremost, it is necessary to determine which "nineteenth century" is being referred to: Napoleon Bonaparte's Empire? The Restoration of Charles X? Louis-Philippe's July Monarchy? The Second Empire and Napoleon III? Or the Third Republic and the Belle Epoque? Second, and of even more telling importance, how can a century be said to "have" an "everyday"? The final sense of a century becomes defined, retrospectively and provisionally, at the end of its hundred-year reign as it moves into a new cycle of a hundred years. The task of the new century is to define repeatedly the cultural and social history of the century just ended, especially as new modes of looking at that past are conceived. It is clear, however, that the practice of historical reconstruction is inhospitable to the idea and experience of the everyday. When subjected to the historical gaze, the movement of the day-to-day is stopped dead in its tracks. Once highlighted for analysis, it is removed from the temporal flow that at one time defined it as the "everyday" in all its ephemeral regularity. It is probable, therefore, that the everyday has no history, or that, if it does indeed possess one, this history is essentially and continuously different. The mere act of telling the history of the everyday encircles its monotonous repetitiveness in an aura of uniqueness. The spotlight of singularity highlights what at one time had been no more than an ordinary, unremarkable drabness. Today cannot be fully perceived through the lens of tomorrow. The passage of time transforms what is current, actual, and here-and-now into an immobilized history too general and abstract to capture the flux of successive, monotonous, and trivial gestures, which at one time had composed an endless series of unremarkable "todays." Despite the invaluable ways by which history has resurrected the past and transformed that past into knowledge, it has lost—how could it be otherwise?—the present whose very immediacy forms the crucible of history; "daily living [le vécu quotidien]," writes Thuillier "is time that passes and is worn away."[2] It is this loss of the present's presentness that history tries to reverse.

The Napoleonization of Perfume

The nineteenth century, primarily the years from 1804 to 1871, could be called the century of Napoleon, or more precisely of the two Napoleons. Even when Napoleon I and III, Napoleon Bonaparte and his nephew Louis Napoleon, had lost their power and gone into exile, the governments that came in their wakes were forced to confront the history, myths, and iconography that they had bequeathed. In the years after their fall from power (1815 and 1870 respectively) the two Napoleons continued to reign, albeit as phantom-emperors. In the realm of perfume they and the courts they dominated left an indelible trace, a Napoleonic scent, its imperial notes floating over a good part of an entire century.

Perfume and Napoleon I

During the last half of the twentieth century the French perfume house Roger et Gallet used an image of Napoleon Bonaparte to advertise its eau de cologne. Accompanied by a slogan declaring the fragrance to be "the Emperor's scent" "since 1806," the advertisement may have raised some eyebrows, since the claim boasts a longevity, going back to the first decade of the nineteenth century, of a product known to be as ephemeral as the aromas it emits. It has been estimated, for example, that between 1884 and 1984 over 6,000 perfume names were distributed in France alone; of these, very few have survived. Yet, strange and rare as it may seem, the Roger et Gallet advertisement is apparently free of exaggeration. For their eau de cologne, although known to the emperor under the name of another perfumer (Jean-Marie Farina), was most assuredly Napoleon's preferred essence. He consumed on average sixty, half-gallon bottles a month—despite his aversion to heavy perfumes—and imposed its use on his family and court. According to his sister, Pauline, the Princess Borghese, there existed "no scent able to make the skin so pleasantly youthful." Every morning the emperor asked Constant, his valet, to rub the cologne on his back and shoulders and even apply it to his celebrated forelock. He carried with him a specially designed perfume bottle (cylindrical in shape) that he could easily hide in his boot while on military campaigns. Claiming that the scent stimulated his mind—or perhaps like Lear sweetened his imagination (*King Lear*, IV, vi, 132ff)—he would, when under particular stress, consume a piece of sugar moistened with the cologne. On his death bed in exile on the British island of Saint Helena, 1,200 miles west of the coast of Africa, he requested, it is reported, that perfumed pastilles of this scent be burned.[3] Like many of the larger-than-life stories surrounding the myth of Napoleon, this one may not be completely true.

The eau de cologne that Napoleon enjoyed on Saint Helena—among the few pleasures of his last years—was in all likelihood as much in a condition of exile as he was. The aromas that filled his death chamber were possibly not the very same ones that floated in the air of his sumptuous rooms at Versailles. When Napoleon was exiled to Saint Helena on the order of the Duke of Wellington—he arrived on October 15, 1815, and died there on May 5, 1821—his servants Ali the Mameluke (Louis-Etienne Saint-Denis) and Louis Marchand, both of whom accompanied the emperor to the island, had, before departing France, slipped bottles of the emperor's eau de cologne into their baggage. The supply did not last long. Because shipping from England would have taken too long and because Napoleon was in great need of his fragrance, he asked the aides and companions who had accompanied him to try to remember the scent as it had smelled back in France. With the help of books and treatises in the library at Longwood, the house Napoleon occupied on the island, Ali came up with a homemade eau de cologne, containing locally grown ingredients like lemon, citron, bergamot, and rosemary. Another version of the story recounts that Ali wrote Fargeon, one of Napoleon's perfumers in Paris, to ask for the formula; once dispatched to Saint Helena, the formula was used, along with substances available on the island, to reconstitute the cologne.[4]

A History of Eau de Cologne

That Napoleon's scent in exile was not the equal of the eau de cologne produced by Jean-Marie Farina, which he had used unsparingly in France, is most certain. Farina's product had a long and interesting history and was recognized as the "scent sensation of the age." In 1709 the Italian barber Gian Paolo Feminis, who had been born in a town near Santa Maria Maggiore, left for Germany to market a distilled herbal "water," light and citrusy in aroma, which had been in use among Italian families for generations. The scent, whose formula was later enhanced by the addition of rectified grape spirit and a blend of oil of neroli (from flowers of the bitter orange tree), bergamot (from the peel of the bitter orange), lavender, lemon, and rosemary, was given the name Aqua Mirabilis. In an early attempt at self-promoting hyperbole, Feminis's "marvelous," "miraculous" water was advertised as a remedy for problems of the skin, the stomach, and the

In 1931, Molinard, an old nineteenth-century Grasse perfume company, launched its Napoleon-inspired fragrance *1811* in a bottle topped with a stopper resembling the emperor's celebrated bicorn hat and tricolor cockade. The fragrance celebrates, in all likelihood, the year that finally saw the birth of Napoleon's first heir by his new Austrian wife, Marie-Louise.

gums, as well as a cure for headaches, toothaches, strokes, jaundice, ringing of the ears, difficult childbirths, and unrequited love.[5] Since the alcohol of the time was not yet denatured—that process would arrive in the late nineteenth century—the "eau" could be diluted in wine, water, or broth and thus even drunk. So well received was Feminis's scent that he needed assistance in marketing the product and called on his nephew, Giovanni Maria Farina (1685–1766), to join him in Cologne. Once in Cologne, Farina took care to write down his uncle's formula; and in 1732 he took over the direction of the business. Twenty-five years later, French troops stationed in Cologne during the Seven Years' War, which saw France, Austria, Russia, Saxony, Spain, and Sweden doing battle against Great Britain, Prussia, and Hanover, discovered the scent. They carried it back to France where it was appropriately and accurately named after the city of its discovery. It was an immediate success. Madame Du Barry, for one, spent a fortune acquiring it.

For the maison Farina, this popularity was a mixed blessing. Its eau de cologne inspired many imitators, all of whom claimed to be descended from Feminis and to possess his authentic formula; indeed, by 1865 nearly thirty-nine establishments in Cologne carried the name Farina. In 1809 Farina's grandson, Jean-Marie, relocated to Paris, opening a shop at 331 rue Saint-Honoré where he sold the emperor's cologne. At the same time, he vigorously defended his family's rightful claim to the scent by taking to court a host of self-designated "Farina" imposters. To dissuade counterfeiters and to assure his faithful consumers that they were buying the genuine cologne, Farina had his signature, accompanied by the image of an imperial eagle and the coats of arms of the French and German Courts, stamped in green wax on the cases of his product.

Promoting Farina's Eau de Cologne

Farina's advertising prospectuses made different claims for his cologne. Some engravings advertised the "Seul Véritable Eau Admirable de Cologne de G. F. M. Farina" and were illustrated with the royal crests of European monarchies and with images of chemists stoking small distillation furnaces and setting up alembics and *essenciers* (distillers). Another engraved, hand-colored, legal-looking prospectus, which is included in a leather-bound trade catalogue (circa 1815–1820) of perfumes, eau de cologne, soaps, creams, pomades, hair dyes, and other cosmetics manufactured by the Farina firm (in the collection of the Oak Spring Garden Library), touts the virtues of Farina's "Eau Admirable, dite de Cologne" (fig. 17). Dating from the early Restoration, it announces that Jean-Marie Farina has been granted the exclusive patent and registered trademark for the eau de cologne which carries his name and that his firm is the only one licensed as the "official purveyor to the French, German, and Prussian Courts." Images

of three royal crests decorate the prospectus along with the portrait of a man—either that of Jean Paul (Gian Paolo) Feminis (identified in the border above as the "inventor") or that of Jean-Marie (Giovanni Maria) Farina (identified in the lower border as "his successor")—who is flanked by two winged angels, one with a horn, the other with a smoking torch. Two mythological emblems—the caduceus, symbol of the god Hermes and of the medical profession, and a stick around which is entwined a serpent—hover at the margins. Occupying half of the prospectus is a text which first recounts the history of aqua mirabilis and then offers examples of the flattering testimonials the cologne has received from "the premier doctors and best known chemists of Paris." One such testimonial, taken from the *Journal du Commerce* of March 31, 1818, is cited at length:

> We have just received a précis concerning the medical properties of Jean-Marie Farina's Eau de Cologne. If one is to believe the author, and we have no reason to doubt his veracity, his Eau de Cologne, available at the stores on the rue Saint-Honoré, no. 331, has been widely distributed among all civilized peoples and is to be found in the pharmacopeias of Philadelphia as well as on the dressing tables of Moscow. "It alone," M. Farina says, "sustains and preserves the grace and freshness of youth and gave the enchantress Ninon the gift of charm at eighty". . . We know that it is the best [eau de cologne] in Europe. This is the opinion of several celebrated physicians. Their testimony is printed at the end of the précis in question. It alone justifies the confidence of consumers and of women who wish to walk in Ninon's footsteps.

Before retiring to Italy, Farina sold his original formula to Leonce Collas who, after adding a total of 800 new products (eaux, extracts, creams, pomades, and cosmetics), sold the business in 1862 to his cousins Armand Roger and Charles Gallet, to this day the legal owners of the original and authentic eau de cologne of Jean-Marie Farina.[6]

Other stories exist to explain the invention of eau de cologne. One of these affirms that a soldier returning from India gave Feminis the formula for an antiseptic, which the perfumer then reworked. Another version asserts that Feminis obtained the secret formula from a nun in the convent of Santa Maria Maggiore. A third story explains the provenance and popularity of yet another brand of eau de cologne. When Wilhelm Mülhens, the son of a Cologne lawyer (or banker), was married in October 1792, he received a wedding gift from a monk of his acquaintance: a parchment containing the formula for a so-called "aqua mirabilis" (composed of lemon, neroli, rosemary, and lavender). The young man improved the formula and began to produce the scent in a small factory that he established on Glockengasse, one of Cologne's streets. Four years later, after the city of Cologne had come under the control of the French army and the municipal authorities decided

DÉPÔT
D'EAU DE COLOGNE
DE JEAN-MARIE FARINA,
Fournisseur Breveté
DES COURS DE FRANCE, D'ALLEMAGNE, DE PRUSSE.

PAUL FÉMINIS fut le premier Inventeur de l'Eau de Cologne, surnommée *l'Admirable*, à cause de ses merveilleuses propriétés. JEAN-ANTOINE FARINA, l'un des plus anciens distillateurs de Cologne, et son unique successeur, transmit le secret de sa composition à lui seul connu, à moi JEAN-MARIE FARINA son petit-fils; mes veilles et mes travaux m'ont fait porter cette Eau au plus haut degré de perfection; et je justifie sa perfectibilité et ses qualités supérieures à toutes autres, par les divers brevets de Fournisseur que j'ai successivement obtenus des Cours de France, d'Allemagne, de Prusse, etc. etc. Les suffrages flatteurs que j'ai reçus des premiers médecins de Paris, de ses chimistes les plus renommés, et le constant emploi qu'ils en font tous les jours comme cosmétique ou comme remède, me donnent les droits les plus incontestables à la confiance générale; l'expérience, la raison et la vérité se réunissent donc pour garantir les précieux et salutaires effets *de mon Eau.*

« Nous venons de recevoir un *Précis* sur *les propriétés médicales de l'Eau de Cologne* de Jean-Marie Farina. S'il faut en croire l'auteur, et nous n'avons aucune raison de révoquer en doute sa véracité, l'Eau de Cologne qui sort des magasins de la *rue Saint-Honoré*, n° 331, se distribue avec profusion chez tous les peuples civilisés, et on la trouve dans les pharmacopées de Philadelphie comme sur les toilettes de Moscou. « *C'est elle seule*, dit M. Farina, *qui perpétue et conserve les grâces et la fraîcheur de la jeunesse, et qui donna à l'enchanteresse Ninon le don de plaire à quatre-vingts ans.* »

Une telle propriété doit assurer à ce cosmétique une prodigieuse consommation. Au surplus, la réputation de l'Eau de Cologne de Jean-Marie Farina est faite depuis long-temps. On sait que c'est la meilleure de l'Europe. C'est l'avis de plusieurs célèbres médecins. Leurs témoignages sont imprimés à la suite du Précis dont il est question. Ils suffisent pour justifier la confiance des consommateurs et des femmes qui veulent marcher sur les traces de Ninon. (*Extrait du journal du Commerce*, mardi 31 mars 1818.)

Jean Marie Farina

NOTA. Voyez l'article du journal de Paris, du 5 janvier, 1818, le portrait de l'inventeur et le nom de JEAN-MARIE FARINA.

Toutes les caisses seront cachetées en cire verte, représentant les armoiries ci-dessus, le portrait de l'inventeur et le nom de JEAN-MARIE FARINA.

Chaque boîte portera une semblable gravure à celle en tête de ce Tableau et renfermera un Précis sur les propriétés médicales.

Fig. 17 Royal crests, mythological symbols, winged angels, and a laudatory text of testimonials advertise the effectiveness of Jean-Marie Farina's original, eighteenth-century "Aqua Mirabilis," or *Eau Admirable, dite de Cologne*, in this engraved, hand-colored prospectus from around 1818.

to give numbers to all houses and buildings, Mülhens's factory was assigned the street address "4711." After 1875, the number became the registered trademark of what was to become one of the world's most consumed and ubiquitous colognes: *Echt Kölnish Wasser No. 4711*. Richard Wagner adored it, consuming a liter a month.[7]

Napoleon's sensitivity to odors and the subtlety of his sense of smell were legion. With eyes shut, he once boasted, he could recognize his native Corsica by smell alone. "I have seen him," his personal secretary once wrote, "move away from more than one servant, who was far from suspecting the secret aversion he had inspired." During one of his military campaigns Napoleon is purported to have written

Josephine, whose smell he found immensely seductive, asking her not to wash until his return in two weeks' time. By imperial request the vast chambers of Versailles were purified and scented with the aromas of aloe wood, sugar, or vinegar burning in small silver-gilt bowls. Napoleon's love of the bath, at a time when the general custom of using water and taking partial (foot or seat) baths was growing among the elite, although it remained uncommon among the other classes of French society, equaled his love of cologne. Napoleon bathed often, probably to relieve his chronic dermatitis; from time to time, he would take lunch in the bathtub. It is recorded, for example, that on June 12, 1817, he spent four and a half hours in the tub, an exposure to water far greater than what was advised at the time; twenty years later the Comtesse de Bradi would counsel women to take only one bath a month. The emperor's favorite soap, a British product, was called Brown Windsor, a blend of bergamot, cumin, clove, lavender, rosemary, storax, castoreum, and other aromatic ingredients. Even in exile Napoleon's obsession with smell continued. The odor of fresh paint prevented him from moving into Longwood while the house was being renovated; four times he sent aides to smell the air and give him an assessment.[8]

Surviving the Revolution

Napoleon's fondness for cologne extended into the political and economic realms as well. During the Revolution, perfume along with many other objects considered frivolous luxuries—symbols of the excesses of the ancien régime—had all but disappeared. A few scents with patriotic names, although ephemeral lives, like "parfum à la Guillotine" and "parfum à la Nation," were still available. Under the Terror, choice of scent indicated political affiliation, a kind of odorous password. Such a "politically correct" scent could literally save one from execution: "You braved banishment and the guillotine by impregnating your ruffle and handkerchief with essence of lily or eau de la Reine," one commentator observed nearly a century later. A number of perfume establishments that had been founded before the Revolution and had supplied scents to the ancien régime, found ways to survive the difficult years of the Revolution. One such establishment belonged to Jean-Francois Houbigant. His "A la Corbeille des Fleurs" at 19 rue du Faubourg Saint-Honoré opened in 1775 and supplied wig powders, scented pomades, and floral extracts to Madame du Barry, Louis XV's mistress, and to Marie-Antoinette, Louis XVI's queen. Houbigant even delivered perfumed garter belts to the countess Saint-Hermine. The evening before the royal family fled Paris, only to be captured several hours later outside of the capital (the famous "night of Varenne" of June 20–21, 1791), Marie-Antoinette visited Houbigant's store to have her perfume bottles refilled before the journey. During the Revolution—in about 1792—Houbigant became a gathering point and supplier for a group of politically reactionary fops and elegant dandies called "les muscadins." They cut quite a figure with their tight-fitting, extravagant clothes and their passion for dousing themselves with heavy fragrances like musk, from which they derived their name, as well as ambergris, oliban, and spirits of tuberose, thyme, jonquil, and sandalwood. Under the Empire, Houbigant created captivating perfumes for Josephine, whose taste for heavy animal scents was not at all to Napoleon's liking. He was physically incapable of remaining more than a few minutes in the same room with the odor of musk, ambergris, and civet that filled the air of her apartments at the château de Malmaison, outside Paris. It was a smell that would linger

in the château for at least sixty years, even after the empress, whose nickname was "la folle du musc," had departed. The long-lasting wake left by her, once she was summarily "dismissed" as Napoleon's wife for having failed to give him an heir, was an act of olfactory revenge on her part.[9]

Another perfumer who came into prominence a year before Napoleon was named First Consul was Jean-Francois Lubin, whose store Aux Armes de France opened in 1798. Princess Borghese was a faithful customer and Lubin named a perfume after her. During the Empire, the court was particularly fond of *L'Eau de Lubin.* Created from citronella, lavender, and civet, it was used to refresh and soften the skin. Generally speaking, the years of the Consulate (1799–1804) and the First Empire (1804–1814, 1815) saw the renaissance of strong perfumes, whose structure was built on a base of heavy animal notes, like musk and civet. The fascination with all things Greek and Roman, which characterized the new Empire style in decor and fashion, inspired the reappearance of unguents and perfumed baths. Madame Tallien, a great beauty of the early days of the Empire, bathed in a watery blend of strawberries and raspberries and had her body gently massaged with sponges full of milk and perfumes. Napoleon's court, it was widely agreed, was even more perfumed than that of Louis XVI.[10]

Saving the Perfume Industry

Despite the slowdown in perfume production and consumption, which coincided with the end of the ancien régime and its "cour des parfums," the houses of Houbigant and Lubin as well as those of Antoine Chiris (1760), Jean-Louis Fargeon (1773), and Dissey (1774)—it would become L. T. Piver in the next century—somehow found ways of surviving both the Revolution and the Terror, even though their most wealthy and faithful customers had lost their perfumed heads under the blade of the guillotine. But as the new empire dawned and the refined customs and habits of the aristocracy began to reappear, Napoleon, recognizing the importance of French manufacturing to the glory of the nation, offered aid to the lagging perfume and soap industries. He granted imperial commissions and encouraged scientific and technological research in the field of organic chemistry, a science that would completely revolutionize perfume creation and the perfume industry in the last half of the century. Along with Madame Récamier and Madame Tallien, noblewomen of stunning beauty, and Josephine, whose need for exotic scents, high-waisted, semi-transparent gowns, and exquisite fashion accessories (flasks, combs, bottles, and the travel cases, called "nécessaires" they were carried in), Napoleon helped to resuscitate the traditional luxury industries which under the ancien régime had contributed to making the adjective "French" inseparable from the noun "civilization." Josephine, like her husband, loved baths, especially those perfumed with rose water and cognac, and she did her part in encouraging the manufacture of soap.[11]

Once available only to the aristocracy, these luxury products, under the new empire, had a more general and populist allure. Along with the abolition of social and political hierarchies founded on blood and heredity, the Revolution ensured that luxury itself would leave the narrow confines of the Court to take up residence among the newly emerging bourgeoisie. The availability of fragrances to the bourgeois class can be seen in a tongue-in-cheek list made by a Frenchman in 1807 of his wife's annual expenses. With obvious exaggeration he calculated that she had bought 600 dresses, 365 hats and bonnets, 500 pairs of stockings (in white and in different colors), and 1,200 francs' worth of "essences, perfumes and other drugs to make her young and pretty." After the Revolution the old aristocratic models of appearance, beautiful manners, and "bon ton" did not just disappear; they continued in phantomlike ways, behind the scenes.[12] Aristocratic style found new, albeit more muted, forms of expression in a bourgeois environment that valued distinction and quality, yet sought to possess them in a more moderate and less public manner; perfume labels of the period from 1815 to 1820 for products manufactured by the Farina firm reflect this subdued, yet nostalgic, even mythic view of an elegant, refined monarchy (figs. 18, 19, 20, 21, 22).

woman of the Court, whose aristocratic nobility and distinction were already established (by blood or heredity or royal decree) and in no need of further signs of legitimacy, the luxury with which the bourgeois woman now surrounded herself—her colorful clothes, rouged face, floral perfumes, and the decor of her ornate apartment—changed the very meaning of her identity as a woman. Feminine luxury had become the sign and emblem of wealth and upward mobility. The success of the man—husband or lover—was displaced onto his companion—wife or mistress—at a time when the idleness, wealth, and lavish consumption represented by such success could not, because of the dictates of bourgeois moderation and sobriety, be conspicuously displayed on or by his person. In the social world of the Second Empire (1852–1870) the bourgeois woman was not so much a woman of luxury as a feminized object of luxury, along with many other possessions, like the piano or the heavy curtains and ponderous furnishings—the poufs, cushions, frills, and prudish leg coverings—decorating the bourgeois apartment of the time. Whether courtesans, mistresses, or wives, elegant women were, Philippe Perrot observes, "money-pits exalting the glory of their protectors who were rich and powerful enough to turn these avid collectors of diamonds, these expenders of fortunes, into diamonds, their own diamonds."[13]

The coat of arms for the Guild of Gantiers-Parfumeurs [Glovemakers-Perfumers], 1729, features a glove flanked by what appear to be two jars of scented pomade, which were symbols of the trade.

Perfume and the Bourgeois Woman

The mentality of the bourgeoisie hid luxury behind a veil of sobriety and seriousness. The spectacle of ostentation once associated with the Court was refashioned within the more limited and private space of the domestic apartment. "The bourgeois who came into ascendancy with Louis Philippe," remarks Walter Benjamin, "sets store by the transformation of near and far into the interior. He knows but a single scene: the drawing room." Luxury was no longer a stable sign referring to itself, to its reality as an elegant, refined, or beautiful objet d'art; it was now a sign of the useful labor—the intellectual, managerial, and capitalist labor of the seriously dressed, black-suited bourgeois man—that had produced it or that could purchase it. Luxury had undergone a displacement: from the Court to the home, from the public to the private, from the indolent aristocrat to the working man, from the colorful foppery of male attire to the sober and uniform black suit. Where luxury had once been only an accessory for the fashionable

The Perfumer's Guild

Thanks to Napoleon, perfumers adopted a new code of professional comportment. Since the Middle Ages perfume makers had been ruled by the strict laws of a guild primarily dominated by and oriented toward the interests of glove making. Because of the toxic and putrid substances (urine was not uncommon) needed to tan hides, leather gloves had to be scented before they could be worn. The medieval guild that encompassed artisan perfumers was the "confrérie des Maîtres Gantiers et Parfumeurs," whose charter was established by an edict of King Philippe-Auguste in 1190 and reconfirmed in letters of patent issued by King Jean in 1357, by King Henri III in 1582, and by Louis XIV in 1658. For six centuries the corporation of master perfumers (gantiers-parfumeurs), whose patron was Saint Anne, regulated the practices of the profession and protected the interests of its artisans. It established the credentials of those who could sell gloves as well as perfumed goods and dictated the kinds of products they could

Fig. 18 A woman of healthy, pink-cheeked mien from the kingdom of Georgia, considered at the time to be a far-off, if not exotic, land in the Caucasus, lounges in a loose-fitting gown in this engraved, hand-colored perfume label for *Eau de la belle Georgienne, c.* 1815–1820.

Fig. 19 The classical proportions of this lifelike statue, the abundance of flowing and standing water, and the half-shell dimensions of the basin suggest the presence of the goddess Venus in this engraved, hand-colored perfume label for *Eau de Beauté, c.* 1815–1820.

manufacture. The list was long. In addition to simple toilet waters, glovemakers had the exclusive right, a monopoly of sorts, to sell: sachets filled with perfumed powders; pastilles and other compositions for use in perfume burners; potpourri; scented powders and pomades for the hair; soap; cosmetics; scented gloves; tobacco; and "oyselets de Chypre." These were cloth birds in bright colors decorated with real feathers and stuffed with aromatic powders; placed inside ornate cages and hung from ceilings or walls, they added fragrance to the air of a room.

Members of the corporation—there were 250 master perfumers in 1750—were obliged to serve four years as apprentices followed by three years as "compagnons" before becoming master perfumers. They were not free, until the Revolution that is, to work outside the confines of the guild or to develop their own trade and commerce. An exception was made, however, for two artisan perfumers who had the clout to receive royal protection. The first was René Le Florentin, Catherine de Medicis's personal perfumer, reputed to be as talented in creating scents as in fabricating poisons, who, once he had left his native Italy and set him-

self up in Paris, ran a boutique on the Pont au Change. The second was Martial, perfumer to Louis XIV, a king so enamored of strong scents (ambergris, musk, heavy floral odors)—until they gave him headaches and he could bear only the odor of orange blossoms—that he was known as the "sweetest smelling" monarch in French history. In the wake of the Revolution and with Napoleon's encouragement, perfumers, now free of the demands of glovemaking, could go their own way and create any scent or perfumed product they wished, as long, that is, as the market displayed interest. They had gained autonomy, and perfumery would henceforth no longer be an accessory, used only to enhance other luxury products like gloves, boxes, handkerchiefs, and fabrics. Having moved to center stage, perfume manufacturing would never again stand in the wings. This change provoked an explosion of new perfume houses. No longer constrained by the protectionist rules imposed by the guild of master perfumers, no longer forced to imitate the same uninspired perfume formulas year after year, but now stimulated by the rise of a moneyed class and the availability of new perfume ingredients, the perfumer was on his

Fig. 20 The three Graces of Greek mythology, representing beauty, charm, and good cheer and known for "giving life its bloom," according to the classicist Edith Hamilton, dance gracefully in this engraved, hand-colored perfume label for *Extrait des Trois Graces,* c. 1815–1820.

Fig. 21 Venus in the company of a mythological fish appears on her sculpted half-shell floating on the waves in this delicately engraved, hand-colored perfume label for *Eau de Vénus,* c. 1815–1820.

way, thanks in some degree to Napoleon, toward becoming an artist, a true creator of scents.[14]

Napoleon and Aromas of the Past

Napoleon, as the historian of his exile, Jean-Paul Kauffmann, has written, "exhausted himself trying to rekindle the ashes of the past." That those ashes were perfumed, that they filled the rooms of his mind with the scents of glories, victories, and pleasures now gone, and that they emitted traces of lost memories goes without saying. It was the very aroma of the past that Napoleon craved: the odors of boudoirs and ballrooms, of battlefields and chambers of state. It was the smell of a France now lost which he sought to revive. Eau de cologne for Napoleon had been a kind of eau de vie (brandy); the alcohol in both gave him life. It refreshed his mind through scent and exhilarated his spirit through taste, but only insofar as he could, from his island prison and while dictating his memoirs, remember the immediacy of such freshness and exhilara-

tion. This was a difficult task, for "the smell of melancholy and sadness is the smell of Longwood," Kauffmann observes. The effort of memory came at a steep price, especially to a man who had an extremely acute sense of smell. At Longwood Napoleon inhaled and ingested a past that was also a poison. "Day after day for five-and-a-half years, he took the hemlock of regret, desperately seeking to recover the consistency of events and the essence of things."[15] Eau de cologne had become for the emperor less the sustaining water of life than the debilitating water of death. Kept too long in the flask, the fragrance had turned stale, rancid, and sour. Memory now released only "the incense of melancholy and the musk of depression." It was "the smell of tragedy," one of many odors, like the smells of loneliness, boredom, desolation, oblivion, and decay, among which Napoleon was forced to live out his last days. On Saint Helena as in Versailles the great emperor was surrounded by odors he could not dissipate or efface. But at Longwood the valence of these smells had dramatically changed. They were now scents of loss and death: the ultimate aroma of defeat that eventually we all shall breathe.

Fig. 22 Members of the royal family, starting with King Louis XVI (1754–1793) on the right, are shown in profile in this engraved, hand-colored perfume label for *Eau de la famille royale*, c. 1815–1820.

The Smells of Streets and Bodies

The Paris of 1815 was still in great part a medieval city. With its 700,000 inhabitants living in a space equal in size to the first six arrondissements without the other fourteen, Paris was not yet the imperial capital of which Napoleon had dreamed. Air circulated poorly in narrow streets, which remained as dirty and dangerous as they had been near the end of the ancien régime, when Louis-Sebastien Mercier called Paris "the dirtiest city in the world." No sidewalks existed until 1823 when property owners of new constructions were required to build them; yet in the last years of the July Monarchy, in 1847, many city streets still had no such pedestrian paths. The mud, dust, and dirt were aggravated by the garbage thrown into public spaces by the ever-growing population. Butchers allowed blood and bowels from slaughtered cattle to run into the already filthy streets, reddening the shoes of those brave enough to cross;

sometimes entire carcasses were left for dogs to consume. Several streets were covered with boards to allow pedestrians to avoid the piled-up mud. This mud, according to Mercier, was tinged black by the iron and grease falling from passing wagons, and it stank from the runoff from kitchens and the droppings of horses. A spot of this awful mixture falling on the clothes of any unlucky pedestrian could burn a hole in the cloth. The street is, Mercier notes, "a terrible cesspool," where one must walk through "a liquid muck, black and stinking, and reaching to one's calf." Sewers were rare. Parisians emptied their chamber pots into the street, or their excrement was collected in tanks located beneath each house and emptied regularly at night, which did not prevent the fetid odors of the tanks from infecting the air of an entire quarter. In order to save themselves the effort of carting fecal matter beyond the city, the men who nightly emptied the tanks dumped the raw sewage into streams, which flowed down streets and eventually into the Seine. The principal water supply of Parisians was taken untreated from the Seine by porters who, for a price, carted it in buckets up narrow stairways to households. Direct-to-sewer drainage in Paris did not arrive until after World War I (and in some provincial cities not until after World War II), although a law imposing such connections had been passed in 1894. By 1903 only one Paris house in ten was connected to a general sewer system.[16]

While Mercier describes the Paris of the last days of the ancien régime, conditions fifty years later, after the Revolution, had not changed much. Visiting the city in 1835, Fanny Trollope was disconcerted by the bizarre juxtaposition of elegance and filth. In a city, she wrote, that transforms everything visible into graceful ornamentation, where the cafes and stores resemble "fairy palaces," and where "women seem too delicate to exist in this world and men too meticulous and cautious to allow the wind to ruffle their clothes, one is shocked and disgusted at every step by sights and odors I dare not describe." To experience the Paris street was to submit to an "unending attack on the senses." Such barbaric conditions indicated how far Paris had fallen, Trollope observed, behind cities like London, where pumped water already ascended to second- and third-floor apartments. The unhealthfulness of the urban scene could not continue for long without a signal of alarm, which had, in fact, been sounded three years before Trollope's visit, when 20,000 people perished in the cholera epidemic of 1832. This and a subsequent epidemic seventeen years later, along with a mortality rate of around 30 percent, finally persuaded the bourgeoisie that the miserable living conditions found in the poorer neighborhoods of the city constituted a direct threat to their own comparatively cosseted lives. Everyone had henceforth a vested interest in cleaning the city and instituting codes of hygiene.[17]

Against the odors of filth, waste, and human corruption "all the perfumes of Arabia" (*Macbeth*, V, i, 57–58, 48) were powerless. The war against the medieval smells of early nineteenth-century Paris inspired equally antiquated strategies of attack, some of which had been in existence since the seventeenth century, if not earlier. In the classical age of Louis XIV (whose reign lasted from 1643 to 1715), cleanliness had been associated with distinction, with the visible signs of one's appearance. In a court where everything was spectacle and theater, cleanliness was part of a general "art of representation" in which the way one dressed and the look of things took precedence. Merely to seem clean was sufficient, and there were many ways to accomplish this: powder for the face and hair, which gave a clean look without recourse to the much feared, weakening effects of hot water; cinnamon water, held in the mouth to sweeten the breath; vinegar, believed to ward off the plague and which pedestrians sniffed from the vinegar-impregnated sponges they held in their hands as they crossed the foul streets; and perfume, which emitted the aroma of cleanliness and disguised body odors. Fragrance was thought of as therapeutic; it strengthened the body and renewed the mind as well as disinfected the contaminated air.[18]

The Scents of Cleanliness

In the seventeenth-century art of semblance and mask, perfume played a complicated role. It was used not only as an agent of seduction and pleasure but as a force of purification: "Washing came down to a question, a strategy, of perfuming." The objects or materials judged to be healthful because they were perfumed grew. Royal inventories at the end of the seventeenth century revealed nearly forty objects of everyday use—combs, mirrors, linen, powders—that had been perfumed. Such objects were "supplementary instruments in the cautious game of appearances." Small sachets, called "coussine" or "coissine," had for several centuries been used to scent piles of linen and the insides of

clothes closets. Henri IV (1553–1610), the King of France and Navarre, paid his apothecary ninety-six pounds in 1578 for violet powder to be placed inside of his clothes chests. Men and women wore perfumed sachets in the space between their linen undergarments and their outer clothing; these were sewn into the inner folds of their dresses, tucked beneath their armpits, or attached by belts to their hips. Some individuals preferred to wear caps the linings of which contained a scented powder. They walked about the city, whenever obligated to do so, carrying a pomander—a small silver or gold ball shaped like an apple ("pomme," in French), its several compartments filled with aromatic substances like musk, civet, or ambergris ("ambre," in French)—which they would sniff

as an antidote, a counter-odor, to the stench of the street (fig. 23). Parisian hospitals like La Charité burned perfume in cassolettes (incense burners) all day and night to purify and render fragrant the air of the wards. And the great courtesans of the ancien régime, in particular those who frequented the "cour parfumé" of Louis XV at Versailles, changed their perfume every day following a calendar of 365 scents, each scent of their own creation.[19]

Perfume Burner. Eugène Rimmel, *The Book of Perfumes,* 1867. (London: Chapman and Hall, 1867).

Fig. 23 The "apple" of scent, each ornate "slice" filled with a different aromatic substance, was carried about to keep disagreeable odors at bay. Pomander open (above) and pomander closed (top), gilded silver and lapis, nineteenth century.

Perfume burner/diffuser, with gilded coiled snake, style Charles X (1824–1830).

For the aristocracy of the seventeenth century, perfume was a cleansing agent; it embodied freshness and purity in opposition to all that was dirty, repugnant, and malodorous in the streets or on the body. The very presence of scent signaled the absence of dirt and the fetid smells associated with it. To smell clean was to *be* clean. While literally invisible to an aristocratic society that had created an art of the visible, perfume, nonetheless, shared with the fashion, painting, and architecture of the court of Louis XIV(who reigned from 1643 to 1715) a quality of spectacle and theater. To the linen undergarments and silk dresses lavishly enveloping the aristocratic body, perfume added yet another covering, another furnishing; the body was made beautiful (and clean) through the mask of art. Slowly turning its back on the aesthetics of appearance and refinement—which, nevertheless, in some aristocratic quarters retained a certain power of attraction—the eighteenth century clearly showed its dislike for the excessive artificiality of Louis XIV's reign. In place of the delicacy, affectation, and love of disguise of the seventeenth-century court, the new century substituted a vigor, simplicity, and spontaneity more in accord with the natural world. Powdered wigs, starched hair sculpted into gigantic pyramids rising above the head, colored makeup on the cheeks, lead- and arsenic-based cosmetics, and the overuse of perfume weakened, it was now believed, the spirit and corrupted the purity of nature. An encyclopedia of beauty from 1806 advised women to have pure white skin, a recommendation that would lead to the cult of pallor favored by the Romantics. The deleterious and detestable use of "powders and odoriferous pomades," wrote one observer in 1791, were signs of "weakness and vanity." The superficial values of a society of appearances were denounced in favor

of more inward and spiritual qualities. "The state of the skin was more important than what might color," cover, or perfume it. Rousseau, for one, insisted on the natural cleanliness of his heroine Sophie in *Emile* (1762); the only scents she knows are those emitted by flowers, and the sweetest perfume her husband will ever inhale comes from her breath. For the first time, a connection between cleanliness and hygiene announced itself. The use of water was feared less and less, although baths when taken were only partial or localized. As the nineteenth century arrived, the most common instruments of cleanliness were washbasins: made of bronze or porcelain for the rich and stone or clay for all others.[20]

At the beginning of the nineteenth century the popularity of bathing grew, although the generalized anxiety about water did not abate; hot water, it was believed, weakened the body's vigor and stole its energy. After 1830, however, the temperate, lukewarm bath was considered the most hygienic form of cleanliness because it facilitated the respiratory function of the skin. With this new concept of "hygiene" came a new functionalist vision of the body and of its mechanics. The skin was conceived of as a breathing machine. By blocking and "choking" the pores, dirt prevented the body from "inhaling" oxygen and "exhaling" carbonic gas. A new representation of the body, taking the steam engine as its metaphor, began to spread through the collective unconscious of the century. As the 1800s progressed, a new perspective on the body, hygiene, health, and illness developed, in large part thanks to the discoveries of Louis Pasteur. Pasteurian microbiology changed the image and ideology of dirt. Another new system of images, based not on the combustive energy of the steam engine but on the invisible menace of natural organisms, of germs, now appeared. The rituals of cleanliness were envisioned as waging a defensive war, through weapons of water and soap, against invisible forces. Staying clean was an affair of privacy, demanding greater surveillance in more intimate spaces, and requiring more secret gestures than ever before. An interior cleanliness and a psychological cleanliness deepened the idea of what it meant to be clean. More than the body and skin, cleanliness involved the soul and spirit. To suppress the proliferation of germs both inside and outside the body, a regimen of daily washing had to be practiced. The body was a reality, a space, an organism that needed to be policed. And so beginning in 1880 the number of bathrooms with bathtubs, most often constructed off the bedroom, proliferated, especially in multi-floor Parisian apartment houses. Most bourgeois homes had running water on every floor after 1870. Thanks to the appearance of natural gas around the turn of the century, water heaters were installed above the tub. Yet, when the Duc de Broglie, one of France's richest men, acquired a hôtel de ville (townhouse) in Paris in 1902, it had no bathroom, and only one water faucet per floor.[21]

A new image system for the body arose from the growing popularity of bathtubs. The bathing space was a realm of intimacy, a sanctuary of total privacy into which the woman entered in full knowledge that she would not be disturbed by either her maid or spouse. As a space into which the male gaze could not penetrate—a hidden, secret world of feminine self-indulgence—the bathroom gave birth to voyeuristic fantasies, heating the imagination of certain fin de siècle male writers who fantasized the sensuality of warm water and scented soap touching the skin of a naked body. Cut off from the world, protected from furtive glances, the bathing space became a sensualized, feminized no-man's-land, where the woman's body and her pleasure were, unlike so much else in her daily life, potentially, if not completely, her own. Of course, internalized social, religious, and patriarchal prohibitions governing the chasteness, morality, and behavior of the female body could not help but follow the woman into the tub.

Aristocratic and Bourgeois "Airs," 1815–1851

The French court had for several centuries determined perfume taste. In place of the delicate scents of violet and iris root favored at the beginning of the seventeenth century came the strong, heady animal odors of ambergris and musk loved by Louis XIV, until he developed an antipathy for perfumes; his court, in complicity with his change of heart, pretended to faint at the very sight of a flower. The beginning of the reign of Louis XV in 1715, especially during the years of the Regency (1715–1723), revived among the French aristocracy the love of strong, spicy fragrances. The heavily incensed Catholic mass, celebrated before dinner at the Sainte Chapelle in Paris, was called the "messe musquée" (the "musk-mass"). By the middle of the eighteenth century, however, musk and civet had lost their respectability, and only pleasant, suave, indistinctive scents were encouraged. Madame de Pompadour, Louis XV's mistress, favored a blend of iris, sandalwood, and rose called "l'huile de Vénus" ("Venus oil"). In fact, the use of heavy musk fragrances could arouse suspicion about the state of one's cleanliness. The presence of too much perfume signaled a desire to hide something. In reaction to the use of animal scents, a preference for essential oils and scented waters extracted from flowers began to emerge. The emphasis was now on "good taste," and some men and women of elegance used nothing more than a perfumed handkerchief. Particularly popular were rose, lavender, and rosemary waters as well as delicate, discrete concoctions like "eaux de la maréchale" and "eaux de la duchesse."[22]

Perfume's Therapeutic Powers

The rise of Napoleon, who favored light scents like that of Farina's eau de cologne, nevertheless encouraged the short-lived renaissance of animal scents, only because Josephine and her entourage adored such smells and used them to excess. Once again, with the fall of the Napoleonic Empire, the tables turned, and delicate scents reasserted themselves in the courts of subsequent monarchies: those of Louis XVIII, Charles X, and Louis-Philippe from 1814 to 1848. The rise of Romanticism nourished the taste for light, gentle, and floral fragrances in harmony with the delicate odors of nature; a perfume, it was believed, should have the aroma of a bouquet. In the arts of perfumery as well as makeup, the natural was paramount. "I forbid the use of prepared perfumes," counseled the countess Bradi in 1838; "but those derived from natural flowers seem quite acceptable as long as they do not disturb others." With the arrival of Napoleon's second wife, Marie-Louise of Hapsburg, in 1810, the court turned its back on the excessive use of makeup, particularly of rouge; this was a major change since Josephine had, in one year alone, spent around 3,500 francs for her rouge. From the 1820s on, the delicateness of flowers and their vaporous, ethereal scents were linked to the physical condition of women, now seen as fragile beings, pallid of visage, white of skin, hollow of check, and subject to fits of fainting. Against such spells, smelling salts, carried in small flasks with a chain and a ring to be worn on the finger, or hung from the neck or belt, or slipped into sleeves and handbags, were of great relief. Scented waters also were believed to have a curative effect. In a prospectus for an eau de Cologne from around 1825–1830 (fig. 24), the image of a seated woman who has just fainted and to whose aid an elegant man is running flask in

Fig. 24 Abundant were the images, symbols, and stories brought together in advertising prospectuses for early-nineteenth-century scents as in Cosnier's lithograph for *Eau de Cologne de Dufour,* c. 1825, in which a fainting woman, an angel, garlanded portraits of nineteenth-century beauties, a snake, and a perfumer's tools share the stage.

hand, is followed by a text that first touts the cologne's medicinal aroma—"the Cologne Paul Gr. Dufour . . . is valuable as a restorative after a fainting spell: it is tonic, penetrating and animates the circulation of vital fluids"—and then celebrates its cosmetic powers: "The Cologne Paul Gr. Dufour . . . is perfect for all uses of the toilette: it is astringent, refreshing, makes the pores elastic, and is a pleasant perfume." Moreover, a host of images around the central panel suggest the perfumer's technical and spiritual knowledge, even his magic. On one side, a winged angel, surrounded by plants and flowers and an arrange-

ment of different-sized vials and bottles, studies a book. On the other, a mortar and pestle, an intricate network of alembics, distillers, serpentine tubes, funnels, boiling pots, and a large snake create a modern and mythic still life. The art of perfumery is represented as a blend of angel and reptile: at once spiritual and material, angelic and chthonic, natural and man-made.[23]

As the prospectus for Cologne Dufour indicates, perfumery in the first half of the nineteenth century, especially during the Restoration and the July Monarchy, was linked to medicinal and pharmaceutical uses: not only as a

64

Fig. 25 Nineteenth-century prospectuses were often as extravagant in the rhetoric of their claims as in the artistic beauty of their designs as in this poster-prospectus, a work of art in its own right, for *Eau de Cologne de Vourloud*, c. 1820s.

means to bring one back from a state of unconsciousness but also to whiten hands or grow hair or calm nerves. Several prospectuses for similar colognes call on medical testimony to support their claims. A prospectus for Eau de Cologne de Vourloud (from late in the 1820s)—a work of graphic art (fig. 25) that lavishly uses colors, symbols, images, and detailed allusions to Greek and exotic motifs—claims that it has been "approved by the Royal Society of Medicine" and that the Medical Society of Lyon has declared "in its meeting of July 22, 1823" that the cologne was "not only well made but had a level of perfection greater than any such colognes known to the Society up to this day." Similarly, the prospectus for one of Pierre-François Pascal Guerlain's earliest scents, *Eau de Cologne Impériale* (from 1830) presents the fragrance as both cosmetic and therapeutic, a pleasant toilet water and a medicinal agent for use in maintaining health: "Used as a rubbing solution in the bath or for partial ablutions, it admirably strengthens the entire organism as much by its lively and penetrating scent as by its impressively tonic action upon the skin." Ten years later in a bilingual prospectus presenting its "crème de fraises" (strawberry lotion) for the "softening, cooling, and beautifying of the skin," Guerlain appeals once again to the medical community to bear witness to the superiority of its product in the treatment of such "epidermal affections" as sunburn, dryness, blemishes, and other skin irritations.[24]

During the reign of Louis-Philippe the number of active perfumeries in the city of Grasse, renowned the world over as the center for the harvesting of flowers and the production of primary perfume ingredients, doubled from the twenty artisan manufacturers that had existed in 1806 under Napoleon. But despite this increase in perfume manufacturing, despite the growing number of perfume emporiums in Paris, despite the variety of perfumed objects available for sale (colognes, scented waters, sachets, creams, powders, toilet articles, and room disinfectants like Guerlain's *Ruban de Bruges*, a scented ribbon designed to burn slowly and release balsamic vapors into the air), and even despite the somewhat outrageous idea from the 1840s of using a Guerlain scent to perfume an issue of the newspaper *La Sylphide*, the revival of perfume in the first half of the nineteenth century moved slowly indeed. In fact, it took until 1835 for the French perfume industry to regain the volume of trade it had enjoyed at the start of the Revolution. This may account for the observation in an 1818 issue of the fashion journal *Observateur des modes* that the perfumery of the times "offered nothing new." "No women of class would dare to use perfumes today," opined the *Petit courrier des dames* in August 1830. "On the other hand," the article went on, "it is acceptable to scent one's linen and silks with the odor of vetiver or other kinds of herbs that one puts in a sachet." The popularity of these sachets had nearly eclipsed the use of liquid perfumes among polite society, reported the *Journal des dames et des modes* in 1829. Moreover, the traditional master perfumer of the Restoration and the July Monarchy was, generally speaking and with a few notable exceptions, an anonymous nose, whose talent for innovation, if he had any, was hampered by a stock of over-used formulas and whose palette of scents suffered from a limited number of existing ingredients and an equally limited reserve of knowledge. As the Restoration came to an end, there was no hint that perfume would grow into the industry it would eventually become, nor that a taste for smell-related sensations would be raised to the "height of art by the Baudelaires and Huysmans" of the second half of the century, although the fashion-conscious dandy of the period (of whom Baudelaire and Huysmans would come to represent the finest examples) already knew well the value of perfume and other fashion accessories.[25]

Guerlain Changes Attitudes

The first hint of the dramatic change in perfume creation to come, although there was no way at the time to foretell it, was the opening in 1828 of a perfume shop on the rue de Rivoli on the ground floor of the Hotel Meurice by Pierre-François Pascal Guerlain. His first compositions—*Senteur des champs*, *Esprit de fleurs*—recalled his youth in Picardy. *Bouquet du jardin du roi* and *Parfum des rois* were scents created in homage to the royalty of England and France. They continued a tradition of naming perfumes after noble men and women of European courts, a custom that would intensify through the nineteenth century and then continue into the twentieth, with names of actresses and other celebrities replacing those of kings, queens, and duchesses. At the start, Guerlain was a "parfumeur-vinaigrier"—vinegar waters ("vinaigre de toilette") were much in demand—but he soon created other fragrances of note, like *Eau de cologne impériale* (1830), which in 1853 earned him the much coveted designation of "Perfumer to Her Majesty the Empress Eugénie." During the Second Empire, Guerlain, whose store had in the meantime been relocated to the rue de la Paix, produced several popular perfumes: *Bouquet de l'Impératrice, Bouquet Napoléon, Parfum de France, Parfum Impérial, Eau de cologne russe*, and *Bouquet de l'Exposition* (named for the world's fair of 1867).[26]

By the turn of the century, Guerlain had already produced two hundred fragrances, and the company, now run by the founder's sons Aimé and Gabriel, created several well-known perfumes, especially during the last years of the century: *Fleurs d'Italie, Rococo, Belle de France, Le Jardin de mon curé*, and in 1889, *Jicky*. This was a subtle, truly new fragrance which would move perfumery in an

Guerlain's *Véritable Eau de Cologne impériale,* first composed in 1830, is presented here in the so-called "bee bottle," designed by Pochet & du Courval in 1853. The bottle is decorated with a colony of hand-painted bees, a Napoleonic symbol, and carries a label displaying the imperial arms of Her Majesty the Empress Eugénie, the wife of Napoleon III and a faithful client of Guerlain.

altogether different direction, abandoning the floral single-note world of the "bouquet" for scents—the components of which were impossible to identify—that had no resemblance to anything in nature. *Jicky*, whose notes start out as those of an eau de cologne and then deepen into the animal scent of civet, was, Elisabeth Barillé and Catherine Laroze note, as "troubling in its own way as the Eiffel Tower" constructed the same year.[27] During the 1830s and 1840s, Guerlain's perfumes were admired and used not only by French nobility and the haute bourgeoisie now beginning to evolve, but by writers like Balzac, for whom fashion was the very "expression of society," a necessity "touching all of life" and not a mere luxury. At the moment in the early 1830s that he began to put pen to paper and compose his novel *César Birotteau* (1837), the story of the trials and tribulations of a perfumer-capitalist during the First Empire and the subsequent Restoration, Balzac had Guerlain make a specially designed toilet water, which he kept on his desk during the writing of the novel. The novelist, who once wrote that only those who visited Paris often could ever be considered completely elegant (with the exclusion of "businessmen and professors of the humanities") was particularly sensitive to the "poetry" of fashion as practiced by what he dubbed "elegantologistes" and "modiphiles" (stylephiles). More than a social practice, elegance for Balzac was a philosophical and aesthetic experience creative of order, unity, harmony, and simplicity. Moreover, the growing popularity of baths among upper-class Parisians during the 1830s did not leave the elegant Balzac indifferent. He bathed often but along with his bourgeois compatriots worried about the deleterious effect that water might have on his physiology as well as his creativity: "I am fearful of weakening the fibers of my body through overheating," he wrote.[28]

An Entrepreneur of Scent

Balzac's César Birotteau is a dyed-in-the-wool monarchist for reasons having as much to do with politics as with cosmetics and perfume. As one who begins his career working for the perfumer Ragon, supplier of powder to King Louis XVI and his queen, Marie Antoinette, César vigorously opposes the Revolution, fights against Napoleon, is wounded at a royalist insurrection on the steps of the church Saint-Roch on October 5, 1795, and never lets himself forget the memory of the two royal heads decapitated two years earlier only a few steps from his boutique.[29] "Loving the King is the same as loving France!" he proudly declares (6). After being wounded César resolves to be "purely and simply a royalist perfumer . . . devoting body and soul" to his homeland (23). As the monarchy is restored and France enters a new period of unheard-of prosperity coterminous with the rise of the bourgeoisie, César's political fidelity, moral rectitude, and entrepreneurial spirit are rewarded. From the hands of the new king, Louis XVIII, he receives: financial

assistance—when his perfume business goes bankrupt; political patronage—a judgeship and the mayoralty of his arrondissement, which he turns down for a position with less political exposure; and national recognition—the prestigious Légion d'Honneur. But just as important in the formation of his passionately royalist sentiments and his hatred of all that Napoleon has represented is his professional feeling that as a true perfumer he could not but detest "a revolution that gave everyone a fringe à la Titus [a Roman-inspired coiffure] and did away with hair-powder" (22).

The story of César Birotteau's rise and fall as perfumer and businessman (his "grandeur" and "decadence" to quote the words Balzac uses in the novel's subtitle) is succinctly recounted in the titles the writer has given to the first and second parts of the novel: "César at His Zenith" and "César Grapples with Misfortune." The high point from which the seesaw of fate will descend, tipping César from the summit of success into the abyss of financial ruin, arrives during a scene of momentous celebration at the very end of the novel's first part. César arranges a majestic ball to fete his becoming a chevalier (knight) in the Légion d'Honneur—a ball that costs him the equivalent of between 250,000 and 300,000 in modern-day francs—and to celebrate symbolically the fulfillment of a rags-to-riches dream: that of a poor country peasant who had come to Paris on foot with little more than his walking stick and his hobnailed boots (128). At the end of a ball where the bourgeoisie rub elbows with a few token members of the aristocracy whose dress, in contrast to that of their bourgeois counterparts, shows no marks of excess, no labored signs of work, but manifests, rather, a naturalness derived from long exposure to elegant gatherings, Balzac reaches for a musical metaphor—the finale of Beethoven's *Fifth Symphony*—to emphasize, not without the irony that hyperbole offers, the happiness that a bank account stocked with newly acquired money and a buttonhole colored with the red ribbon of the Légion d'Honneur can bestow. The final, surging leitmotif of Beethoven's symphony into which, according to Balzac, converge all the musical powers of the piece, has the same intense, harmonious, and sublime effect on those poetic souls who hear it as César's ball has on his life. Money, the true subject of Balzac's novel, is equated with music. All the possessions that a substantial bank account can buy come together in the symphonic fusion and transcendent harmony of a marvelous paradise, where chords charm the listener as magically as commercial transactions bedazzle the businessman. It is a sublime ideal of rich and lavish things: "A radiant fairy darts forward, raising her wand. You hear the rustling of purple silk curtains, parted by angels. Gold doors, sculpted like those of the Baptistry of Florence, turn on diamond hinges. The eye plunges into splendid vistas and embraces

La Cueillette Du Jardin de mon Curé
à Paris, chez Guerlain Parfumeur 15 Rue de la Paix

Reviewing Guerlain's *Jardin de mon curé* (1895), three years after its appearance, *Le Figaro*, the Parisian newspaper, compared it to a "scent rising from a true garden where rare and exquisite flowers bloom. Is it lily-of-the-valley or verbena or heliotrope that dominates? It's impossible to tell . . . But just one drop of this ideal blend on a handkerchief is all that is needed." This ad for *Jardin de mon curé*, based on a watercolor by the French artist Louise Abbéna (1858–1927), shows a priest ("un curé") picking flowers in the garden ("le jardin") behind his church.

a succession of marvelous palaces from which creatures of a higher species emerge" (136). Prosperity has brought César's life to the heights of mercantile splendor, in which the aesthetic quality of the things that money acquires envelops and colors the reality of money itself. The clinking of metal coins and the crinkling of paper money are transformed like the vulgarity of César's life into the melodious notes of Beethoven's grand symphony. Prosperity becomes a work of art, like music and perfume. In keeping with the success it represents it has a smell all its own:

> The *incense* of prosperity *fumes*, the alter of happiness *flares up* and a *scented vapor swirls* around! Beings with divine smiles, dressed in white tunics trimmed with blue, lightly *flit* before your eyes, exhibiting faces of superhuman beauty and figures of infinite grace. Amoretti [cupids] *flutter* around, *scattering* the flames from their torches! You feel loved, you are *imbued* with a happiness that you *inhale* without understanding it, *bathed* in the *torrents* of this *flowing harmony* that *pours* out for each person the *ambrosia* of his choice. Your heart is smitten with secret *aspirations* which, for a moment, are realized. After leading you through the *heavens*, the *enchanter*, by means of a profound and mysterious transition with the basses, returns you abruptly to the slough of cold reality, only to raise you from it again when he has awakened your *thirst* for his *divine melodies* and your soul exclaims, "Encore!" [italics mine] (136)

Interestingly, Balzac uses words that do double service, describing in one and the same breath the outpouring of music and the emanation of scent, both of which serve here to represent the elevating, sublime power of prosperity. Balzac's literary reinterpretation of Beethoven's *Fifth Symphony*, with its emphasis on verbs like "fume," "flare," "swirl," "flit," "flutter," "scatter," "inhale," "bathe," "flow," "pour" and nouns like "incense," "scented vapor," "torrents," "harmony," "ambrosia," "heavens," "aspirations," "enchanter," "divine melodies," describes the dynamic action and the interpenetrating motion of three simultaneous realities: music, perfume, and money. The bliss created by an exquisite chord or by a delicate scent is no different, Balzac seems to say in a tone of deliberate exaggeration, than that state of superior, "spiritual" being that money creates.

But every crescendo has its decrescendo, every trace its dissipation, every fortune its ruin, and every ideal its cold, hard reality. The finale of Beethoven's uplifting symphony—in Balzac's imagination an allegory for the upwardly mobile aspirations of the new bourgeoisie—represents the finale of César's "commercial symphony" (136): the beginning of the end of his personal success and prosperity. Before his fall from financial grace occurs, César has had a successful career as a purveyor of scent whose establishment, La Reine des Roses, sells perfumes and cosmetics of his own invention. César's *Double Pâte des Sultanes*

("The Sultana's Double Hand-Cream") for whitening the hands and his *Eau Carminative* ("Carminative Water"), a lotion for giving color to the face, have generated a substantial profit, primarily because of the perfumer's savvy skill at advertising and his innate understanding of consumer psychology, which are far more subtle and advanced than his knowledge of chemistry and perfumery. César's promotional skills have been inspired by a style of advertising just beginning to appear in Parisian novelty shops and dry goods stores, like Le Petit Matelot where Constance, his wife-to-be, works. Here, ingenious displays of painted signs, hanging streamers, posters, cravats structured like card-houses, ribbons, "illusions and optical effects," and other kinds of "commercial attractions" turn a shop window into a "poem" celebrating trade. The first perfumer to see the promise of spectacle, César uses a "wealth of bills, announcements and other means of noising things abroad that are, perhaps unjustly, known by the term 'quackery'" to promote his perfumes and cosmetics (24, 28). Both products, the *Double Pâte des Sultanes* and *Eau Carminative*, invented with the assistance of the celebrated chemist Vauquelin, are brought to the attention of the public through colored advertisements (*affiches*) which boldly announce that these products have received the "approval of the Institute!" (28). This kind of authoritative endorsement, which César is the first to use, casts over consumers a magical spell only slightly less successful than César's strategy of tying his cosmetics to an exotic orientalism, especially in a France where "every man wishes to become a sultan and every woman a sultana" (28). The allusions to foreign places like Constantinople or Cologne are, as César observes with a canny understanding of bourgeois taste, nothing but "tricks contrived to attract the French who could not stand whatever was from their own country" (34).

César Advertises His Wares

Balzac, arguably "one of the first to have divined the power of the advertisement," invents a fictional prospectus for the *Double Pâte des Sultanes* and the *Eau Carminative*, which in form and structure closely follows authentic promotional materials of the period. César's prospectus begins with a six-line headline mostly in caps, announcing the names of the products, heralding their newness and efficacy—they represent a "wonderful discovery"—and assigning them the scientific authority that the approval of the "Institut de France" can alone accord (29). This is then followed by a long prose text the tone of which is simultaneously rhetorical, promotional, and pseudo-scientific, not unlike today's advertisements for cosmetic and skin-rejuvenating products. The first paragraph of César's prospectus makes several claims: first, that the sultana's hand cream (*Double Pâte*) and the carminative lotion (*Eau Carminative*) fulfill the desire of European men and women for a product superior to cologne that would enhance the "softness, pliability, luster, and smoothness of the skin" (29); second, that the *Pâte* and the *Eau* have been developed from a long, careful study of the dermis and epidermis of both sexes; third, that the two products have been deemed "wonders" by elegant Parisian society; fourth, that they both possess "astonishing" propensities for acting on the skin and for avoiding premature wrinkles; and fifth, that the cream and lotion, since they have been specifically designed for two different kinds of personalities, have been color-coded so that those with "lymphatic" constitutions would need to choose the pink *Pâte* and *Eau* and those with "sanguinary" temperaments the white (29). Cleverly, César ties the sultana's hand cream to three esteemed authorities: first, the past, since the initial discovery was made by an ancient Arab doctor for use in a sultan's harem; second, the state, since the august French Institute has given its approval; and third, science, since the cream has received from the illustrious chemist Vauquelin an enthusiastic and learned report. César then turns his attention to the aesthetic, cosmetic, and dermatological effects of his concoctions: in particular, their ability to efface freckles and pimples and their success in whitening the skin, in drying sweaty hands, in reviving one's coloring by opening or closing the pores, and in resisting the attacks of time. Grateful to César for this new weapon of epidermal defense, women, the prospectus proclaims, call *Eau Carminative* "Beauty's Friend" (30). This is a friend to men as well, for it is beneficial in the treatment of razor burn, chapped lips, rough skin, migraines (by balancing the humors), and skin irritations.

César's publicity prospectus for his *Pâte* and *Eau* are, however, nothing compared with the advertisement that he commissions for a new formula, a product certain to assure his comeback after the bankruptcy which his own stupidity, greed, and excessive spending have caused. *Huile Céphalique* ("Cephalic Oil"), a hazelnut concoction designed to protect hair, will compete fiercely against and ultimately dominate—this is César's hope and that of his future son-in-law, Anselme Popinot—a popular product already on the market: *Huile de Macassar*. In fact, Macassar oil was an authentic hair preparation fabricated in Great Britain and popular not only during Balzac's time but well into the century. César's prospectus for "Cephalic Oil," created by Andoche Finot, a writer whose lack of literary success has pushed him into the nascent world of advertising— what Balzac, tongue-in-cheek, calls a "literature with a purpose" (115)—reveals Finot's talents at getting "inside the shopkeeper's head" (98). The finesse of Finot's psychological acuity is evident from the advertisement's first sentence, a seemingly self-defeating statement asserting the inefficacy of hair treatment preparations in general. Science has proven, Finot proclaims, that no cosmetic product known to humankind can ever grow hair, or prevent its loss, or for that matter reverse graying. Candor is wedded cunningly to scientific authority in order to steal the stage (and the thunder) from Macassar Oil, which had been advertised as a fail-safe cure against hair loss. Having thus announced the brutal fact that aging is irreversible, the prospectus carves out new terrain for *Huile Céphalique*, not as a cure for baldness, but as a way to slow down the inevitable. With its hazelnut oil and exceptional fragrance, "Cephalic Oil" will nurture the hair roots and the beneficial "liquors" they contain, protecting them against the action of the outside air and the noxious effects of cold and heat, and by extension (since the oil touches the scalp and keeps the inner temperature of the head stable) warding off colds, rhinitis, and other afflictions of the brain (114). Hair will thus be preserved to an advanced age, maintaining the "brilliance, fineness, and luster which endow the heads of children with such charms" (114).

Once again the arguments of the prospectus are rhetorically "scientific," and once again they invoke different forms of authority. Not only is the awarding of the "Gold Medal at the Exhibition of 1824" to *Huile Céphalique* proudly announced in the advertisement's heading, but the two sides of the medal are visually reproduced. One side represents a Greek goddess about to bestow a laurel wreath on the head of another figure. Behind them lie technical instruments (the alembic frequently used for distillation by perfumers and chemists of the age) while above them, engraved in a hemispheric arc, are the words: "Encouragement et récompense à l'industrie." The medal's recto portrays the profile of "Charles X. Roi de France."[30] The appeal to royal authority is matched by the invocation of scientific approbation. The oil is "manufactured according to principles laid down by the Academy of Sciences" (114). Even its pretentious name, "Céphalique," nothing more than a synonym for "head," suggests a scientifically developed product endowed with "miraculous" if not hermetic powers. Finot, as the writer of the prospectus, is keenly aware that a new style of advertising has dawned: "The age of the light-hearted, jocular prospectus has passed," he observes. "We are entering a scientific era, so we need a learned tone, a note of authority to impress the public" (115–16). In addition to invoking the authority of learning, Finot appeals to the authority of the past as well, although Balzac presents it more as parody than reality. In protecting the hair root from all external effects of the atmosphere, Cephalic Oil rediscovers a secret "prized in classical times by Greeks, Romans and the Peoples of the North, who set high store by their hair. It has been proven by scholarly research that the nobility, formerly distinguished by the length of their hair, used no other method than this" (i.e., Cephalic Oil) (114). The confidence with which ancient practices are interpreted anachronistically and presented as consonant with, if not prophetic of, contemporary habits defines the authority that the past has for Popinot, Finot, and César. In fact, the idea for a hair oil is César's alone. While the names suggested for the product evolve in César's mind from *Huile Comagène* ("Comagenous Oil," from the Latin word, *coma*, signifying "hair of the head") to *Essence Comagène*, to *Huile de Birotteau*, to *Huile*

Césarienne, in honor of César's daughter, Césarine (Popinot wisely drops it because of its allusion to a Caesarian section), and finally to *Huile Céphalique*, the evolution of the name reflects a series of decisions more concerned with design, commerce, and advertising (even poetry) than with either chemistry or perfumery: "Absorbed in his calculations" César, according to Balzac, "walked along the Rue Saint-Honoré thinking about his duel with Macassar Oil, considering the labels and shape of his bottles, and working out the texture of the corks and color of the posters. And they say that there is no poetry in trade!" (78).

The inspiration for César's hair oil, which at first he strongly believes will grow new hair, a supposition of which he will in short order be disabused by the chemist Vauquelin, comes to him in the same way as his discoveries of the *Double Pâte des Sultanes* and the *Eau Carminative*: namely, by chance. One day, opening a book, he comes across the engraving (based on an 1814 painting) of the Greek priestess, Hero, pouring oil on her lover's, Leander's, head, an irrefutable sign for César that even the ancients loved hair and detested baldness (16). His lack of chemical and biological knowledge and his innate conservatism, which regards all figures of authority—the Greeks, the Bourbon monarchy, and the past in general—as embodiments of truth, push César toward the conviction that if the ancients "used as much oil on their hair … they must have

Fig. 26 Despite the names given to early-nineteenth-century scented products, the images used to represent them were often incongruous; neither the inhabitants nor the trees resemble a Canadian scene or landscape in this engraved, hand-colored label for *Admirable Graisse d'Ours du Canada*, c. 1815–1820.

had some reason for doing so. After all, Antiquity is Antiquity!" (85). The engraving serves as the central image for 2,000 enormous red notices invented by Popinot and Finot and placed in the most prominent spots in Paris, including the doors of hairdressers, wig makers, and perfumers: "No one could avoid being confronted with Cephalic Oil" (160). Nor could Parisians avoid the claim,

printed as an epigraph to the engraving, that "the ancient peoples of Antiquity preserved their hair through the use of cephalic oil" (160). The hair oil is an immense success; and César earns enough money to pay off the debts incurred through his earlier bankruptcy.

If an engraving of Hero and Leander was the stimulus for César's invention of Cephalic Oil, one can assume that a similarly graphic artifact, seen in the Paris of his day, was the inspiration for Balzac's creation of the prospectus for *Huile Céphalique*, as he describes it in the novel. Prospectuses using similar language to tout the hair-growing power of different products were common during the late Restoration and throughout the July Monarchy (1820s to 1840s). One such notice for the prevention of hair loss, a prospectus for *Pommade du Sieur Allian*, dating from the first half of the nineteenth century, vaunts the receipt of a royal patent and the approval of the Faculty of Medicine. Not only is it "a pleasantly scented pomade," but it performs better than its competitors, which it mentions by name just as the prospectus for Popinot's Cephalic Oil claimed superiority in its "duel" to the death with Macassar Oil. Several houses, so the prospectus for *Pommade du Sieur Allian* affirms, sell Lion and Bear oils (*Graisse de Lion et d'Ours*), but "it is well known that these two oils heat the brain and occasion the loss of hair. If Lion and Bear oils possessed the properties attributed to them, the forests of Russia would not hold enough animals for those who use these products everyday." A beaver pomade and oil, another product actually created during the same period, advertised its achievements in a prospectus showing the engraved image of two Indians, their heads encircled by a crown of plumes, standing on each side of an engraved panel displaying the figure of a large beaver crossing a stream. Manufactured by the Parisian perfumer Pigeau, the substance was purported to prevent hair loss and encourage rapid hair growth. Of similar inspiration was a label for Farina's "Admirable Canadian Bear Fat," a pomade created to "maintain beauty and the head," which pictured two native North Americans (with clearly European faces) looking on as a tamed bear sniffs at (and bows before) a young woman's foot (fig. 26). Hair growth (both in animals and humans) appears to have been associated with cold northern climes: those not only of North America (the Canadian wilderness, in particular) but of the mountainous regions of the Greater Caucasus of Russia as the label and name for *Huile Circassienne* manufactured by Pinaud indicate (*3000 ans*, 143, 147) (fig. 27).

In Balzac's *César Birotteau*, perfume and cosmetics are points of departure for a more incisive and critical analysis of the excesses of salesmanship, advertising, and consumer fetishism, which were in their infancy in the bourgeois society of the Restoration. Money and speculation, of course, are social forces or "machines" whose functioning Balzac examines in depth not only in this novel but throughout his multi-volumed *La Comédie humaine*. César is exemplary of a certain merchant mentality recognizable by its preoccupation with commerce, advertising, and money and its attraction to ridiculous dreams and comic schemes. And César is exemplary of honesty as well (although the outlandish claims he has made for his cosmetic and perfume products are anything but honest), for he repays his creditors the enormous debt his bankruptcy has caused and raises himself and his family out of financial ruin. As he dies suddenly of an aneurysm in the novel's final pages—a scene of exaggerated glorification in which the death of "the just man" is given a figuration worthy of Rembrandt (whom Balzac mentions)—he is presented, not without a mixture of sympathy and irony, as "a hero of commercial probity" (263), a "righteous man" (264), and "a martyr to honest dealing, worthy of his eternal crown" (264). As a capitalist, and generally speaking an honest capitalist at that, César Birotteau receives at the hands of Balzac a portrait at once mocking and celebratory. The grandeur of his success as a businessman followed by his descent into financial ruin and followed, in turn, by the restoration of his family's honor and fortune make for a cautionary tale in which César represents one of many social types, but the only perfumer, in Balzac's "human comedy."

The Growth of Advertising

When Balzac describes César Birotteau's reliance on advertising—the posters, prospectuses, announcements, and other printed materials the perfumer uses to sell his hand cream, face lotion, and hair oil—he remarks that such promotional media are "perhaps unjustly" criticized as "quackery" (28). At almost the same historical moment, the caricaturist Honoré Daumier portrays the bufoonery of a perfumer in his satirical series of drawings entitled *Robert Macaire* (1836), an excoriating portrait of the hypocritical pretensions of certain middle-class types like the financier, the lawyer, and the businessman. Wearing a monkey's face and speaking with pompous self-righteousness, the perfumer disingenuously tells a male client to whom he is hawking one of his scents, "Sir, I despise the charla-

Fig. 27 The thickness and abundance of the woman's calf-length hair in this label for Pinaud's *Huile Circassienne* offer testimony to the product's magical effectiveness.

tanism of the Affiche, I despise the puffery of the advertisement, I abhor everything that smells of the quack, the vacillator, the tightrope walker." Daumier's mistrust of and hostility toward advertising seem to have accompanied the modern development of advertising in France from the start of the nineteenth century until the 1930s. In the form of "a commercial message diffused by means of an organ of mass communication," advertising can be said to have begun with the start of newspapers; the first paper (*La Gazette*) was published in France in 1631, and the first "advertisement" in the form of a small notice (*petite annonce*), designed to bring together the seller of a good with a buyer, appeared just two years later. Yet, the true development of modern advertising does not really get underway until the beginning of the nineteenth century. In the wake of the Revolution, which witnessed the diffusion of information through widely circulated posters, bills, and periodicals linked to political but not yet commercial ends, the nineteenth century vigorously set about to extend the reach of publicity into economic and business spheres. By 1830 advertising had come to mean "the laudatory presentation of a product for the purposes of attracting a buyer," and it was disseminated primarily through newspapers, posters, and prospectuses. Prospectuses were favored because, unlike newspapers, they could describe the advertised product in detail and at great length; they could also target pre-selected categories of people (hunters, priests, grocers, functionaries) whom the merchant wished to attract. Such prospectuses, some printed on expensive vellum, others on rag paper, could be sent directly to the homes of potential customers. To facilitate this distribution, new enterprises—the first was founded in 1829—specialized in assembling lists of names and addresses and delivering prospectuses to them.[31]

Newspapers and Advertising Agencies

Stimulated by the economic prosperity of France, the spectacular growth in the circulation of newspapers, and the development of new commercial and industrial opportunities at the beginning of the Second Empire in 1852, advertising began to flourish, becoming a business in its own right. The liberalization of laws governing the press between 1868 and 1881 produced a proliferation of newspapers. In 1867 there were twenty-one dailies in Paris and fifty-seven in the provinces. Thirteen years later that number had grown to sixty dailies in the capital and 190 in the provinces. The press runs for the Parisian papers went from 200,000 in 1863 to 5,500,000 on the eve of World War I. In this time, newspapers became the primary vehicle for the diffusion of ads. By the beginning of the Third Republic in 1870, for example, advertising composed a quarter to a third of the space in the large Parisian political dailies, a prosperous situation that would not recur until the next century. With the proliferation of newspapers came the creation of advertising agencies. Charles Havas founded his firm in 1832, and it would become a gigantic empire lasting well into the twentieth century. By selecting newspapers popular among different social classes advertisers targeted their messages to different groups of potential consumers. Because its readers came from the lower or middle ranks of the bourgeoisie, *Le Journal,* created in 1892, published twice the number of ads than *Le Petit Parisien,* founded in 1876, whose readership was centered primarily in the working class (Martin, *Trois siècles,* 91–92, 16–17, 404, 99, resp.).

A variety of different kinds of advertisements appeared in these newspapers. On the eve of World War I, the small notices placed by individuals for the goods or services they offered slightly outnumbered the larger *annonces-affiches* (commercial ads), which were the primary instruments of mercantile advertising. Commercial ads were concerned with food and drink (wines, apéritifs, mineral water), pharmaceutical products (tisanes, cough drops, purgatives, miraculous cures), books, jewels, and toiletries. Relegated to the newspaper's last page where they were thrown together pell-mell, these advertisements were distinctly drab and boring. From time to time the commercial ad occupied several columns. The only advertisers to buy a whole page in a given issue were usually the large Parisian department stores, by far the most important advertisers at the end of the Second Empire, although by the close of the century they had begun to withdraw their advertising from the dailies. A third type of advertisement, designed to call attention to a new product or brand, was directly inserted as a news item (a "fait divers") into the contents of a newspaper, and even into the middle of an unrelated news article. More expensive than any other kind of advertisement and considered the most sophisticated form of publicity, it was an early form of today's "infomercial." Among specialist newspapers the women's press was by far the most popular. Whereas in 1852 there were forty fashion newspapers, by 1870 the number had doubled. The largest of these women's papers, *Le Petit Echo de la mode* (Fashion Gossip), a Catholic weekly with a run of 300,000 copies, carried ads for chocolates, jellies, syrups, clothes, fabric, sewing machines, and after 1893 offered sewing

patterns. Not to be outdone by the popularity of these specialist periodicals, the large Parisian dailies began to create their own fashion supplements, like the monthly *Figaro Modes* launched in 1903. On the whole, however, fin de siècle newspaper advertisements were monotonous, dreary, and unimaginative. The text alone was paramount, and a drawing, sketch, or image, if included, was merely an accessory. There were no colors, and it was not unusual for the same black and white images to run for twenty or thirty years. Newspapers, especially from the Second Empire to the beginning of World War I, were not the only medium for advertising in France. The nineteenth century witnessed the birth of two uniquely French advertising inventions: the catalogue and the billboard poster or *affiche,* which in the last decades of the century turned Paris into the "shop window of modern France." With the creation of the *affiche* and later with the opening of the Paris subway in 1900—its good lighting and its nearly 33,000 yards of wall space specifically reserved for posters made it a superb venue for ads—French advertising became part of the daily reality of the cosmopolitan city.[32]

Billboards and Catalogues

The billboard and catalogue began their rise in the 1860s, the latter linked to the soaring popularity of the new department stores popping up all over Paris. At first these stores advertised abundantly in the Parisian dailies, but in the years following 1865 they made the catalogue their primary medium of advertisement. The first catalogues, those from before 1850, were prospectuses of one to a few pages in length or small brochures with printed lists of prices; bookstores were the first to use these price catalogues. But printed in great numbers and widely circulated, the catalogue became the organ of preference for the large department stores; it was the best vehicle for sales by mail, especially among the bourgeois consumers living in the provinces or abroad. All the large Parisian stores, like Le Bon Marché (created in 1852), Les Grands Magasins du Louvre (1855), Le Printemps (1865), La Samaritaine, and Les Galeries Lafayette (both founded in 1869), used them. The 1866 catalogue for Le Bon Marché ran to nearly one hundred pages. Three years later, it displayed the first black and white drawings of women's clothing; color was not featured until the early 1900s. From the start Le Bon Marché catalogues were the most attractive and the most illustrated. By the turn of the century the torch had passed to the Grands Magasins du Louvre, which used the most modern processes of photographic reproduction. Interestingly, the photographs, which replaced drawings in catalogues, were considered at first too direct and "raw." They were therefore only used to display men's clothing and women's furs. Of the two and a half to three million francs a year Le Bon Marché and the Grands Magasins du Louvre spent on advertising (according to Martin), nearly two-thirds were set aside for catalogues.

As for the poster or placard, it had been in existence for a long time. Theaters and politicians had used it in print form without illustration. Color had appeared in the eighteenth century, but the engravings were done according to a process that severely reduced the sharpness of the image and limited the print run. In the middle of the nineteenth century, *affiches* were primarily text, usually presenting "laudatory celebrations of the merchandise they vaunted." Such were the "advertisements" that Balzac's hero César used for his products and the perfumer Farina and other vendors created for their eaux de cologne. The principal disseminators of the *affiche* in the first half of the nineteenth century were bookstores, trying to make new literary works known to a wider circle of readers. Newspapers used placards as well to advertise the launching of their new serialized narratives and hired both men and women to plaster these posters all over the city. Balzac's *La vieille fille* (The Old Maid), the first serialized novel, was published in the newspaper *La Presse* in October 1836. The first commercial posters for perfumes, modeled after the small black and white lithographs printed by bookstores, began to appear in the final years of the Restoration; they advertised such scents as *Bouquet Français* (1825), *Entrepôt de parfumerie Marius Isnard aux senteurs d'Orient* (1836), and *Aux parfums d'Arabie* (1839).[33]

In relaxing constraints on free speech, the Revolution boosted the popularity of billboards and posters. With the invention of lithography in Germany at the end of the eighteenth century and its introduction as a printing technique in France in 1807, the billboard found a new and rapid form of reproduction. But the first lithographic poster was not created until 1836 (to advertise a book), and placards using chromo-lithography only began to appear toward the middle of the century. The great revolution in the commercial poster, its elevation to the status of an art form, occurred at the end of the Second Empire when the creative graphic designs and decorative illustrations of Jules Chéret began to appear. Born in France in 1836, Chéret studied English lithography in London, where his career was launched by a perfumer who commissioned him to decorate bottles. Upon his return to Paris in 1866 Chéret inaugurated a new style of publicity using bold colors, tonal oppositions, flat tints, and strong delineating outlines in an effort to "produce a visual shock." With the appearance in 1878 of the first machines capable of printing large-size posters, large-format billboards became a decorative motif of the Parisian street, although there were those who denounced them as "mural madness," a sign of creeping decadence. The law of 1881 establishing the liberty of the press, notes Eugen Weber, also "changed the aspect of the street in France and made the illustrated placard . . . commonplace." It was not long before other artists like Manet and Alfons Mucha, Sarah Bernhardt's favorite poster designer, created illustrated *affiches*, along with Steinlen, Bonnard, Valloton, Toulouse-Lautrec, and in the 1920s the great illustrators Paul Colin and A. M. Cassandre.

Posters invited the masses to participate, Weber writes, in "the visual language and perceptions of the educated elites," a difficult offer to refuse:

> Whereas the Impressionists had wanted to catch the moment on the wing, advertising artists had to capture the attention at a glance. They did it by marrying bright colors and stylized forms to images of the shows, stores, sewing machines, or bicycles that they sought to sell. Their placards flashed out not from walls alone, but from special pavement columns (*colonnes Morris*, still to be seen in Paris), sandwich boards, public lavatories, and omnibuses. Whenever possible the product advertised was combined with the erotic appeal of a feminine image. "Wherever the crowd stops, wherever it passes [Vicomte d'Avenel writes], the poster follows."[34]

During the Belle Epoque (1870–1914) Paris became the "paradise of the advertising poster." Baron Haussmann's major renovation of the city between 1853 and 1870 and the destruction of certain neighborhoods during the Commune (1871) uncovered great expanses of wall waiting to be decorated by *afficheurs* (postermen). Walls, however, were not the only site; sandwich men, an imported British invention, and cars kept advertisements in perpetual motion on the city's streets. Other urban spaces, like the music hall, the circus, the theater, and the subway, were colonized for the advertising message of the billboard, a message often designed, especially before 1914, to introduce the French to new inventions and diversions, like the bicycle and tourism. The lithography of the *vignette-chromo* (colored vignettes), a smaller version of the poster, created eye-catching images as well. A few inches square, it popularized brands of chocolate and those of children's food products; it helped to make the names of the large Parisian department stores household words in the most remote regions of France. Beginning in 1853, Le Bon Marché used these colored card-sized pictures to produce a series of collectable images with different views of French châteaux. Every year a new series was introduced so that over a sixty-year period more than 2,000 of these vignettes, devoted to a host of subjects, were created. The chocolate company Suchard attached such images to its bars of chocolate in 1880. Cookie companies, like Biscuits Lefèvre-Utile, edited a series of vignettes illustrating the Czar's visit to Paris in 1896, while the drink company, Ricqlès, printed images of pre–World War I French army uniforms in tandem with its advertisements for alcoholic products. It goes without saying that with the growth of photography and cinema interest in these images declined dramatically after 1918 (Martin, *Trois siècles*, 112–13, 115–17).

Despite the respectability and cachet bestowed on advertising by the art of the poster, the French advertising industries, as the twentieth century dawned, were decidedly underdeveloped in comparison with the publicity media of other countries. Most French newspaper advertisements were relegated to the last page of an issue; they were unremarkable, repetitive, and generally mediocre. Still more deleterious to the development of advertising was an ideological antipathy toward advertisements among the general French populace. Professional groups were suspicious of them. Grocers, for example, who were numerous in French villages, avoided advertised name brands. Doctors rejected, for obvious reasons, advertisements for miracle cures. Druggists favored their own preparations over advertised laboratory products. The Church identified advertising with a sinful passion for lucre, and different worker-movements (socialism, communism, anarchism) saw in advertising a capitalist ploy. Moreover, the narrowness of the French national market in what was still a substantially rural nation, where villagers spent little of the little money they earned, worked against the widespread adoption of advertising throughout the country. Such hostility led one commentator in 1925 to bemoan the paucity of perfume posters visible on city streets when compared to the more common billboard ads for soap products. "As a luxury product does perfume scorn advertising?" he asks. "Is it because perfumery, proud of the high prices of its articles of luxury, disdains using modes of vulgarization [which] it prefers to leave to those who cater to more plebian classes?" The indiscriminate exposure of wall posters to every passerby may, he suggests, compromise the illusion of elitism perfume seeks to create. But this, he argues, makes no sense. In a large city, are there, he wonders, any male and female members of the petty bourgeoisie who do not use perfumes and cosmetics? The time has come, he asserts, for the greatest artists of the period to design posters as tasteful and refined as the products of perfumers. Discreet and subtle, eschewing the "aggressive and crude style" of certain gigantic placards, they would be posted only in those places—restaurants, hotels, theater lobbies—frequented by a "high-class clientele." A poster, he concludes, "can be a work of art just like a perfume vaporizer or bottle. They are made to function together."[35]

Yet, only in the 1930s did a radical change in attitude

toward French advertising occur, thanks in great part to the prosperity of the 1920s and to a gradual disarming of the ideological opposition to advertising on the part of professional groups. Large companies, like the auto manufacturer Citroën and the cosmetic and perfume company L'Oréal, made a point of involving small businesses in their advertising campaigns, the former by persuading auto repairmen to sell its cars, the latter by enticing coiffeurs to use and recommend its products. But the greatest neutralizing of the anti-advertising sentiment was accomplished by radio. In the 1930s a new kind of private broadcasting, which favored advertising jingles and humorous slogans, captured the attention of the French public. In the years preceding World War II the "principal cultural barriers" to advertising disappeared once and for all. Advertising now enjoyed a newfound respect, reflected in the appearance for the first time of an advertising pavilion at the 1937 Paris International Exposition.[36]

The popularity of the billboard and the poster from the July Monarchy (1830s to 1840s) until its golden age during the Belle Epoque is, for the historian, literally a writing on the wall. The history of nineteenth-century French culture is partly inscribed in these advertising messages for chocolate, wine, cookies, soap, corsets, perfume, and bicycles, which like a modern-day medusa transfixed the wandering pedestrian's glance. "The best historian of Paris, if he ever set his mind to it," the historian Richard Cobb once wrote, "would be the *afficheur*. The damp, blistered sides of Paris houses have screamed with the strident history of the capital for at least two centuries: red on black, black on yellow, black on white, blue on white, in butterfly variations of anger, denunciation, self-justification, promise, threat, command, information or cajolery."[37] On these walls was painted and written the collective history of the desires, longings, and dreams of an entire people at a given moment of its existence. Although uttered as criticism, Walter Benjamin's remark that "the advertisement is the ruse by which the dream forces itself on industry" is on the mark. The advertisement signifies the creation of a double need: that felt by

Fig. 29 Flat German bottle
(a *flacon à sels*) in the shape of a
powder f ask; Germany, early
eighteenth century.

the pedestrian-consumer to possess an object of desire and that fulfilled by the industrialist-manufacturer to provide a dream object of desire. Colored and decorated by posters, placards, and images, the walls of streets, boulevards, and squares become a museum of invisible image systems: those of the female body (as flower and sylph); of the home (as a bourgeois nest of warmth and comfort); of intimacy (as evoked in fantasies of dress); of food (the pleasures of chocolate and wine); of speed (the freedom and mobility promised by bicycles, cars, and trains); of cleanliness (the body purified by sweet-smelling soaps and perfumes); and of landscape (those bucolic and picturesque vistas waiting to be visited). Nothing short of poetry lies at the heart of the constellation of images that advertising brings together, as Benjamin recognized: "Many years ago, on the streetcar, I saw a poster that . . . would have found its admirers, historians, exegetes, and copyists just as surely as any great poem or painting . . . And didn't that poster furnish an image for things that no one in this mortal life has yet experienced? An image of the everyday in Utopia?"[38]

Scenting the Everyday: Bottles, Labels, Cards, Calendars, and Fans

If the billboard casts onto the fissured, grimy walls of urban streets an image of what is utopian and if ordinary objects— light bulbs, bicycles, soap—are represented encircled in an aura of dreamlike possibility, then everyday life becomes a place of magic. Utopia, as Benjamin, declared, takes up residence in the quotidian, and, as the surrealist Louis Aragon once observed, the "sense of the marvelous suffuse[s] everyday existence." Manufactured things take on an aesthetic, erotic, and hedonistic suggestiveness that transcends their functional and utilitarian reality. Even though produced in the tens of thousands, they become—for the consumer who has purchased and wedded his or her identity to them— unique, personalized objects, redolent of a mysterious intimacy. Perfume and perfume advertising, along with advertisements for corsets and bath paraphernalia, and other previously unseen objects of dress and beauty, were one of the first instances of the public dramatization of the experience of intimacy. Staged on walls, on billboards, in

shop windows, the private becomes spectacle. Within common public spaces, it projects authorized images of the erotic and the forbidden. An object, like the perfume bottle, and an image, like the advertising poster, serve as symbolic surrogates for the displacement of hidden eroticism. On a symbolic level, sexuality becomes yet another vapor blending with the perfumed fragrance floating around a female body. Perfume, the historian Marylène Delbourg-Delphis writes, "is certainly one of the very first objects of consumer society to explicitly appeal to the pleasure principle, to take society out of the private sphere of books and dark theaters and into the elegant glow of shops. The beginning of the century exhibited intimacy in its windows."[39] As a spectacle of intimacy perfume also allows for the visualization of intimacy. Eros, even though still sublimated, is brought out into the open, in accord with authorized protocols of seeing, as structured by the decorative arrangements of store windows, by the stereotypical (and morally sanctioned) poses of the female body in advertising images, by the suggestiveness of perfume names, and by the play of transparence and opacity, glass and label, and form and color in bottle design. One of the consequences of the scenting of the everyday, it would appear, is the eroticizing of the everyday. The ordinary object is ripe for fetishization, and the aura of singularity and hyperbole that the object carries, thanks to its elevation as a "good" (the word is meaningful) to be bought and consumed in a bourgeois society, turns the ordinary into the extraordinary, makes the habitual and the mundane unique, and scents the everyday world with the perfume of the remarkable.

Perfume Vessels

While a clear glass bottle may be nothing more than a clear glass bottle, a perfume bottle is no such thing. It is a bottle made distinctive through art, technique, and invention; as such it has its own complex reality. It projects an association of images all its own, and yet complementary to, although not always synonymous with, the poetic image of the perfume generated by its smell, name, slogan, packaging, and advertising. Like the history of perfume, the history of the glass perfume bottle goes back in time to Venice. As a major sea and mercantile power geographically located at the crossroads between Byzantium and the West and as the commercial terminus for convoys carrying perfumed substances like musk from

Fig. 30 Bohemian glass bottle, late seventeenth to early eighteenth century.

Ball-shaped, lacquered bergamot box, eighteenth century, made from the dried bark of the bergamot tree, which produces a non-edible variety of orange. The tree made its first appearance in Calabria, grown by Italian arborists who grafted a lemon branch on to the trunk of a bitter-orange tree (*bigardier*).

Tibet, aromatic gums like incense from Arabia, fragrant woods like sandalwood from India, and spices like cinnamon, cloves, and pepper, the Venetian Republic was the birthplace of, or at least the point of entry for, perfumery in Europe during the Middle Ages. Venetian perfumers sold and exported sweet-smelling waters as early as the twelfth century. Committed to pursuits of pleasure as they were, Venetians soon took to perfuming everything they touched—gloves, shoes, stockings, shirts, rolls of money, even the mules they rode—and to mixing their bathwater with scents of musk, ambergris, myrrh, cinnamon, and aloe. Long before perfumes started to float through the air of the labyrinthine canals and narrow streets of the city, Venice had, as early as the seventh century, begun to manufacture glass and later mirrors, following a technique so secret that any glassblower leaving the city did so under the penalty of death. By the early sixteenth century Venetian glassmakers had discovered the process for making clear crystal glass; perfume now had a container in which it could be seen. Exported throughout Europe such transparent bottles and other iridescent Venetian glass flasks (fig. 28) were in great demand. By the seventeenth and eighteenth centuries, glass bottles were made all over the continent with major

centers growing in England, Ireland, Belgium, Germany, and Bohemia (fig. 30). In 1673 a London glassmaker created a new lead-glass crystal soft enough to allow for complex cutting and faceting. Popular in the next century were bottles of colored glass as well as glass overlaid with repoussé and filigree. Cobalt blue bottles became the specialty of English glassmakers in Bristol and South Staffordshire. The first perfume bottling plant was built by Bernard Perrot in Orléans, and by 1672 was in full production, suggesting that in France "even before the Revolution, liquid scents were by no means worn exclusively by the nobility." Perrot's bottles were recognizable by their flattened, molded tear-shape and their distinctive amber hue incised with a raised fleur-de-lis motif.[40]

In the eighteenth century the French aristocracy, already attracted to bergamots (small perfumed boxes made in Grasse from hardened bergamot orange peel or bark) became infatuated with a new kind of perfume container: the vinaigrette. Called a "boîte-à-parfum" or "étui-à-parfum" it was derived from the pomander. A piece of cotton wool or sponge inside the small vinaigrette absorbed drops of vinegar, known for its antiseptic and tonic power, which had been blended with rose, orange,

Flacon-vinaigrette pendant, seventeenth century. The pendant holds a small sponge saturated with aromatic vinegar.

cloves, and rosemary; held beneath the nose, the vinai-grette could quickly bring a lady out of the depths of a fainting spell. The absorbent sponge was usually placed behind an inner grill, which was at first made of perforated metal and then later, as the vinaigrette evolved into an objet d'art in the early nineteenth century, of miniature fil-igree decorated with arabesques, scrolls, and floral motifs. To protect the inside of the vinaigrette from the acidic action of the vinegar, the container was lined with gold, sil-ver, glass, or porcelain, and to protect the contents from an all-too-rapid evaporation, the container was hermetically sealed. In the late eighteenth century different components of the vinaigrette became the locus for ornate designs, and some smelling salts bottles (*flacons à sels*) were molded in interesting shapes (fig. 29, see page 75). The lid was embossed, engraved, or made from bloodstone, agate, or jade. The stopper was composed of glass or sometimes cork; in later, more technologically sophisticated models, the stopper was replaced by a spring-activated cap. Shaped as ornately bejeweled rings, bracelets, earrings, and pocket watches, or sometimes as flowers, purses, books, and musi-

cal instruments, or even as mummies and harlequin fig-ures, the vinaigrettes could be carried and displayed in several different ways; at the end of the nineteenth century hat pins were designed to contain small vinaigrette com-

Fig. 31 Meissen porcelain bottle, Germany, c. 1750.

Fig. 32 French flacons were molded in different shapes and forms as in this bird bottle, c. 1825.

Crystal opaline bottles, France, mid-nineteenth century.

partments. By this time chemical discoveries had rendered the vinegar-soaked sponge obsolete, and vinaigrettes now contained smelling salts of crystallized ammonium carbonate mixed with eucalyptus oil, menthol, lavender, and rose scent. In the last half of the nineteenth century special smelling salt bottles of glass or porcelain with an attached ring or chain were introduced. Women could now fix the vinaigrette to a belt or a finger, carry it in a bag or a pocket (which dresses started to show in the 1870s), or keep it tucked into a sleeve. Some of these smelling-salt bottles in colored or transparent glass contained double compartments: one for perfume, the other for the salts; for obvious reasons, they were called "jumeaux" ("twins").[41]

Well into the nineteenth century most perfume in France was sold in cheap, plain, undecorated bottles plastered with large gaudy labels, which sometimes covered the entire surface of a bottle's side. In fact, the design for bottle molds was standardized in the last third of the century to allow for the display of these large labels. Most often sold in apothecaries, these flasks were taken home and their contents decanted into smaller toilette bottles. Even perfume stores of the time functioned as a kind of domestic perfume service. Women who did not prepare their own scents saw in their perfumers a type of "valet." Until the beginning of the twentieth century, when Lalique started to mass produce bottles that were distinctive as singular works of art in their own right, most fragrance companies used the same standard bottle design for different perfumes; only the label indicated the different contents. An illustrated commercial catalogue for its handkerchief perfumes, distributed by the Bourjois company in 1897, shows a series of seven different "essences"—*Essence Prima Violeta, Essence Idéal Oeillet, Essence Prima Rosa, Essence Fougère Impériale Russe, Essence Prima Mimosa, Essence Royal Acacia, Essence Royal Muguet*—all using the same bottle but distinguishable one from the other by the color and floral design of the label (violet for *Prima Violeta*, red for *Idéal Oeillet*, light blue for *Prima Rosa*), by the color of the bow-tie ribbon encircling the bottle's neck, or by the

geometric shape (diamond versus rectangle) of the stopper. The general simplicity and homogeneity of bottle design at this time went hand in hand with the perfumer's own lack of professional distinction. The nineteenth century "nez" ("nose") was mostly anonymous and not particularly talented. His inventions were limited by the ingredients available and were simple combinations either dissolved in water or in a solution of alcohol; their smell was uncomplicated and easily identifiable. Many companies offered the same scents with the same formulas and names; *White Rose* was produced by fifty-seven companies and *Jockey Club* by forty-six. The time of the artist-perfumer had not yet arrived, nor had developments in chemistry yet proceeded to the point that would fundamentally change perfume creation forever. Scents popular in 1870, like *Parfum de l'Alhambra, Le Bouquet de Bosphore, Le Bouquet de Buckingham Palace,*

PERFUME VENDING MACHINES

Above:
"Whiffs of Fragrance," Mills Novelty Co., American vending machine, patented 1916. Decorated with cupids and flowers this machine perfumed handkerchiefs in one of four different scents. Customers were instructed to "turn indicator to odor desired; hold the handkerchief in front of proper [flower]; place penny in slot and pull handle down."

Opposite:
The "Lady" Perfume Sprayer, Mills Novelty Co., American vending machine, 1905. This life-sized (nearly eight and a half feet tall) machine instructs users wishing "to perfume your handkerchief etc." to "hold same over spray of lilacs in hand of figure and drop one cent in slot of purse."

LANCE PARFUM "RODO"
BREVETÉ   S.G.D.G.

Le "RODO" Automatiquement
Parfume et Rafraîchit
nous mouiller ni tacher.
SE VEND PARTOUT

Fig. 33 Since perfume was usually applied to clothing like handkerchiefs and linen and only rarely rubbed on the body, even as late as the beginning of the early twentieth century, unique devices and delivery systems were invented as in the perfumer Rodo's "Lance Parfum" advertised in this poster (1898) by the artist/affichiste Alfons Mucha.

Le Bouquet de baisers dérobés (The Fragrance of Stolen Kisses), were, despite their exotic, poetic, royal, and romantic names, stunningly uncomplicated. The base note never changed; only a certain tone or a different mixture of simple ingredients distinguished one scent from another.[42]

Fancy Bottles

Beginning in the latter half of the eighteenth century and continuing over the course of the nineteenth century, perfume bottles became thicker and more opulent, as artisans

sought a container more resistant to evaporation and heat conduction (fig. 31). In 1828 a Bohemian glassmaker created a polished marbled glass that was opaque and had the look of semi-precious stones; it was called Lithyalin glass. Baccarat, the French crystal maker founded in 1816, became an expert in the manufacturing of translucent or opaque opaline glass. Metallic oxides gave the glass a milky white color popular for making perfume bottles. Along with the changes in taste and fashion, as nineteenth-century France moved from republic to empire, to monarchy, to republic again, to empire once more, and finally, a third time, to republic, the styles of perfume bottles and the decorative motifs they exhibited kept pace with the changing preoccupations of the larger culture. The return of the Bourbon monarchy under the Restoration coincided with an interest in medieval and Renaissance jewelry techniques, like niello, repoussé, enameling, and inlay which were reflected in the perfume bottles of the time. In the second half of the century, insect, butterfly, reptile, and exotic fauna motifs dominated, along with oriental themes, the latter perhaps inspired by the opening of Japan to the West in 1853. Bird and serpent designs were popular until the 1840s (fig. 32). During the Belle Epoque, flacons shaped like pocket watches started to appear. Bottles, *flacons à sel*, and vinaigrettes in the form of opera glasses, pistols, daggers, quivers, and horns of plenty were not uncommon.

Sometimes bottles were engraved with images of public monuments or architectural structures. Automatons served as perfume recipients as well. From the barrel of a miniature pearl-studded pistol, a set of gilded petals popped out when the trigger was pulled, releasing a squirt of scent. *Pisseuses à parfum* (from the French word "pisser," to pee) were tiny atomizers in the shape of a half-naked woman from between whose legs a tiny hole emitted a spray of perfume. One particularly fanciful perfume recipient, called the "*bague à jet d'odeur*," became popular around 1870. It was a ring attached to a small rubber bulb that the wearer hid under the inside base of her thumb and which, when squeezed, forced a jet of perfume, usually frangipani, out of a hole in the ring and into the face of the man kissing her hand. An eyewitness of the time reports that "in bending over the hand of a lady, a gentleman was showered with [a dose of] the long-lasting 'Kiss Me Quick' to the general pleasure of the crowd which was delighted to see him so easily discountenanced." The perfumer Rodo even designed a gadget, for quickly perfuming sheets, linen, and handkerchiefs. It was a squeezable syringe called a "lance-parfum" guaranteed to "automatically perfume and freshen without wetting or staining" for which in 1898 he asked the artist Alfons Mucha to design a poster (fig. 33). Perfumed buttons, mounted on absorbent velvet pads, existed as well in the last third of the century.[43]

81

Fig. 35 "This scent's richness and softness has earned it the approbation of the Fashionable world" announces the perfume label for L. T. Piver's *Eau de Cologne des princes*, c. 1850.

Perfume Labels

Standard and unremarkable bottles in clear glass containing a monochromatic perfume did not (and do not) promise anything out of the ordinary. Enter the label, which covers the flat surface of the bottle with image, color, name, character, and identity in the way a city wall is animated by the posting of a billboard. In many ways, the perfume label is a miniature poster, a writing traversing a space (glass) not usually inscribed with words. The use of labels on perfume containers goes back to the sixteenth century. From the start, the names of products on labels were accompanied by vignettes and ornamental designs that sought, as they do today, to attract attention to the product. An early label from 1760 contains a rounded ornate crest, encircled with a molding of braided rope and surmounted by a shell, in the middle of which a perfume burner gives off four thick puffs of vapor. Below the image of the perfume burner lies a large empty space reserved for the handwrit-

ten identification of the product, which the perfumer, in this case "Antoine Artaud, Marchand Parfumeur à Grasse," would sign once he had filled the bottle with scent. At the four corners of the label are etched small emblems of the profession: an arm, a bottle, a pot, and a few pills. Artaud was probably an apothecary, a profession closely linked to perfumery at the time. Among some of the oldest perfume labels known in France are a series of small étiquettes (labels) framed by scrolled borders and printed in the plainest type; these appeared around 1765 for a number of products like *Eau d'ambre de Paris*, *Eau à la Belle de nuit*, *Véritable Eau Sans-Pareille*, *Eau à la Dauphine de Paris*, and *Eau à la Coquette flatteuse*, among others.[44]

Other perfume labels were decorated with interesting subjects, motifs, and scenes. *Eau des montagnes russes* created by Laugier and Sons (fig. 34) sometime between 1815 and 1830, showed a snow-covered landscape near the Ural Mountains where a Russian peasant, his wife, and their dogs converse in front of a wood hut while a landlord and

Fig. 36 A pastoral scene of airborne sylphs and human butterflies collecting the dew from flowers graces this engraved, hand-colored perfume label for Dissey et Piver's *Eau de la rosée des fleurs*, c. 1830.

his wife pass by in a horse-drawn sled and a warrior on horseback surveys the entire scene. *Eau de fleur d'orange*, from Grasse, presents an aproned worker standing before a steaming alembic and removing a distilled liquid. Towering over him on each side are two gigantic pots holding immense orange trees. The entire design is framed by orange branches and buds. While the label contains the printed name of the product, a space has been left empty for a perfumer to write his own name in hand, for this is a generic label, possibly of potential use to several distillers of orange blossom water at the same time. Eighteenth- and nineteenth-century labels were illustrated by scenes even more exotic (and colonialist in spirit) than the wintry Russian countryside. *Pommade de Jocko* shows a young man playing a guitar and sitting under a coconut tree while offering something to a monkey, undoubtedly the "Jocko" of the pomade's name. Less exotic labels presented close-up portraits of beautiful faces. *Double Eau de Cologne* offered a reproduction of the facial features and hair style

as well as the fashionable clothes of a First Empire beauty. L. T. Piver's *Eau de Cologne des Princes* (c. 1850) displayed the noble visages and lavish robes of a young prince and princess (fig. 35). *Extrait de Fleur d'Italie* featured a brown-haired Italian woman, her head crowned with ostrich feathers, delicately holding a rose whose color perfectly matches the carnation of her skin. Historical figures and events were frequently represented on labels, especially during the Second Empire and later when the desire to commemorate in stone the great men of the nation—a kind of "statuomania," as Philippe Perrot calls it—took hold of French consciousness. As the self-declared "Perfumery of Nobility," a claim boldly displayed on its labels, the house of Pinaud marketed handkerchief perfumes called *Bouquet favori de l'Empereur* and *Bouquet favori de l'Impératrice*, each showing portraits of Napoleon III and his Spanish-born wife, Eugénie, in full dress. Under the heading of "Parfum Impérial et Royal," the label for Pinaud's *Bouquet de Solférino* displayed side by side the proud, arrogant,

Fig. 37 The perfume label not only records a scene but tells a dramatic story as in *Eau des Grecs*, L. T. Piver, c. 1830, engraved, hand-colored perfume label.

mustachioed portraits of Napoleon III and the king of Sardinia, Victor Emmanuel II, allies in the battle of Solferino in 1859 against the Austrians. In addition to historical and mythological motifs and iconography—cupids, angels, nymphs, the goddess Flora, and two-headed eagles—perfume labels were not hesitant about illustrating religious themes. The engraved label for Piver's *Eau du Damoisel et Bergerette*, framed by Gothic architectural motifs (vaults, arcs, and statuettes) and flowering branches, shows two lovers (Damoisel and Bergerette) attired in the clothes of the period standing in a garden and peering intently at a statue of the Virgin Mary lodged in a small niche, while two pigeons fly toward the towers of a castle in the distance. Finally, a less idyllic but more religiously edifying representation from the nineteenth century appears on a label for a perfumed sachet called *Sachet des Vertus Chrétiennes*. A young bride accompanied by a well-dressed female companion places a coin into the hat of a bald and bearded beggar kneeling before her. The scene is encircled by a decorative border in which religious emblems (Gothic window arches, statues of saints, a cross) vie for attention with the word, "Charity."[45]

Cultural events and icons were not foreign to perfume labels either. On March 12, 1832, the ballerina Marie Taglioni danced onto the stage of the Paris Opera to star in *La Sylphide*, the first extraordinarily successful Romantic ballet. Set in Scotland, considered an exotic and wild country at the time, and based on a tale by Charles Nodier, the

ballet tells the story of an impossible love between an air sprite and a young Scot. The dance begins with James, the Scot, asleep in an armchair, by a fire, the very morning of his marriage. Suddenly, there appears a winged spirit, a sylph, who gazes at him, awakens him with a kiss, and then flees. James eventually pursues the sylph into the forest, abandoning his fiancée and committing his love to this elusive supernatural creature. He succeeds in enveloping her in a magical scarf, a witch's gift. But the scarf has been poisoned, and the enveloped sylph loses her wings and dies. Considering its romantic theme, it is not surprising that the ballet inspired several cultural artifacts not the least of which were perfumes. *Elixir des sylphides pour la toilette*, produced by a Parisian "distillateur chimiste" probably in the late 1830s or 1840s carries a label illustrating the opening of the ballet. A kilted Scotsman slumbers in a chair before a fireplace while a winged sylph, with an air no more exotic than that of a delicate woman with wings, hovers over him. The better-known house of Lubin launched a *Parfum Taglioni* probably about the same time; its label displays the image of a delicate, graceful dancer attired in a gossamer dress, ballet slippers, and wings (*Les Parfums à travers la Mode*; *Parfumerie française*).

The image of women pictured in the hand-colored engravings of perfume labels during the July Monarchy and into the early years of the Second Empire accorded with a certain Romantic iconography. Women were presented as sylphs, fairies, sprites, winged angels, delicate like

EAU DES INCAS.

Composée par DISSEY et PIVER Rue St Martin 6 à Paris

Fig. 38 When represented on early-nineteenth-century perfume bottles the customs of distant civilizations and the features of their inhabitants were imagined as European, as seen here in the engraved, hand-colored perfume label for *Eau des Incas*, Dissey et Piver, c. 1830.

the flowers and blossoms displayed around them (fig. 36). This *femme-fleur* motif would continue well into the Belle Epoque. The ethereal, unearthly representation of the woman was enhanced by the settings in which she was found: romantic woods and hidden glades, overgrown with flowers and branches, the air slightly disturbed by the quiet flight of birds. The image was idyllic and Edenic. The label for Dissey et Piver's *Eau Printanière* from 1845 shows a demure woman in a flowing gossamer robe, one breast uncovered, placing a bouquet of flowers on her head while holding a flowering branch with her other hand. She stands in a wooded glen filled with branches, flowers, and birds. Kneeling beside her a male fairy with prominent mothlike wings, his hips draped in a light cloth, offers her a bouquet of flowers. The woman is at once in nature and at the same time de-natured. Her romanticization depends on a sublimation which removes any trace of the erotic. She is not a woman but a fairy, not a body but air; she is more sensual as flower than as female. Other images of women are more mundane and less sentimental. A series of different illustrations for a variety of scented oils from the middle of the century—*Huile à la Rose, Huile à la Vanille, Huile à la Fleur d'Orange, Huile à la Violette*—reproduces a miniature image of a woman wearing different costumes, hats, and coiffures of the day. The stylish clothes are rendered in vibrant and sumptuous colors—chromolithography has been used to good effect—although the woman's face is indistinctly, one might even say naively, drawn (fig. 39)

(*Les Parfums à travers la Mode; 3000 Ans,* 101). Still other labels are more technical in nature, representing the equipment of the distiller-perfumer—his alembics, *essenciers,* infusers, heated ovens, vaporizers, *vases florentins* (Florentine vessels), pipes, jars—and showing him at work extracting fragrant liquids.

Finally, nineteenth-century labels tell stories. The colored label for *Vinaigre des Quatre Voleurs* from 1838 presents a quartet of panels each depicting a different type of robber furtively departing the scene of his crime. One carries sacks of money, one a clock, one a number of small boxes, and one lifts something from a chest of drawers. Another panel for the same product shows a man applying drops of vinegar to the mouth of a woman passed out on the ground. Exotic colorful scenes are imagined for labels having exotic names. The label for *Eau du Sérail* (Fragrance of the Harem) by Dissey et Piver displays an oriental palace with minarets. *Eau des Grecs* presents turbaned warriors with sabers and lances, pillaging a church before an outraged priest (fig. 37), while *Eau de la Belle Aspasie* contains the image of Aspasia, the beautiful fifth-century Greek courtesan and advisor to Pericles, seated at her mirror while she talks with two men. On the hand-painted engraving that serves as the label for Dissey et Piver's *Eau des Incas* (c. 1830) dozens of European-looking personages in feather headdresses, colorful skirts, and white robes kneel, pray, trumpet, and burn incense under the guidance of a high priest who celebrates the rising of the sun (fig. 38).

Fig. 39 Some of the first generic perfume labels (early nineteenth century) for scented oils like *Huile à la Rose*, *Huile à la Vanille*, *Huile à la Fleur d'Orange*, *Huile à la Violette*, *Huile à l'Oeillet*, etc. indicate the preference during the first half of the nineteenth century for single-flower ("soliflore") compositions.

Parfum d'Afrique by the same perfumer shows a clothed odalisque holding a smoking perfume burner while a slave waits besides her. A hieroglyph-inscribed obelisk, pyramids, a temple, statues, palm trees, a village with domed roofs and minarets, and the desert all crowd onto the "orientalist" label for *Eau des Pyramides* by Dissey et Piver as well. The label for *Serkis du Sérail*, the "Favorite Powder of Sultanas" (from Piver) shows an elegant, and apparently European, noblewoman at her toilette aided by her maid. Seated on a rug (or a marble floor) decorated with blue, red, yellow, violet, and green geometric designs, the noblewoman occupies the very center of a vivid blue and gold tent opened to reveal the minarets of a distant palace. At a corner of the room an ornate blue and gold perfume burner spews forth a scented vapor.[46]

Perfumed Cards

Another form of nineteenth-century perfume advertising, making its appearance around 1879 and widely distributed, was the perfumed advertising card (*cartes-réclames parfumées*). At first, these cards were used to advertise more than one product. One such card from the end of the nineteenth century, for example, represents a tropical field with natives harvesting sugarcane; at the bottom is written the legend "Carte parfumée aux Fleurs des Tropiques." On the other side, however, the image of a large bottle of Jamaican rum stands beside the oversized letters of the

product's name, "Fox Land." It was not unusual for perfumes to be advertised in bizarre combinations with other products and establishments; wine, food, shirts, cobblers, hat shops, and sewing goods stores were indiscriminately combined. One advertisement for the scent *Incroyable Bouquet* and its Parisian manufacturer, the "Parfumerie de la Société Hygiènique," is composed of an engraving of a woman wearing a plumed bonnet and holding flowers. Turn the card over, however, and there stands the engraved figure of an elegant eighteenth-century man holding a shoe; here is one of the first advertising "tie-ins," associating scent with a French chain of shoe stores, both sharing the same brand name: "Incroyable" ("incredible").[47]

In general, perfume cards had clear and concise text, an odorous scent, and a colorful and attractive design. Their thematic orientation followed the same romantic trail as perfume labels of the day, and like these, exhibited a marked preference for the names of flowers. As perfume creation became more chemically sophisticated and involved a greater use of synthetic materials, perfume cards accordingly became more magical and mysterious in concert with the names of the fragrances they advertised. The evocation of exotic places, the presence of humor and playfulness, and the appearance of clever puns and wordplay reflected the changes in style associated with fin de siècle fragrances and their names. On the back of one card, produced by Gellé Frères for the 1900 Paris Universal Exhibition, the perfume's name and an exquisite drawing were hidden so that in order to see and smell them one had first to scratch away the covering surface. The influence of art nouveau made itself apparent in perfume cards as in other cultural artifacts of the fin de siècle. Art nouveau style was especially apparent in the association of images of women's bodies with flowers, leaves, and sinuous design motifs. Surrounded by a variety of floral arrangements, women were depicted wearing flimsy, diaphanous, free-flowing gowns or draped in dresses enveloping their bodies in serpentine folds and abundant fish-tail hems.[48]

Delicately printed and redolent of fine scents, perfume cards were distributed at hair salons, perfume shops, and haberdasheries. Bourjois and other perfumers slipped the cards free into orders sent to their distributors. The early twentieth-century couturier Paul Poiret offered his best clients lavish cards decorated with ribbons, which served as excellent bookmarks. In 1906 Piver inserted a perfume card into an issue of the daily *La Tribune de l'Aube*. Much later, Jean Patou had the entire run of 146,640 copies of the March 16, 1987, issue of the *Quotidien de Paris* perfumed with his new fragrance *Ma Liberté*. Around New Year's, perfume cards often took the form of beautifully illustrated calendars, the most luxurious of which, especially during the second half of the nineteenth century, were constructed of folding panels. The English-French perfumer Eugène Rimmel (1820–1887) was a master of this kind of perfumed almanac. He was also the author of a historical study of fragrance, *The Book of Perfumes*

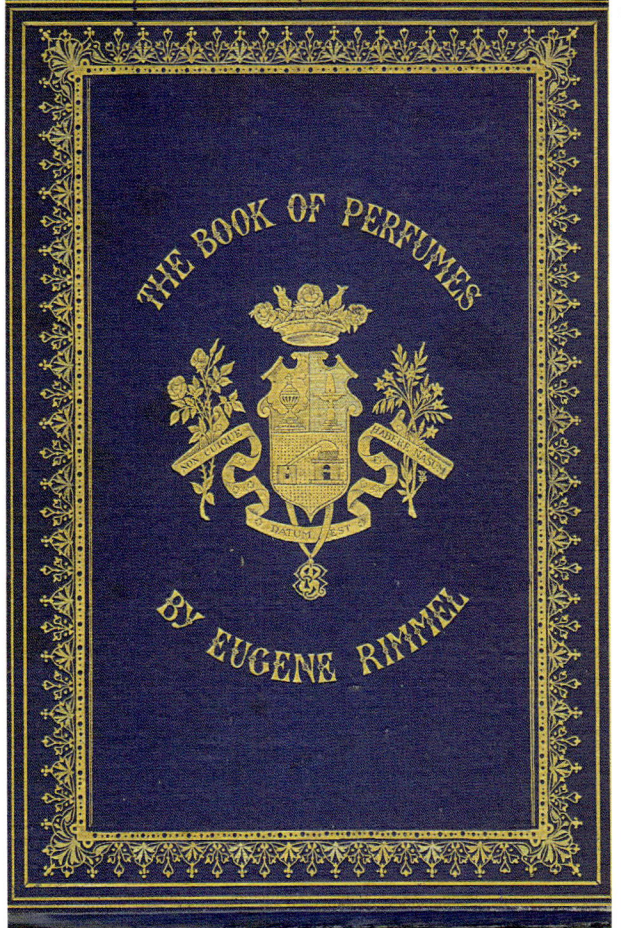

Cover of Eugène Rimmel, *The Book of Perfumes,* 5th edition. (London: Chapman and Hall, 1867).

Fig. 40 A long line of people stand under the arcing ceiling of London's Crystal Palace waiting to dip their handkerchiefs into Rimmel's perfume fountain as the front cover of this foldout perfumed calendar (*Rimmel's 1861 Perfumed Almanack*) shows.

(c. 1865–1870), a best seller originally serialized in a women's magazine and eventually published in a leather-bound first edition impregnated with scent. A gifted publicist and entrepreneur, as well as a close friend of the writer Victor Hugo, Rimmel created and distributed promotional gifts and souvenirs to celebrate different social or seasonal events, like Valentine's Day, Christmas, and birthdays; he even invented perfumed firecrackers. He was the first to facilitate the scenting of rooms with his invention of a particular kind of perfume diffuser. In the entrance pavilion of the 1851 London World Exhibition Rimmel installed a giant "Perfume Fountain." He successfully scented the entire Lyceum Theatre with a rose perfume for the performance of a play entitled *Crystabelle,* or *The Rose Without a Thorn.* One of his perfumed calendars for 1861 was composed of several individual fold-out panels, listing the months and days of the year. The colored front panel pictured the outside of Rimmel's London store while the back displayed a colored engraving of Rimmel's Crystal Palace "fountain" surrounded by a long line of people (fig. 40).[49]

Another accordion-fold calendar, this one for 1880, was designed with French music lovers in mind; it was thematically organized around well-known operettas. Entitled "Perles d'Opérette," it joined eight panels into what it called a "comic portfolio" (figs. 41, 42). The versos of the panels featured a calendar of months and days as well as lists (reminders) of the "Principal Specialities" and the "Principal New Creations of the Maison Rimmel." The eight recto pan-els, however, displayed humorously designed color drawings by the artist Faustin, six of which illustrate scenes from popular operettas by Offenbach, Hervé, Lecocq, Sullivan, Planquette, and Cellier. On the covering panel, a seated muse (perhaps Euterpe) with a lyre in one hand and an unwound scroll inscribed with the names "Rossini," "Beethoven," and "Meyerbeer" in the other, sits majestically on her throne. Dressed in a colorless toga, her head crowned with an olive wreath, the sober-looking muse appears, somewhat incongruously, next to a long-haired woman in a bell-trimmed, red, yellow, and green dance-hall costume set off by calf-high red and yellow boots. This dancer is shown on the verge of placing a red buffoon's hat, ridged with bells and decorated with yellow polka dots, on the muse's head. Rimmel seems to suggest that 1880 will be a year in which frivolity and sobriety, opera and the dance hall, myth and the everyday will collude.[50]

Along with the scientific changes in perfume chemistry and design, brought on in the latter part of the century by the invention of new synthetic ingredients, the fabrication of perfume cards became more technologically efficient. For one thing, synthetic scents were better absorbed by paper; perfume cards now held these scents for longer periods of time. Moreover, technical improvements in the fabrication of paper improved the physical quality (the "feel") of the cards. The first perfume cards

Fig. 41 Music and scent join hands in Rimmel's accordian-fold belle époque calendar celebrating the gems (in this instance, the "pearls") of comic operetta. *Almanac Rimmel, 1880*, "Perles d'Opérette," drawings by Faustin.

had interacted bizarrely with certain kinds of fragrances. The paper had a tendency to turn a strange hue of red when touched with jasmine or a dark lemon-yellow color when in contact with synthetic musk. Satiny, glossy, and powdery papers were eventually eliminated—they tended to spot—in favor of grosgrained papers, which allowed for very good reproductions especially when fast-drying inks, not affected by alcohol-based fragrances, were used. To impregnate the cards with the desired scent, several techniques were employed. At the beginning of the twentieth century the cards were plunged one by one into perfumed baths and then left to drip and dry. Another process, called

"à sec," took longer, but the results were far better. Large sheets of paper (the uncut, blank cards) were placed in specially designed placards. These closets held trays of concentrated perfume which were heated at a low temperature to make them evaporate and pass slowly into the paper sheets; the sheets were then printed and the cards cut. This "dry" process was inexpensive, and it produced more uniform and dependable results than was the case with cards perfumed by immersion. However, as the nineteenth century yielded to the twentieth and electricity became the "goddess" of the new machine age, a more efficient technique came into common use: namely, an

OFFENBACH.

ORPHÉE AUX ENFERS.

Fig. 42 The fires of hell burning around him, an unfazed Orpheus serenades Eurydice not with a lyre but with a violin in Faustin's illustration for a panel celebrating Jacques Offenbach's operetta, *Orphée aux enfers*, in Rimmel's 1880 calendar, "Perles d'Opérette."

electrically powered machine that carefully deposited a drop of perfume on each pre-printed card. Metal sleeves or cylinders lined with felt absorbed the perfume from a glass bottle affixed to the machine; the cards, at a rate of 5,000 per hour, passed through the machine's cylinders and were scented.[51]

Other Perfumed Objects

Cards and calendars were only some of the common objects from the middle of the nineteenth-century to about 1930 that were perfumed. The scenting of everyday life included menus, blotters, theater programs, *carnets de bal* (dance cards), train schedules, and, above all, fans. For centuries, fans, especially those used by noblewomen at court, had been perfumed. By the end of the nineteenth century, fans not only were scented but were decorated with aesthetic and advertising images similar to those printed on perfume cards. Rimmel designed oval-shaped calendar cards joined together at the base by a ribbon and tassel to form a fan. Not infrequently, fans told a story. When fully opened, a Rigaud fan showed the colorful and animated image of the perfumer's storefront on the rue de la Paix before which a short doorman stands ready to help clients enter and exit; a car with lights illumined waits at the curb. An elegant woman in a large feathered hat (a style popular in the early 1900s), her long scarf billowing behind her, catches the doorman's eye as she walks toward the entrance, while several passersby stare into the store's windows. For his line of perfumes created in 1911 and sold under the name "Rosine," the couturier Paul Poiret, the first designer to create his own signature scent, produced elaborate perfumed fans, some inspired (as were his couture designs) by the Ballets Russes, which had mesmerized the Paris of 1909. One such fan, for "Les parfums de Rosine," represented an elegant woman in a tunic dress and a turban hat, seated on a bed of brilliantly colored pillows and cushions decorated with intricate geometric designs (fig. 43).[52]

Perfume Becomes Napoleonized Again

The Second Empire which came into existence on December 2, 1852—Louis-Napoleon Bonaparte having been declared Emperor Napoleon III by the newly reconstituted French Senate—and which abruptly ended on September 4, 1870, after the emperor had been forced to surrender to the Prussian army at the battle of Sedan, lasted longer than any other French regime since 1789. The Second Empire carried many reminders of its earlier incarnation, the First Empire. In the magnificence of Napoleon III's Tuilieries was reflected the sumptuousness of his uncle's Versailles. In Louis-Napoleon's financing of free public baths for the poor of Paris was mirrored his uncle's ablutionary practices and concerns for personal hygiene. The new emperor's difficulty in conceiving a child—Napoleon II was born in 1856, the imperial couple having been advised that innumerable sea baths in Biarritz would be aphrodisiac—forces a comparison with Napoleon I's own procreative problems. But there are striking cultural differences as well between the First and Second Empires. The simple, high-waisted "Empire" dresses inspired by Greek and Roman clothing contrasts vividly with the excessive, tasteless, if not often ugly, fashions of *le style Napoléon III*, described by Zola as "this opulent bastard of all styles" and by Flaubert as this "wave of shit that submerges us." The plethora of historical references to the past, as evidenced in the Second Empire's fascination with museums, antiquities, and collections, and the overstuffed interiors of bourgeois apartments with their bazaarlike accumulation of curios, bric-à-brac, objets d'art, furniture, cushions, fringes, poufs, and rugs, departs dramatically from the more simple, refined elegance and the more restrained commemoration of the past—the Revolution after all had sought to destroy the ancien régime—that distinguished the First Empire.[53]

Economically, the period of Napoleon III was decisive in French history; it was characterized by "a brilliant prosperity and a rapid expansion occasioned by the rise of capitalism and culminating in 'the birth of modern France'" (Plessis, 80). During the Second Empire, especially in its first phase from 1852 to the end of the decade, the rhythm of expansion and the development of capitalism were seen in two striking areas, each of which would have a permanent and significant effect on the modern French economy: the growth of the railroad and the organization of large urban centers. Yet for all this modernization, France remained in certain areas a rural, traditional country with

motor of capitalism." The city provided the form, vehicle, and locus for the appearance of capital. Henceforth, everyday life in the city was to become a matter of consumption not industry. Paris was therefore not only the "capital of the nineteenth century" (in Benjamin's expression); it was "the *sign* of capital" in the nineteenth century, as Clark observes: "There one saw the commodity take on flesh— take up and eviscerate the varieties of social practice, and give them back with ventriloqual precision."[54] The bourgeoisie of the time was not by any means a homogeneous class. It comprised three general groups: first, the "bonne bourgeoisie" of merchants, manufacturers, lawyers, teachers, and public officials; second, the world of shop owners; and third, the "petite bourgeoisie" whose difference from the working classes was not always easy to define (Plessis, 167–68). The stylish, worldly life of the Second Empire was often criticized for its immorality and debauchery. Money was made quickly and dishonestly through real estate speculations and stock market investments and spent just as quickly by a frivolous society dedicated to the pursuit of all kinds of pleasure. Paris was called a "new Babylon," as celebrated for its cafes and Bohemian life as for its women of easy virtue. Second Empire Paris, the historian Joanna Richardson has written, was "a place for the *parvenu* and the *nouveau riche*. It was a place for the dynamic, the resolute and versatile, for the *arriviste* and the unscrupulous. It was a place for those who remained undisturbed by graver issues, and could afford to live a life of pleasure." The allure and seductiveness of "la vie parisienne," as well as the term itself, from the title of an operetta by Jacques Offenbach, dates, not surprisingly, from the Second Empire.[55]

High Fashion, 1852–1870

While the reign of Louis-Philippe through the 1830s and 1840s had been remarkable for the lack of splendor of its fashions, the Second Empire with its innumerable receptions and balls encouraged a magnificence in dress rivaling that of the ancien régime. Empress Eugénie, Napoleon III's wife, bought her first dress from the couturier Charles Frederick Worth in 1859; her court followed suit, although she was the only woman who did not need an appointment to meet Worth face to face. Corresponding to the renewed passion for ornamentation and luxury in dress was a renewed interest in makeup. When Marie-Louise had become Bonaparte's second wife in 1810, she and the women of her court had turned their backs on the use of rouge, preferring the white pallor that was the fashion of

Fig. 43 Paul Poiret, the first designer to sell his own fragrances, although under the name of his daughter Rosine, advertised his products in different ways, including this perfumed fan designed by the artist Georges Lepape and inspired by the Ballets Russes and the garçonne look of post–World War I. *Les Parfums de Rosine*, fan, c. 1920.

deep attachments to the past. During the Second Empire a conflict between vestiges of the ancien régime and new signs of modernity continued unresolved. The new capitalist spirit never completely wiped out or replaced older forms of production and exchange. "This is a period of striking dualism where an eighteenth century that cannot end and a twentieth century laden with all possible contemporary problems cohabit and clash," Plessis writes (230).

Even though France remained a deeply rural and agricultural country—in 1856 nearly three-quarters of the population lived in the country and half made their living from agriculture—urbanization grew strongly and steadily during the Second Empire (Plessis, 159, 230). Following Napoleon III's desire to make Paris the equal of London and the capital of all capitals, the city's prefect, Baron Haussmann, initiated a brutal urban transformation which would separate Paris into two distinct and antithetical cities: a "city of wealth"—at the center and in the western arrondissements—and a "city of poverty"—to the north, east, and south (Plessis, 166). Such public works represented, as the art historian T. J. Clark has observed, "the

the time. Similarly, the Empress Eugénie was not quite as enthusiastic as other Second Empire women about makeup, and she attempted to set a conservative example that would rein in the trend. Rice powder continued to be widely used, although it contained, as it always had, potentially harmful chemicals (talcum, magnesium, and zinc oxides). Nevertheless, the demand for beauty products and beauty services continued unabated through the Second Empire. A "salon d'embellissement" was opened for women by Rachel, a British enameler in 1867; Sarah Bernhardt was a client. The first beauty salon, given the name "institut de beauté," opened on the place Vendôme in 1893.[56]

Life, especially for the upper classes, became easier during the Second Empire; a desire for greater comfort and pleasure, which showed itself intermittently during the 1830s and 1840s, took greater hold. It was, Perrot notes, "a kind of slow slide into delight as a mode of life. The repression of pleasure lost ground. The old pressure to avoid excessiveness ceased. All that was enjoyable joined with all that was useful to create a life of ease." Linked to this search for an easy (or easier) life, particularly among the bourgeoisie, was a fantasy of ennoblement. Behind the appearance of moderation and sobriety and in opposition to the leveling effect of social democratization, the bourgeois of means was obsessed by a dream of distinction and privilege associated with a bygone aristocratic era, as if "material enrichment were accompanied by a certain symbolic deficiency that only the 'nobility' could correct." Such ambivalence was visibly represented in the difference between men's and women's fashion. Democracy was perfectly embodied in the uniform black suit, modest, simple, and self-effacing, which successful bourgeois men wore. They had the "look," at least, of sameness and egalitarianism, although discreet signs of individuality were visible in the choice of accessories (vests, shirts, watch chains, stickpins) that men added to the uniform. Women's fashions, however, were anything but democratic in spirit, for they bespoke nostalgia for royal and aristocratic luxury. The bourgeois obsession with nobility and distinction had, to be sure, its vociferous detractors. In 1865 the president of the Senate proclaimed the pursuit of luxury to be the cause of prostitution and, as a result, the source of the declining birth rate. Luxury, so his argument ran, contributed to the dissolution of marriages and therefore to the reduction in the number of births. Octave Uzanne, the author of a study of Second Empire fashion published in 1898, was not opposed to luxury per se or to the pleasure lavish clothes could give: "Dress for women is the first of arts," he wrote, "the one that contains all the others. It is her offensive armor. Her harmonious palette." But he found very little to praise in the way luxury was put into practice in the design and couture of fashion: "With the Second Empire we reach the most hideous period in female dress that has ever vexed the artistic eye . . . Never, all through the century . . . were beauty and grace, and elegance so openly defied."

Crinolines were "frightful," colors testified to a "screaming vulgarity," and fashion was in general "diseased."[57]

Like the eighteenth century, the Second Empire was nevertheless considered a golden age for women. But for what type of woman, one might ask? The historian Pierre Guiral supplies the answer: "For the bought woman, the woman as object, the woman as the site where pleasure and possession meet: in short, the woman both slave and courtesan." No better signs of the woman as imprisoned seductress, at once passively obedient and aggressively predatory, existed perhaps than the corset, constraining bodice and waist, and the crinoline, enveloping the lower torso in a domed cage. The latter was popular among Parisian women starting in 1850, and the Empress Eugénie wore one in 1856 to hide her pregnancy. The steel frame or hoop invisibly supporting the crinoline gave women the shape of a bell and seriously curtailed their mobility. Getting in and out of carriages or buses was enormously difficult. One woman and her daughter attending a masked ball in Nice had their skirts catch fire when they passed too close to a fireplace; both died. Women in the middle and lower classes also wore crinoline hoopskirts, hand-me-downs from wealthy employers or items obtained through the popular used-clothes' trade. Crinolined women from all social classes were also required to wear corsets. In the Paris of the Second Empire 10,000 seamstresses manufactured over a million corsets annually, some costing as little as three to five francs. The overwhelming popularity of the bicycle in the 1880s would eventually sound the death knell for the crinoline and corset and revolutionize not only fashion but the social condition of women. Freeing women from the constraints of their clothes was a first step toward liberating them from the bonds of a patriarchal society. The corset, one doctor remarked in the first decade of the new century, was "a new Bastille to be demolished."[58]

Society's regulation of the female body and its control of female eroticism were facilitated by crinoline and corset alike. The body became a stage for the theatrical display (through clothes) of wealth—masculine wealth, in particular. The luxuriously and brightly attired woman bore witness to her husband's financial success. She walked by his side as an object of display, offering a spectacle of color. The Second Empire, "an age of opulence rather than taste," favored vivid, bizarre, sometimes crude colors with strange names like "cockchafer brown and sun yellow," or "solferino" in honor of Louis-Napoleon's victories during his Italian campaign of 1859. The wife or mistress was a show of lavish excess set in motion; the simplest dress required no fewer than seventeen yards of material; one gown worn at the Imperial Court had a train four yards long. The velvet, satin, muslin, and silk used in the making of dresses were considered rich and sumptuous fabrics as were the three to four different kinds of trimmings—lace, flower garlands, ribbons, frills—with which a dress could be adorned. The crinoline, moreover, was a symbol not only of "the supposed inapproachability of women," but of a certain moral ambiguousness, since it was a garment full of restlessness and agitation. In swaying from side to side and tipping up in the front and then the back, it risked revealing the ankle. "The crinoline was not a moral garment," the fashion historian James Laver has observed, "and the period in which it reached its greatest development, Second Empire France, was not a moral period."[59]

Second-Empire Scents

Compared to the modest, even chaste scents women wore between 1814 and 1848 (the years of the Restoration and the July Monarchy), the perfumes characteristic of the Second Empire (1852–1870) could not, generally speaking, be called "moral" either. The heady, animal-based scents of Josephine's apartments and of the Bonapartist court in the first decade or so of the nineteenth century were effaced by the light eaux de cologne (one modern perfumer has called cologne the "watercolor of perfume") and the floral, sweet, and soft scents of the Restoration and July Monarchy where, in keeping with the growth of Romanticism and with the modesty of the new bourgeois class, perfume etiquette was determined by protocols of subtlety, refinement, distinction, naturalness, and "l'art de la dose." It took forty years and another Napoleon, along with his spouse, to restore to France a passion—one historian calls it a "veritable orgy," another "an unparalleled vogue"—for strong, captivating scents, in particular those composed of musk, jasmine, and ambergris. Once again "heavy, animalic perfumes imposed their lyricism" on the nineteenth century. This renewed fascination for perfume and for the air of luxury with which it enveloped the wearer was helped by technological advances and chemical discoveries, as we shall see, and by the invention of the vaporizer, especially the "hydrofère" through which scented preparations were diffused in the bath. Along with the showy, exuberant, and colorful fashions of the period, perfume became a popular vehicle of display, a way of showing off wealth and a taste for luxury. The Paris Chamber of Commerce estimated in 1848 that there were 110 perfume manufacturers working in the city with a collective annual turnover of nearly ten million francs. Perfume exports in 1853 reached thirteen million francs per year, a figure that would balloon to twenty million by 1862. The Paris Universal Exposition of 1855 contained a fountain perfumed with eau de cologne, and its popularity with the public was not without its humorous and cautionary aspects, as an ink drawing possibly published in a newspaper of the time showed. The caricature presents the backs and legs of at least six men and women who have thrown themselves head and torso into the fountain. Coming to the rescue, a perfumer pulls the legs of one of these avid scent lovers. A caption below the illustrated scene emphasizes the dangers of the "Eau de Cologne Fountain"; "the unfortunate manufacturer," it notes, "ha[s] put too much faith in the discretion of the public."[60]

Brands much in demand during the Second Empire included *La Boîte de Jouvence* (Box of Youth) by Violet; *Lys des Vallées*, a cream by Delettrez; and aromatic pastilles for burning by Coudray. Entire bottles of violet-scented vinegar or jasmine water were spilled into baths. The mouth

Fig. 44 Ylang-ylang flowers grow in Madagascar, the Philippines, and the Comoros. With its rich and intoxicating aroma the essence of ylang-ylang blends well with jasmine (it is sometimes inaccurately called the "poor man's jasmine") and adds warmth and volume to some floral scents. The ylang-ylang pictured here was picked in Mayotte, Comoros, near Combani.

was sweetened with an iris powder and the body rubbed with lemon juice before being massaged with tuberose oil. The aroma of Indian vetiver, appearing on the scene in the late 1820s, was used to scent white linen stored in the cabinet de toilette. A bundle of vetiver, according to the *Journal des dames et des modes* (The Ladies' Journal of Fashion), cost five francs in 1827. Balzac's perfumer, César Birotteau, found the scent powerfully evocative of "women dancing in Turkish baths" (33). Another intensely aromatic fragrance, patchouli, originally from Indonesia, appeared in the West around 1830, not as a perfume ingredient but as an early form of "insecticide." In order to protect the colorful cashmere shawls women wore to offset their white Empire dresses, Indian weavers enveloped the cashmere in dried patchouli leaves before shipping the shawls to Europe. The delicate wool absorbed the fragrance and patchouli scent turned out to be as popular among the French as the shawls it protected. The courtesans so dear to Baudelaire were fascinated by patchouli's devilish, sulfurous powers. Other captivating scents, like Mexican rosewood and ylang-ylang (the Tagalog word for "flower of flowers" with an odor of wintergreen) (fig. 44), arrived later during the Second Empire and the Third Republic: ylang-ylang, for example, at the Paris Universal Exposition of 1878.[61]

French military campaigns and the nation's colonialist expansion during the 1850s and 1860s brought the Middle East and Far East to the attention of the French

"Grasse, La Ville des Fleurs et des Parfums," travel poster by Julien Lacaze, 1910. Grasse was a center for the tanning industry during the Middle Ages. Because tanned leather gave off horrible odors, which had to be removed through the application of aromatic scents, Grasse grew in the sixteenth century into an important center for the production of perfumed leather gloves and, given its mild Mediterranean climate, an important region for the cultivation of aromatic plants. During the second half of the nineteenth century and into the twentieth Grasse became the perfume capital of the world.

LA VILLE DES FLEURS ET DES PARFUMS

public. A fascination with an exotic East redolent of amber-gris, heliotrope, musk, sandalwood, patchouli and chypre worked its dream magic on the French imagination, especially that of writers like Baudelaire and Flaubert. At the same time, perfumery was becoming accepted as an "art" and the perfumer (like Rimmel, Piesse, and Guerlain) was seen as a unique "artist," an "author," a "composer" possessed of a genius for olfactory creativity equal to that of the painter and musician. When the English fashion designer Worth came to Paris from London in 1858 to set up his atelier, he was overwhelmed by the overuse of perfumes. Being surrounded all day by the heavily perfumed grandes dames who came to his shop for fittings gave him, he complained, terrible migraine headaches. And yet, the popularity of intoxicating perfumes, like the trend toward lavish clothing, had its vehement and vociferous critics. Manuals of beauty and savoir-faire at the beginning of the Second Empire—like those by Madame Celnart and the Comtesse de Bradi during the earlier July Monarchy—counseled women to avoid musk, civet, tuberose and other intoxicating fragrances too closely associated, according to certain prim bourgeois minds, with the *odor di femina* of prostitutes and other women of easy virtue. Even a perfume that Queen Victoria wore on a royal visit to Paris in 1855 was heartily criticized for the compromising hint of musk it gave off.[62]

Second Empire perfumes were described in 1925 by those old enough to remember the scent of their grandmothers as "appealing . . . to the imagination." These were products laden with exoticism, Jean Robiquet recalls, fragrances that "appeared to have been collected on the banks of the Ganges or in the harems of Ispahan; whether called nard or patchouli, they were, all of them, fine scents as long as their aroma was strong." A truly feminine woman wanted only "intoxicating odors . . . It mattered little if they sometimes gave her a tiny headache." A new olfactory mindset, a full-blown Romanticism of exotic scents, evocative of "Spanish serenades and Venetian moonlight," had surfaced. The taste for heavily accented perfumes, Robiquet remembers, continued into the second half of the nineteenth century, as evidenced "by the carriages along the Chaussée d'Antin [in Paris] and the coaches at Compiègne [Napoleon III's favorite residence] whose cushions gave off an odor of musk, patchouli, or opoponax, every time a stylish woman [*une lionne*] or a great lady sat on them." Robiquet's Proustian memories lead him to compare the perfumes of his grandmother's time to those of the jazz age in which he is writing: "If the olfactory memories of my earliest youth are exact, it seems to me that women back then often still allowed themselves certain bold compositions of which a Parisian woman of 1925 would be rightly terrified."[63]

A Changing Industry

Like his uncle, who after the Revolution had freed perfumers from the control of an excessively monopolistic guild thereby according them a new professional status and identity, Napoleon III took steps to enhance the autonomy of perfume creation and production. He was, perhaps indirectly, responsible, Edwin Morris writes, "for finally separating perfumery from pharmacy" by passing a law requiring pharmaceutical companies to list ingredients on

Fig. 45 The acknowledged great and classic jasmine fragrances of the twentieth century are Chanel's *No. 5* (1921), Lanvin's *Arpège* (1927), and Jean Patou's *Joy* (1930). While the production of jasmine in and around the city of Grasse began in the mid-nineteenth century and peaked in the 1920s and 1930s, it has declined dramatically today; most jasmine is now imported from Egypt, North Africa, and India. The jasmine flowers pictured here were harvested at Plascassier, near Grasse.

the labels of their products. Strongly opposed to disclosing the secret constituents of their formulae, perfumers turned their backs on their pharmaceutical colleagues and went their own way. During the Paris International Exhibition of 1867, moreover, perfume and soap products were for the first time allotted their own section, completely separate from the pharmaceutical and chemical products with which they had been traditionally grouped at previous exhibitions.

Under the July Monarchy and then the Second Empire the perfume industry developed aggressively. Near the end of the First Empire, in 1812, perfume had accounted for twenty-two million francs of total commercial sales in France. By 1855 it comprised more than forty million francs. The number of perfume houses in that time doubled as well. By mid-century, Grasse, now known as

Fig. 46 Since antiquity, lavender has been used to scent linen and bath water, a usage evoked by its name (from the Latin verb "lavare," to wash). It blooms from the end of June to the end of August, and the entire plant is harvested and used. Here rows of lavender color the landscape in Sénanque, Provence.

the "city of perfumes," saw the family-run, artisanal operations of earlier times transformed into full-scale industries. Cannes was upgraded as a port for exports, and a rail link between Grasse and Paris encouraged the commercial distribution of perfumes throughout the country. In the 1850s the development of an irrigation system and the construction of the Siagne Canal permitted large plantings of flowers in Grasse and surrounding villages. By the end of the century nearly six tons of flowers were being processed in the Grasse region annually: rose, jasmine, violet, tuberose, and orange blossom, in particular. Eighty tons of jasmine were harvested in Grasse in 1856 and nearly two hundred tons by the turn of the century (fig. 45). Grasse also controlled a world monopoly on the production of lavender essence (fig. 46). Accompanying this heightened production was the increased importation of primary ingredients, like vetiver, ylang-ylang, patchouli, sandalwood, iris rhizome, and geranium. Some perfume houses established their own plantations in foreign countries in order to standardize and control the cultivation of flowers.[64]

Another important area of capitalist innovation, revolutionized by major scientific discoveries and technological discoveries in both France and Europe during the second half of the nineteenth century, was the transformation of the chemical industry, which more than any other factor occasioned the radical modernization of perfumery. "There is only a hand's breadth between the chemist and the perfumer" (86), the scientist Vauquelin announces flatteringly to César Birotteau in Balzac's novel. The flattery is substantially less hyperbolic than it may appear. The emergence of organic chemistry around 1828 helped to improve the quality of perfumes, allowing composers to reproduce through purely chemical means the essential identifying constituents of natural flowers. After having succeeded by mid-century in replicating certain molecules found in nature, nineteenth-century scientists turned their attention to the invention of chemical substances with no

"Initial U: A Nineteenth-Century Perfumer at Work." Illustration from Eugène Rimmel, *The Book of Perfumes* (London: Chapman and Hall, 1867).

known natural equivalents. Their discoveries enabled perfumer-artists to create for the first time combinations of smells with no existence in the floral world. Earlier improvements around 1826 in the design of steam furnaces and alembics reduced the incidences of explosions and made distillation considerably safer. In 1835, H. E. Robiquet succeeded in extracting essential oils from flowers, like jonquils, too delicate to withstand the withering effects of steam distillation. His process, called "solvent extraction," involved, nevertheless, the use of highly flammable substances, like ether; but later experiments produced more stable, less volatile solvents, like benzene. At the Universal Exhibition of Vienna in 1873, the French industrialist Claude Roure presented a new form of solvent extraction, called "concrete essence," which his brother, Louis, had created in Grasse. Concrete essences provided perfumery with highly concentrated substances completely soluble in alcohol. The first factory specializing in the manufacture of synthetic scents—the production of synthetic vanilla (vanillin)—was constructed in Paris in 1876. Other companies, some of which are industrial giants to this day, followed: Givaudan, Rhône-Poulenc, and Descollonges. By 1880 it was clear that the use of synthetic ingredients in combination with natural substances offered rich, unheard-of possibilities for the future of perfumery. Scents, previously resistant to extraction from natural sources, were now successfully isolated. Yet, certain natural fragrances proved much less costly and easier to create from scratch. Totally original and synthetic substances, like vanillin, were found to be even more potent than their natural forms (vanilla). Finally, the color of perfume, which earlier had had the unfortunate effect of leaving stains on clothes, was dramatically improved.[65]

Synthetic Additions

Year after year, a host of new synthetic chemicals were discovered or invented, thus expanding in unprecedented ways the richness of the perfumer's palette. In 1837 benzaldehyde, the fragrance of peach kernels and bitter almonds, was invented. In 1868, the odor chemical coumarin, the smell of new-mown hay, was derived from the tonka bean by the English chemist William Perkin. It would become a constituent note in Houbigant's classic perfume of 1882, *Fougère royale*, historically the first perfume to contain synthetic scent materials and, incidentally, the French novelist Guy de Maupassant's favorite scent. Vanillin was derived in 1874, not from vanilla beans but from pine sap; this was a major event in perfume history because vanillin, in combination with coumarin, would give birth fifteen years later to "the first great modern perfume" and the first truly "oriental" fragrance: Aimé Guerlain's *Jicky*. 1876 saw the invention of a synthetic rose scent and 1877 that of a synthetic hawthorn odor, essential to Guerlain's 1906 scent *Après l'ondée*. A family of synthetic substances called

"Interior of a Perfume Manufactory at Nice." Illustration from Eugène Rimmel, *The Book of Perfumes* (London: Chapman and Hall, 1867).

quinolines, an odorous blend of leather and smoke indispensable to perfumes marketed under the name "cuir de Russie," was synthesized in 1880. The next twenty years witnessed one new discovery after another: heliotropine, a basic element in amber and oriental perfumes, in 1885–1886; synthetic musk, extraordinarily cheaper than the natural substance, in 1888–1891; ionone or synthetic violet in 1893, a key note in Roger et Gallet's *Vera Violetta* and in Coty's 1905 fragrance, *L'Origan*; and finally amyl salicylate in 1898, a synthetic clover with a soft, sweet hay odor. This synthetic inspired Piver's unique scent *Trèfle incarnat* of 1898 ("the first synthetic perfume to produce a totally new odor," writes Delbourg-Delphis) and an essential ingredient in perfumes belonging to the class of fragrances known as "fern" ("fougère"). Three years into the new century came the invention of the all-important aldehydes without which *Chanel No. 5* could not have been conceived by the perfumer Ernest Beaux in 1921. And on the eve of World War I, chemists discovered nerol, which Beaux described as having "the fresh notes of the sea and of oysters bathed in lemon juice."[66]

From the beginning, the reaction to synthetic substances was hostile; there were two reasons for this. First and foremost, synthetics were expensive; a kilo of vanillin cost 8,800 francs in 1876, although the price would fall to only forty-five francs in 1913. Second, elegant consumers of perfume initially mistrusted substances so avowedly "unnatural," even though the synthetic chemicals were almost always blended with natural ingredients. One newspaper in 1895 decried the rise of artificial scents. Even the perfume house Lenthéric took steps in its advertising for *La Feria* in 1904 to assure consumers that it was a "natural" fragrance, "completely different from those artificial perfumes that make you sick after they evaporate." Lenthéric may have had a more honest motive in alerting its customers to potential problems with synthetic scents. Perfumes of lesser quality or of merely ordinary quality were beginning to appear on the market in large part due to the advances in chemistry. Moreover, a certain myth of the "natural" had taken hold of the French imagination. The nostalgic return to the past and the illusion of a lost natural paradise could not possibly be served by a product dependent on synthetic materials. Aimed at city women rather than at the inhabitants of the agricultural countryside, perfume advertisements of the period were keen on maintaining—and on encouraging their customers to embrace—the myth of "la bonne nature." Until World War I only a sophisticated elite was ready to accept synthetic scents. Only later, when perfumes began to vaunt the "art" of their chemistry and flaunt their originality as creations "beyond nature," did they successfully project a seductive allure. "Reconstructed through chemistry" writes Delbourg-Delphis, "nature becomes once again the repository of magic."[67]

It is often noted that modern perfumery, which changed our ways of smelling things, was born at nearly the same time as impressionism, which altered our ways of seeing things in the world. The perfumer now had at his—perfumery was still very much a masculine profession—disposal a scale of perfume notes and accords, an "immense register of scents," completely unknown to his predecessors. Perfume creation was no longer a question of combining plain, simple scents but rather one of orchestrating fragrances into symphonic chords and melodies. The complex interaction of light, the overlapping of its iridescences, and the shimmering dazzle of its reflections as perceived and rendered by Monet and his fellow impressionists paralleled a perfume's harmonious interplay of scents, its consonance of varied accords, and its architecture of juxtaposed notes. Perfume introduced a new mentality to the French public, a new culture of scent. Nature was now seen and smelled as it had never been before—through the magic of art and the medium of the imaginary. The perfumer, like the poet, was nature's rival, for he was the creator, as Baudelaire noted in his essay, "In Praise of Cosmetics," of "the incomparable majesty of artificial forms." Perfume, fashion, and poetry shared the same goal, Baudelaire believed, which was to invent an ideal that surpasses nature, that lifts men and women "above Nature": "Fashion should thus be considered as a symptom of the taste for the ideal which floats on the surface of all the crude, terrestrial and loathsome bric-à-brac that the natural life accumulates in the human brain: as a sublime deformation of Nature, or rather a permanent and repeated attempt at her reformation."[68]

JICKY: Blending the Natural and Synthetic

If modernist art in the guise of impressionism coincides with the appearance of an authentically modern style of perfumery, one that will change the landscape of scent for the next one hundred years, it is fitting that the launching of "the first great modern perfume," Guerlain's *Jicky*, should have occurred the same year (1889) as the inauguration of that icon of modernism, the Eiffel Tower. Until Aimé Guerlain conceived of *Jicky*, notes Colette Fellous, fashion demanded that perfume be "the photograph of a flower," resembling as closely as possible the smell of a rose or a jasmine blossom; with *Jicky*, one no longer "dreamed of imitating nature but of transforming the real." It was indeed "a perfume-manifesto," for in offering an artistic, man-made, and artificial composition it announced, the perfumer Jean-Claude Ellena has observed, the beginning of a modern "emotive perfumery, [one that] no longer attempted to imitate the scent of flowers, but sought instead to arouse emotion."[69] Named for Aimé Guerlain's nephew Jacques, whose family nickname was "Jicky," the perfume represents a bridge between nineteenth-century eaux de cologne like Pierre-François Pascal Guerlain's *L'Eau Impériale,* created in 1830 but dedicated to the Empress Eugénie in 1853, and Jacques Guerlain's *Shalimar* of 1925. *Jicky* made use of a new solvent, sulfuric ether, which because it comes to a boil at 86 degrees F. does not damage the odor molecules of the flower, a perpetual problem with processes of pure distillation, where flower and water had to be heated to 212 degrees F. Eventually, sulfuric ether, because it was volatile and dangerous to handle, was replaced by petroleum ether.

The great achievement of *Jicky* is found in the harmonious balance it achieves between natural and synthetic ingredients. Its sophisticated composition makes it unarguably the "first modern perfume," although Houbigant's *Fougère royale* (1882) was the first perfume to use synthetic materials. Unlike a single-note scent, like rose water or a nineteenth-century eau de cologne, the components of a modern perfume like *Jicky* cannot be broken down and identified, at least to any nose other than that of a perfumer. *Jicky* begins with a head note that is fresh and aromatic, an eau de cologne scent but with touches of lavender, bergamot, rosewood, and herbs like rosemary, verbena, and thyme. Its spicier heart note is intensified by the odors of geranium, jasmine, and rose. Deep in its interior, *Jicky* smolders with warm and sensual base notes generated by a blend of vanillin and coumarin. Strangely—or, perhaps, not so strangely considering its masculine name—*Jicky* was not at first accepted by women. Its scent was too "ferociously modern," too great a departure from older fragrances with their simple, easy-to-define, single-note aromas. It remained much more popular with men until 1912, when women's fashion reviews gave it their seal of approval. Appealing as it did to both sexes, *Jicky* prefigured perhaps, as Barillé remarks, "the disturbing aura of androgynous perfumes."[70]

The modern perfumer whose knowledge of science inspires his fertile imagination, whose lyrical sensibility informs his musical and sensual bouquets, and whose artisanship expresses his fluid emotions is both poet and chemist: an interpreter and a technician of scents. One of the first of this breed, part seer and part perfumer, although fictional, is Des Esseintes, the dandy hero of Joris-Karl Huysmans's novel *A Rebours* (Against the Grain) published in 1884, five years before the inspired creation of Guerlain's *Jicky*. Although Des Esseintes is modeled after Baudelaire and although *A Rebours* contains several allusions to Baudelaire's poetry and his belief in the power of artifice to surpass nature and create an ideal state of blissful being, Huysmans's dandy has the unmistakable vision of the fin de siècle perfumer. Like Baudelaire, Des Esseintes is a *grand olfactif* (gifted "nose"); he is an ingenious composer of fragrances. Suffice it to say here that Huysmans clearly points to the magical, world-transforming illusions that Des Esseintes's mastery produces. In his castle at Fontenay, Des Esseintes is surrounded by the technology of beauty. Bottles, flasks, vials, vaporizers, and burners for processing new fragrances are scattered about. Samples of tuberose, vanilla, styrax, jasmine, and verbena to be used in new perfume combinations lie helter-skelter on shelves. A clutter of porcelain pots, Chinese boxes, jars, lotions, vials of rosewater, brushes, pincers, scissors, powder puffs, files, and other instruments of makeup left behind by a former mistress—a woman whose understanding of the artifice of cosmetics was, like the work of the perfumer himself, as much informed by knowledge as by art—fills the bathroom. The transformation of mundane reality through the scenting of the everyday falls within Des Esseintes's powers.

One idle day at Fontenay he starts to daydream and then to remember a long-ago afternoon when, in the company of his former mistress, he visited her sister in the industrial Paris suburb of Pantin. As the two women talk, Des Esseintes looks out the dirty window at what is a desperately bleak and depressing sight: a long, muddy street which echoes under the "incessant impact of galoshes splashing through the puddles."[71] This, a Baudelairean vision of urban desolation, melancholy, and spleen, is reinterpreted by Huysmans:

> The season of heavy rains is here: under the pavements, the down-spouts spew forth their melodious burdens; horse-dung steeps in the bowls of milky coffee that hollow the macadam; foot-baths are available everywhere for the use of the lowly passer-by. Beneath the lowering sky, in the clammy air, the walls of the houses sweat black filth, their air-shafts stink; the disgust of existing is ever more acute, the spleen more overpowering; the seeds of vice which lie in every man germinate (100).

Against this depressing reality of everyday life stands the resurrectional beauty of poetry, art, and perfume. No sooner has Des Esseintes finished describing the loathsome cityscape outside the window then he thinks of the warm room in which he is standing, of the basket of flowers on a table filling the air "with the scent of benzoin, geranium and vetiver" (100). April, he tells himself, has come to mid-November Paris. What enables the illusion of spring to dominate the reality of winter is technology, artifice, and human invention. "Harsh nature has no part in this extraordinary phenomenon," he realizes. "It is to industry alone that Pantin owes this artificial spring" (100). This is because the flowers in the room are in fact artificial—made of a glossy silk fabric mounted on brass wires—and the spring fragrance he smells "comes filtering in through the joints in the window-frame, emitted by local factories where the Pinaud and Saint James perfumes are manufactured" (100). Industry, commerce, and perfumery, Des Esseintes recognizes, have succeeded, as much in the realm of existence as in that of aesthetics, in disguising, if for only a moment, the brutality of everyday reality. Thanks to these perfume manufacturers, the laborer exhausted by his work and the employee fatigued by long hours shut up in a store or office are given "the illusion of breathing a little good clear air" (100). Des Esseintes even imagines the medical potential of an artificially manufactured climate in which the fragrance of spring never disappears. No longer would a Parisian man have to go south (to the Riviera) for his lungs or liver. He could "take the waters," as it were, without leaving home, thanks to the fabulous subterfuge of imaginatively replacing his illness with a perfumed surrogate, namely the scent and "atmosphere of the Paris brothels and their prostitutes" (101). Seeking to cure himself with "a fairly fertile imagination" (101) the sickly man could purchase a dose of illusion transported to his home by a spray of scent.

Reality, a wasteful, costly, often harmful experience, would, thus, surrender to illusion and art, far better investments for the soul. And so, through Des Esseintes, his fictional counterpart, Huysmans examines the role of perfume and of advertising in the fragrant metamorphosis of reality, although like perfumes dissipating in the wind, such illusions could never have permanence. At the end, Des Esseintes is assailed once again by the nauseating odor of frangipani, an obsessive smell reaching him from the outside world and not from his own imagination; it brings him to the edge of insanity (101–02). The dandy-perfumer, the dandy-artificer, the dandy-technician loses his mastery over nature, a loss Baudelaire will also attempt to reverse.

Charles Baudelaire
and the
Music of Perfume

Chapter 3

*I was no longer aware of
whether I was breathing
music or hearing perfumes.
Guy de Maupassant*

*If perfume leads us to the future,
it never forgets to hold
open the doors of yesteryear.
Louise de Vilmorin*

HOW CAN A POET SAY of women that they are "*natural, therefore vile*," that they are as simple-minded as animals, that they present the "greatest stupidity married to the greatest depravity," that they could not possibly have anything meaningful to say to God, and at the same time celebrate the voluptuous sadness of their faces, inhale the mysterious scent ("le parfum") of their blood, and glorify the intoxicating power of their fragrant hair to transport his soul to a sensual paradise?[1] Was Baudelaire confused? Incapable of knowing his own mind? Detached from his feelings and desires? A victim of bouts of terrible, if not pathological, ambiguity? Yes and no.

Nothing is simple in Baudelaire's universe where everything seems to have double, often contradictory, meanings. Women are creatures of nature, and they are also creations of artifice born of the images the poet assigns to them or of the images they create for themselves through the use of perfume, cosmetics, and clothes: in other words, through those human artifices of makeup that also make over. "On her tawny brown skin the rouge was superb!" (I: 158), Baudelaire remarks in a manner that emphasizes the cosmetic and artistic transformation of the skin into a canvas of colors (tawny brown and red). In the Baudelairean world art often masks physical and material realities. These are hidden behind an aesthetic embellishment that changes the seductive feminine body into an incarnation of ideal, statuesque Beauty, turns urban hovels into "artificial paradises," transforms sensual scents into airy, spiritual vapors, and gathers everyday words and sounds into timeless poems. Ambiguity strikes at the heart of all things and all experiences in Baudelaire's world; there is no escaping it. His poetry testifies to the presence of a terrifying mortality, to the audible ticking of a relentless clock, and to a melancholy and a boredom of infinite and yet tangible dimensions.

At the same time, however, his poetry offers the dream and illusion of escape—through reverie, drugs, wine, sensuality, beauty, poetry, imagination, even, paradoxically, death itself—into an ideal, otherworldly realm of spiritual and ecstatic bliss, which, as the English title of one poem promises, is "any where out of the world" (I: 356). The physical in all its time-bounded and sensuous reality exists but always at a tangent to the *meta*-physical. And the metaphysical, despite the eternity and ideal felicity it promises, is never fully separated or distanced from the physical realities of love, melancholy, and loss. What is material flows in and out of what is spiritual. The everyday coexists with the extraordinary, the natural with the supernatural, time with eternity, beauty with melancholy, and elevation with baseness. At every turn of a street, during every encounter with a woman, whether he is smelling an exotic perfume or watching the sun set from a balcony, ambivalence laps Baudelaire's hand like a faithful dog. It defines his experience of the world and dominates his perception of sensory phenomena: smells, colors, textures, tastes, sounds. It is an experience of the uncanny and the bizarre which impels the poet to look into the eyes of a woman, a stranger he passes on a Paris street, and see staring back at him "La douceur qui fascine et le plaisir qui tue" ("The sweetness that charms and the pleasure that kills") ("To a Passerby," I: 92). No simple or basic colors, uncomplicated by the hues of ambiguity and paradox, could possibly exist in the Baudelairean universe, as the poet himself recognized: "As a child, I felt in my heart two contradictory sentiments: horror for life and ecstasy for life" (I: 703; Fowlie, 261). "La douceur qui fascine et le plaisir qui tue" ("The sweetness that charms and the pleasure that kills")—this is a line that demonstrates the auditory acrobatics that Baudelaire's ear sought and the verbal associations his poetic genius conceived. Is there any reason not to reverse the two verbs in the line and imagine a rewriting that presents, with admittedly less remarkable euphony, "la douceur qui *tue* et le plaisir qui *fascine*"? The words "fascine" and "plaisir" assert their resemblance through the close, although not perfectly identical, sibilance of consonant and vowel: the blend of "s," "c," "i" sounds. But beyond structural or auditory links, the interchangeability of the two nouns and two verbs—*douceur, plaisir, fascine* and *tue*—are evident. Sweetness can be as much a delight as delight can be a sweetness; what fascinates can kill as potently as what kills can fascinate. And sweetness and delight are both able, like a swaying, entranced cobra, first to fascinate and then to strike. Where there is pleasure, delight, and sweetness, there death can be found, too, as the metaphors and images associated with perfume illustrate so persuasively. Where the horror of life appears, the ecstasy of life cannot be too far away.

A sweetness that fascinates and kills, a delight that kills and fascinates, sweetness that is delight and delight that is sweetness—the permutations affirm and disaffirm almost simultaneously the ambiguous perception of love, of woman, of memory, and of spirituality that identifies Baudelaire's encounter with reality. This is a vision that experiences no presence without a counterbalancing absence, no possession without an equalizing weight of loss, no joy without an equivalent dose of sadness, and no "there" without a countervailing "here." Moreover, the overlapping, intertwined associations of sweetness, delight, fascination, and death capture in profoundly important ways Baudelaire's experience of perfume and his olfactory perception of the world.

To the scented imagination perfume is a sweetness, a delight, a pleasure; it fascinates, entrances, charms, bewitches, and kills. It provokes ecstasy through the spiritual elevation, vertiginous expansiveness, and sensual intensity it creates; and it inspires horror, because it is derived from the secretions of animals and flowers, from roots with magic and poisonous properties, and from base matter susceptible to organic decomposition. The language of flowers, as the philosopher Georges Bataille has remarked, expresses a human ideal literally grounded in baseness, squalor, and filth: "Even the most beautiful flowers," he writes, "are spoiled in their centers by hairy sexual organs ... The interior of a rose does not at all correspond to its exterior beauty." The "sordid tuft" lying within the interior of the flower reveals a plant that "rots indecently in the sun," withering garishly—its "roots swarming under the surface of the soil, nauseating and naked like vermin ... loving rottenness just as leaves love light"—while it bravely ascends from the "stench of the manure pile" toward the sky and the clouds.[2] What desire seeks in the ephemeral beauty that the flower presents in its form, color, and scent is death itself: the most base aspect of material reality. Paradoxically, perfume once distilled from this very baseness works to mask the repulsive odors produced by such baseness. Perfume is the transformation of mortal and material substances—destined for decomposition and "garish withering," as Bataille says—into a liquid and a vapor that preserve the floral aroma beyond the natural span of the flower's life. Perfume spiritualizes the flower's matter, raising it to a higher plane of being and elevating baseness to an angelic purity. Yet, it still contains traces of the natural ingredients of that baseness. For this reason perfume, as Baudelaire was one of the first poets to recognize, has a dual suggestiveness. It is both material and spiritual, noble and perverted, natural and artificial, ephemeral and lasting; its ambiguity could not help but attract the Baudelairean nose.

The double-edged nature of fragrance—both sweet and fatal, fascinating and murderous—not only defines Baudelaire's preoccupation with olfactory sensation—he is one of the greatest poets of perfume—but reflects the fashion protocols of French society during the Second Empire (1852–1870) and into the Belle Epoque (1870–1914) of the Third Republic. The social imagination, which unconsciously dictated the protocols for the use of perfume among the French bourgeoisie and aristocracy, also reveals the unbridgeable ideological divide between this conservative society and Baudelaire, an avant-garde dandy strangely in and out of step with his times. For Baudelaire was exceedingly knowledgeable about the fashion customs of his day—fashion, he wrote in *The Painter of Modern Life*, should be "considered as a symptom of the taste for the ideal"—and rabidly disparaging of the political realities of the Second Empire. He regarded "the imbeciles of the Bourgeoisie" (I: 707) with contempt, Napoleon III with hatred—"Yet another Bonaparte! What a disgrace!" (I: 679)—and the French populace with disdain: "The Frenchman is a barnyard animal ...; the filth of his domicile does not displease him and in literature he eats dung, infatuated as he is with excrement" (I: 698). And yet, Baudelaire's poetry reflects the interest in perfume that continued to grow and intensify during the Second Empire, captivating a bourgeoisie intent on adopting the tastes of the aristocracy and of Napoleon III's court; "Baudelaire's theory of 'correspondances'" as Alain Corbin observes, "reflected something that was actually taking place in contemporary civilization."[3]

It is not surprising then to discover Baudelaire "experimenting" poetically with different combinations of scent. He juxtaposes their names as if he were seeking to create an olfactory chord that would evoke sensations of self-indulgent pleasure, sensuous idleness, and blissful love. In certain lines of verse Baudelaire acts like a "nose." Musk mixes with tobacco in one poem ("Sed Non Satiata," I: 28), rose with musk in another ("Les Projets," I: 315). Incense, spikenard, and myrrh join together in a third ("Benediction," I: 8), while rare floral scents are combined with ambergris in a fourth ("L'Invitation au voyage," I: 53). But his real olfactory skills rise to the challenge in "La Chevelure" ("Her Hair") where the poet, drunk with ardor, imagines himself sated "On the mingled smells / Of coconut oil, of musk and tar" (Fowlie 43). While this combination of scents generates dream, intoxication, and bliss—in other words, the felicity of an ideal world brought into being through the scented imagination—Baudelaire in another prose poem, "The Double Room," drastically changes the blend of aromatic ingredients in order to represent, in aromatic terms at least, the loss of an idyllic paradise and the sad return of sordid everyday reality: "And that perfume of another world, on which with perfected sensibility I had gotten drunk, alas, was replaced by a tobacco stench mingled with a nauseating moldiness. Now we breathe here the rancidness of desolation" (I: 281; Fowlie 123). If the experience of "spleen," melancholy, and despair has an odor for Baudelaire, in contrast to the incense of the ideal for which he perpetually searches, then its olfactory signature is identified by this blend of tobacco, mildew, and rankness.

The Scents of Sight

If beauty, as Baudelaire believed, is always bizarre—always contains a strangeness alone capable of forming the uniqueness of the beautiful itself (II: 578–79)—then perfume, invariably associated by Baudelaire with feminine beauty and seductiveness, promises an uncanny and mystifying experience of exoticism. In naming one of his many poems on perfume "Parfum exotique" (Exotic Perfume) Baudelaire stresses the fundamental otherworldliness of the perfumed creations that the scented imagination perceives. In this poem several of the themes common to Baudelaire's poems of scent commingle; for example, perfume as a form of perception and apprehension, a second "sight"; perfume as a sensual and ethereal music; perfume as transport and displacement; perfume as the expansion of reality; perfume as the confusion of interior and exterior spaces; perfume as respiration and inspiration; perfume as carnal aroma, the beguiling emanation of a woman's body, her flesh made spirit; perfume as reverie and intoxication;

perfume as the unfolding and opening of imaginary sites, scenes and narrative scenarios; perfume as pleasure, as "luxury, calm, and delight" (I: 53); perfume as vagueness and airiness; perfume as knowledge; and so on.

In "Exotic Perfume" Baudelaire captures the poetic essence of olfaction: how perfume explodes within the imagination and how it provokes moments of erotic sensuality, intoxication, bewitchment, and physical as well as spiritual presence. Baudelaire's poem reveals and enacts the process by which the perfumed imagination gives rise to the poetic imagination. For it is not only the poet's consciousness that takes flight on the wings of fragrance; it is poetic language itself which ascends on the waves of scent. The meanings of words are volatilized and spiritualized, like primary ingredients (jasmine, iris, bergamot) of a perfume, expanding, intermingling, and mutating under the heat of a poetic fire. The unfolding of perfume images in Baudelaire's poems and especially in "Exotic Perfume" (I: 25–26) coincides with the unfolding expansiveness of poetry itself, which moves simultaneously upward, outward, and inward, like perfume, permeating air and soul, invading world and spirit. Not only is there something poetic about scent, there is something aromatic about poetry:

> When, on our late, hot autumn afternoons,
> Eyes closed, I breathed your breast's warm, heady scent,
> I see a sun, fixed in the firmament,
> Shining on dazzling shores: strand, rolling dunes;
>
> One of those lazy, nature-gifted isles,
> With luscious fruits, trees strange of leaf and limb,
> Men vigorous of body, lithe and slim,
> Women with artless glance that awes, beguiles.
>
> Lured by your scent, led on to charming clime,
> I see a port, all mast and sail,
> Battered and buffeted by tide and time;
>
> And all the while green tamarinds exhale
> Perfumes that fill my nostrils and my soul,
> Blending with sounds of sailors' barcarole.
>   (Shapiro, 47)

From the first line, "Exotic Perfume" announces, even requires, a new way of "seeing" the world. The exotic is already at work, demanding that the familiar, the conventional, the comfortable strategies of perception be dismissed for new, untried modes of sensory experience: a sightless seeing, a blind vision, with no dependence on eyesight. Eyes closed, his attention focused on the scent of the woman's body, the heat of which corresponds to that of the autumn evening outside, the poet is transported on the wings of scent to another world: an exotic, odorous, languid dreamland. It is only after he has breathed the woman's fragrance that he begins to see (ll. 2–3); smell makes vision—an interior, dream vision—possible. For

the poet can sense the outside world, can even "see" it, but only at the moment paradoxically when, eyes closed, he takes this world, as shaped by the scent of a woman's body, into himself, internalizing it through smell. Scent literally transforms sight into in-sight. It can be said that the poet "sees" through the nose. His vision is no longer visual. By comparison with sight, today the primary sense of human survival, smell can be considered the "exotic" sense, the one that millennia of evolution have made the most degraded, forgotten, and unused of the five senses.

Moreover, the highlighting of the scented imagination in "Exotic Perfume" at the expense of sighted vision—an interior "vision" does indeed develop in the poem, but it is mediated first and foremost through smell and not sight—starts at the beginning of the poem. The first sentence (ll. 1–2) announces that normal sight has been suspended, that the poet has chosen, figuratively speaking, to blind himself. From the beginning, the poem proclaims that any sight or act of seeing, any dream vision or act of reverie, as reported in the lines to follow, will result not from the perception of the eyes, but from the perceptual work of the nose. The exotic dream world to which the poet is carried and the languid, indolent movements of the men, women, trees, and boats on this imagined island unfold according to the rhythms of breath and smell: "Lured by your scent, led on to charming clime, / I see." This is all the more surprising considering that the first stanza makes such a strong case for conventional sight by referring in the French poem to the fires of a relentless sun ("les feux d'un soleil monotone") whose unwavering light dazzles the blissful shores on which it falls. These intensely visual realities, so eloquently evoked by the sounds of Baudelaire's words, are, however, not seen but felt—and felt through smell. The world of scents and odors eclipses the world of sights (a port, sails, masts, waves, trees) and, until the final line, of sounds. Or put another way, odors and aromas alone make vision possible; they open the world to, and prepare the way for, visual perception.

Linking Sight and Smell

Throughout "Exotic Perfume" vision and smell are inextricably linked, as if each sense were a shadow of the other. In fact, there is a determined, if not programmed, alternation between the visual and the olfactory throughout the poem. This is primarily because, for Baudelaire, vision is a form of smell by other means. The first stanza begins by referring to the poet's closed eyes, but then follows this image with an allusion to the act of breathing (l. 2), which is itself followed (l. 3) by a reference to seeing. Similarly, the second stanza presents fruits (l. 6), described in French as "savoureux" ("luscious")—taste and savor being closely linked to olfaction—in tandem with the image of a beguiling "artless glance." This is followed, in the next stanza, by allusions first to the beloved's "scent" (l. 9) and then, in the

Attar of roses ("attar" coming from a Persian word meaning perfume essence) is shown here being distilled in Delhi, India.

very next line, to the poet's act of seeing. The final stanza, however, breaks this see-sawing dialogue between the olfactory and the visual, as if the mention of the one demanded the immediate iteration of the other. The image of seeing in the third stanza ("I see a port . . .") is replaced in the fourth by the evocation of the scent of tamarind trees (l. 12), an allusion to smell, at once strengthened and intensified in the following line by the expansive power of scent circulating in the air and invading the poet's being. Given the pattern up to this point of alternating pairings of smell and sight, the reader now expects that this allusion to olfactory sensation ("green tamarinds exhale / Perfumes that fill my nostrils and my soul") will be followed by a reference to vision. And yet, the final line disappoints the expectation. The allusion is not to visual but to auditory experience; it links perfume—and the ultimate spiritualization it undergoes as it enters the poet's soul through the nose—to music, song, and poetry: namely, to what the French poem identifes as the "chant des mariniers" (the sailors' song). Scent is musicalized and poeticized; perfume becomes lyric poetry as poem becomes scented sound. The expansiveness of fragrance, provoking the poet's nose to swell and his olfactory imagination to surge, explodes into perfumed song, into words ascending on intermingled waves of scent and sound. And this fusion of sight, smell, and sound, propelled by the oscillation between experiences of olfaction and vision, as it occurs nine times in fourteen lines, reiterates the interiorization which "Exotic Perfume" has sought to establish from the shutting down of conventional, and the privileging of poetic, sight which began in the poem's first line.

Perfume is the poet's guide in "Exotic Perfume." It leads him toward unknown, unseen realities. Even though attached forcefully to an intense, intimate and sensual present (the warm evening air, the closeness of the beloved, the odor of her skin), perfume takes him away from the here and now, moving him out toward distant, uncrossed horizons. It opens an imaginary world. It forces him to make use of another, not quite familiar, mode of perception: i.e., smell. In all these ways, perfume is truly "exotic." It renders the familiar unfamiliar; it mystifies the commonplace: an autumn evening of love. It exiles the poet from the everyday, turning the ordinary into the extraordinary; and it accomplishes a transformative estrangement, through which the poet experiences an ecstasy, at once exorbitant, esoteric, exilic, extravagant, and extraterritorial, terms reflecting the root of "exotic" in *exotikus*, the Greek world for "stranger." The expansive power of perfume is creative of strangeness, a delightful disembodiment whereby the poet's body and soul become an airy, vaporous reality. This strangeness is provoked by an amalgam of sensory colors, sounds, tastes, smells, and surfaces fusing into the secret being of the universe: the "dark and profound unity / Vast like night and like light," which Baudelaire evokes in his great sonnet "Correspondences" (I: 11).

A Symphony of Sight, Sound, and Scent

The exoticness of perfume is clearly evident from the first lines of "Exotic Perfume." With a quick leap, the poet's consciousness surges from the beloved woman and her warm

105

breast (an odorous emanation, if not "reflection," of the evening's warmth) to a vision of a blessed faraway landscape: the felicitous, sensual shores of an island warmed by a radiant sun, welcoming to ships and sailors who, exhausted from their voyages, hope to be restored by the vigor, candor, and richness of the island and its inhabitants. The poet's imagination jumps from an odor to a world, from a person to a universe, and from a woman to a paradise of blissful warmth, pleasure, and fullness. What begins as odor ends as perfume: namely, the scent of green fruit trees ("tamarinds") permeating the island air, expanding within the poet's nose, and invading his spiritual being, where it mixes with other sensations (the sailors' songs) in a symphony of sight, sound, and scent. The outside world—that of the beloved's body, of the autumnal evening, of the imagined island, of its port, its ships, its fruit trees—is interiorized. Interestingly, what had begun as a physical experience, involving respiration ("I breathe"), odor, and the body (the woman's breast) only to expand into a landscape and universe—the island paradise—comes full circle, returning at the end to the body (i.e., the nose), although now this body has become a cosmos unto itself. The initiating power of the woman's fragrance, circulating throughout the poem as the inspiration for the imagined island and for the poet's reverie—causing nose, imagination, and mind to swell—reaches the apogee of its olfactory trajectory in the poem's final line. So, what began as body ("breast") returns as body ("nose"), although by the poem's end this body has taken on a strangely spiritualized corporeality.

This is because the abundance of physical and sensual images in the poem—the references to eyes, nose, breast, and body, the represented acts of seeing, breathing, smelling, and the intimations of a naturalized sensuality associated with the island's fruits, trees, men, and women—do not only translate an experience of physicality but that of its opposite: spirituality. These concrete sites of material phenomena are the spawning ground for the imaginary. It surges and rises, like a potent scent, from the world of everyday, sensual reality, opening matter to dream, body to spirit, and nature to soul. This spiritualization of the physical, which perfume accomplishes so well, this opening of the everyday to the exotic, this immobilizing of the ephemeral in the eternal circulation of scent and sound, and this movement outward (toward the universe), which paradoxically figures a fundamental inwardness (toward dream and self-consciousness), all signal in Baudelaire's poetic imagination the coincidence of physicality and spirituality, of matter and air, of the sensual and the essential: in other words, the ambiguous duality that perfume—as the coexistence of liquid and gas, substance and vapor, the contained and the dispersed—evokes. Moreover, the tendency of perfume to go from a state of concentration to one of dispersion recalls one of Baudelaire's observations about the nature of the self: namely, that it is in constant motion between "vaporization" and "centralization" (I: 676).

"Exotic Perfume" makes clear that for Baudelaire seeing involves a more expansive form of apprehension, a more intense way of capturing the world, through a form of perception called "synaesthesia," whereby one sense impression (a smell, like that of a rose) evokes another (a color, like red). Through synaesthesia seeing can be coincident with smelling, smelling with hearing, and hearing with seeing; there are no longer clear-cut demarcations between sensations and the senses that stimulate them. In "Exotic Perfume" Baudelaire's synaesthetic imagination determines the poem's images. From the beginning, traditional vision is shut down; the poet begins to "see" through smell not sight. The experiences that his desire imagines—of happy shores, a dazzling sun, the indolent island with its fruits, trees, and delightful weather—are experienced through the inspiration that respiration and smell have allowed. Even the image of vision and the perception of the island's women whose "artless glance . . . awes, beguiles," come into being through the poet's olfactory imagination, since everything in the poem, once the poet has closed his eyes to the real world in the first line, transpires under the sign of smell. Like a blind man, the poet is guided (synaesthetically) by the "touch" of the olfactory; he is led on and "lured" by smell to sight (ll. 9–10). Everything in this dream world is animated by the trail of scent, as if fragrance awakened the island's flora and fauna to life the very minute it touched them.

Yet, the many images representing the experience of smell undergo further intensification in the poem's final stanza. Endowed with a scented air, from the moment of the poet's initial act of respiration (l. 2), reality undergoes a penetrating olfactory transformation. What had been a continuous dream of scent, initiated by the aroma of the woman's skin, is further interiorized, further perfumed, when the poet realizes that the odor of the "green tamarind" trees, already an olfactory experience within his reverie of the dream island, causes the air of his nose to expand; the perfume swells "my nostrils," he writes. The poet's representation of the movements of his olfactory unconscious and of the allure an imagined scent has had on this unconscious becomes even more complex. The poem spirals through layers of greater and greater inwardness, through more and more complex "phantasmagorias of the interior" (Benjamin, *The Arcades Project*, 9). The fragrance the poet inhales at the end of the poem—the scent of the tamarinds—after his having inhaled a different fragrance earlier in the poem—the scent of the woman's skin—is the olfactory "reflection," so to speak, of an earlier "reflection": one scent-image echoing a second scent-image, which echoes a third scent-image, and so on. This is a perfume so folded upon itself and so concentrated as to resemble the endless reflections of two mirrors standing face to face. A further consequence of this infinite reflexivity is the way phenomena are progressively deepened and interiorized: the way, for example, perfume first triggers a dream, then is incorporated into the dream, and finally is drawn more deeply into the poet's soul.

This overlapping of different layers of reality and fantasy, blending one into the other, which the fluidity and airiness of perfume so perfectly represent, is evident in the poetic transformations the woman's body experiences in the poem. When we first meet her, she is already reduced to the status of an object. Although she has a real body ("breast"), possesses a real scent (identified as "heady"), and lives in the real world of changing time ("late, hot autumn afternoons"), she is quickly transformed into vapor, reduced to an intoxicating aroma, which lifts the poet out of reality and into reverie and imagination. The feminine body has been distilled into perfume. Her being is her aroma. But this scent is then re-embodied and re-concretized as an imaginary landscape: namely, the island of delight where the woman's fragrance continues to "lure" and "guide" the poet's desire. In the final stanza, her perfume floats in the air. Passing through the poet's nose into his soul, it becomes even more vaporous and spiritualized. As the accomplished perfumer that this poem suggests he could be, Baudelaire subjects the woman's fragrance to increasing degrees of distillation and vaporization. As flowers are distilled to create what perfumers call a concrete essence and as this "concrete" is distilled yet again to produce a purer, rarer, more potent scent called an absolute essence, so Baudelaire's poem enacts a movement toward an absolute of sorts: that of pure bliss, harmony, and spiritual union. Thus does the scented imaginary attain the apogee of imagination itself.

"Exotic Perfume" suggests a new way of experiencing love, dream, and poetry. By first reducing the power of sight and then privileging the power of perfume, insofar as vision and smell contribute to his physical contact with the temporal world and, more significantly, with the woman he desires, Baudelaire reveals that vision—particularly, an inner, spiritual vision—is governed by the rhythms of respiration, as if images, sights, and dreams—sensations of the optical conscious and unconscious—necessarily depend on the cadences of inhalation, inspiration, and olfaction: on the body's "flair," so to speak. As the nose inhales scent molecules transported by the air and as the lungs take in oxygen, according to a regular pattern of breathing, so poetry, one might suggest, follows breath rhythms attuned to the body. The body *speaks* in the poem, usually subliminally and unconsciously. Its trace hides in the meter of verses, in pauses and breaks, and in the play of consonants and vowels. In offering a description of the mechanics of perfume's dissemination and expansion—the exotic unwinding of scent—as a metaphor for the unfolding of a dream vision redolent of desire and passion, Baudelaire appropriates the physical reality of the body to represent spiritual and metaphysical experiences. The body and the world are never far away, even when the poetic imagination finds a momentary haven in a distant island of blissful fantasy, a dream space where unimpeded perception permits the spontaneous understanding of what Baudelaire in the poem "Elevation" calls "the language of flowers and voice-less things" (I: 10; Fowlie, 27). Whether as a concentrated presence or a vaporous absence, whether as a physical emanation of the body's sensuality or a vestige of a lost, evaporated scent, perfume is, according to Baudelaire's olfactory imagination, a phenomenon deeply connected to the earth and air of existence and inseparable from the "body" of the world and the soul.[4]

The Simulation of Perfume

While "Exotic Perfume" ties perfume to breath—to the rhythmical respiration of the world, the body, and lyrical song—the poem "Perfume" links it to reading. In Baudelaire's *Flowers of Evil* the reader is ever-present. The collection's first poem, "To the Reader," a greeting at the threshold of the volume in the form of a title and an invitation, is meant as a homage, a dedication, and even a warning to the reader opening the book. Putting him or her on notice that the catalogue of human sins and evils and the melancholic representation of the despair of human existence—"An oasis of horror in a desert of boredom!" ("The Voyage," I: 133; Fowlie, 101)—which will follow, may not be appreciated, Baudelaire makes the reader fully aware of what she or he should expect. So that there will be no doubts about the universal and representative quality of Baudelaire's depiction of humankind and no self-serving rationalizations by the reader, who may wish to dismiss the poetry as the ravings of a mad poet, "To the Reader" ends with a hug of complicity, the poet vigorously reminding the reader of their profound resemblance: "Hypocrite reader—my twin—my brother!" (I: 6; Fowlie, 21).

In a similar fashion, "Perfume" (part of a four-sonnet sequence entitled "Un Fantôme," I: 39) directly addresses the reader, appealing to her or his olfactory experience; once again the reader is made to collude in the poet's fantasy:

> Hast thou inhaled—O reader say!—
> With zest and lazy greed, the old
> Incense that chapel arches hold
> Or the stale musk of a sachet?
>
> O magic spell, O ecstasy!
> —To make the present yield the past!—
> Thus, from and on a beloved breast
> Love culls the flowers of memory.
>
> From tresses long about her face
> —A living sachet, censer and bedroom of the place—
> Rose strange wild odors all astir,
>
> And from her velvet, muslin, lace,
> Permeated with her youthful candor
> Emanated a perfume, faint, of fur. (Mathews, 48–49)

Fig. 47 Near the end of the eighteenth century, light, transparent dresses of cotton muslin or chiffon ("mousseline") became the rage in France, encouraged by the new Empire style of fashion with its emphasis on simple, loose-fitting, high-waisted shifts. Napoleon's wife Josephine wore Indian muslin so fine and translucent that she appeared to be, one commentator observed, clothed in a "robe of mist," an airiness that inspired diaphanous floral fragrances like Farina's *Extrait de mousseline*, c. 1815–1820, represented here in an engraved, hand-colored perfume label.

"Perfume," like "Exotic Perfume," begins with a breath, the inhaling of a scent. Baudelaire appeals here to the recognition of odors and perfumes inseparable, as the poem will show, from the recognition of memories. The first stanza of "Perfume" is dedicated to describing the phenomenon of smell as a physical act, a sensual experience, a heightened perception of reality, and a poetic condition of being. (In fact, each stanza will offer aromatic or odorous substances for the reader's delectation.) The first stanza, moreover, does not only describe the perceptual act of smelling—the long inhaling breath, the slow filling of the lungs to savor greedily the pleasurable fragrance, the feeling of intoxicating lightheadedness—but moves to offer an evocation of two precise substances of odorous fascination: frankincense and musk, aromas that have embodied spirituality and sensuality since antiquity. Given that frankincense has always been linked to religion and divinity and musk to amorous dalliance (the third stanza's allusion to a bedroom confirms this), the potency of these aromatic substances is clearly emphasized here. The reference to the odor of a grain of frankincense able to fill an entire church (l. 3) affirms perfume's power of expansion. And the allusion to a sachet capable, after many dormant years, of restoring an intense aroma of musk (l. 4) underscores perfume's power of permanence and its power to work magic like an amulet or charm.

It is also obvious that Baudelaire knew his "sachets." In the nineteenth century these perfumed objects took the form of silk bags or ornamental envelopes filled with fragrant powder. They were placed in drawers to perfume linen and clothing. The fragrant substances within the bags were ground into powder in a mill or mortar and then sifted. Only those primary materials capable of retaining a scent in a dried state were selected for use as powders. Thus, lemon, thyme, mint, and the leaves of orange or citron trees were often chosen. Since few blossoms other than lavender, rose, and cassie preserve their original fragrance when dried, classical perfume ingredients like jasmine, tuberose, violet, and mignonette were never placed in sachets. A nineteenth-century powder, enveloped in what was called a muslin sachet, was, according to the late nineteenth-century perfumer Septimus Piesse, composed of powdered vetiver, sandalwood, orris, black-currant leaves, powdered benzoin, and attar of thyme and of roses. Moreover, there is a correspondence, based on a common lightness and airiness, between muslin or chiffon fabric and perfume. A jasmine fragrance called *eau de Mousseline* was first created by L. T. Piver in 1812 and sold by perfumers like Farina (fig. 47).[5]

In Baudelaire's "Perfume" two forces characteristic of the mobility and mutability of perfume compete: namely, emanation and penetration. The number of aromas, fragrances, and scented fabrics mobilized in the poem is considerable: frankincense and musk, flower and hair, sachet and censer, clothes and fur, velvet and muslin. Even the woman's youth has its own signature scent (l. 13). The incidence of olfactory impregnation is nearly total. Almost all of the phenomena and personae mentioned are penetrated by scent: first, the reader who is called on to remember the experience of inhaling perfume as she or he "inhales" ("breathes in") the poem, as it were; second, the church saturated to the rafters with frankincense; third, the sachet impregnated by musk; fourth, the present penetrated by the resurrected odors of the past, the flowers of memory; fifth, the woman's hair alive with a savage and wild scent; sixth, the bedroom alcove redolent of a sensual odor of femininity and love hovering like burnt incense; seventh, clothes impregnated with the scent of youth; and finally, the "perfume of fur," which, as we shall see, embodies for Baudelaire the primordial scent of erotic femininity and maternity. Objects, places, events, decors, fabrics, parts of the body—the material reality of the world itself—are all invaded here by the *spirit* of scent.

Fragrant Music and Fragrant Memory

"Perfume" presents the phenomenon of emanation not only by highlighting the movement of aromas into the air—the incense permeating the church, the miasma of musk enveloping the sachet, the heavy, suggestive scent of hair floating in the bedroom, the odor of fur emanating from muslin and velvet—but by presenting the poem itself as a kind of "perfumed music." I am referring to the way the poem appears to have the structure or architecture of a fragrance: in particular, the combination of suggestive and harmonious forms it brings together and the layering of richly associative notes it blends into a sensual whole, into a composition at once poetic, musical, and aromatic. Like scents emanating from the different substances described in the poem, the syllables, words, lines, and stanzas of "Perfume" flow into and emanate out of one another. A ubiquitous and suggestive musicality, a fragrant lyricism, floats over the poem; it determines the repetition of words ("sachet" in stanzas 1 and 3 and "incense" and "censer" in lines 3 and 10), of syllables (in French the sounds "li," "or," and "auv" are repeated in several words in lines 3, 7, and 11), and of syntax. It is here in the syntactical structure of the poem that what may be called a poetry of emanation is most evident. More than is common for a Baudelairean sonnet, "Perfume" is saturated with connections, associations, and prospective and retrospective allusions. With references to breath, intoxication, incense, sachet, musk, the interior of a church, a magical amulet, and the resurrected past, the first six lines compress into a few verses a host of powerfully evocative objects and phenomena. This rich hoard of associations, circulating in the atmosphere of the poem's first lines and in the reader's mind, is connected to the remainder of the poem's images by the simple conjunction "thus" ("ainsi," l. 7). It is a conjunction of organization and concentration at the very midpoint of the poem; it draws together into a whole, and gives closure to, the disparate although exemplary fragments which have preceded it.

In "Perfume" the conjunction "thus" focuses and magnetizes the poem's initial allusions, builds a bridge of transition between the first and second parts of the poem, and links the reader, who was addressed in the first line, to the lover and the beloved of the third stanza: the latter, a woman known for her anatomy (breast, hair) or for the precise texture of what covers that anatomy (clothes, muslin, velvet). Yet another syntactical device for creating connection and suggesting emanation is the structurally important use of the modest, usually unnoticed, preposition *from* ("de") here given the responsibility of representing a process of extraction. Moreover, several words, like "rose," "permeated," "emanated," describe not only the perfumed imagination active in the poem—the reader's memory of perfume, of the smells adhering to places and things, of the real or remembered aromas of love—but also the structural movement and activity of the poem itself. Not only is "Perfume" about perfume; it moves like a perfume as well, each image permeating and then mixing with another: each stanza offering a rich, heady, perhaps even hyperbolic, description of perfume's mobility and its power to create plenitude. Almost iconically, the poem simulates the way a scent rises, saturates, permeates, remembers, and turns objects and spaces into aromas; the bedchamber, for example, becomes a room-sized censer. Through images of extraction, expansion, dissipation, and saturation the poem mimes the movement of perfume. In the overlapping of words, the mixing of sounds, and the associations of images, it attempts to represent the way invisible, mute scrolls and curls of scent float through the air, envelop objects, and trigger a remembrance of things past.

In addition to simulating the movement of perfume, "Perfume" represents the movement of memory, for perfume works as much like memory as memory operates like perfume. Both provoke a flowering, as Baudelaire suggests—"O magic spell, O ecstasy! / . . . / Thus from and on a beloved breast / Love culls the flowers of memory"—although what memory triggers is, more precisely, a *re*-flowering. In fact, the lover's act of "picking" this memory-flower sets in motion a figurative process of aromatic creation. The movement in the poem from "the flowers of memory" (l. 8) to wilder, stranger "odors all astir," (l. 11), and finally to an elegant "perfume, faint, of fur" (l. 14) recalls, albeit unintentionally, the traditional stages of perfume production: first, the harvesting of petals, then the distillation and extraction of floral substances, and finally the ultimate creation of an absolute essence, which for Baudelaire becomes the "absolute essence" of the past restored to the present. The memory of the floral scent of an "adored body" and "a beloved breast" returning like a vaporous trace from the past and permeating the present, arrives as if through smoke: *per-fumum*, in the original Latin. Paradoxically, the past passes through and disappears into a distillation and vaporization which preserve it. It is as fragrant smoke evaporating into air that perfume and memory endure. A trace, or an indistinct trail, or an incomplete fragment of the past achieves fullness by means of the lover-poet's memory. He performs an act of creative selection (of picking), which is then followed by distillations of greater and greater refinement until a pure and absolute floral scent, the essential spirit of the

past (and of his love), alone remains. This is what memory wedded to the power of poetic imagination accomplishes for Baudelaire. This is what the metaphor of perfume in "Perfume" represents: namely, the purification of memory, the distilling from the past of precise, exquisite, and sensuous images expressive, in concentrated yet expansive ways, of the essential reality of that past, now resurrected in the present.

For the lover in the poem the question of what (and who) is actually present is critical. His position vis-à-vis the past and the beloved is ambiguous to say the least, and this ambiguity depends on the simple preposition "on." What does the poet mean when he situates the lover "*on* a beloved breast" (l. 7)? Doubtlessly, he is not actually lying on the woman's body. Rather, he focuses mentally on her memory: on his remembered experience of her body in the past. It is not a real body he touches but the memory of that body: an image. And here the mechanics of memory connect with the mechanics of perfume. The lover moves from the body now lost in time to the image of that body re-imagined in the present; he moves from the material to the immaterial, from a physical reality to an imagined reality, a simulacrum. And yet, at every stage in this process of remembering, the image which replaces the body has a concrete substance of its own, especially when it is embedded as language and memory in a poem. At this higher stage of representation image and scent re-materialize in different concrete forms, a reconfiguration not unlike the changes in state the scent of a flower undergoes during the production of perfume: for example, from vapor to solid, through the process of cold *enfleurage*, by which the aroma of petals is absorbed by the fatty substance on which they lie; or from solid to vapor, by boiling flowers immersed in water; or from vapor to liquid, by cooling the resulting steam and separating the denser water from the perfumed essence which rises to the top; or from solid to semi-solid, by submitting petals to the extracting action of solvents like hexane or benzene and then decanting and concentrating the resulting mixture to form a pasty substance, called a "concrete"; or finally from solid to liquid, by washing this concrete with alcohol, filtering it several times to remove paraffin, wax, and other impurities, and then evaporating the alcohol to produce the liquid "absolute."[6]

Memory in "Perfume" travels along invisible pathways already cleared and marked by fragrance. When it comes to rediscovering the past, air and breath become favored media of return. Waves of memory coincide in Baudelaire's imagination with waves of sound or scent or with phenomena of respiration or emanation. Scent in Baudelaire's oeuvre is generally a metaphor, according to Benjamin, for involuntary memory: "If the recognition of a scent can provide greater consolation than any other memory, this may be because it deeply anesthetizes the sense of time. A scent may drown entire years in the remembered odor it evokes."[7] This simultaneity of remembrance and scent, of memory and breath, is clearly announced in the

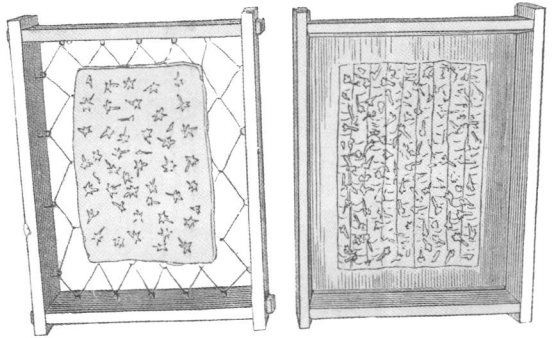

"Oil and Pomade Frames," used in "cold enfleurage," an old and costly process of extracting natural odors from flowers by spreading blossoms on a layer of cold animal fat that absorbs their scent. Illustration from Eugène Rimmel, *The Book of Perfumes* (London: Chapman and Hall, 1867).

first line of "Perfume." The question that the poet asks— "Hast thou inhaled—O reader, say!"—compels the reader to remember and inhale at the same time: to think back to the past and to do this recalling through his or her olfactory experience. Similarly, the lover who appears later in the poem must also experience memory through smell; the image of the beloved's body comes alive again through the fragrant flowering of memory. The restoration of the past coincides with the immediacy of scent; past and present become one. Thus, respiration and reminiscence are mediated through olfaction. To remember is to smell by other means. "Perfume" represents the recapture of the absolute essence of past experience; a remembered love returns in all its potency. From the visual and sensual oblivion of the past, a phantom-memory and a phantom-scent float into the present. Perfume resurrects the physical image of a body, of a boudoir, of a flower and the sensual notes— floral, epidermal, even existential—of a woman's scent, thus reestablishing the presence of her being in the everyday world. And from each odorous reality touching her body—from memory, hair, clothes (as mentioned in the second, third, and fourth stanzas)—something irreducibly essential and powerfully expressive surges forth: a "flower," an "odor," and a "perfume." Moreover, the image of memory as a flower picked from the past reveals the concentrated and compressed power that recollection possesses. This is not a mere trace of the past but its very heart and soul returning on the wings of perfume. This is the enduring base note at the center of the scent, outlasting the more ephemeral head and heart notes which only envelop and transport the fragrance.

The Perfume of Velvet, Muslin, and Fur

Thus, "Perfume" presents a variety of aromatic, floral, and animal odors: from the scent of frankincense and musk to that of a flower and from the aroma of human hair to that of clothes. The most intriguing fragrance of all, however, seems to be the one with which the poem concludes: the perfume of fur. What is this scent? How does it emanate from clothes made of velvet and muslin? And what similarity does it have to the candid smell of youth? One of its most unique attributes is the tactile quality it seems to have acquired: qualities of softness, pliability, and transparency derived from its association with the lightness of muslin, the rich smoothness of velvet, and the warm sheen of fur. This elegant scent stands in marked contrast to the more aggressive and primal smells of the woman's hair. Historically, fur as clothing and adornment remained out of style during most of the eighteenth century but returned to favor in the second half of the nineteenth century due in large part to the founding of the house of Reveillon in 1839. Culturally and symbolically, fur as a sign of sexual fetishism can be traced, according to Julia V. Emberley, to the middle of the seventeenth century.[8] It goes without saying that, like perfume, hair, and jewelry, fur functions as a marker of erotic fetishism in Baudelaire's poetry. As an odor, it resurrects for him the smell of all that is feminine. Thinking back to his childhood, he once admitted to "confus[ing] the odor of fur with the odor of the woman," that of his mother, in particular (I: 661).

This confession, from the poet's private journal, is extraordinarily revealing. The juxtaposition of fur and femininity is clear. But the jump from the poet's experience of fur to the memory of his mother reveals the sexual ambiguity that fur holds for Baudelaire: on the one hand, soft, protective, caressing, and therefore maternal; on the other, elegant, mysterious, and feline. The fur of Baudelaire's cats, for example, when caressed would give off "a sweet fragrance" or "a dangerous scent" (I: 35, 51). This overlapping of the maternal and the feminine, the oedipal and the sensual, the human and the animal, as linked to Baudelaire's fantasy of fur, is more clearly revealed in a passage from a letter the poet wrote to his friend Auguste Poulet-Malassis in April 1860:

> What is it that the child loves so passionately about his mother, his maid, his older sister? Is it simply the being who nourishes, combs, washes, and cuddles him? It is also the caress and the sensual delight.... He loves his mother, his sister, his nurse, therefore, for the pleasure of the tickling their satin and fur give, for the scent of their breast and hair, for the jingling of their jewelry, for the playful arrangement of their ribbons, for this *mundus muliebris* [world of feminine dress] which expresses itself as much in their choice of blouses as in their selection of furniture, and where a woman leaves the mark of *her sex.*

The women who domestically surround the child, Baudelaire suggests, do so in an ambivalent manner at once nourishing and seductive, maternal and voluptuous. All pleasurable and therefore "passionate" transactions with the feminine world, according to Baudelaire's imagination, are mediated by the senses: through touch (in the titillating sensation which fabrics like fur and satin provoke), through smell (in the scent emanating from skin and hair), through hearing (in the ringing of silver and gold bangles, an erotic experience evoked in the poem "Les Bijoux" [Jewels]), and finally, through sight (in the beribboned ornamentation of bonnets, shawls, blouses, and dresses). In this synaesthetic representation of the feminine, Baudelaire envisions the woman as spectacle, one in which nearly all the senses are made to correspond, intersect, and intermingle. The woman imprints everyday reality with her existence; in the air, on the body, in fashionable society, in the home, she leaves a trace of her (sexual) presence. The world of the feminine is that of *mundus muliebris,* from a Latin expression meaning "feminine adornment" or "toilette," to which Baudelaire gives his own interpretation; it is, he writes, "atmosphere, odor, breast, knee, hair, clothing, bath unguents" rolled into one.[9]

In the final stanza of "Perfume," the woman has become the sum of her adornments. She is an amalgam of clothes, fabrics, and fragrances, all of them delicate and ethereal. Enveloped in transparent muslin or silky velvet, she is like a life-sized sachet giving off the pure scent of her "youth"; she is all lightness and vapor, what another poem calls "A being made of light and gold and gauze" ("L'Irréparable," I: 55; Mathews, 71). Behind this vision of the woman as a sublimated being, as a perfume in her own right, lies Baudelaire's belief that matter—the clothes, the velvet, the muslin, the scent of fur—exists as an outward sign of an inner essence. In his poem "Le Flacon" (I: 47–48) Baudelaire describes this transition from inside to outside, this flowing of spirit into world:

> There are some powerful odors that can pass
> Out of the stoppered flask; even glass
> To them is porous. Oft when some old box
> Brought from the East is opened and the locks
>
> And hinges creak and cry, or in a clothes press
> In some deserted house where the sharp stress
> Of odors old and dusty fills the brain,
> An ancient flask is brought to light again.
> (Mathews, 61)

Perfumes penetrate the walls which separate them from the world; a soul surges from a bottle; a flask tumbles out of a dark clothes closet; an object remembers. This is not merely an instance of Baudelaire's supernaturalism, by which the inanimate becomes animate; rather, it his vision of the world's permeability. Matter is porous to spirit. Consequently, because they are spirits, essences, and emanations, perpetually impalpable and amorphous, given to invisibly expanding and changing shape, perfume and memory (as well as poetry) are in a state of perpetual reawakening. They return and renew, bringing with them a breath that holds the scent of the new.

At the beginning of our examination of "Perfume" we suggested the possibility, based on the poem's initial line, that reading may be a form of smelling. But are inhaling a scent and reading a poem similar activities? Outside of the fact that one could not read if one could not breathe, what possibly links breathing to reading? The resemblance may be found in the fact that the experience of a text, like that of a scent, takes *flair*. One must be sensitive to nuances of expression, to subtle turns in meaning, to meandering and spiraling complications of sound, sense, and scent, to the combining of different images and notes, and to hidden suggestions and phantom presences. One must develop not only a flair—the ability to smell and sense keenly and knowingly—but both a corporal consciousness, sensitive to the body's rhythms of inhaling and exhaling, and a spiritual consciousness, attuned first to the emotional effects of word and fragrance and second to the delight, fantasy, and desire they awaken. In reading, the reader follows the blended scent of sense, sound, and image, the union of metaphor, music, and association. In inhaling an aroma, the perfumer follows a similar blend of sensations, memories, and associations. While Baudelaire, under the sway of perfume, experiences *scent as song* and sings "the transports of the mind and senses" ("Correspondances," I: 11), the reader, under the sway of the poem, experiences *song as scent,* breathing rhythmically with the music of the poem and the music of the perfume.

Perfumes of Paradox

Many and various are the epithets Baudelaire attaches to scents. Perfumes, he writes in various prose and poetic works, are "horrid," "dangerous," "singular," "otherworldly," "acrid," "angelic," "sweet," "heavenly," "dirty," "virtuous," "potent," "mysterious," "subtle," "delicate," "bewitching," and dream-inducing. But no poem offers the accumulation of adjectives describing the action of perfume as does "Correspondances." Here perfumes are revealed to be fresh, soft, green, corrupted, rich, triumphant, expansive, infinite, rhapsodic, errant, spiritual, and sensual. With half of its fourteen lines directly concerned with perfume, this sonnet is, it could be said, literally possessed by fragrance:

> All Nature is a pillared temple where,
> At times, live columns mutter words unclear;
> Forests of symbols watch Man pass, and peer
> With intimate glance and a familiar air.
>
> Like distant, long-drawn calls that seem to be
> Obscurely, deeply blended into one—
> Vast as the dark of night and as day's bright sun—
> Sound, perfumes, hues echo in harmony.
>
> Perfumes! Some fresh and cool, like babies' skin,
> Mellow as oboes, green as meadows;
> —And others, rich and exultant, decadent as sin,
>
> Infinite in expanse, like benzoin gum,
> Incense and amber, musk and benjamin,
> Sing flesh's bliss, and soul's delight therein.
> (Shapiro, 13).

The spiritual and mystical properties of perfume are suggested from the first line. Nature as a temple where vertical, upward-thrusting forms (pillars, trees, forests) emit confused and vaporous messages calls to mind, among several possibilities, the temples in which Egyptians, Hebrews, and Greeks burned incense as offerings to the gods. Considering that sacrifice, as the classical scholar J.-P. Vernant writes, signifies "the human race's definitive separation from the race of the gods," sacrificial rituals present a normal channel for communication between heaven and

"The Altar of Incense," as God possibly wished Moses to construct it in *Exodus* (30:1–10). Illustration from Eugène Rimmel, *The Book of Perfumes* (London: Chapman and Hall, 1867).

earth. While man's share of a sacrificed animal was the dead, corruptible meat, the gods' part was the smoke arising from the charred bones. Because the Egyptian word for incense (*sonter*) was traditionally preceded by the ideogram for god or divine kingdom, it came to mean "divine odor" or "the odor that pleases the gods." In fact, the Egyptians believed that incense was the very "sweat of the gods which had fallen to earth." Perfumes and spices represented, Vernant observes, "the portion allotted to the gods alone, the portion that men could never assimilate." Fragrant incense, myrrh, and spices designated "the inaccessible character of the divine." The gods, moreover, were themselves endowed with signature fragrances; their presence was, Vernant writes, "made manifest not only by intensely bright beams of light but also by a marvelous smell." In all ancient civilizations perfumes were reserved first and foremost for the gods; the Old Testament offers recipes for the preparation of ritual perfumes, and God is not above advising Moses on how to prepare a fragrant holy oil (see *Psalms* 133, *Exodus* 40).[10]

The power to separate the divine from the human world and celestial from terrestrial spheres of activity

belonged for many centuries to the mythic aura assigned to perfume by the ancients. This myth continues in *The Flowers of Evil*. Baudelaire's allusion to nature as a potentially transcendental site of being and as a crossroads where the signs of heaven and earth commingle confusedly reveals the ambiguity of an earth dominated by wispy traces and imprecise emanations. As a perfume bottle may allow confused scents to escape into the air (or even through its glass as in Baudelaire's "Le Flacon"), so nature's temple with its living architecture ("live columns") allows confused, indecipherable words to soar on the wind. Language has come to possess the immateriality of scent; words are clouds of incense rising into the sky, their meanings amorphous and fugitive to those humans who hear or smell them. Yet, this confusion soon changes into a fusion; the confounding of reality initiates the founding of reality. And what was trace, trail, particle, dispersion, and dissemination coalesces into a whole, a unity "Vast as the dark of night and as day's bright sun."

But how unified and seamless can this oneness be? Can the center hold together the confused structures, words, symbols, glances, echoes, and scents circulating in this world? It can and cannot. Baudelaire insists on the fundamental ambiguity inherent to the cosmic unity he imagines. For this is a unity composed not of original events or realities but of their echoes—in other words, their traces and aftereffects. While perfumes, colors, and sounds will, according to the poet's desire for the mingling of senses—for a heightened experience of synaesthesia—correspond and respond to each other, they will do so in a continually fragmented, multiple, and diasporic manner. Rather than presenting an odorous harmony of fragrances or the presence of a master scent which would create a sublime synthesis of disparate notes, the two final stanzas of the poem describe several different kinds of unassimilated fragrances. The poem's emphasis on a "confusion" of words and echoes reinforces the notion that the correspondence of perfumes, colors, and sounds forms not a permanent union but an unstable equilibrium among sensual and spiritual forces, ready at any moment to come undone.

What is a poet, Baudelaire asks in his essay on Victor Hugo, "if not a translator and decipherer"? In the world of nature and everyday reality, there is "a mathematically exact" relationship between a "metaphor, a comparison, and an epithet" and the actual reality it designates. This is true because these linguistic forms "are rooted in the inexhaustible depths of the *universal analogy*" (II: 133). Insofar as it is grounded in the same universal analogy, language touches the structure of all that exists; thus, it expresses the one-to-one correspondence between sensual and spiritual, natural and heavenly, and mortal and eternal realms of being. World and spirit converse; they respond to and correspond with each other: "Everything—form, movement, number, color, perfume—in the *spiritual* as well as in the *natural* world is meaningful, reciprocal, converse, and *correspondent*," Baudelaire declares (II: 133). As echoes rumbling in the distance draw together into a choral unity, so in "Correspondences" "sound, perfumes, hues echo in harmony." The paradoxical spectacle of colors, as dazzling in their scent as in their sound, and of scents animated by an odorous spectrum of colors and by a scale of aromatic notes—as resonant with hues of red, blue, and yellow as they are with chords of jasmine, iris, and patchouli—fulfills Baudelaire's dream of a sublime poetry generated by the experience of synaesthesia, which, as we have seen, is a perceptual process through which information provided by one sense is filtered, interpreted, and "read" through the medium of another.

Perfume and Metaphor

Considering the pride of place it enjoys in "Correspondances," perfume may be the synaesthetic agent par excellence, impelling the other senses towards a superior and keener perceptiveness, provoking a sensory experience of unknown harmonies, and creating, in the poem's ultimate line where sensuality and spirituality finally correspond, a song of intermingled colors, sounds, and scents. The French poem's final nouns—"transports," "esprit" (spirit), "sens" (senses)—precisely identify the physical reality of perfume, which is, indeed, "transported" through the air as body and as vapor and which is never more sensual and erotic (the other meaning of "les transports") than when spiritualized. During religious rituals, for example, Egyptian users of incense felt enveloped in an otherworldly halo, detached from time, space, and the world's spectacle. This was a drug-induced "transport," according to the historian Paul Faure, where incense, acting as both stimulant and narcotic, heightened and numbed the senses. The ecstatic song of rapture ("flesh's bliss," "soul's delight") that scent—in the form of ambergris, musk, benzoin, and incense—sings at the poem's end is the culmination of several verses in which Baudelaire celebrates the evocative and analogical power of perfume. And not just one class of perfumes—that of floral, sweet fragrances, for example—but of several classes grouped together under the general, non-specific rubric he identifies as "others," all of which share, vis-à-vis the aforementioned sweet, innocent scents, a fundamental difference; they are not light, floral fragrances but, rather, heavy, animal scents (musk and ambergris) or gummy, aromatic resins (benzoin and incense).

The first group of scents, the "floral" aromas, that Baudelaire mentions are as fresh, sweet-smelling, and dewy as the flesh of children, as soft, gentle, velvety, mellow, (and reedy) as the sounds of oboes, and as green, lush and pastoral as fields. These fresh green scents share in common certain qualities. Each is inherently expansive, because the moment the poet identifies the scent as either "fresh," or "cool," or "mellow," or "green," he propels (one might say, transports) the freshness, coolness, mellowness, or greenness evoked by the adjective on to a particular reality ("child," "oboes," "meadows"). The process by which meaning expands through metaphor (here, the repetition of "like" and "as"), which these lines self-consciously dramatize, coincides with the process by which perfume expands to infiltrate other spaces and touch other senses. Scent possesses the same quality of expansiveness as metaphor does. At the threshold of the adjective and the simile a new and *other* world of intensified associations and blended meanings opens. Perfumes are *as* fresh, innocent, milky, dimpled, smooth, cool, soft, rosy, and chubby—the list can go on—*as* the skin of children. While such an association may, at the start, favor one sense—here it would be the *freshness* confirmed by touch or sight—the comparison expands to include other senses, like smell, hearing, and taste. Similarly, the softness or mellowness of the oboes, beginning as an auditory sensation, deepens insofar as it evokes the experience of touch (the velvetlike quality, for example, of the oboe's sound). Finally, the pastoral greenness of fields, an image unquestionably dependent on vision, also evokes smell (that of grass or hay or even the category of perfumes often referred to as "green" scents), while at the same time calling to mind—through the rhyme of "chairs" (flesh) and "verts" (green)—the constellation of tactile and odorous images surrounding the freshness of the child's skin. The scope of metaphorical relatedness or correspondence is immense and the permutations of overlapping comparisons endless. As the accomplished poet-perfumer that he is, Baudelaire "blends," so to speak, different "ingredients"—word-associations, images, comparisons, metaphors (of touch, sound, and color), repetitions of consonants and vowels, and recurring syntactical structures—to produce lyrical effects. "Correspondances" is a tone poem of sorts, except that the "notes" evoked by the words are those not only of music but of perfume.

Families of Perfumes

That the color "green" can describe a perfume indicates how prescient Baudelaire's understanding of perfume was, for "greenness" is, today nearly 150 years later, an important identifying quality of certain classes of perfume according to a system of classification first created in 1984 and revised in 1990. According to this system a fragrance is determined and defined by the "more or less overriding fragrance concept" it embodies (H&R, 8). The seven such concepts, or families, according to which feminine and masculine perfumes are categorized are: 1) citrus; 2) floral; 3) fougère (the French term for "fern"); 4) chypre; 5) woody; 6) amber or oriental; and 7) leather. The family of citrus fragrances (also called *hesperides*) includes the first eaux de cologne, those eighteenth and nineteenth-century fragrances composed of essences of bergamot, lemon, mandarin, grapefruit, and orange. The floral family, the most important and largest of the seven groups, contains fragrances derived from a single flower (what are called "soliflores") as well as more complex floral bouquets. The fougère class of fragrances may be a misnomer of sorts, since ferns are odorless plants; however, the designation is used to suggest scents with a fresh, woodland, lavender odor in which can be detected notes of oakmoss, coumarin (the smell of fresh mown hay), patchouli, and bergamot. Although the fern family began as a predominantly feminine class of perfumes, especially after the creation of such classic fragrances as Houbigant's *Fougère royale* (1882) and Guerlain's *Jicky* (1889), it refers today mostly to masculine scents. The chypre class, named after François Coty's

groundbreaking perfume of 1917 of the same name, is a spicy, powdery fragrance composed of an accord of oakmoss, labdanum, patchouli, and bergamot notes. Like the perfumes of the oriental (or amber) family, chypre scents are rich in complex base notes and have, from the moment the bottle is uncapped, a powerful and explosive "départ" (start), as perfumers like to say. Scents classified as woody are primarily masculine fragrances derived from sandalwood and cedar as well as from patchouli and vetiver. Amber or oriental fragrances have a soft, voluptuous, spicy, and musky intensity with sensual vanilla overtones. Lastly, the family of leather scents—of the seven groups it contains the smallest number of fragrances—includes perfumes whose dry and smoky aroma comes from essences of birchwood and tobacco. Each of the seven fragrance concepts—citrus, floral, fougère, chypre, woody, amber/oriental, and leather—is in turn further classified according to the different variations and orientations that give it a more complex and often more subtle interpretation within "the perfumistic bounds of the concept."[11] This refinement has generated subgroups which indicate the affinity of one class of scent for another. So, for example, citrus fragrances may be classified as floral-green citruses; chypre scents may, depending on whether they are feminine or masculine fragrances, have either floral-animalic, or green, or citrus qualities. Finally, floral perfumes may be classified in several ways: as green, fresh, fruity, sweet, or marine.

Dark Fragrances

That the scents in the third stanza of "Correspondences" are fresh, soft, and green, that they figure a pastoral innocence and fertile abundance, and that they evoke the soft echoes of a reedy, velvety sound lazily floating in the air is all the more paradoxical considering the substantially different kind of scent Baudelaire then goes on to describe. Not only are these new odors different or "other" in as much as they symbolize the very opposite of innocence, freshness, softness, and greenness and in as much as they possess an almost baroque sumptuousness or decadence, since they are described as rich, corrupted, decomposing, triumphant, dominating, expansive, excessive, infinite, and transporting, but they are different as well in the form and structure of their poetic representation. The metaphorical

"The Principal Perfumes of the Hebrews, taken from a Twelfth-Century Arabic Manuscript from Persia." Illustration from Eugène Rimmel, *Le Livre des parfums*, Paris: E. Dentu, 1870 (page 64, facing). According to the accompanying text, the bottom panels show two varieties of spikenard, the most precious of biblical scents, while the panel on the upper left pictures a cinnamon tree. The only human being in the four panels is shown in the upper right extracting what appears to be gum resin from the trunk of a Judean Balsam tree.

quality of the earlier pastoral scents, so evident in the unique imaginary worlds (of child, oboe, and fields) onto which these fragrances opened, is strangely absent from the lines naming ambergris, musk, benzoin, and incense: aromatic and animal scents, dark and profound fragrances, whose fundamental difference is signified visually and graphically by the interruptive dash setting them off from the rest of the stanza (l. 11). Because these scents are literally "other," they cannot be "like" a child's skin, or a musical instrument, or meadows, or anything else for that matter. If they are indeed "like" something, it is themselves. Their metaphorical power—their ability, that is, to explode into a series of figurative comparisons and expansive, complex associations, a kind of imaginative riff—is limited. All that the poet can give us in the way of metaphorical outreach is a list, a catalogue, an enumeration of names with little potential for further development. Ambergris, musk, benzoin, and incense ("benjamin" is not mentioned by Baudelaire in the French poem), as scents, are metaphorical dead-ends, referring only to their names: in other words, to themselves.

Why is the presentation of these scents, then, limited to a mere enumeration of names and not subject to greater elaboration and development? Why does the poet's dependence on enumeration here seem to prevent him from using metaphor and image to expand the meanings of his enumeration, something he was not shy about doing in the first part of the poem? One possible explanation might lie in the very nature of these dark, decadent, animal perfumes. For in their state as richly corrupted, masterful odors, taking dominion everywhere and possessing "the expansiveness of infinite things," ambergris and musk—rare and costly scents, excreted from the intestines of a whale, on the one hand, and extracted from the excretory follicles of a small exotic male deer, on the other—as well as benzoin and frankincense—aromas used in religious rituals and derived from the resinous gum secreted from the bark of trees or bushes—lie beyond the power of metaphorical language. Certainly, these corrupting scents subvert the metaphors of softness and freshness used to figure the first group of floral perfumes; for what could be further from the smell of a child's skin than the odor extracted from the excretory organ of a Himalayan musk deer! The expansiveness of these decadent fragrances touches an "infinite" that no words can capture. Unlike fresh, green perfumes, these "other" aromatic scents fall into the realm of the incomparable, where analogy holds no sway. At once inexpressible and absolute these fragrances emanate from Baudelaire's "flowers of evil" or from the dark void of existence with its "taste for nothingness" (I: 76) and its aroma of absence. Only the enumeration of their names can represent the olfactory experience of bliss, ecstasy, and "transport" that the four "exultant" scents of ambergris, musk, benzoin, and frankincense can provoke, especially when conjoined with rhapsodic language and song. In their infinite state the four "rich" scents arrive at a

vertiginous, sublime point where they "Sing flesh's bliss, and soul's delight therein" (l. 14).

Thus does Baudelaire signal the resemblance of perfume to music. Like music, scent is nearly unrepresentable in language. Since antiquity, the words available to describe odors have been invariably limited in number, scope, and suggestiveness, for one of the deficiencies of our humanity, as Faure observes, is to be "incapable of defining or designating our deepest, darkest sensations; at most, we can distinguish, and then only in the grossest terms, a few basic tastes and odors": namely, what is salty, bitter, sweet, or acidic to the tongue or what smells good and bad. These are nothing more than "purely subjective sensations which vary from individual to individual" (Faure, 11). Insofar as Baudelaire's poetry aspires, paradoxically, to the wordless condition of music—an aspiration which Mallarmé and the symbolist poets will intensify—so it seeks to make audible the silent condition of perfume.

The Aromas of "Infinite Expansion": Musk, Ambergris, Benzoin, and Frankincense

The nature and history of the animal and resinous scents—ambergris, musk, benzoin, and frankincense—to which Baudelaire refers in "Correspondences" needs to be discussed. The four aromas described are scents central to the composition of aromatic substances and are associated with the mythical, historical, and poetic properties of the scented imagination. Ambergris, a substance with a faint wood odor, is produced in the stomach of the sperm whale where it protects the intestinal lining against the tough, horned snout of cuttlefish, a kind of squid that the whale swallows whole. It was once considered the second most precious treasure of the sea, after pearls, and was, accordingly, nicknamed "the gold of the ocean." Excreted by the whale, ambergris was at one time harvested from the surface of the ocean near the islands of Sumatra, Molucca, and Madagascar. Its hardened shape was likened to that of fossilized lumps of amber sometimes found on the shore, except that the material was usually grey in color; hence the origin of its name, "grey amber" (fig. 48). Certain kinds of ambergris have been known to float in the ocean for up to a hundred years. More practically speaking, ambergris is to perfume creation, observes the perfumer Jean-Paul Guerlain, what cream is to haute cuisine: an exquisite binding agent. His observation is more than metaphorical, since ambergris was added like a spice to food in the Middle Ages. To chocolate, according to the testimony of Casanova, Madame Du Barry, and Madame de Pompadour, it gave an indispensable aroma which inspired the early

LORIGINE DES PARFVMS

"The Origin of Perfumes," frontispiece, Simon Barbe, *Le Parfumeur françoys* (re-edited as *Le Parfumeur royal, ou L'art de parfumer*), Paris, 1699. Illustration from Eugène Rimmel, *Le Livre des parfums.* Paris: E. Dentu, 1870. The engraving shows ambergris floating on the water, a civet cat in a cage, and a musk deer about to be eviscerated.

nineteenth-century gastronomer Brillat-Savarin to create a recipe for ambergris-laced chocolate in 1826. In the sixteenth century, Nostradamus, the astrologer and physician to Charles IX, believed ambergris could increase the production of seminal fluid. A century later, the nonagenarian Cardinal de Richelieu, having perhaps learned of Nostradamus's hypothesis, was rumored to chew on small amounts of the substance. Among the Chinese, ambergris was at one time considered a potent aphrodisiac as well.[12]

In perfumery ambergris is used as a fixative; it delays the rate of volatility of the other scented ingredients with which it is blended. While by itself ambergris has a smell reminiscent of balsam and leather, in perfumes it adds a velvety, warm, even carnal note. During the eighteenth century, when single-scent fragrances were popular, ambergris was used to produce a one-note perfume (as were jasmine and neroli). The aristocracy of eighteenth-century France, which regarded ambergris as the very "perfection and soul of *les toilettes*," was beholden to a Swedish noblewoman who had brought ambergris back into style by touting its aphrodisiac qualities. One of the first "delivery" systems in Europe for aromatic scents—the earliest and

Fig. 49 Unctuous in texture and reddish-brown in color, musk, according to the nineteenth-century perfumer Eugène Rimmel, had such a violent smell that before removing the musk glands from the killed musk deer Chinese hunters had to cover their noses and mouths to avoid hemorrhages. Musk pods from China, Roure Distillery, Grasse.

simplest forms date from the fourteenth century—derives its name from ambergris. It was, as mentioned in Chapter 2 (see fig. 23), an apple-shaped globe, ornately decorated in gold or silver and made up of small individual sections, held together at their base by a hinge. The touch of a spring at the top of the globe caused the compartments to unfold, like quartered pieces of an apple. Each segment was filled with a different scented paste and powder. It was called a pomander, from the French *pomme d'ambre* ("apple of ambergris"); in its original incarnation it was nothing more than a pungent ball of compressed ambergris. Carried in the hand by both sexes, the pomander would be sniffed at timely moments to ward off the malodorous smells of the street or those of an unventilated room. Larger pomanders were hung from a belt around the waist or from chains around the neck. Smaller versions, some no larger than a thimble, were connected by a chain to a finger ring or to bracelets and jeweled collars or even used as cape buttons. Like musk, ambergris has a persistent, insoluble scent, which, according to Septimus Piesse, the nineteenth-century English chemist-perfumer, "clings pertinaciously to woven fabrics and . . . is still found upon the material after passing through the lavoratory [*sic*] ordeal."[13]

Musk, like ambergris, is a scent that leaves a potent wake. It is removed from the excretory follicles located within a small sack or membranous pod situated beneath the navel of the male musk-deer (*Moschus moschatus*). A small animal about the size of a greyhound, it inhabits forested elevations above 8,000 feet in the Himalayan mountains. Since the secretion of musk in the male deer is most abundant during rutting, it has an important sexual and reproductive function. In fact, it was the location of the musk sack, immediately anterior to the deer's penis, that inspired the Sanskrit name for the animal, "mushkas," meaning testicle; the word subsequently moved through Persian and then into Latin as "muscus." The chemical composition of musk, according to some, is similar to that of human testosterone, and its odor has been described as "intense, fecal, oily, and clinging." Musk was once valued as a medicine, and it was reported that the last thing swallowed by the Emperor Nicholas of Russia before his death in 1855 was a potion of musk. The substance was also rumored to possess aphrodisaic powers. Chinese courtesans were given bland foods flavored with musk. As their skins were caressed during lovemaking, their heated bodies, so the story goes, gave off a musk-tinged sweat.

"Musk-Deer Hunting (from a Chinese drawing)." Illustration from Eugène Rimmel, *The Book of Perfumes* (London: Chapman and Hall, 1867).

Victorians "linked musk with lasciviousness and banned it," favoring in its place toilet waters made from light floral scents like lavender, rosemary and strawberry. Yet, when Queen Victoria made an official visit to Paris in 1855 she wore an expensive perfume which the elegant upper crust of Parisian society found in bad taste because, as the papers of the time reported, a light scent of musk had been detected.[14]

There are three kinds of musk: Chinese musk from Tonkin and Tibet, which is the most prized (fig. 49); Assam musk from Bengal which is somewhat inferior; and Russian musk, which is of the lowest quality. Musk, as Piesse observes, "is remarkable for the diffusiveness and subtlety of its scent: everything in its vicinity soon becomes affected by it, and long retains its odor." For this reason, the East India Company ordered its captains not to carry musk when their ships were carrying tea. The musk itself lies within its enveloping pod in the form of tiny round or oblong grains. Before it was synthesized and before safe methods for extracting the musk from live deer were developed in the twentieth century, a kilo of musk required the slaughter of a hundred and forty animals. Musk entered Europe in all probablilty during the eleventh century when Crusaders returning from Islamic lands brought with them Arabian spices and solid forms of odorous animal scents. These pungent scents could not have arrived at a better time. During the different plagues that struck Europe, especially the Black Plague of the mid-fourteenth century—it wiped out a quarter of the continent's population—musk, as well as ambergris and civet (fig. 50), were believed to disseminate a protective barrier of vapors and were thus the favored of all aromatic defenses. The Empress Josephine, as already mentioned, was fascinated by musk and earned accordingly the nickname "la folle du musc"; the curtains and furniture of her dressing rooms were redolent of the scent. Piesse, in a similar vein, reports the story of a wealthy Turk who had the cement of the walls of the harem he was constructing mixed with a musk which remains "fragrant to this day."[15]

These stories reveal what science would later discover: that amounts of musk as infinitesimally small as 0.000,000,000,000,032 of an ounce are still potent enough to be detected by the human nose. For this reason among others, extract of musk is used as a fixative in perfume creation; it gives permanence to volatile compositions. Because of the extreme violence of its odor, musk in eighteenth-century France was looked upon, according to Diderot's and D'Alembert's *L'Encyclopédie,* with detestation or admiration depending on one's national sympathies: "Italians have a strong taste for it but the French vilify it." But musk's unpleasantness could be transformed into a suave and gentle odor by combining the grains with other scents. The *Encyclopédie* also mentions the use of musk for medical purposes—to fortify the stomach, to remedy headaches, to increase semen—but indicates that such uses are no longer common. Moreover, the *Encyclopedia*

Fig. 50 Civet and horn containers, Roure Distillery, Grasse.

attests to the existence in France of a live musk-deer, a gift to Louis XV from the Count of Maurepas in 1726; placed in the King's menagerie, it survived for over six years.[16]

The passion for musk was kept alive during the French Revolution by a group of young, overdressed, and ludicrously elegant royalists. Calling themselves the musk-lovers ("les muscadins") they bathed in musk (as well as civet) and replenished their stock of the scent at A la Corbeille de Fleurs, the perfume establishment founded in 1775 by Jean-François Houbigant. A late nineteenth-century advertising poster for Vaissier's *Parfumerie du Congo* (a name undoubtedly designed to celebrate France's colonial triumphs) imagines a perfume store under the Directory (the mid-1790s) in which an excessively dressed *muscadin* helps a woman choose her scents (fig. 51). The fascination with musk among elegant women of this time and into the nineteenth century bordered on the obsessive, for, as Balzac reports, they applied musk even to their hair.[17]

The industrial and chemical uses of musk in the production of fine leathers and perfumes have been in evidence for many centuries. Fifteenth- to seventeenth-century Spanish tanners prepared fine kid skins by impregnating the hides with musk as well as other aromatic substances like ambergris, thus producing "peau d'Espagne." The first chemical synthesis of musk by the German chemist Albert Baur occurred between 1888 and 1891. Despite an initial mistrust in the late nineteenth century for synthetic fragrances by a public reluctant to adopt anything that was not "natural," the usefulness of artificial musk in perfume composition as well

Fig. 51 In this late-nineteenth-century poster by Van Hessel, a foppish "muscadin" of the 1790s, his clothes, one imagines, reeking of musk, helps a lavishly dressed woman select a fragrance called *Parfumerie du Congo*, by Victor Vaissier.

as its indispensability to the survival of the musk deer as a species—hunting or trapping the animal is banned today—became increasingly evident as the twentieth century evolved. In 1895 the French chemical company Givaudan produced only ten and a half ounces of artificial musk a day; by 1925 the company's daily production had grown to 440 pounds. Not the least of considerations in the increased dependence on synthetic musk has been the prohibitive cost of natural musk, known to sell at one time for as much as $700,000 for a little over two pounds of absolute.[18]

Musk helps to harmonize and stimulate associations among the different fragrant ingredients which make up a perfume, adding a sensual, fleshlike warmth and density. It remains one of the most important ingredients in luxury perfumes, found almost exclusively in synthetic form in about 90 percent of fine fragrances. In the late 1960s "musk oil" appeared in the hippie stores and head shops of New York and San Francisco and then exploded into an international phenomenon, the message having been passed among members of the counterculture that musk, even in

Fig. 52 Viscous tear drops of Peru Balsam, native to Central America, drip from an incision cut into the trunk of a tree as illustrated in this engraved, hand-colored perfume label for Farina's *Extrait de baume de Pérou*, c. 1815–1820. Used in the past as a stimulant for the skin, Peru Balsam serves today as a fixative for floral and oriental fragrances.

its synthetic form, possessed extraordinary powers of sexual attraction. For women, moreover, musk has functioned, according to Corbin (who in this instance cites Havelock Ellis), as an olfactory equivalent to the corset. Like its form-fitting counterpart, musk accentuates the "salient contours" of the body, highlighting the woman's aromatic silhouette; it gives odorous definition to her figure. Women, Ellis argues, have used it not to mask but to emphasize their odor. Accordingly, the evolution of a spirit of modesty among women at the end of the eighteenth century led to a general discrediting of musk (and all other animal scents, for that matter). Through the nineteenth and into the early twentieth centuries, according to Ellis, a woman was as unwilling to call attention to her figure as she was to advertise the salient points of her odorous sensuality. This decline in the use of musk represented a new, more conservative, attitude toward the olfactory realities of the female body.[19]

The third scent that Baudelaire mentions in "Correspondences," benzoin, is derived from a tree (of the species *styrax benzoin*) native to Sumatra and Malaysia and has a sweet balsamic odor of vanilla character. It is obtained through incisions made in the tree's trunk, from which oozes a sticky, white gum resin with an acrid, balsamic odor. (A similar aromatic and viscous resin, Peru Balsam, is also collected from the incised bark of a tree as a colorful perfume label from the early Restoration represents the process, fig. 52). Benzoin, considered the frankincense of the Far East, has long been used in rituals of the Roman Catholic, Hindu, Muslim, Buddhist, and Hebrew religions. In the nineteenth century it was the principal ingredient, according to Piesse, in all substances sold for the purposes of disinfection and "sweet fumigation." Heat turns benzoin into the highly volatile benzoic acid, which, when diffused in a house or church, adheres to the "walls and penetrate[s] every nook and cranny."[20]

Frankincense, Baudelaire's fourth scent, sometimes called olibanum (from the Hebrew word *lebonah*, meaning milk), is a gum resin also obtained by slashing the bark or the branches of a terebinaceous plant belonging to the *Boswellia* family and native to the hot, arid regions of the southern coast of Arabia ("Arabia Felix," as the Romans called it), Eastern Africa, and India. The sticky resin that oozes from the tree in whitish drops has a bitter taste but when burned becomes sweetly balsamic in odor. Twenty-three varieties of *Boswellia* (named for James Boswell, the biographer of Samuel Johnson) have been identified, and they correspond to the frankincense of the ancients and of the Arabs. In antiquity, the land of Sheba (corresponding more or less to the area covered today by Yemen and part of Oman) produced the finest frankincense, to which even the Bible attests (*Jeremiah* VI, 20) as well as several Latin writers. Herodotus described Arabia as giving off a "marvelously sweet fragrance," one so pervasive that Alexander's fleet could smell it far out at sea. Plutarch remarked that Alexander's mouth and all his flesh "exhaled a fragrance so sweet that his garments were filled with it." The Egyptians used frankincense in embalming. Also, it was much valued among the Hebrews as revealed by the gifts given to Solomon (tenth century B.C.) by the Queen of Sheba (I *Kings*, X: 10) and, of course, later offered (along with myrrh from the same region) to the infant Jesus by the three Magi. Interestingly, a small bowl of incense was found when the tomb of Tutankhamen was opened in the 1920s; after 3,500 years it still gave off a pleasant odor when it was burned. The preciousness of incense is revealed in the commerce it generated, which recent archeological study suggests extended from 5,000 B.C. through the Roman Empire. In addition to the silk and cinnamon trade routes coming from the East, there existed an "incense road," with Petra as one of its trading centers and Shabwa (an ancient Arabian city) another. Pliny the Elder, in the first century A.D., describes not only the route in his *Natural History* but names eight small fortresses which served as rest stations along the way.[21]

Like other valuable aromatic perfumes and spices, incense was no stranger to myth and fable. Herodotus reports that the "incense" tree was protected by hundreds of small winged serpents of different colors. The Romans used incense to calm skin irritations and make pimples disappear. It was also valued as a remedy against the inflammation of the eyes and commonly drunk as a stimulant in wine. It is said, moreover, that for the funeral of his wife, Poppea, the emperor Nero had ten years' worth of Arabia's incense production burned. The practice of using incense—sometimes blended with benzoin—during the celebration of the Mass in the Catholic religion dates from around the fourth century, although in the early years of its history the Christian Church banned the use of any kind of aromatic offering. Moreover, the rise of Christianity, once Constantine had proclaimed it the official religion of the Roman Empire in 323, cut deeply into the market for frankincense. By the ninth century the swung censer (the thurible) came into widespread use, and four centuries later it was to become an integral part of the Mass. A secondary, though not insignificant, aspect of the censer, was, as Piesse remarks, to neutralize "the cadaverous odors of our old cathedrals and abbeys, formerly used as burial-places." The English word "incense" derives from the Latin verb *incendere*, meaning "to burn." The most valuable and finest incense, much prized by cultivators, is taken from the trunk of the frankincense tree not after the initial cut but when a second secretion has been allowed to overtop the first deposit. Olibanum, whose Arabic and Hebrew names refer to its "milky white" color, is a form of frankincense strongly balsamic in odor and with a slight floral scent. Twentieth-century chemists have observed that this incense produces a smoke that acts on brain cells in a manner similar to cannabis oil.[22]

In Baudelaire's "Correspondences" perfumes shimmer like colors and reverberate like sounds. They intermingle; they "speak" to each other; they "correspond." Borrowing qualities from one another they coalesce momentarily into sensually symphonic harmonies. Though it is but a sonnet, "Correspondences" offers a wealth of details about the sensual, spiritual, and poetic nature of scent. In fact, the poem describes seven qualities of perfume. First, perfume is presented as expansive, possessed of a plasticity that allows it, at least in Baudelaire's imagination, to connect with flesh, childhood, music ("oboes"), fertility ("green"), pastoral abundance ("meadows"), and a host of other overlapping, interrelated realities. Second, perfume is seen as musical, moving through the air like notes of a song and speaking melodiously to the other senses and to the spirit: "My soul," Baudelaire writes in a prose poem, "voyages on the wings of perfume as the soul of other men on the wings of music" (I: 300). Third, perfume is described as mobile, initiating movement, transport, and elevation. Fourth, perfume is double-edged: at once sensual and spiritual, and of the body and of the soul. Fifth, perfume is ambiguous, if not contradictory, creating syntheses of aromas in which the individual notes are never totally integrated into the whole. Sixth, perfume is ethical insofar as the trail it leaves has moral weight, for there exist fragrances of good and evil—"virtuous perfumes" (I: 294) and "terrible perfumes" (I: 155)—as there are flowers of good and evil. Seventh and last, perfume is ultimately non-figurative, for it defeats the efforts of language and metaphor to encompass it; tautologically, it signifies only itself. The sense of scent—its meaning and its perception—is, ultimately, scent.

The Music of Perfume

Arguing strongly in "Correspondences" for a synthesis of different kinds of sensory experience, Baudelaire's imagination dreams of a "confusion" of sounds, a unity of vastness and depth, a fusion of night and day, and a reciprocal mingling among senses, as summarized in the eighth line: "Sound, perfumes, hues echo in harmony," a fine example of the phenomenon of synaesthesia. Though Baudelaire's ideas concerning synaesthesia were influenced by the eighteenth-century Swedish philosopher, Swedenborg, the notion of applying musical structures to other realities, like color and perfume, was very much in the air in the London and Paris of the nineteenth century. The theory of smells put forth by chemists and perfumers of the time identified odors as vibrations perceptible to the sensorial apparatus of the body in ways closely resembling the perception of colors and sounds. A scientific work by Septimus Piesse, written first in the 1850s and subsequently published in several revised editions and translations during the next four decades, concluded, inaccurately as future discoveries based on molecular theory would reveal, that "we can best understand the true theory of odors by viewing them as imponderable agents, affecting the nervous system by special vibrations, as colors affect the eye, and sounds the ear."[23] The link between sound and color had long been recognized, Piesse observed; it can be traced as far back as the ancients who associated the musical gamut with the chromatic scale. More recent work, according to Piesse, had discovered close analogies between musical notes and particular colors: for example, "*do*" has a blueness, "*mi*" a red hue, and "*sol*" corresponds to yellow. Since blue, red, and yellow are the primary colors and in combination or contrast produce "the most perfect harmony," then a similar euphony will occur when the corresponding notes, *do*, *mi*, *sol*, are combined. For Piesse, this correspondence, or "agreement" as he called it, "proves the existence of some universal law of harmony," a finding with which Baudelaire would have heartily agreed. In an effort to extend this universal law to the phenomena of odors and to describe the principles determining their harmonious combinations—

there being at the time no "accepted criterion for measuring the intensity of an odor as that of a sound is measured"—Piesse began a series of experiments in which he succeeded in identifying the "velocity" of certain common odors, or what he called "the force of [their] volatility"; he discovered a direct relation between this force of evaporation or dissemination and "the manner in which an odorous substance affects the sense of smell." He concluded as follows:

> The force of volatility of essences, or the rapidity with which they evaporate, would always be in proportion to the velocity of the vibrations produced, or the rapidity with which the odorous waves might be propagated. If this velocity were not high enough, there would be no perceptible odor; just as with sounds, which remain inaudible unless they correspond to at least sixty vibrations per second.... Thus bodies possessing a very low degree of volatility are those known as strong odors; those, on the contrary, which have a high degree of volatility, are feeble and delicate odors. In this respect we note an analogy between odors and sounds. The loudest sounds are produced by sonorous waves which are the most slowly propagated; and the most powerful odors are produced by the most slowly propagated odorous waves.

Piesse's most original and most bold, if not most eccentric, hypothesis concerns the musical structure of scents. Identifying an "octave of odors," a scale of scents akin to that in music, he assigns different fragrances to different notes, through a process more subjective than musical, for its rationale is no more rigorous than Piesse's decision to place "the name of the odor in its position corresponding to its effect upon our olfactory sense." How he has observed and determined that "effect" scientifically is not explained. Piesse invents a gamut of scents organized in groups of octaves. The smell of rose, for example, is assigned the note of middle C, while that of camphor lies one octave above middle C, that of jasmine two octaves above, and that of pineapple three octaves above. On the descending side of middle C lie geranium (one octave below), sandalwood (two octaves below) and patchouli (three octaves below). While musk is F, that is, four notes below middle C, and benzoin a still lower F (two octaves below middle C), ambergris and lavender are assigned the notes of F and A (two octaves above middle C) respectively. Scents of a lower bass note, Piesse observes, will appeal more to the young than odors of the upper treble which will mostly attract people "of age." In all, Piesse assigns to forty-six odors—those most commonly used in perfume composition (heliotrope, vanilla, citron, orange peel, verbena)—a different note in his idiosyncratic scale of scents.

The structuring of scents does not stop there. Piesse identifies "semi-odors," like rose and rose-geranium, to which he assigns half notes. Then there is the rich possibility of harmonious combinations or chords of scent: "From the odors already known, we may produce, by uniting them in proper proportion, the smell of almost any flower, except jasmine.... I know of no odor in a chemical laboratory— and they are pretty numerous—to which I could not assign its corresponding key." While odors exist to which no sharps or flats can be assigned, there are other scents whose variety of differences would constitute a scale unto themselves, like lemon, which constitutes, according to Piesse, "the most numerous class of odors in nature." The goal for the perfumer, as Piesse conceives it, is to choose primary scents whose musical notes promise harmonies: "If a perfumer desires to make a bouquet from primitive odors, he must take such odors as chord together; the perfume will then be harmonious ... As an artist would blend his colors, so must a perfumer blend his scents." To assist the neophyte Piesse offers sample "recipes": the bouquet of chord F, for example, would include the following musical and aromatic notes: *F*: musk; *C*: rose; *F*: tuberose; *A*: tonka bean; *C*: camphor; *F*: jonquil. How this would sound (or smell, for that matter), is anyone's guess.

Although Piesse's ideas were known in England and possibly in France during Baudelaire's life, it is doubtful the poet was acquainted with them; there is no available data that can confirm or disconfirm such a possibility. What is known, however, is that Baudelaire's notions about synaesthesia were inspired by Swedenborg and by notions of "audition colorée" (sound-color), well known among French poets of his generation. Such theories, regarding the interaction of different sensations and the mingling of different senses, would play a considerable role in the development of symbolist aesthetics in the last three decades of the century, especially among poets like Mallarmé, who sought to create a language of poetry aspiring to the suggestive and conceptual reality of music.

The Flowers of Evil opens the way for the music of poetry both to resound in and to color the world. When Baudelaire imagines that "music hollows out the sky" (I: 653), he dreams of a musical verse sailing into the ether of ideal worlds in the same way as he imagines perfume penetrating the spiritual regions that exist "any where out of the world" (I: 356). Considering its interrelatedness with music, scent shares a similar power of ascension and cosmic penetration. Other poems by Baudelaire like "All of Her" ("Toute entière") refer to the synthetic and sensorial metamorphoses that fragrance and music together create: "O mystic blend of senses mine, / Fused in one perfect harmony! / Her voice, a fragrant perfume fine; / Her breath, the sweetest melody!" (I: 42, Shapiro, 79). But Baudelaire admits in the poem that the ability to distinguish clearly the intertwined sensual threads composing the "exquisite" music—to separate the olfactory from the auditory, let us say—is made impossible by the inappropriateness, if not weakness, of analysis. Mind and thought cannot sunder what sense has physically joined, and what is now completely whole. This extends to the auditory perception of odors—the *hearing* of breath—as well as to the odorous

sensation of sounds—the *smelling* of notes or syllables.[24] They cannot be reduced to or divided into their components. The mere rhyming of "parfum" in the French poem's final stanza with the somewhat unusual end word "un" (the indefinite article) confirms the power of scent to create an irreducible oneness.

The interchangeability of breath and voice as media for odorous and auditory sensations and the harmonious interdependence of music and perfume are confirmed by Baudelaire in a metaphor from his poem on hair ("Her Hair") that links sailing and swimming: "As other spirits sail on music, / Mine, O my love, swims on your perfume" (I: 26, Fowlie, 43). Ship and swimmer, adrift in an openness far from shore, rocked by the rhythmical surge of waves, pulled helplessly in the direction of powerful currents, frightened by the thunderous menace of swelling whitecaps, represent two physical responses to sensations of music and scent: on the one hand, the drifting, floating, and somewhat passive reverie which musical sounds provoke in the poetic spirit and, on the other, the more aggressive, concentrated, masterly activity which the act of moving through and being enveloped by water (and fragrance) calls to mind. Yet, it is the very point of Baudelaire's comparison that the physical actions of sailing and swimming, the sensory realities of audition and olfaction, and the harmonious compositions of music and perfume be essentially interchangeable.

While images of swimming and sailing evoke the waves which scent and sound produce and the voyage toward unfamiliar shores which their notes promise, Baudelaire makes use of yet another metaphor—one evoking turning and twirling—in his representation of the coexistence of smell and sound in the poem "Harmonie du soir" (I: 47):

> Now comes the time when quivering on its stem
> Each flower exhales like a censer;
> Sounds and perfumes turn in the evening air;
> Melancholy waltz and languorous vertigo
>
> Each flower exhales like a censer;
> The violin sobs like an afflicted heart;
> Melancholy waltz and languorous vertigo.
> The sky is as sad and beautiful as a great altar of rest.
>
> The violin sobs like an afflicted heart,
> A tender heart, which hates the huge black void!
> The sky is as sad and beautiful as a great altar of rest
> The sun drowned in its blood which coagulates.
>
> A tender heart, which hates the huge black void,
> Welcomes every vestige of a luminous past!
> The sun drowned in its blood which coagulates ...
> Your memory shines in me like a monstrance!
>   (Fowlie, 57)

In a poem where whole lines are repeated according to a set pattern (the second and fourth lines of a stanza become the first and third lines of the next, with the result that twelve out of sixteen lines are repeated), Baudelaire literally creates a poem of echoing sights, sounds, and scents. The choreography of twirling lines, a kind of waltz of verses, suggests an auditory and olfactory reverberation. The repetition of a line recalls its earlier appearance. Making it come again makes it last, makes it memorable, like the trace of a persistent perfume. Everything in the poem is echo, resonance, vibration, and rhythm. The harmony of evening becomes musical and perfumed; it possesses its own particular scent. The aroma of a flower volatilizes into air, like the aromatic cloud emanating from an incense-burner. This perfuming of the air is further suggested by the consonance of words phonetically brought together in the French original—through the repeated voicing of the consonant "v" (as in "venir," "vibrant," "s'évapore," "valse," "vertige")—into a constellation of meanings which suggest the volatility, languor, and trembling fragility of fragrance: a precariousness it shares with the quivering, plaintive sound of a violin. All that vibrates does so either musically (the violin) or odorously (the flower). And the evocation of the graceful turns of a waltz hides both an auditory and olfactory allusion to the rustle of ball gowns, on the one hand, and the heady perfume of elegant women, on the other. Into this sonorous and odorous atmosphere, where music and perfume perform a dance of turns and arabesques, lightheadedness and sadness intermingle. Under the sway of spiraling smells and notes, the poet's head turns in rhythm with a poem whose many twists and twirls reproduce a similar sensation of vertigo. Repetitions (of sounds, words, lines, images) become, the second time round, trails of the already-spoken, as emanations (of sounds and scents) become traces of the already-perceived. The transformation of physical states—so clear in the poem's conversion of flower into perfume, of music into airborne sounds, of dance into the vibrations of evening, of sun into blood, and of the past into a luminous memory—possesses a religious and sacred aura, which the abundance of religious objects ("censer," "altar," "monstrance") affirms. Fundamentally, this transformation is a volatilization, through which all that is solid—flower, incense-burner, violin, sun, heart, past, memory—melts into the thin air of evening. It transpires in harmony with the transubstantiation suggested by objects which turn the host into the body of Christ ("altar," "monstrance") and incense into the Holy Spirit ("censer").

Such spiritualization, moreover, bears witness to the permanence of the transformations the poem accomplishes. The image of the heart, repeated four times as well as twice more in the image of blood, is an agent of these transformations. At once tender and afflicted, it seeks to reverse the nothingness of night, death, and the encroaching blackness into which the sun, in the throes of its daily suicide, will soon fall. To accomplish the undoing of this "huge black void" the heart must go inward, seeking refuge within the illuminated subjectivity of the poetic self. It salvages traces and vestiges from the past, rescuing them from the annihilation of nothingness, internalizing and preserving them in the interior of the poetic self and, by extension, of the poem, as the final line attests: "Your memory shines in me like a monstrance!" That the heart suspends the sun's death, replacing its cold emptiness with the musical and perfumed harmony of evening, is literally figured by the points of suspension added to the end of the poem's next-to-last line, which, when it first appeared in the previous stanza, contained no such signs of suspension. The light appearing at the poem's conclusion is the light of transubstantiation and incarnation, an illumination that preserves memory through language, music, and aroma. The harmony of evening, created by the vaporization of fragrance and music which turn and dance in the air—an evaporation foreshadowing the transubstantiation to follow—also prefigures the preservation, within the harmony of light and the brilliance of perfume, of the vestiges of memory the poem has captured.

Fragrant Vessels of Memory

The nineteenth-century perfume bottle, stoppered or uncorked, in cut crystal or enameled porcelain, made of Limoges china or Bohemian glass, possesses an evocative power to which Baudelaire was immensely sensitive. Two of his poems, one in verse celebrating the power of memory, ("The Flask") and the other, a satirical piece in prose ("The Dog and the Flask"), are uniquely concerned with the bottle as object and as symbol. In the prose poem, "The Dog and the Flask" written in 1862, Baudelaire offers an allegorical critique of the impoverishment of bourgeois sensibility in all areas of art and poetry. The public is represented by a dog to whom the narrator presents a superb perfume purchased at one of Paris's finest perfumeries. In horror the dog recoils from the flask and barks a vociferous reproach. With scathing bitterness the narrator observes that had he presented the mutt with a "packet of excrement" the animal would have sniffed it with exquisite ardor and might even have eaten it, just like—and this is the point of Baudelaire's satirical parable—French bourgeois men and women to whom "one must never offer delicate perfumes [and poems!], which only make them angry, but garbage, carefully chosen garbage" (I: 284).

For Baudelaire the perfume flask is, in general, expressive of a certain poetics of the vestige, of that which remains present solely through signs of absence made odorous. For absence has substance—and fragrance—in Baudelaire's world. It materializes in the form of decomposing, decrepit objects whose bare existence—the very embodiment of nostalgic melancholy—looks back longingly to a lost magnificence and plenitude: "An old boudoir am I, / Strewn round with faded roses, and where lie / Yesteryear's bygone fashions; where, pell-mell, / Pallid

Bouchers and many a sad pastel / Are left, abandoned and alone, to quaff / The lingering scent from an uncorked carafe" ("Spleen," I: 73, Shapiro, 141). From the bedroom, the wilting roses, the out-of-style clothes, the muted colors of the painting (by the eighteenth-century artist François Boucher), and the empty bottle of perfume flows the very fragrance of a lost past. Absence hovers over the scene like a scent whose turns and spirals, determined by chance currents of air, powerfully dissipate all that was once present.

Perfume bottles in the nineteenth century, at least up until 1840, remained objects of luxury that were not widely circulated among the general public. These flasks were considerably less refined and well-crafted than they had been in the previous century. Porcelain bottles revealed considerably less magnificence and pomp as those French, German, and Austrian flacons so much in demand during the ancien régime. Yet, the popularity of glass, particularly the cut crystal that had begun to appear in the eighteenth century, increased considerably in the flurry of industrialization which took hold of all aspects of perfume manufacturing in the second half of the 1800s. The most common crystal flacons in England and France at the beginning of the nineteenth century were, as was seen in Chapter 2, long, narrow, flat, sticklike bottles, called "lavande d'Oxford," manufactured in Bohemia and most often filled with rose water. For sale at fairs, these bottles were made of transparent glass and decorated with simple floral or scroll motifs either in gold or enamel. Some bottles were made in a dark blue glass called "Bristol blue." Others in transparent and facetted crystal had a flattened teardrop shape, in keeping with a style that had begun during the English Regency (1800–1820).[25]

Most crystal flacons were made with lead (in percentages from 24 to 30 percent) to give the glass a supple and dazzling effect. Such flacons, capped with embossed and stylized silver tops, were widely distributed in the second half of the century. Original bottle designs (from the middle of the century, for example) included ornately chiseled and ground crystal flasks shaped like hunting horns or cornucopia and topped with silver fittings and gold filament. Other unusual bottles of thickly cut crystal (from 1820–1830) took the form of tapered test tubes or vials with screw tops in gold; some were fan-shaped, flat, round bottles in blue opaline glass. There were bottles decorated with two or three layers of different colors, a process called "overlay" (popular beginning around 1850) and still others (from 1830–1840) that were created from a pink and transparent glass decorated with scrolled arabesques and small flowers delicately painted in gold and silver. Of popular interest as curiosities in the early 1800s were complex flacons, of gold or enamel, with mechanized parts made in Switzerland. They were combined with clocks or automatons or small carillons in ways that gave another dimension—musical, chronological, animate—to the scent they contained. One such device in the form of a pistol sprayed perfume into the air to the accompaniment of music.

Bohemian crystal was immensely popular during the nineteenth century, because of the glass's brilliance and the ease with which it could be shaped, engraved, and its surface bonded to or overlaid with opaque layers or motifs. The bottles came in deeply rich colors: ruby red, periwinkle blue, emerald green, and uranium yellow. In the second half of the nineteenth century, as the romantic image of the delicate and fragile "femme-fleur," subject to spells of faintness and fits of swooning, took hold of the cultural imagination of French society, smelling salts became increasingly popular, and vials and flasks for carrying them were designed. Made of porcelain or glass, but rarely of silver, these bottles were equipped with small chains and rings so that women could hang them from their belts, their necks, or even their fingers; models without chains were carried in a pocketbook, a hand, or inside a sleeve. As a reflection of the stylistic evolution of the other plastic arts during the course of the century, the perfume bottle enjoyed moments of baroque, rococo, Biedermeier, and art nouveau inspiration. Bottles decorated with art nouveau forms began to appear around 1860 when the first oriental motifs from Japan—bamboo, poppy, iris, stork, frog, carp, butterfly, and dragonfly images—were incorporated into bottle design, eclipsing such traditional forms as baroque and rococo spirals, eighteenth-century rose patterns, and idyllic romantic scenes.

Baudelaire offers his own description of a perfume bottle in "The Flask" (I: 48); but the object lacks precision, the poet's imagination being more focused on the effect of the perfume bottle than on its appearance. The flask is presented as the instrument of memory, par excellence, as a singular force of resurrection, transforming absence into presence and materiality into spirituality within an environment seemingly hostile to such restoration, since the objects in the poem (an oriental wooden box, rusting locks, creaking hinges, a sinister armoire, an empty house) speak only of loss and ruin. And yet, "there are some powerful odors that can pass / Out of the stoppered flask; [for] even glass / To them is porous" (Mathews, 61). In the poem, perfume volatilizes matter—the glass of the bottle, the wood of the box, the metal of the lock—into haze, mist, aroma, and soul. Liberated from its container, scent is no longer a "liquid prisoner." Awakened from its slumber, it takes off explosively, filling a space simultaneously physical and mental with exquisite sensations and sunset colors of azure, pink, and gold: "And forth the ghosts of long-dead odors creep— / There, softly trembling in the shadows, sleep / A thousand thoughts, funereal chrysalides, / Phantoms of old the folding darkness hides, / Who make faint flutterings as their wings unfold, / Rose-washed and azure-tinted, shot with gold. / A memory that brings languor flutters here." The scented imagination reaches vertiginous heights as memory is reborn. The intoxicating aroma of the past floats in the troubled air. Fragrance reaches a crescendo as the poet's physical being—his eyes now closed to the world, as they had been in "Exotic

Perfume," his will suspended, his energy diminished, his soul detached from the body and fully transported by scent—rises to an apogee of abstraction and dissociation synonymous with a memory that, because it recalls a passion paradoxically charming and funereal ("the ghost / Of an old passion, long since loved and lost") is the essence of ambiguity. Under the sway of memory's perfume, the poet himself risks becoming a disembodied scent, his identity and distinctness increasingly absorbed into a threatening cloud of polymorphous being. Vanquished by the scent of the past, the soul is pushed toward a yawning abyss of confused aromatic diffuseness where memories and odors are absorbed indiscriminately one into the other. It is, as the poem observes, "a pit darkened by the noxious exhalations of men" or as a variant line which Baudelaire discarded affirms, "a pit whose air is full of human scent" (I: 921).

In "The Flask" Baudelaire imagines the aromatic volatilization not only of the past but of the self. Phantom memories and ghostly scents sweep over him threatening to absorb the soul in a terrible cloud of unconsciousness. Perfume's overpowering sensuality, its qualities of absorption and adherence, and its tendency toward diffusiveness and compression represent the confusing ambiguity of a past returning to and absorbed into the air of the present. But the poet avoids the menacing abyss; his soul stops just short of its edge. The abyss turns out to be "secular," for it is associated with human love and not infernal damnation, although love and sin are neighboring lands in the Baudelairean moral universe. The porosity of matter announced in the opening line is reiterated in the image of an odorous Lazarus tearing open his shroud and releasing into the world the sweet (if not sickly sweet) aroma of his resurrected body, an image suggestive of perfume's power to revive a lost reality in the present.

To this image of resurrected memory linked to an aromatic revival, "The Flask" contributes, in its two concluding stanzas, an altogether new element. The fixative powers of perfume (through which volatility is reduced and intensity somewhat prolonged) and the lasting images of memory (through which the indelible face of a beloved is preserved) are rendered even more intense and indelible through the inscribing power of poetry. The bottle is clearly an image for the poem, a vessel containing the past and the beloved, from which their conjoined aroma spills out in word and sound. The poem's scent is the scent of a woman and the scent as well—translated into feeling and poetic statement—of the poet who has been touched by the remembered odor of that woman. The poem is enveloped and haloed by aroma. And so Baudelaire ends "The Flask" by calling attention to the metaphorical nature of a poetic conceit through which the past reappears as perfume, the flask as memory, and poetry as glass vessel:

So, when vanished from man's memory
Deep in some dark and somber armoire I lie,

An empty flask they have cast aside,
Broken and soiled, the dust upon my pride,

I'll be your shroud, beloved pestilence!
The witness of your might and virulence,
Sweet poison mixed by angels; bitter cup
Of life and death my heart has drunken up!
(Mathews, 61–62)

The first line of this passage announces a conclusion that turns the preceding stanzas of "Le Flacon" into prophesies. It shows the flask to be a symbol of two kinds of resurrectional memory: first, the poet's subjective remembrance of the beloved, as she once existed in the past and as she has reappeared in the present, like a long-lost scent dormant, yet vibrantly alive, within the hollow of an empty bottle; and second, the poem's future commemoration of that memory, its recapturing of that lost fragrance, and its "rebottling" it for generations of readers to come. While memory, as "The Flask" reveals, has, figuratively speaking, its own distinctive type of perfume, scent has its own unique form of memory. The odors of tea, autumn leaves, smoke fires, and rain become olfactory impressions pressed together like dried flowers in a book. They disclose a potentially explosive atom of remembrance.

The relationship in the poem between objects that contain and objects that are contained reaches a final resolution at the end of the Chinese box of images that "The Flask" constructs. Without exception, pride of place is given in the poem to contained things: for example, the soul lying *in* the old flask which is found *within* a dark armoire *inside* an empty house; or Lazarus's body *inside* its shroud; or the poet lost *in* the memory of future readers, his book of verse discarded *in* a "somber chest." But certain things escape their containers: "long dead odors creep" out of the bottle, "ghosts" of lost loves arise from "the gulf of sleep," Lazarus steps out of his shroud. This triumph of objects or phenomena escaping the confines of their vessels and moving freely into the world is undone, however, by the poem's final stanza. Here, the poetic self, the speaker, identifies with the old flask, albeit in a self-deprecatory manner, for both self and bottle have been seen throughout the poem as old, decrepit, dusty, dirty, abject, sticky, and cracked.

Despite the physical ruin of the vessel, the containment of the beloved is complete and final. An open flask becomes a closed casket. The earlier expansion of objects into the air and the world is now replaced by a "bottling up," which coincides with what could be called the "containment" that writing and poetry in general accomplish. The scent of the beloved is now held *within* the walls of the poem (a flask in its own right). Words preserve the presence of the woman as she once was in the world and as she now is in a poem. But more than a scent or aroma, the woman has been restored to liquid form. She is a "liqueur," a "sweet poison," not only inhaled but ingested. The poetic self and the poem are vessels filled now with *both* the vaporous *and* the liquid presence of the other. Once she has become enfolded within the poet's imagination, the beloved becomes encapsulated in fragrance, enshrined in memory, and entombed in poetry; she has truly become "a liquid prisoner" but pent not "in walls of glass" as Shakespeare imagined, but in walls of words. From the poetic space she now occupies the woman continues to gnaw at the poet from within his language, as it were, trying to erode the walls of her poetic cell so as to make them porous once again. Although flask gives way to casket and perfume to acid, the scent and spirit of the other, at once nourishing and mortal—she is, the poet declares, his heart's "life and death"—are preserved by the poem containing them. The "I" that speaks in the poem keeps the presence of the "you" alive just as musk and ambergris, odorous fixatives in their own right, ensure that the more volatile fragrances with which they are blended will not disappear too rapidly, but will impregnate the air with an enduring and heady wake.

If writing encloses and fixes the memory of the beloved woman in the poem, thereby assuring her future, then reading will eventually unleash her preserved presence. To open the vial of the poem is to liberate the odor of the other traced within: the phantom of the beloved "you" to whom the poet addresses himself and the voice of the poetic "I" who speaks for her and for himself. In "The Flask" the expansiveness of perfume and the explosiveness of memory are equally powerful forces, generating sensations, images, and stories which demand interpretation. The reader has to be "on the scent" and has to make sense of the scents—those clues and hints—he or she discovers. Smelling and reading demand, as the earlier discussion of "Perfume" showed, that one be conscious both of a fragrant and a textual spirit alive within the bottle and the poem. "The Flask" is a vessel filled as much with memories as with perfumes and created as much from words as from glass.

The Perfumes of Otherness

In "Correspondences" Baudelaire describes what he calls "*other*" perfumes—ambergris, benzoin, musk, frankincense—as if they were emanations of exotic realities situated outside the bounds of the familiar and the ordinary. These perfumes are literally extravagant; they evoke what is otherworldly, representing for Baudelaire the otherness associated with life itself: in particular, the sin, guilt, melancholy, death, beauty, and desire which he experiences and then turns into poetry. Perfume is explosive, exorbitant, eccentric; it moves away from the center of things toward other spheres on the margins of existence. It is literally transportive and ecstatic, carrying consciousness beyond the here-and-now. Perfume opens worlds for Baudelaire, worlds of alternate existence, realms of spiri-

tual fullness, and paradises of sensual pleasure. Usually the cosmogony perfume establishes emerges from a simple objective phenomenon: from a perfume flacon ("The Flask"), or from the texture of cloth or fur ("Perfume"), or from the body of a woman (the scent of a lover's warm breast in "Exotic Perfume"). But one of the more sensually odorous objects in the Baudelairean universe, one of the more suggestively fragrant inspirations for the poet's scented imagination, inspiring dreams of voyage and delight as well as desire and possession, is hair. The strong scents of a woman's hair would have most definitely impressed a poet as attracted to odors as Baudelaire. During the Second Empire women rarely washed their hair—shampooing would only begin to catch on during the Third Republic—and so hair remained, Corbin observes, "one of a woman's strongest (and most seductive) trumps."[26] The opening stanzas from Baudelaire's verse poem "La Chevelure" ("Her Hair," I: 26) leave no doubt about the erotic power of fragrant, albeit unwashed, hair to provoke sublime dream-worlds, where scent and memory intermingle: "O fleece which covers her neck like wool! / O curls! O perfume heavy with nonchalance! / Ecstasy! Tonight, in order to people this dark alcove / With the memories sleeping in this hair, / I want to shake it in the air like a handkerchief!" (Fowlie, 43). Similarly, in the prose poem "A Hemisphere in Tresses" (I: 300)), hair and cosmos, as the title makes clear, are one: "Your hair holds an entire dream, filled with sails and rigging; it holds huge seas whose monsoons carry me toward enchanting climates, where space is bluer and deeper, where the atmosphere is perfumed with fruits, foliage, and human skin."[27]

Hair is a site for creation, that of new universes—"A whole distant world, absent, almost defunct, / Lives in your depths, O aromatic forest!" the poet writes—because hair, once combed, arranged, and scented, once touched, that is, by a human hand, becomes artistically shaped. As the woman fashions her hair, so the poet's experience of hair passes through the combing and arranging mechanisms of his language. The interactions of sound, sense, syntax, rhythm, cadence, meter, and music comb out a meaning from the curls and tresses the poet imagines caressing and smelling. For most of his life Baudelaire was horrified by all that was natural, uncontrollably natural, that is; only art and artifice, he believed, could contain the wild, unpredictable tendencies of nature. Like the dressed and made-up woman, her body covered by silk and jewels, her skin masked by rice powder and rouge, her being transformed into an animate work of art, scented hair signals mastery and domestication; here is a dream-universe created by imagination out of a living body. Not only does perfume work to inspire a reverie of sensual paradises or "faroff oases" (I: 99); it serves appearance and to that end masks nature with artifice. Sight, contemplation, even speech and knowledge are secondary pursuits in comparison to the one singular activity superceding them all: namely, the commitment to beauty, the faithfulness to art, and the worshipful submission to aesthetic subterfuge, which neither sight, nor contemplation, nor even speech or knowledge, but only adoration, can accomplish: "But is it not enough that your looks prevail / . . . / I adore your beauty. Mask or semblance, hail!" ("The Love of Lies," Mathews, 126). Perfume is this artifice masking the body's raw odors, this decor the skin wears to disguise its perpetual decomposition. Fragrance is the voice of sweetness the body adopts to capture and enrapture. In perfume, which is designed to inspire dream and to provoke escape, artifice is all.

A vaporous substance like perfume, so dedicated to appearance and illusion, so possessed with dream, and so committed to change and evasiveness, exists in a state of transitoriness. Despite the architecture which structures it, despite the interactive blend of top, middle, and base notes, and despite the presence of fixing agents which reduce its volatility, scent remains ultimately unfixed and formless, subject to the spiraling, meandering motions chance imposes on its ephemeral life. Fragrance moves ineluctably toward disappearance. Perfume is thus pure passage, itself always *en passage*. Either passing momentarily through the present or brushing past or against someone or some thing, it is, as Baudelaire writes of a striking woman who passes him on a street, an "elusive beauty" ("To a Passerby," 92).

When it comes to postponing the passing away of scent so as to preserve the traces of its precarious presence, Baudelaire's two poems on hair offer strategies of sensual appropriation. Breathing, seeing, smelling, hearing, even an intoxicating dizziness, which the prose poem "A Hemisphere in Tresses" mentions, are not, when taken individually, acts that explain the intensity of the passion inspired in the poet by the woman's physical proximity. Even the poet's experience of the sound, color, smell, and taste of hair—it is described in "Her Hair" as "A resounding port where my soul can drink / In long draughts perfume, sound and color"—only goes so far. For what Baudelaire's fantasy requires more than anything else, as he reduces a woman to her hair and her body to one of its parts, is to consume her totally. He will not be content until he can inhale her odor, drink in her sensuality, and cannibalize her being, as the final paragraph of the prose poem—"Let me bite ever so long into your tresses heavy and black"—and the final verses of "Her Hair"—"Are you not the oasis where I dream, and the gourd / From which I draw in long draughts the wine of memory?"—assert.

That Baudelaire is given to impressive feats of inhalation—sniffing and absorbing scents of different potencies and varieties—only confirms the reality that he is subject to fantasies of ingestion: moments when the only means of possessing the other is through her internalization inside the poet himself. After six prose paragraphs affirming the aromatic sensuousness of the universe that hair alone creates—lines signaling the poet's need to bury his face in hair "like a thirsting man into the water of a spring," or to shake it with his hand "like a fragrant handkerchief," or to become dizzy inhaling its exotic odors of tobacco blended with opium and sugar or of tar mixed with musk and coconut oil—nothing less than biting, chewing, and eating the hair will give the poet the chance to possess the cosmos emerging from its aroma. For the ingestion of the beloved's existence and the inhaling of her scent represent the internalization of memories: "when I nibble at your elastic and unruly hair, it seems I eat memories."

What began in "A Hemisphere in Tresses" with the desire to "inhale ever so long, ever so long, the odor of your hair" ends with a true act of inwardness. Interiorization is Baudelaire's sole means of preservation. Absorbing into himself what exists in the world—fragrances, sights, sounds, colors, tastes, objects, landscapes—guarantees that what is taken in will escape the ravages of time. And strange as it may seem, the poem, despite its physical presence on the page, is fundamentally an interior vision, an imagined possibility, forged within and then projected onto the world. Few poets, if any, have ever given such rapturous and rhapsodic expression to the oceanic feeling that fragrance—musicalized, sensualized, eroticized, poeticized, and memorialized—awakens within the soul. When, in "A Hemisphere in Tresses," Baudelaire admits to the beloved that he has entered a uniquely odorous universe to which each of his senses responds—"If only you could know everything I see! everything I feel! everything I hear in your hair!"—he underscores the all-encompassing power of perfume. And when at the beginning of the same poem he admits to his beloved that "My soul travels on aromas like other men's souls on music"—thus uniting scent to symphony and perfume to displacement—he prefigures what in the prose poem's concluding words ("I eat memories") will become nothing short of a self-fulfilling prophesy about perfume and the poet's absorption of it.

The Scent of a Woman: Perfume and Passion

The ambiguity of perfume, so expressive of the ambiguity of being and of poetry out of which Baudelaire constructed a fundamentally binocular vision of the world, reveals itself in the idea of perfume's materiality. A substance as vaporous, evanescent, and spiritual as fragrance possesses simultaneously a heavy, dense reality. This ambiguous blend of the carnal and the spiritual is voiced with a vacillation characteristic of Baudelaire in two lines from "Her Hair": "O perfume heavy with nonchalance! / Ecstasy!" The paradoxical union of heaviness and airiness, common to perfume aesthetics, is subtly suggested by the contrast between the phonetic similarity and the semantic difference of the French words "*chargé*" (heavy) and "*nonchaloir*" (nonchalance). While both expressions share a rhyming syllable ("*cha*") creating a momentary phonetic resemblance, they semantically express very different, if not opposite, experiences. Encumbered with meaning and  heavy (*chargé*, in other words) with motivation, perfume is nevertheless associated with an opposite reality: namely, *nonchalance*, an experience suggestive of languor, indolence, and a certain lightness of being. Thus, Baudelaire's scent is, paradoxically, heavy with lightness, carnal in its spirituality, and active in its passivity. It is "loaded" with an aroma provoking a state of bliss which the poet identifies as "Ecstasy!"

The fleshiness, density, and opacity of perfume is often suggested by Baudelaire. In fact, the association of perfume with women and with the female body gives fragrance its own singular body, its own substantiality. The body grounds scent in reality. The woman *embodies* perfume; in other words, she lends it her body as a mode of transport, a vehicle of expression, and the medium through which it can move into and out of the world. The body's solidity, which animates fragrance, becomes the point of departure for a voyage and a liberation. Anchored by gravity to the earth, the body in itself has no possibility of transcendence, except insofar as its scent can detach itself from the constraining surfaces of skin and sail forth as a vapor into the air.

Invisibly, perfume in Baudelaire's poetry prowls, sneaks, tiptoes up and down, and floats over the body, haphazardly enveloping the arms here or the neck there, moving outwards and upwards with the same freedom as fragrant smoke curling from an incense burner: "Perfume swims around your naked breasts," he writes in "Causerie" (I: 56). Yet, Baudelaire does not limit his perfuming of the female body to lyrical fantasies of skin, hair, bust, flesh, or clothes. The body's envelopment in perfume does not stop at the epidermis. It penetrates the skin. This is revealed in the image of an extraordinary intimacy with the beloved, one expressive of the poet's amorous need to internalize the lover, absorbing her into his own being: "As I bent over you, queen of worshiped women, / I believed I could smell the perfume of your blood" ("The Balcony," I: 37; Fowlie, 51). What fragrance, one may ask, does blood transformed into vapor or spirit have? Passing through the opaque density of the beloved's skin, like a perfume escaping the bounds of its flacon, blood, the very force of life, is transformed into the scent of the woman, the aroma of her being. In this state of sublimated spirituality she is inhaled by the poet. Perfume becomes the medium of an appropriation, the instrument for a kind of vampiric possession.

In the poem "Hymn" (I: 162) Baudelaire offers a song of praise and celebration to a loved woman; it is a hymn that uses the metaphor of perfume to express the spirituality of a love whose essential truth the poet wishes to capture. Addressing the beloved, the poet asks her how he can impart truth to "Your purity and keep it whole?" To which he seems to answer, "through perfume." His poem is a hymn rising not only through word and song to God, as hymns are wont to do, but through smell and scent to a realm of sublime being, which love has created. As in his other poems of scent, where perfume serves either as the metaphor for love, passion, desire, woman, travel, escape, music, memory, poetry, self-consciousness, and exoticism, Baudelaire in "Hymn" (as well as in his other poems of scent) makes perfume, whether a grain of musk, a cloud of frankincense, or a drop of ambergris, the essence and spirit of his poetic—that is to say, his scented—imagination.

Traces, Vapors, and Arabesques: Woman as Scent in the Fin de Siècle (1880–1914)

Chapter 4

I am the sovereign of transitory things.
—Robert de Montesquiou

A poet must leave traces,
not proofs, of his passing.
Traces alone make us dream.
—René Char

FOR POETS LIKE BAUDELAIRE and writers and artists who in his wake gave symbolism its definition, like Huysmans, Mallarmé, Robert de Montesquiou, Gustave Moreau, and Odilon Redon, nature in its truly "natural" state was an imperfect reality: base, formless, savage, even criminal. Nature, Baudelaire observes in his essay *The Painter of Modern Life* (1863), "incites man to murder his brother, to eat him, to lock him up and to torture him." In whatever is natural, that is to say "all the actions and desires of the purely natural man, you will find nothing but frightfulness." But nature, a truly mediated nature that is, reshaped by a human hand, corrected by imagination, and adorned by art could be changed into a sublime, ideal reality. Beauty, as well as fashion, cosmetics, and perfume, Baudelaire argues, is a "symptom of the taste for the ideal which floats on the surface of all the crude, terrestrial, and loathsome bric-à-brac that the natural life accumulates in the human brain: it is a sublime deformation of Nature, or rather a permanent and repeated attempt at her *reformation*" (31–33).

Here is nature raised to the level of Art, humanized by acts as commonplace as a woman applying makeup, or as private as a poet channeling a cry of pain or joy into the music of language, or as magical as the transformation of jasmine and rose petals into a complex perfume. And when artifice becomes more real than nature itself, when nature has no reality outside of the artifice that masks and transforms it, when the world is "reformed," if not replaced, by imagination and fantasy, then aestheticism and eventually decadence take precedence. A forest is no longer an assemblage of trees but a congregation of symbols. Natural things are not what they are, but what artifice makes them seem to be. They are inhabited by symbols that speak of anterior, lost states of existence, by signs that point to a spiritual world beyond themselves, by sensations that transcend the senses, and by a music of the spheres. Nature becomes theater where art, beauty, and fashion, having substituted new scenes and decors for old visions, institute an "artificial paradise" of pleasure, elegance, and beauty.

Nature as Decor

Sequestered in his castle at Fontenay and thus protected against any and all intrusions from the everyday world of bourgeois mediocrity, Duke Jean Floressas des Esseintes, the dandy, misanthropic, and neurasthenic hero of Huysmans's *Against Nature* (*A Rebours*) delights in the sensuous pleasures of an imaginary world whose sights, sounds, savors, and scents art and taste have transformed into a decor. The creative blend of colors and fabrics has been selected by Des Esseintes, an obsessive night owl, for their propensity to become more intense and mysterious under the artificial light of lamps and candles (12–13). The walls of his living quarters are covered, like bound books, in smooth, grosgrain Moroccan leather and the moldings overlaid with dark

indigo enamel. The domed ceiling is surrounded by an orange border—Des Esseintes's favorite color—which softens the blue of the woodwork. As for the furnishings, Des Esseintes has filled his rooms with books in ebony cases and with rare flowers designed to harmonize with the wild animal skins and blue-fox furs placed helter-skelter on the parquet floors. Through leaden windows of opaque glass, distorted in places by tiny bulges and bubbles, a weak daylight penetrates; what light that does enter is further darkened by thick, russet draperies (14–15).

Everywhere artifice dominates. The house is an "artificial paradise" completely in tune with Baudelaire's ideal dreamscapes. This is as it should be, for Des Esseintes (as well as his creator) are Baudelairean devotees to the core, and the apartments at Fontenay offer an architectural and decorative homage to the poet of *The Flowers of Evil*. On the mantelpiece of his living quarters Des Esseintes has installed a sacred altar in tribute to his forefather's memory: a framed triptych of "three works by Baudelaire copied on genuine vellum in exquisite lettering" (15). Of the three poems one, in particular, occupies a central place, its title signaling the ultimate goal of Des Esseintes's aesthetic imagination: namely, to be "Anywhere out of the World." Des Esseintes's fascination with the aesthetics of decor appears at different moments in *Against Nature*. One of his more ingenious, if not bizarre, decorative additions, turns out, alas, to be ephemeral. Intrigued by the glints of silver, gold, and plum threads running through the woolen weave of an Oriental carpet covering the floor of his Paris apartment, Des Esseintes decides that the vividness of the hues could be much more successfully set off by the addition of something dark moving across and contrasting with the surface of the rug. This decorative fantasy haunts him for weeks. Then, one day, passing in front of the window of a pet store in the Palais Royal he spies an enormous tortoise; at last, he believes, he has found the solution to his decorating problem. Like a consumer infatuated with a purchase in the store but then disappointed when it is delivered to his or her home, he discovers to his chagrin that the tortoise does not "go" (35). His attempt to intensify the rug's colors by the addition of a contrasting darkness (that of the tortoise) was a serious mistake. The colors, he realizes, should have been softened, not darkened; a touch of brightness is what is now needed. But the tortoise in its natural form cannot supply this radiance.

Such problems, however, do not easily defeat an aesthetically clever mind like Des Esseintes's. He sends the tortoise to a gilder to have its brackish shell completely overlaid with a gold patina. The tortoise is returned "blaz[ing] like a sun, shining triumphantly over the subjugated tones of carpet" (36). But still Des Esseintes's creation remains, to his mind, a hair short of perfection. He sends the creature to a jeweler, this time to have its gilded shell inlaid with precious stones. Insisting that the jeweler not use diamonds, emeralds, rubies, topazes, and amethysts—they are common and bourgeois, in his

Fig. 53 Baccarat, the French crystal maker founded in 1764, produced some of Guerlain's standard perfume bottles starting in the mid-1850s, a collaboration that would continue into the following century with more innovative and fantasist designs like this tortoise bottle of 1914 for Guerlain's *Parfums des Champs Elysées*.

opinion—he instructs him to select only rare gems like peridots, chrysoberyls, azurite, cat's eyes, and sapphirines (37). Arranged on the animal's back in a configuration that enhances the harmonies and contrasts of iridescence, fieriness, and opalescence, the jewels give the tortoise a sublime otherworldliness. They also give him an unreal immobility which soon, tragically, becomes a self-fulfilling prophecy. When Des Esseintes kneels to touch the motionless tortoise, he finds it stone-cold dead. Alas, this common animal from an ordinary, everyday world has been forced to carry too great a weight of the sublime. There are, Des Esseintes learns, terrestrial phenomena and living realities, which cannot be fashioned into works of art or made "to bear the dazzling splendor thrust upon them" (43).

In its fatal incarnation as a mobile decorative object, Des Esseintes's turtle was not entirely a figment of Huysmans's vivid imagination. The Count Robert de Montesquiou-Fezensac, whose love for the aesthetic life and taste for the decorative arts Huysmans had first learned about in 1882 from the poet Stéphane Mallarmé, owned a similarly gilded amphibian. Not only did Huysmans use Montesquiou's dandyism as the model for Des Esseintes's aestheticism, but several of the Count's decorative creations—not least of which was the golden tortoise—were featured in the rooms of Fontenay-aux-Roses, where, as in the Count's apartments on Paris's Quai d'Orsay, dark interiors, ecclesiastical ornaments, leather-covered walls, a sled lying on a polar bear rug, and a church bell at the front door for visitors to ring, combined to make of decor an unique form of *writing*.[1] The sinuous lines, swirls, and spirals of ornamental motifs, whether incised in glass or embroidered in fabric or carved in wood, described a spiritual landscape of the soul. Vases, bottles, brooches, necklaces, chandeliers, sconces, tables, cupboards, headboards, stair railings, covered with or molded in the form of insects, birds, reptiles, flowers, vines, leaves, and other organic figures, narrated the fantasies of a dream world where the Beautiful existed in perfect harmony with the exotic and the symbolic (Bertrand, I: 92, 95, 117). This farrago of period styles "written" in the designs of wallpaper, rugs, candelabras, and other furnishings and captured in a variety of decorative motifs— the peacock feathers and spider webs in wood and leather, the roses, bats, dragonflies, and hydrangeas drawn or painted on objects of varying sizes and shapes, and the rainbow of colors, each imparting to a particular room of the Count's *hôtel de ville* a singular spiritual and mystical aura (mauve in the bedroom, blue, gray, and silver in the "moon" room, red and gold in the "sun" room)—was, as Montesquiou remarked in his memoirs (*Les Pas effacés*, 1923), "permeated with symbols" (Bertrand, I: 91–93), thanks to which this decorative heterocosm became a unified and harmonious whole. Under the Count's guidance, the rooms of his quai d'Orsay residence were made to reflect an *état-d'âme* (a spiritual state) expressing through the harmony of decorative and structural elements a subjective and eccentric sensibility. Such rooms spoke to the senses like works of art and works of nature. Emerging mysteriously from furnishings, ornaments, and decorative objects, a host of strange messages—musical, auditory, visual, and olfactory—joined in a symphonic and symbolic experience of synaesthesia; each room was a "theater of sensations" (Bertrand, I: 97).

As for Montesquiou's gilded tortoise, it was no less symbolic than other decorative objects in the quai d'Orsay townhouse. Subject to the same fate as Des Esseintes's creature, it died from the very embellishment it was made to embody and transport. Symbolist ornamentation turns fatal as decor becomes, in the Count's words, "a funeral monument at once metallic and jeweled" (Bertrand, I: 74). Yet, Montesquiou's tortoise was not his own creation. He had taken the idea from his friend Judith Gautier, the daughter of the nineteenth-century poet Théophile Gautier, and a friend to Hugo, Flaubert, and Richard Wagner; Judith had herself borrowed the idea from a Japanese drawing she had once seen. Such ambulatory golden turtles were believed to bring good luck in Japanese households (Bertrand, I: 74). While Montesquiou did no more than have his animal covered in gold, Gautier went a step further and had jewels glued to the turtle's gilded shell, which gave off a shimmering radiance as the reptile ambled around her rue de Berri apartment (Jullian, *Robert de Montesquiou*, 78). Huysmans, whose tortoise was fictional from the start, allowed his imagination even more extravagant latitude. To Madame Gautier's use of randomly placed gems he added a complex symbolist design in which leaves and petals, fashioned from artfully arranged gem stones, represented a thin stalk culminating in "a cluster of flowers" (*Against Nature*, 36). Around 1891, in homage to Des Esseintes's aesthetic imagination, the jeweler, Templier, in whose shop on the Rue Royale a stylish Parisian clientele liked to congregate, created a "*tortue-bijou*" (turtle-jewel) covered in platinum and tied to a chain eight inches long. It became the "creative sensation of the year" (Bertrand, I: 75), signaling again that the poetry of the beautiful and precious object in which art takes nature to unimagined heights of sublime perfection could have popular and consumerist appeal.

The tortoise as art nouveau ornament did not end with Templier's popular jewel, however. In 1914 Guerlain marketed a new perfume bottle in the shape of a turtle designed by the French luxury glassmaker Baccarat (fig. 53). This *flacon tortue*, as it was (and continues to be) called, contained a fragrance, "Parfum des Champs-Elysées," which Guerlain had launched ten years earlier.[2] Rendered in cut, chiseled glass, Guerlain's bottle imitates the oval, slightly tapered form and mottled patterning of a turtle's back. At each of the flacon's corners four pawlike protuberances, decorated with tiny scales and sometimes colored in tortoiseshell amber or in gray, protrude. The stopper, an elongated, tapered wedge of clear, cut glass, captures the thickset, reptilian shape of the turtle's head. The bottle, along with its satin-lined red box, is an objet d'art designed to be as evocative and symbolic as the perfume it encloses, and yet the object has a practical function. Nature, enhanced through fantasy and art, is made social and bourgeois. The turtle becomes part of an everyday, albeit sumptuous, decor.

Fragrant Walls of Glass: The Art Nouveau Bottle

The perfume bottle as an exquisite art nouveau ornament did not have to wait until Guerlain's and Baccarat's rather late 1914 tortoise bottle. The production of such artistic objects had occurred in the two decades preceding the 1900 Paris World Exhibition, which in architecture, interior design, glassblowing, woodworking, metallurgy, and the art of lighting saw the glorification of art nouveau style and of the modern decorative arts. One of the first glassmakers along with Baccarat to create art nouveau perfume bottles, which were also works of art in their own right—delicate objects designed to decorate a woman's dressing table much as an ornate vase might beautify an end table—was Emile Gallé and his Ecole de Nancy glassworking atelier, founded in 1901. Born in 1846, Gallé was a learned botanist and an artist for whom nature in general and the "eloquence of the flower" in particular, as he wrote in his essay "Le Décor symbolique" (1900), were more suggestive sources of inspiration than the human figure. As much a poet as a glassmaker, a spiritualist as a craftsman, and a symbolist as a woodworker, Gallé was strongly influenced by Baudelaire's mystical vision of nature as expressed in *The Flowers of Evil,* as well as by other symbolist representations of the natural world. Soon Gallé had formulated his own brand of organicist symbolism, which looked in nature for the hidden sounds, scents, and signs of a secret, mysterious language: the "nuances, contours, and perfumes," he writes, that coincide with Baudelaire's "language of flowers and voiceless things." To allow this language of flowers, trees, and insects to speak in wood, metal, and glass was Gallé's spiritual and artistic mission. It was an act of expression not lost on his friend Montesquiou, who wrote a number of poems describing in precise detail Gallé's hallmark forms and motifs. In "Murrhins" and "Galerie" (the latter punningly evokes Gallé's name) Montesquiou gives new life to green, pink, blood-red, golden-yellow, and black vases, fashioned from materials like "enamel, gemstone, ivory, metal / Alabaster, marble, wood, lacquer, bamboo, crystal / Kaolin, China stone, porcelain, stoneware." Gallé, writes Montesquiou, makes "dream sing in glass" and this song, uniting flower and fantasy, fills the "crystal" work of art with spirit and matter, "thought and vitality." The language of vases, cups, goblets, drinking bowls, chalices, pots, pitchers, bottles, and flacons—as translated by Montesquiou's imagination—speaks through carved or enameled images representing "snow weep[ing] on the moon," an "octopus splaying its terrors," and the sinuous movements of insects, fish, frogs, and slugs. In Gallé's works nature whispers the "confused words" Baudelaire in his poem "Correspondences" imagined the poet would hear when walking through a forest of trees suddenly filled with symbols. Gallé possesses, according to Montesquiou, the magical power to pull confessions from the "heart of a felled tree"; the tree's "very essence talks through him" and "sings its own story."[3]

Beyond the inspiration he took from Baudelaire's poetry, Gallé, through his amorphous, vaporous, and protean creations—their blend of streaked and marbled blown glass resembles lava fixed in a molten state—sought to multiply the nuances in brilliance, translucence, and reflectivity that the play of light and color accomplishes. In this, his inspiration was the American dancer Loïe Fuller who fascinated Gallé—he called her a "magician of reflected light"—when he, along with all of Paris, witnessed her debut at the Folies Bergère in 1893. Fuller resembled one of Gallé's vases made flesh. Like his bottles she was a mobile, protean field of concentrated and diffused light emanating from a center of continually changing radiance and reflection. Writing in *The Architectural Record* of March 1903, the English critic Charles Anet observed that Fuller had been a model not only for artists but also for those artisans working in the applied arts. "Her influence is discernible in the revival of the decorative styles," he writes. "The glassworking art owes her a great deal. Emile Gallé, the best master glassworker in France, freely admits that he was led to seek new coloring for his glass by seeing the beautiful light effects invented by Loïe Fuller."[4]

The iconography of floral, entomological, and ornithological motifs which adorn Gallé's works is complex and diverse. Among insects, he favors dragonflies, grasshoppers, bees (in the act of pollinating flowers), spiders, butterflies, and even a stag beetle. Flowers are represented by roses, lilies, columbines, and orchids, while plants and trees are evoked by images of mushrooms, onions, windblown autumn acorns, vines, tendrils, hanging fruit (grapes and apples), and gourds. Flying creatures are identified by the bats, the pelicans, even a pterodactyl, whose wings overspread the surfaces of his creations. Among marine and lake life, seashells, fish, tadpoles, and frogs proliferate. This diversity of motifs is matched by a richness of coloration. By 1889 Gallé's artistic arsenal included over one hundred distinct colors which could be blended into different hues, including a new black glass, "hyalite," used to create Gallé's somber, mournful "vases de tristesse." His perfume bottles were, generally speaking, non-commercial works. They had neither been commissioned by a particular perfumer for the purposes of marketing a particular scent, nor were they destined for wide distribution among the public. Rather, they appear to have been one-of-a-kind bottles made to decorate the elegant dressing table of a woman, who transferred her favorite scent to them from the nondescript, generic bottles she had brought home from her perfume store.

Some of Gallé's clear glass scent bottles from the 1880s are overlaid with enameled decorations. In one, a large praying mantis is seen spreading its long legs and ample abdomen over the bottle's ovoid surface where they intertwine with vines, tendrils, and other similarly sinuous lines. A second clear glass scent bottle from the same period is covered with thin branches and delicately figured

Fig. 54 Emile Gallé
perfume bottle, glass
and enamel with a
silver stopper, 1886.

leaves near to which a large, finely drawn fly hovers. On the face of another turn-of-the-century scent bottle, made of an opaque yellow and amber glass, a large red "rose de France" decoration is carved in relief. Other flasks from the late 1880s and 1890s sport etched decorations of bats or dragonflies with spread wings (fig. 54) or impose the vertical, upwardly spiraling shape of a flower on the entire bottle; some use a milk-white background to set off a simple landscape "en grisaille" around which seashells are carved in relief. Often, the name "Gallé" would be subtly and harmoniously integrated into the petals or foliage of the design. A perfume atomizer decorated with a large morning glory, fabricated by the Gallé company around 1920 (Gallé died in 1904), is composed of industrially produced cameo glass, a process of glass engraving using fluorohydric acid which Gallé had been producing on a limited scale since the mid-1880s. Gallé's handmade pieces sold for 300 francs

and some even for as high as 1,500 francs. But in keeping with his strong belief, as inspired by William Morris's Arts and Crafts movement, that art and the beautiful should be accessible to the public, his industrialized vases and bottles could be bought for as little as 5 francs.[5]

Perfume also figures as a theme in some of Gallé's works of furniture. One extraordinary piece, a commode designed in 1894 and given the title *Les Parfums d'autrefois* (Perfumes of Yesteryear, fig. 55), combines a pagoda-shaped dressing table and a tall mirror whose wood frame, in a trilobe motif common to Gallé's furniture of this period, is decorated with vines, branches, and flowers (roses, in fact) placed in relief and, in some instances, extending beyond the commode's edges. Little shelves supporting perfume bottles asymmetrically border the mirror. Exhibited at the Salon du Champ de Mars in 1895, the commode attracted the attention of one commentator, Louis de

Fig. 55 The spirit of art nouveau brings perfume and furniture together in Emile Gallé's commode *Les Parfums d'autrefois*, 1894.

Fourcaud, who was sensitive to the work's nostalgic evocation of the scents of yesteryear. *Les Parfums d'autrefois,* he wrote, displayed the "mosaic surfaces of a complete garden of bygone scents." This garden is, at least iconographically if not nominatively, present in the images of flowers and the Latin names of plants and herbs delicately inscribed in the marquetry of the table's three panels. Written in a sinuous art nouveau script, botanical terms, like *Asperula* (sweet woodruff), *Vervena* (verbena), *Reseda* (reseda), *Lavundula* (lavender), *Rosmar* (rosemary), *Svaveol* (from the Latin *suaveolens*, sweet-smelling), *Orchi Odoratisisma* (fragrant orchid), and other scientific names, along with the title of the piece (*Parfums d'autrefois*), compete with the windblown forms of branches, petals, and leaves. Gallé's commode, moreover, creates an interesting contrast between the absence and the presence of scents insofar as the images of flowers fashioned from wood or cast in metal, and thus literally odorless, contest the floral fragrances, arising in reality from the small perfume bottles set on the mirror's tiny shelves.[6]

Gallé conceived of his vases and bottles as delicate poems cut in glass. "With what talent," Victor Champier writes in 1902, "he combines his bits of glass to form those veritable little poems of shape and coloring which captivate the mind." Sometimes, his bottles and vases were indeed poems, engraved with verses by Hugo, Montesquiou, and others; Gallé called them "verres parlants" (talking glass). Like poetry, and music also, which Mallarmé and the symbolist poets sought to conflate, Gallé wished to make glass speak, sing, and cry and to endow it with a power of suggestion able to evoke sensual experiences beyond the reaches of language and other forms of representation. Gallé proposed that the modern decorative arts function "like secret voices that respond to our inner vibrations," that they offer tremulous landscape visions of the soul, and that they give form to the world of the dream, to what the historian Debora Silverman calls the "unstable field of vibration and fluidity." Flowers for him were not merely organic phenomena; they were presences, persons, and women. The rose, he wrote, was "the eternally adorable queen" whose "velvety feel" caresses us.[7] Moreover, Gallé's attempt to have glass reproduce dreamscapes, or to evoke musical harmonies, or to suggest the vague symbolist "Idea" buried behind the cameo image of a water lily or a dragonfly, or finally to interchange spirit with matter and matter with spirit reveals the extent to which his symbolist aesthetic achieves in glass what the scented imagination attempts to realize through the emanations of perfume. Dreams chiseled in glass are matched by fantasies, olfactory in nature, unfolding and vaporizing into thin air.

Thus, in the surging forth of an enchanted dream world set in motion by glass forms and aromatic smells; in the presence of a crystalline prism (glass, air) through which light, reflection, and scent pass; in the unfolding realities of memories and the memories of unfolding realities generated by the power of glass and perfume to provoke a play of mirrored light and contrasting odor; in the fullness of pleasure derived from visual and olfactory experience; in the flowing out of inner being, sensual feeling, and erotic desire released by the dynamic operation of visual and olfactory stimuli; and finally in the enjoyment and voluptuousness which dreams in glass and dreams in scent offer—lies a compelling correspondence, if not identity, at the turn of the century, between symbolist and art nouveau aesthetics and the constellation of imaginary associations generated by the experience of perfume.

Woman as Objet d'Art

When Des Esseintes gilds and bejewels his tortoise transforming it into a mobile work of art, he achieves a denaturalization of nature: its aesthetic transformation, or in Baudelaire's word, its "re-formation." The fin de siècle woman, at least insofar as the system of images surrounding and embodying her goes, fares no better. It is as an aesthetic object, an ornament, and a decor that woman is figured in the images and creations of symbolist and art nouveau styles. She is, as the art critic Gustave Coquiot called her at the time, the "ultimate bibelot [decorative object] and the consummate *article de Paris*," a term referring to fancy accessories (gloves, artificial flowers, feathers) used to personalize an outfit during the last quarter of the nineteenth century. She is, as one writer remarked in 1910, "a living poem, a painting that walks, a statue that breathes, a form of music that can be seen." Why not even, one might ask, a perfume that can be heard? In which case, she would have to be seen as both flask and scent, glass and odor, prison and prisoner. Decorating guides of fin de siècle France presented women not only as "artists" of the home, but, according to the historian Lisa Tiersten, as "an integral part of the interior, a decorative object to be coordinated with the other objects of the home." As both the subject and object of the creative process, as both the spirit and the matter of artistic production, and as both the designer and the designed, woman has no identity other than the ambiguous forms she comes to adopt; this self-contradicting identity destabilizes her very existence. Transformed into a sylph, a vase, an aroma, or a trace she is made to sacrifice the naturalness of her femininity. She is always other than what she is or appears to be. Never just a woman, but always a woman-flower, or a woman-nymph, or a woman-cloud, her being can never escape the hyphenated hybridity that society uses to define and control her condition. The woman-flower motif so prevalent in art nouveau imagery evokes, as fashion historian Rhonda Garelick argues, "a purely decorative female, prettified but insubstantial, sexual but only florally so, not corporeally." It represents an "aesthetic evacuation of female bodiliness."[8] This is the woman as designer item, as rare and precious artifact, and as a manufactured product of the French luxury industry.

One of the latent purposes of symbolist and art nouveau fantasies of the woman, primarily for the male artists and writers who held these feelings and channeled them into their paintings and poems, was to transform into art, thus "re-form" and master, the menace of a sinister and morbid femininity, perceived as closely linked to the dark, carnal side of nature. The flower, the plant, the woman, like their odors, undergo spiritualization; they must be dematerialized. The physical decay, rot, and death of the floral world are discarded so that a pure scent, a lasting fragrance, or a delicate flask may take their place. Hallucinated as scent, her body enveloped in a diaphanous emanation, the woman loses her sting as well as the medusa-like powers the masculine imagination fears she possesses. Aestheticized, fetishized, and commodified, like some exquisite, though dead, butterfly arranged in a collection or like some rare bird of paradise costumed in sumptuous dresses and displayed as a trophy on the arm of a sober, black-suited, older gentleman (as in James Tissot's celebrated painting, *The Political Lady* of 1883–85), the woman becomes an ornament; she is pure decoration.

This aestheticist image of the fin de siècle, symbolist, and art nouveau woman coincides, as we shall see, with the imaginary associations and cultural realities of perfume. For many turn-of-the-century artists and writers, the woman resembled a dancer, and her body, flowing through a space in which it appears vaporized, was seen as undergoing the kind of dissemination and sublimation associated with scent. The female body is abstracted; it becomes a distillation, a spirit, an Idea, as Mallarmé hoped it would. Like perfume, the woman is at once sensual and spiritual, organic and immaterial, earthbound and airborne. Vaporous in her gossamer gowns, sinuous in her movements, and protean in her metamorphic incarnations, the woman is an emanation, not unlike those nebulous clouds of smoke spiraling up from an incense burner, or the ephemeral traces of moonlight dotting a dark landscape, or the disembodied tresses of flowing hair—all so eminently figured in art nouveau painting, sculpture, glass design, jewelry, interior decoration, and advertising.

The Dance of Perfume

The iconic image of the art nouveau woman—and the one that best connects to the scented imagination—is that of the celebrated American dancer, Loïe Fuller whose dances during the 1890s helped to set the direction for the evolution of art nouveau style in the decorative arts. Turned down for a job at the Paris Opera in 1892, she was quickly hired by the director of the Folies Bergère, where she gave 600 successive performances to wildly enthusiastic crowds (Bertrand, II: 625). The stage she occupied was devoid of conventional scenery. Fuller, the "Electric Salomé," as Garelick calls her, filled the empty stage with fabrics, lighting mechanisms, and optical devices, all of her own invention. One such apparatus was a glass pedestal placed on the stage and lit invisibly from below. When she had mounted this pedestal in an entirely darkened theater, Fuller gave the impression of being "suspended mysteriously above the stage, dancing in mid-air." A more complicated device used beams of light and mirrors to create a tiny octagonal space in which Fuller gave the illusion of "a small crowd of identical dancers in a self-enclosed, mirrored room" (Garelick, 102–04).

Loïe Fuller was a woman-dancer who, paradoxically, during her performances was neither woman nor dancer, but a vortex of concentrated light, a node of fluid energy, and a whirling spiral of colored fabric. Mallarmé would even argue in his essay "Crayonné au théâtre" (1887) that as an art of spirituality dance gives visual form to absence, to what he calls "a spiritual nakedness."[9] The dancer is like "a bird impatient to fly away into the regions of the Idea" (II: 173). She is, he writes, not a woman "but a metaphor" (II: 171); as such she is already an abstraction, a creation of mind and imagination. She is also a symbol, her movements evoking elementary forms of reality: a "flower, wave, cloud, jewel." (II: 163). The dancer is pure suggestion and pure concentration. In one lightning-quick movement of her body—a flick of the wrist, a thrust of the leg—she compresses what in writing would require multiple paragraphs to express. For this reason, the dancer is a poem, or more precisely "a writing of the body" (II: 171), the words and gestures of which are, like perfume, written on the wind and inscribed on the air before disappearing; hers, it seems, is a writing unable to hold on to its signs. Fuller, Mallarmé notes in a later essay (1893), moves like some wild "snowflake pushed hither and thither by a furious wind" (II: 175). Enveloped in fabrics, which take on an ecstatic life of their own, and propelled into the very space that her body has just created from the whirlwind turning of skirt and cloth, she performs a choreography notable for the mobility and metamorphosis of the forms she adopts and then abandons. Overwhelmed by the "intoxication of art," Fuller allows herself to become a vapor, an emanation, even a scent, insofar as she surrenders to what Mallarmé calls "a vertigo of the soul made airborne through artifice" (II: 174, 175).

Mallarmé's description of the mobility, volatility, and dizzying upwelling of Fuller's dance, especially his suggestion that what one witnesses is the sublimation of an evanescent body, uses metaphors of volatilization and distillation that could easily figure the ascension, dissemination, and permeation associated with perfume. Loïe Fuller, if one were to develop further Mallarmé's image, performs a dance in which her body, while seeming to disappear into thin air, lives on in a pure state of essential being; her "spiritual acrobatics," he writes, "exist, albeit invisibly, as pure movement and silence" (II: 177). Is Fuller's dance not experienced, then, as an airborne scent—mute, invisible, and yet ever present ? Does she not *have* perfume," in the way the great ballerina, Alexandra Danilova, once used the term to refer to the genius of a gifted pupil?[10] In calling Loïe Fuller the "inexhaustible fountain of her own being" (II: 177), Mallarmé points to the unending potentiality of a dancer's movements and, in the same breath, to the virtuality adhering to the as-yet unrealized Idea, or the as-yet unwritten poem, or the as-yet unformed scent. If one takes at face value, moreover, the illusion Fuller created when, dancing behind a transparent wall, she seemed as if caught in a glass display case—"a prisoner pent in walls of glass"—then the "vitrification" or "bottling" of her choreographic essence may point to yet another aspect of the fin de siècle, symbolist imagination: namely, the effort to spiritualize the world's body—floral, animal, corporeal, or feminine—and transform its reality into scent.

In fact, the theatrical use of perfume in nineteenth-century France and England—a mise-en-scène of scent dating back to antiquity when Roman spectators at the theater or the circus sat under an awning (a *velarium*) from which a fine rain of perfume fell—was not uncommon (Pillivuyt, *Histoire*, 77). The dramatic mingling of different sensations in Fuller's performances, for example, and the ambiguity by which one sense (hearing, let us say) might merge with another (vision) would have been of substantial appeal to those symbolists and decadent writers who firmly believed in synaesthetic works of literature. In 1891 a production of *The Song of Solomon*, blending color, sound, and perfumes, was mounted by a group called the "synesthesiasts." In England, Oscar Wilde considered using odors emanating from perfume braziers strategically placed throughout the theater as substitues for the sounds of an orchestra; clouds of a new scent would express a new emotion, and perfume would take the place of music. Fire ordinances of the time, however, prohibited the spectacle (Garelick, 195, n. 17, 148).

With names like the "Dance of the Thousand Veils," "The Fire of Life," "A Thousand and One Nights," and "Radium" (a tribute to the Curies's discovery) Fuller's dances are full of paradoxes (bound to appeal to a poet like Mallarmé), in which plenitude arises from nothingness and life from death. This tornado of interchangeable forms and sensations, segueing into each other, generates a performance where light, color, smell, and sound come together in fits and starts of varying duration. These give rise to rapid and slow-burning jumps in association, to what Mallarmé calls "decorative bursts of skies, sea, evenings, *perfume*, and foam" (II: 176). Surrounded by hundreds of yards of cloth—yet to Mallarmé's mind reduced to "near-nudity" (II: 177)—Loïe Fuller surrenders her sensuality and carnality to the purity of spirit, essence, and soul; her art, like the poetic word itself, becomes a "direct instrument of the Idea" (II: 178).

Loïe Fuller: The Fairy of Electricity and Scent

The words often used to describe "La Loïe"—dynamic, protean, volatile, fluid, undulating, serpentine—are, one could say, terms applicable as well to a description of the emanation and permeation of scent. Fuller's choreography turned her body and her costumes into an ineffable, otherworldly presence. It was as if the air around her had suddenly caught fire and eclipsed her presence as a person, a woman, and a body. Like a perfume dissipating and impregnating the atmosphere with its odor, Fuller was vaporized, her being diffused into space. An aura of light, color, and reflection arose from this space evoking the movement of a butterfly, or the growth of an orchid, or the undulation of seaweed, images dear to the art nouveau spirit. No longer was it a body that moved across the stage, but a trail of curving smoke, or a trace of vapor, or the trembling of a flower brushed by the wind. Not only were her performances "electrifying," they were also, literally speaking, electric. Aided by her own team of electricians Fuller made such powerful use of the magic of stage lighting that she came to embody the fairyland beauty associated with electricity. This was a new technology which, in the words of the Hachette Guide of the time, became the "living, active soul" of the 1900 Paris Exhibition and, in particular, its gigantic, baroque Palace of Electricity, with a facade illuminated by the "changing lights of 5,000 multicolored incandescent lamps."[11]

Rather than erecting over the exhibition grounds, as in fact they did, the monolithic, buxom, twenty-foot-tall statue of a fin de siècle goddess crowned with a tiara in the shape of a ship (the symbol of Paris) and wearing a corseted, full-length dress and ermine evening cape (created by the designer Paquin) the organizers of the 1900 Paris Exhibition might have commissioned a statue of Loïe Fuller. Her physical image and her sinuous movement were more in harmony with the fluid dynamism of the Exhibition, especially with its celebration of "La Fée Electricité," than was the straitlaced, wasp-waisted, bourgeois grande dame rising 120 feet from the pavement, to which visitors at the Exhibition gave the name, *la Parisienne*. Fuller's image of androgynous femininity, her dynamic metamorphism, and her dramatic manipulation of swirling veils, flowing lengths of silk, and electric light made her a "fairy of electricity" in her own right (Garelick, 99). Moreover, Fuller was "reflected in all the truly modern parts of the exhibition, in bronze, in glass, in fresco or in terra-cotta. Her fluttering veils inspired the glass tulips enclosing the electric bulbs and also the precious ornaments of Lalique" (Jullian, *Triumph*, 90). Her own pavilion at the Exhibition, moreover, offered a performance that, in addition to the souvenir ashtrays and lamps offered for a price, was itself a marketable product, not all that different from the thousands of other goods presented by the 76,000 exhibitors, half French, who participated (Garelick, 116, 120; Jullian, *The Triumph*, 203). Fuller was a commodity and in this respect satisfied the desire of the Exhibition's organizers to advertise beautiful and artistic French luxury and cultural goods. Pavilions, exhibits, and little museum-quality collections could be found all over the fairgrounds. They displayed toys, wallpaper, clocks, jewelry, stationery, furnishings, arms, costumes, hunting paraphernalia, perfume (its pavilion was located on the Champ de Mars), and other products of the artistic industries that, it was believed, expressed the spirit of the French republic. "Nothing is more conducive to intimate knowledge of a people, its manners, its character, its temperament, its moral and intellectual life, than its ornaments and jewelry," Victor Champier observed in 1902; "show me the jewelry of a nation, and I will tell you its character": a boast that could as easily apply to a nation's perfumes.[12]

This fascination in the fin de siècle with the ornamental and decorative object—brooch, bracelet, vase, flask, chair, wallpaper, even woman—reflects a poetics of the *thing* that gives dominance to craft, manufacture, and construction—in other words, the arts of the hand—over the uncontrollable forces of nature. As the result of a desire to humanize nature, the decorative object is a symbol, as well as a fact, of mastery; it has both moral and existential authority. The decadent ethos of a Huysmans or a Montesquiou, so fundamentally elitist, and the decorative impulse of art nouveau artists and artisans, so fundamentally democratic—Gallé wished to make the beautiful object a part of the everyday life of all social classes—revolve around the power of *things*, as the historian Rosalind H. Williams demonstrates in *Dream Worlds,* her study of mass consumption at the end of the nineteenth century. Consumer objects, it was believed, "both express and mold the individual," she writes. They had magical power. Things take on a life of their own, and when brought together to furnish a room or to create a collection for display, as Des Esseintes learns in his castle-fortress at Fontenay, they "create a material refuge, an illusory universe, preferable to a less attractive or even hostile social reality." Des Esseintes, along with the decorative arts reformers, the bourgeois buyers, and the mass consumers of his time, share one thing: "they *all* seek dream worlds of the consumer": objets d'art that doubled as objects of fantasy.[13]

The Symbolist Poetry of Perfume: Albert Samain and Stéphane Mallarmé

Through an iconography of tendrils, flowers, leaves, insect wings, and other organic forms fashioned from wood, glass, iron, and gems, symbolist and art nouveau artists and designers, in an effort to suggest the whiplash lines, gossamer webs, trembling tresses, and undulating waves of a nature redesigned by art, succeeded in creating a dream world of enchantment, beauty, and fantasy. Yet, in this illusory world the languorous fragrance of melancholy, the fetid smell of decadence, and the menacing whiff of madness were never far away. One need only look at the lyric poetry of the somewhat forgotten symbolist poet, Albert Samain (1858–1900), whose first work, *Au Jardin de l'Infante* published in 1893, enjoyed an immense success, including the admiration of Montesquiou. By 1925, this work had sold 75,000 copies, and sales showed no signs of slowing (Bertrand, II: 540). Samain, whom a contemporary called a "poet of the autumn and of the evening," wrote lyrics that gave off a "feeble and melancholic odor, the scent of farewell associated with the chrysanthemums of the feast of St. Martin" (Bertrand, II: 541). Despite its overt simplicity and modesty, in keeping with Samain's severe shyness, the poetry of *Au Jardin de l'Infante* is nonetheless an encyclopedia of symbolist sensitivity and sensuality. Roses wither and fall; objects (a harp, a flower) sigh languorously; dying coals tremble; an infinite silence reverberates; hair emits an aroma of forgetfulness; nymphs cavort at twilight; and far-off music dies away into the air.[14] Mists, clouds, smoke, pale moonlight, and ghostly presences whirl within a poetic landscape in which Samain's obsession with the ephemeral and its melancholic beauty gives pride of place to the verb "éteindre" (to fade, to deaden). The world is struck by an unending and unexpected changeability and an indistinct "farawayness." Reverie emerges from the mystic mists arising from an erotic intermingling of water, perfume, and music. Moving like butterflies through the illusory landscape, dreams become spiritual realities.

In traditional symbolist fashion, Samain describes the fragrances that perfume his world. Love exists among "irritated perfumes" (13). The hour, as well as time itself, broadcasts its scent (17). The soul exhales "suffocating aromas" (17), while sexuality revels in its "lakes of perfume" (183). The beloved's lips are heavy with the fragrances of love and shadow (30). The woman's scent is "subtle, obsessive and complex" (53), and the fan she waves at a ball moves back and forth in cadence with its own "perfumed rhythm" (80). The odor of her disappearing gown floats away toward the horizon like an "ardent breath" (138). When love attains its most intense and elusive moment, the heart fails like "an aromatic flask / that breaks" (192), suggesting that shards of glass (and lost love), although permanently broken, continue to emit traces of a lost aroma. The beloved's green eyes dream in "a fragrant darkness," where "full-bloom jasmine / trembles"; but this is only a fragile memory. If "Perfumes alone reign ... over vanished gardens," it is only because, as phenomena of death and loss, they spread a scent of mourning over the land (19–20). In the poem "Cleopatra" Samain imagines the Egyptian queen under the influence of the "bewitching spell of perfume braziers" burning in her rooms. Suddenly, Cleopatra is overwhelmed by love. Tearing her tunic from her body she stands naked on the high terrace of her apartments offering herself as pure scent to the wind and the world: "Her wild eyes flashing with bolts of lightning, she desires / That the world this evening possess the perfume of her flesh" (109). Often, Samain transforms the female body into an eroticized objet d'art, a fetish-object of man-made poetic beauty. Flesh becomes opalescent mother-of-pearl overlaid with "liquid enamel"; it shimmers and drips with "crystalline pearls" (134). The woman is an erotic object, mastered by the poet-designer or the poet-collector who fetishizes her.

Sensuousness and spirit coexist in Samain's extraordinary long poem "Luxure" (Lust) written in 1889. Lust is the alpha and omega of matter and spirit. It is "the blood of our blood and the marrow of our marrow," the entwining of "sensuality and splendor" (179–80). The odors of sexual pleasure compose a "black perfume," whose caressing aromas lead to a loss of consciousness (181). Sexual pleasure—"the paradise of flesh which makes the soul cry"—unites love with death, a death synonymous with scent, for it is "inhaled from the most fragrant of flowers" (184). The double nature of sexuality, at once physical and spiritual, base and sublime, violent and calming, is revealed in the contradictory juxtaposition of opposites that "Luxure" presents. Sexual pleasure is a "wine" that provokes frenzy; yet it possesses calming powers. It is a "balm," composed of the scented resins—benzoin, olibanum—found in certain perfumes. (186). Sexuality gallops headlong like a "rider's horse . . . towards nothingness," and yet it is "A spasm towards oneness. A nuptial within the absolute" (187–88). Simultaneously a "consoling" and "devouring" power, lust is the "Immortal Empress of the world"; it is "Our Lady of Hell" (188).

"I adore what is indistinct," announces Samain in his poem "Dilection" (Spiritual Love, 58), and he defines this state of mirage as follows: "I adore what is indistinct, faint sounds, colors, / Everything that trembles, waves, shivers, and shimmers: / Hair and eyes, water, leaves, silk, / And the spirituality of slender forms / . . . / The smoke where dreams spiral and curl." Within this ghostly, wavering reality—not unlike the whirling of protean forms Loïe Fuller's body projects onto the stage—the poet identifies several material phenomena (sounds, colors, hair, eyes, leaves, silk, smoke) which, when touched by the blurring power of dream and fantasy, come undone. They have lost the clarity of their contours, transformed into a kind of smoke or perfume that is now only a trace of what it once was, more aura than object. In this symbolist distillation of reality there is a movement toward evanescence coinciding with the volatilization of organic things which the power of perfume accomplishes. A symbolist poet like Samain welcomes the experience of smell, since it enables him to turn solid objects into vaporous scents: signs and traces of things that have disappeared. Thus he can call attention to the process of transformation itself, to a world suddenly made unstable by synaesthetic fusions (golden sobs, black perfume) or by metamorphic combinations where one reality (smoke or perfume) adopts the form of another (the female body).

Similarly, Mallarmé, who had the greatest influence of all nineteenth-century French poets on the development of symbolism, was fascinated by evanescences: by those amorphous things (the changing contours of a vase) and those transformative movements (a woman's hair or the colors of a setting sun) best able to give "form"—ghostly, ephemeral form—to an abstract world of ineffable ideas compressed into a poetry whose power of evocation was equal to that of music. Mallarmé was sensitive to the material and sensual object (a bed, a vase, a flower, a book, a swan) but only insofar as this object could be experienced as the starting point for the sublimation and spiritualization of the world. Mallarmé accepts the object but only in order to flee its rawness and the weight of its matter. He withdraws, the critic Jean-Pierre Richard writes, from "the brutality of things" because at the heart of his aesthetics is found "an existential refusal of *matter*." What attracts him in an object is "less the weight of its presence than the trembling of its disappearance."[15]

The key to Mallarmé's aesthetics, it would seem, is the phenomenon of vaporization: How, in other words, to vaporize the word so that the images and associations it evokes become mobile and unstable and therefore more evocative? Where is "the power capable of lightening the heaviness common to language and of making this language transparent and permeable to every dream fantasy," Richard asks (391)? How to ensure that the word, while remaining formally anchored in the poem, shifts, turns, and disappears (like vapor and scent) within an ephemeral constellation of meanings? How to vaporize the movements of a dancer's body so that the changing forms it enacts will poignantly write themselves into and then out of being? How to vaporize an object, like a flower or a cigar, or hair or even the sun, so that as the object moves from a material to an immaterial state, or from a sensual to a spiritual condition, or from life to death, it becomes a breath which, at the moment before being exhaled and disappearing into nothingness, expresses the plenitude of an existence that can only be intimated because it is impersonal and ideal? Mallarmé's poetics of vaporization is rooted in the phenomenon of respiration. The acts of inhaling and exhaling enact a drama of spiritual creation where breathing is tantamount to living and dying.

Mallarmé's aesthetics of vaporization and respiration and his poetic dramatization of vaporous emanations contain a clear, though latent, allusion to the scented imagination. In using music to make the object volatile, to turn it into air or "ambiance," as Richard remarks (394), Mallarmé envisions a poetry of dispersion where every thing solid has the potential to melt into thin air, becoming no more than a trail, a trace, or a wake of what it once was. In many ways, perfume is a bottled ambiance awaiting release. The constellation of elements constituting the imaginary associations generated by a given perfume—the scent, the bottle, the name, the romantic or erotic image, the concept or idea—gives rise to an aura that infiltrates and then imposes itself on the world. That Mallarmé sees music as the means to accomplish this metamorphosis of the object into atmosphere suggests the similarity between the way both song and scent fill the air. Moreover, Mallarmé's desire to possess (through its "transposition" into language) "a phenomenon of nature in its almost final quivering evanescence" and to reveal the pure idea "emanating" from this self-abolishing disappearance calls to mind the events of absence and presence characteristic of the volatilization of perfume. Disappearance wedded to the idea of permanence, so common to the aesthetics of perfume, suggests a typically Mallarméan paradox: namely, the reality of something potently filling a space which it empties (and from which it disappears) at the same time. The odor molecules that define the olfactory reality of a flower (a true "phenomenon of nature," if there ever was one) are captured and then "transposed" into a liquid (perfume) whose production has necessitated the disappearance (in more technical terms, the distillation or maceration or decomposition) of the material object (the flower). And the odor molecules defining the sensory reality of a bottled scent (also "a phenomenon of nature") are, once they are exposed to skin and air, dispersed and "transposed" into a vapor through a volatilization totally dependent on the disappearance (namely, the evaporation) of the liquid. In both instances, the presence of one state of being requires the annulling—the abolishing (to use a favorite Mallarméan word)—of another.

Ultimately, what Mallarmé seeks is not the transformation of one state into another (solid into gas, let us say) or of one object into another (flower into perfume). Rather, what intrigues him is the elevation of the object through its spiritualized dispersion, its act of absenting itself, to the level of idea and symbol and its consequent purification as an abstraction. Mallarmé does not seek a purer scent or a purer flower. What he desires is the universal, abstract, and pure Idea of scent or of flower which transcends the particular, material, and sensual experience of scent or flower. "I say: a flower!" Mallarmé writes. "And out of the oblivion, where my voice consigns no contour [or form] other than the sepals [seen and] known, there arises musically—an idea at once selfsame and fragrant—the absent flower of every bouquet" (II: 213). In other words, not only should the saying of a word ("flower") give rise to the image the word evokes (of a flower) or the associations (to the flower's scent or color) the word brings to mind; but the saying of "flower" should call into being out of emptiness ("oblivion") the pure notion or idea, the pure "flowerness," of the flower. Curiously, the sublime appearance of the flower as idea—an idea that despite its spiritualization still has the sweetness of music or the pleasantness of fragrance—comes into being as music: that is, as an art, unlike poetry, with an infinity of non-linear, synthetic, and choral combinations. And what this music of pure form expresses, according to Mallarmé, is the Flower of all flowers—evoked but never stated, hidden but never formed, present but forever absent—to such a degree that within every real bouquet it becomes its sublime, ineffable, and phantom symbol. The withdrawal of the flower from the sensual world, its literal abstraction, produces an emptiness; but this gap is soon filled by the fullness of the emptiness that has just taken place. The generation of this absence coincides with and is translated through the wordless abstraction, the symbol, which has been evoked.

Perfume in Mallarmé also has a cosmic resonance. Recalling a childhood dream the poet re-imagines a flower exploding into a multitude of petals which snow like "white bouquets of perfumed stars" ("Apparition," I: 7). The metaphor links an experience of bliss to a vision of snow, flowers, constellations, and a sensation of milky-whiteness, all enveloped in a scent that is literally "heavenly" or at least astral; the stars emit perfume; the snow is fragrant; even whiteness has its own aroma. Moreover, perfume in Mallarmé's poetry has a repressed and latent eroticism. In "Eventail (de Méry Laurent)" (I: 68), a late, short, dedicatory poem describing the to-and-fro movement of a fan whose rhythmic waving recalls the beating of a wing, the poet celebrates the power of the fan (and by implication the power of the cadenced to-ing and fro-ing of his poem) to express the scent, and therefore the spirit and essence, of a beloved woman. The waving of the fan stirs the woman—Mallarmé calls it a liberation—from a state of lethargy and "frigidity," awakening her to life and laughter and intensifying her desire to "flower drunkenly." So the fan, impregnated with perfume as was the custom in the late nineteenth century, is praised by the poet for being a better, more appropriate "container" for the beloved than a perfume bottle could ever be. Yet, the fan does more than just contain; it disseminates and impregnates the air with "the emanating aroma" of the woman, Méry. The poem-fan holds the essence of the beloved within the fabric and structural stays of both the fan and the poem. Such containment involves as well a paradoxical opening out, a deployment, by which Méry's scent is propelled and literally expressed into the atmosphere. Through the unfurling of the fan, the best perfume bottle imaginable according to Mallarmé, and through its rhythmic beating, which is also a kind of breathing out, a process of volatilization occurs. Aromatic spirits, poetic words, and melodic sounds rise all at once into the air. The poem, for Mallarmé, is not merely a bottle, but a process of dissemination and dispersion. Writing produces words and sounds from which a spirit, once unfurled, emanates into the world, assisted by the waving, cadenced motion inherent to the music, imagery, and meaning of the words. Not only is the poem a fan, or even the rhythmic beating of this fan; it is a perfume and the point of departure for this perfume as it impregnates the air with the scent of its sounds and the fragrance of its meaning: "The aroma emanates from Méry," the poet writes alliteratively. In "Eventail" Mallarmé figures a drama of expression, through an allegorical image of perfume, here imagined not as a static, contained fragrance but rather as one that is spiritually poetic, because it breathes itself into the substanceless air of the world. From the waving of the fan, perfume arises as a trace, a spiral, an arabesque, and a melody: in other words, a writing on the wind.

The trajectory of Mallarmé's thought, as we have seen, moves inexorably toward spiritualization even when the poet contemplates a trivial object like a cigar, a common animal like a swan, or an everyday occurrence, like fashion. In *La Dernière Mode* (*The Latest Fashion*), the short-lived fashion magazine he founded between September and December 1874, Mallarmé, writing under three pseudonyms, praises the couturier Charles Frederick Worth, the first designer of haute couture and the first to use live models to show his dresses, as the creator of "a *toilette* as fleeting as our thoughts." Ball gowns may begin with fabric, Mallarmé observes, but they soon evoke ethereal, conceptual realities. "By elevating the act of walking to

that superior form called dance," they "render light, ❧ (*Baume de la Mecque*), endowed with the magical power of
vaporous, and airy the goddess who appears in their preserving youthful skin, removing crow's feet, hiding
cloud."[16] The search for Beauty through the tangible and rings around the eyes, covering freckles, age spots, and
sensual realities of fashion (fabric, cut, feel, and smell) sunburn, and, finally, turning a beard blue and hair green.
demonstrates the fundamental spirituality of women. "A But if one really wishes a potent scent, Montesquiou drolly
woman," he writes, "isolated from politics and gloomy concludes, one need only distill an extract of cow paddies
cares has the necessary leisure, once her *toilette* has been and name it "bouquet de mille fleurs" (*Le Chef*, 216–17).
brought to completion, to satisfy her need to adorn the
soul." Women "love verses as much as perfumes and jewels." Generally speaking, Montesquiou was rarely so flip-
Considering that "there are no longer any male readers, only pant or droll about perfume in his poetic work *Le Chef des*
women readers," a book of verse, writes Mallarmé, has the *odeurs suaves* (The Master of Fragrant Scents), the title of
same power of fascination as a bottle of perfume. It is an which he had borrowed from the name of a character in
object of refinement, elegance, and distinction; it enters Flaubert's novel, *Salammbô*, of 1862. Montesquiou's *The*
memory as scent enters the nose. One has only to "let a vol- *Master of Fragrant Scents*, a title that plays on the double
ume stay a week half-opened like a scent bottle, resting on meaning of the French word "le chef" (the human head
silken cushions embroidered with imaginative fantasies" and, by metaphorical extension, a leader or chief) is com-
and the spirit, perhaps even the essence, of both bottle and posed of nearly four hundred pages of erudite, precious,
book will fill the room and the mind (II: 495–96). In the sometimes mediocre, symbolist-inspired poems about
"Gazette de la Fashion," which the pseudonymous Miss flowers and their "suave" or sweet fragrances. "Montesquiou
Satin writes in the last number (20 December 1874) of *La* polished off a thousand sonnets, his hand ringed with
Dernière Mode Mallarmé shows how aware he is of the spir- black pearls," the writer Paul Morand observed nastily,
itual and ghostly elevation that the poetics of perfume wed- "and will leave only a few modern style curiosities and
ded to the poetics of naming sets in motion. He counsels his Mallarméan pastiches written in red ink and powdered
feminine readers to try scents like "*Eau de Toilette au Lait* with gold dust." Yet, Morand misjudges the importance of
d'Hébé" or "*Oppoponax . . . Exora, Ylang-Ylang*, or *Celtic* Montesquiou as a cultural presence, an arbiter of elitist
Spikenard" with powers both olfactory and poetic: these taste, and a "Professor of Beauty," as Proust once called
fragrances are "strange but pleasurable fancies whose scent, him. Indeed, Montesquiou was both an expert in the ele-
when inhaled, inspires dreams just as their names do when gance of dress and an impresario of decadence and aes-
merely spoken." To give perfume to a woman as a gift, sug- theticism.[17] These qualities were not lost on the crowds of
gests Mallarmé, promises a more intimate and meaningful young women and men, enamored of Beauty, who fervently
relationship: "Does a container of perfume," he asks in a admired the Count, despite his eccentricities, and attended
voice more that of a salesman than that of a poet, "not the poetry readings he gave in various Paris salons or the
enclose a sensual delight completely different from the joy soirées he organized in his apartment on the rue Franklin
afforded by a bag of bonbons?" (II: 640–41). or at his estate in Versailles where Sarah Bernhardt often
read his poems aloud (Bertrand, II, 809–11). If truth be
told, Montesquiou lived the symbolist and the art nouveau
aesthetic on a daily basis; he transformed it into a decor
and a home. He made it habitable for those with the financial means and the spiritual imagination to make of Art a

Poetry, Perfume, and Suavity: Count Robert de Montesquiou

refuge and a life—as well as a form of dress. For his morning sorties, for example, the Count favored suits of white
serge with a black boater. He was one of the first Frenchmen
to wear a tuxedo in the evenings, although it was made of
velvet and colored scarab green or bordeaux red (Jullian,
The symbolist attitude toward perfume had, as Mallarmé's *Robert de Montesquiou*, 120).
advice demonstrates, its pragmatic, if not humorous,
side. Even a dandy like Robert de Montesquiou-Fezensac Montesquiou is important also because, more than
exhibits a sense of humor, touched by sarcasm, of course. any other poet of his time, he knew how to articulate the
After satirizing in a poem the witches' brew that had once cultural and symbolic images associated with perfume—
passed for perfume and cosmetics in medieval times, he its blend of exoticism, enchantment, violence, eroticism,
pokes fun at the hyperbole of the advertising prospectuses and dream—which belle epoque women, art nouveau
from the 1830s—like the ones Balzac spoofed in *César* designers, and symbolist writers were perceiving in the
Birotteau—which had been used to convince the public wind of fin de siècle France as well as in the air of the 1900
that perfume had regenerative powers. A mixture of pigeon Paris Exhibition. Given his exquisite skill at naming and
entrails, dragon's blood, a thigh of veal, beef gall, white describing scents and his extraordinary knowledge of
honey, egg white, fish paste, frog spawn, candied sugar, gold flowers Montesquiou was commissioned by Madame
leaf, wine vinegar, and milk from a black cow is crushed, Klotz, owner of the Pinaud perfume company, to write a
ground, heated, and cooled in a variety of distilling appa- report on the exhibition of perfumes, scented boxes, per-
ratuses. The result? An exotic balm, named for Mecca

fume burners, and various types of bottles belonging to the perfume in general, is, he recognizes, both fleeting collection of her husband, Victor Klotz, which was to be exhibited at the Exhibition's Perfume Pavilion. Under a wordy title—*Retrospective Exhibition of Perfume (Its Primary Ingredients, Materials, Processes, and Products) at the 1900 Paris World Exhibition. A Report by the Count Robert de Montesquiou*—the text gave readers a short history of perfumery from the Greeks to the end of the nineteenth century. The Klotz collection, along with a few other objects lent by Guerlain and other perfumers, comprised, according to Montesquiou's *Retrospective*, a total of 488 objects. Bottles cast from twenty or so different kinds of glass and in Louis XV and Louis XVI styles were displayed side by side with scented balls, composed mostly of ambergris, and necklaces of small "pearls" each made of similar hardened ambergris paste. Particularly attractive to Montesquiou were the mottos (what we would call slogans today) inscribed on the neck or other surfaces of the bottles; they ranged from "You trouble my sleep" to "Love guides my steps" and "I hold the secret of beauty." Equally alluring to him were perfume labels like the one for the Restoration cologne *Eau des montagnes russes* (see fig. 34, page 81), which he reproduces in his text. The report also included a list of the perfume exhibitors displaying their wares at the Perfume Pavilion or, as Montesquiou preferred to call it, "our museum of scents." Montesquiou ended his written text with a full-page illustration of Larmessin's *The Perfumer's Costume* (see fig. 8, page 38). When eventually republished in an expanded edition, the *Rapport*'s title was blessedly shortened to the more poetic, *Land of Scents (Pays des Aromates)*, a work Proust greatly admired.[18] Indeed, Proust's praise of the book becomes dramatically more meaningful when his words are taken as a prefiguration of what, a decade later, would become the major theme of his *Remembrance of Things Past*:

> From these scent boxes whose odors once perfumed rosy faces, long ago turned to dust, from these perfume fountains which no longer retain their "scented memory," and above all from these infinitely graceful and profound pages, it seems that something troubling and delightful, although supremely intangible, escapes: namely, the melancholic odor, the "imperishable Perfume," of the Past.

The past continuously emits an odor of sadness. But suddenly and quite unexpectedly, as Proust's protagonist, Marcel, will learn from smelling and tasting the *petite madeleine* or from tripping on a cobblestone in *Remembrance of Things Past*, melancholy may turn to joy when the past, made odorous by its "imperishable perfume," returns. It is interesting that for Proust, reading Montesquiou in 1901, the odor of the past is already simultaneously "melancholic"—the result of a loss caused by oblivion—and "imperishable": the result of a resurrection provoked by involuntary memory. The past, not unlike perfume in general, is, he recognizes, both fleeting and tenacious.

Montesquiou, like Mallarmé, experienced things—a fragrance, a flower, a glass vase, furniture, clothing, a bat, a peacock—as endowed with physical and spiritual being; they possessed, he believed, "an exquisite soul" (*Le Chef*, 95). They were symbols that could speak of other places, other realities. Montesquiou's poetic imagination prized what in the world was most ephemeral and fugitive. "I am the sovereign of fleeting things," he wrote in his 1892 collection, *The Bats* (*Les Chauves-Souris*), a work that valued what was most subtle and suggestive in life: "I am" he boasts, "the sharp-eyed stenographer of nuance." In other words, Montesquiou's imagination moved like perfume. It danced through the world, silently and dreamily, expanding and rising with the lightness and grace of a scent. It sought to capture the elusive signs and nuances of a fleeting reality and to seize, stenograpically as it were, the traces and arabesques of its evasive writing. Montesquiou was captivated by the elusiveness of objects, by how much like a perfume the things of the world could be in their movements and metamorphoses. Faithful symbolist that he was, Montesquiou was drawn to phenomena touched by that loss of being which perfume enacts and which art can express but never arrest: "I continuously seek, oh I who move from side to side without respite, / the stream one cannot grasp."[19]

That Montesquiou was what the French call an "olfactif," a man with a refined sense of smell, cannot be denied. Poetry is for him a garden where he works as a "gardener-poet" (*Le Chef*, 279), a "florist of delights" and of "ecstasies," cultivating "hyacinths / Of the Unreal," "Tulips / Of Infinitude," and "clods / Of the Ideal" (*Le Chef*, 381–82). Few are the things, objects, and natural phenomena that Montesquiou fails to perfume in *The Master of Fragrant Scents*, a work that makes reference to over one hundred different kinds of flowers and scents. Prayers smell "balsamic" (xiii) as does lightning (279). Kisses express "arôme" and "amour" (255) all the more so considering that the word "amour" is a nearly complete anagram for "arôme." Laughter has its own kind of incense (213); floral expressions of anger and rage thunder in the air like "perfumed storms" (36); the scents of flowers, sounding the passage of the hours, make "perfuming and speaking simultaneous" (292); and poems, as the refuge of scents, the place where they survive, learn to speak odorously: "In my rhymes, I inhale again / What these rhymes have taken from perfumes" (264). In Montesquiou's world, fragrances see, hear, speak, touch, breathe, tell time, and of course smell; they "speak to the five senses which become one" (277). In addition to being audible, this olfactory speaking can produce a unique writing. Perfume has its own grammar. The rules of its vocabulary and syntax dictate how to go about conjugating the language of odors and poems. Thus scents emerge from "infinitives of odors"; they can make the present tense of verbs aromatic. The poem is a container, a vase, a bottle where new effusions are blended, new sensations created, new meanings generated, and "where syntax lives / bursts forth, blooms, takes on color, becomes nuanced, / Gives off fragrance, evaporates, impregnates, penetrates" (312–13). All in all, a poem is "un bal des odeurs," a gala of scents.[20]

Enfleurage

Imagined as a vase or a bottle, the poem can be said to propel scents into the air as does a flower or Mallarmé's waving fan. Yet, the poem can also absorb fragrances. In "Enfleurage" ("Inflowering") Montesquiou poetically describes one of the oldest and most costly (and therefore now abandoned) methods of perfume production (see page 110). In this process, petals, most often of jasmine or tuberose, are spread across a glass plate which has been framed in wood. Cold animal fat of a high quality (usually pork) is spread in layers one-centimeter thick across both sides of the glass and then covered with flowers. Fresh petals are added every two days until the fat has become saturated with the floral scent; this fragrant, fatty substance is called a "pomade." A solvent of alcohol is then used to separate the precious floral essences from the fat, resulting in an *essence absolue*, or simply "absolute," the most concentrated jasmine and tuberose extracts available (*H&R*, 68, 78, 98–99).

Montesquiou begins "Enfleurage" as if he were a perfumer spreading floral substances over a fat-encrusted glass plate, except that the fat corresponds here to the surface of the white page onto which the poet presses petals that are his words: "Onto the virginal leaves where my verses will come alive, / Each morning I place a leafy foliage or flowers" (*Le Chef*, 11). The "fatty" page will absorb the sentiments marked thereon by the words, which themselves will surrender the poet's essential feelings to the paper. Poetry is thus figured as a process of extracting essences from words. Absorption by the page allows for the transfer of these feelings to a new medium and space of expression. The feelings are made to "flower inside" or "within" (to "inflower," *en-fleurer*), and the poem records the act by which this expressing, this pushing outward, occurs. In this manner, nature literally passes into the written text. The poem becomes saturated with the world which has been pressed into it: "My art, infused with the force of life, is saturated / With an outline of the full sky, with an echo of true sound." On the chassis or frame of the poem, different flowers come together and different scents meet: the odor of verbena, the "lively, peppered scent of the carnation," the exotic "Japanese soul" of prune trees, the "pale strangeness" of hortensias (the Count's favorite flower), the purple of tulips, the sadness of irises, the gaiety of roses, and the glow of sunflowers.

Montesquiou's metaphor of enfleurage imagines flowers "inseminat[ing] the page"; but this fertilization also saves the flower from extinction. Absorbed by the poem, the rose or the hortensia is reborn in the music of words. Aroma is translated into sound and speech, as the flower "breathes its soul / Into the touching hemistich of my sovereign verse." And so mannered is Montesquiou's conceit of a flower finding refuge in lyrical song that he imagines a "buzz," namely, that of the "bee of rhyme," coming from within the poem's lines. Redolent of fragrance, the poem, like the flower, attracts insects, except that in Montesquiou's imagination these insects are sounds; the aromatic pollen of speech and the fragrant honey of poetry are carried from word to word by this busy bee of rhyme.[21] The poem "Enfleurage" demonstrates skillfully, despite its mannered style, how perfume becomes poetry, how scent reawakens as music, and how, finally, a poem speaks through the dilation of its own vocal and audible wake. For Montesquiou, therefore, flowers are noises and scents sounds. Roses reverberate like brass instruments and from them "a pure voice evaporates" into the air until an ear "voluptuously . . . inhales" that voice (126). Olfaction and audition exchange roles so that perfumes become "melodic," flowers sonorous, and aromas "bruited about." One must listen to a flower, Montesquiou believes, as one listens to "incense sighing / And a *song* inhaled" (127).

The synaesthesia of perfume, music, and poetry, so eminently evoked in Montesquiou's poetry, played a significant role in his social life and inspired the Count's creative forays into the decorative arts. Decoration wedded to music and to writing informed the design of the domestic interiors he occupied (Bertrand, I: 94). A journalist writing in *La Liberté* in 1901 asserts that the Count was "the first to make perfume part of the decorative arts":

> The visitor entering his home feels his olfactory nerve stimulated by agreeable odors each of which has a symbolic meaning. A perfume burner had been installed in the room where one eats; another in the room where one smokes; another in the room where one sleeps; another in the room where one converses. And I believe that the scents varied depending on the nature of the discussions: those that inspired flirtatiousness were not those that encouraged talk of politics. All these emanations accumulated without blending together. In an atmosphere of sensual delight they enveloped all beings animate and inanimate: that is to say, the master of the household and his collection of hortensias (Bertrand, I:94).

Scents, moreover, were used, as Morand testifies, as a decorative motif at Montesquiou's celebrated parties. Guests would arrive after the dinner hour and once seated would listen to the young pianist Delafosse, Montesquiou's protégé, play the *Quintet of Flowers* "while perfumes, as if in response to the musical sounds, permeated the room."[22]

Fig. 56 While designing the art nouveau entrances to the Paris métro between 1899 and 1904, with their intertwined tendrils and leaves, architect Hector Guimard created this crystal perfume bottle, literally bulging with life, for Félix Millot's *Kantirix* (1900), named for a Mexican flower.

❧ *Perfume at the 1900 Paris World Exhibition*

If Montesquiou had really been the first to conceive of perfumes as decor—there is indeed a long tradition going back to Hebrew and Egyptian times of filling rooms with scents—then the custom must have reached its operatic apogee in the spectacular party for three hundred guests given by the Paris fashion designer Paul Poiret at his Faubourg St. Honoré home on the night of June 24, 1911. Poiret's dress designs were freeing women from the constraints of corsets and from the masses of crinolines that had made them look like ships under sail. Inspired by the Russian impresario Sergei Diaghilev's *Ballets Russes*, which began its performances in Paris in 1909, Poiret designed exotic, brilliantly colored tunics or haremlike dresses in a striking "orientalist" motif; he encouraged women to give up their voluminous hats for turbans and bobbed hair. To his June 1911 costume party, a giant theatrical production of Persian inspiration, he gave the name "One Thousand and Second Nights." Despite the freedom of movement that the uncorseted Poiret woman was beginning to enjoy, the theme of Poiret's costume party—the allusion to Scheherazade and the seraglio—was hardly liberating. Upon entering the garden of Poiret's townhouse guests were confronted, the designer recalls in his autobiography, by "an immense golden cage latticed with twisted fittings inside which I had locked my favorite woman (Madame Poiret), surrounded by her maids in waiting." Water flowed in thin jets around plants, and pink ibises shared the garden with live monkeys, macaws, and parrots. At a predetermined moment Poiret rose from his seat and advanced to the cage where his wife, "the queen of the harem," waited. As he set her free, a tearing sound suddenly reverberated in the night air, and a cascade of golden and silver fire burst forth running down the steps of the terrace. Into this colonialist mise-en-scène of costume, color, fire, and music came perfumes: "As twenty black men and twenty black women kept perfume burners supplied with myrrh and incense, scenting the atmosphere in bluish smoke, a flute and a cither played in a copse and clouded everyone's senses." Perhaps among other things, it was the memory of this remarkable party, as much a creation of Poiret's imagination as were the different scents his perfume company (Parfums de Rosine) would launch a few years later, that inspired the fashion and perfume designer Marcel Rochas to offer the following tribute to Poiret and his innovative fragrances: "His perfumes are the lavish dreams, it seems, of a poet. A whole imaginative world surges forth as if by enchantment from the dream of One Thousand and One Nights. Sometimes it is *Aladdin* and all the wonders of magnificent Moorish palaces or . . . *Antinéa*, the sharp fragrance of algae at the bottom of the sea . . . [or] the childish whims of Rosine, his precious daughter, in 'Le *Mouchoir de Rosine*,' . . . a rainbow of attributes, the very medium of Modern Art."[23]

While perfume and fragrance were only bit players in Poiret's 1911 extravaganza, their presence was not overlooked by a Parisian society driven for many years by a fascination with the exotic fragrances of the Orient. The Paris Exhibition of 1900 had released a plethora of strange aromas into the air of the city: scents that were olfactory equivalents of the exotic sights, sounds, and tastes offered to the forty-eight million French and foreign visitors who flocked to the Exhibition between April and November. Again, Paul Morand is a reliable historian, this time testifying to the enticing smells that stimulated his twelve-year-old's imagination. Twice a week he drank tea at the Ceylon pavilion. Ambling through the villages and other installations which foreign exhibitors had constructed beneath the Eiffel Tower and on the heights of the Palais du Trocadéro, or stopping to watch natives at work in front of their huts, or consuming fragrant foods at different ethnic restaurants, Morand was passionately moved by the sensual blend of scent and sound, sight and taste, and more than a bit impressed, it should be added, by the chauvinistic spirit of French imperialist and colonialist history which the Exhibition glorified: "The entire hill was nothing but perfumes, incense, vanilla, the aromatic fumes of the seraglio. I followed this opiate mixture, this perfume of Javanese dancing girls, sherbets and rahat-lakoum, as far as the Dahomean village." In addition to scenting the air of the Champ de Mars and its environs with heavily aromatic and opiate fragrances, perfume at the 1900 Exhibition inspired a new kind of invisible, although no less potent, decor and architecture.[24] At the Perfume Pavilion, luxuriously constructed around a central fountain from which the different exhibition spaces radiated, perfume was not only decor but also ornament. Several perfumers hired talented art nouveau decorators to design their spaces and their bottles. Piver engaged Edouard Colonna, the designer of a celebrated room in the Bing Pavilion, a small mansion especially constructed for the Exhibition whose interior has been called "one of the most elegant and avant-garde examples of Art Nouveau furniture and hangings" (Jullian, *The Triumph*, 116–17). To design and decorate its stand Houbigant hired the poster artist Alfons Mucha whose art nouveau posters for Sarah Bernhardt's performances, for "Job" cigarettes (1896, 1898) and for beer, chocolate, and railroad companies during the last half of the 1890s were widely popular. The perfumer Félix Millot commissioned Hector Guimard to design not only his exhibition stand but also a special bottle incorporating the architect's sinuous, floral lines, which were beginning to appear in the wrought-iron entrances Guimard was creating for Paris métro stations. Guimard's bottle, strikingly vertical except for a large, rounded exuberant bulge protruding from one side of the flacon, was incised with sinuous tendrils and what seems to be the image of a plume-tailed bird or other creature (fig. 56). Another somewhat similar Guimard design, also for Millot's perfume *Kantirix*—in a bottle decorated with abstract, curvilinear lines, possibly imitating the floating tendrils of seaweed—was presented as well. Houbigant, in contrast to the perfume it had produced for the earlier 1889 Paris Exhibition—called *Souvenir de l'Exposition,* it featured on its label a bird's-eye view of the Eiffel Tower—launched a more romantic scent, *Coeur de Jeannette,* created by its owner Paul Parquet to commemorate the start of the 1900 Exhibition; on the perfume's red and green label, a stylized heart-shaped flower was prominently displayed. Incidentally, Houbigant's scent *Parfum Idéal,* a name most certainly consonant with symbolist aesthetics, also appeared in 1900 as did Rigaud's *Modern Style,* yet another name by which art nouveau was known.[25]

Economically, perfume had by 1900 become a good-sized industry with 300 manufacturers employing more than 2,000 retailers and providing a livelihood to a total of 20,000 people. A third of the industry's revenues came solely from exports. It is not surprising, therefore, that the 1900 Exhibition would feature a host of perfumers, like Piver, Lubin, Rigaud, Houbigant, and Guerlain, exhibiting large displays of their many products. The two decades preceding the Exhibition had witnessed the development of a new marketing strategy involving the organization of fragrance products in groups of "families" or "lines." The perfume or "extract," usually endowed with a distinctive, eye-catching name, represented the "matriarch," so to speak, of the line. The bath oils, creams, lotions, talcum powders, and other scented products (including the box and other packaging)—"offspring" spawned by the primary perfume—carried the same image and decorative detail; they displayed a replica of the name, label, and overall design of the perfume bottle. Roger & Gallet's *Violette de Parme* (1884), created to respond to the late nineteenth century's obsessive taste for violets (from the 1850s on women had even injected infusions of the scent under their skin) could be purchased, for example, in several different formats: extract, toilet water (for the bath), soap, oil, brillantine, pomade, cosmetics, and sachets. Roger & Gallet's famous *Vera Violetta* (True Violet), created in 1892, was available thirteen years later in sixteen different coordinated products. Behind this marketing strategy was the concept, already widely practiced among fashion houses, of attracting the consumer through an unending production of new scents, which, since they were not designed to have a long commercial life and in fact did quickly become obsolete, shows how truly remarkable the survival of perfume "classics" like Guerlain's *Jicky* from 1889 or Coty's *L'Origan* from 1905 was. To give an idea of this expanded perfume production, in the decade from 1890 to 1900 Guerlain launched an unheard-of ten perfumes a year. According to certain experts, the perfumes on display at the 1900 Paris Exhibition were abundant but not, aside from a few technically innovative scents, all that original. "It did not display,"

a former curator of the Musée de Grasse observed, "a creative spirit corresponding to the bold inventions of Art Nouveau," although this would change dramatically when, in 1904, Coty, "the Napoleon of perfume" as he would be called, began selling his first fragrance.[26]

In addition to the many precious and rare objets d'art displayed at the Perfume Pavilion during the Exhibition, there was one item that attracted many curious visitors and the attention of Montesquiou, for he makes mention of it in his report. It was a simple glass perfume bottle from the Restoration called "Vrai Vinaigre des quatre voleurs" (Authentic Vinegar of the Four Thieves) manufactured by the company of Maille et Aclocque, official vinegar-distillers to the king, and filled with an alcoholic mixture known for its stimulating, restorative, and pharmaceutical properties. Maille, an eighteenth-century distiller, had been the first to add perfume to the vinegar that, since the early seventeenth century, had replaced water as a means of fortifying the epidermis and refreshing the skin. The bottle was displayed at the Perfume Pavilion, Montesquiou reports, with a notice to the effect that "This bottle has never been opened and still contains the well-known scent." The bottle's label, which may not have been displayed when Montesquiou visited the exhibit, is composed of four panels, each showing a different thief in the act of committing a different crime. All four thieves look furtively over their shoulders to see if they are being watched. The first robber lifts bags of money or gold from a strong box; the second exits a house with a valuable clock in hand; the third furtively removes some item from a bureau or desk; and the fourth carrying small suitcases steals away from a coach. The fragrance and its label date from 1838. The attraction of this bottle for visitors to the Perfume Pavilion must have resided in the imagined longevity of the scent's power, although there was no way, the bottle having never been opened, to verify that the odor was still refreshing. Yet, the bottle and its scented vinegar were "relics" of a faraway time, and the allure of its history and the myth of its imperishability must have impressed the public. Moreover, here was an early form of scent which carried with it its own narrative and legend going back to the seventeenth century. During one of the plague epidemics which ravaged Toulouse early in that century, there were, so the myth goes, four thieves, seemingly untouched by the disease, who were arrested in the act of robbing the homes and looting the bodies of the dying and dead. Their immunity had come, they admitted, from an unguent called "Vinegar of the Four Thieves" which they had applied to their hands and face so as to avoid contagion. The vinegary, alcoholic mixture—its formula continued to appear in the French pharmacopoeia well into the 1880s—was composed of absinthe, lavender, mint, rosemary, and rue (some say garlic as well). The city immediately distributed posters informing the public of the prophylactic potential of the new substance; but its antiseptic qualities, alas, were not sufficiently potent to prevent the thieves from being summarily hung.[27]

"Perfumed Flutterings": Scents and Memories in Charles Cros and Émile Zola

A scent's persistence and longevity can have a powerful, almost mythic seductiveness. At the time Montesquiou came across the bottle of "Authentic Vinegar of the Four Thieves," the fragrance was already enveloped in an aura of magic: namely, the power to cleanse, refresh, and ward off disease, something with which perfume had habitually been associated during the plague years. If perfume disappears into thin air, it also survives. This permanence makes perfume an ideal metaphor for the endurance of love, the eternality of life, and the immortality of the soul. The Parnassian poet Leconte de Lisle, whose love of Greek and Indian civilizations was often expressed in his poetry, published a poem in the early 1880s, "Le Parfum imperissable," (Immortal Perfume) to which Proust in 1901 made reference in his praise of Montesquiou and for which Gabriel Fauré composed a musical score in 1897. De Lisle imagines a perfume, composed of roses and contained in a bottle made of clay or crystal or gold, which is poured onto an expanse of burning sand. The absorbent sand becomes yet another, larger container for the scent, one that covers an extensive space, both geographical and psychological. The perfume remains indelible. Rivers and the ocean, in their vastness and with all their destructive energy, wash over the beach, but in vain. The "divine aroma" of the "perfumed grains" of sand is protected. De Lisle's description of perfume's dispersion, expansion, and preservation is only a metaphor, however, for the imperishability of the poet's love. From his pierced heart wounded by a woman, a "celestial liqueur," the indelible scent of love, flows. The beloved may have departed, but love ("inexprimable amour"), intensely alive within the poet's being like sand imprinted with the ineffaceable perfume it has absorbed, remains eternal: "My heart," the poem concludes, "is embalmed with immortal odor!"[28]

Having "poured" the perfume of his heart onto the "sand" of his poem, the poet transfers the undying odor of love from the self to language; the poem is the new flask. Similarly, for Charles Cros, an impressionist poet and symbolist before symbolism became a full-fledged movement, whose most important work *The Sandalwood Chest (Le Coffret de Santal)* was published in 1873, it is not just the poem but rather an entire collection of poems that must serve as the container, the perfumed "coffer," that a poet offers to his beloved, in this instance a woman named Nina. "Your captivating summer scent," he writes in the work's dedication, "Alone, among others, has remained."[29] The fragrance that becomes word is the fragrance that does not disappear. This can be a disadvantage, especially when the poet wishes to forget. The beloved stays with him "like a warm perfume incapable of decay" (137); even when she

has angered him, he cannot escape her "foul smoke" (137). Glancing at his empty bed Cros is overcome by the odors, the "persuasive perfumes," which the memory of lovemaking recalls (155). The sensuality and physicality of perfume—and Cros was a daringly erotic poet for his time—awaken life, illuminate the night, disperse sadness, and inaugurate presence in the place of absence: "Smiles, flowers, kisses, essences, / After such insipid concerns / After such dull absences / Perfume the air of my nights! / Illuminate my fantasy / . . . / And drench me in your ambrosia, / Your long glances, lilies, lips, sandalwood" (88). Cros's universe is fragrant in different ways: his "mouth scented / From the warm touch of her breasts" (93); his face caressed by the wind carrying the "perfume of her kiss" (93); his mind possessed by "an earlier life / Whose scents pursue me" (125); and his entire being "intoxicated with vetiver and ambergris" (136). Perfumes, like the art of decor and furniture, are, truly, "doors opening on to the imaginary" (200).

Cros, like Mallarmé, turns a perfumed fan into a poem. Entitled "Madrigal: Translated From the Top of Lady Hamilton's Fan" (204–05), it opens with a statement—"Time, that implacable alchemist, will consume the warm scent of sandalwood"—which the poem will ultimately contradict. This is so because the words written on the fan (and, by implication, recorded in the poem) will survive the passage of years. After the scents have disappeared, after youth has lost its radiance, and after flesh has "withered slowly in the wind of old age, to be dispersed finally in the brown earth," words will give birth anew to the "immaterial scents of memory." Memory as an odor and words as the writing of that odor will replace the real fragrances that had once perfumed the present. This is an ephemeral moment coincident with the poem in which the woman's body has the color of dawn, her hair the insolence of flame, and her eyes the transparence of an unearthly beauty. Even the fan is not immune to decrepitude. "Sold, bought, resold, dirtied in drawers, broken by children, a worthless curio among bric-à-brac, burned perhaps," it will fall to pieces and then into oblivion. Except that the woman's fan, flesh, and perfume—the material objects of the poet's world—once recast as poetic language will triumphantly endure; they will become "sovereign." The woman's allure, as seen by the poet and captured in his poem, is "the visible ring in the perpetual chain of her beauty; what has shone once shines forever, in the absolute." Cros concludes with a celebration of the immortality of poetry, especially its power to recall memory and resurrect the aroma of the past: "These words that speak of you, having passed from memory to memory, will unendingly give new life to the sovereign hand that held this fan and to the flesh it caressed with its perfumed flutterings." That the poem flutters with the beats of its own rhythms and sounds and that the woman's body is enveloped by the aura of perfume emanating from the fan as well as from the poem point to the to-and-fro movement of words, envisioned by Cros as floating like scents between a lost present and its resurrection in the future. The woman's "sovereign hand," waving the fan and diffusing perfume, turns into the poet's sovereign hand. The poetic word triumphs for Cros as it did for Mallarmé. The poem-fan like the poem-flacon internalizes the spirit of the past despite the evanescence of that spirit and that scent in the mortal, everyday world.

Although Cros admits that "carnal things die / Or fade away in the real air" (89), they do not become extinct. Poetry, through spiritualization and vaporization, as we saw in Mallarmé, transforms them into presence: "Forever does your beauty remain / In its immaterial cloud" (89). However, there are moments when for Cros the immaterial and spiritual are not enough. The poet wishes, poetically, to embrace the beloved, not as an idealized being but as a carnal, sensual presence—a difficult task given poetry's inherent tendency toward sublimation. He may wish to lose himself in an Eden of dreams, its "garden filled with blooming roses" and blue lakes (154). But in place of this illusory universe he prefers reality: the sensuous reality of the woman's laughter and the erotic carnality of her body. So her lips and teeth are "roses and lilies of the valley," her eyes are "sapphire lakes," her body an emanation of musk. The woman has a physical presence, but the more he describes her corporeal reality the more she takes on the presence of an objet d'art. As he evokes her sensuality, he starts to dream again. His intoxication becomes "oriental" as hashish and "rash desires" take control of him. Paradoxically, the beloved's beauty appears both erotic and aesthetic. Exotic, lapidary, and enveloped in a drug-inspired haze, this beauty seems otherworldy; yet, it remains anchored to a body: "More than in my most longed for fantasies / I found perfumes in the gold of your hair / And intoxication in your beautiful, wiry, enveloping arms."

This combat between fantasy and reality, imagination and the senses, and dream and carnality is lyrically dramatized in Cros's beautiful prose fantasy, "Distrayeuse" (The Distracting Woman, 197–99). Committed to writing a poetic celebration of the beloved, the poet strenuously resists the erotic befuddlement provoked by her body. He struggles to forget that she is in the room and that she is "beautiful," "white and undressed." Against her encroaching presence he concentrates on creating an abstract and otherworldly work of art, a poem. To that end it is necessary for the poet to cleanse his bedroom of the distracting scents emanating from a basket of "reseda, jasmine, and small red, yellow, and blue flowers." The sudden appearance in his imagination of a series of visions accomplishes this purifying task, and the poet surrenders to the dominating allure of their unreality. In taking control of the poet's spiritual being and bracketing his everyday world, these visionary images seek permanent and protected residence within the rhymes and rhythms of his art. So, grabbing pen and paper the poet begins to scribble away in an effort to capture these hallucinations. But the demands of his unworldly visions and his efforts to immortalize them on paper quickly come into conflict with the powerful reality of the here-and-now. The present moment works to reestablish its intrusive primacy and succeeds, indeed, when the scratch of pen on paper provokes a disturbingly unpoetic sound, rending the air like the "cry of a swallow skimming across a still lake." The bubble of dream and art has burst. And so in the wake of the screech and scratch of writing, a second sensual event interrupts the ethereal trajectory of the poem. The woman, unnoticed and marginal, calls attention to herself by shaking the bouquet of reseda and jasmine so that its petals and scents fall on to the page of paper. The distraction—of the prosaic world, the body, the senses, and eros—grows increasingly intrusive. Under active threat from flower and fragrance, the visions counterattack. They try to re-impose their empire by compelling the poet to blow away the floral blossoms which have come to rest on the page. Symbolically, the poet's exhalation has dissipated fragrance and dismissed the world in the same breath, restoring dominance to dream, fantasy, and, of course, art. Even as he is about to kiss the woman the poet feels the seductive, otherworldly visions with their "faraway odors" dancing once again in his imagination. And yet, the poet recognizes that, despite his having already captured one of these visions in the vise of a "tight stanza," the woman is much too physically present to be ignored, for as "she places her elbows on the low table next to me . . . her disturbing breasts caress the smooth paper."

The battle between the ideal and the real continues at a quickened pace. Like Ulysses, the poet closes his ears to the siren's erotic call. He pushes away the body, which in caressing the page of paper has interrupted his work; he reclaims the page which still awaits his hand and the completing of the poem's last line. But the woman finally extends her whole body over the sheet of paper and into the poem. Once and for all, the visions and fantasies disappear. Sensuality triumphs. Abandoning his self-involved concentration and writerly impulses, the poet loses himself in the woman's aromatic loveliness. His eyes become blind, his ears deaf, and his nose insensitive to everything but the body he embraces, a flesh-and-blood being enveloped by reseda, jasmine, and the fragrances of other flowers. Body thus negates poem, eros resists the sublimating power of art, and the physical experiences of smell and touch eclipse all forms of written expression.

Zola's Scents of Paris and Paradise

Cros's erotico-spiritual and erotico-aesthetic conception of scent and his ambivalence regarding the relationship between the real and the ideal, the physical and the aesthetic, differ from the ideas of the novelist Émile Zola, arguably one of the great sociologists of olfaction in literature. The description of urban smells in Zola's *Le Ventre de Paris* (The Belly of Paris, 1873), his novel about Les Halles, Paris's sprawling nineteenth-century market, are unmatched, as is

Fig. 57 The fragrant emanations of this perfume fountain (c. 1880), probably on display in a Parisian department store, attract a fashionable clientele to its four founts of scented water, all, alas, beyond reach.

his depiction of the exquisite scents hovering over the perfume department of Au Bonheur des dames (The Ladies' Delight), a fictional Parisian store which is the subject of Zola's novel of the same name (1883). Among the myriads of luxury goods filling the festive and sacred interior of this paradise and "chapel" of desire, which is the modern department store, can be found cases and shelves displaying pots of pomades and vials of fragrance. But even more wondrous and seductive to the ardent consumer of scents

is an ornate silver fountain "with a shepherdess seated on an abundance of flowers, and a continuous thin stream of violet water running from it and tinkling harmoniously into the metal basin." Here ladies dipped their handkerchiefs as they shopped (fig. 57).

Two years after the publication of Cros's *Sandalwood Chest*, and nearly a decade before Zola would write his novel about the department store, the novelist published *The Sin of Father Mouret* (*La Faute de l'abbé Mouret*) in

1875. The book recounts the fall from purity and innocence of a village priest seduced by the scents and aromas emanating from a private park and forest (a country paradise Zola names "Paradou") inhabited by Albine, a sixteen-year-old woman who is not only nature incarnate but the very embodiment of flower and scent. Her smell is that of "a great rose," "a large deeply aromatic bouquet"; her dress is described as capturing "the scent of the entire garden."[30] Emanating from her skin are the essential odors of the countryside which penetrate deeply into the psyche of the priest, Serge Mouret. Albine is a walking sachet and the brazier (cassolette) from which smoldering nature dispels into the air vapors of heady and sinful scent. Given Mouret's avid and obsessive love for the Virgin Mary—he prays for hours on end to her—and his keen sensitivity to smell—the Virgin is for him the celestial "mystic Rose" (126)—the priest will eventually surrender to the temptations of the flesh. Convalescing in the Eden of Paradou from a serious illness from which he is saved by Albine's ministrations, Mouret is literally reborn. He experiences a sensual reawakening, opening himself for the first time to "the smell of the earth, of dappled woods, of warm plants, of living creatures, a full bouquet of odors whose violent intensity pushed him to the edge of unconsciousness" (176).

In the early days of his convalescence Serge cannot support too much sensory reality: "The odor of roses is too strong for you," cautions Albine, a warning that will become prophetic (179). The garden and its surrounding forest are overrun with roses of all varieties, colors, and odors. Scent, not only of flowers but of love, is ubiquitous. It eroticizes the landscape. Sexuality becomes botanical; roses show off their nakedness like "bodices disclosing the treasures of the bust" (184). The aroma of roses expresses the aroma of the lovers' breath (189). Albine, her hair, ears, neck, and shoulders enveloped in a "cloak of roses," her feet, knees, and skirt, submerged in roses, her entire body "drenched in roseness" (181–82), becomes the "absolute essence" of florality and femininity. From her body emanates "the scent of the passionate woman," the natural woman (353). She is transformed not into a spiritual sublime but a physical, sensual sublime. The incense-laden atmosphere of the church yields to aromas of rose, lavender, reseda, jasmine, carnation, violet, tuberose, verbena, and to the scents of eros these flowers release. Moreover, in Albine's bedroom, where faded, nearly invisible representations of eighteenth-century lovers encircled by cupids cover the upper reaches of the walls, Serge and Albine feel the disquieting odor of the past, for the room seems "to tremble still from the rustle of a musked skirt, and the floor still preserved the scented softness of two satin slippers" (253).

In his dramatization of this tragedy of sensuality Zola conceives of scent as a fundamentally non-spiritual phenomenon corresponding to the primeval power of eros itself. Unlike Montesquiou, Mallarmé, or other symbolists, Zola looks at scent as unmediated reality, as nature at its most sensual, primal, and earthly. Fragrance is life at its most elemental, the very "odor of … fecundity" (369). Zola's scents do not go beyond the physical immediacy of the here-and-now; they are not signs of an otherworldly universe, invisible, ideal, and spiritual. Rather, they symbolize the kind of procreative pleasure that leads to the continuation of the species. No wonder then that, when Serge and Albine consummate their love in the dark shadows of a gigantic oak tree, all of nature applauds their physical union: "it was a triumph for the animals, the plants, the things that desired that these two children enter the eternal kingdom of life" (269). But such a kingdom is not to be. At the end of the novel, Albine submerges her deathbed in flowers of all kinds. Lying down to await the darkness, she "listens to odors that whisper" to her and play a "strange scented music." Strange, indeed, are these sounds, for they fuse into a music of perfume. Zola imagines scent and song, flower and fragrance, as inseparable. This symphony of scents begins with a "gay, childlike prelude," which, suddenly expanding on the "musked notes" of a flute, explodes into the peppery aroma of the brasses. The sharpness of the brasses is calmed by the chanting melody of a canticle composed of vanilla-scented heliotrope and by the whispering of "a discrete trill" which emanates from the petals of the mirabilis (belles-de-nuit). As it approaches its finale, the entire choral arrangement of odors swells into a "fanfare of roses," before descending into the "final sigh" of hyacinths and tuberoses, now enveloping the dead Albine (401–02).

The Spectacle of Scents: Woman as Advertisement

The fin de siècle, according to a number of observers, celebrated the cult of the woman. "Rarely," the historian Philippe Jullian states, "has an epoch been more obsessed with breasts and backsides. All stages of undress are displayed on walls by means of posters, on the stage and in the pages of magazines. . . . Courtesans are national figures, adultery an inexhaustible theme [for playwrights like] Feydeau and Bourget" (Robert de Montesquiou, 144–45). Proof of this fascination with the feminine is found in the 1900 Paris Exhibition, dominated as it was by female images: from the gigantic "La Parisienne" towering over the Porte Binet, the exhibition's main entrance, to Loïe Fuller herself; from the orientalist, rococo "Salammbô style" of certain statues (like those of Salome or the "goddess" Electricity) to the "Jugendstil Valkyries" dotting the park's grounds (Jullian, The Triumph, 39, 173). With his usual penchant for hyperbole the cultural critic Octave Uzanne, writing in 1902, praises women's ingenuity in perfecting the art of coquetry, for since the beginning of humanity feminine flirtatiousness "has displayed more forms, given rise to more innovations, fought more battles than the accomplishments of the greatest conquerors, the most illustrious men of science, and the deepest philosophers." Twenty years later in an essay devoted to advertising, the Viscount D'Avenel celebrates the feminization of the Parisian landscape, in particular those larger-than-life, audacious women who stare down at passersby from walls and kiosks:

> Where the colored *affiche* [billboard] . . . shows confidence, where it triumphs, is in the representation of a female being whose features show a bit of wear: half fairy princess and half strumpet, lips slightly apart, hair flopping bizarrely on her forehead, eyes filled with promises. . . . An illusive type, sometimes swaying her hips in a gauzy cloud, sometimes astride a horse (to advertise a racing daily); now and then, seen in a bathing suit surrendering herself to the caresses of the waves (to celebrate the opening of a new beach resort) or pictured smoking (to tout a brand of cigarette paper). . . . In expression always the same, yet in attitude indefinably different, she lends to all these commercial come-ons the charm of her person, even if she appears a bit too frivolous and, as it were, too brazen in the display of her seductiveness.[31]

The city had been transformed into a place of spectacular and specularized femininity, where the female body, long privileged as an impassive *objet d'art,* was elevated to the status of an erotic *objet de publicité.* Still offered up for consumption, the body, in the democratic spirit of advertising, was no longer available to the elitist collector alone, at one time the only person wealthy enough to afford the objet d'art, but to the masses.

Symbolist and art nouveau–inspired perfume advertisements, mostly in the form of multicolored posters or placards (*affiches*) displayed in the salons of hairdressers or in other public spaces from the late 1890s into the new century, portrayed the same ethereal, willowy, dreamy, flower-woman seen in other decorative and artistic representations of the fin de siècle. Although the mistrust of advertising, so widespread during the Second Empire and early Third Republic during the last half of the nineteenth century, continued among turn-of-the-century French businessmen, it became less intense with the introduction of the poster as an art form. Yet even marketing reformers of the time found artistic advertising defective because it placed too much emphasis on the artist to the detriment of the product or company. One journalist for an advertising trade publication observed in 1905 that French advertisements were uniformly similar, portraying "a pretty, suggestively clad woman before a mirror, engaged in her toilette" regardless of what product was being sold, whether "L'Absinthe Alphonse" or "Biscuits Gaston."[32]

The images of women featured in perfume advertisements of the Belle Epoque are of two types: either that of a prim, proper, high society grande dame dressed to the nines in the corseted, wasp-waisted, high-bosomed,

décolleté dresses of the 1880s to mid-1890s; or that of a sylphlike, airy waif in a flowing gossamer gown, her body enveloped by thick coiling tresses of hair more evocative of floral than human form, which, under the influence of art nouveau aesthetics, came to dominate the artistic imagination of advertisers during the last years of the nineteenth century. The grande dame and the sylph are the two poles between which fin de siècle perfume, cosmetic, and soap advertisements appear to oscillate. In fact, these two feminine types are the iconic, allegorical figures dominating the landscape of the 1900 Paris World Exhibition. There was the imposing statue of La Parisienne, queen of the home hearth, arbiter of fashion, and symbol of bourgeois femininity who, forever visible in her haute couture by Paquin, looks down from on high on to the millions of visitors moving through the main entrance of the Exhibition. There was also Loïe Fuller, the shape-shifting, ethereal femme-fleur, image of an aesthetic and rarified femininity, who dances and floats like an invisible presence, like an aroma, through the spaces of the Exhibition itself.

Posters and the Female Body

The bourgeois grande dame imposes herself in an advertising poster from around 1886 for Viville's *Parfums des Femmes de France* by the poster designer Pal (Jean de Paléologue). It shows a stylish Parisienne with an extremely thin waist, dressed in a purple décolleté dress with mutton-leg sleeves and holding a white lace handkerchief in one hand and a perfume atomizer in the other. Her raised, slightly turned head with its pursed lips and its confident, somewhat haughty expression of pleasure, suggests that she has just sniffed the scented handkerchief. A sentence beneath her raised arm declares "Oh! what exquisite perfume this is." It should be remembered that even late into the century perfume was not applied directly to the body; it was sprayed onto handkerchiefs, hair ribbons, lace, or the linings of dresses as it had been in the past. The illustrated "Commercial Catalogue" for 1897 published by the perfumer Bourjois displays nearly thirty different kinds of handkerchief perfumes, in such scents as white rose, chypre, peau d'Espagne, white lily, violet, mimosa, Imperial Russia, and so on; bottles of toilet water, cologne, lavender water, scented vinegar, and bars of soap are also advertised. Guerlain's *Le Mouchoir de Monsieur,* bottled in a distinctive triangular flacon molded to resemble the curving shape of a snail's shell, was created even as late as 1902 for handkerchief use alone. Infrequently, and not without risk to their reputations, more audacious women might apply a drop or two to an ear lobe or the hollow of the neck. It was only as the twentieth century came into being, however, that the generally accepted site of perfume would move from "the handkerchief . . . to its owner."[33]

A poster from around 1895 for Delettrez's *Supra Violetta* (fig. 58), "the only veritable violet perfume," shows

Guerlain, "Triangular" or "Snail" Bottle ("Flacon Escargot"), designed by Pochet & du Courval, 1902, for *Mouchoir de Monsieur* (*His Handkerchief*).

Fig. 58 A poster for the house of Delettrez, "the perfumery of elegant society," advertises a violet-based fragrance called *Supra Violetta*, c. 1895.

a society woman dressed in a chocolate-brown low-cut dress, smiling broadly as she inhales the violet scent from the small perfume bottle she has raised to her nose. Her other hand holds a bouquet of violets which are also profusely displayed on a nearby table. The advertisement for Delettrez's *Parfumerie Imperator* (fig. 59) from 1892 takes the same kind of grande dame and mythologizes her in keeping with the allusion to Roman emperors of the perfume's name. Clad in what appears to be a loose-fitting toga, this woman rides like a goddess on a red and gold chariot, surrounded by little winged cupids throwing flowers. Yet, only five years later Delettrez, calling itself the "Parfumerie du Monde Elégant," advertises its scent,

Vrais Parfums de Fleurs, by means of a poster where pride of place is given to a large bouquet of flowers, leaves, and stems above which hovers a half-naked woman, her neck garlanded in flowers, her hair adorned with petals, and her body from elbow to feet covered in a white, gossamer gown which almost doubles as a pair of wings. The floral theme may be a bit overdone, since she holds close to her nose yet another bouquet of flowers while a swirling mass of clouds or vapors amass above her head.[34] In a short period of time during the 1890s the iconography of perfume advertising had moved from the image of the corseted grande dame to that of the free-spirited, floral, toga-clad, art nouveau sylph.

Another revealing perfume poster from 1889 (for the company Gellé Frères) in pastel tones of red and pink and orange (fig. 60) replaces the portrait of a grande dame with that of an actress or dancer in her dressing room busily applying makeup. It is a poster that hides a narrative, not unlike Manet's 1877 painting, *Nana*, to which it bears an uncanny resemblance. Wearing an extremely low-cut, wasp-waisted costume, highlighted at the waist, the hips, and around the bodice with red ribbon, the actress-dancer holds a powder puff in one hand and a container of powder in the other (again like Manet's *Nana*). On her dressing table a mirror, a light, and a perfume atomizer stand. Another table holds hairbrushes, a plate filled with calling cards, a rectangular red box inscribed with the words "Brisas de Palermo" (Palermo Breezes), and three different-sized bottles of Gellé Frères's perfume *Régina*. The wall is decorated with a statue, a framed portrait, a feather, a small lute, and a faded theatrical poster for the play *Les Pilules du Diable*, a work popular during the 1830s and 1840s and remarkable for its use of spectacular scenic effects involving music, buffoonery, and magic. However, an indication at the bottom of the poster places Gellé Frères at the Paris Universal Exposition of 1889. The most interesting aspect of the poster concerns the presence of two smiling gentlemen—Manet's painting shows only a single individual—attired in black tails, who converse easily with the flirtatiously smiling actress. Clearly, the narrative of seduction expressed by the scene—it was acceptable for upper-class fin de siècle men to visit the dressing rooms of the dancers and actresses (even if the latter were changing their clothes) who would become their mistresses—is meant to enhance the erotic aura of the advertised perfume. No surprise, then, that a few years into the new century Gellé would advertise as "a sophisticated perfume" a fragrance called *Séduction* (Delbourg-Delphis, 14). Gellé's suggestive image of the actress-dancer did not, however, prevent the perfumer from employing a more maternal and socially correct image to market its scent, *Le Royal-Mondain*, in 1894 (fig. 61). The representation of a loving mother at play with her children contains once again the dramatization of a small, this time endearing, narrative. On a terrace opening on to the sea a mother sits on a love seat. In this place of bourgeois comfort, wealth, and leisure she wears a long and luxuriously draped day-dress. Her young daughter leans over and covers the mother's eyes with her hands. Her son, wearing a sailor's suit and with atomizer in hand, stands before his mother spraying a jet of perfume in her direction. "Mother," the children ask, "what is this perfume?" Confused for only a moment the mother, regaining her aplomb, replies, "the best of all perfumes, my children, the Royal-Mondain of Gellé Frères." Not only is perfume the agent in a playful game of detection between mother and child, a kind of olfactory hide-and-seek; it is the sign of a certain bourgeois sophistication. Of course, it also brings the mother down to the level of her offspring: the child-woman who lets herself become the plaything of the perfume she wears.

A similarly light-hearted and sophisticated series of illustrations, again produced by Gellé Frères for several of its products, is found in a humorous calendar for the year 1902.[35] Composed of several folded panels, the calendar

PARFUMERIE GE[...]

Fig. 60 Actresses and dancers of the Belle Epoque were often the mistresses of wealthy men who had easy access to their dressing rooms. These pillars of society, as the heroine-courtesan of a popular play of the Second Empire observes, are "drawn not to our qualities but to our weaknesses, our extravagances; it is our taste for luxury [and that would include perfume] that attracts them as light seduces moths." Parfumerie Gellé Frères, Exposition Universelle, 1889, poster.

Fig. 61 Perfume
becomes the
inspiration for a
domestic game
between a mother and
her children in this
poster for *Le Royal-
Mondain*, Parfumerie
Gellé Frères, c. 1894.

was designed by the caricaturist and poster designer Albert-André Guillaume. One of the panels, called "On the Nile," shows a well-dressed couple on a sailboat watching the desert shore pass by as they engage in a witty dialogue. The man observes that it seems to him that "the perfumes of the enchantress Cleopatra still float over the banks of the Nile" to which the woman teasingly replies: "Ungrateful man! You think about Cleopatra while it is I who scent the air with my perfume *Nilsis*." A second panel portrays an elegant man, dressed in a pink-striped shirt, white collar, a bow tie, a black jacket, white pants, and a yellow hat, who, leaning nonchalantly against the railing of a boardwalk as he looks out at the sea, declares to the woman by his side (she carries an open parasol and wears a large hat): "The dazzling immensity is less profound than my tenderness for you, my dear fiancée.

What has seduced me first and foremost is your perfume of innocence and candor." To which the woman replies: "My friend, it is the perfume *Idylle-Bouquet*." A third panel, entitled "In a Private Dining Room," offers the picture of a couple sitting at a table where a bottle of champagne cools in a bucket, and two glasses of bubbly wait to be consumed. The man and the woman are elegantly dressed, but the woman wears a black mask. Their conversation involves a repartee that would be used again in several perfume advertisements, especially during the 1920s (in particular, one of Bourjois's "Babette" advertisements): *She*: "How come under the mask and the domino, without hearing my voice, you recognized me? I can't guess what sign gave me away." *He*: "The sign that betrayed the elegant woman you most certainly are, Marchioness: namely, your lovely perfume *Sylvanis*."

162

The portrait of the grande dame in perfume advertisements reaches one of its most stylish levels in a multicolored advertising lithograph from the 1890s for the perfume house Bourjois (fig. 62).[36] On the reproduction of a large open fan set against a Louis XV rococo floral background, the oval portraits of four different women from different historical periods are painted: an Egyptian courtesan wearing an ornate headdress; a seventeenth-century noblewoman dressed in a stunning blue and gold gown; an elegant, possibly eighteenth-century Austrian noblewoman, her gloved hand applying color to her lips or a tiny, taffeta beauty mark called a *mouche* (fly) to her cheek; and finally, a late nineteenth-century Parisienne, puff in hand, who is about to powder herself with "Poudre de Riz de Java," a Bourjois product. Beneath the middle two portraits a still life of various perfume accessories—an incense burner, an inlaid coffer, a small box of perfume vials, and several scent bottles and pomade jars—has been painted. Less exotic but no less stylish is a Bourjois poster (from the 1890s as well) picturing a corseted, wasp-waisted belle epoque woman standing before her dressing table powdering her face (fig. 63); the table displays instruments necessary for la toilette (scissors, tweezers, a perfume vaporizer) and three distinct Bourjois products: a flat box of rice powder, a tall bottle of the scent *Prima Violeta* (c. 1890), and a smaller flacon of *Bouquet Manon Lescaut* (c. 1890) with a delicate bow at its neck.

Another decorative motif favored by perfume advertisers during the fin de siècle evolved from a fascination with orientalism, not all that surprising considering the ubiquity of colonialist representations at the 1900 Paris Exhibition. To advertise its new perfume *Amaryllis du Japon* in the early 1890s Delettrez made use of a poster picturing a somewhat Westernized portrait of a Japanese woman wearing a red kimono and standing in front of a Japanese landscape of pagodas and boats (fig. 64). The exoticism of antiquity replaces that of the East in a small 1899 poster for the scent *G. Ugo Stefani* created by the Florentine perfume company Officina Profumo Farmaceutica; it portrays an ancient Greek priestess in a white toga, her arm encircled by bracelets, who touches a vase of flowers with one hand and a golden chalice surrounded by a coiled snake with the other, at the same moment that fragrant smoke from a perfume burner arises from below and a statue of Hippocrates, the Greek physician, watches from above. The medicinal and magical powers of perfume to chase away foreign, unhealthy odors are also the subject of a poster from around 1890, designed by Beaussart for an aromatic product called *Papier d'Arménie* (fig. 65). This was a paper scent strip, heavily impregnated with the odor of benzoin, that was burned slowly in order to disinfect the air of homes or the rooms of the sick. The poster shows a saintly woman seated in a red armchair in front of the facade of a Gothic cathedral. Her head is enveloped in a halo as if she were dreaming; she holds a burning scent strip from which arises a thin trail of smoke. The fumes expand as they ascend until they become a whirlwind of vapors sweeping a horde of terrifying skeletons, winged demons, and even the Grim Reaper himself, scythe and all, into the night sky. The presence of the cathedral in the background and of the halo around the woman's head links *Papier d'Arménie* to the holiness and purity of incense. Odor, as the advertisement graphically shows, is a question of morality. Bad odors are not only immoral; they are evil, satanic. The purifying whirlwind of effluvia becomes nearly audible at the very center of the poster where bright red words announce to the consumer that "perfume cleanses."[37]

To these Asian, Greco-Roman, Armenian, and Gothic images of exoticism must be added those associated with Egyptian antiquity. A picture of the Egyptian Sphinx, supported by a large winged green scarab and surrounded by a frame whose lines are constructed from the intertwined coils of art nouveau flowers and tendrils, stares out from the surface of one of Lubin's perfumed cards for its scent *Enigma* (c. 1898), an image designed to bring the exotic mystery of the Egyptian desert to the Parisian fin de siècle (fig. 67). It is possible that the association of the perfumed woman with enigma (and even her association with the indecipherable riddle of the sphinx) corresponded to the ideology that Lubin developed for its perfumes in the years leading up to World War I. It was its mission, Lubin stated, "to give birth to 1001 voluptuous fantasies, to call into being 1001 dreams of sumptuousness, grace and gallantry, . . . to create around the one who inhales the intoxicating charm of Lubin perfumes an atmosphere of poetry and ecstasy." The cautionary tone of some of these perfume advertisements, like that for *Papier d'Arménie*, which emphasizes the moral quality of scent as an agent for ensuring the health of the body and therefore the purity of the soul, takes on an ambiguously striking aspect in an advertisement for the beauty products offered by the company Icilma (fig. 66). Designed by Pal this poster, probably from the last ten or so years of the nineteenth century, makes use of a biblical theme to link perfume with transgression and then to undo or trump the association. Standing under a dark tree, its boughs hung with bottles of scent, a voluptuous Eve, naked except for what the tresses of her ankle-length hair cover, looks up to a large perfume bottle hanging from the mouth of a thick serpent; written on the snake's coils are the words "Hygiene" and "Beauty."[38] That hygiene and beauty are associated with the serpent of the Garden of Eden would suggest, it might seem, a morally questionable link between scent and sin, especially in late nineteenth-century consciousness. Yet, while the poster uses this association to emphasize the powerfully seductive allure of perfumes (they make "beauty" indeed possible), it signals at the same time the salutary power of perfumes' seductive allure (they make "hygiene" possible, too). The ambivalent image of woman as both saint and temptress, Eve and Lilith, is carried over to the beauty products she uses.

Previous pages:
Fig. 62 Four noble-
women belonging to
different historical
periods are shown
using Bourjois rouge,
perfume (applied to a
handkerchief), lipstick,
and powder in this
color lithograph
poster, after Charles
Verneau, from
the 1890s.

From Grande Dame to Sylph:
Fin de Siècle Perfume Advertisements

As the nineteenth century came to its end in the all-important 1900 Paris Exhibition and as the clothing styles of the time underwent an evolution toward the looser fitting, less-constrained dresses of the new century, the images of perfume advertisements also experienced a significant transformation. The corseted grande dame of the bourgeois interior, as we have noted, yielded the scene, albeit slowly, to the free-spirited, disheveled sylph of symbolist and art nouveau fantasy. Even the original combinations of floral and animalic notes conceived by certain gifted perfumers of the time began to express the ethereal and vaporous world of symbolist dream experience. Praising the perfume artistry of Jacques Guerlain, who had already invented *Le Jardin de mon curé* (1895) and *Voilà pourquoi j'aimais Rosine* (1900), a journalist noted, in a 1900 number of *Printemps parisien*, that "the banal decor [of the everyday] has been made poetic. . . . We are reborn, we breathe, we fall into the delightful ecstasy of the *parfumeur d'opium.*"[39] We need only look at a few perfume

Fig. 63 A fin de siècle woman at her toilette. Parfumerie A. Bourjois et Cie, Paris, 1890s, poster.

advertisements from the early years of the twentieth century to remark the extent to which the neat bourgeois salon and its matronly inhabitant were replaced by a pastoral landscape of vestal princesses, although it is not possible to date the precise moment when the grande dame of the bourgeoisie became the ghostly sylph of opium dreams.

A woman in a white dressing gown sits before her dressing table sniffing perfume from a bottle while she delicately holds the stopper in her other hand (fig. 68). A second woman in a blue gown stands behind her smiling and holding a small box. There's nothing particularly remarkable about this scene, an advertisement for Coty's perfumes, except for the impressionistic manner in which each woman is represented. While the hair, face, neck and shoulders of the two women are precisely rendered in telling detail, the gowns covering their bodies appear increasingly imprecise, vague, and ghostly; they are more sketched than drawn. The lower parts of the women's dresses disappear into the pastel ocher of the paper. The chalky white gown of the seated woman and the deep blue dress of her friend appear to arise (like vapor) out of invisibility. Even the blue swirls around the shoulders of the standing woman and the trails of gauzy blue fabric extending from the back of her dress suggest protruding wings. From the bodice down, these women are thin, immaterial creatures, more butterfly than human being. And the words "Parfums de Coty" at the bottom of the poster, written in sinuous, insubstantial letters, the edges of which appear to be eaten away by the darker, smudged, brown color surrounding them, have the look of an ephemeral writing fashioned momentarily out of clouds or smoke.[40]

Similarly, a poster from 1897 for *Eau de Lubin* by the artist Eugène Grasset has a decidedly art nouveau (as well as pre-Raphaelite) look in the sylphine woman it portrays (fig. 69).[41] Long, thin, her body arced slightly backward under the folds of a loosely fitting yellow gown, her brown hair undone and floating backward through the air in an S-curve, the sylph looks directly into a tilted mirror on a marble table cluttered with perfume bottles, an atomizer, and a white and green porcelain washbowl. The woman's alabaster skin corresponds to the white of her peignoir at the same time that it sets off the darkness of her long, thick ribbon of hair. Her statuesque, upright grace is enhanced by the mannered posture of her arms, one of which, pulled back to form a "v" at the elbow, allows her hand to rest on her falling hair. The other arm, which appears classically perfect (even stylized) in the facture of its sinuous form and in the stillness of its suspended extension, reaches out toward the mirror. The hand at the end of this arm delicately tilts an elongated clear glass bottle from which a thin arc of scent or oil falls into the washbowl. The room's decor reveals several art nouveau motifs: a potted tree with orange blossoms, the folds of white lace lying over a table, a beige curtain imprinted with the pattern of a flower's corolla, and large arcing windows through which are visible a garden, the statue of a winged god, tall green trees, and a blue sky. A mass of clouds forming in the distance serve as a backdrop against which the woman's head and hair are highlighted. Lightly covering and blurring the scene is an indistinct patina of greenness which washes out the overall yellow, blue, and brown colors of the poster. Everything here, including the many references to arcing

AMARYLLIS
DU
JAPON

PARFUM
NOUVEAU

DELETTREZ
15, Rue d'Enghien

PARIS

175501

Parfumerie du Monde Elégant

F. CHAMPENOIS _ PARIS.

Fig. 64 *Japonisme*, the influence of the Japanese arts of glass-making, printmaking, calligraphy, and metalworking on the development of impressionism and art nouveau in Europe during the second half of the nineteenth century, exercised an influence as well on perfume creation and advertising, as this poster from 1893 for Delettrez's *Amaryllis du Japon* reveals.

and curving forms, has become either pale or veiled. The entire representation is framed by a thick, ornamental border of green-beige leaves and flowers. This floral design is composed of ambulating tendrils which move in two directions: scrolling upward through clustered leaves and blossoms to form a decorative panel containing the words "Eau de Lubin" and spiraling downward to outline a panel inscribed with the words "La Reine des Eaux de Toilette" (The Queen of Toilet Waters). The woman at her toilette in Lubin's poster is stately, otherworldly, even divine; she is a kind of sublime Loïe Fuller. The graceful flow of her hair, the sinuously falling folds of her gown, the graceful contours of her extended arm, the angular form of her bent elbow, and the curving cascade of perfume dropping into the bowl create a choreography expressive of the concentrated self-awareness that the act of perfuming demands.

Fig. 66 The tree of the knowledge of hygiene and beauty as imagined by Pal (Jean de Paléologue) in this undated poster for "Hygiène Beauté Icilma."

Fig. 65 In the late nineteenth century a certain morality of cleanliness made it as important to scent one's home as to perfume one's clothing, thus chasing away not only evil odors but the odors of evil, as this poster by L. M. Beaussart for the paper scent strip, *Papier d'Arménie* (c. 1890), makes so dramatically clear.

One other poster from the turn of the century—an all-purpose advertisement for Rimmel's Perfumery—offers a pastoral landscape as the backdrop for the image of the graceful, feminine, dreamlike elegance associated with the experience of perfume (fig. 70). Rimmel's advertisement depicts two goddesses, their bobbed hair overflowing with flowers, who stand or kneel near an ornate perfume burner, which has been placed in a wide meadow abloom with roses, irises, violets, and lilies of the valley; a blue bay lies in the distance. One goddess drops petals into the smoking censer while winged cherubs fly toward it with their own floral offerings. Trails of smoke from the censer form gossamer ribbons of scent which float over the meadow.

The stylized thick, curved lines of art nouveau design, highlighted against a background of geometrical motifs and forms, which the artist Mucha favored in his advertisements, is evident in the one poster the Czech designer created not for perfume per se but for a perfume accessory. In 1898 he was asked by the Rodo Company to design an advertisement for their "Lance Parfum," a tube-shaped bottle that, when squeezed, propelled a fine jet of perfume on to a handkerchief, linen, or sheets (see fig. 33, page 80). Against an ornamental circle of small green rectangles divided by yellow lines and pink roseate forms, a woman with short blond hair is shown wearing a white silk peignoir the collar and sleeves of which spill out in folds of intricate lace. Her attention is fixed on the "lance-parfum" she presses with one hand and on the spray of scent directed toward a crumbled handkerchief she holds with the other. A text informs the consumer that "The 'Rodo' automatically perfumes and refreshes without wetting or staining." Perhaps, a "Rodo" and not an atomizer might have been of greater use to the late-nineteenth-century aristocrat, the Princesse de Sagan. Not wanting to be unevenly perfumed, she had her maid spray her with scent as she was spun around on a stool (Jullian, *Robert de Montesquiou*, 106).

The "theater" of scents in which women participated and performed during the fin de siècle, especially in those dramatized spectacles—the posters, billboards, and cards—that we call advertising, reveal the extent to which a woman through the medium of her body and her clothing was transformed into a "lance-parfum" of her own. She projected onto the imagination of consumers the images of perfume that the advertising poster sought to embody. She was the delivery system for the imaginary world of perfume: its erotic seductiveness, its bourgeois luxury, its natural florality, its auratic magic, its hygienic and disinfectant power, and its exotic potential for social and mythic reincarnation. She was the iconic image of a magical and ambivalent femininity whose multiple and protean forms ranged from the grande dame, the sylph, the vestal virgin, and Eve in the Garden of Eden to the butterfly, the flower, the vine, and the Egyptian, Greek, Indian, or Asian princess. The French aura given to these images corresponded to the ecstatic wave of national chauvinism expressed throughout

Fig. 67 *Lily of the Nile, Queen of Egypt, Scarab, Ramses, Nubian Amber*—such were the evocative Egyptian allusions influencing the names of perfumes created from the 1890s to the end of the 1920s. Lubin's *Enigma,* as advertised on this perfume card from 1921, recalled perfume's Egyptian origins.

the 1900 Paris Exhibition, a world's fair symbolizing not only the culmination of art nouveau style but also the pantheonization of French artistic and industrial ingenuity. There were few more adulatory expressions of the glory of France than that put forth by the perfume house of Piver, which proudly and fervently declared the primacy of French fragrance: "The superior product of superfine quality in any market anywhere comes from France; it has no rival. It is France that exports its tools to foreign lands; it is

A modest fin de siècle woman would never apply perfume directly to her body but would scent her linen and handkerchiefs, using this clever device called the "Lance-Parfum."

Aux Armes de France was founded in 1798 by Pierre-François Lubin and during the first decade of the nineteenth century counted among its faithful clients the empress Josephine and her sister-in-law, Pauline Bonaparte. Until the 1960s Lubin produced several celebrated perfumes like *Nuit de Longchamp* (1935) and *Lubinette* (c. 1925) pictured here in the form of a doll hiding a perfume bottle beneath its skirt.

she who has produced all [perfume] creations; it is she ... who, through the perfume's note, the perfume's elegance, and the artistic taste of the label, sets the style."[42]

Oedipal Scents

As a nine-year old child, Joseph Rouletabille, the hero of a series of mystery stories written by Gaston Leroux from 1907 to 1917—Leroux would go on to write *The Phantom of the Opera* in 1910—is sent to a private boarding school in Eu, a small town in Normandy. A gifted journalist turned amateur detective, Rouletabille had already successfully solved a complicated crime in *The Mystery of the Yellow Room* (1907), Leroux's first detective story. In *The Perfume*

of the Lady in Black (1908), the sequel to that novel, Rouletabille is again called upon to use his impressive powers of logical deduction to confront his arch enemy, the evil, demonically clever Frédéric Larsan, a former agent of the French Sûreté pushed for a variety of reasons into a life of crime. Although during his childhood Rouletabille has no idea who his parents are, he often wonders why a beautiful, veiled woman, stylishly dressed in black, visits his boarding school from time to time to see him. Passionately, he lives for these visits, recalling the mysterious woman's potent presence through his memory of her extraordinary perfume:

Until I did see her again, the memory of her presence and of her perfume was continually with me. As I had never seen her dear face distinctly, I used to try to absorb her perfume while she held me in her arms,

Fig. 68 The ethereal sylph-woman perfumes herself in "Les Parfums de Coty," an early-twentieth-century poster.

Fig. 69 A regal, graceful, and long-limbed art nouveau beauty, "the queen of les eaux de toilette," prepares her scent in this advertising poster by the artist Eugène Grasset for Lubin's *Eau de Lubin,* 1897.

and I lived more with the memory of that than with her image. During the days following her visit, I used to . . . go into the parlor, and when it was empty . . . I'd take long, deep breaths of the air she had breathed and I'd go away again, my heart steeped in her perfume. It was the most delicate, the subtlest and certainly the sweetest, most natural perfume in the world, and I was convinced that I should never know it again.[43]

At the very beginning of *The Perfume of the Woman in Black*, the action of which takes place in the 1890s, the adult Rouletabille along with his good friend Sainclair, returns to the boarding school, as Sainclair explains, to "find the trace of a perfume, to revive a memory, an illusion" (26). Not a day has gone by that Rouletabille has not thought of the woman in black. He needs, especially now that he has become an adult, to find her again and make sure that she really did in fact exist, that she was not a creation of his child's imagination; he "must [breathe] her identity as a dog [breathes] its master's" (38). Rouletabille's commitment to the remembrance of things past coincides with his and Sainclair's presence at the wedding of Mathilde Strangerson and Robert Darzac, whom they follow several days later to a château in the south of France. No sooner does Rouletabille enter the empty room of Mathilde Darzac then, suddenly turning frightfully pale, he asks Sainclair: "Can't you smell the perfume of the Lady in Black?" (121). The fragrant signs of her presence are everywhere: in the stairway leading to the château tower, in the garden, in Sainclair's room, and on the terrace, even when the pounding rain of a thunderstorm would seem to have washed away all trace. It is here that Sainclair experiences for the first time the dolorous fragrance of the Lady in Black: namely, her "sorrowful perfume, sweet and melancholy, like the perfume of tears, something like the perfume of an abandoned flower condemned to bloom alone in some desert waste. Alone!" (130). And this olfactory recognition happens quite dramatically when Madame Darzac runs to Sainclair in the pouring rain to ask him, her voice full of desperation, where she may find Rouletabille, who is, it is now evident, her son:

> It was a delicate, haunting perfume that suddenly intoxicated me in the midst of the battle between the wind and the waters and the thunder. It was an extraordinary perfume. Yes, extraordinary, for I had passed close by the Lady in Black twenty times or more and never smelled it, and it came to me at a time when the most persistent perfumes on earth— even perfumes so heavy they make your head ache— are swept away by the breath of the sea. This captivating, adorable perfume was one that would cling to you and me for a lifetime. One's heart became somehow laden with its infinite sweetness for ever. It tugged at the heartstrings of a son when that son was

Rouletabille, or it fired the heart of a lover, if that lover was Darzac, yet it poisoned the soul of a scoundrel, if that scoundrel was Larsan. Ah, once under its mysterious and wholly enthralling spell you could never tear yourself away from it. Thus I understood more fully Rouletabille and Darzac and Larsan, and all the misfortunes that had befallen Professor Strangerson's daughter [Mathilde] (130–31).

Sainclair makes the perfume the alpha and omega of the mystery; it determines and explains the son's, the husband's, and the criminal's passionate love for Mathilde. For a good part of the story, except for the dénouement, it is the dominant note in Leroux's mystery of detection. This is a symbolist mystery of deduction because it demands a search for hidden signs and meanings, a decoding of reality. If, as Baudelaire had observed, "All Nature is a pillared temple where, / At times, live columns mutter words unclear" ("Correspondences," I: 11; Shapiro, 13), then the poet-detective must attempt to understand and interpret the babble of that muttering. If, as Baudelaire had written in the same poem, "Forests of symbols watch Man pass, and peer / With intimate glance and a familiar air," the poet-detective must decode those symbols and discover why they look upon him like old friends. If there is a "correspondence" between the visible world and its hidden, immaterial counterpart and if symbolism seeks to find a hidden meaning behind the appearances of reality, then the poet (like Baudelaire and the symbolists) and the detective (like Rouletabille) are called on to detect the traces of the lost, other world buried in the forest of the present or afloat in the scented air of the everyday The fiction of detection in *The Perfume of the Woman in Black* is, in other words, dependent on a symbolist view of reality.

The Aroma of Maternity

Beyond the multiple repetitions of the refrain, "The perfume of the Lady in Black! The perfume of the Lady in Black" (131 and passim) which resound throughout the novel, beyond the poignant recognition scene precipitated solely by scent—"How they must have hugged each other to make up for lost time! How he must have breathed his fill of the perfume of the Lady in Black!" (136)—and beyond the twists and turns of the complicated plot reuniting Mathilde with her husband and leading Larsan to suicide, the representation of the scented imagination in *The Perfume of the Lady in Black* has a psychoanalytic resonance as new to the fiction of the time as it was to the kinds of fragrances launched during the first decade of the century. During the course of the narrative Rouletabille learns to his horror that Larsan is his father and to his joy that Mathilde is his mother. To free the mother from the evil which the father has invented to ensnare her and to be rejoined with her in a scene (the parlor) beyond the sphere

RIMMEL'S

PARIS PERFUMERY LONDON

Fig. 70 The London- and Paris-based perfumer Eugène Rimmel evokes the mythical and angelic fragrances of the Elysian Fields in this advertising poster by Deupé for *Rimmels' Perfumery*, c. 1900.

of the father's destructive power, Rouletabille has to arrange the father's death, which, although a suicide, is most certainly caused, albeit involuntarily, by the son's actions. The Oedipal conflict is evident, and perfume becomes a powerful symbol of its psychic drama. Through the agency of scent the child's closeness to the mother—in that dark, womblike parlor of yore—is relived. Perfume restores the immediacy of the mother, recapturing her essence as the child enveloped in her arms once felt it. Perfume regenerates an impossible fusion, initiating an unmediated, uninterrupted oneness, which is, given the nature of scent, short-lived, since the mother in leaving the parlor abandons the young child to olfactory memories which may be no more than an illusion. Behind her in the parlor floats an aromatic wake, an indelible trail of being that in auditory terms corresponds to the rustle of invisible

175

wings. Perfume is fundamentally maternal. It expresses the experience of joy—that of possession and intimacy—encircled by sadness, that of loss. "Once under its mysterious and wholly enthralling spell you could never tear yourself away from it," Sainclair remarks. Whether as an experience of blissful union or one of melancholic separation, perfume throbs unforgettably, living on in the heart as an ineffaceable memory.

Sainclair's testimony to the storm at sea and to the emotional tempest provoked within his and Rouletabille's soul by the scent of the Lady in Black reveals perfume's nearly cosmic power. Here is a force that rivals that of the monstrous waves. It comes to dominate the "battle" between heaven and earth and that between wind, water, and thunder. Olfactory experience triumphs over the sight, sound, taste, and touch associated with the storm-tossed elements composing the landscape. Smell is the *sense* of senses. The storm cleanses the scene of all odors, turning the site into an olfactory tabula rasa ready to welcome the re-blossoming of the mother's fragrance: the only scent that can now exist in the world and the only one capable of "taking hold" of Rouletabille's consciousness. Wedded to the flesh of the mother's body—a scent not from nature but from a stylish, self-made woman, a *lady* dressed in black—perfume empties the earth of all natural odors. It re-forms nature, as Baudelaire and the symbolists had wanted it to do. It effaces sea, sky, and earth replacing these natural forces with a creation of artifice and imagination.[44] The odors of the earth having finally disappeared, Sainclair smells at last the powerful fragrance of the Lady in Black; it is an epiphany. The wealth of description and the plethora of adjectives he gives to this perfume highlight its magical intensity. It is delicate, haunting, intoxicating, persistent, captivating, adorable, clinging, sweet, enthralling, and mysterious. It penetrates deeply into the human heart, where it tugs at the heartstrings, or triggers sparks of erotic love, or poisons the soul. Perfume casts a spell, a consequence of both white and black magic, from which escape is impossible. Yet, perfume, as Sainclair makes clear, is a means of understanding, a mode of detection, and a form of knowledge, leading him, the narrator, to an explanation of human desire and leading Rouletabille, the protagonist, to an understanding of his childhood past and the desperate longing it had provoked.

❧ *Symbolist and Art Nouveau Perfumes: 1880–1914*

The Oedipal reality of fragrance in *The Perfume of the Lady in Black*, with its insistence on the mirage of a phantom mother whose scent is the only trace, although illusory, of her past reality, signals the growing awareness on the part of perfumers, advertisers, and consumers in the fin de siècle of the potentially powerful role that psychology could play in the creation, naming, and marketing of perfume. That Lenthéric launched a perfume called *La Dame en noir*, a year after Leroux's novel was published, is not in and of itself compelling evidence for the place of Freudian notions of conscious and unconscious experience in perfume composition and bottle design. What is, however, is the importance given to perfume names that were expressly designed to evoke feelings of inwardness or call to mind scent images corresponding to dream fantasies. This is perhaps what the perfumer Jacques Guerlain (1874–1963), the creator of *Parfum des Champs-Elysées*, *Après l'ondée* and *L'Heure bleue* in the first decade of the twentieth century, had in mind when he observed that "a successful perfume is one whose odor corresponds to an initial dream." In the last years of the nineteenth century a new conception of fragrance had begun to appear. The acceptance of what Delbourg-Delphis has called "a psycho-esthetic perfumery," bringing the inner world of the psyche into closer contact with the outer world of beauty and fashion, became more and more widespread. From a host of scientific discoveries about the way nerves worked and the processes by which cognition affected the senses, a "new psychology" began to infiltrate French culture. This scientific conception of human inwardness went hand in hand with efforts by the decorative arts reform movement to make interior space the new locus of artistic expression. The arts of decor and of perfumery, which are arts of intimacy and domesticity, took on a psychological depth they had never had before. Nineteenth-century psychology, Silverman observes, "had invested the enterprise of interior decoration with new meanings and transposed the eighteenth-century associations of modernity, intimacy, and interiority into the new key of nervous vibration,

Opposite page:
Fig. 71 From sylph to moth, the art nouveau woman was subjected to continual stages of metamorphosis as in René Lalique's extraordinary glass perfume bottle for D'Héraud's *La Phalène*, c. 1919.

Left:
Fig. 72 Ancient Greek motifs and the peplos worn by Grecian women are highlighted in René Lalique's glass perfume bottle for Coty's 1910 fragrance, *Ambre antique*.

A maison Lalique bottle with tiara-shaped *Bouchon Mûres* [stopper with mulberries], 1920.

spatial self-fashioning, and unconscious projection." Modern style and art nouveau were now seen as forms of "psychological interiority." Even symbolists like Des Esseintes favored leaded windows, thick curtains, artificial light, and heavily patinaed objects because such artifacts created an interior that was, Silverman notes, "no longer a refuge from but a replacement for the external world."[45]

Perfume: The Abstract Art

The addition of a psychological dimension to the image-system associated with perfume was achieved primarily through a more poetic form of naming. No longer was it enough to give a perfume the simple designation of *eau de lavande* or *eau de violette* or "eau" of this and "eau" of that. Perfumes were no longer single-flower compositions. They had become more chemically complex and more dependent upon the imaginative intuition and genius of their creator. If perfume composition is indeed, as the postwar perfumer Edmond Roudnitska has declared, "the abstract art par excellence," then perfumes required names that would suggest this complexity and this aesthetic abstractness, identities made evocative through images of sensual, poetic, and symbolic phenomena. Perfume manufacturing had moved away from nature and entered the domain of the artisan and artist. Fragrances with no equivalents in nature came into being; they were synthetic creations, objets d'art, inspired by human desire, imagination, and the unconscious. Even perfumes for different times of the day (morning or night), for different seasons of the year (summer or winter), and for women of different hair color—Coty advertised *L'Or* (1912) for blonds and *Chypre* (1917) for brunettes—signaled a more subtle and sophisticated understanding of the psychological effects of scent on the woman who wore it. Moreover, the perfume bottle itself underwent a conceptual change, becoming more psychological, idiosyncratic, and poetic. From 1885 to 1900 bottles were still geometrical, unexceptionally shaped, and unadorned forms made of clear glass. They came in standard sizes and shapes—square, rectangular, cylindrical—and resembled apothecary vials. Only their colorful labels gave them personality and uniqueness. But in the early years of the new century glass bottles, now created by sculptors, jewelers, glassmakers, and artisans like Gallé, as we have seen, displayed new shapes, colors, and designs.

The perfume bottle was being transformed, like so many other artifacts of everyday life, into an objet d'art with symbolist and fantasist properties. Paper labels were becoming much less prominent; the name of the scent was now etched directly onto the surface of the glass or the stopper.[46]

Changing Bottle Design: René Lalique and François Coty

When the glassmaker René Lalique and the perfumer François Coty combined their talents around 1907 and 1908—the first Coty perfume in a Lalique "dragonfly" bottle was *Cyclamen*, launched in 1909—flacon design experienced a sea change. The bottle's material beauty and symbolist evocativeness realized Coty's singular vision of perfume as "that which goes beyond perfume." "In the choice of a perfume," he wrote, "the quality of the juice plays only a part; a perfume is seen as much as it is smelled." Sometimes referred to admiringly as the "Napoleon of perfumery" and more derogatorily as "the dictator of modern perfumery," Coty—born with the name Spoturno, he adopted his mother's more poetic maiden name, Coti—was the major, seminal force in the industry during the first thirty years of the twentieth century. Not only did he create new types of perfume, but he was the "first true professional in perfume marketing," revolutionizing the way perfumes were bottled, packaged, advertised, and delivered to stores. His factories in Suresnes, which he called "la cité des parfums," employed 4,000 workers who occupied 54,000 square feet of workshops and laboratories. His glass factories could produce 100,000 bottles a day. His first perfume, *La Rose Jacqueminot* from 1904, named after a variety of *rose centifolia*, earned a million francs in two months, a success due as much to his skills as a perfumer as his talents as an entrepreneur. Coty had been making the rounds of department stores in the Paris of 1904 trying to interest buyers in this new rose scent. At the Grands Magasins du Louvre he deliberately struck a counter with a bottle of *Rose Jacqueminot*, breaking the glass and causing a host of women shoppers (some say friends of his wife who had been planted there by the perfumer) to come running toward the delicious fragrance now permeating the store. Coty was unceremoniously booted out by the manager. By that evening, however, he had received orders for twelve bottles. This would be the first of many advertising coups (including the assembly-line

Fig. 73 The fascination of art nouveau style with the sinuous curves of reptiles is evident in this witty glass bottle designed by Maurice Dépinoix for Lubin's *Au soleil*, c. 1910.

production of singular, "luxury" perfume bottles and the free distribution of miniature perfume "samples") orchestrated by the perfumer. By the 1920s Coty was one of the wealthiest men in the world, rich enough to start buying up French newspapers—*Le Figaro* was acquired in 1921— which were humorously nicknamed "les Cotydiens," a pun on "les quotidiens," the French word for "dailies."[47]

The Tales Perfumes Tell

Often perfume names had historical, biblical, mythological, literary, theatrical, and exotic associations. Gellé Frères's *Le Mikado* (1889), Rallet's *Le Lys du Nil* (c. 1890), Delettrez's *Oryalis* (c. 1908), Roger & Gallét's *Narkis* (1912), and Poiret's *Nuit de Chine* (1913) its label displaying the name in French and in Chinese characters, evoke Asian and Middle Eastern places or imagine poetic-sounding names, real or invented, in order to suggest Baudelairean sites of "luxury, calm, and delight." The influence of successful theatrical plays of the day, along with their decors, sets, costumes and even the personalities of their actors, were sources of perfume inspiration. There were Rigaud's *Mary Garden*, named for a famous opera singer, and Caron's *Isadora* (1910), its bottle engraved with three different poses of the dancer Isadora Duncan. Gabilla's *La Vierge Folle* (The Mad Virgin, 1911) borrowed the title of a popular play of the previous year by Henry Bataille—and more esoterically, an allusion to Rimbaud's sarcastic name for his lover Verlaine— which dramatized a young girl's unhappy liaison with an older man. D'Héraud's fragrance *La Phalène* (c. 1919), bottled in a moth-shaped flacon engraved with the spectral outline of a fantastic moth-woman (fig. 71), also alluded to a play by Bataille of 1913 dealing with sex and suicide. Romantic love, of course, still remained a significant and powerful theme in the choice of perfume names and designs. Richard Hudnut's *Eros* appeared around 1910 and Lenthéric's *Désir princier* was created two years later. Coty's *L'Entraînement*, also known as *Le Baiser* (1913), appeared in a fascinating Lalique bottle, which on one side showed a man leading a woman (both wear diaphanous robes) and on the other the couple kissing. One of the most striking bottles to represent perfume not only as an expression, but as a physical offering, of love is

Guerlain's fragrance, *Voilà pourquoi j'aimais Rosine* (This Is Why I Loved Rosine), which debuted at the 1900 Paris Exhibition. Here was a scent whose sentence-long name left no doubt (the "why," the "pourquoi," is self-explanatory) about the sentiments ("aimais") of the man who presented it as a gift. *Voilà pourquoi j'aimais Rosine* was sold in what Christine Mayer Lefkowith has called the "first 'representational' perfume bottle": a vase-shaped container from the neck of which a large silk bouquet of reddish-white begonias and green leaves protruded. Guerlain called the bottle a "flacon fleuri." Indeed, it did seem as if flowers were sprouting from the bottle cap and that the offering was as much a perfume as a bouquet.[48]

Mythic Names and Capricious Bottles

Perfumes were often named or their bottles designed with the express purpose of evoking a traditional myth, symbol, or icon of early Western culture. Examples abound, like Dralle's *Illusion* (1908), Giraud's *Dans les nues* (1912), and Delettrez's *Laïs* (c. 1914). Coty's *Le Styx* (1910–1913) came in a bottle, designed by Lalique, whose unique gold-leaf stopper displayed the image of four bees, their open wings joined together at the center. The Greek motif continued in his *Ambre Antique* (1910), in a cylindrical Lalique bottle, picturing graceful Grecian women in long, pleated robes, holding bouquets of flowers (fig. 72). Piver's *Rosiris* (1899) joined in its one-word title references to rose, iris, and the Egyptian god Osiris. *Scarabée* (1909), also by Piver, was bottled in a scarab-shaped vial, while the bottle for Roger & Gallet's *Cigalia* (1910) displayed two identical, upright art nouveau cicadas, their long, translucent wings colored like stained glass windows. The unique apple-shaped bottle of Poiret's *Le Fruit défendu* (Forbidden Fruit, 1915) iconically suggested the possible dangers of the scent. These perfumes and their bottles are rich in allusions. References—to phenomena of spiritual immateriality (like illusion and clouds), to the mythical Greek courtesan (Laïs) murdered by her lovers' jealous wives, to Hell (the river Styx), to the Egyptian symbol for the sun (the scarab beetle), to the mysterious cry of the longest living insect (the cicada), and to the forbidden apple of the Garden of Eden—abound.[49]

Fig. 74 The words "flower," "flirt," and "effluvium" echo in the name of Coty's *L'Effleurt*, its glass perfume bottle incised with the wispy figure of a sylph as designed by René Lalique, c. 1908.

Fig. 75 With many extraordinary bottles and in particular this glorious crystal masterpiece with its tiara-stopper for D'Orsay's *Leurs Âmes*, c. 1913, René Lalique realized François Coty's dream of turning perfume bottles into works of art. "A perfume," Coty declared, "needs to attract the eyes as much as the nose."

Moreover, these scent names were made more mysterious through a poetic, erudite, sometimes exotic play on words. Thus, "cigale" ("cicada") receives an added last syllable (*Cigalia)*; or the word "arôme" (aroma) is given a more fanciful and musical pronunciation in Roger & Gallet's *Aromis* (1894); or "fleur" and "ami" are combined to become Piver's neologism, *Floramye* (1903).

The most striking and innovative use of a portmanteau name is Coty's richly allusive and clever *L'Effleurt* (c. 1908) (fig. 74) advertised at the time as a scent offering "the enchantment of Spring flowers, [the] sweet memories of that first meeting . . . [and] a perfume for lovers." The phonetics of the word echo several other terms associated with flowers, women, and love. Most evidently, there is, for example, the word *fleur*, flower. There are allusions to the noun *effluve* (emanation), a word used in French to refer to

perfume, and to the verb *effleurer*, to touch lightly or caress as if a hand were to tickle a cheek by delicately drawing a petal across the skin. *Effleurer* can also mean to scratch or remove a very thin layer of skin; it suggests a renewal of beauty, a purification, and an effacing of any kind of defect.

Related to *effleurer*, moreover, is another verb, *effleurir*, which means the flowering or opening of blossoms. There are still other hidden associations in *l'effleurt*. First and foremost, one hears the echo of a word of English derivation (*le flirt*)—it entered French in 1879—referring to an amorous yet more or less chaste, if not superficial, relationship. *Le flirt* in the plural (*les flirts*), and spoken the way the French pronounce words imported across the Channel, has a close phonetic resemblance to *l'effleurt*. Flirtatiousness had already been evoked in French perfume names, most particularly in Pinaud's *Flirt* (1891) and Roger & Gallet's

181

A maison Lalique square bottle called *Le Carré d'Hirondelles* engraved with downward flying swallows, 1920s.

"essence" for handkerchief, *Miss Flirt* (1896). Finally, the noun *l'effluent,* the cascading of water from a well, lake or glacier, reverberates in *l'effleurt,* suggesting the flowing of water, perfume, and love. In addition to the images brought to mind by *L'Effleurt*'s rich web of verbal allusions, several visually inspired images were evoked by the engraved label that Lalique molded into the side of the *L'Effleurt* bottle. No longer were perfume labels mere pieces of colorful paper glued to glass. With *L'Effleurt,* Lalique designed what Lefkowith has called the "quintessential Art Nouveau perfume label," although its appearance in 1909 coincided more or less with art nouveau's decline. The label of the *L'Effleurt* bottle shows a sylph rising like a vaporous plume of smoke from a swirl of plant stems, leaves, and tendrils. The lower limbs of this frail sprite, seen in silhouette, display the same plantlike consistency and the same "voluptuous arabesques" as the tendrils out of which the limbs emerge. "Like Venus arising from her shell or Daphne metamorphosing into a tree," the historians of glass Mary

Lou and Glenn Utt observe, "this erotic flower creature is very much at one with magical, even mystical nature." A similar Grecian-inspired motif with art nouveau overtones is evident in the bottle Lalique designed four years later for D'Orsay's *Ambre* (1913). Each of the bottle's four corners is engraved with the gossamer figure of a standing caryatid draped in a flowing gown.[50]

Another art nouveau bottle, this time for Lubin's *Au Soleil* (1909–12), was designed by Maurice Dépinoix in the shape of a lighthouse, or more specifically an upright smokestack, arising from a wide, shallow base (fig. 73). A large green lizard climbs up the phallic cylinder of the bottle, its long tail curved around the shaft and onto the base where it ends. The lizard's head and its large paws are pointed upward to the top of the bottle and to the object of the reptile's desire; for engraved in the stopper is a small fly. Yet, another art nouveau bottle, by Lalique for Piver's *Misti* (1912), was circular with a flattened convex base which made the flacon rock from side to side thus "creating the

A stunning maison Lalique serpent bottle with an open-jawed snake stopper, c. 1920.

impression of fluttering butterfly wings," according to Lefkowith. Lalique designed spectacular art nouveau–inspired bottles for D'Orsay as well. One such flacon, with dancing nudes chiseled on one side of the bottle, lived up to its name, *L'Elégance* (c. 1910). A second, cylindrical bottle with a stunning tiara-shaped stopper held D'Orsay's scent *Leurs Âmes* (1913) (fig. 75). The tiara-stopper curved around the outer contours of the bottle like an enveloping fan until it reached a point a few scant inches from the base. Engraved onto the tiara's transparent glass was the design of a plant, its thick root arising from the bottom of the stopper and giving the impression of emerging from the mouth of the bottle. The plant's flowering branches move up the width of the tiara and then begin to move down its sides. Hanging from the branches and descending on each side of the tiara's wings are the profiles of two nude nymphs, their bodies completely extended. Despite the volume of glass composing the bottle, a spirit of lightness and transparence emanates from the flacon: a spirituality in harmony with the perfume's name: "Their Souls." Finally, Lalique's bottle for Coty's *Au coeur des calices* (1905), made of delicate blue glass in the form of a dome with, as the Utts write, "a regular three-tiered pattern of ovoid dewdrop petals molded on the outside," has the cup-like shape of a flower, except that the cup, the calyx (*calice*) of the flower, from which essential oils composing a scent are usually extracted, is inverted; this unusual stopper is entirely formed out of a "solitary plump bumblebee."[51]

The Flowers of Perfume

If the names of perfumes during the fin de siècle are an index of the psycho-aesthetic images that perfume manufacturers sought to evoke in the hearts and minds of potential customers, then those images, despite the allusions to insects, mythic figures, exotic places, contemporary plays, historical personages, and illusory, immaterial realities, would, almost incontestably, be floral in nature. Just a list of the different designations indicates the botanical as well as syntactical variety of these names: *Fougère Royale* (Royal Fern) and *Quelques Fleurs* (Houbigant, 1882, 1913); *Vera Violetta*, *Fleurs d'amour*, and *Rêve fleuri* (Roger & Gallet, 1892, 1903, 1904); the crocus-based *Safranor* (L. T. Piver, 1902); *Kantirix* (Millot, 1900), the name of a Mexican flower; *Avril en fleurs* and *Fleur qui meurt* (Guerlain, 1883/1905, 1901); *La Rose Jacqueminot*, *L'Origan*, *Jasmin de Corse*, *Le Muguet* (lily-of-the-valley), and *Cyclamen* (Coty, 1904 to 1913); *Narcisse noir* (Caron, 1911); and so on. One scent from the first decade of the twentieth century, Guerlain's *Après l'ondée* (After the Rain, 1906), carries a name that is also an impressionistic poem: an evocation of a wooded landscape dripping with the aftereffects of a gentle shower, a dream image intensified by the aromas of orange blossom, violet, and hawthorn contained in the fragrance. A journalist for the newspaper *La Liberté* wrote in April 1906 that the

perfume's "exquisite delicateness" had "something of the melancholy of a poet's mind" (Atlas and Monniot, 160).

The new psychological and spiritual orientation of perfume names and bottles, the aura of poetry, mystery, and romance surrounding them, and their evocation of a floral, pastoral, almost blissful dreaminess correspond to the appearance at the turn of the century of a new constellation or system of scent-images, which conceived perfume as a more layered, intimate, and musical reality. This new way of perceiving scent (what the perfumer Roudnitska has called "penser en odeurs," to think, literally, via smell) could not have possibly developed, in its usual unconscious way, without the technical advances that revolutionized the chemistry of perfumery and gave birth to modern perfume creation. The increased use of synthetic scents, as was mentioned in Chapter Two, allowed perfumer-artisans not only to imitate scents as they existed in the natural world, but to go beyond nature and create nonexistent, abstract, conceptual fragrances corresponding to an emotion, a memory, an idea—even the psychic reverberations of a sound or a caress—that had suddenly surfaced in the perfumer's imagination. No longer did the composer need to "translate" what already existed in the outside world; he could now articulate what existed inside the world that was the self. And those natural floral scents that had resisted reproduction, like lily-of-the-valley, honeysuckle, gardenia, magnolia, lilac, and other aromas, could finally be created synthetically.[52] Yet, synthetic scents were never put to the service of creating completely artificial perfumes. They were used as vital complements to other natural notes, like rose, jasmine, and tuberose, with which they were blended and whose odors they amplified and intensified in never-before-imagined ways.

JICKY, L'HEURE BLEUE, and L'ORIGAN

Jicky, often called the first great modernist perfume, was created by Aimé Guerlain (1834–1910) in 1889 and was as revolutionary a creation in the world of perfume as the Eiffel Tower constructed the same year was in the world of architecture. Until the invention of *Jicky* the fashion of the fin de siècle demanded that perfume, as the writer Colette Fellous observes, "be a kind of photograph of a flower." But the advent of impressionism blurred that photograph, revealing the flower as a reality at once vaporous and out of focus. Monet had given nature a shimmering, imprecise subjectivity. Painting had become "the search for pure emotion," and perfume composition, especially the "emotive perfumery" that *Jicky* was to inaugurate, was not far behind. *Jicky*, remarks Jean-Paul Guerlain, Aimé's great-nephew, "is emotion translated into perfume." At first, women did not take to *Jicky*. They found its fragrance to be not only a radical departure from the easily recognizable, single-flower perfumes of the past, but too "resolutely modern, indefinable," and brutal a scent. Men, however, liked it, even though it may have been, frankly, too avant-garde for either sex. Not until 1912 did the French feminine press begin to pay it homage and women begin to use it on a regular basis. Because of its distinctive blend of synthetic and natural ingredients—head notes of lavender, bergamot, and rosewood wedded to soul notes of vanilla, coumarin, civet, and opopanax—*Jicky*, a scent of the fougère (fern) class of perfumes, was a watershed fragrance in the history of perfumery. It symbolized "a change in attitude" toward fragrance and a radical transformation of the image system associated with scent. It was the first perfume, Philippe Guerlain, a descendant, remarks, "to combine natural and synthetic materials to create a perfume with many different facets: fresh, flowery, spicy, oriental, animalic." In the history of Guerlain perfumes it was also a bridge-scent, linking the nineteenth century to the twentieth, and the 1830 *Eau de cologne impériale* of the first Guerlain to the *Shalimar* (1925) of Jacques Guerlain (1874–1963), whom Aimé, Jacques's uncle, liked to call "Jicky." All in all, *Jicky* represents a paradigm shift in scent corresponding to the technological, industrial, and aesthetic inventions of the dawning century. The "quadrilobe" stopper in the form of a champagne cork, which Gabriel Guerlain designed for a new *Jicky* bottle in 1908—it was modified by Baccarat after World War II—captures the celebratory mood and festive optimism the perfume came to express in the first decades of the new century.[53]

The other great, innovative Guerlain fin de siècle perfume, *L'Heure bleue*, was in many ways an art nouveau scent. "In this perfume [Jacques's] love for nature," observed his wife Lily in 1912, was "sublimated through Art, an art called Nouveau." Even its bottle, with curvilinear "shoulders" etched with curlicue commas as designed by Raymond Guerlain, displayed a definite art nouveau spirit. *L'Heure bleue*, observes Phillipe Guerlain "is an attitude! It is a symbol of the Belle Epoque, that peaceful twilight before the terrible storm of the First World War." Inspired by Coty's 1905 *L'Origan*, the first "oriental" floral perfume, *L'Heure Bleue* uses soul notes of iris to give the perfume a soft, powdery quality, recreating in scent that sensation of soft, vaporous blueness which emerges from what the French like to call the "blue hour." The warm, velvety, sensual feel of *L'Heure bleue* comes from the blend of iris and vanilla mingling, according to Roja Dove, a Guerlain spokesperson, with "the richness of musk and the warmth of carnation and aniseed."[54]

L'Heure bleue was created by Jacques Guerlain as a gift to his wife and as a tribute to the impressionist painters "who reveal through a new light what our eyes have not seen," writes Lily Guerlain ("Autoportraits"). The perfumer sought to evoke his subjective experience of that peaceful, blue, twilight hour, when the summer sky remains softly and dimly blue and when this velvety blueness floats down to envelop Notre Dame and to hover over the Seine. It is a moment, fleeting and disquieting, "when the sky has lost its sun but has not yet found its stars," Madame Guerlain observes. The *L'Heure bleue* woman was, according to Fellous, very much of her times; she was "sensitive to the passionate accord of musk and Bulgarian rose, to the tender blend of iris tinged with heliotrope, and to the evocation of woodlands and wet earth." After the excitement of the opening of the new century, it was the moment for repose, calm, and discretion. It was also the time, Fellous remarks, for the "femme-fleur buried under tassels, frills, pleats, and lace" and the time, as Lily Guerlain asserts, for the woman who "keeps the fullness of her strong, uncontrollable emotions under wraps" ("Autoportraits"). The scent for such a woman was *L'Heure bleue*, "a chaste perfume with just a hint of insolence." It emitted the aroma of "foreshadowed happiness," as the perfume's slogan announced and as the flacon with a stopper in the shape of

Guerlain's *Jicky*, created the same year as the Eiffel Tower (1889), was as revolutionary in spirit—it is the first perfume to incorporate synthetic ingredients—and as challenging to French fin-de-siècle taste—women in particular were put off by its oriental and musky odor—as the Tower itself. This ad of a woman at the steering wheel of a vintage car dates from the 1990s, but the square black bottle is late nineteenth century.

a heart ("bouchon coeur") suggested. *L'Heure bleue* was for "the woman who wants [to have] everything and nothing, yesterday and today" ("Autoportraits"). For it is an ambiguous scent in conflict with itself: on the one hand, timid and shy—a reticence conveyed by its soft, powdery notes—and on the other bold and insolent—an audacity conveyed by the overlapping of aniseed with the subtle animalic note of musk. "'I'm shy,' says the powder. 'Draw close,' says the aniseed. 'I'm sensual,' says the musk," as Dove describes the perfume's unabashedly mixed message.[55]

L'Heure bleue is an evening scent; it expresses that moment when a woman feels the kind of disquiet that emanates from the suspension of time, from the troubling sensation of "living between two worlds," and from the unsettling feeling that "a fraction of a second can change everything, that a story begun in a dream can suddenly descend into real life," as Madame Guerlain notes ("Autoportraits de femmes"). In an effort to represent the conceptual idea as well as the visual image he had in mind while creating the scent, Jacques Guerlain jotted down in his notes the following poetic description of the imaginary associations that *L'Heure bleue* brought to mind:

> The sun has set, but night has not yet come. It is an uncertain hour. In the deep blue light everything—the trembling leaves, the lapping water—coalesces to express a love, a friendship, an infinite tenderness. Suddenly, in the brief time of a second, the brief time of a perfume, man is in harmony with all things.[56]

The other great masterpiece of perfumery in the first years of the twentieth century was François Coty's *L'Origan* (1905), a word meaning "oregano," although there is no hint of such a spice in this carnation-intensive scent. Coty was "the mastermind who turned perfumery from a rough sketch into a work of art," as Roudnitska has remarked, and his greatest, groundbreaking works were *L'Origan* and *Chypre* (1917), both of which inaugurated two brand-new classes of perfume. *L'Origan* was indisputably the first, so-called "floral-oriental" scent, while *Chypre* gave birth to a perfume family (of the same name) that had never before been imagined. Coty was committed to using synthetic ingredients to enhance and highlight the aromas of the natural floral and animalic scents he blended into his scents. He was fascinated by synthetic violet (ionone), synthetic iris blended with violet (iralia), and ambreine, a floral accord made with labdanum and used as a base to give a distinctive amber note to a fragrance. Coty was equally committed to using the best distillation and extraction techniques available so as ensure that these natural raw materials were of the finest and purest quality. Among such raw materials were highly purified absolutes containing as little waxy material as possible. Called "parfums naturels sans cires" ("natural waxless perfumes"), or PNSC, these absolutes were not unknown to other perfumers like Houbigant, Lubin, and Guerlain. But these houses refused to use them because the odors of the PNSCs were much too strong for their own compositions. Coty, however, was intrigued, and he based his innovative perfume creations on the use of PNSC. Moreover, his composition of *La Rose Jacqueminot* (a species of rose named for a French general) in 1904 testified to an ingenious and harmonious balance between natural rose absolute and two synthetic ingredients—rhodinol (a warm rose note) and ionone (violet)—which made this scent one of the most original and tenacious rose perfumes ever conceived.[57]

L'Origan was advertised as a "warm, rich, and luminous [perfume which] suits all women and yet is different on each one—the perfume of fashionable society." The fragrance, Roudnitska believes, translated a fauvist sensibility. From the flamelike, swirling lines, and the smoldering passion of fauvist painting *L'Origan* borrows "all the vividness, violence, and audacity." It is a complicated and daring composition made up of the harmony of six fundamental notes: orange blossom, violet, jasmine, rose, carnation, and the odor of sweet grass. Its architecture is constructed around two synthetic bases: the "sweet, floral woody notes" of iralia and the "spicy carnation bouquet" of dianthine. To them has been added the top notes of bergamot, neroli, and ylang-ylang, heart notes of jasmine, rose, and orange blossom, and a base note of vanillin, coumarin, musk, and sandalwood. The success of *L'Origan* was instantaneous, and its influence on modern perfumery long lasting, generating a host of imitations not the least of which was Yves Saint Laurent's *Opium* (1977), which, as Roudnitska remarks, is an *Origan* "without the flowers, a reminder that this Coty fragrance was the first intense perfume of the century."[58]

Of the seven recognized families or groups of perfumes—the citurs, floral, fern, chypre, woody, amber/oriental, and leather fragrances—the most fecund and rich are the "chypres," a class that had not existed until Coty's groundbreaking creation of the eponymous *Chypre* in 1917. This composition made him one of the giants of twentieth-century perfumery at the very moment that Picasso in the world of modern painting and Coco Chanel in the world of haute couture were becoming giants in their own right. Coty's aim was a scent that would be "discrete and tenacious, brisk and yet sensual." The top notes are indeed buoyant, while the heart notes, asserts Roudnitska, are delicately enveloped in "a cloud of jasmine" carefully blended with vanillin and coumarin. The striking originality of *Chypre*, however, is found in the stunning scale of woody notes—patchouli, vetiver, sandalwood, bergamot, oak moss—perfectly blended with floral thrusts of jasmine. For Roudnitska, *Chypre* is a true masterpiece with all the extraordinary qualities—character, vigor, delicateness, clarity, volume, volatility, and "the capacity of scent to expand as it dissipates"—of a truly great perfume. With unimagined perfection, Roudnitska continues, Coty brought into being "a composition, in the most noble sense of that word: that is to say, an olfactory form, conceived abstractly, elaborated by the work of sensuality and intellect, and powerfully nourished, as in the other arts, by imagination and intuition." To the soul note of oak moss ingeniously amplified by floral heart notes and citrusy top notes, a composition that points to *Chypre's* uniqueness, several classical perfumes of the modern era owe their existence: namely, Guerlain's *Mitsouko* (1919), Chanel's *No. 5* (1921), Millot's *Crêpe de Chine* (1925), Rochas's *Femme* (1944), Grès's *Cabochard* (1959), Hermès's *Calèche* (1961) and Roudnitska's own creations for Dior, *Eau Sauvage* (1966) and *Diorella* (1972).[59]

During the fin de siècle years extending from 1880 to World War I, years that encompassed the Belle Epoque as well, the art nouveau image of woman in art, poetry, dance, design, glassmaking, advertising, and perfumery was often expressed through figures of curves, arabesques, curlicues, and other sinuous, sylphlike traces. The woman was a form of writing. Her calligraphy coincided with the whiplash tendrils and intertwined vines found in the iconography increasingly displayed on objets d'art and in the decor of interior spaces, which had become, among symbolist poets, dandies, and art nouveau decorators, a fortress of aestheticism designed to keep at bay the vulgar realities of the everyday world. This was a calligraphy that corresponded as well to the trails of smoke and vapor associated with perfume. In order to represent the otherwise invisible diffusion of scent, floating lines and circles of smoke were shown rising from a perfume burner or a bottle of fragrance. Flesh became vapor, breath spirit, and the female body a volatile, abstract symbol written invisibly, although fragrantly, on the wind that carried it away. It was as much *sign* as *sigh*. Like the ephemeral traces left in the air by a dancer or by a perfume, woman became ambiance.

Within the collective unconscious of fin de siècle culture the constellation of images enveloping the "idea" of woman was no different from the image-system associated with the experience of perfume. Woman and perfume represented presences turned into absences and bodies transformed into air: the "luxury of air," as the late-eighteenth-century writer, Madame de Staël, once described perfume. They were emanations like that trail or wake of

perfume the French call "sillage," which a woman and a fragrance leave behind as the tenacious sign of their disappearance, their abstraction, and their transformation into pneuma and soul. This was a new state of being which Coty believed essential to a woman's experience of scent. In a beauty guide published by his firm, Parfums Coty, in 1924, he wrote:

Each woman should be surrounded by a fragrant ambiance—one which will suit her style and be the true expression of her personality. She must use it to express what kind of woman she is—her emotions, her moral character, her deepest aspirations—as much as to enhance her outward appearance. It is essential that Coty perfumes be the expression of a woman's soul.[60]

187

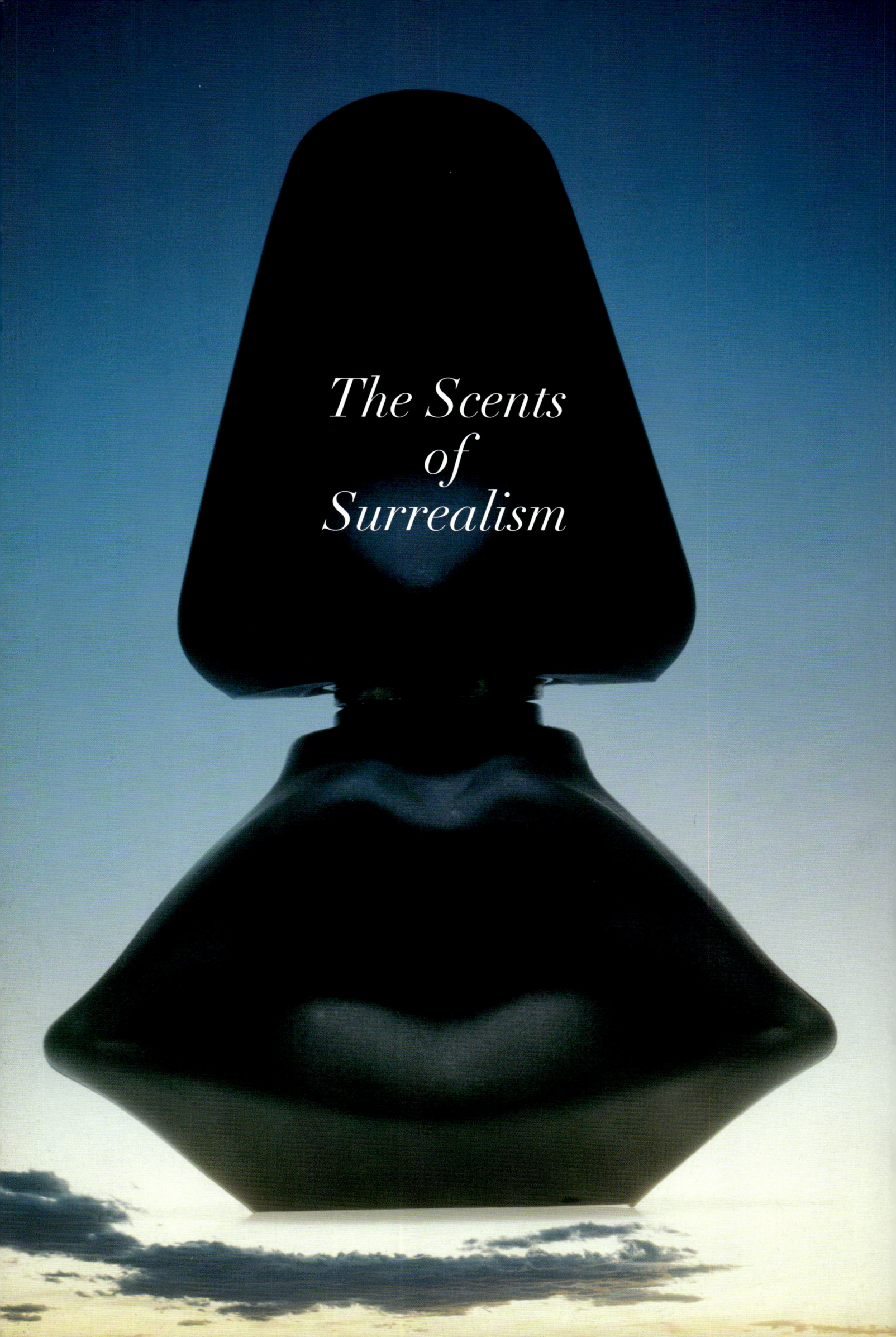

Chapter 5

Fashion is the predecessor—
no, the eternal deputy—
of Surrealism.
—Walter Benjamin

The amusement, as well as affliction,
of the most noble of our senses,
the search for perfume follows
no other path than that of obsession.
—Colette

Squeezed from the reproductive glands
of plants and creatures, perfume is the
smell of creation, a sign dramatically
delivered to our senses of the Earth's
regenerative powers—a message of
hope and a message of pleasure.
—Tom Robbins

The Knowing Nose

IF "EVERYTHING IS FIRST PERCEIVED by the nose, everything is within the nose, the world is the nose," as Italo Calvino asserts in his story "The Name, The Nose," then to be is to smell (71). Of course, Calvino is thinking, with a modest degree of hyperbole, of the prehistoric past when to survive one indeed had to detect odors. Almost everything that could be considered "world," in this time before time when the nose was the primary sensory organ, existed by grace of smell and odor. By means of the nose, one fed, preserved, defended, and protected oneself. The universe was fundamentally a complex network of overlapping natural odors: those that attracted and those that repulsed; those that charmed and those that sickened; those that increased appetite and those that took it away; and those that promised pleasure and those that signaled danger to the humanoid quadruped, our ancestor, who, with nose to the ground and avidly breathing a strong concentration of odorous signs, made his or her way through the world. That the "world is all nose"—that air is impregnated with smell, that the past comes alive from the explosion of a perfume, and that love is triggered by the release of sensual odors—is an irrefutable truth in which Napoleon, Josephine, Flaubert, Baudelaire, Huysmans, Zola, and others strongly believed.

For Guillaume Apollinaire, the early twentieth-century poet, the world was nose as well. One needed the sense of smell not only to experience and interpret the modern reality of the city but to provoke and inspire imagination. With a keen sense of smell and taste and a powerfully creative imagination, the poet could reinvent the universe. Orpheus, with whom the bon vivant and insatiably life-loving Apollinaire often identified, was more than a mythic Greek poet whose music and song moved rocks, changed the flow of rivers, and awakened life in an inanimate world. In Apollinaire's vision, as the poem "Vendémiaire" (1913) phrases it, Orpheus is a sensualist. He listens to polyphonic voices arriving from all the capitals of Europe; he gulps down rivers of wine from vineyards all over the Continent; and he inhales the odors of different places and different peoples. The modernist orphic poet, who sings the vibrant, dynamic life of Paris into existence and whose modern incarnation Apollinaire declares himself to be, ingests a universe now transubstantiated into wine. With Dionysiac abandon he sings "songs of universal drunkenness" celebrating the ecstasy of the world's sounds, scents, and tastes. Literally drunk on the world, Apollinaire-Orpheus acquires a knowledge grounded in sensual being and intoxication. "I know," he confidently declares, "the savor of the universe."[1] The taste and odor of the world come to him not as a rational form of understanding but as a sensuous, primal, even irrational knowledge. Experienced and known through a fusion of the senses, the world is mouth, eye, ear, hand, and, of course, nose; and this nose truly "knows."

Similarly orphic in his power to celebrate the dynamic modern world through poetry and similarly sensitive to the vibrant intensity of odors is the surrealist poet Robert Desnos. Written three decades after "Vendémiaire" Desnos's stirring poem of resistance to the Nazi Occupation, "The Watchman of the Pont-au-Change" (1944), dreams of a confluence of odors, at once delicate and horrible, coming together from different points of the universe like armies of comrades. As they march to liberate Paris these odors clamor in "A language that has only one word: Freedom!": "Cries, songs, sounds of the dying, sounds of riot, they come from everywhere. / . . . / From the four corners of the horizon, across the barriers of earth, / With the scent of vanilla, of wet earth and blood, / Of saltwater, of powder and funeral fires, / Of kisses from an unknown giant." Desnos perceives the arrival of his comrades through a union of the senses that matches the solidarity of the liberators: "Friends, friends and brothers of friendly nations. / I heard your voices in the scent of African orange trees."[2]

Poet of sensuality and sensuousness, of sensitivity and sentimentality, and of sense and senselessness, Apollinaire was the self-elected poet of a new century whose modernist rhythms and cadences he sought to express: from the noise of cars passing on the bridges beneath the Eiffel Tower and the loud proclamations, the "cries," as he called them, of billboard advertisements to the fragments of conversations overheard one Monday morning in a Parisian cafe. Voice of the air of modernism—its music, smell, flavor, savor—and poet of the senses and scents of the everyday, Apollinaire continuously opened himself to the exterior world and to the otherness of modernist life. In fact, the poetic self, he argued, could not exist without the scent of the other, as the autobiographical poem "Cortège" ("Procession") from *Alcools* (his collection of 1913) asserts: "One day / One day as I invited my soul / I said to myself Guillaume it's time to come / So I at last may find out who I am / I who know the others / I know them by fives senses and by some others" (66–71). This commitment to self-knowledge is followed by a catalogue of the poet's sensory powers of imaginative creation, testimony to his magical gift for constructing the other from the minimal sensations and disjointed signs the world gives him. "If I see their feet I can recreate those people by the thousands," he boasts. And not even feet. As Picasso, Braque, and other cubist painters—Apollinaire was close to them—attempted to recreate our perception of reality by rearranging fragments of a bottle, a table, or a woman's body, so the poet, watching the procession of the "others" who come forward to represent him, takes one of their hairs, or their tongues, or their children and recasts these elements into a new image. And sight is not his only faculty of poetic or artistic invention; the other four senses are equally powerful. Hearing their footsteps he can determine the road these people have taken; touching their clothes, he can sense whether they are cold; tasting the flavor of the laurel they cultivate he can know whether to love or to ridicule. Of all five senses, pride of place (eight lines' worth) is given to sight. This is not all that surprising considering that vision, from the moment humans began to walk on two legs nearly two million years ago, instead of crawling on all fours closer to the ground where smells naturally congregate, has become our most powerful sense, the one that has assured our evolutionary survival by triggering the "flight or fight" instinct, as once, long ago, the sense of smell, before it became degraded and weakened, had determined many of our most primitive reactions.

While Apollinaire devotes one line or sometimes two to the senses of hearing, taste, and touch, his appreciation of smell is greater. After sight, it is the most powerful faculty in his sensory arsenal, if the number of lines in "Cortège" devoted to its description is any measure; there are seven, one fewer than for vision: "It's enough that I smell the odor of their churches / The odor of the rivers in their cites / The fragrance of flowers in the city parks / O Cornelius Agrippa the scent of a little dog would have been enough for me / To describe precisely your fellow citizens of Cologne." Smell for Apollinaire becomes a faculty of detection and of imaginative creation: in other words, a form of knowledge. From simple and complex odors—a geography and landscape of scents—he can reconstruct an entire population, that of Cologne, a city not hostile to fragrance, as we know. Even Apollinaire's erudite allusion to Cornelius Agrippa, a sixteenth-century doctor and alchemist, depends on a knowledge of the history of perfume. By blending blood with certain aromas Agrippa believed he could create scented balms that would inspire love. This is the kind of perfumed aphrodisiac for which humankind has been searching from the time of the Egyptians to the scientists of our own day who investigate the existence of so-called human love pheromones. Moreover, perfumes, as Agrippa wrote in his major work, *Occult Philosophy* (1531), are a kind of cosmic "open-sesame"; they make "the gates to the elements and to the heavens open, so that through these gates man may glimpse the secrets of the Creator" (Le Guérer, *Les Pouvoirs*, 192, 305). Like the medieval alchemists who influenced him and like Apollinaire who follows him, Agrippa discovers in perfume a path to knowledge and revelation.

The link between knowledge and smell, as Apollinaire shows in "Cortège" (does he not willfully assert his intention to know the citizens of Cologne by their smells), places him squarely in the tradition of Baudelaire, Mallarmé, and Montesquiou, poetic predecessors sensitive to the complex and subtle affinities between scent and poetry. "Enveloping, atomizing, enrapturing, perfume resists being signified," the contemporary philosopher Julia Kristeva remarks. "It confuses words; it forms alliances with metaphors. . . . Poetry is the true language of musk, ambergris, and incense." Although most twentieth-century poets, and particularly the surrealists, tended to favor the visual—namely, those experiences susceptible to representation and to the "tyranny" of the image as seen or read—they did not, despite the odorphobia of a sanitized and deodor-ized society, turn up their noses at the scents and smells of modern life. With the rise of surrealism in the years between World Wars I and II—André Breton's first *Surrealist Manifesto* appeared in 1924—came several creative interactions between the sensuality of perfume and the sensibility of poetry, especially in the areas of advertising, bottle design, poetry, and the plastic arts. Despite sometimes naively idealistic manifestoes and overheated theories, surrealism in general (and the surrealist creations of poets and artists like Louis Aragon, André Breton, Paul Eluard, and Marcel Duchamp) never abandoned the realm of experience, whether sensory or imaginary. The real is always real in surrealism, and experience, even when fantasized and imagined, is consistently sensorial if not sensual. In surrealist terms, the "imaginary," as Breton declared in 1930, is "what tends to become real."[3] Within surrealist poetry, art, design, event, performance, and theory there never was a retreat from experience. There may have been a departure (primarily by disaffected members) from surrealism as a movement, or a way of living, or a philosophy of being, especially after that explosion of super-reality, which the horrors of World War II produced and from which surrealism never recovered. But the insistence on lived experience—whether love, poetry, imagination, politics, or the streets of Paris—remained an unwavering dimension of surrealist life. The use surrealism made of perfume, as we shall see, was in keeping with this commitment to life lived at a higher level of the real: namely, the surreal. The ambiguity of perfume as the fusion of the sensual and the spiritual and of the real and the imaginary provoked surrealists to juxtapose the kinds of contradictory realities they sought to draw up from the dark well of unconscious life and to expose to the light of (the every) day. The power of perfume to generate overlapping movements of dissipation and concentration and to merge fusion with diffusion and confusion produced the chance encounter of opposites (the celebrated coincidence, for example, of an umbrella and a sewing machine on a dissecting table) which the surrealists so passionately sought.

The Surrealist Nose

Smell, as one scientist has remarked, is "the inarticulate sense." Unlike the world of colors, there are no words in the realm of scents comparable to red, blue, or green to designate different qualities, values, tones, or hues of smell. Beyond the principal descriptive classes of perfumes as categorized by perfumers (according, as mentioned above, to their floral, oriental, chypre, citrus, fougère, leather, and woody properties) and despite the Fragrance Foundation's efforts in the 1990s to identify five basic, although highly subjective, scent categories ("exhilarating-energetic," "relaxing-understated," "romantic-sensitive," "erotic-mysterious," "sophisticated-confident"), there are not many evocative words readily available to describe smells.[4] Small, by comparison with other sensations, is what historian Paul Faure calls "the lexicon of osmology" (15). There may be, he observes, no more than a hundred or so adjectives—like delicate, sweet, weak, strong, heavy, heady, intense, pungent, insidious, penetrating, powdery, smooth, dry, vigorous, piquant, expansive, fugitive, ethereal, intoxicating, tenacious, captivating, suave, repulsive, wild, exciting—and no more than twenty verbs—to breathe, inhale, savor, sniff, smell, scent, perfume, deodorize, waft, permeate, emanate, stink, reek, and so on—relating to the sense of smell and the experience of odor (15). And yet, in spite of the fundamental indescribability of smell, Baudelaire, Mallarmé, and other nineteenth-century poets and artists, as we have seen, discovered ways of articulating the very inarticulateness of jasmine, musk, rose, and other aromas. They turned the silence of perfume, its resistance to representation, into metaphor by means of which the past as memory and as scent could be recaptured in writing. What past there is, their poems seem to say, exists only in the aroma of that past, only in the mnemonic wake (the "sillage") it has left behind, which words trace and to which they give voice.

The Sensual Poetry of Perfume Slogans

Thus, perfume is a language with its own unique rhetoric and its own distinctive syntax or combination of associations, which give rise to a kind of poetry where feelings of love, desire, seduction, romance, and bliss come together to create a sensual fantasy. This is a reality that advertisements for many contemporary fragrances never let us forget, as the following examples show: "The perfume of precious moments" *(Trésor*, Lancôme); "A tribute to the beginning of love" (*Shalimar*, Guerlain); "The secret of charm is in not revealing everything" (*Mitsouko*, Guerlain); "Life is more beautiful when one writes it oneself" *(Champs-Elysées*, Guerlain); "Put it *where* you want to be kissed" *(Ici*, Coty); "Never has perfume provoked such emotion" (*Opium*, Yves Saint Laurent); "A drop of perfume . . . an ocean of love" (*Hanae Mori*); "The secret world where every woman is a sun" (*24 Faubourg,* Hermès); "The perfume is within" *(Eau d'Issey*, Issey Miyake); and "*Yvresse,* for women who bubble" (*Yvresse*, Yves Saint Laurent). There are even slogans that favor the unconscious, giving pride of place to the dream experience which the surrealists found so fascinating: "The best dreams happen when one is awake. Who needs night?" (*Dreams*, Tabu); "Perfume is the music of my dreams" (*Anick Goutal*); "When fantasy becomes reality" (*Caroline Herrera*); "Share the fantasy" (*Chanel No. 5*); "The unconscious has its scent" (*Fantasme*, Ted Lapidus); "There is no life without excess" (*XS*, Paco Rabanne); "Create your dream" (*Image,* Cerrutti); "For the sensualist who believes in making her dreams a reality" (*Beyond Paradise,* Estée Lauder); and "Fantasy: everybody has one" (*Fantasy*, Britney Spears*)*. One

recent slogan, for Giorgio Armani's *Sensi*, employs a strange juxtaposition of passion and logic which the surrealists in their war against reason would have greatly appreciated: "I sense, therefore I am," declares this new, perfumed version of the *Cogito*, the seventeenth-century philosopher René Descartes' celebrated dictum, "I think therefore I am."

Such rhetorical intensity as the scented imagination possesses, such magic to inspire dreams, fantasies and desires, and such force to make us love or even to provoke acts of collective violence, as happens at the end of Süskind's novel, *Perfume,* were recognized by writers, pre-surrealist and surrealist, early in the twentieth century. Mallarmé, whose knowledge of the Parisian fashion world was extensive, even sensed a poetic threat coming from fin de siècle practitioners of the perfume arts. "They have taken all our words," he admitted to the poet Paul Valéry, who passed the comment on to Breton in a letter of March 1916. And in "Le Musicien de Saint-Merry," a poem from 1914, Apollinaire offered the following advice to his fellow wordsmiths: "Poet emulate the labels of perfumers." Breton, also, was captivated by advertisements, in particular those for the beauty products created by Saint-Ange ("the most beautiful ads one could possibly read in newspapers," he observed), going so far as to claim in the first *Surrealist Manifesto* "that the world would end, not with a good book but with a beautiful advertisement."[5]

While Apollinaire and Breton admired advertising in a passive, armchair sort of way, Desnos took a much more active interest in this new art form, inventing poetic slogans, rhymed proverbs, and catchy jingles for the chocolate, soap, fur, and Cinzano products, among others, which sponsored his popular radio programs during the 1930s. A series of jingles for the Sauzé perfume house used one simple rhyme to link the final syllable of "Sauzé" to words like "efficacité," "qualité," "beauté, and "aisée" (easy). To advertise a Sauzé perfume, called *Pour Soi* (For Oneself), which probably came in a refillable bottle, Desnos invented a dialogue between two voices: "What would you say of someone who threw her wallet away when it was empty?" one person asks. "She'd be crazy," the interlocutor answers. "Then why do it with your perfume bottles?" queries the first voice. Another advertisement poses a similar question to make the same point about the advantages of refilling: namely, that one would never buy a brand-new pen if it ran out of ink or a new cigarette lighter were it to run out of fluid. Finally, in his essay, "Publicité = Poésie" written in 1927, the poet Blaise Cendrars praises advertising as one of the "seven wonders of the modern world." Advertising, he writes, is "the most beautiful expression of our times, the greatest novelty of the day, an Art. . . . What characterizes advertising the world over is its lyricism. Here advertising intersects with poetry. . . . That's why I call on all poets: 'Friends, advertising is your domain. It speaks your language. It gives form to your poetics.'"[6]

How did surrealist poets like Breton, Aragon, and Desnos, who came after Apollinaire—and whose mission

Fig. 76 Rigaud,
Un Air embaumé,
c. 1915, glass perfume
bottle designed by
Julien Viard.

and aesthetic were modeled after what he had defined as a modernist "new spirit" of adventure so harmoniously in tune with the poetry of streets, posters, advertisements, telegraph messages, and perfume labels—react to his command that they compete with the "poetry" of perfumers? Did they ultimately develop a surrealism whose world would be simultaneously cosmos and "osmos" (the Greek root for words referring to smell, like "osmology," the science of smells, "osmometry," the measurement of odors, and "osmothèque," a library of scents)?[7] Can surrealist desire be awakened through olfactory stimuli or must it always, considering the surrealists' idolatry for and subservience to the image, be provoked by sight, glance, and the visual imagination? Did surrealist painters or poets ever discover an *arôme trouvé* (found odor) as imaginatively suggestive and prophetic as an *objet trouvé* (found object), the bizarre, sometimes magical, things they discovered by chance in Paris flea markets? Did the surrealist poet ever follow a seductive scent through the streets of Paris, surrendering to the caprices of an olfactory *flânerie* (wandering), the outcome of which was not just the chance encounter with a woman but the chance discovery of a sensually overpowering odor? Let us look at the poets and artists who signaled an interest, either Dadaist or surrealist, in perfume, starting with a poem by Aragon, moving to the "readymade" constructions of Marcel Duchamp and the writings of André Breton, and then concluding with a poem by Paul Eluard, whose latter-day reincarnation appears as an advertisement for Lancôme perfumes.

The Scented Air of the Poet

Louis Aragon (1897–1982) was one of the first poets after Apollinaire to jump on the perfume bandwagon and coincidently to have done so in a poetic homage to Apollinaire himself, written one year after Apollinaire had died of Spanish influenza in the 1918 pandemic. The sonnet in question, whose first line emphasizes the scent or taste of "fruits with the savor of sand," was originally published without a title. Seven years later, however, as he was organizing the manuscript for his collection *Le Mouvement perpétuel* (Perpetual Movement), Aragon decided to give the poem the title, "Un Air embaumé" ("Scented Air"), the name of a popular French perfume before and after World War I.[8] While the poem makes no direct allusions to perfume, aside from its title, it nevertheless gives off hints and whiffs of olfactory phenomena and intimations of effervescent and exalting phenomena, all of which are designed to evoke Apollinaire's energetic personality and forceful poetry.

Having floated in the air of the past, Apollinaire's work continues to endure, give off scent, and sing in the posthumous atmosphere of what the final verse of Aragon's poem calls, linking Apollinaire to two of the greatest innovators of poetry (the Greek demi-god, Orpheus) and love (the infamous libertine writer, the Marquis de Sade), "Mon Sade Orphée Apollinaire." The air inhaled by the young poets of Aragon's generation remains "scented" ("embaumé") by Apollinaire's spirit, saturated with the discoveries that he, this "handsome plunderer of secrets," had revealed, and perfumed by the changing fragrances that his poems had diffused and would continue to diffuse. The reverberating echoes of Apollinaire's verses, which continue to make themselves heard, the sparkling of his imagination which passes like odorous bubbles of champagne into the air of the future, the savor of the fruits of his imagination still there for the tasting—all constitute the scents, exhalations, and effervescences of what the poem calls the "unique canon," the oeuvre, both fragrant and embalmed, which Apollinaire had created and, in the wake of his death, had left as his legacy: his "scented air," in other words. The bubbles arising from his genius, the emanations given off by his poetry, and the sounds issuing from his verses are traces passing into the air of the present where the wind of history carries them on to the next generation of poets, like Aragon, who will try to ensure in their own poems that Apollinaire's "scented air" remains symbolically vibrant, intoxicating, and provocative. The auditory, odorous, and prophetic emanations of Apollinaire's poetry with its "lyrical echoes"—do not echoes in the world of sounds correspond to what "sillages" (trails) are in the world of perfumes?—construct what Aragon calls a "memorial tomb," an enclosed object (at once monument and bottle) out of which the sounds, sensations, and scented airs of Apollinaire continue to emerge.

Rigaud's "Scented Air"

While the allusions to perfume in Aragon's poem are not numerous, the title's reference to the fragrance, *Un Air embaumé* (Scented Air), is decidedly unambiguous. Launched in 1912 by the house of Rigaud and sold in 1915 in a bottle (fig. 76) designed by Julien Viard—a sculptor who created more figural bottle stoppers than any other flacon designer—*Un Air embaumé* was an amber-scented perfume created from a distinctive blend of floral and woody notes; it would inspire other perfumes later in the century, like Schiaparelli's *Shocking* in 1937 and Guerlain's *Chamade* in 1969. Founded in 1854 and located near the Palais Royal, Rigaud was the first perfume house to exploit France's colonial interest in Asia by introducing fragrances with names evoking Far Eastern associations, like *Melati de Chine, Kanaga-Osaka,* and *Pagoda Flowers*. Like Rigaud's other perfumes—*Parfum sentimental* (1900), *Mary Garden,* one of three scents named after famous prewar opera singers—*L'Heure charmante,* and *Le Parfum tendre* (1924)—*Un Air embaumé* was much in demand thanks to an aggressive advertising campaign. Benefiting from what today we would call "brand identification," the fragrance remained popular for over forty years in France as well as in the United States where it first appeared in 1915. Advertisements for *Un Air embaumé* were widely disseminated in women's magazines and published in theater programs.[9]

There are two such advertisements of interest. The first, from around 1915 (fig. 77), shows a woman in a long flowing gown or toga with a garland of flowers (roses perhaps) around her neck. From the flacon at the bottom right, curved waves or emanations of perfume rise. The vapors encircle the woman in a curve that echoes the shape of the bottle, suggesting that she, whose ethereal look signals a semiconscious reverie, is enveloped in the scented air designated by the fragrance's name. The woman appears contained, even "bottled," one might say, by the vaporous and undulating trails of the fragrance. Other advertisements and perfumed cards of the period show

this intoxicating vapor curling upward to the woman's nose, giving her a faraway look of otherworldly bliss. The typography of the perfume's name set at the head of the advertisement has a character in keeping with the airy, floating forms inscribed at the center of the ad. Calligraphy and perfumery reinforce each other through a sinuous and slightly bulging script in which the different curves of the letters composing the fragrance's name intertwine and blend. This calligraphic entwining repeats the vaporous forms of the swirling spirals which beneath the words "Un air embaumé" figure the emanations arising from the bottle and dispersing into the air. The "a" of "air" and the "e" of "embaumé" are uppercase, but the first word, "un," and the letter "u" are presented in an awkward lowercase type. Of all the letters, the "u" is the most deformed, rounded and billowy, suggesting the expansive and deforming power of a perfume, which can change the very air one breathes, the landscape one inhabits, and the shapes one perceives. Even the air becomes calligraphic, thanks to the similarity (as pronounced in French) between the sound of the word "air" and the sound of the letter "R," a resemblance Rigaud used to its advantage. In 1910 the company produced a luxurious advertising catalogue in art nouveau style, the white cover of which revealed a half-sentence elaborately written by hand in black ink—"Un Air Embaumé Parfume le Monde...C'est ..." ("An *Air Embaumé* Perfumes the World ... It is ...")—which the next page completed: "... L' *R* de Rigaud, sa firme, ses parfums" ("... the *R* of Rigaud, its company, its perfumes") (fig. 78). A dozen pages tied together by a thin white string offered nine original color compositions by well-known illustrators, depicting medieval, eighteenth-century, fin de siè-cle, Egyptian, and Russian scenes, filled with romantic and floral motifs and surrounded by a border of swirling perfume vapors; the illustrations represented Rigaud's nine most fashionable perfumes. The ini-tial color illustration on the cata-logue's second page displayed an enormous capital "R" (a letter that is pronounced in French like the word "air"). The letter's curves, arabesques, serifs, ascenders, and descenders were composed of intertwined flowers and leaves; above it hovered a similarly garlanded crown.[10]

Another advertisement for *Un Air embaumé* (fig. 79), this time from 1920 and in all likelihood destined for an American audience, presented an alto-gether different theme, strangely both Egyptian and Venetian. Standing at the prow of what appears to be a gondola and costumed *à la Pharaonne*, a woman, under a night sky illumined by a crescent moon, guides a bark laden with the full line of *Un Air embaumé* beauty prod-ucts, from toilet water to rouge and face powder. Against

Fig. 77 (*top*) Tendrils of scent envelop the woman in this adver-tisement for Rigaud's *Un Air embaumé*, c. 1915.

Fig. 78 This art nouveau advertising catalogue from 1910 (entitled "Un Air Embaumé Parfume le Monde, C'est L'R de Rigaud ...") for nine Rigaud perfumes uses the letter "R," pronounced "air" in French, to make the initial letter of Rigaud's name rhyme with the very *air* of fragrance.

the stern sit two individuals lost in reverie—two lovers? two maidens? Who can be sure?—dressed in long flowing gowns and at whose feet four muscular rowers propel the ship toward its unknown destination. However, the typography, still in Gothic script, is more formally regular than that found in the 1914 advertisement. The first word is drawn on the same scale as the other words, although there are more mannered curlicues evident in some of the letters—the "*u*" of "un," the "*a*" of "air," and the "*e*," "*b*," and "*a*" of "embaumé"—as if the orientalist motif of this advertisement required a more exotic typographic tone.[11]

As for the connection between the title Aragon gave to his poem and the subject of the poem itself, and as for the link between this particular surrealist sonnet and the advertisements distributed for Rigaud's perfume, there is not a great deal that can be said—this is surrealism, after all—other than to put forth the following hypothesis: namely, that Aragon sought to give his funerary poem in praise of Apollinaire a very contemporary and modernist aspect. Like perfume itself, impregnating the air around the wearer with an aura of mystery and beauty, with echoes of a tenacious and penetrating fragrance, and with a music and "air" suddenly made odorous, the sound, music, and air of Guillaume Apollinaire's poetic legacy leave in their wake a trail, which will enchant, seduce, and give direction to all French poets to come. Aragon's "Un Air embaumé" takes possession of the work of Apollinaire in an effort to embalm it through the scent of words and contain it in a kind of "poem-bottle." Thus, a young poetic admirer (Aragon) preserves the spirit of a great poet at the same time that French modernism transforms this spirit into a patrimonial presence: a poetic "scented air" hovering over

twentieth-century French culture. Aragon assures for Apollinaire a future renown, guaranteeing him an afterlife as permanent, tenacious, and captivating as the scent of a great and classic perfume.

The Eros of Rose

Un Air embaumé, the perfume, enjoys an afterlife too. Its bottle reappears in another work of avant-gardist spirit, a Dadaist creation by Marcel Duchamp: one of his famous "readymades" from 1921. These "readymades" were originally everyday objects of the most commonplace sort, turned away from their original function and, by the artist's (i.e. Duchamp's) mere selection of them, made into works of art: for example, Duchamp's giving the title *Fountain* to a urinal and displaying it in a gallery, or his turning a simple snow shovel into a sculpture by writing along its handle the words "In Advance of a Broken Arm." Duchamp's perfume readymade involved his transforming Rigaud's well-known perfume bottle, with its imposing oblong stopper and wing-shaped lines etched in the form of a horseshoe as designed by Viard, (fig. 80), into an incarnation of his feminine alter ego, "Rrose Sélavy," a pun on the phrase "Eros, c'est la vie," ("eros is life"). The label, its oval form repeating the shape of the bottle and even that of the female silhouette, the notorious "S-curve," shows Duchamp cross-dressed as Rose in a photograph taken by Man Ray. The perfume's name, *Belle Haleine,* represents an ironic, tongue-in-cheek act of subversive iconoclasm, a Dadaist mockery of Western mythology and perfumery. It refers to the odor of breath ("*haleine*")—not a smell that would inspire the olfactory imagination of a traditional perfumer nor an appropriate name for anything but a mouthwash—as well as the image of classical feminine beauty expressed in Western culture by the myth of "la belle Hélène": namely, Helen of Troy, whose "face … launched a thousand ships" and whose image has influenced poets, like Homer, Ronsard, and Pierre Jean Jouve, and a composer like Jacques Offenbach, whose operetta *La Belle Hélène* (1864) was a runaway success during the Second Empire.[12]

Puns and wordplay swirl around Duchamp's subversive object. This readymade appropriates, for its own cheeky and iconoclastic ends, both the iconic quality of perfume—its status as a luxurious, sensuous object to be collected and consumed—and the imaginary quality of perfume: the fantasy it evokes of all that is romantic, erotic and mysterious, and the promise it makes to create "a complete aura of irreversible fragrant femininity," as a late-twentieth-century advertisement for *Chanel No. 5* claims (*Elle,* May 1999). At the same time, Duchamp's artifact deconstructs the very object it has perfectly imitated and parodied. It is not only that eros is life, but that all scents and all flowers, in particular the "rose" (R-O-S-E), which the four letters of *eros* are rearranged to spell, are life as

well. Rrose Sélavy's initials, "RS," written below the perfume name on the label, evoke an imaginary association as well, calling to mind experiences of sensuality, intoxication, and death which the symbolism and mythology associated with roses traditionally express. In an effort to give his "readymade" a refined, dignified look in keeping with the high cultural status of perfume in society, and to make the bottle as real, authentic, and accurate an object as possible—though he refuses to fill the bottle with, let's say,

jasmine absolute from Grasse at $12,500 a pound or iris absolute at nearly $40,000 per pound—Duchamp designs an elegant and aesthetically pleasing logo. As the great French couturier Paul Poiret, who had been the first fashion designer to make the jump from couture to perfumery and who, in 1912 as a tribute to his daughter, had created one of his first fragrances, *La Rose de Rosine*, in a bottle (fig. 81) decorated with an elaborately gilded and hand-painted "R"—it was designed by the art deco artist

Georges Lepape—Duchamp in *Belle Haleine* artfully highlights the initials of Rrose Selavy's signature scent. First, he reverses the "R" of her name and then elegantly makes the ascending arm of the letter "S" (on the right) mirror the graceful descending leg of the now backward "R" (on the left).[13]

Aside from the humorous substitution of "haleine" for "Hélène," by means of which insubstantial "breath" replaces, but never fully evacuates, the image of the mythic woman, and aside from the surprising photographic portrait of a woman who replaces and veils, but never fully effaces, the image of a man, what informs the observer that this is most definitely not an authentic flacon, despite an initial second of doubt, is the label's announcement that this "fragrance" is not an "eau de toilette" (toilet water) but an "eau de voilette" (veiled water), the "*v*" replacing the "*t*" and turning not only *toilette* into *voilette* but *toile* (canvas) into *voile* (veil). Duchamp's "assisted readymade," as he called it, engages in acts of veiling and unveiling; it creates its own dance of veils. There are possibly six turns or revolutions contributing to its choreography. First, in the hybrid, cross-dressed image of himself and of Rrose Sélavy, Duchamp veils, though he never effaces, his own masculine sexuality. Second, he "takes the veil," as it were, but in doing so his commitment is not as much to the new feminine presence which hides the old masculine reality as to the veil itself, the subversive subterfuge and dissimulation. He unveils the very process of veiling, that very metamorphosis by which male and female, self and other, Rose (as the name of a woman) and Eros (as the name of love) morph one into the other on the label. Third, the "readymade" object, at once what it is and what is other than it is—both an authentic perfume bottle and a bottle made into a readymade through the intervention of a creative and conceptual artistic act—presents itself as a veiled object: the ironic surrogate for a familiar, everyday object which it appears to embody but in reality disembodies. Fourth, the bottle, which is and is not a bottle, as the woman is and is not a woman, and Duchamp is and is not Rrose Sélavy, calls attention to the ambiguity of perfume: namely, its function as a mask and a veil, worn on and over the skin, mixing with the body's natural odor in order to disguise and aestheticize it. Fifth, since the verb "voiler" (to veil as well as to rig a ship with sails) refers to any object having a convex form (a billowing ship's sail or a fluttering face veil), it pointedly signals the full, curved, and rounded shape of Duchamp's and Rigaud's bottle. Finally, replacing the first syllable, "*toile*," of the word *toilette* with the first syllable, "*voile*," of *voilette* (so that the customary designation *eau de toilette*, toilet water, is transformed into *eau de voilette*, veiled water), Duchamp, with a humor as fierce as it is ironic, illustrates the iconoclastic playfulness of his avant-garde aesthetics.[14]

Yet, this Dadaist mischievousness produces even more ingenious linguistic pranks, for Duchamp suggests that in the expression "eau de voilette" lies hidden a repressed "eau de violette," violet water, produced by the reversal of the letters "o" and "i" in "voilette." This fragrance, however, is no simple violet water, as one might expect to find in any run-of-the-mill eau de toilette. No, this "eau de violette" is unusual, because suggested in the syllable "viol" (the French word for "rape") is the reality of a violation: namely, the transgression of gender boundaries, or artistic conventions, or protocols of taste, which Duchamp's readymade has committed and which it has also worked to veil. The alternation between concealment and revelation and the manner by which one reference hides an allusion to its opposite (haleine-Hélène, voilette-violette) can be summarized by the following tongue-twister: *Belle Haleine* expresses the veiling of a violation (*le voile d'un viol*) that is also the violation of a veiling (*le viol d'un voile*). Subtly, Duchamp reveals, moreover, how the visible surface of a canvas, the *toile*—for centuries the point of departure for traditional artistic production—is effaced and replaced by the veil, the *voile*, of a new, iconoclastic process of artistic creation that produces hidden, or disguised, or subversive works which may no longer be works, or even art, for that matter. Rather, the readymade is born from common objects of everyday life, like a perfume bottle, a snow shovel, or a urinal, which have been randomly selected and "made ready" to become "art," only because the artist has deliberately chosen them for conversion and has by means of the imaginative power of this choice, conceptually reconfigured them. The readymade, as Duchamp defined it late in his life, is, as the art critic Francis Naumann remarks, "a work of art . . . without an artist to make it."[15]

The subversion of reality and the confusion of expectations concerning the world, as realized by the Dadaist and surrealist juxtaposition of objects, divested commonplace things of their familiar everydayness and enveloped them in a transformative strangeness. The effect was literally iconoclastic. Whether the objects were part of a mixed media construction (like Breton's *Song-Object* from 1937, where pipe cleaners, a handwritten poem, a seahorse, and a small opaque perfume bottle share the inside space of a box bordered with lace), or whether they were Duchampian readymades (like his French window from 1920 with its glass panes covered in black leather and renamed *Fresh Widow*), or whether, finally, they were images in a poem (like Breton's verbal collage from the early twenties in which he imagines dark edelweiss and car brakes serving as the resting place for "subterranean forms resembling perfume stoppers") the effect was consistently the same: to trouble and shock the conscious mind with revelations from the unconscious or dream imagination. Dadaists and surrealists were equal-opportunity employers of objects, words, and artifacts. No matter what acts of unconscious, chance, automatic, and free association the surrealists provoked through their practice of automatic writing or automatic thought ("automatism")—whether historical, religious, natural, or consumerist in nature—the goal was consistently to undermine in the most revolutionary manner possible the conventions of bourgeois reality. And yet

Fig. 81 The calligraphy of perfume and the letter "R." Paul Poiret and Les Parfums de Rosine, *La Rose de Rosine*, 1912–1916, glass perfume bottle designed by Georges Lepape.

surrealists were not reluctant to include in their works allusions borrowed from the popular bourgeois culture of the time, like advertisements, consumer products, perfume bottles, and names of popular fragrances. Capitalist, industrial artifacts were welcome in Dada and surrealist constructions; but once incorporated in these new settings the objects underwent a destabilizing of context and meaning which turned the commodity object against itself and against the bourgeois class that had fetishized it. This removal of a capitalist patina from the object's surface revealed a hidden poetic dimension, as Walter Benjamin observed. Surrealists (and Duchamp included), he wrote, "treat words like trade names. . . . Nesting today in trade

names are figments such as those earlier thought to be hidden in the cache of 'poetic' syllables."[16]

Anti-Fragrances and Scentless Perfumes

It is indeed a shame that Duchamp did not live to see and experience *Odeur 53* (late 1990s) from the Japanese designer Rei Kawakubo for her fashion house Comme des Garçons. The "fragrance," if that is the correct word, was designed to be an "abstract scent, [an] anti-perfume" "meant to confound the nose." Made from totally inorganic materials, more evocative of burned rubber, nail polish, and wash drying in the wind than roses, it contained fifty-three ingredients "purposely drawn from the poetics of common experience"; a later fragrance, called *Comme des Garçons 2,* was based on the scent of ink. In a similar manner, the quintuplet of Kawakubo perfumes sold as an ensemble under the name *Synthetic* offered "anti-fragrances" based on man-made materials like Tar, Soda, Garage, Dry Clean, and Skaï (imitation leather). Even more enjoyable for Duchamp would have been a whiff of another anti-scent, *Viktor & Rolf, le parfum* of 1996, created by Viktor Hörsting and Rolf Snoeren, two Dutch couturiers-conceptualists for whom "art and fashion are similar if not identical impulses." Their scent, most definitely Duchampian in spirit, is a scentless perfume, designed to offer nothing more than the idea of a fragrance, a concept-in-a-bottle. If conceptual art began with Duchamp, then conceptual per-fumery has followed his aesthetic trail. By "bottling" the potential absence and disappearance that perfume will become—capturing, in other words, the very fragrance of its loss—and by promising the consumer that she or he will have the pleasurable though contradictory experience of wearing a fragrance with no smell, Viktor and Rolf rein-terpret perfume as a virtual reality. They capture and mar-ket absence. Because of its conceptual quality, this perfume captures the spirit of Duchamp's readymades. Both are manufactured objects which, through the artist's act of intellectual and imaginative thought, have been made to turn against themselves and to subvert the raison d'être of their conventional functionality. An upturned bicycle wheel mounted on a stool, a bottle rack placed in an exhi-bition, a urinal renamed "Fountain," a perfume bottle that is not the Rigaud bottle it seems to be, a perfume label for *Belle Haleine* displaying the picture of a woman who is not a woman, and finally a Dutch fragrance that has no fra-grance although it is advertised as one—all these creations question and subvert the aesthetic (in Duchamp's case) and the consumerist (in Viktor & Rolf's case) worlds in which they exist.[17] With *Viktor & Rolf, le parfum,* commod-ity fetishism is reconceptualized as readymade. Or put another way, the ready-to-wear—and perfume is always *prêt-à-porter*—becomes the readymade.

Woman as Atomizer

Based on the number of allusions to perfume that appear in the two volumes of his complete works in the Bibliothèque de la Pléiade edition, André Breton (1896–1966) may have possibly been the greatest lover of odors among surrealist poets, claiming in one poem (from 1926) that "An under-ground passage unites all perfumes" (II: 70), evoking in another (from 1934) the "jasmine field I saw at dawn on a road outside of Grasse" (II: 408), and discovering one Paris night in 1930 inside a pharmacy window at the corner of la

rue du Faubourg-Montmartre and la rue Lafayette a "per-fume bottle tied with a pale ribbon inside which a faded rose floated, its stem and leaves equally lifeless" (II: 52). There is, however, one glaring lapse in the poetic fascination Breton reveals toward perfume and smell, and it indicates that while he was a poet who could forge powerful images of perfume and could describe the scent of flowers and even the shape of atomizers, he was, like other surrealist poets, sometimes at a loss for words when it came to articulating the intense sen-sory feelings and the complex aromatic sensations charac-teristic of fragrance. The lapse in question is the *blason*—a traditional form of Renaissance love poetry celebrating in detail different parts of the beloved's body—which Breton wrote in 1931 and entitled "Free Union" ("L'Union libre").

With its lyrical litany in celebration of the female body "Free Union" most definitely falls within the tradition of the *blason.* Moreover, its images are liberated by surrealist free association, as the following lines reveal: "Woman of mine with champagne shoulders / And shoulders of a fountain of dolphin heads under ice / Woman of mine with matchstick wrists / Woman of mine with fingers of chance and the ace of hearts / With fingers of mown hay," and so on.[18] In this evocative dissection of the body in which Breton signals out for particular attention (and fetishization) the woman's feet and breasts (each mentioned three times), her tongue and genitals (each mentioned four times), and her eyes (five mentions), he never once refers to the woman's nose nor makes any reference to the phenomenon of smell, other, perhaps, than to evoke "Woman of mine with armpits of marble and beechnut," an image more visual and tactile than odorous. What smell, even surrealist, does marble have, for example? There are just no odors to speak of in the erotic landscape of "Free Union." It is stunningly poetic, lyri-cal, and passionate, but, alas, deodorized.

Yet, Breton's writing, in general, does not manifest an insensitivity to odors; it is not "anosmic," to use the scientific term for the inability to smell (anosmia). In an early auto-matic prose poem constructed of free and unconscious asso-ciations, written in 1920, he, like Aragon, gives his work a title that is a not-so-oblique advertisement for a perfume. And like Aragon's poem, there is little evident connection between the perfume reference in the poem's title and the images or nar-rative the text sets in motion. While Aragon's sonnet indirectly publicized Rigaud's fragrance, *Un Air embaumé,* although the scent hardly needed Aragon's poetic endorsement, Breton's short poem, entitled "Parfums d'Orsay" (I: 412), goes a step beyond that of his surrealist colleague, giving, as it were, free advertising space not to a particular scent but to an entire perfume house, one of the largest and most renowned in the first forty years of the twentieth century.

Parfums D'Orsay

Parfums D'Orsay was established in 1908 by a German-Dutch group of investors who named their establishment

for the Count Gabriel Alfred d'Orsay (1801–1852), an aristocratic dandy and social charmer who divided his time between Paris and London from the 1820s to the end of the 1840s. D'Orsay's theatrical style of dressing—he favored velvets, silks, perfumed gloves, diamond jewelry, and high hats—attracted attention and admiration from even the lower classes, who were much taken with his "look" when he appeared on horseback (an often repeated image that Parfums D'Orsay used as a trademark). This "archangel of dandyism," as the poet Lamartine called him, and "perhaps the first modern media celebrity," as a recent biographer describes him, d'Orsay was a painter, an inventor, and a friend of Lord Byron, and other artistic, literary, political, and theatrical luminaries of the 1830s and 1840s.[19] He is even reputed to have invented a fragrance, *L'Eau de Bouquet D'Orsay,* which only further enhanced his reputation as a man of extraordinary amorous and artistic skills.

D'Orsay's signature fragrance, reconceptualized and renamed *Etiquette bleue* in 1908, was launched as one of the first fragrances of the newly created company, Parfums D'Orsay. From 1908 to the eve of World War I, D'Orsay created and marketed several new scents, all manufactured at the D'Orsay factory, which employed over 500 workers, in a converted château at Puteaux-sur-Seine, a western suburb

of Paris. Reflecting the trend of fin de siècle and prewar perfumers to give their compositions names that were romantic, floral, and aristocratic and to offer consumers luxurious fragrances in deluxe editions with bottles created by the great French crystal manufacturers (Lalique, Baccarat, Süe et Mare, Saint-Louis), D'Orsay's perfumes carried such intriguing names as *New Mown Hay* (c. 1910), *Milord* (1911), *Le Rêve* (1912), *Rose ambrée* (1912), *Mystère* (1912), *Le Porte Bonheur* (Good-Luck Charm, 1913), *Leurs Âmes* (1913), *Nelly* (1913–14), *L'Aveu* (Confession, 1914), *Poésie* (1914), *Grâce* (1914), *Le Parfum d'antan* (Perfume of Yesteryear, 1916), and *Toujours Fidèle* (Forever Faithful, c. 1909)—the latter, one of D'Orsay's longest selling perfumes, with a stopper in the shape of an obedient bulldog (see page 214). It could be said that there was nothing here to interest a surrealist. Even the D'Orsay fragrances which appeared after World War I—with patriotic names like *Fleurs de France* (1918) and *Triomphe* (1920) or more stylish appellations like *L'Elégance* (1922), *Bijoux* (Jewels, 1924), and *Le Dandy* (1925), a hit with flappers—offer no surrealist inspiration or provocation. The only possible exception might be *Belle de Jour,* a perfume D'Orsay produced in the late 1930s, which may have a link, perhaps in name alone, to the surrealist director Luis Buñuel's film of

1966, starring Catherine Deneuve. Of course, some perfumers and couturiers were friendly with the surrealists and called on their genius for the design of perfume bottles and the conception of advertising posters. It should be noted that perfumery had become one of France's most important industries, boasting at the end of the nineteenth century a work force of 20,000 people, over 300 individual manufacturing companies, and more than 2,000 perfume stores.[20] The Paris Art Deco Exhibition of 1925 officially recognized the importance of perfume manufacturing as a uniquely French art.

An industry, as rooted in the bourgeois culture of France, as associated with the ideology of high style and national spirit, and as exploitative of the working classes as the perfume industry was, would, one would expect, have been an anathema to the revolutionary and Marxist orientation of 1920s surrealism. It may very well be the case that in the war between poetry and politics, the lyrical and erotic qualities of perfume won out. Given that few surrealist poets express themselves on the subject of the production or manufacturing of perfume, with the exception of an Eluard poem more lyrical than critical, about the jasmine pickers of Grasse, it is difficult to judge whether the surrealists let political principle overcome sensual experience; often, they did not. What is clear, however, is that as a substance provoking images of reverie and unconscious imagination, as an object energized by feminine interest and obsession, as a form of poetry-on-the-wind, and as an intoxicant deepening love and desire (the rose that becomes eros), perfume attracted the surrealists in varying degrees. Fascinated perhaps by the ephemeral and illusory reality that fragrance creates, the surrealists were sensitive to the compelling links between poetry and scent, agreeing with the poet René Char's statement that "a poet must leave

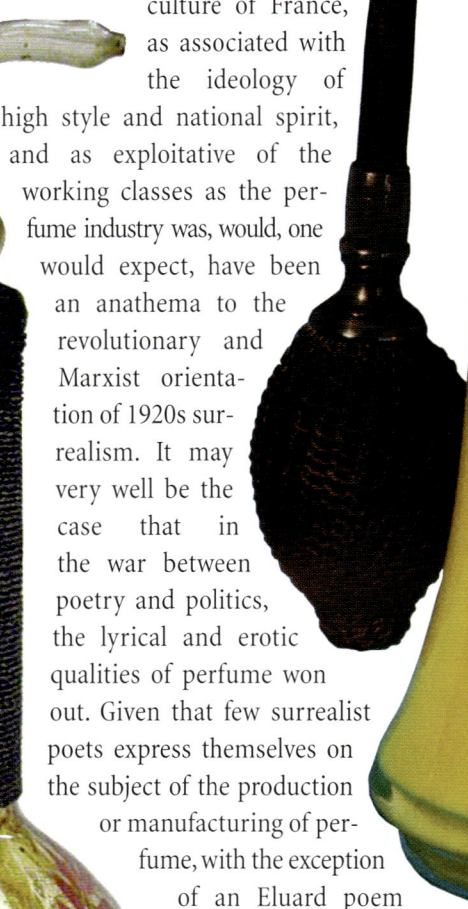

Fig. 82 The bizarre shape of perfume vaporizers, at once phallic and feminine, android and mantislike, appealed to the surrealist imagination in the twenties and thirties. Bohemian double crystal atomizer, c. 1925.

Perfume atomizer created by Parfums de Rosine, 1920s.

traces, not proofs, of his passing. Traces alone make us dream."[21] If one seeks traces, then perfume is most definitely the medium in which to live.

The Erotic Strangeness of Vaporizers

Breton's freely associative and "automatic" poem of 1920, "Parfums d'Orsay," does, indeed, make metaphorical allusions to perfume—to a perfume bottle, to roses (and the echo of "rose" in the verbs "se poser" and "se reposer"), to an orange, and to a woman named Germaine. Interpreting these references creates, however, the same insurmountable difficulties one invariably encounters when reading any automatist surrealist text. Breton's opening line announces with enthusiasm: "The newcomer looks at, but does not see, the sexually feminine vaporizer [*vaporisateur de sexe féminin*] which stands unmoving on the communal dining table" (I: 412). From the outset, a perfume bottle is evoked, one that Breton has clearly feminized. But surely the surrealist unconscious with its penchant for excess and hyperbole has gone too far here, for few are the vessels containing perfume that are, in reality, "feminine" in size and shape; most are indeed rather phallic. Vaporizers and atomizers were first invented in the late 1850s for medical purposes. In fact, the first vaporizers were used to spray thermal water and cure respiratory ailments at Pierrefonds, a French mineral spa. They were then appropriated by flower growers and other cultivators for use in spraying pesticides. Around 1870, barbers started using them to scent men's beards. Relieved of its heavy awkward form and its original pharmaceutical look, the vaporizer in transparent, opaque, engraved, or painted glass became a staple of a woman's toilette in the 1880s. At about the same time, Leopold Franck invented a sophisticated vaporizing system, which with the help of his son Marcel he sold to coiffeurs, pharmacies, and then to the large Parisian department stores.[22]

Because of the culturally determined association between perfume and women and because as a container the bottle lends itself to fantasies of envelopment and containment, Breton's feminization and sexualization of the atomizer exoticize the obvious. It presents a confirmation of what, in his mind, is already known: namely that a perfume vaporizer is always already feminine, in spite of the fact that its initial use in perfumery was designed primarily to scent men's beards and that its physical form is usu-

ally phallic, or at least bisexually ambivalent.[23] In Breton's hands the atomizer reveals the erotic strangeness which any common object may suggest to the surrealist imagination. Certain atomizers (fig. 82), with their thin shapes or, in some instances, curved, swelling, even anthropomorphic bodies, could be seen as structurally or iconically feminine or as imitations of female silhouettes. Or with their long, snoutlike spray heads they could be interpreted as resembling female praying mantises, whose habit of devouring their mates after sex intrigued several surrealists who kept these insects and enjoyed watching them perform.[24] Beneath the reality of the phallic or android atomizer lies the surreality—and the threat, considering Breton's masculine gaze—of a "sexually feminine vaporizer" as his "Parfums d'Orsay" poem conceives of it. His feminization of the phallic bottle—even its possible transformation into the feminine sexual organ—is not, however, an empowerment. The atomizer-woman, as the prose poem represents her, is passive, immobile, and objectified; she is a thing unworthy of attention. The male observer glances at her or at her reincarnation as atomizer, and yet he sees nothing. Even in a surreal state of extraordinariness, the woman in the poem is no more than an object set among other instrumental and possibly utilitarian objects on a dining room table. And there is, moreover, no wind in Breton's poetic scene; it has been absent for years, the poem reports.

Thus, the expressive potential of the atomizer-woman is severely curtailed: no wind means no dissemination, no possibility of perfume permeating or traversing the ambient air. Furthermore, two other allusions in the poem—one to a butterfly, an image of elegant ephemerality and frail sublime beauty, and the other to a tear "longer than the Seine" falling from the narrator's eye—refer possibly to perfumes or perfume bottles popular right before and after World War I. The first is the wing-shaped flacon for the perfume *La Phalène* (referring not really to a butterfly, but to a flame-seeking, self-destructive moth) that D'Héraud launched around 1919 to celebrate, as mentioned in Chapter 4 (see fig. 71, page 176), a scandalously erotic and

macabre play of the same name by Henry Bataille which had debuted six years earlier. Etched in the Lalique-designed glass is the frail silhouette of a woman from whose skeletal torso thin lines expand outward to form the wings of a moth. The second bottle, designed by Viard for Caron's *Parfum précieux* of 1910 (fig. 83), is molded in the form of a glass teardrop or stalactite.[25] It may possibly be linked to Breton's image of a long and, one would suppose, crystalline tear.

Finally, in Breton's "Parfums d'Orsay" a female character, named Germaine, is presented as the object of the male protagonist's thoughts and desires. In an attempt to regain her love, the male protagonist decides to make her the gift of the past: "he was going to present her with lost time like an orange before turning it into a hat store [*chapellerie*] where one could go to rest and contemplate the sun" (I: 412). Breton associates the lost past with the aroma of an orange (although he fails to clarify whether the orange exists as a rounded whole, or is cut into portions, or is merely an odor). He may also be aware of the importance of orange blossoms in the fabrication of certain expensive perfumes. But most interesting is how the image of the citrus fruit suggests that lost time will be given the shape and smell of an orange and then presented to the woman as a gift. The past, thus, becomes an odor; what has been lost emits a distinctive scent which hovers over the scene. Absence is given sensory form; it is made both present and presentable: "he was going to *present* her with lost time." Absence now turns into a perfumed presence. And the lost past, magically resuscitated by the orange scent, suddenly changes into a hat store, a place of fashion, where millinery metaphorically replaces perfume bottles and a hat maker's boutique (*chapellerie*) replaces a perfumer's store (*parfumerie*). That this fashion site is associated with a place of calm, repose, and meditation—more chapel [*chapelle*] than *chapellerie*—and that scent accomplishes this return of a lost past, signal Breton's sensitivity to perfume's explosive power of restoration and immediacy, not unlike the blinding, metamorphic energy of the surrealist image. Within reality itself, scent and aroma (as well as poetry and love for the surrealists) are "open-sesames," unlocking hidden realms of desire and revealing that what the surrealists called the "wonder" or "marvel" ("le merveilleux") of life is also a wondrous experience of fragrance.[26]

The "Lancôm-ization" of Poetry: Paul Eluard and Poême

The marvelous experience of sensual wonder which fragrance expresses and disseminates is found in the surrealist poetry of Paul Eluard (1895–1952) as well. The scented imagination, like all forms of imagination in surrealism—and let us not forget Breton's dictum that "the imaginary is what tends to become real"—is not, as Breton also reminds us, a gift, but rather an "object par excellence of conquest" (II: 49, 50). Surrealist poets attempt to find and master the images that will release those particular powers of imaginary experience which perfume and scent can unconsciously trigger. Because they work directly with physical scents, perfumers possess the artistic power to compose this imaginary experience. But for poets, distanced by words from direct contact with the realities they seek to articulate in their poems, even if words do "make love" as Breton declared (I: 286), the scented imagination is more difficult to invoke and evoke; it exists beyond language and representation. This difficulty is evident in the poetry of Eluard, arguably the most passionately sensual of surrealist poets and the most lyrical and poetically erotic, but who also appears from time to time to be the least sensitive to odors. In the hundreds of texts and the two thousand pages of his collected works there are surprisingly few allusions to perfume. Why is this so? One possible explanation is that Eluard is primarily a poet of vision, of visibility, and of the image. Sight is fundamental to his experience of being in the world; writing, to quote him, means "giving sight."[27] In the Eluardian poetic universe, space is inscribed through glance and gaze. It becomes the very medium of sight, an omniscient and voyeuristic place of transparence where seer and seen intermingle: "Between trees and gates / Between walls and jaws / . . . / Space has the form of my glances" (I: 175). Light literally speaks in this poetry, and the surrealist image mediates this luminous speech. In the Eluardian cosmos, "to see is to breathe and desire," and poetry is "the art of light" (I: 1074, 527). Consequently, Eluard's poetry favors any experience, event, or condition involving glance, visibility, and contemplation and any physical or mental activity that requires eyesight or other forms of optical perception.

The smells of daily life, of course, are not absent from the work of this sensual and materialist poet, who fervently declares that "I have passionately conjugated the verb *to be*" (II: 133). Eluard speaks of "the jasmine of hands opening on to a star"; of "great floods of sunlight washing out the colors of perfumes"; of the beloved's breasts "more delicate than the scent of frozen grass." He imagines "the odor of sound," "the aroma of intertwined lovers," the "perfumes of great love," "the bouquet of flesh," and the "fragrant orange" aroma of day (I: 181, 248, 375, 422, 604, 1036, 1270; II: 118). Yet, in a poem about a jasmine picker (I: 808–9), Eluard offers no description of the heady scent of the flower, no evocation of the imaginary and poetic associations that jasmine evokes. He prefers instead to emphasize the movement of the picker's hands, the landscape surrounding her, and her participation in the physical world of stars, water, and fire.[28] In the poem, "Blason des fleurs et des fruits" (A Blason of Flowers and Fruits, I: 1084–88), which lists about eighty floral and fruit phenomena along with a concise surrealist description of each, including some of the classic ingredients used in perfume composition since the nineteenth century (like tuberose, lilac, orange, honeysuckle, jasmine, iris, bergamot, verbena, datura, lavender, and hawthorn, among many others), not one single line describes or evokes a scent or an odor. It is surprising that Eluard, a poet who stressed the imagination's ties to the concrete world, to physical, sensual experience, and to the body's impulses, was not also more intensely aware of the world's odors; after all, as he once wrote, "My reason refuses to negate the experience of my senses. The object of my desires is always real, always tangible" (I: 979).

There is, however, an explanation for this poetic form of anosmia: namely, that instead of avoiding odors, Eluard's keen and hypersensitive visual imagination acts like an organ of smell. Visual phenomena are presented as odors. They become transparent and ethereal, and they rise to permeate the air of the landscape enveloping them. The face and body of the beloved, once love has made them pure, diaphanous, and radiant, undergo a fundamental change of state; a solid turns into a gas, as it were. The body is spiritualized as it moves out into the world, flowing effortlessly through material barriers, embracing the universe, and finally fusing invisibly with it. Without directly saying so, or even referring to the sense of smell, Eluard presents the beloved and her movements as if they were scents. The woman becomes the perfume emanating from her skin and the scented aura surrounding her body. Her being is coextensive with her scent; to see her is also to smell her, and vice versa. A fine example of this transcendence via fragrance and this sublimation of the body, which turns it through osmosis into a perfume, is found in the poem "Celle de toujours, toute" [She Who Is All Things, Forever] : "The fan of your mouth, the reflections of your eyes / I alone speak of them / I alone am encircled / By this empty mirror where the air circulates through me / And the air has a face, a loved face / A loving face, your face" (I: 196–97). The metamorphosis of the beloved's face, its vaporization into the air which it marks and impregnates, and the way the scented air now expresses the woman's essential reality indicate the workings of an imagination that is fundamentally olfactory. Perfume literally expresses the skin of the person wearing it, giving voice to that skin. "Without perfume, the skin is silent" announces an advertisement from the 1980s for the French Council on Perfume.[29] What Eluard suggests in his poem is that the beloved writes herself on the air through a process of osmosis, fundamentally poetic in nature. Does this transformation of the woman from a physical body to a vapor and from visibility to invisibility not enact the same process of poetic expression by which the beloved whom the poet sees and caresses becomes the beloved about whom he sings and writes? Her being is now expressed in words, in the "aroma" of syllables. Is this osmosis which spiritualizes the woman, transforming her body into air through olfaction and transmuting her being into song through vocalization, not of the very nature of poetry itself? Eluard most definitely thinks so: "I sing the great joy of singing you, / . . . / I sing only to sing, I love you only to sing" (I: 197).

Curiously, of all surrealist poets, Eluard, despite his moments of forgetting to describe odors, became during the final years of the twentieth century (through no choice of his own) the one most intimately linked with perfume. Thanks to the advertising campaign that Lancôme conceived for *Poême*, the fragrance it launched in 1995, Eluard's name spread throughout the world, from large, chic Parisian department stores to modest malls in small towns in the United States. Lancôme's decision to call a perfume "poem" was not a new marketing strategy. D'Orsay had launched the perfume, *Poésie D'Orsay* in 1914, three years after the house of Oriza-Legrand had conceived "*Poéma,*" and fourteen years before the Franco-American perfumer, De Musset, whose name honors the nineteenth-century French poet, had invented the scent "Poème" (1928).[30] In the 1950s Guerlain continued this lyric theme with its fragrance *Ode*, and Forvil with its brillantine *Poème*, which gave hair a kind of poetic aura. While Lancôme's *Poême* may be pronounced the same as De Musset's fragrance and Forvil's pomade, the two names—*Poème* and *Poême*—are distinctly different, despite how they sound. This is because Lancôme, as part of its general marketing strategy and for aesthetic as well as commercial reasons, modifies ever so slightly the spelling of the words it appropriates for its perfumes and cosmetics, adding whenever possible the signature circonflex appearing over the "o" in the company's trademark name and logo: Lancôme. Both their fragrance *Ôui* and their toilet water, *Ô*, the latter a pun on the sound "o" and the word *eau* ("water"), carry the trademark "o-circonflex," as do *Une*

Rôse de Lancôme, a perfume released in 2000 and *Hypnôse* (Hypnosis), launched in 2005. Thus, in keeping with its desire to appropriate or colonize vowels through "*circonflexion,*" Lancôme spells the name of its 1995 perfume: "Po-ê-me."

Lancôme was founded in 1935 by Armand Petitjean, who, after training with François Coty, became the managing director of Parfums Coty. Petitjean sought a name for his company, one that would have a certain elegant softness and would rhyme with Vendôme and Brantôme, and other well-known French names. A friend suggested "Lancosme," the name of a château in the Indre, a region of central France. The silent "s" was easily changed to a circonflex, which now flew "like the proud flag of French savoir-faire" over a name that was graphically and sonorously attractive. The singular nature of the circonflex as an icon and sign of Frenchness is expressed as well in one of the company's slogans: "France has a word for beauty: *Lancôme.*"[31] Moreover, the circonflex in certain French words is a linguistic sign and trace of something lost. In words like "tête" (head) or "fenêtre" (window) the circonflex points to a phantom letter, an old, long-lost "s," dropped from the original "teste," "fenestre," and for that matter "Lancosme."

Poême is a fragrance whose name leaves no doubt about the poetic power of perfume. The advertisements created for it, at least the following text from the American edition of *Elle* (April 1996), celebrate "A poetic bouquet . . . of modern sensuality and luminosity. A scent of contrasts: the icy, transparent Blue Himalayan poppy embraces the intoxicating desert Datura flower . . . for the first time in a fragrance. *Poême* is a cascade of flowers, composed with no beginning . . . no end . . . just echoes." Can one imagine any advertising copy more lyrical? The blend of poetic associations that intertwine and overlap to turn *Poême* into a "perfume of light" is evocatively complex and provocative. The suggestive contrast between sensuality and luminosity, cold and heat, ice and sun, mountain and desert, torrents and flowers, as well as the evocation of intoxication, transparence, blueness, contradiction, and even a postmodernist indefiniteness (there are, declares the advertisement, neither origins nor ends) all come together to declare the fundamental correspondence of poetry and scent. *Poême* asserts poetry's unique power to evoke the transcendental states of sensual being which perfume initiates. Moreover, the name of Lancôme's scent—*Poême* with its hovering circonflex—hides a telling pun. The perfume is not only poetic and erotic; it is poetically and erotically epidermal. *Poême*, the perfume's name, must also be read as "*peau-aime,*" that is, "*la peau qui aime*" (the skin that loves). It testifies to a skin made erotic and amorous by the application of perfume, a skin awakened and revived for love and for loving. "The amorous state [of being]," notes Kristeva, is "a perfumed state, par excellence."[32]

Even if the poetry of the advertising copy for *Poême* and the romance associated with its portmanteau name were not sufficiently evocative to seal the link between poetry and perfume, several other advertisements published in France and the United States established the relationship once and for all, by quoting in full a poem by Eluard. It is a love poem written in 1950 and entitled "I Love You" ("Je t'aime") the first line of which—"I love you for all the women I haven't known"—celebrates one of the key concepts of surrealist experience: namely, the epiphany of the one-and-only love ("l'amour unique") and the encounter with the one-and-only woman whom fate has chosen for the poet, as Eluard's first and last stanza reveal:

I love you for all the women I haven't known
I love you for all the times in which I haven't lived
For the scent of the open sea and the smell of hot
    bread
For the melting snow and for the first flowers
For the innocent animals which haven't been fright-
    ened by man
I love you for love
I love you for all the women I don't love

(...)

I love you for your wisdom, which is not mine
For health
I love you against everything that is mere illusion
For that immortal heart over which I have no power
You think you are doubt and you're just reason
You are the powerful sun that rushes to my head
When I am sure of myself.[33]

The poem's title "I love you," which becomes its refrain, creates a litany that by means of a form of poetic repetition called anaphora (consecutive verses beginning with the same words) builds like a crescendo. Of the twenty-one lines in this three-stanza poem, ten begin with "I love you for" (or simply the preposition "for") and one with "I love you against." These eleven lines dominate the first and third stanzas and passionately celebrate, through the resounding echo of the "I love you" refrain and two other appearances of the verb "love," Eluard's feeling for Dominique Lemor, whom he met in Mexico in 1949 and married two years later. The poem overflows with a passion experienced within a time and place that this love has made cosmic and universal. "I love you," the poet affirms, *for* a host of reasons and realities: *for* other women I have neither known nor loved; *for* other moments I have not lived; *for* other roads not taken; *for* other odors—of bread and sea—I smelled and found unsatisfying; *for* snow and flowers; *for* wisdom and health; *for* truth and certainty; and finally *for* reality: the reality of love, of the woman, and of

her fertile light. Presented from a narcissistic, one-sided perspective, characteristic of Eluard's way of poetically seeing and imagining the other—for it is most often the "*je*" who does the loving in "Je t'aime"—love and poetry affirm the importance of the masculine self over the feminine beloved, the "I" over the "you." From a purely grammatical point-of-view, the continual reiteration of "I love you" graphically illustrates over and over again the degree to which the "you" has become the direct object of the act of loving (and of the verb "love") for which the "I" is responsible and which he alone, as masculine subject, accomplishes.

However, in the final stanza and the penultimate line, the "you" regains her power. In what is the most celebratory and cosmically powerful image of the poem—one indicating the woman's life-giving, sun-inspired power over the amorous poet—Eluard announces that "You are the powerful sun that rushes to my head" ("Tu es le grand soleil qui me monte à la tête"). It is this line that has brought Eluard the posthumous fame that only Lancôme and contemporary fashion could have given him. Advertisements for *Poême* use this line as the perfume's slogan and, more important, to express the fantasy of sublime love that the fragrance promises. As advertisement and as perfume *Poême* circulates an image in which the visibility of light is joined to the liquidity of scent, and rays of sun dance in the air as sensuously as waves of perfume. *Poême* gives to this luminosity the same power of volatility, intoxication, and lightheadedness as the scent which invades the poet and through its captivating emanations turns his head. Perfume and sun, odor and light, smell and vision, drunkenness and ecstasy all become one. Thus, the poet's vertigo and dizziness, suggested in the French expression "monter à la tête" ("to rush to the head") and expressed by the woman's identification with solar power—she is the dazzling center of the cosmos, the high noon of the poet's existence, and her light sustains him and the world they inhabit—indicate that the intoxicating headiness generated by her freshness, beauty, and allure can be had through the simple act of wearing *Poême*, as the smiling, jubilant, blissful countenance of the French actress Juliette Binoche, the "face" of *Poême*, guarantees in one advertisement (*Elle*, 15 Jan. 1996). The conjunction of Eluard's poem with the image of Binoche's face creates a powerful juxtaposition, almost symphonic in the poetic, corporeal, sensual, and romantic associations it successfully orchestrates.

What has just been described applies primarily to the advertisements of *Poême* conceived for the French market, because, as one would expect, Eluard's verse— "Tu es le grand soleil qui me monte à la tête" ("You are the powerful sun that rushes to my head")—could not have been a successful trademark slogan for English-language advertisements, although translations of the entire poem were indeed displayed at Lancôme stands in several American department stores. In place of the identifying headline, "Tu es le grand soleil qui me monte à la tête,"

More than words can say

Poême

LANCÔME
PARIS

LANCÔME
PARIS

Fig. 85 "Love," "sun," "smile," "light," "stars," "sea"—a bouquet of words come together to compose a calligram of love in this advertising pamphlet designed by Philippe Dapsance for Lancôme's *Poême* as part of a promotional contest: "Composez votre plus beau Poème d'Amour," "Jeu-Concours *Elle* / Lancôme," 1997.

Fig. 86 Mae West's torso served as the model for this Bohemian crystal bottle created for the designer Elsa Schiaparelli's *Shocking* by the surrealist artist Léonor Fini in 1937.

American advertisements proclaimed that "Sometimes words are not enough / to reveal your heart, to describe your love." Still other versions in English as well as French insisted in a similar vein that "Sometimes words don't say everything," or that *Poême* expresses "More than words can say" (fig. 84), or that it can "Say everything without a word" ("Tout dire sans un mot"). Finally, in a multi-page advertisement with the overall title of "Planète-Parfums,"(from a 1999 issue of French *Vogue*), which associates nine different perfume brands with nine different planets, *Poême*, linked to Mercury—"Planet of Thought, / of Words and Language / Star associated / with Expression / in all its

In the fashion designer Elsa Schiaparelli's torso-shaped bottle for her perfume, *Shocking*, haute couture is represented by the red velvet tape measure crisscrossing the bodice of what resembles a dressmaker's dummy.

Most of Schiaparelli's fragrances were given names beginning with the letter "s," but none came in a bottle as inventive as this one for *Snuff*, 1939.

Forms"—is presented once again as a sublime fragrance: "*Poême.* . . . Beyond words, a message of love made sublime by a tumult of flowers and emotions."[34] The expressive power of words is transcended—even annulled here—by a perfume purported to inhabit the "beyond." Mercury is indeed a planet of expressivity, but the thought, words, and language it expresses take place beyond words. Language is transcended by a tumultuous experience of love that sublimates any linguistic message or discourse. It is silently, only through flowers and feelings, that expression occurs.

Another advertising effort to show that words cannot by themselves capture the intensity of sensual experience, especially that initiated by perfume and *Poême*, is a *calligramme* (calligram) of sorts (fig. 85) designed by Philippe Dapsance and composed of words taken straight from Eluard's poem. Words are not enough, the calligram suggests, unless they also have a visual dimension, the very shape of the thing they evoke. This calligrammatic advertisement was part of a pamphlet announcing a poetry competition (sponsored by Lancôme in conjunction with *Elle* magazine) and inviting readers to submit their "most beautiful love poems" to a jury presided by Juliette Binoche. First prize was announced as a weekend for two in Venice, while the next four winners were to receive a year's supply of Lancôme beauty products; the best twenty poems were to be published as an insert in one of the forthcoming issues of *Elle*. In Lancôme's calligram, yellow letters cleverly arranged against a blue background (the signature col-

ors of *Poême*) represent a laced bouquet of stems, flowers, and petals whose curves and arabesques are given visual form by the turns and twists of the words "lumière" (light), "mer" (sea), "fleurs" (flowers), "sourire" (smile), "étoiles" (stars), "amour" (love), "soleil" (sun), and "je t'aime." The two key words of the bouquet—"soleil," serving as the ribbon tying the stems together, and "aime" of "je t'aime," descending vertically toward the center—are written in the largest type face.[35]

What can we make of a perfume named *Poême* which pays homage to poetry, which appropriates the power of lyrical language, and which evokes in its publicity "a poetic bouquet . . . of . . . sensuality . . . luminosity, . . . contrasts," and yet in the same breath, the same whiff, paradoxically reverses or deconstructs the power of the poetic by announcing that "Sometimes words are not enough," or that *Poême* is beyond language, or that it says "More than words can say"? *Poême*, the perfume, exploits all the connotations that the word "poem" evokes in popular culture. But once having brought those meanings to the surface, once having unleashed the rich associations evoked in public and popular imagination by an allusion to whatever is "poetic," *Poême* takes the gambit a step further, suggesting that perfume can go where no poem could ever possibly venture, into the ineffable, silent, more spiritual and erotic realms of scent: into the world, that is, of the scented imagination. The interplay of the poetic and the fragrant, of word and scent, of text and image (in particular that of

Fig. 87 A perfume bottle replaces an African mask in this Man Ray–inspired advertisement for Jean Paul Gaultier's *Le Classique de Jean Paul Gaultier*, photo Jean-Baptiste Mondino, model Ninja Sarasolo, *Elle*, February 22, 1999.

Juliette Binoche's confident, radiant face, as captured by the photographer Richard Avedon against a sometimes blue, sometimes purple background and juxtaposed with the image of a large yellow bottle of *Poême*), is heightened by Lancôme's complete appropriation of the idea of the poetic. The "poème" undergoes, one could say, a "lancômization"; its spelling and meaning are changed by the addition of the "lancômian" circonflex. The notion of the "poem" is transformed through contact with its own perfumed replacement (all the more striking in that the only mention of "poème" in the advertisement is on the bottle). Once under the spell of a scent, the poem can no longer "spell" itself, as it were. Experiencing a radical change in state, volatilizing into air and vapor—the very media through which sound and odor move and hearing and smell function—the "poème" is, as it traverses the sensual world on the other side of language, rechristened "poême." This is because *Poême*, the perfume, initiates a difference: that of another language, which has been dispossessed of its words, sounds, and writing so as to give priority to a poetry that is body, a language that is emanation, and a word that is scent, as another Lancôme advertisement makes clear: "Discover a body of poetry . . . Immerse your body in the language of *Poême*" (V-NY, Nov. 1996.). Poetry's body and woman's body are one, fused through the wordless "language" of a scent named *Poême*.

Surrealism's "Sex Perfumes"

The borrowing of Eluard's poem "Je t'aime" by Lancôme came long after the poet's death in 1952; whether he would have been pleased or displeased by the poem's revival is anyone's guess. However, there were several surrealist artists and creators who collaborated enthusiastically with perfumers either in designing perfume bottles or creating advertising posters. In 1937, the artist Leonor Fini created a bottle for Elsa Schiaparelli's fragrance *Shocking* (1937) (fig. 86). Molded in the shape of a corseted bust—with crisscrossed pieces of a tailor's tape measure over the bodice, a gilded floral brooch covering the stopper, and a box lined with shocking pink satin—the sinuous S-curved bottle lived up to its name and to that of Schiaparelli as well. In fact, Schiaparelli had a fondness for fragrance names beginning with the letter "S": there were *Schiap* and *Soucis* from the mid-thirties, *Salut* and *Spanking* from 1939 and 1942, and *Si* and *S* after World War II. In designing the *Shocking* flacon, Fini was inspired by the mannequin of Mae West's torso, which Schiaparelli kept in her atelier and used to tailor clothes to the actress's proportions, especially when West could not come to Paris for fittings. But it is also possible that Fini recalled the bust of the Venus de Milo that Mae West had given Schiaparelli. The design of the *Shocking* bottle was taken up and revised in 1993 by the

212

Fig. 88 Man Ray (1890–1976), *Black and White* (*Noire et Blanche*), 1926; gelatin-silver print.

couturier Jean Paul Gaultier (Madonna may have replaced Mae West as the model) for his signature scent *Le Classique de Jean Paul Gaultier* (fig. 87). Gaultier's advertising for this fragrance also appropriated surrealist images: namely, the close-up photograph, entitled *Noire et Blanche* (fig. 88) of the head of the model known as Kiki of Montparnasse, which the American photographer Man Ray had taken and published as an advertisement in a 1926 issue of Paris *Vogue*. In the photograph Kiki holds an African mask (from the Ivory Coast) next to the jaw of her horizontal, "decapitated" head.[36]

As for the scent of *Shocking* it was not made for the timid woman. No shrinking violet would be attracted to the warm, sensual animalic notes of ambergris, civet, and musk and the fruity and spicy tones of patchouli and vetiver blended with such classic perfume ingredients as rose, jasmine, syringa, magnolia, and gardenia. In accord with the surrealist goal of freeing love from the constraints of bourgeois prudery and making erotic desire the prime mover of existence, *Shocking* may indeed have been, as Jean-Marie Martin-Hattemberg has claimed, "the first sex perfume." Less than a decade later, Mae West's body would once again serve as a muse—this time her hips—for the rounded, curvaceous bottle Marcel Rochas created for his 1944 perfume, *Femme*. Schiaparelli's friendships with the surrealists (and other poets and artists like Jean Cocteau and Christian Bérard) and her sympathy with the surrealist project of

giving free rein to desire and of blurring the distinction between reality and imagination inspired other humorous, surreal, or fantasy bottles. *Sleeping* (1939), advertised as a night perfume, was cast in the form of a crystal candlestick topped with a flame-shaped stopper, while the lavender-scented *Snuff* (also from 1939), Schiaparelli's first fragrance for men, was a crystal-shaped pipe packaged in a cigar box. *Zut*, presented to the American market in 1949, turned out to be more shocking than the original *Shocking*. Fashioned in the shape of a woman's lower torso, which had been tastefully omitted from the earlier *Shocking* design, the bottle sported only a pair of painted-on panties; it so offended American women that the perfume was quickly taken off the market. For even more surrealistic designs Schiaparelli called on Salvador Dali. In 1946, he designed an extraordinarily beautiful bottle for her *Le Roy Soleil* (fig. 89). Displaying a large sunburst stopper decorated with the silhouettes of flying birds, the Baccarat crystal flacon was set atop a base molded in marbled glass and enameled in blue to resemble ocean waves; a large golden box in the form of a scallop shell housed the bottle.[37] Another Dali perfume creation in glass—a dark, ponderous flacon, its spherical stopper as massive as its triangular base—hides a phantom image of parted lips and a tongue (fig. 90, page 188); this is a flacon that is also a mouth.

Even surrealism's last gasp, as the movement went into decline, was perfumed. In December 1959 at the

To be faithful to one's love as well as to one's perfume is suggested by D'Orsay's *Toujours fidèle* (Forever Faithful), c. 1909, a pillow-shaped Baccarat crystal bottle with a bulldog-shaped stopper.

Daniel Cordier Gallery in Paris the eighth "International Surrealist Exhibition" devoted to "EROS," as conceived by Duchamp and Breton, opened its doors. Visitors entered the exhibition through a shadowy, low-ceilinged, narrow tunnel called a "Love Grotto," leading, as the art historian Alyce Mahon has described it, "into a warm and comforting rose-colored chamber. Here the ceiling, designed by Duchamp, rhythmically breathed in and out by means of hidden air pumps, and the floor was covered by a layer of sand." In another room a tape of the recorded moans and sighs of women making love played endlessly, while mists of a perfume by Houbigant, called *Flatterie*, scented the air. A celebration of Sadean love in painting, sculpture, music, performance art, and design, the exhibition fused the eros of Rrose Selavy, the eros of marvelous scent, and the eros of Eluard's blinding and intoxicating "sun" with the surrealists' desire, according to Breton, to face "with open eyes the bright daylight of love" and to see in "the idea of *love* ... the only idea capable of reconciling any man, momentarily or not, with the idea of *life*."[38]

Fig. 89 A surrealist dream fantasy of sun, sea, birds, and a shell inspire Salvador Dali's crystal Baccarat perfume bottle for Elsa Schiaparelli's *Le Roy Soleil*, 1946.

The
Fragrant
Garçonne
(1920–1950)

Chapter 6

*Perfume is the medium by which
the lady magically usurps the
sexual powers of the blossom.*
— Tom Robbins

*Perfume, that conqueror of
the most subtle of our senses,
that informer of our unspoken desires,
perfume which from out of the
unreliable depths of human memory
uncovers the fount of tears,
the secret of pleasure.*
—Colette

The Perfume Pavilion

IT WAS A LONG TIME IN COMING, almost seventeen years. But when finally, in April 1925, it did rise up in the center of Paris for a six-month run, the Exposition Internationale des Arts Décoratifs et Industriels Modernes (International Exposition of Modern Decorative and Industrial Arts), from which forty years later the term "art deco" would come, was an explosive celebration of modernism in primarily French decorative and interior design. The idea of an international decorative arts fair, conceived early in the first decade of the century by the Société des artistes décorateurs (Society of Decorative Artists), a group formed in the wake of art nouveau and the 1900 World Exhibition, had been presented to successive French governments until an official committee was appointed in 1912 with the goal of mounting the exhibition three to four years later. But the outbreak of World War I canceled the entire project, and it was not until after the armistice that the idea was revived as a way of rekindling the glory and economic power of a devastated France. The exhibition was announced for 1922, postponed to 1924 because of serious postwar shortages, and then delayed yet another year by a series of construction problems. Yet, over these many years of organization, postponement, and disappointment, one idea remained unchanged: namely, the fact, as the art historian Victor Arwas notes, that the 1925 exhibition would not be an historical exhibition, celebrating achievements of the past, but "a forward-looking one" where, according to the exhibition committee's stringent rules of submission, only "works that fulfilled the criterion of being 'modern'" would be accepted. The Information Handbook of the Exhibition left no doubt about this: "Reproduction, imitations, and counterfeits of ancient styles will be strictly prohibited," it declared. And so from the cascading fountains, glass tables, exquisite lighting fixtures, and perfume bottles created by René Lalique to the domestic interior designs by Jacques-Emile Ruhlmann who, in collaboration with a group of other craftsmen, artists, sculptors, architects, and furniture, textile, carpet, and object designers, conceived the rooms of a model Townhouse of a Wealthy Collector (L'Hôtel d'un Collectionneur), the aesthetic imagination of high art deco style was celebrated in an explosive burst of modernist design.[1]

Many of the exhibition's pavilions, along with the sophisticated products they displayed, showcased this new French modernism. Each of the design studios of the four large Parisian department stores erected its own stone pavilion, decorated on the outside with eye-catching leaden glass or wrought iron facades and on the inside with different examples of interior settings. In addition to these pavilions there were individual exhibits (130 in all) dedicated to French cities (Lyon and Nancy), to French provinces (Franche-Comté and Provence), to French industries (the Paris Gas Company, the National Wine Bureau), and, finally, to French crafts. The stone, wood, metal, ceramics, and glass arts had their own collective pavilion as did artisans working in linen, gloves, furniture, jewelry, and stained glass. Decoration and fashion magazines of the time (Art et décoration, Art, Goût, Beauté, and the women's journal Fémina) as well as L'Intransigeant, one of Paris's most important dailies, were also represented. The jeweler and silver maker Christofle shared a pavilion with the glassmaker Baccarat. And of course, foreign countries had their own buildings.[2]

In all ways and regards, the 1925 Exhibition was a French creation designed to show off (as the 1900 Art Nouveau Exhibition had done so successfully) the industrial artistry and accomplishments of the modern Gallic imagination. Accordingly, it was unthinkable that fashion, one of France's great artistic and industrial achievements, would not be in evidence; of course, it was. Seventy-two haute-couture fashion houses participated. Among the general decorative arts groups represented at the exhibition—architecture, interior design, ceramics, and glassware—one was devoted to "la Parure," the art of elegance, appearance, and beauty. This group was further divided into five specialized classes: clothing, accessories, fashion, perfumes, and jewelry. In the minds of the exhibition's organizers, fashion was not only an important decorative art; it was a uniquely French art, one of luxury and refinement par excellence. "Is clothing insofar as it is associated with feminine style," Henri Clouzot asked in a guidebook written for the exhibition, "a decorative art? It is, without a doubt, and the most venerable: the one that leads all the others." On the eve of the exhibition, women's clothing was regarded as a major French industry, with annual exports amounting to 2.5 billion francs. Three well-known couturiers—Jeanne Lanvin, Jean Paquin, and Paul Poiret—were members of the exhibition's board of organizers. Luxury had become a product of Gallic artistry and genius, and Paris, as one traveler wrote in 1919, was the only city in the world with "luxury boutiques," a metropolis committed, as another observer noted, to the "commerce of vanity."[3]

Situated close to the Porte d'Honneur, the principal entrance to the approximately 377,000 square feet of the exhibition's grounds and a stone's throw from the Grand Palais, stood the Fashion Pavilion. Yet, it was not the only display dedicated to French style and chic. Within the Grand Palais itself individual sections, spread over two vast floors, were devoted to jewelry, textiles, embroidery, hairdressing, and other aspects of fashion, including perfume. Designed by the architects Raguenet and Maillard, the perfume section was an octagonal room, its center occupied by a series of display cases all of which radiated from a center over which a magnificent glass waterfall by Lalique, the "fontaine des parfums," was suspended. Fashion was also evident in the Parisian "street" that had been constructed on the upper floor of the Grand Palais to display the latest in shop-window design and street advertising. Just down from the Grand Palais and along the Pont Alexandre

III stood a shopping mall, which some compared to a "cramped medieval Italian town" or a modernized Venetian "Rialto Bridge." Here, the simultaneist painter of pure color Sonia Delaunay had a shop called *Simultané*, where visitors could purchase her fabric and clothing designs (in colorful geometric motifs of cubist and simultaneist inspiration) as well as furs by the couturier Jacques Heim and leatherwork by Gilbert Girau. In addition to the perfume pavilion, an attractive stand-alone building in stone with the air of a small, delicate temple was built by the architect Eric Bagge for the perfume company Fontanis.[4]

Fashion was also in evidence beneath the Alexandre III Bridge. Floating at anchor along the left bank of the river, between the Pont Alexandre and the Pont des Invalides, were the unusual exhibition barges created by Paul Poiret. Poiret, of course, had been the first fashion designer to envision perfumes as an integral aspect of fashion style and the first couturier to market fragrance under his own direction, although he named the line Parfums de Rosine, after one of his daughters. Decorated in various styles and designed to fulfill different functions, Poiret's barges, named *Amours* (Loves), *Délices* (Pleasures), and *Orgues* (Organs), were created to boost his declining reputation and reverse a series of recent financial difficulties. While the interior of *Orgues* had been created by the painter Raoul Dufy, that of *Amours* displayed a series of comfortable art deco living spaces designed by Poiret's own in-house firm, Atelier Martine, named after another daughter. The Martine School and Workshop taught local twelve- and thirteen-year-old girls to draw, paint, weave, and embroider and then encouraged them to create naïve and naturalistic works in fabric, glass, ceramics, wallpaper, tapestry, and furniture design for use in homes, shops, restaurants, offices, and theaters. In fact, the Atelier Martine designed a distinctive perfume bottle for Parfums de Rosine's scent *Le Balcon*; the fragrance's name perfectly matched a miniature iron balcony that encircled the glass bottle. Rosine perfume bottles, moreover, were decorative accessories in the sitting room Poiret designed for his barge *Amours*. Against the wall in a corner of what was a "lush, joyful, jungle-like" interior, complete with soft sofas, puff pillows, and palm trees, stood a green-yellow lavatory table on which were set perfume bottles and an atomizer similar to those hand-painted by the Atelier Martine and sold by Parfums de Rosine.[5]

Perfume Reigns

On the evening of June 16, 1925, the imposing staircase inside the Grand Palais was the scene of an extravaganza involving over 2,000 participants, some of them great theatrical and music-hall celebrities of the day. The actress Eva Le Galienne and her company, the dancer Ida Rubinstein, a friend of the Count de Montesquiou, the actors of the Comédie Française, Loïe Fuller and her students, the singers of the Paris Opera and other companies, showgirls from the Moulin Rouge and the Folies Bergère, clowns from all the Paris circuses, as well as 300 members of the corps de ballet of several Paris dance troupes, performed a succession of spectacles, processions, and tableaux as beautiful, according to participants, to hear as to see. While opera, dance, theatre, music, and song were celebrated until the early morning, a good part of the gala was devoted to fashion:

> Thirty mannequins modeled ermine coats with endless trains held by an army of page boys. . . . A number of tableaux followed. Each color of "the Rainbow" was made up of leading mannequins from each of the main haute couture houses, while other tableaux included Napoleon's "grande armée" and a symbolic representation of perfumes.

This tableau of perfumes offered the audience in a few minutes an experience of elegance and sophistication that the display of French perfumery on the upper floor of the Grand Palais would give them over the coming months: namely, an appreciation of the beauty, artistry, and imagination—all modern—of a distinctive French creation. Perfume would have a watershed year in 1925. In addition to giving pride of place to perfume creation and to designating perfumery as one of the most important of the French luxury industries—something that earlier world exhibitions including that of 1900 had never done, at least not to the same extent—the 1925 Paris Exhibition was witness to the launching of *Shalimar*, whose distinctive bat-wing bottle (despite its art nouveau echoes) had been expressly designed by Raymond Guerlain to be the central point of attraction at Guerlain's exhibit. It was also the venue for the launch of one of the best-selling perfumes ever created, Millot's chypre scent *Crêpe de Chine*. Jean Patou's trio of perfumes, *Amour Amour* (Love, Love), *Que Sais-je?* (What Do I Know?) and *Adieu Sagesse* (Good-bye Reason), their names suggesting a sentimental drama of indecision followed by capriciousness and then commitment, also debuted in 1925. The Baccarat bottle for *Amour Amour* was designed by Louis Süe, one of the most important interior designers of his day, who with his partner André Mare created all the rooms and the furnishings in the exhibition's Museum of Contemporary Art; two years before, Süe and Mare had designed the art deco gilt-bronze work for the facade of D'Orsay's perfume store on rue de la Paix. Also presented with great fanfare at the Perfume Pavilion was a unique set of six exquisite tiny perfume bottles shaped like pearls and arranged to resemble a "Perfumed Necklace," for which the perfumer Isabey was awarded a gold medal for design, although Delettrez had created a similar ensemble named *Parfum XXIII* in 1923, which featured a set of thirteen tiny graduated bottles nested upside down in a green leather jewelry box.[6]

Conceived by the architects Raguenet and Maillard and the sculptor René Binet (the creator of "La Parisienne," the immense statue dominating the 1900 Paris Exhibition),

Delettrez, *Parfum XXIII*, 1923: graduated pearl flacons (each cork-stoppered) set as a "string" of pearls and presented in a leather-covered box.

the pavilion or palace of perfumes boasted a stunning ensemble of architectural and decorative motifs designed to give to the art of French perfume and bottle making the elegance and distinction they deserved.[7] Under a high, cone-shaped ceiling covered by a gauzy, pleated awning of white muslin—like "an eight-sided pope's hat or a belfry with its point lobbed off," Georges Bourdon observed at the time—a vast room was built to house part of the exhibit (figs. 92, 93). Around the upper half of the room, descending diagonally from the awning, six painted panels in a metal "neither as shiny as silver nor as dull as tin," writes Bourdon, stretched along the walls. Etched or painted in light relief these panels were filled with abstract, stylized motifs—compressed lines in the shape of waves, delicate seaweed branches, overlapping arcs, and what appears to be the naturalistic form of a seal or manatee—vaguely suggestive, according to Bourdon's eye-witness report, of a "chaos" which he associated with "the depths of an Asian jungle or those of the ocean." Beneath these panels and dividing the outside wall at regular intervals were a series of small alcoves; it was here that the classic French perfumers (Bourjois, Gellé Frères, Houbigant, and others), their names in bright lights, mounted their personal exhibition spaces.[8]

Fig. 91 The art deco, frozen-fountain motif. Guerlain, "Flacon Petit Beurre," 1916, 1929, crystal perfume bottle designed by Baccarat and Poche & du Courval for *L'Heure bleue*, featuring a fountain-design label.

At the center of the Perfume Pavilion stood the eye-catching pièce de resistance, designed by Lalique, arguably the most ubiquitous designer at the Exhibition.[9] Arranged in the shape of a star, a constellation of six vertical display cases rose up. Each display, in keeping with art deco style, was bordered by colored panels of deep purple, inset with silver fluting. Each was triangular in form, and each exhibited, behind glass doors, the perfumes and flasks of a particular French perfumer. Crowning this ensemble of glass showcases and rising upward toward the cone-shaped awning on the ceiling, there loomed a majestic, multi-tiered sculpture of arcing, interlaced, ribbonlike sheets of frosted glass, the very imitation of a cascading fountain, or, as Bourdon observed, of "a giant palm tree with large hanging palms." Appropriately named the "fountain of perfume," it soon became a symbol of the 1925 Paris Exhibition and, accord-

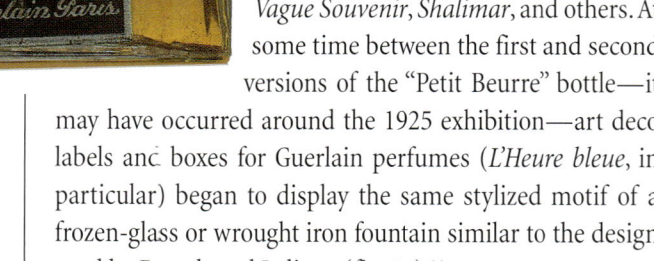

ing to Bourdon, represented, along with the "magnificent hall of Couture and the enchanting room of Jewelry, one of the triumphs of the section devoted to Fashion [La Parure]."[10]

With its cascading arcs of grooved glass (in harmony, it should be noted, with the fluting on the edges of the display cases it dominated), Lalique's fountain was a fine example of high art deco style. It calls to mind the metal designer Edgar Brandt's polychrome wrought iron folding screen, called "Oasis," which also debuted at Brandt's own stand at the exhibition (fig. 94). The tightly rendered, finely etched metal lines of falling water in the work's central panel along with the curling palm fronds at the bottom of all five panels echo the forms of Lalique's glass fountain as well as recalling some of the design motifs represented on the Perfume Pavilion's walls. Yet, the gushing-fountain motif was not only observable in works of glass sculpture. In 1916 and again in 1929 Guerlain asked the Baccarat and then the Pochet & du Courval glassmaking firms to invent a new standard perfume bottle named "Petit Beurre" (after the popular, rectangular-shaped cookie made by the firm LU) which was to be filled with several already marketed Guerlain scents like *Une Rose*, *L'Heure bleue*, *Vague Souvenir*, *Shalimar*, and others. At some time between the first and second versions of the "Petit Beurre" bottle—it may have occurred around the 1925 exhibition—art deco labels and boxes for Guerlain perfumes (*L'Heure bleue*, in particular) began to display the same stylized motif of a frozen-glass or wrought iron fountain similar to the design used by Brandt and Lalique (fig. 91).[11]

Exotic Perfume Alcoves

The individual exhibition alcoves had their own charm, according to Bourdon. They were decorated in different styles which gave each its own idiosyncratic elegance. One, of Chinese inspiration, displayed a vaulted ceiling in the shape of a golden conch shell; the glass display cases were

220

Fig. 92 Not only did René Lalique, the crystal maker, have his own pavilion at the 1925 Paris Art Deco Exhibition in which he exhibited vases, bowls, light fixtures, wall and floor tiles, and other decorative ornaments; but he designed extraordinary glass fountains like this showpiece *Fontaine des parfums* at the exhibition's Perfume Pavilion.

colored green, the rope-molding gold, and the walls black lacquer streaked with golden lines. Another cubicle completely in gold was filled with mirrors. A third, decorated with furniture and a polished wooden display case, was ringed with wall panels on which flowers and exotic scenes had been painted. In still another, where green and gold dominated, a lovely set of arching glass showcases vied for attention with a beautiful green, blue, and gold mosaic. In these alcoves of green silk fringed with gold and of wine-red carpeting heavy with the lushness of a tropical rainforest, how, Bourdon asked, can a writer express "the form, the color, the presentation of so many bottles, boxes, sachets, atomizers: . . . that is to say the charming and powerful arsenal to which, for our pleasure, the elegant, seductive woman goes to find her irresistible weapons"? The

Fig. 93 Architect's drawing for René Lalique's *Fontaine des parfums,* Pavillon de la parfumerie, Art Deco Exhibition, Paris, 1925.

Perfume Pavilion was, above all, an aesthetic space: "it is artists that we are visiting here," Bourdon remarked. Although the scents displayed were sealed in what Bourdon called their "prisons," "chastely withdrawn behind the splendor of their crystal walls," the space was nothing less than a "land of enchanted forms and ravishing inventions." Exhibits of the utmost simplicity competed with others that veered toward baroque excess. There was one exhibit filled with nothing but blue flacons—large, small, tiny, flat, curved, rounded, bulging—but all in a stunning "intense blue, a 'night-blue,' dotted with points of gold that call to mind the starry firmament," Bourdon rhapsodized. Beyond

the principal room of the pavilion, passageways with their own perfume displays and their own charming mysteriousness led in other directions:

An obscure corridor, a short gallery like a tunnel or a burial chamber (*hypogeum*): where are we? It is dark, cool. The walls are covered with an old flowered fabric. Look on the right, on the left, it is pure delight. At eye-level, like portholes . . . are narrow glass windows behind which repose, bathed in light, perfume bottles of all sizes and all forms, among which I tend to prefer the tiniest.[12]

Fig. 94 The art deco frozen fountain motif in metal. Edgar Brandt, *Oasis,* polychrome metal screen, Art Deco Exhibition, Paris, 1925, private collection, Paris.

Perfume and French Nationalism

The experience of the pavilion was not merely decorative or aesthetic; it was one of charm, delight, elegance, mystery, and ravishment. And, above all else, it was an experience of nationalistic pride. "There is no Parisian woman, no Parisian man, no visitor of taste," wrote Bourdon,

who will not inhale the enchantment of the section devoted to Fashion. Among so many beautiful things which have been brought together at the Exhibition of Decorative Arts, there is not one that can give a

clearer and more contemporary idea of what is universally accepted to be the charm of Paris. And within the Fashion Exhibit, the Hall of Perfumes has a standing, an elegance, and above all a style that confer the greatest honor to this French exhibition.

Such chauvinism was restrained in comparison to that of R. Bienaimé, president of the French Perfume Union (Syndicat de la Parfumerie Française) and head of the organizing committee for the perfume section of the exhibition. In an introductory essay, "La Parfumerie Française à l'Exposition des Arts Décoratifs" (French Perfume at the

Art Deco Exposition) appearing in a nearly 500-page, hardbound promotional book, *La Parfumerie française et l'art dans la présentation* (French Perfume and the Art of Its Presentation), published to coincide with the opening of the exhibition by the trade group responsible for the French perfume and soap industry, Bienaimé wastes no time in asserting the importance of perfume as an art unto itself. "To compose a perfume," he wrote, "is to create with fragrant elements a work analogous to a painter's canvas with its colors, a composer's musical phrase with its notes." The year 1925, he continued, would go down in the history of French perfumes as significant because it not only represented the fact that the exhibition had placed perfumery in "the first rank of industries specializing in the production of luxury goods," but showed the acceptance of perfume's "true place and precise role . . . in our country where French moderation and taste manifest themselves as hallmarks of the fine arts industries and as invaluable boons to France's expansion throughout the world." The pre-eminence of French perfumery "is the result of a concatenation of natural circumstances and human efforts that only France could have brought together." What were these natural conditions accounting for the supremacy of French perfumes in the world? They were, Bienaimé answered in an exaggerated style which gave no quarter to anything *not* French, "the richness of her soil and the gentleness of her climate," for "no country is so varied and yet so balanced, no earth possesses a flora so rich in aromatic plants." Of course, it is the region of Grasse he had in mind, where flowers have "a fragrant power and finesse found nowhere else in the world."[13]

As for the human effort (the French ingenuity and talent) which has contributed to the superiority of French perfumery, it can trace its origin to "those two distinctive qualities of our race: taste and diligence." Taste, Bienaimé suggested with haughty condescension, was the result of several centuries of civilization and refinement, especially in the evolution of the perfumer's art, which over the years had become "more subtle, more intellectual, and far beyond the crude sensations that *less developed peoples* experience" (my emphasis). Diligence, which Bienaimé defined as a certain knowing attention to detail, was the result of scientific inquiry. "French science" had already made discoveries in perfume composition as worthy as those made by other nations in the fields of physics and chemistry. In joining their forces, French taste and diligence had, he argued, produced extraordinary creations. All the "artistic qualities of our race," Bienaimé concluded, "have produced new and infinitely varied ways" of manufacturing glass crystal, of printing paper labels, of making carton packaging, and of fabricating perfume bottle cases. His final sentences rang with a pride and chauvinism that only the stirring chords of *La Marseillaise* could possibly equal:

> A French perfume is thus a small work of art created from the riches of our soil, from the intellectual qualities of our race, and even to a certain extent from our

long centuries of civilization. No country in the world can bring together at once so many varied elements; this is why the date of 1925 . . . has to be seen as a point of departure toward the future realization of the works of this great French industry.

Bienaimé's paean to the Frenchness of perfume composition is merely the preface to *French Perfume and the Art of Its Presentation.* His words introduce pages upon pages of promotional and historical literature, including photographs of the individuals responsible for the exhibition and the Perfume Pavilion as well as two-page spreads advertising the stands and products of the exhibitors. All the major houses, some tracing their roots back to the eighteenth and nineteenth centuries—Houbigant, Lubin, L. T. Piver, Guerlain, Gellé Frères, Bourjois, Rallet, Rimmel, Rigaud, D'Orsay, Gabilla, Rosine, Cheramy, and Callot Soeurs—were represented, along with companies working at the margins of perfume manufacturing: an engraver, a papermaker, a specialist in the fabrication of luxury packaging, a manufacturer of bottle caps, and a certain Monsieur L. Marboeuf, whose company at 39 rue de la Grange-aux-Belles would, as his advertisement indicated, fabricate upon request perfume labels "de grand luxe." The historical section of the book is composed of several essays dealing with a host of specialized and timely subjects: old and new perfume labels, the development of the atomizer, the decorating of perfume stores and display windows, and the fabrication and use of sachets, perfume cards, bottles, advertising posters, perfume boxes, and trademarks. The city of Grasse and the daily routines of its perfume industry—the handpicking of flowers, the extracting of fragrance—are discussed in detail. Moreover, individual chapters are devoted to particular flowers and their scents—the rose, the orange blossom, lavender, mimosa, jasmine, tuberose—as well as to aldehydes, the class of synthetic scents just beginning to revolutionize the chemistry of perfume composition. Even the use of cellophane in perfume packaging merits a brief chapter.

From Art Deco to Modernism: Perfumes of the Roaring Twenties and the Hollow Years.[14]

Insofar as art deco favored "lavish ornamentation, superlative craftsmanship and fine materials" it can be said to have evolved from art nouveau and the latter's culmination in the 1900 Paris Exhibition. From its conception in the years 1908–1912, art deco opened itself to the influence of many artistic movements, design motifs, and aesthetic styles. Fauvism, cubism, futurism, Russian constructivism,

Diaghilev's Ballets Russes, haute couture, oriental exoticism (China, Japan, Africa), the *Revue Nègre* (as created by the American dancer Josephine Baker in 1925), and even Egyptology (King Tutankhamen's tomb was discovered in 1922) contributed forms and motifs to the iconography of high art deco, as did the move in artistic figuration toward abstraction, simplification, distortion, angularity, and geometric patterns like zigzags, lightning bolts, arcs, chevrons, and circles. In many ways, art deco's exuberant eclecticism and avid embrace of contemporary fashion and style were modernist to the core. Art deco was a cornucopia of styles, a movement that sought, in the words of one art critic, "to unite architecture, fine decorative arts and the cheapest consumer goods" in a "decorative response to modernity." From 1925 on, the growing presence of the machine and of machine aesthetics along with, in the 1930s, the appearance of streamlined forms derived from aerodynamic design pushed art deco modernism in a less ornamental and more industrial direction.[15] "Modernism" or "Modern Style," or "Jazz Modern" or simply "Moderne" were the names given to this new kind of radically purist functionalism with its reliance on simplicity of line, form, and volume, its passion for steel, chrome, leather, and glass materials, its use of diagonal or aerial perspectives, its juxtaposition of geometric and machine elements, its love of speed, power, and technology, and its taste for sober colors, clean, precise lines, and sharp, eye-grabbing sans serif typography.

The Roaring Twenties did not seek to eliminate the sensual and aesthetic pleasures, the so-called "superfluities," that already in the wake of World War I's devastation had taken so many years to re-establish. During the 1920s twelve couture houses, following Poiret's revolutionary example, added perfume creations to their fashion offerings. Chanel did so in 1921, Lanvin the following year,

Worth and Vionnet in 1924, and the luggage-maker Louis Vuitton between 1925 and 1927. Perfume would not be suppressed during the Roaring Twenties, nor for that matter would fashion, jewelry, or decorative design. Even in America, between 1911 and the end of the war, an elderly Sarah Bernhardt made a great display of her faith in perfume when in the middle of her public lectures she would dab one of twelve perfumes she carried with her onto a handkerchief and then apply the scent to her neck, face, and arms. Bernhardt had always taken her love of luxury to exaggerated extremes. During her world tour of 1891 one whole trunk alone (of the 120 she traveled with) held perfume and makeup.[16]

The increased attention paid to the sensory effects of smell and perfume in the post–World War I period is evident from the number of perfumes produced in the 1920s. In that decade alone Guerlain introduced twenty new scents, while Coty launched thirteen. Although in the 1930s Guerlain's production fell off a bit (to seven new fragrances), Coty's twenty-one new scents represented an increase of slightly more than half. The postwar period, writes Delbourg-Delphis, witnessed "an unprecedented olfactory explosion" brought on by the incorporation into perfume composition of chemical innovations, discovered before the war but not yet applied, and by a new desire to democratize perfume consumption and spread its use beyond the confines of the upper classes. Deodorants were introduced in the mid-twenties to the chagrin of conservative, antifeminist writers, who saw in the "deodorizing of women" the same move toward defeminization that they abhorred in the boyish "garçonne" look with its shapeless dresses and short bobbed hairstyles. One critic, Guy (Georges) de la Fouchardière, in his novel *Cherchez la femme* (1927), was particularly hostile. Women, he suggested, had lost a certain carnal expansiveness. Alas, they no longer possessed, he complained (with not an iota of tongue-in-cheek irony), "the natural hills and valleys that make landscapes so attractive." In addition to being troubled by the unnatural look created by the popular flapper-style dresses with their flat bodices and loose, shapeless backs, de la Fourcadière worried about a growing tendency toward deodorization, clearly evident in the desire of women to disguise their natural "incommodious odors," as he put it. "Poets," he wrote, "will no longer sing of the natural *odor di femina*: the wild odor, the spicy odor, the amber odor, the musk odor that have inspired so many lyrical lovers."[17]

A Revolution in Perfumes

The sheer number of extraordinary perfumes, "so numerous that they defy classification," which were launched during the twenties, along with their provocative and imaginative compositions, names, themes, and bottle designs, gave scent a new eroticism and along with it a new amorous identity which, according to Delbourg-Delphis,

Fig. 95 The slender verticality, the minimalist simplicity, and the geometric symmetry of art deco style are reflected in this glass and bakelite, tasseled bottle designed by Julien Viard for Les Parfums de Rosine's *Arlequinade*, 1924.

was "strangely solipsistic and totally feminine" (187). Instead of meekly waiting for men to approve, women at the beginning of the 1920s, Delbourg-Delphis writes, decided to take the lead in teaching men about the new captivating scents they were wearing. Many traditional men of the time felt "trapped by the new, mysterious perfumes" that had left them bewildered. They needed instruction. The ease and comfort with which men had perceived , understood, and appreciated the simpler (more "logical") floral bouquets launched between 1885 and 1914 were challenged by the complexity and uniqueness of the perfumes—and the fragrant sensations they produced—created after World War I. While a few, now classic fragrances had indeed revolutionized perfume composition from the fin de siècle to the end of the war—*Jicky*, *L'Origan*, *L'Heure bleue*, *Chypre* to name a few—the extraordinary profusion of new scents that began to appear almost the day after the armistice—*Mitsouko*, Guerlain's peach-scented chypre, was launched in 1919— possessed a completely unknown character. Because these new fragrances made unprecedented use of aldehydes, because they deepened the floral, citrus, and oakmoss accord Coty had invented in his innovative 1917 fragrance *Chypre*, because they harmonized exotic blends of amber, spice, and vanilla notes, and because, finally, they juxtaposed the smoky aromas of tobacco and the essence of birch bark—a new class of more masculine fragrances for women called "cuir" or "leather" scents introduced in Caron's *Tabac blond* of 1919—the revolutionary new olfactory forms of the 1920s were for certain men, already confused if not "de-virilized" by the consequences of the war, truly discomfiting. The role played by chemistry in this "paradigm shift" was, as it had been at the end of the previous century, remarkable. The years 1923, 1927, and 1928 witnessed several important discoveries, which replicated synthetically the odors of natural substances: for example, *Flosal*, a floral-based aldehyde; *ambrettolide*, the synthesized floral-musky fixative fashioned after the musk plant; and *civettone*, the essence of civet, an extremely tenacious fixative in oriental and chypre perfumes and in citrus colognes. *Cinnamylal*, synthetic honeysuckle, was created by Edmond Roudnitska in 1932, *muscone*, a synthetic musk, appeared in 1934, and *jasmone*, a warm-spicy, somewhat fruity synthesis of jasmine, followed soon after.[18]

The revolutionary intensity and the distinctive, sometimes troubling, aromatic signature of these new fragrances were matched by the exotic, mysterious, and theatrical presentations they received. Operas, ballets, and music hall performances (notable for their fairy-tale scenarios and romantic imbroglios) provided themes and names for certain perfumes during the 1920s. Poiret's "Rosine" brand produced *Arlequinade* (1924), a perfume whose name was derived from a popular Russian Ballet, *Harlequinade,* playing in the Paris of 1922; its geometric art deco flacon topped with a stopper molded from bakelite, a favorite art deco material, had been designed by

Julien Viard (fig. 95). At the 1925 Exhibition Parfums de Rosine debuted a stunning heart-shaped ruby-red perfume bottle adorned with a pair of frosted and clear glass wings which came in a red heart-shaped box; the scent was named appropriately *Coeur en Folie,* the title of a Folies Bergère show of the previous year. Moreover, in the mid-1920s perfume houses organized their own spectacles and performances to publicize their products. At the Hotel Négresco in Nice, D'Orsay sponsored a Second Empire–styled gala in March 1925. In London, a year later, the English division of Coty participated in a show called *The Review of 1926,* in which one striking, erotically charged scene, called "The Scents of Coty," moved a member of the audience, clearly male, to write as follows:

> One watched as the principal creations of this famous perfumer walked on stage in the enticing form of divinely beautiful creatures. The monumental tiaras they wore in their hair called to mind the forms and ornaments of the perfume bottles of Coty's precious scents. The scant clothing, enveloping these Olympian goddesses like a halo, evoked the petals or flowers found at the heart of Coty's fragrances. In turn, there appeared *la Jacynthe, l'Or, la Violette, la Rose Jacqueminot, l'Origan, l'Eméraude* and *l'Ambre antique.* One personality, whom many women want to emulate, dominated the group: it was Mademoiselle Spinelly, the living incarnation of grand Parisian sophistication, who, clothed in a filmy costume like a tuft of swan's down from which her soft bosom and shapely legs appeared, embodied "The Perfume of Paris" (Lefkowith, *Art,* 12, 99–100; Delbourg-Delphis, 88).

In keeping with this theatrical and dramatic spirit, several perfumes at the beginning of the decade adopted the mask, the masquerade, or the *bal masqué,* with the inevitable associations to Venice and Carnival as their theme. Marcel Guerlain (no relation to the creators of *Jicky* and *Shalimar*) conceived *Masque Rouge* in 1925, while Piver created *Mascarade* two years later. In 1929, *Les Parfums du Lido* appeared in a square, domed box decorated with romantic night scenes of Venice and a label featuring stylized art deco representations of the Venetian skyline. In response to the increase in the number of chic women willing to be seen smoking in public, Piver released a purse-sized perfume bottle shaped like a cigarette lighter (Lefkowith, *Art,* 99, 123, 125, 71).

A Chaplinesque Atomizer

Encouraged by the fashion magazines of the twenties, women began in fact to carry small portable bottles of perfume as they moved around the city. Marcel Franck, the son of Leopold, who had begun to market the first modern atomizers in the 1880s, displayed a new invention at his stand at the 1925 Paris Exhibition. A small pocket atomizer (two and a half inches long and three-quarters of an inch in diameter) called "Le Kid," after the Chaplain movie of 1921 (fig. 96), it was an immediate success. "Should not a woman, at any moment, in any place" wrote Franck in *French Perfume and the Art of Its Presentation* "be permitted to create a lingering, perfumed wake?" Available at different prices (from 22 up to 200 francs) and in several different finishes (brass, nickel, gold plate, mother-of-pearl, lacquer, enamel, tortoise shell, lizard, eel, snakeskin, and sharkskin), "Le Kid" was marketed, in a cubist-inspired advertisement from 1925 by the art deco designer Cassandre (fig. 97), as the "indispensable pocket atomizer." One expensive enamel model was adorned with the miniature image of an elegant woman walking in the rain, dressed boyishly *à la garçonne* in cloche hat and scarf. "Le Super Kid," sold in 1931, was a deluxe miniature atomizer created by Franck to compete with the "L'Aiglon" series of atomizers for purse and travel that Aromys began to sell in 1929. "L'Aiglon" came in three sizes and eighty different styles; there were twenty mother-of-pearl models alone.[19]

Art Deco's Fascination with the Exotic

The postwar interest in exploration and colonization produced an air of mysterious exoticism and a fascination with otherness, not unlike that which had attached itself to perfume presentation at the turn of the century. In addition to the Slavic influence, which came by way of Diaghilev and Bakst and their Ballets Russes, the impact of the Egyptian pyramids—the excavation of which was well underway at the time—on art deco style was considerable. Cinemas, for example, were being constructed in the shape of pyramids ornamented with friezes of ochre and gold. Women wore what were called "Cleopatra" earrings, and furniture makers used palm wood and parchment to create chairs resembling Egyptian thrones. The same Middle-Eastern and oriental influence was clearly reflected in the Egyptian, Babylonian, Indian, Japanese, and Chinese motifs decorating perfume bottles or inspiring their names during the early years of the twenties. This is evident in scents like *Nuit Etoilée de Bagdad* (c. 1927 from Diamant Bleu), its dark blue glass bottle (as designed by Julien Viard) trimmed with gold and shaped to resemble the step-down, zigzag pyramid form (also called a ziggurat) characteristic of the terraced architecture of the Hanging Gardens of Babylon; or in Lubin's elephant-shaped Baccarat bottle for *Kismet* (1921); or the pyramid bottle inscribed with the

Fig. 96 A Chaplinesque purse atomizer, c. 1925, named "Le Kid" in honor of the "Little Tramp's" widely popular film of the same name.

profile of a partially Greek, partially Egyptian, gold sphinx that Viard also created for the reissue of Lubin's 1898 scent *Enigma*. In or around 1925, L'Institut de Beauté launched a perfume called *Djavidan* (a Turkish-Armenian name) that, according to Lefkowith, "represented a curious combination of many foreign elements, ranging from Turkey to Greece to Egypt." Shaped in the form of an ancient Greek vase and sitting on a tripod decorated with the Egyptian figure of a vulture, its wings fully extended, the bottle displayed a coat-of-arms clearly Turkish in origin. It was packaged in a box on which was pictured an Egyptian princess dressing herself, assisted by two attendants. Moreover, Chinese motifs were featured in flacons molded to resemble ginger bottles, and Chinese-styled calligraphy was turned into a design motif in the vertical lettering Violet gave to its bottle of *Jasmin* (1922) and Guerlain to its flacon of *Liu* (1927).[20]

This stunning rectangular bottle in cobalt blue and gold for Bryenne's *L'Heure Exquise*, 1926, features a side-mounted stopper typical of art deco perfume bottles.

Liu is an interesting case of orientalism on several levels (fig. 98). Structurally, the flacon was designed to resemble a Chinese tea box. Typographically, the three letters of the scent's name in jet black are arranged vertically on a gold label affixed to the black bottle; the calligraphy is simple, stylized, and linear, a combination of cubist, art deco, and Chinese styles. Narratively, *Liu* recreates a Chinese story which, in moving from East to West and ending up as Puccini's last opera, *Turandot* of 1926, undergoes a sea change. Liu, the heroine of the opera, is the slave of a prince, Calaf by name, whom she secretly loves, but who is himself smitten by the dazzling beauty of the heartless Princess Turandot, the emperor's daughter. Because of the murder in the past of one of her female ancestors, Turandot has vowed never to give herself to any man, a resolve that has not, it appears, dissuaded many suitors. But Turandot has invented what she believes to be a fail-safe strategy for turning away those who have become enamored of her. Before she will give her hand in marriage, her suitors must

solve three enigmas which the princess knows are beyond solution. Those who fail are beheaded, and their heads displayed on the walls of the Imperial Palace as a warning. As the opera begins, twenty-seven suitors have already died.

Calaf, who to protect his identity from his enemies calls himself the Unknown Prince, is the only suitor who does indeed finally succeed in explaining the several enigmas. But Turandot immediately refuses to honor her pledge. Calaf then offers his own challenge. If she can discover his real name before dawn, then he will agree to die and release her from her oath. The crafty princess attempts to extract the secret name from Liu. Out of love for her master, Liu chooses to kill herself rather than risk revealing his name under torture. In a moving aria before plunging a dagger into her chest, she explains to Turandot that "it is love that has given her strength, a secret love for the prince who is her lord." Despite Liu's sacrificial death on his behalf, Calaf, whose real name, as it turns out, is "Love," cannot exist without Turandot. His passionate embrace of

Fig. 98 A Chinese tea box and a Puccini opera about a slave girl who commits suicide rather than betraying the man she loves inspired Jacques Guerlain's *Liu*, created in 1927 and presented in this black glass perfume bottle.

Folds, pleats, drapery, a curtained alcove, and a dreaming woman combine in this ad for Lucien Lelong's *Indiscret* to evoke visually what the ad's words make clear: namely, that the scent is by nature "indiscrete," peering behind curtains and invading the woman's private realm where it "joins with the odor of [her] skin, caressing it like a scented, musky madrigal, and creating an air of lazy, languid dreaminess." *Votre Beauté. Revue de la beauté féminine*, Paris, November 1, 1936.

her at the end of the opera signals his victory; he has won her heart.

Affirming the feminine virtues of faithfulness and love embodied in Liu's example, the Turandot story serves as the narrative and iconographic backdrop—exotic, colonialist, moralizing, and romantically misogynist—for *Liu*, a scent Guerlain describes as "a veritable hymn to femininity."[21] Despite her confident power, her resistance to patriarchy, and her proto-feminism, Turandot is a much less attractive figure than the self-sacrificing, obedient Liu, especially for the kind of glorification of feminine stereotypes demanded by the traditional, somewhat retrograde, nature of the scented imagination of the 1920s. And yet, as the decade progressed, women with their short, bobbed hair styles and their boyish "garçonne" look were indeed becoming more empowered and more emancipated, not only in French society but in the images they were given on the labels of different beauty products. One such label, circa 1925, for Rimmel's *L'Heure du Rimmel* (The Rimmel Hour) pictured a young woman in a loose-fitting gown sitting at her mirror and applying makeup (a perfume bottle sits at the ready on the table), while she seems to sip from a drink glass (fig. 100); clearly, the "hour" in question is the cocktail hour.

Art deco interior design as celebrated at the 1925 Paris Exhibition also influenced the very materials used to fabricate perfume bottles. Many of the model living spaces constructed by the large Parisian department stores at their own pavilions, as well as the lavishly decorated alcoves sur-

Fig. 99 Art deco style sought to capture the speed of fast cars and ships, so in 1935 it was only natural for Jean Patou to celebrate the maiden voyage of the steamship *Normandie* by creating a fragrance of the same name and by commissioning the designer Louis Süe to reproduce the liner's profile in this metal flacon.

rounding the Perfume Pavilion, displayed wall coverings, draperies, carpets, furniture, and objets d'art made from rich, sumptuous, and exotic fabrics, woods, and other materials. Some of these, like black Chinese lacquer, silk, mother-of-pearl, ivory, and sharkskin (called "galuchet" in French) were later incorporated into perfume bottle design. "Le Kid" was, for example, made in many of these materials, including sharkskin. And Piver produced a perfume called *Galuchet* around 1927, which was sold, quite appropriately, in an imitation sharkskin box. The avant-garde designer Madeleine Vionnet, one of the most important couturiers of the century, who was known for her sculptural, often geometric, bias-cut dresses, included a piece of ivory-colored crêpe-de-chine, her favorite fabric, on the top of the box of her first perfume, *Temptation*, (c. 1924). Rather than making cloth itself an integral part of his perfume presentations, the fashion designer Lucien Lelong preferred to represent the delicateness of falling pleats and folds in the drapery design (a parted curtain) sculpted on the front of his bottle for *Indiscret* (1935) along with a glass stopper in the form of a bow. Not adverse, moreover, to incorporating authentic materials into his presentations when he felt they could add drama, Lelong placed the bottle of his *Mon Image* (1933) in a stark, abstract, industrial box composed of cubes of mirror glass, reflecting, in more ways than one, the sleek geometric art deco style popular in the early thirties.[22]

L'HEURE DU RIMMEL

Fig. 100 For the liberated garçonne of the twenties, known for her short hair and her devil-may-care femininity, applying makeup and having a drink were not mutually exclusive activities as this chromolithograph advertisement and label, c. 1925, for *L'Heure du Rimmel* illustrates.

The Dynamic, Sleek, Streamlined Art Deco Perfume Bottle

Aside from bottles that, like a collage, appropriate real materials or those that imitate them through abstract sculpted designs, there were perfume bottles designed to be functional objects in their own right—like the flacon-cum-champagne flute for Guyla's *Divin Narcisse* of 1926, hand-painted by the Atelier Martine—or bottles that miniaturized an elegant, luxurious object. Examples of these "representational" trophy bottles were Marcel Guerlain's over-the-top *Rolls Royce* (1926) and Jean Patou's *Normandie* (1935). The Rolls Royce bottle was fashioned in the shape of the automobile's distinctive grille, with a metallic stopper resembling the car's celebrated hood ornament (the "Spirit of Victory"); it was set on a black

bakelite base molded to represent mudguards and tires. Patou's souvenir-bottle (fig. 99), a gift to all first-class passengers on the maiden voyage of the liner *Normandie*, which left Le Havre for New York on May 29, 1935—its sumptuous salons, dining rooms, and other interiors designed by the leading art deco decorators of the day—was cast in the shape of a miniature metal replica of the boat, created by the designer-architect Louis Süe. The glass perfume bottle was hidden inside a large silver column resembling the ship's central funnel.[23] The fact that these two bottles take the shape of luxury modes of transportation testifies to the impact on art deco design of the dynamic functionalism, machine aesthetics, and fascination with speed that characterized the linear, sleek, industrial style popular during the 1930s. Worth's tall, fluted bottle in blue glass for *Je Reviens* (I Return) of 1931,

231

designed by Lalique, embodies this kind of streamlined linearity and skyscraper verticality, although the romantic and nostalgic implications of a name announcing a return to a past state of love (*je reviens*) appears at odds with the modernist thrust of a bottle evoking the futuristic dynamism of the city.

Not all "representational" bottles, however, aimed at reproducing luxury objects. Sometimes the most ordinary and everyday artifacts were transformed into bottle designs. Take, for example, Piver's *Volt* of 1922 (fig. 101); it was sold in a bottle shaped like an inverted French light bulb with a stopper that exactly replicated the bulb's metal base. Or consider Lubin's *Fumée* (1934), a bottle covered with a white label that, when nestled in its box, resembled a row of five cigarettes (Lefkowith, 152). Even such a widespread art deco motif as the bolt of lightning found its way into perfume presentation. *Coup de Foudre* (in French it means to be struck by lightning or by "love at first sight") was created by Parfums de Rosine (sometime between 1925 and the 1930s); the front of its box was divided by a sharp zigzag. Numerous perfumes during the 1920s and 1930s, moreover, came in boldly colored, smooth-surfaced, opaque glass with lacquer finishes in green, blue, red, orange, purple, jade, turquoise, and black. The striking simplicity of these bottles, the sleek, geometric forms they favored, their flattened, minimalist shapes, and the paucity of mannered ornamentation, evident, for example, in the white, opaque crystal bottle decorated with a gold lacquer sun and zigzag edges that Caron had made for its scent *Alpona* in 1939 (fig. 102), accorded with the decorative aesthetics of art deco modernism. Rimmel's appropriately named *Art Moderne* from 1925, in the shape of one of those rounded "milestones" called "bornes," which are still found along old French highways, was such a bottle. A smooth, opaque jade surface culminating in an arcing black lacquered top, embossed with a subtle floral motif, *Art Moderne* was notable for the economy of its ornamentation, which still could not match the purely functional flacon, made of unadorned thin sheets of metal, created by Hermès for Guerlain in 1918.[24]

Jazz Age Ads: From ARPÈGE to CUIR DE RUSSIE, VOL DE NUIT, and GOLLI-WOGG

Arguably, one of the most stunning of colored opaque bottles, in jet black glass (or sometimes burgundy or blue Sevres porcelain), was the standard "house" bottle designed for Jeanne Lanvin by the art deco poster designer Paul Iribe (a celebrated illustrator who had created advertisements for Poiret, Lanvin, and Chanel) and the interior decorator Armand Albert Rateau. Lanvin, a milliner who eventually become known in the early 1900s for her "distinctive style of mother-daughter dressing," began to market perfumes in 1922. Rateau, who had redecorated Madame Lanvin's Paris townhouse on the rue Barbet-de-Jouy between 1920 and 1922 and had designed her stand at the 1925 Paris Exhibition, was commissioned by the fashion designer to create what would become the signature bottle of the house of Lanvin: a black spherical flacon referred to as the "boule noire" (black ball). On the front of the bottle was engraved and hand painted in gold a schematic, stylized representation of Jeanne Lanvin wearing a turban, a floor-length ball gown, and a cape that covered her shoulders and arms before falling down her back in a series of cascading arabesques and elegant soft folds. Madame Lanvin leans over to embrace her young daughter, Marie-Blanche, also attired in turban and flowing dress. Based on a 1922 drawing or painting of the Lanvins (mother and child) by Iribe, the representation soon became (and still remains) the logo for Lanvin products. While the logo may have first appeared in 1924 on the labels of Lanvin's clothes, it became inseparably linked to perfume once the celebrated "boule noire" of 1927 became the container for Lanvin's celebrated *Arpège*, a perfume gift from Jeanne to her musician-daughter on the latter's thirtieth birthday. *Arpège* was indeed a resonant floral symphony. Its inventors, the perfumers Paul Vacher and André Fraysse, blended sixty-two different notes to create a scent in which the dominant accords of rose, jasmine, and lily of the valley are

ALPONA CARON

enhanced with spices like pepper and nutmeg and fortified with base notes of vanilla and vetiver.[25]

Arpège: Perfume, Music, Romance

The link between perfume, music, and romance is highlighted in a photographic advertisement for *Arpège* from 1936 (fig. 103). At the keyboard of a white Gaveau piano the hands of a woman, her arms emerging from the intricate folds of a white gown or cape, play a musical piece. Over the keyboard a bouquet of fully bloomed roses hangs, a few fallen petals on the keys below. The scene is illuminated by a large white lamp. At the corner of the piano, his black tuxedo contrasting sharply with the general whiteness of the scene, lean the slightly out-of-focus hand and arm of a man whose vested shirtfront (white) and pants (black) are, along with his chest and arms, the only visible parts of his body. With the exception of the massive piano keyboard, the slightly withered roses, the base of the large lamp, and the woman's scarf with its folds and pleats draped upward to frame the foreground of the image, the scene is composed of cropped fragments—*her* arms and hands, *his* hands, chest, hips and legs—of two anonymous, depersonalized, partial bodies. This impersonality contrasts strangely with what one imagines to be the charged air of the room, heavy with the notes of music, fragrance (the roses), and love. But the strangeness is not all that strange when one realizes that each of the constitutive elements of the photograph has been reduced to the common denominator of a sign. Like

Fig. 103 The image of perfume and love, released into the air of a boudoir by "the magnetic caress of a hand giving birth to music," takes on poetic and visual form in this suggestive magazine advertisement for Lanvin's *Arpège*, published in *Votre Beauté. Revue de la beauté féminine*, Paris, November 1, 1936. The Lanvin "boule noire" bottle, imprinted with the turbaned mother-daughter logo, is pictured in the upper right.

the flowers and the piano with their clear reference to aroma and music, the two human figures have been reduced, concentrated even, into symbols of human interaction and dialogue, albeit silent: the woman who plays, the man who listens, during a quiet yet intense moment before fragrance and music lead to passion and lovemaking, an eventuality about which the text of the advertisement leaves no doubt: "Profound, . . . subtle, . . . it is the magnetic caress of a hand giving birth to music in the soft atmosphere of a flowered bedroom during an extraordinary night evoked by . . . *Arpège* de Lanvin."[26]

CUIR DE RUSSIE:
The Perfume of Adventure

The elegant, decorative details of the *Arpège* advertisement—the piano, the roses, the hands, the intense contrast of shadow and light (common to the kind of modernist fashion photography perfected by Edward Steichen and George Hoyningen-Huene, chief photographer for French *Vogue*)—evoke a luxurious and comfortable interior, a protected domesticity. The mystery here (and mystery, there is, indeed) is not exotic; it comes from another quarter, from

the whisper of an intimate interplay of music and fragrance. Other advertisements from the mid-thirties evoke more adventurous tales, in particular a publicity photograph for Chanel's *Cuir de Russie* (Russian Leather), a scent invented in 1924 by Ernest Beaux, the creator of *Chanel No. 5*. Perfumes designated as "cuir," or "leather," are dry and smoky compositions, whose unique aroma comes from the blend of the essences of tobacco and birch bark to

which spicy, amber notes have been added. Moreover, the animalic ingredient, castoreum, organizes the scent's base note to give the fragrance greater tenacity. When provided by the Siberian beaver, castoreum possesses an inherent "cuir de Russie" note coming from the birch bark on which the animal feeds. In Russia, precious jewels were at one time stored in wrappings of fine leather, which tanners had prepared by using birch bark. The first "cuir de Russie" scent, Caron's *Tabac blond*, appeared in 1919. It was created to appeal to women who smoked and would therefore be attracted to the perfume's woody, even opiate, aroma, characteristic of the strong cigarettes of the time. It is clear that the scent was designed to attract only certain unconventional women, for as one Chanel advertisement makes clear, "well-bred ladies will find [its scent] improper."[27]

Other houses followed Caron's lead: Lanvin had its *Scandal* (1932) and D'Orsay its *Trophée* (1935). A warm, masculine, somewhat gamey scent, the "cuirs," according to one professional perfume critic writing in 1936, brought to mind "feelings of comfort and memories of travel." But it owed a great part of its success, he observes, to "a certain masculinization of women caused by sports and outdoor life" as well as by the allure of travel, an activity women could now undertake alone, if they wished. Advertisements of the thirties suggested that the mere dream of a voyage could be as powerful and poetic as the reality. Jeanne Lanvin was fascinated by travel, according to her grandnephew Bernard. She "never went to the ends of the earth," he remarks, "but if she had lived in the age of air travel, all her perfumes would have been souvenirs of her journeys." Her fragrance *Le Sillon* [Wake] brings to mind a ship at sea, and *La Dogaresse* evokes the isle of Venice. One publicity photograph for Chanel's *Cuir de Russie* from 1936 (fig. 104) shows a woman in a hotel room, seated on a bed, her overcoat still around her and her valises and a vanity case open, as she holds up a bottle of *Cuir de Russie*, checking perhaps to assure herself that her supply has not run out. "Fine leather suitcases," the text declares "evoking adventurous departures; love letters still redolent of the odor of the desk drawer where they had been forgotten: these are the two symbols enlivening the deep, somewhat uninhibited scent of Chanel's *Cuir de Russie*."[28]

The images of leather, smoke, and the Russian steppes thick with stands of birch sustain the poetic images on which *Cuir de Russie* depends, an image-system that draws its power from other imaginary associations as well—those associated with international travel and the exoticism of foreign lands as captured in one of Chanel's advertising slogans for the scent: "the poetry of action expressed in perfume." An interesting example of the dramatization of these different yet interlocking systems of images is given in the typewritten manuscript of a publicity text for *Cuir de Russie*, written in November 1936 and prepared either as a press release or, more likely, as part of an information brochure for use by Chanel's sales staff. From the first sentence, it is evident that the travel suggested

Fig. 104 That the independent, resourceful woman of the thirties travels by herself throughout the world but would never forget her favorite fragrance is suggested by this print advertisement for Chanel's *Cuir de Russie*, published in *Votre Beauté. Revue de la beauté féminine*, Paris, November 1, 1936.

Opposite page:
Fig. 105 The garçonne, wearing the chic cloche hat and voilette typical of the style of the twenties and thirties, happily inhales a fragrance in this striking advertising poster from 1934 by André Wilquin, in all likelihood created for a large Paris department store since different products ("Gloves-Perfume-Lace-Flowers-Stockings-Brushes") are mentioned by name.

GANTS
PARFUMERIE
DENTELLES · FLEURS
BAS · BROSSERIE

But for a woman, this perfume, this bewitching perfume, at once meditative and dynamic, is also the very scent of travel, of the transatlantic cabin, of the hotel room where she closes sumptuous suitcases, her heart filled with the vigorous joy of promising discoveries and rich tomorrows. And this is why I easily imagine this perfume floating in the wake of a tall, slender brunette, whose moves are confident, whose voice is accustomed to giving orders, and whose fingers are slightly darkened by tobacco. She is one of those women who always wears a suit, even at midnight at the Savoy; one of those women captivating to watch at the casino in Monaco who, after having lost a sum of money, takes bills and a money order from a love letter hidden in her fine leather handbag, where they have taken on a pungent, slightly wild odor, and with great calm throws them on the green baize of the gaming table. Chanel's *Cuir de Russie* is a cocktail of purebred refinement, of pungent sources, of quiet happiness, of bold seductiveness, of an invitation to a journey. It is all that remains of poetry in our time.[29]

is of the armchair variety and the mode of transport that of reverie. It is on the wings of dream and fancy as provoked by scent (and by narrative) that one takes flight. The poetic and Baudelairean echoes are apparent, even if the spelling of the poet's name is faulty. There are images and turns of phrase—allusions to the pungency of leather, old love letters, a hotel room—which recall the text of the publicity photograph of the woman on the hotel bed scrutinizing or admiring her upheld perfume bottle:

Several images and allusions in this text have been marshaled to create a distinctive mood, one that suggests elegance, sophistication, class, adventurousness, romance, nostalgia, poetry, and, above all, the image of a powerful, independent woman. This is a woman who travels alone, who knows how to ride horses, who smokes and drinks, who knows exactly what she wants, who speaks in a voice accustomed to giving orders, who acts unemotionally, who has her own money, and who does not worry about what she loses at the gambling table. As the final sentences announce, *Cuir de Russie* is an "invitation to a journey," yet another allusion to the title of one of Baudelaire's poems. And it is also the invitation to an imaginary narrative: that of the empowered, self-reliant woman, "tall and slender," who in traveling annuls time and space, who inhabits the here (her transatlantic cabin) and the there (her memories of past love), the inside (the comfortable chairs of hotel lobbies), and the outside (the wild Russian countryside seen from a galloping horse). But this conquistador is also a dreamer who remembers poetically the ideal, otherworldly, Baudelairean spaces of perfect love and bliss. No wonder the final line declares that *Cuir de Russie* is "all that remains of poetry in our time."

> The only perfumes worthy of love are those that lead the imagination toward a journey *sur place* [*in situ*]. *Cuir de Russie* possesses this magical quality. No one better than Chanel has captured its mysterious evocativeness which extends from long, wild rides across the Russian steppes, redolent of the pungent odor of birch bark coming from tanneries, to the peaceful ambience of rich interiors filled with comfortable chairs, leather bound books, and expensive prints. During certain rare, quiet moments, at night, she goes looking without regret in a desk drawer for love letters that have still not grown old. They have taken on the aroma of fine leather transformed into an intensely pure scent. The emotion they once expressed has made them precious; no longer does she think of situating them in time or space. Leaning her head on the back of a chair, a slightly opiate-smelling cigarette between her lips, a glass of whiskey within reach, she abandons herself to the quietness of life as enhanced by memory. "There, all is order and beauty, / Luxury, calm, and delight," as Baudelaire [*sic*] wrote. And reigning "there" as well should be an odor of Russian leather.

Despite this empowerment, however, the garçonne-conquistador cannot escape subservience to and domination by one particularly powerful force: perfume. (Interestingly, André Wilquin, the art deco artist, captures this contradictory blend of potent scent and chic, sleek, empowered woman in an advertising poster from 1934: fig. 105.) Clearly, in Chanel's *Cuir de Russie* advertisment it is not really the woman who is in charge of things, but fantasy itself. "The only perfumes worthy of love," the advertisement asserts, "are those that lead the imagination toward a journey *sur place*": a journey that is essentially imaginary. Made captive to the magic of perfume and its bewitching spell, strangely both "meditative and dynamic," passive and active—after all it is "a cocktail" of contradictions—the woman no longer makes the decisions. *Cuir de Russie* is the dominatrix here; it provides a fantasy in a bottle. Chanel controls the imaginary associations that are in play because, as the text affirms, "no one better than Chanel has captured the mysterious evocativeness" of scents like "*Cuir de Russie*."[30]

Baudelaire is present, if not in name at least in spirit, in another publicity photograph linking perfume and travel, this time for Worth's 1935 *Projets* (*Plans*), marketed in the United States under the less poetic name of *Clear Sailing*. The photo depicts an overly exposed (possibly even solarized) close-up of a woman's face in profile holding a globe of the world close to her cheek. "This is the smell of lands of adventure," the text declares, "of small faraway ports where light breezes are filled with the bouquet of mimosas and of unknown flowers gorged on sunlight, through which Worth's *Projets* inspires the most exquisite

dreams." Once again, as in the advertisement for *Cuir de Russie*, the only real voyages are imagined ones, an idea that also appealed to Baudelaire. In his prose poem "Les Projets," the poet walks through Paris and dreams of the blissful life he and his beloved might have under the roofs of three different dwellings. One possible life could be lived in a palace, a second by the sea in a tropical cabin filled with "the powerful scent of rose and musk," and the third in a small inn. Returning home, the poet realizes that imagination alone has the power to put the entire world within his reach (like the woman holding the globe in the perfume advertisement); there is really no reason to travel. "Why," he

asks, "force my body to change location when my soul travels so nimbly? And what good is it to carry out plans, when planning itself is a sufficient delight?"[31] Perfume is this "sufficient delight," inspiring, as Worth would have one believe, fantasies that are enjoyment enough. The imagination, like the aura of scent enveloping the wearer, is sufficient unto itself.

The Odors of Speed and Sport

Linked to the allure of travel in the late 1920s and 1930s was a fascination with speed. A dynamic style of purist lines, streamlined forms, and uncomplicated, functional shapes, associated with the power of automobiles, trains, luxury liners, and airplanes, became a hallmark of 1930s modernism. "Speed aesthetics" now replaced machine aesthetics in the advertising posters of the time, including those for perfumes. The designs that A. M. Cassandre, the great art deco artist, typographer, and poster designer, created for trains like *Etoile du Nord* (1927), a representation of nothing more than bands of sleek steel tracks plunging forward through a vast expanse toward a star on the horizon, and for ocean liners like *Le Normandie*, pictured majestically, yet gracefully, slicing its way through waves, significantly changed the calligraphy, typography, and forms of advertising. Speed, in general, and the speed of light, in particular, are given an interesting interpretation in a 1938 advertisement for Coty's *Météor*, described as the "perfume you will never forget" (fig. 106). Here the volatility and velocity of both light and scent are underscored. Against the abstract black and white background of an immense solar eclipse stands a bottle of *Météor*. From the edges of the black lunar disk, flamelike rays and bursts of the sun's corona explode into pencil-thin, meteoric trails of light that envelop the perfume bottle.[32]

For his new 1933 fragrance, *Vol de nuit* (Night Flight), a tribute to the French author and aviator, Antoine de Saint-Exupéry, whose book of the same name had been published in 1931, and a celebration of the founding of Air France in 1933, Jacques Guerlain created a perfume designed to embody the aerodynamic spirit of the age. The result was the "flacon rayonnant," a rectangular bottle etched with fluted spokes radiating outward like a sunburst from a center composed of two gold circles, the outer one of which displayed the scent's name in clean art deco letters (fig. 107). The design immediately called to mind the whirring blades of an airplane propeller and of course the idea of flight, escape, and voyage. A publicity photograph for the perfume in the mid-1930s shows two elegantly dressed women and a man, all in evening attire, standing in a field at night next to a small plane they are about to enter. *Vol de nuit* is described in the accompanying text as a perfume for women who are "at once athletic and knowingly elegant," a juxtaposition of qualities reinforced by the fashionable attire the women are wearing in the photo and the

Fig. 106 The explosive, blinding flash of light and scent suggested by this advertisement for Coty's *Météor*, 1938, serves as a possible image for François Coty's meteoric success not only as a great perfumer but as one of France's richest capitalists.

Des exhalaisons un peu sauvages, un léger rappel
de lavande, des accents très frais sur une trame
d'une profondeur luxueuse réservent aux femmes
à la fois sportives et d'une savante élégance,

"VOL DE NUIT"
de GUERLAIN

Fig. 107 The propeller-
bladelike incisions
radiating outward from
the center of this crystal
bottle, known as "le
flacon rayonnant," as
designed by Pochet & du
Courval for Guerlain's
Vol de nuit, 1932, constitute a perfume homage
to French aviation, which
in five years' time would
attract over 10,000 men
and women to local
flying clubs. The black
and white ad (above)
claims that *Vol de Nuit* is
designed for the woman
who is both "athletic and
knowingly elegant," a
combination of qualities
seemingly corroborated
by the photograph,
where "aviators" appear
dressed as much for a
soirée as for a plane ride.
*Votre Beauté. Revue de la
beauté féminine*, Paris,
November 1, 1936.

sport in which they are about to take part: namely, flying. In the 1930s women's aviation was at its height.[33]

"Sports," announced the press release for Jean Patou's lavender-scented *Le Sien* (His) of 1929, "is a field where women and men are equals." Beneath a boldface headline—"For the athletic woman, a masculine perfume"—and a drawing of a woman in a grey and pink wool ensemble swinging a golf club, Patou confesses that an "overly feminine perfume" for a sportswoman would definitely ring a "false note." Even though composed of the "fresh, healthy, and outdoorsy notes" usually associated with men, *Le Sien* will nevertheless accord with the "personality of the modern woman who plays golf, smokes, and drives her car at 75 miles per hour." In this image of the athletic and forceful woman, Patou, the creator of the first so-called "perfume bar"—a professional barman-perfumer mixed different "cocktails olfactifs" (scented cocktails) on request—was following in the footsteps of the novelist Victor Margueritte.

La Garçonne, Margueritte's widely popular and scandalous novel of 1922, had single-handedly created the image, if not the full-blown myth, of the fashionably boyish woman for whom all the stylish Paris couturiers of the time were designing clothes. The garçonne was often seen as a woman with an androgynous figure and an innocent, childlike face, but with a seductiveness and sexiness intensified by her use of lots of makeup, jewelry, and perfume. With her short skirts and body-revealing clothes, she came to embody the moral permissiveness that had burst forth

in the wake of the war. Monique Lerbier, the boyish heroine of Margueritte's novel, is a robust, athletic woman who spends a quarter of an hour each day doing physical exercise and who feels pleasure and confidence at her "muscled torso, flat stomach . . . long legs," "a gymnast's body from which emerges naturally and rhythmically Beauty itself" (115, 120). Like Patou's declaration of the olfactory equality between the sexes in the *Le Sien* advertisement, Monique looks at her body and sees the "flesh of a beautiful animal," realizing that "by dint of wanting it [and working at it] she had physically and morally become the equal of men" (120). As for *Le Sien*, Patou conceived it as a unisex perfume, perhaps the first of its kind, and as a sports perfume, a scent unimaginable during the previous decade. Although since around 1912 women had been wearing perfumes during the daytime, the image-system to which perfume owed its mystery and aura still associated scent, as Delbourg-Delphis notes, with the pleasures of the night. That changed with the 1930s, for "while still depending on the same traditional images associated with scent, the new decade brought about a more casual use of perfume."[34]

Images of the active, athletic sportswoman, golfing, running along the beach, playing tennis were seen in the pages of 1930s fashion magazines, thanks to the snapshot realism, the blurred motion, the informal spontaneity, and the active if not exuberant poses captured by the Hungarian sports (turned fashion) photographer, Martin Munkacsi. A publicity photograph for D'Orsay's *Trophée* (Trophy, 1935) influenced, but probably not taken by, Munkacsi, shows a short-haired, smiling woman in shirt, shorts, and calf-high boots carrying a rifle while projected behind her is the gigantic head and exposed canines of a snarling tiger. In a short text accompanying the photo, the open, unassuming, yet forceful character of *Trophée* is described by epithets that apply to the perfume as much as to the woman stalking big game: "Young, accentuated with leather and iris, evocative of the huntress Diana, bold and athletic, with a straightforward glance, a smiling mouth, and simple charm."[35] Despite the image of competence and self-reliance, the athletic woman is hobbled, nonetheless, by ambivalence. She is a huntress, yet her charm counts more than her aim. She carries a gun but never stops smiling. She is bold, perhaps even fearless, but also naïve, simple, and maybe too candid for her own good.

Despite the tennis matches won by Suzanne Lenglen in the twenties—she was world champion in singles from 1919 to 1923 and again in 1925 and 1926—and by Madame Mathieu the following decade, and despite the active participation of women in tennis, flying, swimming, rowing, and gymnastics during the 1930s, French women still remained "conditioned to keep away from sports events believing that it was more fitting . . . to take care of the children when their husbands were at the stadium." But Lenglen's great popularity and the new emphasis on the sports-oriented woman in 1920s advertising signaled not only a growing female presence in different sports

Left:
No longer considered to be *the* trophy, the woman in this ad for D'Orsay's *Trophée* has become (if only for a moment) an athletic huntress, the goddess Diana, looking for game (shown in the background as many times larger than herself) to bag and bring back from the wild. *Votre Beauté. Revue de la beauté féminine,* Paris, November 1, 1936.

activities but the desire as well for a different kind of daytime dress. Lenglen's somewhat daring tennis outfits—her signature bandeau in the form of a wide swath of orange chiffon and the all-white tennis dresses that added elegance to her athletic image—attracted the interest of Chanel and Patou; the latter designed the sophisticated tennis attire Lenglen wore during the Wimbledon championships of 1921 and 1922. Even Cadolle Frères, the elegant lingerie makers credited with inventing the first brassiere (despite Poiret's claims to have done it earlier), got into the act, creating two perfumes in 1927: *Après le Tennis* and *Suzanne Lenglen*. It is clear that in the 1930s "the French were becoming more interested in sports and in fresh air," despite the opposition of Pope Pius XI, who in 1933 proclaimed that female sports produced "indecent behavior and display."[36]

Perfume and the Art of Pleasing

The ambivalent image of the sportswoman, a confusing hybrid of feminine and masculine, carries over to images surrounding perfume. In a revealing essay, "Perfume: A Seductive Weapon . . . A Necessary Luxury" published in 1936, Michel Arbaud expresses confusion regarding the female sex, an ambivalence he then projects on to women themselves. Women and the accessories (perfume, clothing, jewelry) with which they adorn themselves are enveloped in an ambiguity assigned to them by men. According to Arbaud, perfume is a powerful weapon of seduction in the arsenal women employ to perfect the "art of pleasing," an activity with its own "immutable laws." Under the influence of a woman's perfume, men feel "an untranslatable enchantment," "an involuntary caress," and "a secret need for tenderness that surrenders them, bound and gagged, to a woman's desires." Faced with the "ambiance" that perfume creates and with the "climate" of refinement women establish through perfume, men are helpless. Because their senses have been degraded by the banality of daily life, men are easy targets for the sensual ravishment that perfume initiates.

Yet perfume, this weapon of seduction, is also a necessity, a fragrant, luxurious, and expensive necessity, because, as Arbaud argues, women must, in order to maintain their commitment to the "art of pleasing," use perfume to mask the natural odors of their bodies. Fragrance is absolutely necessary for this reason. (Coco Chanel would beg to differ when she remarked that "luxury is a necessity that begins where necessity ends."[37]) Women must look at perfume as a function of their being, as something that completes them. "You must have your own perfume," Arbaud advises,

> as you have your own smile, your own way of walking, your particular way of looking at each circumstance of your life. . . . Madame, from now on you

must plan to make perfume one of your beauty expenses.... Save money by taking it from some place else, but do not at all deprive yourself of smelling good. You often open your purse for trifles which serve your charm much less. It is your duty to please. It is your duty to be perfumed. It is even the most feminine of your duties.

The downside of women's involvement in sports for Arbaud as well as for Parfums Coty was that as women spent more time in the sun and wind, closer to an unspoiled, natural world, their desire for simplicity and for the natural risked turning them away from all kinds of artifice, including, of course, perfume. In an article of February 1937 in the *Revue Coty*, the company's in-house journal, the anonymous author felt it necessary to remind readers, most of whom worked for the company, that "for the sportswoman, wearing perfume is a duty. With physical exercise and sports has come the mystique of a certain return to nature which has pushed women to the paradoxical conclusion that there is an incompatibility of temperament between perfume and sports. Nothing could be less accurate" (Delbourg-Delphis, 193). On this point, Arbaud was in total agreement. Perfume, the instrument of seduction, which transforms the banal into the sublime, is also an agent of day-to-day hygiene. Exercising one day in the most elegant sports club in Paris, Arbaud takes the time to observe ten young women who are also working out. Although he can tell that they are accustomed to bathing everyday and "scrupulously caring for themselves," they had nevertheless just finished a half-hour of gymnastic activity and had worked up a sweat. This was noticeable "even though the windows were wide open." And so he concluded his personal anecdote with the declaration that "Yes indeed, perfume is a real necessity." From his point of view, it is necessary for three reasons: first, it must be worn as an instrument of seduction affording men the heightened experience that their sensual life does not ordinarily receive in the everyday, commonplace world; second, it must be worn to disguise the odors generated by physical activity; finally, it must be worn to imitate nature. In all three instances, the perfumed woman succeeds in fulfilling the obligation imposed on her by the "art of pleasing." The idea of returning to nature is praiseworthy, Arbaud states. Yet, "one must not forget how prodigious nature is in creating exquisite scents. . . . Would you accuse the lowliest of landscapes of using artifice? Perfume is an attribute of landscape: it completes it and is in tight alliance with it." Perfume thus becomes as natural as nature. Such a contorted and distorted argument is favored as well by the anonymous author of the *Coty Review* article, worried as he is that perfume consumption may decline with the popularity of sports. But he finds a persuasive argument to protect Coty's interests. It may indeed be the case, he suggests, that sports add to the pleasure of perfume by deepening and intensifying its aroma. This is perhaps so because "physical activity, and in particular winter sports, by pushing women to a higher level of excitement and animated movement give their perfume unforeseen contrasts which surprise and delight them."

Fig. 108 The elegance and beauty of perfume invention and design offer no guarantees against the insensitivity of colonialist and racist images as revealed by this glass and fur perfume bottle designed by Michel de Brunhoff for Vigny's *Golli-Wogg,* 1920.

One final aspect of perfume advertising during the 1920s and 1930s concerns its relationship to French colonialism. Many of the expensive ingredients used in the finer, more luxurious perfumes were imported, although not exclusively, from different French colonies. For example, from Madagascar, came vanilla, cinnamon, marjoram, clove, ylang-ylang, and patchouli; from the island of Réunion, geranium and spices like pimento; from Tunisia, coriander; from Morocco, neroli, tuberose, narcissus, cedar, oakmoss, and rose; from Algeria, cypress, jasmine, thyme, and petit grain; from Laos, Cambodia, and Vietnam, benjoin; and from Haiti, vetiver. In conjunction with the importing of perfume ingredients from the colonies came the caricatured image of colonial subjects in general and of West African people in particular, which for a short time was an integral, and clearly racist, aspect of perfume presentation. One perfume bottle for Vigny's 1920 scent, *Golli-Wogg* (fig. 108), created by Michel de Brunhoff (1892–1958), had a stopper that was a puppetlike head of a black man with large exaggerated white-rimmed eyes, thick red lips, grinning white teeth, and a massive, unruly head of black hair made of real fur. The clownish appearance of the bottle was reinforced by a polka-dotted collar encircling the neck and a label over the bottle's bulging "stomach" on which the outline of two black hands was printed. Placed at each corner of the bottle's base were two small black feet. Three identical bottles of *Golli-Wogg*, with the English names "Jack," "Junior," and "Jill," were packaged in a red-satin box and marketed in 1925.[38]

The inspiration for both the name and the bottle design came from a storybook character created by Florence K. Upton, an illustrator, who in collaboration with her mother, Bertha, the author of the accompanying text, wrote thirteen children's books from 1895 to 1909 with such titles as *The Adventures of Two Dutch Dolls and a Golliwogg* (1895) and *The Golliwogg in the African Jungle* (1909). Florence Upton, who had been born in New York in 1873 to English parents and had returned to England in the late 1880s, based her Golliwogg stories on the rag doll that as a child she had played with in New York City, a doll that was a grotesque caricature of American blackface minstrels. Although ultimately of American provenance, the Golliwogg books were hardly known in the United States. First published in London and distributed throughout the British Empire, they eventually migrated to the Continent, where they enjoyed immense popularity and were reincarnated in 1908 as a mass-produced doll by the German manufacturer, Steiff, ultimately to become as ubiquitous among European children as its counterpart, the teddy bear, did in America.[39]

The advertising text displayed on a perfume card for *Golli-Wogg* around the time of its launch describes the scent as "a fetish-perfume" capable of producing "a subtle evocation of the *Orient* which will satisfy the desires of the Elite through its persistence and great distinction." The allusion to the "Orient" here is somewhat bizarre considering that the racist stereotypes packed into the term "golliwogg" do not apply to the East alone; in fact, the bottle's and the doll's caricatured image is evidently more African than Oriental. "Golli-wogg" (without the hyphen and the final "g") is a Britishism, the shortened form of which, "wog," entered British parlance between 1925 and 1930, as a derogatory reference to "any nonwhite, especially a dark-skinned native of the Middle East or southeast Asia." Moreover, the explanation offered by a few postwar French perfume histories (in particular, *Précieux Effluves* and *Hymne au parfum*) that the *Golli-Wogg* bottle reflects the influence of the American dancer Josephine Baker's *Revue Nègre* and the popularity of American jazz in 1920s Paris would appear to contradict the "myth" of the Orient to which the perfume card had sought to refer. Curiously, these French studies of perfume history, by associating the golliwog with the *Revue Nègre* and jazz—among the many legitimate theories regarding the provenance of the word "jazz" is its homophonic similarity to the word "jasmine," the perfume favored by New Orleans prostitutes—leave unchallenged the doll's inherent racism. There seems little doubt that Vigny's *Golli-Wogg* bottle, given the stereotyped manner with which it characterizes the Other and reduces African peoples to the infantilized "cuteness" of a doll, is racist. Yet, to call it, as these two French histories do, a "humorous bottle inspired by black American rhythms" and an "amusing modern bottle" similar to de Brunhoff's other flacon creations for Vigny—his *Guili Guili* (1926) was an abstract bottle dominated by the oversized, carved head of an African mask—seems highly inappropriate. Closer in time to the Colonial Exhibition of 1931, which the French government organized to celebrate the glory of its imperial past—it attracted six million visitors—was the equally racist bottle for the perfume *Nénufar*, created for Ramey by a popular cartoon artist of the time. The bottle's stopper was sculpted into the clownish and stereotyped features of an oval-shaped African head with large, white-rimmed, exorbitant eyes and thick, red lips. The outline of the man's loin-clothed body and of his large, splayed feet covers the front surface of the black glass bottle.[40]

The Garçonne's Perfume: Coco Chanel's NO. 5

At age twenty, Monique Lerbier, heroine of Margueritte's *La Garçonne*, wears the latest fashions; for the evening she selects a loose-fitting tunic dress which drapes her body in supple and ample folds. "I love it!" she exclaims. "How at ease one feels, as if one were naked; and yet it's as chaste as a Grecian robe," very much like, she thinks, the ancient

statue of Diana she has seen at the Marseilles Museum (37). Monique also likes to wear her hair short and in a bob. Since the war she explains to her mother, "we women have all become, more or less, *garçonnes*!" (40). Short hair is "the symbol of independence, if not force. In the past," she continues, "Delilah emasculated Samson by cutting his hair; today, women believe that by cutting theirs they can make themselves more virile" (98). Another outfit of Monique's is a bit more revealing, for it is nothing more than "a *robe-chemise* of silver lamé from which her bust and arms emerged and offered themselves, while the heavy fabric of the rest of the dress lay flat against her body" (120). Beyond fiction, in the real world, the *garçonne* of 1925 was behaving no differently, as her peers, especially male, were wont to complain: "These beings—without breasts, without hips, without 'underwear,' who smoke, work, argue, and fight exactly like boys . . . these aren't young girls! There aren't any more young girls! No more women either!"[41]

The desire for emancipation and autonomy, so clearly apparent in the unconstrained and revealing style of dress favored by the garçonne—something Margueritte's moralizing tale will finally criticize when, after a year or two of dissolute, forbidden pleasures, Monique lets her hair grow long, rejects the décolletage of current fashion, rediscovers heterosexual love, and feels the return of a lost sense of

chasteness—expresses itself in the fashion that Gabrielle (Coco) Chanel made famous in the early 1920s. The "garçonne look" reached its apogee in 1925 and remained vibrant with only the slightest change until the very end of the decade. At first only a marginal style associated with certain lesbian, cross-dressing groups, the garçonne look moved into the mainstream when a new consumer society came to the fore in the 1920s and began to democratize fashion by means of the image of a liberated woman. The major event of 1925 was Chanel's shortening of the hemline to a point just below the knee, a look modest enough when a woman was standing but revolutionary when she sat down; women had never before shown so much of their legs. The casual ease that Chanel's clothes expressed had been evident since 1916: especially, in the unadorned, uncluttered, full dresses; the simple, unbroken silhouette; the suppressed curves; the straight lines, drop-waists, and loosely hanging belts; the appropriation of men's clothing (blazers, cardigans, tweeds, pants, sailor suits, workers outfits, and ditchdiggers' scarves); the casual and fluid jersey suits (jersey had been a lowly fabric until Chanel got her hands on it); the uneven hemline; and the overall freedom of movement. This was an elegant, understated, nonchalant, almost minimalist look, certainly in comparison with the ornate, corseted gowns of fin de siècle fashion and with even Poiret's prewar high-waisted dresses. Chanel's garçonne style was given its signature look by the introduction of the "cloche" hat in the winter of 1923 (although it had already been seen as early as 1916); women wore it low on the forehead, to the eyebrows, and pulled down to the nape of the neck in back. The hair was bobbed in what was called the Joan-of-Arc style or slicked back in the close-to-the-head gamine style. The deep, oval décolletage of the naked back, setting off the woman's uncovered shoulders, the sleeveless arms, and the décolleté bodice were remarkable for the time, revealing more of the body than had ever been seen, at least since the short reign of Empire fashion in the first decade of the nineteenth century, when women's high-waisted, gauzy dresses had been equally unconstraining. Finally, Chanel's "little black dress" of 1926, the new, standard "uniform of the modern woman"—American *Vogue* predicted it would become as conspicuous as the mass-produced Ford—was designed in an innovatively functional manner. It was a dress in harmony with the modernist, streamlined, art deco aesthetics then coming into vogue and with Chanel's strong conviction that one should "always remove, never add."[42]

"A well-dressed woman is closest to being naked," Chanel is rumored to have said. Monique Lerbier, the ur-garçonne, would have certainly agreed, considering how "naked" and free she felt in her Diana-like tunic dress, a feeling that confirms yet another of Chanel's remarks: that "the elegance of clothing lies in the freedom to move." This was a "civilization [that] no longer has clothes" declared the writer Drieu la Rochelle. On the stage and in music halls the naked body had lost its pornographic character; in 1926, Josephine Baker performed topless wearing only a belt of bananas. This vogue for nudity leads Honoré Paquignon, the perfumer-protagonist of Clément Vautel's 1926 novel, *Je suis un affreux bourgeois* (I Am a Terrible Bourgeois), to the conclusion that, because of sports and the style of "Greco-American dancing" made popular by Isadora Duncan, "woman means flesh. I had discovered skin and soon I will take it away from doctors and pharmacists to make it one of the most fertile domains of modern perfumery."[43]

The increasing visibility of the uncovered body in scanty attire had interesting consequences for both perfume and jewelry, as Paquignon indicates. Poiret, who was not an admirer of Chanel's simple, minimalist designs—he called her garçonne look "poor chic"—did however introduce long dangling necklaces, sometimes dropping as far as the stomach and even to the knees, which were worn to accentuate the vertical line of his tubular, although hobbling, skirts. With her closely coiffed hair uncovering ears and neck, the garçonne inspired the vogue of pendant earrings, which by 1929 hung down to the shoulders. Now that sleeveless dresses exposed the arm, slave bracelets, bangles, and medallions could be worn above the elbow and flat bands and bracelets, four or five in a row, below. Chanel was the first couturier to create sumptuous, ornate costume jewelry, manufactured from modest or synthetic materials like lacquered metal, paste, imitation stones, and pearl-drop colored glass, and thus more affordable to the general female population.[44]

Perfume as a Second Skin

Like jewelry, perfume, too, was seen as an adornment (invisible, although by no means imperceptible) to be applied to the epidermal spaces women now boldly revealed. The exposure of so much more skin gave women new areas to explore for the application of their scents. Femininity became synonymous with a much less discreet and more openly sensual nakedness. As the bejeweled body dazzled with its aura of reflected light, so the perfumed body glowed with the halo of fragrant emanations. While in comparison with the nudity that would dominate fashion at the end of the twentieth century, this modest unveiling seems almost quaint, it did bring into existence a style that conceived the absence of clothes as a new form of dressing, a new manner of presenting the body. At the very time when a certain stylistic minimalism in the streamlining of fashion, interior decoration, and product design was coming into vogue, the removal of clothing from certain areas of the body was yet another move toward simplification. Yet, this modest uncovering of the body in the 1920s reflects two of Coco Chanel's firm beliefs: first, that we must have "the courage to be better and to do better when we seek simplicity" and second, that fashion (including perfume) "is what remains when everything else has been removed," as the slogan for Chanel's 1996 fragrance *Allure* declares. "No elegance is possible without perfume," Coco Chanel would say, according to the perfumer Jacques Polge, for "it is the unseen, unforgettable, ultimate accessory." "Is Chanel No 5," one publicity text asks, "a gown that lingers when a woman is finally naked or is it a foretaste of nudity when she is still dressed?" That perfume can be and is said to be "worn" suggests that a naked body, draped and enveloped in scent, can also be seen as "dressed." As there are "styles" of nudity, by means of which even the naked body is not truly naked but rather "clothed" in its own corporeality and in its ways of moving and occupying space, so perfume can be seen as a "second skin" of sorts. Marilyn Monroe made the point compellingly clear during an airport interview in Tokyo in February 1954. Asked by a reporter what she wore in the morning, she responded, "A sweater and a skirt." "And in the afternoon?" he inquired again. "Another sweater, another skirt." "What about the evening?" he continued. "The same, but in silk." "And at night?" he finally asked. "Five drops of Chanel No. 5."[45]

As she had done with fashion, Coco Chanel revolutionized the design of perfume with her first scent, *No. 5*, created by Ernest Beaux in 1921. From this moment perfume history would be described in terms of fragrances created before *No. 5* and after *No. 5*. A fragrant "incarnation of timeless femininity," *No. 5* realized Chanel's longing for

Fig. 109 A few sketched lines and the simple rectangular form of an unadorned bottle capture the desire for a heavenly fragrance in this drawing, one of the first advertisements for *Chanel No. 5*, by the artist SEM (Georges Goursat), c. 1921.

"a woman's perfume with a woman's scent." The first deeply and inherently aldehydic perfume and the first scent to be marketed by a fashion designer under her own name, *No. 5* was a fragrance both floral and abstract, the opposite of Guerlain's more figurative perfumes. The olfactory drama of opening a bottle of *No. 5* and perceiving its head, heart, and soul notes, as recounted by Chanel's advertising literature, is imagined as an intensely poetic encounter with, what one advertising brochure calls, "the very first olfactory work-of-art":

> At the moment the stopper is removed, there arises the enveloping flight of ylang-ylang from the Comoro Islands and of neroli, both captivating flowers which, once lightened by aldehydes, expand their sensuality towards a seductiveness which, while more refined, is nonetheless fatal. Then comes the sensation of a perfect accord, that of May rose and Grasse jasmine, whose secret is to blend with and conform to each woman. It is what makes every single woman who wears *No. 5* unique. Finally, Indian sandalwood from Mysore and Bourbon vetyver from Réunion live on, like the memory of a faraway place, in the quivering wake of a woody *sillage*.

The uniqueness of the perfume and the woman, collaborating to bring to the surface, as it were, each other's essence, is reiterated in another publicity text, this one from 1993: "There are as many *No. 5*'s as women. On each of them, it transforms itself. It marries her personality, glorifying without altering it, exalting without betraying it."[46]

Minimalist Styling

Not only was the abstract composition of *No. 5* remarkable for its complex blend of over eighty ingredients; so were the perfume's name and bottle. The desire for simplicity and for a minimalist style as expressed by a perfume with a cold mathematical number for a name, especially when compared to the mythic, exotic, sentimental, and baroque designations that had dominated perfume presentation since the Belle Epoque—for example, *Narcisse noir* (Black Narcissus, Caron, 1911), *Chypre Egyptien* (Babani, 1919), *Quand vient l'été* (When Summer Comes, Guerlain, 1910), or *Pierrot Vainqueur* (Triumphant Pierrot, Hygiènof, 1918)—added a completely new, somewhat abstract, character to the naming of perfumes. Here was a high-end luxury product with a down-to-earth name and an unassuming, even austere, rectangular label in stark black and white. Its simplicity reflected that of Coco Chanel's couture and mirrored as well the streamlined aesthetics of "moderne" style. Stripped of all ornamentation and artifice (other than the clean block letters in sans serif type displayed against the label's pure white background), the square, angular bottle and its oversized rectangular stopper were revolutionary in their ordinariness. As she had done for her pants, argyle sweaters, and sailor suits, Chanel again went searching in a man's wardrobe to find the undistinguished toiletry vial (a functional perfume holder common to men's traveling cases of the time) that would become the new vessel for *No. 5*.

Even the package holding the bottle was striking in its plainness. This was no elaborate, sculpted, flowered box in metal or sharkskin or wood, in the shape of a heart or a jewelry case, or with panels that opened and closed by means of clasps, ribbons, cords, or tassels. Instead, it was a monochrome box "fitted to the bottle, as closely as a coat fits over a dress." For Chanel, however, the number 5 was no ordinary number. When in the spring of 1921 Beaux presented her with two series of test scents for the new as yet unnamed perfume, they carried the numbers 1 to 5 and 20 to 24. Chanel selected a sampling of scents from which number 5 was eventually chosen. Since she was about to present her spring fashion collection at her new Rue Cambon boutique on May 5, the fifth day of the fifth month, the number 5 seemed an appropriate name to give to the new fragrance. Thereafter, May 5 would always be the opening day of Chanel's spring fashion shows, and five would remain her lucky number.[47]

A strange description, even criticism, of the *No. 5* bottle comes (tongue-in-check, of course) from Chanel Parfums itself:

> It is a bare bottle, more a thing found in a laboratory than an object of luxury and seduction. It has an almost unbearable sobriety. Square, abstract, empty, it is exactly the opposite of what one expects from a feminine perfume. The entire presentation is rendered even more cold and sterile by the name, the terrible name: No. 5.

The quotation is part of an imaginative publicity publication of almost eighty loose-leaf pages in different colors bound by a black cord and entitled *Mes Recherches* [My Investigations] *1921–1993: No. 5 Chanel*, which was published in 1993. The book is designed to resemble a journal-cum-scrapbook. It contains historical documents and memorabilia: photographs of Coco Chanel, of the 1925 Grasse jasmine harvest, of society balls and of the perfumers Ernest Beaux and Jacques Polge along with artistic "portraits" of the *No. 5* bottle (by Sem in the 1920s and Andy Warhol in 1985), and the celebrated "faces" (Catherine Deneuve, Carole Bouquet) that have represented *No. 5* over the years. In addition, the booklet was composed of a number of fictional texts made to look authentic: in particular, worn facsimiles of telegrams, copies of hotel stationery and envelopes, and personal letters, both handwritten and typed. The anonymous voice of a man obsessed by *No. 5* discusses with an air of sincere perplexity the perfume's history and the reasons for his lifelong research into and obsession with it. He asks and then answers over sixty questions about the perfume, the first dating from his initial encounter with the fragrance in 1921. It happened, he explains, at the Hotel Ritz in Paris as he crossed paths with a woman whose wake was perfumed by a scent that "surpassed all other fragrances" because it gave voice to "her skin, her soul, her very being." From this moment on he promises to dedicate himself to "understanding No. 5."

Finally, on January 9, 1971, the narrator receives a handwritten letter from Coco Chanel agreeing to meet him at 11 P.M. the following night; the letter, written on stationery from the Hotel Ritz (Chanel's residence), is the next-to-the-last of the "documents" reproduced in *Mes Recherches*. "Dear Sir, after serious reflection," the fictive Chanel writes, "I have agreed to unlock for you the enigmas of No. 5." The author shows up at the Ritz Bar, their meeting place, but Coco Chanel is not there; she has died earlier that day. The final document of the book is an envelope, sealed with a drop of red wax, inside which lies a folded letter, the author's "Last Will and Testament," announcing his failure at having "decrypted" No. 5, a scent whose enigma remains "whole, infinite, multiple, and indivisible." He leaves to those who follow the task of "interrogating" *No. 5* which, as he now realizes, is not as much a perfume as a "voyage through the century, one that has hypnotized Time as it has enchanted men," himself included.[48]

As regards the garçonne of the 1920s, would *Chanel No. 5* have been her perfume of choice? Would it have sat on her dressing table next to her powders, lipstick, lotions, cigarettes, and car keys? Would the groundbreaking innovativeness of *No. 5* have appealed to this modern women with her shorter, décolleté dresses and her bold, unconventional, rule-bending spirit, especially when, in 1929, *No. 5* became the largest-selling perfume in the world? One would think so. "*No. 5* does not fear modernity," the fictional author of *Mes Recherches* writes. "It is modernity incarnate. And modernity is the perfume's reflection, its private domain, its prisoner." Sem, the political and social caricaturist and artist of the 1920s (his real name was Georges Goursat), created several advertisements for Chanel's new scent. One lithograph from around 1925 uses the front of a *No. 5* perfume bottle as the "canvas" for a scene in Chanel's *salon d'essayage*. A stylish woman attired in a long, loose, plunging-back, fish-tail evening dress stands in front of a kneeling Chanel who, pins in her mouth, makes final adjustments to the front of the dress. Sitting and smoking on a sofa, near to which bolts of fabric lie, is a second client wearing a loose dress and a long dangling necklace. The women all have short hair and are attired in accord with Chanel's interpretation of the "garçonne" look.[49]

Sem's advertisement, moreover, features a poetic ditty written in hand below the sketched bottle of *No. 5*. Signed by a fictional "Marquis of Bottledom" the text plays with the different French meanings and uses of the word "coco." It refers, for example, to a coconut, to a baby's word for an egg, to cocaine, to a strange or suspicious person, to

a term of endearment for a cute child, to the "land of cocagne," an imaginary, mythic country of riches and pleasure, and of course to Chanel herself, whose nickname, "Coco," came from her days as a chanteuse entertaining soldiers in the town of Moulins. Chanel's best known number involved a song about a lost dog, "Qui Qu'a Vu Coco" (Whoever Has Seen Coco?). Some or all of these meanings are possibly hidden in the advertising text, which reads as follows: "I say it without shame / There is nothing less coco / than a toilette of coco / Perfumed with a scent of coco . . . / of Coco . . . of Cocologne." This "Cocologne" (Cocoland) is an invented place-name ending in the suffix "logne" as in Bois de Bou-*logne*, the forest on the outskirts of Paris or, of course, eau de Co-*logne*. A still earlier drawing (fig. 109), probably the first Sem created for *No. 5*—it was published in 1921—illustrates more clearly the link between the garçonne and Chanel's new perfume. It shows a young woman with closely cropped hair, in a sleeveless, pleated, knee-length slip-dress, raising her arms and head skyward toward a large bottle of *No. 5*. A long scarf floats away from her neck, and the position of her head (it is thrown back) and her arms and hands (they enact an imploring gesture) express joy and ecstasy. *No 5*, as Jacques Polge observes, is indeed "a kind of grammar," a system of signs, for the Chanel style.[50]

Babette and "Bourjois" Chic

The ethics of liberation and the aesthetics of sensual display expressed in the garçonne's comportment and in Chanel's fashion and perfume inventions had intense appeal for certain women who best represented the bold, all-caution-to the wind spirit of the Roaring Twenties. One woman in particular, who, so to speak, "worked" for Bourjois, the largest cosmetics and fragrance firm in France by the early 1920s, went by the simple name, "Babette." The Bourjois company had started as a manufacturer of theatre makeup in 1863, selling colors named for the characters of different plays—a "Romeo," for example, was available—and used by actors like Sarah Bernhardt. The company's face powder, composed of Java rice, was created in 1879 and sold at the rate of two and a half million packs per year. Bourjois was the inventor of compressed powder and, under its *Manon Lascaut* brand of the 1890s, gave the world the first compact makeup. By the turn of the century and the start of World War I, Bourjois, under the direction of Ernest Wertheimer, was producing the first pastel compact blushers and was also moving into fragrance. *Ashes of Roses* appeared in 1911, *Mon Parfum* in 1923, and *Soir de Paris / Evening in Paris*, the firm's greatest international success, composed by Ernest Beaux, the creator of *Chanel No. 5*, in 1927–1928.[51]

In its simple, yet stunning, cobalt blue, art deco bottle, with a triangular silver label featuring a crescent

Fig. 110 Bourjois,
Evening in Paris/
Soir de Paris, in a cobalt
blue bottle with a silver
label, 1927–1928.

moon and a star (blue and silver were the racing colors of the Wertheimer stables), *Evening in Paris* (fig. 110) was first sold in the United States, part of a marketing strategy aimed at a primarily middle-class audience. The hope was that American women would purchase the fragrance as much for the imaginary experience of Gallic romance and Parisian sophistication it promised as for its floral and spicy bouquet of jasmine, iris, carnation, rose, vetiver, and sandalwood. To attract the average American female consumer, for whom, given her financial means, European travel and a firsthand knowledge of French culture would have been unthinkable, *Evening in Paris* tapped into the romantic stereotypes of France. In the 1920s, France was a foreign, even exotic, country known only to all but the wealthiest Americans through its iconic and mythic images. To provoke fantasies of elegance, refinement, and luxury, a series of advertisements from the late twenties through the fifties showed idealized Parisian couples in stylish evening dress engaged in sophisticated activities and events: dancing in a ballroom, sitting in a red-velvet loge during a theater intermission, driving in a limo around the Arc de Triomphe, looking over a balcony at the Paris skyline under a moonlit, night-blue starry sky, standing before the cascading water of the illuminated Place de la Concorde fountain, ascending the grand staircase of a Paris Opera gala, and kissing on a bridge beneath the Eiffel Tower. One advertisement from the 1930s informs the consumer that "elegance without perfume is a body without a soul! Madame, your beauty needs the refined atmosphere of . . . *Soir de Paris*. It is the very scent of Paris, so captivating, full of dreams and love. . . . This evening, be more desirable with the complicity of *Soir de Paris*." Another advertisement in the December 1938 issue of *Marie-Claire* described *Soir de Paris* as a perfume with "all the nocturnal magic of the world's most unique city: PARIS!"[52]

Of course, Bourjois's Paris is more dream than fact, more a sublime ideal than an ordinary reality, with the exception of the architectural icons of "Paris-ness"—the famous bridges, monuments, streets, and cafes—and the stereotyped inhabitants of the city, both of which are depicted with a certain quality of everydayness and a concrete, here-and-now accessibility. It is the constellation of imaginary associations gravitating around the name "Paris" that lends its metaphorical and lyrical power to the presentation of *Soir de Paris*. The box containing the flat, blue perfume bottle was decorated, for example, with a panel of miniature line-drawings illustrating the romance of "Paris-ness." Under a crescent moon and in the shadow of the Eiffel Tower a man and woman tango near a typical kiosk. Another couple dine at a cafe table, next to a violinist and a bassist who are placed besides the Arc de Triomphe, while a painter stands at his easel painting a nude model. Here is commonplace, everyday Paris elevated to myth, the myth of Frenchness which *Soir de Paris* appropriates and intensifies for its stay-at-home American audience. Nor were Bourjois's faithful clients across the Channel

forgotten, as a white plastic Eiffel Tower protecting a "nesting" bottle of *Evening in Paris*, a presentation designed for Great Britain in 1949, makes clear (see page 326).

Babette's work for Bourjois began in 1924, the same year Pierre Wertheimer gained a controlling interest in Chanel and, with Coco Chanel's approval—she was in desperate need of a larger company to mass produce and distribute her creations—formed a new corporation: Parfums Chanel. While the new company would henceforth deal with perfume and beauty products alone, the couture and accessories end of the business continued to remain in Coco Chanel's hands. Babette became the spokeswoman, the "ambassadress," at first for Bourjois's *Mon Parfum* and its pastel blushers; but eventually she turned her advertising talents to *Soir de Paris*.

Who, then, was Babette? Was she a garçonne who drove fast cars, exercised at a physical culture club, and, had there been no conflict of interest, wore *Chanel No. 5*? While Bourjois's *Mon Parfum* did not overemphasize its association with the garçonne look, it was not averse to being linked with it. One advertisement from the 1920s, entitled "La Préférence" integrates a bottle of *Mon Parfum* and its accompanying powder box with the colored drawing of a woman in a flapper dress wearing a garçonne hairdo and standing gracefully beside a basket of flowers. A more daring advertisement for Bourjois's Java Face Powder from around 1928, created only for the American market, links intelligence and chic with the image of the fast-living, in-the-know, "society girl," which the garçonne sought to project. "Are Society Girls Smart?" asks the headline at the top of the advertisement published in *Liberty Magazine*. A positive answer follows: "Be as extravagant as you like about your silk stockings and undies . . . but 50 cents will buy a Face Powder used by Society's Favorites."[53]

Babette, however, is not the kind of woman to speak about her lingerie. If she is a garçonne, then she is a truly ambivalent one. She may wear garçonne fashion—pictures of her reveal a short-haired brunette with an upturned nose, a pursed mouth and bangs down to her eyebrows and with a lower fringe of hair sweeping over her ears and onto her cheekbones like a cloche hat (fig. 112)—but her values and her life style are mainstream bourgeois. Sophisticated, refined, fashionable, charming, romantic, well-to-do, and accustomed to a luxurious and privileged style of living, Babette is also, as no less an authority than the Prince of Wales has observed, "the most beautiful woman in the world" and, as a friend tells her, "the prettiest woman in Paris."[54] Yet, Babette is also contemplative. She asks philosophical and moral questions about the meaning of life, the role of fate in history, the secret of happiness, and a woman's fear of aging. She offers her opinions on a variety of contemporary social and cultural issues: the French system of social security (established by the laws of 1928 and 1930), the radio (officially sanctioned by the decree of 1928 granting government licenses to thirteen private stations), the increase in the cost of living, the difficulty of Parisian

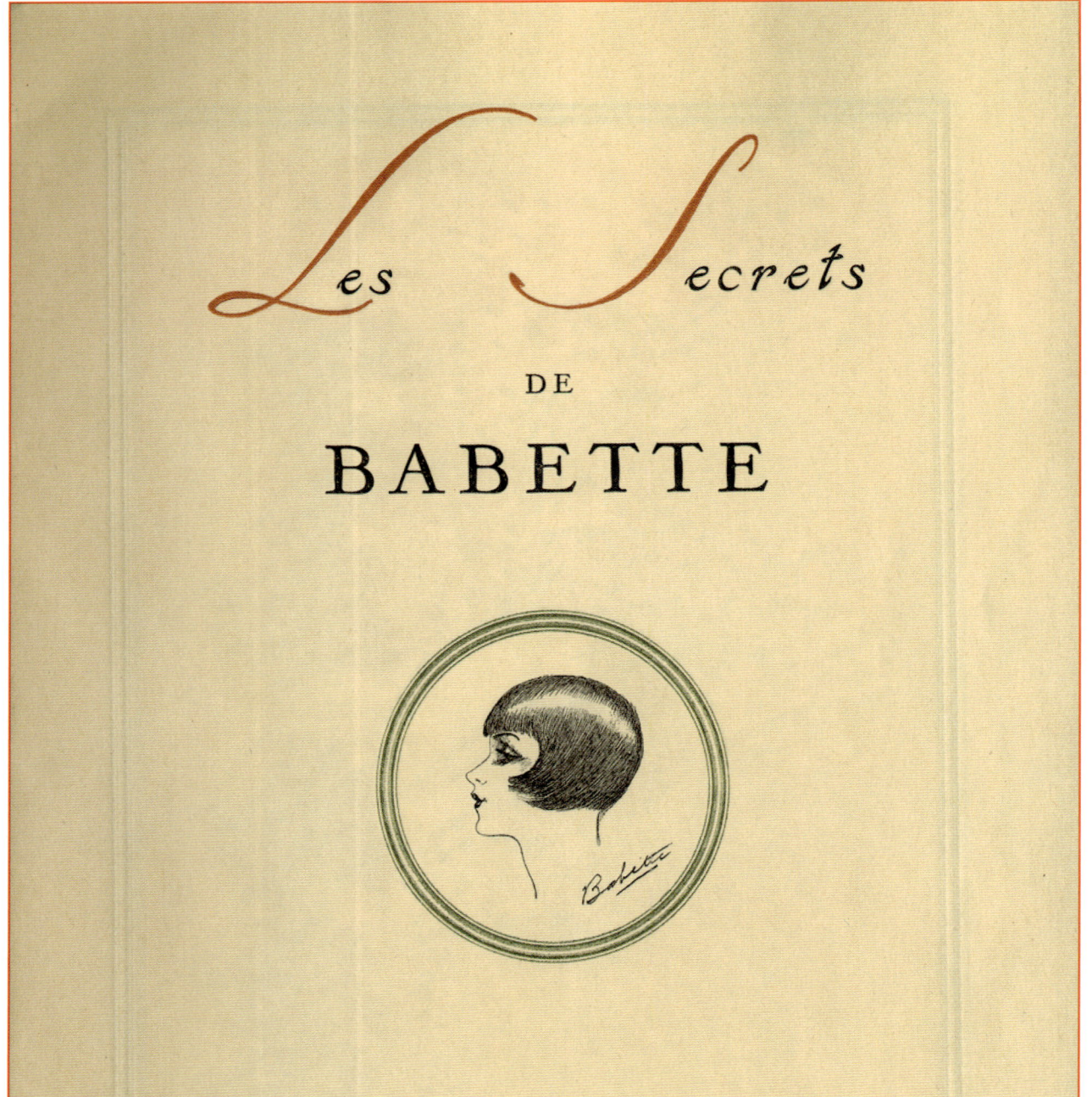

life, the protection of animals, charity for the poor, educational reform, marriage, adultery, and the struggle for power between the sexes.

The elegant, stylish everydayness of Babette's life is filled with activity, excitement, and energetic pursuits. She reads books (*Uncle Tom's Cabin*, poems by Hugo and Lamartine), makes literary allusions (to Ulysses, Kant, and Peter Pan), writes elegant letters, comments on the fashions of the season, and rides horses in the Bois de Boulogne. She gambles at the Deauville casino, sails a boat, goes camping, skis in the Alps, celebrates holidays (New Year's, Epiphany, Easter, Christmas), and goes to a masked ball. She also shops along the rue de la Paix, knits socks for the poor, does crossword puzzles, cleans her house, gardens, sleeps on colored sheets, loses her purse, works at being a good wife, and, of course, without fail, wears Bourjois perfumes and cosmetics. Babette is certainly a woman to take to heart Coco Chanel's dictum that "fashion cannot exist if it does not descend into the street." Married

to Jean, her devoted, supportive, although patronizingly indulgent and paternalistic, husband, with no children (although reference is once made to a son, Didi, who eats a tube of Bourjois lipstick with no dire consequences), Babette, the epitome of mid-to-late 1920s stylishness, is a clever, quick-witted, and intelligent conversationalist. Whether she is teasing, or sparring, or charmingly bickering with Jean, or engaged in a dialogue with her friend Hélène and other female *confidentes*, Babette has "an answer for everything," as one of her friends remarks.[55]

Although she is Paris's or even the world's most beautiful woman, a "petite goddess of true luxury and chic," "the very soul of feminine perfection," a sophisticated member of the upper French bourgeoisie, and "the symbol of the *femme moderne*," Babette is a fictionalized everywoman. A creation of advertising, she was "born" around 1924 and enjoyed a short but full life until the early 1930s as the spokesperson, "interpreter" and "ambassadress" for Bourjois products. Instead of designing an advertising

250

campaign merely praising its products or heavy-handedly dictating what customers needed to buy, the company decided to create a representative who would be a "friend" to the middle-class consumer, "a mirror of your life, a faithful and dependable advisor," as Bourjois's statement of advertising intent put it. Babette, "is she not yourself?" asks Bourjois of its clientele. Indeed, she is, it answers:

> You follow her active, luxurious, elegant life so similar to your own. Babette gets her clothes at your couturier, walks with you, dines at your table, and you meet her at the theater, at the racetrack, on vacation, or traveling. Her delicate profile, her modern figure, her confidant charm become each day more familiar and necessary to you.

And what better proof is there of Babette's resemblance to the average consumer than her makeup and fragrances, for like the woman-in-the-street, she would never think of wearing anything else but Bourjois. This is so because in society, as a friend confides to her, "it's not only the radiant charm of your face that strikes those around you, but also the indefinable charm of your fragrant personality, Babette, you who, among a thousand scents, have chosen once and for all 'Mon Parfum' by Bourjois."[56]

Babette's Creator

Babette was the creation of the novelist, poet, and journalist Germaine Beaumont (1890–1983). Beaumont's mother, Annie de Pène, a novelist, had been an intimate friend of the writer Colette until she died from Spanish influenza in 1918. When Colette, after the war, became literary editor of *Le Matin*, she hired Beaumont (without pay) to be her secretary. At *Le Matin*, Germaine edited a letters column, the women's page, and later part of the Sunday magazine section devoted to literature.[57] Beaumont, who until her death wrote nearly twenty popular, much praised novels (and translated Virginia Woolf's diary), was commissioned by Bourjois probably in 1922 or 1923 to write literally hundreds of short anecdotes, stories, commentaries, and descriptions of the different social situations, cultural events, domestic projects, marital arguments, intellectual discussions, daily dramas, and sports and leisure activities in which a 1920s woman like Babette might participate. Most of these little narratives carried titles that were themselves delightfully intriguing mini-tales of everyday life: for example, "Babette Drives," "Babette Cultivates 'Her Garden,'" "Babette Dreams of Being a Poet," "Babette's Writing Paper," "Babette and Her Photography," "Babette Resists Growing Up," "*Dr.* Babette," "Babette's Toothache," "Babette Has Nothing To Wear," "If Babette Has a Daughter," "After Eve, Babette," "Babette Loses Everything, Except Her Honor," and "Babette and the Psychology of Perfumes." For over six years, from 1924 to 1930, the Babette stories,

no longer than half a printed page in length, appeared daily, weekly, possibly monthly as prose advertisements in such French newspapers and magazines as *Cyrano* (a satirical weekly), *Mode pratique* (a weekly women's newspaper), *Eve* (an illustrated Sunday women's newspaper), and the well-established reviews, *Jardin des modes*, *Femina*, and Paris *Vogue*.

Babette and 1920s' Society

Each Babette story begins with a dramatic or narrative problem. It is interesting to try to guess how the trajectory of the narrative, as it unfolds in all-too obvious or in charmingly clever ways, will eventually lead, ingeniously and humorously, to the advertisement's unwavering dénouement: namely, the resounding endorsement of Bourjois's *Mon Parfum*, its *Soir de Paris*, or its pastel makeup powders. In one story Babette and her husband discuss fate. "When there is a train wreck with ten dead and a hundred wounded," Babette asks, "who's at fault?" "Fate," Jean answers. And when a ship sinks or the overforesting of the countryside creates floods, "whose fault is it?" Again, "fate," Jean replies. But, turning the tables on his wife, he becomes the interrogator: "Whose fault is it," he asks, "when a woman, using her spells and charms, reduces all hearts to her mercy?" Not losing a beat Babette replies: "Bourjois's. Because if great events are governed by fate, the beauty of women can only depend on Bourjois, thanks to its 'Pastel Blusher,' its exquisite 'Mon Parfum' powder, and its divine 'Soir de Paris.'"[58]

Another episode has Babette calling her friend Hélène in tears to tell her that she is certain Jean is having an affair. Babette has overhead a telephone conversation in which Jean tells one of his male friends that "I have never seen a figure like it, wondrous, slender, supple, and submissive. I couldn't tear myself away. I stood there like an idiot completely stupefied. All I wanted to do was to take possession." But since Jean, it appears, has just returned from an auto show Hélène is quick to set Babette straight. And the last sentence is quick to reassure the consumer as well that "Babette is certain of Jean's fidelity, thanks to Bourjois which knows better than anyone how to make a woman beautiful." In another story Babette dreams of becoming a poet and has the fantasy that through her poetry readers would be "moved, ennobled, made happier and better." But, as Jean adoringly points out, there are many ways to be a poet, and even "without writing a line one can indeed move, exalt, enchant all sorts of individuals in one's orbit. Ah, Babette, your beauty is your poetry. When one looks at you, one can't help but realize that you are a gift from heaven, a messenger of dawn. Your face, so pure, so soft, so fresh, is worth all the poems in the world." Modestly, Babette deflects the praise on to her makeup and perfume: "It's not I but Bourjois who is the poet." Jean offers a compromise: "Then Babette, Bourjois and you are the greatest poets of our time."[59]

The Babette stories also offer commentaries on the social scene of Paris during the latter half of the decade and into the early 1930s. One learns about the international character of cultural events—Russian plays, Japanese spectacles, Turkish puppet theater, German operas, Swedish ballets, all performed in the original language—as the background for the assertion that elegant fashion is no tower of Babel; it speaks only one language: that of Bourjois. The sheer number of industrial shows (*salons*) that Babette has to attend during the fall season—the radio, automobile, sewing machine, and Art Nègre salons—prevent her from going to her own beauty *salon*. Yet, the Babette stories offer from time to time a more socially committed and political take on French life. In one such vignette, on the subject of the new laws establishing a nationwide system of social security, Jean affirms the importance of social welfare, identifying it as "one of the highest principles among those honored by enlightened humanity. Mankind believes, and rightly so," he continues, "that the social security of every individual must be guaranteed to its utmost limits." Of course, Babette, responds in a manner that seems to trivialize the philosophical declaration her husband has just eloquently made. "For a long time," she remarks, "women have known about social security, because their own social security involves staying beautiful, seductive, and desirable in order to enjoy an old age sheltered from loneliness and worry. I would like to know what caring for one's beauty is, if not social security . . . especially as offered by Bourjois." Often in these mininarratives, the desire to turn the advertising momentum of the story in the direction of a pedagogical lesson—the value of the new social security system, for example—creates a paradoxical, almost schizophrenic, tale. The seriousness of the end is undercut by the apparent frivolousness of the means. Nevertheless, there is a didactic dimension to these advertisements. They do reflect on the issues of the day; they do express a political and social point-of-view. Beginning with the armistice and extending to the end of the Roaring Twenties, fashion, as the historian Mary Louise Roberts points out, sharpened its political edge, honing it against the ideological whetstone of the social order: "What women wore became invested with political meaning in a profound yet ephemeral way. The political significance of fashion did not inhere in the styles themselves; rather, fashion became political because of the way it was interpreted by contemporaries, how it was understood in the cultural imaginary."[60]

On the whole, Babette does often appear strikingly naïve, gullible, clueless, and, like the automobile Jean desires, mechanically submissive. She has a "childlike sincerity" and, when she is sick, very "plaintive" little-girl eyes. She acts like a "little minx," "or a "little peach of a flirt." She is "flighty," "scatterbrained," and a spendthrift; she is also a "delicate, fairylike creature." When Babette, troubled by an unpleasant encounter with a insane man on the street, announces to Jean that she has something "serious" to tell

him, he responds with the sexist remark: "Serious? For what, . . . my wallet?" These epithets, these so-called "terms of endearment"—no different from the ones Torvald used to patronize Nora in Ibsen's *A Doll's House*—are signs of the crisis in gender identity and the resulting antifeminism of postwar France, especially after Frenchmen, unmanned by the carnage of the trenches, returned to civilian life and found women performing tasks—delivering mail, collecting bus tickets, cleaning streets, running businesses— once uniquely the province of men, as Roberts has shown. All the sexist female stereotypes are to be found in the Babette stories: a narcissistic preoccupation with beauty ("I am nothing without my precious perfume," Babette cries); a difficulty saving money; a lack of seriousness and critical self-awareness; a flightiness; an insecurity about her wifely abilities (she decides to darn Jean's socks in an attempt to better her "performance"); a melancholic moodiness at different seasons of the year; a self-indulgent love of male admiration; a flirtatiousness (she makes Jean jealous by dancing with another man); irresponsibility (she has crashed a new car three times and let the bathtub overflow while she and Jean were on vacation); irrationality; and so on. The coup de grâce of this antifeminist bias is expressed in a story in which Babette complains about how the education of young girls has been neglected and how, had she a daughter, she would teach her that

> Her destiny is perhaps to be quite simply like me, a happy young woman, living in a friendly household with a good husband. This creates an obligation for her: to be pretty, kind, and alluring. And, I would add, there are two things essential to a woman's life: a smile and perfume.

While the smile would be passed down from mother to daughter, the perfume would, of course, come from Bourjois. The secret of happiness for a woman, Babette tells an interviewer, is to guard the love one has inspired and "the only way to preserve the love of a man, especially one who from birth is naturally capricious, is always to be beautiful."[61]

Is Babette then a kind of Barbie Doll before her time? Yes and no. For sure, she is passive, frivolous, and fixated on her charm, beauty, and appearance. As an adored woman-flower she loves the mythic pedestal of reverence and awe on which she is placed. She is an enchantress, a "sorceress," a magical "fairy." Could one expect any less from a creation of advertising that bases its appeal to female consumers on the image of women that postwar society had forged and that women as well as men had unconsciously and unquestioningly internalized? It is true that any suggestion of Babette's sexuality—for example that she might feel passionately about another man or that she might be unfaithful to Jean—is deflected from her on to the Bourjois products she is endorsing. Thus, the specter of female eroticism, so indistinguishable from the allure of perfume,

252

Babette au baccarat

DEAUVILLE. La Salle de baccarat. Babette joue.

Babette gagne. On suit avec une attention troublée, la chance miraculeuse de cette petite créature délicate et féerique dont les mains d'enfant jouent parmi les grandes coupures bruissantes.

— Babette, avoue que tu as un talisman.

— Peut-être.

— Lequel?

— Ah! Voilà.

Et Babette me confie avec une conviction superstitieuse, que « Mon Parfum » de Bourjois est un fétiche; qu'enveloppée de cet arôme suave, elle se sent protégée contre les traîtrises du sort et qu'elle ne se risquerait pas dans la Salle du Baccarat sans avoir vaporisé sa chevelure.

— Ah! Babette, je ne sais si « Mon Parfum » vous fait gagner. Je sais qu'à plus d'un il fait perdre la tête.

BOURJOIS

CRÉATEUR DES FARDS   PASTELS

Fig. 112 Arriving at the gaming tables of Deauville perfumed in Bourjois's *Mon Parfum* and thus haloed in luck, Babette, described here as a "delicate, petite, and enchanting creature," is not shy about gathering her winnings in her "child's hands." "Babette au baccarat," *Les Secrets de Babette*, c. 1924–1925.

surfaces only to see its transgressive power—and its threat to marital and social order—quickly masked through its association with a mere object: a bottle of perfume. In one story, Jean's is the voice of moral order and instruction when he defines faithfulness as "a feeling particularly necessary to conjugal happiness." Babette's sexuality, enhanced by the eroticism of *Mon Parfum* and *Soir de Paris*, does indeed exist, but for her husband alone. When a love letter from a secret admirer turns out to be from a fourteen-year-old, it is Bourjois's fragrances that are blamed. This is an endorsement of perfume's power of attraction, but it also trivializes the threat of adultery by hiding it behind the innocuous naiveté of adolescent infatuation.[62] Yet again, the contradictory encounter between a moral or pedagogical intention clashes with the clearly consumerist mission of the advertisement.

Babette, however, is also *not* a Barbie. She has a clever, wily, intelligent, even independent side, and from this she derives her power. She acknowledges that she is "forthright in her opinions and that my independence and stylishness shock people of reason." She knows men and knows how to manipulate them to her advantage. And she gives as good as she receives, often getting the upper hand: when, for example, she calls Jean, not without affection of course, a "dear fool," or when she tells him that sometimes he almost does act, in fact, *intelligently*, or when she criticizes his love of hunting, or mocks his dislike for the new style of bathing suits (he finds them too daring, impudent, and strange). In one charming episode she shows her superiority (at least in the area of psychoanalysis) by asking Jean if he is "repressed," if he has a subconscious, or if he dreams about stairs. He has no idea what she's talking about and takes her questions as a sign that she's been drinking. "Here I am," she responds, "attempting to discover your problem, and you treat me this way? I try to be a philosopher and you accuse me of inebriation. I try to be a psychoanalyst, and you throw the word 'vermouth' at me."[63]

Babette's personal and spiritual resources give her from time to time a pensive, withdrawn, melancholic, and often mysterious air. The end of summer, the falling of leaves, and the death of young lovers, complains Babette, are no longer subjects for poetic reverie or philosophical meditation. This is, Jean explains, because young people no longer find it poetic to die; they'd rather take good care of themselves and live. "Dead leaves," he unpoetically remarks, "are no longer a theme of literature but a problem of sanitation." Romantic to the core, Babette confesses that "this is precisely why I would have preferred to live in 1830." Such a melancholic and poetic temperament accords well with Babette's love of perfume to which, as one would imagine, there are many allusions in Beaumont's narrative advertisements. Even after two hours of trying on and buying dresses Babette feels the clothes are incomplete until she can renew her supply of *Mon Parfum*: "My dresses will never be mine ... until they will have absorbed the perfume I love above all." Endowed as it is with a first-person adjective, *Mon Parfum*'s very name dramatizes an act of appropriation, personalization, even addiction. Once it is bought, it is *mine*; it becomes *my* scent, an irrefutable expression of the person *I* am. Because of its "discreet, elegant, and chaste name," *Mon Parfum*, may seem, Babette declares,

> a mere nothing! The impression of repose, delight, elegance, and pleasure ... creates a delicate and subtle rapture filtering through one's being; one realizes one can't do without it.... It's a perfume full of tact, a spiritual scent easily wedded to the intimate personality and the grace of a woman. Impudently, other perfumes label and dominate you; this one earns your respect. It is you, yourself.

Mon Parfum is also a good-luck charm. Wearing it while playing baccarat at the Deauville casino (fig. 112), Babette feels its "talismanic," "fetishistic" power merging with her body: "Enveloped by the suave aroma she feels protected against fate's treachery." It may not "make her *win*, but it will certainly make others *lose* their heads." At a masked Venetian ball she is approached by a Harlequin who immediately knows she is Babette from "her unforgettable scent." Yet, when *Soir de Paris* first appears on the French market, Babette has a momentary crisis of indecision:

> At the Bourjois store, I noticed a completely new bottle, a blue one ... I opened it and inhaled. What a perfume, Jean, what a perfume! The only one in the world that could compete with "Mon Parfum" and they call this miracle "Soir de Paris." I'm losing my mind. What will I do, torn between the divine "Mon Parfum" and the intoxicating "Soir de Paris"? "I don't know about you," Jean replies; "but I know I'm ruined."[64]

Finally, perfume leads Babette into an aesthetic and philosophical discussion about the nature of artistic representation. Babette shows Jean a new photograph of herself which she finds extraordinarily attractive, but that he thinks merely okay. He agrees that the photo faithfully reproduces Babette's likeness and that the lighting is fine, the presentation well-balanced, and the image artistic. The

Mystery, danger, the combat of light and dark, and the chiaroscuro of candle and shadow envelop this fearless woman climbing a stairway where the unknown lurks around a corner. If she is indeed Cassandra, the Trojan princess of prophecy, as this ad for Weil's *Cassandra* suggests, she knows what awaits her. Weill's ad celebrates the "encounter of a modern-day woman dressed for sleep with an ancient heroine who possesses the fatal charm of the vamp." *Votre Beauté. Revue de la beauté féminine*, Paris, November 1, 1936.

problem, he explains, is that the photo is her and not her. "Even a perfect photo can never copy the movement, the color, the life, your life, my Babette, in all its quicksilver vitality. Moreover, something, a kind of atmosphere, seems to be missing." Babette understands completely and spraying some *Mon Parfum* on the back of the photo she hands it to Jean saying, "Smell it now; is it better? "Indeed," he replies "I've now found you."[65]

In the end, the Babette stories, like the photograph of Babette, are at once advertisements and not advertisements. They are more than mere copies, simple verbal images, of the products they seek to present, as Babette, the woman, is more than what her photo reveals. An "atmosphere," to use Jean's word, is missing from the photo as it would be from a traditional advertisement of the time. Thanks to Germaine Beaumont, atmosphere is restored to advertising in such a way that the product is invested with a tailor-made image, which goes well beyond the conventional associations (the "cultural imaginary") of advertising. For Babette is a sophisticated woman-about-town who deals with day-to-day cares and she is a role-model who offers sotte voce instruction in the social arts of fashion, makeup, perfume, style, and good manners. Literary imagination has been added to the consumerist demands of advertising through the efforts of a woman of refinement, education, intelligence, wit, spirit, and social consciousness. This woman was not Babette, but Germaine Beaumont.

Colette, the "Olfactory Novelist"

"I am opening my boutique of beauty products on Wednesday, June 1, and the two days following," announced a small handwritten invitation from Colette, sent to selected friends and acquaintances in 1932. "I will be happy, Madame," the invitation continued, "to greet you at 6, rue de Miromesnil, and personally advise you on the most becoming makeup for the stage and for the town." The founding of the Société Colette, the name of her new establishment (and eventually, she hoped, a chain of cosmetic stores) was not as fantastic a dream for a celebrated novelist to realize as it may at first seem. Colette had always been interested in fashion, cosmetics, and perfumes and had been writing on these subjects since World War I. She had been among the first women to cut her hair short, in 1902. In *Trait pour trait* (Line for Line), she admits to having long contemplated the idea of making perfumes. She loved, furthermore, to cut her friends' hair in interesting ways (Francis and Gontier, II: 148) and also considered herself "an authentic makeup expert" having composed her own beauty formulas for thirty years (Thurman, 395). Colette's involvement in fashion, moreover, made her enthusiastic about advertising, for she had already written,

and would continue to write, copy for several designers and perfume houses. For example, there was Colette's seventy-line free verse poem, entitled "Toi" (You), incorporated into a 1926 advertising catalogue for the fur designer Max, who the previous year had brought out his very first scent, *Le Parfum Max*. A fragrance by Carrère (*Signature*, 1946), as well as Eau Perrier, the Ford car, and Lucky Strike cigarettes also benefited from Colette's advertising talents in the thirties.[66] In the back of her mind might have been the success her first husband, Willy, had had with a line of powders and lotions named for Claudine, the heroine of her early novels (Thurman, 394). Finally, the Duchess Sforza, a close friend of Annie de Pène and a role model for Colette, had sold perfumes from an old apothecary she had had redecorated. Her success may have been an inspiration for Colette, who considered buying the Duchess's store and even asked Germaine Beaumont to look into the matter (Thurman, 394, 550, n. 6).

The original idea for the boutique came from a former French minister of defense, André Maginot, a friend of Colette with whom she lunched one day in 1929. Maginot (whose celebrated line of defense would offer France little protection eleven years hence) encouraged Colette to open her own business. Drawing with his hands the imaginary sign he thought should be displayed on the boutique's door, he exclaimed, "My name is Colette and I sell perfume."[67] Colette's store did indeed sell perfume—her scent bottles were decorated with labels displaying a facsimile of her signature and a sketch of her profile (Thurman, 395)—but other products were also available. During the months leading to the opening Colette told a friend that she had already created one perfume and two tonics for different types of skin (Thurman, 395). She spent long hours in a laboratory "choosing, tasting, sniffing, and examining test tubes," one biography notes: "She decided on the shapes and colors of the boxes, the bottles, and the packaging [and] wrote the flyers and drew her own portrait for the cover of the powder boxes" (Francis and Gontier, II: 149). The streamlined, almost clinical art deco look of the store showed the same meticulous attention to detail. Designed by Colette, it was installed, Thurman writes, with "mirrored walls, chrome and leather armchairs, nickel and glass counters, white shelves on simple brackets that displayed Colette's potions in chic black pots" (395). One interesting photograph shows Colette in front of these tiered shelves on which stand tall perfume bottles and stubby cosmetic jars. Across the top of the photograph Colette has written a provocative question: "Are you for or against the 'second profession' of the writer?" (*Colette et la mode*). The affirmative answer, at a time when funding for this kind of business venture was not easy to line up, was given by Colette's wealthy international friends. The princess Edmond de Polignac, heiress to the Singer sewing machine fortune, El Glaoui, the pasha of Marrakesh, Simone Berriau, a singer and actress, Daniel Dreyfus, a Parisian banker and art collector, and Leon Bailby, a newspaper owner, each contributed 200,000 francs to La Société Colette (Francis and Gontier II:131, 149). The opening in June 1932 was a major "media" event. Thanks to the Paris press, Colette received, by her estimate, 50,000 francs in free publicity (Thurman, 395). All of elegant Paris was in attendance including Liane de Pougy, a mistress to kings and bankers and now a princess, and Cecile Sorel, a famous actress (Francis and Gontier II: 150).

The work was hard on Colette. In addition to spending five days a week at the boutique, sometimes not sitting down for hours at a stretch, and opening a branch on the harbor at Saint-Tropez in August of 1932, Colette continued her writing (Francis and Gontier II: 150). Moreover, in the fall there were exhausting promotional tours in France, Belgium, Luxembourg, and Switzerland. In early October she attended an international perfume exhibition in Marseille where she had a stand (Pichois, 328). In Tours, so many women showed up at the hair salon where she was giving a demonstration that they had to be turned away. At the Galeries Lafayette department store in Paris, which had created a window display of Produits Colette, she autographed 650 copies of her books in three and a half hours (Francis and Gontier, II: 150–52). For two days in Luxembourg she made up women's faces for nine straight hours (Pichois and Brunet, 329). Sometimes, Colette would demonstrate cosmetics during the day and then in the evening lecture on her writing (Thurman, 395).

Colette's commitment to the task of helping women "childishly ignorant," as she put it, "of what suited their faces" to overcome bad taste and the rigors of aging, which, from the start, had idealistically informed her idea of a beauty salon, was simply not enough to stem the tide of financial losses the Société Colette was encountering (Thurman, 394). By early 1933, Produits Colette were not selling well; the competition from other more established brands was too great, and Colette was sick and exhausted. Unflattering remarks about the excessive makeovers Colette gave her clients and mean gossip by society matrons did not help the situation. Bankrupt, the Société Colette closed its doors in late 1933.[68]

Quick to accept the label of "olfactory novelist" a critic had bestowed on her, Colette was proud to vaunt the power of smell on her writing. "Whether describing a landscape, recalling a sensual memory, evoking the movement of a crowd, or capturing a city, I give precedence to smell," she wrote in a 1927 issue of *Femina*. "No living being is indifferent to perfume," she asserts in 1942 ("Parfums," *Paysages,* 147), and few French writers of the twentieth century have been as devoted and eloquent a lover of scents as Colette. Arguably, Proust may have been the only one to approach or even surpass her sensitivity, but when it came to Balzac's reputedly prodigious sense of smell it could not support, according to Colette, the all-too-common, and erroneous belief that "the male has the more expert nose when compared to the female." "Mine," she writes unequivocally, "does not yield to many rivals." Even

during bouts of childhood colds she would complain to her mother that she would have preferred a broken arm to her stuffy nose. Smell was clearly for Colette the "most aristocratic of our senses" and the most dominant. Her faith in her innate sense of smell was absolute: "I have followed my nose, which has always led me towards what is best and worst." The sense of smell was not just an intense and pleasurable physical sensation for Colette; it was, she writes, a kind of "listening," the surrendering of the inner ear of the soul to the penetrating "sounds" of fragrances. Smells, she argued, may have a greater effect on our minds than on our bodies, for the olfactory sense is primarily an interior experience, a psychological feeling with clearly somatic consequences: "The excitable man, staggering under the power of perfume, becomes ill and faints. The lover cured of his passion can look unemotionally at his former mistress. But let him fall once again under the heavy yoke of her familiar perfume, and he becomes pale and weeps."[69]

As humans we are sensually impaired; "five senses, that's not many," Colette proclaims ("Luxe I," 249). With the few we have, we must do our very best. And so smell, the most refined and keen sensory apparatus that we possess, opens for us the way to delight, voluptuousness, and sensuality; above all, it reveals, as Colette rhapsodically wrote, the world of

> perfume, that inexplicable allure, as potent on beast as on man, that excess which no one dreams of renouncing, that trap which is the dark, deep source of frenzied loves. . . . Perfume, that conqueror of the most subtle of our senses, that informer of our unspoken desires, perfume which from out of the unreliable depths of human memory uncovers the fount of tears, the secret of pleasure ("Connaissance des parfums," 1945, in *Colette et la mode*, 172).

Perfume: Colette's "Invisible Companion"

Perfume along with couture constituted, according to Colette, the royalty of the French art of fashion. Fragrant, stylish ladies, like bees, moved from street to street, city to city, and country to country transporting what Colette called "the precious honey of French chic" (*Colette et la mode*, 26). "How can one compare," she asks, "heavy, unfinished fragrances from the New World or banal perfume-burners from Asia to the perfect accord that distinguishes a perfume from Paris?" Thanks to French couturiers "perfume has become more than a mere sound within the orchestration of elegance; it can and it must represent the precise and direct expression, the very music, of the styles and tastes of our time." And with her finely developed sense of smell and her expertise in scents—perfume, after all, is hers and all women's "invisible companion" ("Parfums," *Paysages*, 151)—Colette sees herself in tune with this "music" of scent: "I am honored to belong to those groups [of women] who know whether a perfume is for a brunette or a blonde, whether it is for night or day, whether it flows on the austere steps of a temple or floats, like incense, in a secret garden" ("Parfums," *Paysages,* 149). Even the absence of perfume, to Colette's exquisitely perceptive nose, could be a perfume. Her good friend, Marguerite Moreno, the half-Argentine, half-French star of the Comédie Française, had a signature odor, "a personal fragrance," immediately recognizable when one entered her apartment. There was nothing "axillary about it, nothing that derived from human sweat . . . nothing that needed the help of an essence or a lotion," writes Colette. Greeting Marguerite with the customary French double-cheeked kiss (*la bise*), Colette smelled under the back of her friend's ear Marguerite's captivating "epidermal perfume."[70]

In Colette's mind and in her writing, perfume and excessiveness are synonymous. The "pursuit of perfume has no avenue other than that of obsession," she writes in 1929 ("Fragrance," *OC,* 14:36). A profusion of natural smells fills the air of her fictional and personal world. Odor in Colette—whether born from the "wild perfume of dawn" or arising from "a night heavy with jasmine and stars"; whether coalescing from moist soil redolent of mushroom, vanilla and orange blossom into the "forest's very breath" or infiltrating "terrace, garden, and the entire universe" with the suffocating fragrance of gardenia; whether floating up from stacks of new mown hay or emerging from a blend that exists only because the "olfactory novelist" of scents has the lyrical imagination to blend them on the page—is a heady, poetic experience, simultaneous with writing itself. She composes sentences as if she were combining perfume ingredients. "The air, heavy, and musky, barely stirred," she writes, and "a soft wave of scent led us to the wild strawberry . . . ripening in secret here, darkening, trembling and then falling until it softens into a suave raspberry-scented decay whose intoxicating aroma" blends with the fragrances of "greenish honeysuckle and white mushrooms."[71] Scents are nothing short of a revelation; like assaulting armies they travel "in the midnight air, climbing the stairs, forcing open all doors and taking control of our dreams" ("Fragrance," *OC,* 14: 33).

In addition to the many natural scents that waft through Colette's pages there are several varieties of French perfumes which envelop her characters as well as her own person. "What is perfumery after all," she asks, "if not the poetry of hygiene?" This is poetry with moral spirit; it fights all that is foul. The mission of the perfumer is to

> cast over the sad, stale odor of humanity, the greasy rancidness of cramped lodgings, the mildew of closets, and the mustiness of unchanged clothes a suave veil whose folds retain the memory of the damp forest, the garden at noon, the incense of mosques. . . . One must be more or less a poet to devote one's life to robbing flowers of their soul ("Parfums," *Paysages,* 156).

The poetry of this perfumed veil covers all quarters of human life including the spaces one inhabits. The lodgings, closets, and clothes whose odors are changed into those of forests, gardens, and mosques explain perhaps why Colette was given to spraying each room of her apartment with a scent designed to harmonize with its decor. As for perfuming her own body, Colette remained, by her own admission, loyal to one scent: a pure Corsican jasmine fragrance created by Bichara, which she wore for over forty years.[72] Colette personalized the scent, adding certain ingredients to make it heavier and more in harmony with her own personality:

> The only women who love it are those who like me lean towards a group of "white" scents emanating from jasmine, gardenia, bouvardia, pittosporum, white tobacco, datura, all white, pulpy flowers fragrant between six o'clock in the evening and six o'clock in the morning. During the day, they refrain from giving off odors and sometimes even trade their heady aromas for a slight fetidness ("Parfums," *Paysages,* 147, 148, 298, n. 3).

Colette Advises Women on Perfume

Colette favored floral fragrances for herself and for the women readers to whom she offered advice. "Any perfume that does not have a vegetal origin," she counsels, "can be nothing more than a passing fancy of fashion." There are scents around "that could kill a bull. In a restaurant, at the theater, women leave fragrances in their wake that cut one's appetite or detract from what is happening on the screen or the stage" ("Parfums," *Paysages,* 150). Women with "nez fins," like Colette, are too sensitive to embrace perfumes that are not conservative, classic, or what she calls "eternal like the flower that is their inspiration." It is vital that women not flutter like "drunken bees" ("Parfums," *Paysages,* 151, 153) from one perfume to another: "Madame, you who read my words, I hope you never have . . . a 'new' perfume." A woman must practice a certain self-denial by remaining faithful "to a well-chosen perfume, linked to your moral person, to your physical charms, a perfume your friends love and recognize, one that surprises people you meet for the first time and that makes them dream" ("Parfums," *Paysages,* 152). These are, as we have already seen, what Colette calls "white" fragrances (jasmine, gardenia, tuberose, etc.) from mysterious, tenacious, nocturnally blossoming flowers which for many years were resistant to distillation, a kind of spiritual rebelliousness and indomitability that Colette appreciated in general and in women like herself, in particular. It is Colette's goal to teach women about the very nature of perfume: its fragility and complexity, its idiosyncrasies, its capriciousness, and its unforgiving reality. Human skin, she informs her readers, is essentially unstable; "overly rich in effluvia, [it] denatures and undoes a perfume's equilibrium." Therefore, the choice of a perfume is an act of self-knowledge and self-consciousness:

> The pure sensuality of jasmine and its close relative bouvardia, the double odor of gardenia, the integrity of white tobacco depend on the one who wears them. Know yourself, oh woman, madly overcome by so many perfumes. . . . Know what happens to the precious drop when it touches you, when you moisten your ear lobe or the shadowed valley between your breasts. Experiment! Watch, above all, the glance and the wrinkling of the nose of the one to whom you refuse nothing, nothing, that is, except the name of your perfume. Deceive yourself as little as possible, and do not take lightly this serious business of the right scent. As a result of the harmony you will achieve between your changing, warm, living, indiscreet body and your immutable perfume, you will realize through your perfume bottle the happiness of two people . . . at the very least ("Parfums," *Paysages,* 153).

Considering Colette's passion for floral, "white" fragrances, did she, one may wonder, look askance at perfumes composed of synthetic ingredients? A short essay collected in the text "Parfums" is devoted to the fragrances created by Colette's friend Henriette Gabilla, whose store in the Palais Royal quarter of Paris (where Colette lived after 1938) had been established in 1910. Gabilla, one of the first successful female perfumers, was the creator of scents like *La Vierge Folle* (The Mad Virgin, 1913) and *Mon Talisman* (1926).[73] Colette imagines a fictional encounter on a tram with a perfumer-chemist who just happens to work for Parfums Gabilla. Before the perfumer enters the tram, however, Colette finds herself pressed between a man carrying a fish he has just caught, another carrying a block of Roquefort cheese, and a third, a sweating athlete, who has just finished a track meet. All three have descended from the tram by the time the chemist, "the man who smells good" as she calls him, takes his seat. After some initial pleasantries Colette, realizing that she has a specialist in the fabrication of synthetics before her, goes on the attack:

> Sir, I still have my illusions. When I smell a vanilla-scented perfume, I naively want to believe that you've put vanilla in it; I hope that violet smells violet, and that the odor of tuberose will flow from its tight, perennially fragrant calyxes and not from a small, dirty, mineral residue. Chemist, know that we know it, come on, we know it all too well; your flowerbeds are covered by dew that is really tar and the shoots of your plants really coal ("Parfums," *Paysages,* 154–55).

The perfumer is taken a bit back by the passionate agitation of his interlocutor. But with grace he defends himself convincingly. Through the fictional voice of the perfumer Colette again finds a way to instruct her readers in the art—and the science—of perfumery. No perfumer in his right mind would think of substituting coal for flowers, the perfumer-chemist informs her. The modern art of perfume composition, he explains, does not reject but rather embraces the flower, the leaf, the sap, and the root. They are the "noble, ancient blood that galvanizes and adds refinement to the young, inexperienced commoner, which is the synthetic perfume." It is a fine marriage that takes place. The flower "poeticizes" the synthetic creation, while the synthetic element structures and molds the flower's natural, sometimes too expansive, fragrance. Without a synthetic "body" the floral soul can become unstable, errant, and diffuse. Without the flower's civilizing poetry the synthetic element remains crude and tough. Bottled and sold by unscrupulous, inexperienced hands it is these overly synthetic, almost pharmaceutical scents, either rough and coarse or nauseatingly sweet, that attack one in theaters, restaurants, and dance clubs.

Nearly persuaded by the perfumer's eloquence and conviction, Colette, however, ends her imaginary dialogue by insisting twice on the primacy of the natural: its poetry and sensuality. First, she praises the perfumer for the uniquely lyrical way by which he has cast the names of classic perfume ingredients. A description like "Liquid amber, styrax, citrons and citronnelles," Colette points out, has the poetic form and euphony of the classical French alexandrine, a traditional twelve-syllable verse going back to the sixteenth century. Second, she concludes the entire piece with a quotation about perfume from Jean-Jacques Rousseau, the eighteenth-century philosopher for whom nature, the senses, and the heart—there is nothing in any way synthetic here!—were fundamental to human existence ("Parfums," *Paysages,* 157–58). Colette advises the perfumer to affix Rousseau's words to the wall of his laboratory, although, strangely, she cites only part of Rousseau's celebrated sentence: "The sweet perfume of a woman's dressing room is not as feeble a trap as one thinks. . . ."[74]

Interestingly, another much later encounter with a perfumer, this time not at all imaginary, occurs in 1948 when Colette, in a wheelchair, is guided around the Grasse perfume factory of Robertet, a company founded in 1850. Colette watches several different stages in the production of scent: the picking of the jasmine flowers performed so carefully that not even the weight of an ant is allowed to press down on the delicate blossoms; the dumping of about two thousand pounds of jasmine blooms on polished tiles; the dark brown block (the "unctuous chocolate") of the jasmine "concrete" which has been distilled; and the fatally odorous smell of wilting tuberose petals, torpid and barely hanging on to life. Alas, these transformations resonate with the elderly Colette's own unexpressed sense of mortality, giving her visit to the factory a poetic and yet melancholy air (*O,* IV:1022–24).

Colette, however, is not opposed to progress. Given that perfume invention has indeed become too free and

The elegance of Raphaël's *Réplique*, 1947, seems to emanate from the unusual calligraphy of the bottle's label, especially the daggerlike tails of the "p" and "q" and the ornate capital "R."

uncontrolled, that there are too many scents on the market, and that consumer demand has propelled perfumers toward mediocre creations, the advance of chemistry, she realizes, does indeed have its place in perfume composition; in any event, science can and will not be stopped. Colette is no lover of those scents that she calls with ironic exaggeration "tar-based narcissus, . . . creosoted carnation . . . all this imprecise flora where the soot-black soul of coal is . . . poorly disguised." How can one wear perfumes whose existence depends on those "lowly and base servants, *Indol, Skatol*" ("Luxe I," 251). Despite their fancy Greek and Latin names—Colette's knowledge of etymology is matched here by her expertise in modern perfume science—*indole* refers to a coal-tar derivative and *skatol* to a fecal-based compound, both commonly used as fixatives in twentieth-century perfumes. Colette recognizes that the golden age of single-flower perfumes—the blend, for example, of simple jasmine with high-quality alcohol or the violet essence so adored by her mother—is over, and so be it, she declaims ("Luxe I," 252, "Luxe IV," 259). Even though many scents sing off-key and the "woman who buys an expensive perfume is rarely equal to its worth," change can be a good thing. Thus, it is incumbent on women, Colette argues, to develop their knowledge of perfume. A brunette should know enough about perfumes, for example, not to put on the sharp pale fragrance of a blonde, and the blonde should shy away from scents certain to darken her personality. In other words, when a woman "throws herself into the arms of the man she loves," she must take care not to be so disguised by her perfume that "it betrays her in the darkness . . . by clashing with the color of her kiss" ("Luxe I," 252).[75]

In her capacity as social observer, fashion advisor, and friend Colette wishes to give her female readers her own evaluation and recommendation of new perfumes as these appear on the market. She is quick to inform them that these fragrances will neither cut their appetite nor produce a migraine. Rather, the new scents she has it in mind to recommend—there are three—will prove to be "responsive to the natural odor of a well groomed body." To each of these new fragrances a different personality can be assigned, and Colette attempts to evoke the individual qualities of each perfume through dramatic, scenic, and existential descriptions, almost as if she were writing advertising copy for them. The first perfume, she observes, adapts well to life in the outdoors and to physical exercise and sports; it is "forest green and lively." The second scent is more intimate and romantic; "dark like a beautiful night, it evokes the shadowy light of a voluptuous dwelling, with deep armoires, the silky lace of lingerie, linen sheets, and sachets" ("Luxe IV," 260) This is not a "chaste perfume," she observes, like lavender or verbena, fragrances that at one time haloed the skin of young girls or scented the muslin curtains of a room. Such scents are best left in the garden and not brought into the bedroom, because, as Colette asks rhetorically, "What woman today takes it into her head to

choose a perfume because it is chaste?" ("Parfums," *Paysages,* 151). As regards the third of these new fragrances, the most floral of all, it is "younger" in spirit and more contemporary than the other two; it has been created to "scent the steps of this graceful, slender doe—unburdened of any flesh which might slow down her bold rush, her sprightly, adolescent manner—who is the Beauty of nineteen-hundred and twenty-seven" (Luxe IV, 260). Is this beauty, one might ask, not that of the garçonne?

The Shared Scent of Lovers

Sensitive to the dual nature of perfume as a sign of both presence and absence—the beloved may be absent in body but a trace of perfume makes him or her present in spirit—Colette often turns scent into the emblem or sometimes even the ambient air of the cherished other. Perfume becomes a force of presence in "Nuit Blanche" (White Night), Colette's beautiful prose poem of love for Mathilde de Morny, called "Missy," a lesbian marquise ten years her senior, with whom during her early theatrical career Colette—in a stage kiss that went on way too long—had provoked a riot. Missy, who preferred to dress in men's clothing, and Colette began their affair in 1905 (Thurman, 159–60, 171 ff.). The first paragraphs of "Nuit Blanche" are a paean to a bed: "too wide for you, too narrow for both of us, chaste, white, uncovered; no sheet veils, in the fullness of the day, its frank simplicity" (*Sido,* 106). The bed is a sacred, cosmic space: a "star untouched by dawn or loss of light." It is the area of departure for a sublime journey: "our bed never stops blazing until it plunges into the deep, velvet night." It is a point of coalescence where different scents, each an expression of love, embrace:

> A halo of perfume envelops it, embalms it, rigid and white like the body of a cherished woman lying dead. This is a complex perfume that takes one by surprise and which one inhales with careful attention so as to distinguish the blond soul note of your favorite tobacco, the even blonder aroma of your pale skin, and this odor of burnt sandalwood coming from me. But as for this country scent of crushed grass, who can say if it is mine or yours? (*Sido,* 106–07).

The bed's halo surrounds it like a winding sheet. Ephemerality and death are never far. An earlier paragraph had imagined the weight of the embracing couple under a "voluptuous shroud" furrowing the bed with "a valley not much wider than a tomb." Rigid like a dead woman the pale bed is embalmed in fragrance. It becomes more than still earth, inanimate loam, dead matter. It has been transformed into air. It floats on a cloud composed of its own scent and the entwined emanations of the lovers' odors: tobacco, flesh, sandalwood. Transformed into a vessel for different perfumes, the bed, like an opened bottle, exhales the air and aura of Eros into the intimate spaces of Missy's and Colette's life. Yet, despite the perceptiveness of Colette's nose, she cannot detect which lover has contributed the rustic odor of the French countryside to the perfume of their love, a perfume she finds exciting—it takes one by surprise—and complex—it demands concentrated attention. It is no surprise, though, why Colette cannot assign provenance to this particular perfume "ingredient." It comes neither from Missy nor from herself, because it is linked to their shared life in the country, to walks taken together through meadows and grass. Like the simple bed, which they imprint with the contour of their embracing bodies, the perfume takes on a distinctive singularity; it is "personalized," through the commonality of a scent (and a life) shared equally by both lovers.

In "Nuit Blanche" (White Night) perfume establishes presence: that of sensuality, love, and the oneness of two bodies, two spirits, and two beings. But in the novel *La Retraite sentimentale* (Retreat from Love, 1907), perfume expresses separation and loss. Claudine, the heroine of *Retreat from Love*, the last of Colette's series of Claudine novels, goes to stay at the country house of her friend Annie while Claudine's older husband, Renaud, recovers from tuberculosis in a sanatorium. Claudine desperately longs for her husband, whose distance only deepens her love. Claudine is a sensualist—a monogamous one unlike the debauched Annie—and a true lover of smells. Dawn for Claudine has its own peculiarly wild odor (55); a bedroom smells of cut hay which makes her feel blissful one moment and nauseated the next (110). A friend visits, and Claudine, struck by the "stubborn, tenacious, and banal scent that lingers" (235), calls on nature—"oh flowering lime tree envelop me in your fragrance of orange blossom mixed with vanilla"—to cleanse the air which has become "heavy with the odor of tobacco and powdered women" (235).

Although still uncured Renaud returns from the sanatorium and soon dies. Claudine experiences the loss through the keenest of her senses, smell, imagining her husband as present and absent, or more precisely, as present in and through his absence:

> With cold and contrary heart I take care of [his tomb]. There, nothing remains of the one I love, of the one about whom I still speak, in my heart, whispering to myself that "He *says* this . . . He *prefers* that . . ." What is a tomb if not an empty box? The one I love remains whole in my memory, in a scented handkerchief that I unfold, in the sound of his voice which I suddenly remember and, head bowed, listen to for a long while (224–25).

Physically, Renaud is gone; the cold, empty tomb points to his absence. Spiritually, however, he has an everyday presence, the mere spark of which Claudine's memory and imagination fan into a warm, comforting fire. Signs of this presence are everywhere: in a letter he once wrote, in a book he once read, in the garden bench on which he often would sit, and, Claudine suddenly realizes, in the unchanging look and smell of the garden, in particular, the blooming violets, anemones, and chestnut trees, and the animals running about underfoot. In nature, nothing has changed; everything returns as it was. By interiorizing the loss of Renaud she has kept him alive; her mourning is a "costly velvet lining sewn onto the inside of my heart" (241). Absent as flesh but now present as spirit, Renaud has become a presence within Claudine's memory. Strangely, she can only experience this newly found spiritual presence by rematerializing it, by giving it body and substance, through metaphors of physical objects: wall hangings, coat linings, the smell of the earth, chestnut blooms, and so on. These objects are no more than nests, shells, tombs, places of hibernation out of which memory—the spiritual aspect of the absent beloved—may emerge. They resemble the handkerchief from which the scent of Renaud floats upward, entering Claudine's soul and there sparking images, memories, and words which now are no more than signs of a presence-in-absence.

One night, Claudine awakens and calling her animals to her bed promises them that, despite their collective loneliness, the door of the house will be left open so that, as the novel's last, poignant sentence announces, "the night [will] enter, along with its scent of invisible gardenia, . . . and so will the man who cannot leave me, who watches over the rest of my life, and for whom I close my eyes, though I do not sleep, so as to see him better" (243). The aroma of the gardenia floating through the darkened house, followed so closely by Claudine's mental image of Renaud, associates scent with the presence memory creates. Gardenia, however, is just one of two fragrances entering both the house and Claudine's thoughts. Renaud is the other. Like the "invisible" gardenia, Renaud comes to Claudine along a path of odors. He cannot be seen—Claudine's eyes, after all, remain shut—but he does enter Claudine's soul, and there becomes more fully "visible": as an embodiment at once physical and spiritual, as a fragrance at once concrete and essential, and as a reality at once present and absent. In Colette's sensual world, where Eros lives as much in the countryside as in the bedroom, the body has a soul all its own. Like liquid perfume sublimated into an airborne scent, flesh turns into spirit.

That the flesh has a soul and that the body thinks with a "mind" all its own are at the heart of Colette's writings on perfume, whether novels, short stories, journalistic pieces, or even advertisements. Fashion, for Colette, was an assertion of life. It was, Nicole Ferrier-Caverivière observes, "the expression of the adherence of the human being to the world and society." Wearing a certain style of clothing and applying a particular class of scent represented choices that went far beyond the simple, routine, sometimes unconscious acts of dressing. Colette looked at fashion not only as a sign of identity, but as an exercise of free will, the creative act of choosing, Ferrier-Caverivière notes, "the appearance corresponding exactly to what one is, to what one feels one is." Colette studied the perfume, cosmetics, and dress of her time because they gave form to and, as she wrote, "made fast the wavering colors of [one's] epoch and [one's] generation" (*Colette et la mode*, 22, 30). Perfume, fashion, and makeup express the mutability and complexity of human life, an existence where change is constant and the presence (and the present) of the past remains essential to the trajectory of the future.

Proust and the Remembrance of Odors Past

Remembering loss through scent Claudine rediscovers life through scent. In this respect, she is not unlike Marcel Proust's narrator in *Remembrance of Things Past*, another connoisseur of smells who is sensitive to the odor of varnish on stairs, of vetiver in a room, of orris-root in an attic, and of the "aromas of the cupboard, the chest-of-drawers, and the patterned wall-paper." His aunt's house in Combray is filled with "linen smells, morning smells, pious smells," the smells of soot, of a bedspread, and of other objects baked and raised by the morning light until they are transformed into an "impalpable country pie" of odors.[76] The memory of Marcel's entire childhood at Combray returns to him by chance the moment he raises to his lips a piece of "one of those squat, plump little cakes called 'petites madeleines,'" mixed in a spoonful of tea which, once its taste touches his palate and its warm aroma invades his nose, sends a shudder through his entire body (I: 48). Nothing less than "the joy of rediscovering what is real" (III: 913) has been brought about by the collusion of taste and smell: "When from a long-distant past nothing subsists, after the people are dead, after the things are broken and scattered, taste and smell alone, more fragile but more enduring, more unsubstantial, more persistent, more faithful, remain poised a long time, like souls, remembering, waiting, hoping, amid the ruins of all the rest" (I: 50–51).

And yet, since for Proust there exists an "ineluctable law which ordains that we can only imagine what is absent" (III: 905), art by necessity must grow out of loss, imagination out of death, and memory out of the void of forgetfulness. When we imagine the scent of a beloved landscape, a cherished person, or a favorite flower, we have already lost the place, the person, and the flower. The scent of Claudine's husband's handkerchief, the aroma of lime-blossoms in Marcel's aunt's tea, the fragrances of almond, lilac, hawthorn, and violet of the Combray landscape, even the "aromatic perfume" of Marcel's chamber pot after a dinner of asparagus (I: 131) are past and absent realities which indeed return, but as images alone. These images, as their name suggests, are "imaginary," although their origin in absence is brutally real. Perfume is such an image, the presence of something no longer present, like the line of "a roof, a gleam of sunlight on a stone, the smell of a path," an indefinable "something" before which Marcel stands "motionless, looking, breathing, endeavoring to penetrate with my mind beyond the thing seen or smelt" (I: 195), and hoping, by removing it from time, to capture it forever in writing. But deep down Marcel knows that against absence and death images are mere illusions and that the only "true paradises are the paradises we have lost" (III: 903). Perfumes can indeed bring back such paradises; but as they envelop us, perfume and paradise forbid us from forgetting that past, present, and future are endlessly fragrant with nothing if not loss.

Perfume and the Politics of the Far Right: François Coty

One Paris morning, a few years before World War I, the couturier-perfumer Paul Poiret was sitting at his desk when he received a small, elegant man attired in a tailored, light gray suit and a straw boater, a man whom Poiret did not know. Taking a seat, the visitor announced with great assurance, "I have come to buy your perfume house." When Poiret regained his composure after the initial shock of this brash declaration, he informed the stranger that his business was not for sale. "If you continue doing business at the pace you now are," the visitor replied, "it will take you fifteen years to become important, ... but if you join me, you will benefit from my administration, and in two years you will be worth as much as I am." Poiret explained that while this might indeed be true, he knew that after fifteen years of hard work his perfume company would still, at least, belong to him. "You know nothing about business, Monsieur," the visitor angrily observed as he rose from the chair and in a fury left the room. "We watched him depart," Poiret remembered in his memoirs. "Monsieur Coty was the same size as Bonaparte."[77]

François Coty was a brilliant and talented creator of innovative perfumes. He was an artist who radically changed the landscape of perfume composition, an astute marketing genius, a clever, sometimes ruthless businessman, the paternalistic, if not dictatorial, founder of a large perfume factory near the Bois de Boulogne as well as plants in Italy, England, Brazil, Argentina, and New York, and the owner of several important Paris newspapers, including *Le Figaro*, still published today. Coty was also a descendant (by his own genealogical calculations) of Napoleon. He was a reclusive millionaire constantly

protected by bodyguards and a man of fascist leanings. ❧ orable (197). While Guerlain, Patou, and Worth, for exam-
At one time, eight million Frenchwomen were buying ple, introduced only two fragrances each during the 1940s,
his *L'Origan* talc powder at the rate of sixteen million boxes Lancôme only five (one in 1943, 1945, 1946, and two in
a year; four and a half million bottles of his Paris-made 1947), Chanel one (1948), and Lanvin none, Coty brought
perfumes were sold annually around the world. At the time to market twenty-nine scents in the first half of the decade
of his death in 1934, his personal fortune was estimated at alone. From 1941 to 1944, four to five new Coty fragrances
around $250,000,000 (Flanner, 133). The distinctive Coty appeared each year. But this was a mere drop in the bucket
logo—the parabolic "C" reaching out a long arm to touch when 1945 came around, a year that saw the release of
the shoulder of the "o" and the final "y" extending its eleven new Coty scents, including two—*25 Août* and
long, straight tail below the line—is the assertive signature *8 Mai*—commemorating the liberation of Paris in August
of a man with imperial aspirations. "Coty," as one commen- 1944 and the German surrender in May 1945.[79]
tator has remarked, is "a short and catchy name designed
to seduce, whilst [the] signature, with its carnivorous
'C' and a 'Y' the length of a sword, was that of a would-be
conqueror."[78]

Coty was the first perfumer to conceive of perfume as

Coty Caricatured

both a luxury and a necessity—that is, a luxury that nec-
essarily should be available to all. He was the first to recog- One of the most exaggerated and humorous portraits of a
nize the importance of bottle design. A perfume, he rags-to-riches industrialist-perfumer of the stature and
declared, "needs to attract the eye as much as the nose." He style of François Coty reached Parisian readers in 1926
was a visionary who envisioned the creation of a "City of with the publication of the satirical novel, *Je suis un affreux*
Perfumes" situated on the Ile de Puteaux in the middle of *bourgeois* (I Am a Terrible Bourgeois), by the popular jour-
the Seine across from the Bois de Boulogne. But Coty was nalist, editorialist, and novelist Clément Vautel. Not since
fervently anti-Bolshevist. He financially supported several Balzac's *César Birotteau*, nearly a hundred years earlier, had
organizations of the extreme right, like the Croix-de-Feu, a a more opinionated, egotistical, benighted, and ludicrous
paramilitary group of war veterans founded in 1927 to perfumer starred as the major character of a work of fic-
support Mussolini. After the right-wing uprising that took tion. Vautel was a well-known writer and a fervent anti-
place in Paris on February 6, 1934, Croix-de-Feu boasted feminist, antisuffragist, and pro-family advocate whose
a membership of 150,000 men and women. In 1928, Coty propagandistic novel of 1924, *Madame ne veut pas d'enfant*
established the antiparliamentary and anti-Semitic news- (Madame Does Not Want a Child), portrayed the social
paper *L'Ami du people*, which, because it was priced at ten dangers of a woman's refusal to bear children and the dele-
and not the usual twenty-five centimes, had one of the terious consequences of her selfish dedication to a life of
largest daily circulations in France. The paper published pleasure and ease. In *I Am a Terrible Bourgeois* Vautel
more than thirty articles by Coty opposing Bolshevism and depicts the life of the fifty-six-year-old perfumer, Honoré
arguing for a new Bonapartist republic tailored along fas- Paquignon, called, as Coty himself had been, "the Napoleon
cist lines. In 1933 Coty's politics took a step further to the of perfumery" (20). Honoré's beginnings are modest. He
right; he founded Solidarité française, an organization starts his career as a simple salesman at a large Parisian
sympathetic to the Nazi party. For a short time, Coty left department store, is promoted to head of the perfume
the haven of his newspaper and perfume empires and department, invents new scents, and then moves to a larger
entered politics, serving briefly as senator-elect from store. Here he modernizes the perfume section, invents
Corsica, until the French Senate, citing electoral irregulari- more fragrances, and creates a new kind of shaving soap
ties, took the seat away. "A Bonaparte by blood," Janet for men and a revolutionary cosmetic for reducing the size
Flanner writes, "a perfumer by trade, this was his little of women's breasts, called *Pâte de Diane*. Confident of his
Waterloo" (128–29). Finally, it may either have been the talents he decides to make it on his own. His newly con-
wide popularity of Coty's perfumes, which continued structed factories turn out products for "la nouvelle
unabated through the war years, or possibly the cor- femme" of the post–World War I period, a woman whose
rectness of the maison Coty's political sympathies that new sense of style revolves, Paquignon observes, around
accounted for the company's striking productivity, in com- "thinness, hair coloring, and near-nudity" (49–52).
parison with that of other perfume houses, especially dur- "French perfume manufacturing was waiting for a man,
ing the German Occupation of France, when, as one would and I was that man," he boasts (50). Now worth over 30
imagine, there was a scarcity of primary perfume ingredi- million francs, Honoré has unbounded faith in the future
ents. Coty himself, of course, had been dead six years when of the French perfume and cosmetics industries. France, he
the Germans marched into Paris on June 14, 1940. Between recognizes, can barely produce enough perfumes, creams,
1941 and 1945 most perfume companies launched very lotions, compounds, lipsticks, pomades, and powders to
few new perfumes, and most of these, according to satisfy the demand of its large female population, poor as
Delbourg-Delphis, were neither groundbreaking nor mem- well as rich, old as well as young, rural as well as urban.
Perfume is not only a social phenomenon as democratic as
the Fourth Republic; it is tied to militaristic expansion:

The War has made perfume a sensation, the War which liberated women, making them more frivolous, flirtatious and resourceful (a real necessity) in their pursuit of a man. The true victory is that of a tube of lipstick. Gunpowder spoke during the War forcefully, but only to assure the triumph of rice powder! First came poison gas, then fragrant scents (13).

After the carnage of the war, love in all its forms has returned. "Don Juan is in fashion," Honoré observes. The war could not have been more favorable to business; it inspires love, and love, of course, requires perfumes. "Wars and revolutions," he philosophizes, "are aphrodisiac: for women above all, they were occasions to commit a thousand follies, less brutal, it is true, and less stupid than those committed by men" (52). Honoré's allusion to women's so-called "follies" takes up a not uncommon antifeminist view expressed by certain newspapers and novels during and after the World War I: namely, the returning soldier's accusation, according to Roberts, that his wife or lover had "lived it up while I was at the front."[80]

As Vautel's novel begins, Honoré's cashier, Théodore Borax—could there be a name less fragrant for the character who supplies Honoré with the names of all his perfumes?—has just come up with a new appellation for an as yet to be invented perfume. *Moi toute* (All of Me) is the idea Borax presents to his boss, and they both agree that the other names that have come to Borax's mind—"Un Soir, nous deux" (One Evening, the Two of Us) or "Caresse de fleurs" (Flowers' Caress)—are too traditional and stodgy, too much like "slow waltzes." Honoré is ecstatic as he dreams imaginatively of the success and revenue *Moi toute* will bring:

In these two words, there is charm, coquetry, mystery. By themselves, they distill and give off the scent of an intimate, amorous, sensual perfume . . . *Moi toute*! It will look good on the bottles, in the advertisements, on cinema screens, on stage curtains. I already can imagine the image and the text announcing this new creation. . . . A blond with large, languorous eyes, with a smile at once pure and enticing, revealing a deep décolletage, her body barely covered, the entire image framed with roses, dahlias, carnations, little chubby-cheeked cherubs, blue birds, and multicolored butterflies. *Moi toute*. . . It's very good. (8–9)

Because he thinks that he understands women's needs and desires Honoré believes himself to be a skillful, even brilliant, marketer and publicist of his many beauty products: perfumes like *Rose mouillée* (Wet Rose), *Nuit d'amour*, *Feuilles de Rose* (Rose Leaves), and *Une nuit viendra* (A Night Will Come); depilatories like *Filles de marbre* (Marble Ladies); soaps like *Vénusia*; shaving creams like *Rasibus*; beauty creams like *Lys d'amour* (Lily of Love); and even a toothpaste, *Ta Bouche* (Your Mouth), a name that also impolitely tells one in French, to "Shut up."

Honoré leaves the composition of these products to his chemists. His bailiwick is that of perfume presentation. He chooses the styles of bottles and boxes, conceives ideas for posters and colored advertisements, organizes publicity campaigns, and sees to it that no theatrical performance takes place in Paris without a mention of his perfumes and beauty creams. Some of his more successful publicity stunts have involved the skywriting of *Rasibus,* his shaving soap, over Paris, the installation of lights on the sides of the Eiffel Tower flashing the names of his products, and, one festive July 14th—France's national holiday—the scenting of the small fountain on the Place Pigalle (Paris's red-light district) with a heady dose of *Une nuit viendra* (14). A more complicated advertising ploy involves the running of a national contest to find "the prettiest perfume name." Honoré selects the somewhat ridiculous and not very subtle name, *J'en ai mis partout* ("I've put it everywhere"), because in his mind it suggests with simplicity and a certain subtle sensuousness "the voluptuous odor that a women blends with the scents of her own flesh" (11).

Having successfully designed the logo, the text, the presentation, and the central image of his perfume, *Moi toute,* Honoré turns his attention to the all-important problem of "the living symbol," the "face" that will embody the fragrance on the labels, boxes, posters, and calendars he intends to invent (15). Celebrities and movie stars are fine, but their faces are often too ubiquitous and thus overexposed. As for the elegant countesses and marquises who have done perfume advertising for him in the past, they are too demanding, always questioning him about why their images have not been seen on certain billboards around the city. In a pool of applicants for a secretarial position, Honoré accidentally discovers the perfect face for *Moi toute;* her name is Micheline Romanet, and she becomes the symbol of the perfume, as well as Honoré's mistress. With his usual brio and hyperbole Paquignon cannot help but compliment himself on his artistic judgment in selecting Micheline: "When Raphaël saw la Fornarina for the first time he must have felt the same shock, whispering to himself, 'With her, I shall create a masterpiece!' He made a painting and I make an advertisement, two arts that are complementary and equally worthy" (19–20).

The pièce de resistance of Honoré's Raphaëleque artistry will be the advertising film for *Moi toute,* which he intends to have shown on all cinema screens in France. The director, whom Honoré has hired, recognizing that perfume is probably "the least cinematographic reality in the world," suggests that the film be based on a "simple yet poetic scenario." The camera will focus on a Prince Charming walking through a forest and dreaming of love while inhaling the fragrance of flowers. Suddenly, he spies a magnificent rose. He picks it, and as he breathes in the flower's aroma, the rose transforms itself into a woman, Marceline in fact, who gives the prince a passionate, lingering kiss. As the image fades, the following text appears on the screen: "*Moi toute,* the fragrant creation of Honoré Paquignon, a perfume that makes women irresistible" (75–76).

That *Moi toute* translates as "All of Me" is significant, for it suggests Honore's misogynistic view that not only are women irresistible, but that they are incapable of resisting; they cannot help but give "all" of themselves. The perfume's name expresses a masculine objectification of women that is based on the fantasy of female abjection. This is a scenario in which the woman surrenders herself completely (*toute*) and offers up her very identity and self (*Moi*) to the man who in a sense "inhales" her like a scent. In fact, the woman is no longer a woman, but a nameless body that has evaporated into thin air. Although he has not a clue about the meaning of his words, Honoré admits as much when, after Micheline abandons him and he cannot free his mind of her image, he has to admit that the "living symbol" of *Moi toute* is as tenacious as the perfume itself: "This face, this smile, this figure, this nipple, they are *Moi toute,* they are not Michette" (267), Honoré explains to himself, even as he ironically misremembers Micheline's name. Indeed, Micheline is no longer a woman, no longer a real face, but fragments of a body, a self, a human being (whose very name has been forgotten). When all is said and done, she is no more than an image and, most important of all, a product: that is, a perfume who is not a woman but a commodity. Again, Honoré reveals a benighted astuteness: "One does not change the trademark identifying a product. . . . Don't forget that you have spent hundreds of thousands of francs to display this image everywhere and to tyrannize the consumer just as Michette now persecutes you. You must go on . . . It's *business*!" (a word he utters in English) (267).

From salesman to France's premier perfumer and one of its most celebrated industrialists, the president of the French Board of Perfumery and an officer in the Légion d'Honneur (24), Honoré Paquignon, like Coty, has reached the pinnacle of bourgeois success, which confers on him an aura of bourgeois heroism as noble as any other kind. "Men, like me," he declares,

> are responsible for the grandeur, wealth, and glory of their country. My perfumes are known, loved, and preferred all over the world. . . . Five hundred thousand American women apply my lipstick, *Carmencita,* and remove unwanted hair with my compound *Filles de marbre.* Along with their fragrant emanations my creations spread the taste and even the love of our precious homeland. In every perfume bottle marked with the trademark and signature of Honoré Paquignon, there is the essence of France (48–49).

Hyperbole aside, Honoré has accomplished the sublime dream of every Gallic perfumer: he has succeeded in selling France in a bottle. Moreover, he fervently believes that the rights of the bourgeoisie and the entitlements of captains of industry like himself are under attack by the State, the working class, and the Bolsheviks. He waxes lyrical, often to ridiculous excess, about bourgeois values and the work ethic which have built France. Everyone who works for him—of this he is certain—is out to cheat him, from Monsieur Borax to his former secretary turned nemesis, Alice, who mounts a leftist campaign of slander against him under the penname "Vindicta" in the paper *Le Petit Bolchevik illustré* (The Illustrated Bolshevik Bulletin). In one issue he is caricatured under the title "Le Pendu de la Semaine" (The Hanged Man of the Week). Below the figure of a hanged man with an enormous tongue drooping from his mouth Vindicta has written the following menacing description: "Honoré Paquignon, exploiter of the people, cynical pleasure-seeker, perfumer who will soon smell foul in the fullness of the evening air!" (97). After a strike has shut down Honoré's factory, Vindicta will write that "the Napoleon of Perfumery has found his Waterloo" (213).

Paquignon is outraged by these caricatures and offers arguments in his own defense, which only add more fuel to the fires set by his ridiculous, hypocritical personality. "I have been accused," he fumes, "of preparing my perfumes with the sweat of the people, when, to the contrary, it is I who have created an inexpensive antiperspirant cream called *la Palméa*!" (213). When the strike hits his factory and the government refuses to intervene, Honoré finds himself under investigation by the French equivalent of the I.R.S., out to verify whether during World War I he had engaged in tax evasion and profiteering. Insult has been added to injury, and Honoré blusteringly protests that he, one of the builders of French capitalism, has come under simultaneous attack from workers *and* government. "The [fiscal authorities] are threatening me, me, with investigation! They didn't talk to me like that in 1918 when I was making poison gas! And when do they choose to persecute me? Just at that moment when I'm being attacked by revolutionaries!" (166).

Things are just as bad on the home front. As his children never stop telling him, Honoré is out of touch with the modern world. His daughter, Pierrette, favors the bobbed hair, the sportive laid-back style, and the cigarette-between-the-lips pose of the garçonne. She argues for women's rights and resists, quite successfully, her father's patriarchal power (57–58): "I am in favor of women taking their revenge," she yells at her father. "Our time has come.... We have decided no longer to be pushed around by men! ... There are hosts of girls and women who believe the tyranny of men has lasted long enough" (58). "Women," she goes on, "have been forced by men to parade their beauty just as one asks a little dog to sit and beg.... What a job it is to be a girl. Dolls, that's what we are" (67). Pierrette and her wealthy female friends open a garage ("la Femina-Garage"), and she eventually marries a chauffeur. While Honoré's daughter is a garçonne, his son, Maurice, is an effete aesthete, what his father calls a "hothouse flower" (62). Pierrette, he complains, "has a virile appearance, but

Maurice looks like a *fille manquée*" (59). Maurice wears the perfumes created by his father that Pierrette will not touch. He inaugurates an aesthetic review that puts on artistic presentations in Honoré's mansion. All of Paris, "le Tout-Paris," Maurice boasts to his father, will come. But when Honoré sees the audience, he quips that it is "le Tout-Charenton"—all of Charenton, an insane asylum—which has shown up (121).

To defend his interests Honoré financially supports Marc Brifaut, the naïve leader of a group called "The League of Francs-Bourgeois," devoted to protect, with arms if necessary, the interests and privileges of the haute bourgeosie. A sometimes inventor, who had proposed to Honoré the idea of a perfume atomizer that would double as a flashlight, Brifaut leads his ragtag group in a fight against a band of communists during a Christmas Eve "revolution" and loses his life (235, 312). In Honoré's opinion, he has not died in vain but for the honor of the bourgeoisie, a class that is society's "creative and dynamic element, its light, warmth, and movement: its very engine" (220). Not only does "noblesse oblige," but, as Honoré loves to repeat, "grande bourgeosie oblige" (173). Despite moments of grand rhetoric when Honoré praises the bourgeois class—and some of the flattery can be seen as Vautel's own sympathetic nod to the conservative bourgeois family—the perfumer's behavior is rife with hypocrisy. The poor Brifaut, before the Christmas insurrection, confesses to Honoré that his mission has been to resurrect the bourgeoisie, restore its "virility," and revive the traditions and virtues of the moral life it has always represented (136–37). Nevertheless, Honoré, who is having an illicit affair with Micheline, feels no shame or guilt. Yet, anger and humiliation do indeed touch him to the quick when Micheline admits her sexual infidelities in a vituperative language only a perfumer, and a bourgeois perfumer at that, could understand: "Get out of here, you filthy bourgeois ... You are a cuckold, an ultra-cuckold, everything that is the most cuckolded in the world! ... Look at him, the great perfumer, the triple extract of cuckolds, the concentrate of cuckolds" (208).

Paquignon's views on French industry in general and perfumery in particular are colored by his chauvinistic defense of the bourgeoisie and its values; in this respect, he is not very different from Balzac's César Birotteau, except that César's sympathies favored the monarchy of the ancien régime. Civilization, Honoré pompously affirms, "is the work of the bourgeois class" "I am a bourgeois ... and proud of it" (43, 46). Moreover, he thinks his service to the glory of the French nation deserves to be better rewarded, and the reward he has in mind is election, along with lawyers, judges, military men, politicians, and writers, to the Académie Française. Should he, Honoré Paquignon, not be one of the "immortals," as members of the august French Academy are called? Are his perfumes "not as valuable from the perspective of composition, art, and style as all the books of so-and-so? My works, which do not need to be translated, enchant millions of women all over the world: what writer could say as much?" (274). Honoré's egomaniacal narcissism even finds Napoleon at fault. "I have often been compared to him," he admits, "but he was never a perfumer, this Napoleon!" (280). Paquignon's estimation of himself is high, to say the least, and totally lacking in self-awareness. As an artist he considers himself superior to any writer and says as much when, with a bit of defensiveness, he asserts that

> perfumery is an art worth more than many others. To give pleasure to the noses of my male and female contemporaries is as noble, if not more difficult, than to charm their eyes and ears. In order to create, introduce, and launch my products, I must have as much if not more imagination than is needed to write a novel... Even if it is true that Mr. Théodore Borax, my cashier, finds names of perfumes for me, it is I, at least, who select the best ones—and it is in this discriminating choice ... that true genius lies (48).

Clément Vautel's sarcasm and satire—moral salvos fired against the institution of the haute bourgeoisie—are explosive, to say the least. Few social classes come off unscathed in his misanthropic and moralizing *comédie humaine*. Feminist garçonnes, aesthetes, poets, artists, actors, theater directors, filmmakers, journalists, advertisers, industrialists, politicians, government functionaries, workers, revolutionaries, Bolshevists, duchesses, foreigners, mothers and fathers, leftists and rightists, heterosexuals and homosexuals, as well as wealthy members of the upper bourgeoisie are presented as ludicrous, pretentious, and immoral types out to make their greedy fortunes and to dishonor the aristocratic glory of "La France." No wonder, then, that the novel's final sentence announces—in the words of its only moral character, Antoine de Persicot, the head of personnel at Honoré's factory and, as a former army colonel in World War I, a man of few illusions—that "the bourgeoisie is screwed!" (45, 313).[81]

The resemblances between Honoré Paquignon and François Coty are more than coincidental. Both figures are self-made men, both are distinguished creators of perfume, both appreciate the singular importance of advertising (posters, photographs, films, packaging), both are "Napoleonic," both see their industry from a global, international perspective, and both are interested in democratizing perfume and cosmetics by making them accessible to all social classes. On the negative side, both are dictatorial bosses, both treat their workers in paternalistic ways designed to reinforce their own superiority, and both are terrorized by Bolshevism. Certainly, the sophisticated Vautel must have been acquainted with the myths and legends swirling around the personality of the mysterious inventor of *L'Origan* and *Chypre*. Moreover, his novel is prescient in many ways. The kinds of social comportment, political action, and ideological strife he describes in the contemporary Paris of 1926—the street battles between supporters of the right and left, the labor unrest, the crisis of the family, the liberation of women, the decline in the birth rate, the *garçonne* with her short hair and skirts— would by the end of the decade and into the 1930s play a more extensive and subversive role in French society, as Coty would soon learn firsthand.

The Game of Perfume

If seduction is a game, like bridge, then perfume is the trump card, an advantage one must use with savoir-faire and tactical skill. Perfumes, as the poet, novelist, and social commentator, Louise de Vilmorin (1902–1969) whose works were published from the mid-1930s to the 1960s writes, are

> full of ruses, and if you treat them indifferently, they broadcast your secrets to every wind, lay you bare in unbecoming ways, stab you in the back. Like fate, they have a thousand hands, a thousand individual ways to make us endlessly part of their game. We think we have tamed them, because they are in a bottle and we are distracted or feel superior. But barely do we uncork the bottle, barely do we put a drop of the released scent on our shoulder than a new star rises, and chance is prolonged.

Perfume is a game of chance where one must take a chance. With its notes of hyacinth, jasmine, white musk, vetiver, and patchouli *Chance*, "the unexpected new Chanel fragrance" as it was advertised at its launch in 2002, makes the point simply and emphatically: "It's your chance ... Take it!" Perfume coincides with a moment, an opportunity, and an event where luck may change as quickly as a scent fills the air and then dissipates. Fragrance involves an instant or a lifetime, or maybe both simultaneously, as Calvin Klein's 2004 scent, *Eternity Moment* ("just one moment can change everything") proposes. The change or chance desired by Chanel's *Chance* as well as Givenchy's *Organza* ("Something in me [is] eternal.") and Guerlain's *L'Instant* ("A fragrance inspired by the unforgettable moments that can transform your life in an instant") may last forever, or not at all. Moreover, a woman who mistakenly wears a perfume that clashes with her appearance or her personality, Vilmorin observes, can be victimized by the scent; "her cause [is] lost, the perfume ... has taken its revenge," and any hope of mystery or seductiveness she once envisioned is destroyed. But the same perfume on a friend, enveloping her in a "magical aura," may change her destiny; she wins "the lottery, the jackpot," for, as Vilmorin notes, "there are no perfumes without consequences. They awaken intimate echoes, coveted images, nostalgia and

JEU DES PARFUMS

Le jeu des parfums se joue avec 2 dés, comme le jeu de l'oie. Le but est de parvenir au N° 45. Si les points que vous obtenez ne vous conduisent pas exactement au but, retournez en arrière du nombre de cases correspondant aux points en surplus. Chaque case dont le numéro est encerclé, comporte un avantage ou une pénalité.

Fig. 113 "Jeu des Parfums," a game no woman can lose. From square 1 ("Your Hand") to square 44 ("Hope") rolls of the dice lead players along an intriguing and delightful path of fragrances in this clever board game conceived by the graphic designer and illustrator, Raymond Savignac, in 1944–1945.

desire. We seek in them the clarification and conclusion of our dreams. Because they come to us as temptations we must think seriously before surrendering to them." The risk of loss surrounds perfume as it also haunts the act and game of love. Seduction and perfume set in motion an event of disappearance. Its secret lodges in the flashing or hallucination of a presence, as the philosopher Jean Baudrillard observes, which then disappears. This "eclipse of presence," which at first holds out the promise of love but then just as quickly removes it, effaces the promissory image of fullness behind a lingering emptiness. As in a game of chance like roulette, for example, the spark of fortune is extinguished in the darkness of ruin and emptiness. Perfume in the service of seduction is just as tenuous.[82]

Envisioned as a game of seduction and love, a game with the attendant ideas of play, risk, luck, victory, and failure, perfume can be seen as a metaphor. Whether expressed in advertisements or articulated in works of literature, this metaphor is potent. It insists on the irrefutable link, in the minds of many, between scent and love: an eroticization of fragrance that has been essential since Egyptian times to the cultural images associated with perfume. In the mid-1940s, however, the metaphor of perfume as play, as an occasion for winning and losing, turned literal. Perfume became a real game: in fact, a board game. The "Jeu des Parfums" (1944–1945), as created by the poster designer and illustrator Raymond Savignac (1907–2002) in collaboration with Hélène Jarron, was composed of forty-five squares in different colors, numbered 1 to 45, and arranged in a spiral track (fig. 113).[83] To the name of a popular perfume from the 1920s, 1930s, and 1940s and that of the company that had created the fragrance, each square added a cleverly conceived icon or emblem, which served as a coded illustration. For example, the first square, denoting Jean Desprez's fragrance *Votre Main*, displayed the image of a hand and a pair of dice. Square number 2 for Worth's *Je Reviens* showed a sign hanging from a nail—the kind left by a proprietor stepping out of his or her store for an instant—with the scribbled message, "I'll be back" ("Je reviens"). The fifth square, as one might imagine, merely showed the number 5 (repeated five times) and the name Chanel. Lanvin's musically inspired *Arpège* in square no. 6 displayed a harp, while Worth's *Dans la nuit* in square no. 7 was represented by a constellation of stars. In this way, each square was coded with a miniature iconic narrative. Some other distinctive images, signs, and codes were: the outline of Paris against a starry sky (Bourjois's *Soir de Paris*); a leather wallet or bag (Chanel's *Cuir de Russie*); a white swallow with an envelope (Renoir's *Messager*); the top of an electric pole against a starry black sky (Schiaparelli's *Sleeping*); a revolver (Lanvin's *Scandal!*); a hand covering a woman's mouth and eyes (Schiaparelli's *Shocking*); a door opening on to a dark interior (Lelong's *Indiscret*); and a heart surrounded by keys on a chain (Guermantes's *Coeur volé* [Stolen Heart]). The final number (45) and thus the

end of the game showed a large pink rose whose two leaves, having turned into arms and hands, hold an atomizer; the flower is literally scenting itself.

According to the directions, the "Game of Perfume," which resembled the "Game of Goose" (invented in the 1560s) or "Monopoly" (invented in 1935), proceeds by players throwing a pair of dice and then moving their counters the number of squares indicated by the dice. Play begins at the perimeter of the board (square 1) and ends in the center at square 45, which the player has to reach by an exact number. If the number indicated on the dice does not lead exactly to the final square, then players must move their counters backward by a number equal to the extra points indicated. The advantages and penalties encountered when one lands on different spaces make the game interesting. From as early as the third square, for example, luck can be yours because you occupy the space of Pierre Dune's *Fringant*, a word whose meaning, "frisky," is evoked by the large silhouette of a horse's head and mane; you are instructed to mount the horse and with the appropriate "friskiness" advance by double the number of spaces that landed you here in the first place. Similarly, the *Arpège* square (number 6) is a lucky space; it informs players that since the fragrance involves seven notes, they may jump ahead by seven squares. If, however, you have the misfortune of landing on Worth's *Imprudence*, you are requested to start over again at the very first square, because "every imprudence has to be paid for." Landing on Rival's *Poivre* will blind you with pepper and so you have to go back to square 7. However, getting to square 21 (Renoir's *Messager* with its images of a bird and envelope) gives you an errand to perform, and you jump ahead as if on wings to square 32 (Caron's *Pour Une Femme*) where you will find the woman, symbolically represented by a pearl necklace, to whom the envelope, undoubtedly a *billet doux* for which you are the messenger, must be delivered. Square 23 for Lancôme's *Flèches* is decorated with intersecting arrows pointing in three different directions; if you land here, you immediately are propelled like an arrow to square 39 where you will find the woman of your dreams in Lelong's *Elle . . . Elle. . . .* You are stopped in your tracks, however, if you are unlucky enough to land on Schiaparelli's *Sleeping* (square 26); you have to stay in the space until another player lands here and wakes you up. And the same thing happens when, getting to Patou's *Colony* (represented by a explorer's white pith helmet), you are instructed to rest one turn because your voyage has been so long and tiring. No benefit comes from arriving at square 31, Lanvin's *Scandal*, because it only advances you two spaces to Schiaparelli's *Shocking*, a name with which it enjoys a certain consonance and resonance. Close to the end, however, you run into trouble, if you land on square 34 (Lelong's *Indiscret*); for then your indiscretion turns costly, and you are exiled back to the wilderness of number 11, Lancôme's *Tropiques*, with its image of a hot sun. Not quite as costly, though, is square 41, Institut Philodermic's *Doux Sacrifice* (with its skewered,

frying heart); a sacrifice is now exacted from you; happily, it is only the loss of your next turn.

This clever and sophisticated game, like most parlor games, serves to entertain and instruct. Aside from the pleasure it offers, the "Jeu des Parfums" introduced the public to the imaginary and romantic associations con-nected to the names of different scents. It made perfume visual *and* narrative at the same time. Reducing the scent to an ironic, suggestive, or schematic icon and creating metaphorical links between the scent and a dramatic scene (the revolver associated with *Scandal*), a narrative story (the clock hands on a blue background for *L'Heure bleue*),

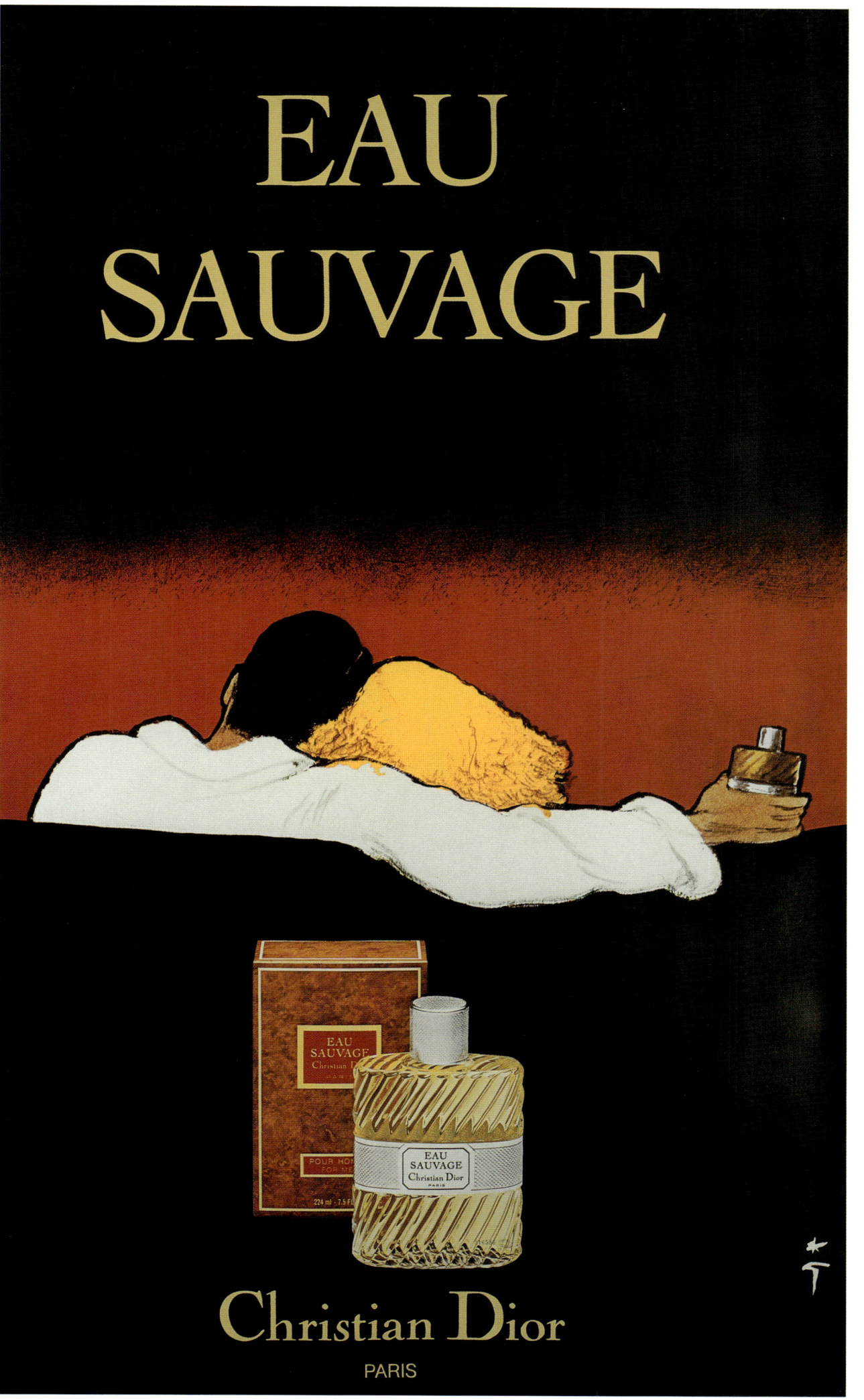

Fig. 115 Born in Italy René Gruau was for over half a century one of the most important postwar fashion illustrators. He had worked for a number of French fashion magazines before Christian Dior asked him to create the simple and elegant advertising images for *Miss Dior* in the late forties, *Diorissimo* and *Rouge Baiser* (a lipstick) in the fifties, and *Eau sauvage* in the sixties, seventies, and eighties, like this advertisement from 1984. Sign of a Gruau creation is always indicated by the artist's hallmark asterisk-over-the-letter-g logo.

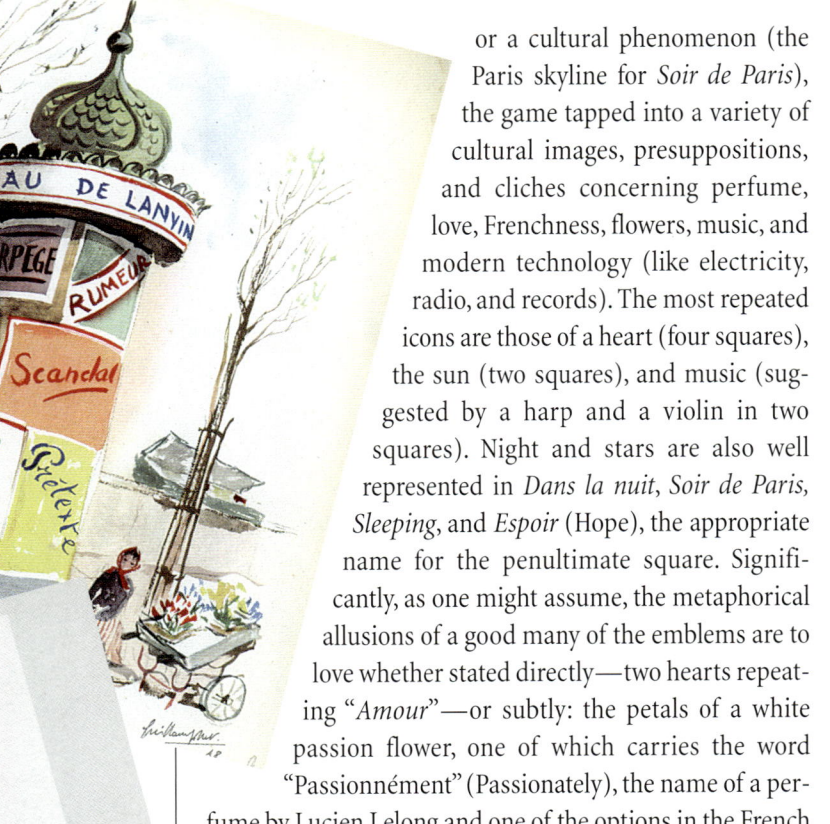

Fig. 116 A kiosk of perfumes as posters. Lanvin, *L'Opéra de l'odorat*, 1949, watercolor by Guillaume Gillet, Chanel archives, Neuilly sur Seine.

Fig. 117 A kiosk of perfumes as a hand-written poem. Lanvin, *L'Opéra de l'odorat*, 1949, written version of "À L'Opéra de l'odorat" by Louise de Vilmorin, Chanel archives, Neuilly sur Seine.

Fig. 118 A kiosk of perfumes as a calligram. Lanvin, *L'Opéra de l'odorat*, 1949, calligram of "À L'Opéra de l'odorat" by Louise de Vilmorin, Chanel archives, Neuilly sur Seine.

or a cultural phenomenon (the Paris skyline for *Soir de Paris*), the game tapped into a variety of cultural images, presuppositions, and cliches concerning perfume, love, Frenchness, flowers, music, and modern technology (like electricity, radio, and records). The most repeated icons are those of a heart (four squares), the sun (two squares), and music (suggested by a harp and a violin in two squares). Night and stars are also well represented in *Dans la nuit, Soir de Paris, Sleeping,* and *Espoir* (Hope), the appropriate name for the penultimate square. Significantly, as one might assume, the metaphorical allusions of a good many of the emblems are to love whether stated directly—two hearts repeating "*Amour*"—or subtly: the petals of a white passion flower, one of which carries the word "Passionnément" (Passionately), the name of a perfume by Lucien Lelong and one of the options in the French game "He / She loves me, he / she loves me not, ... etc."

Perfume and Joy After the War

If the "Game of Perfumes" arrived on the scene exactly in the middle of the 1940s, which seems likely, then it would have most certainly offered the pleasure and the lightness of being the French desperately needed after the long nightmare of war and occupation. Peace was definitely a cause for perfume celebration, as we have seen in Coty's "liberation" fragrances, *8 Mai* and *25 Août,* from 1945, and in Patou's *L'Heure attendue* (The Long-Awaited Hour, 1946). Nina Ricci introduced the celebratory *Coeur-Joie* (Joyful Heart), "a romantic perfume" as it was advertised, in 1946. A floral aldehyde with a dash of musk, it was created by the woman-perfumer Germaine Cellier. The heart-shaped crystal bottle with a heart-shaped hole at its center was accompanied by nearly thirty gouache advertising posters (fig. 114). Painted by Christian Bérard, a famous artist and designer of the period, these posters of demure young girls wearing simplified belle epoque dresses, hats, and veils expressed the nostalgic longing for a return to a more remote and innocent time, one that might efface the horrors of the recent past. This was a perfume expressing rebirth and youth. "I wanted it to be noble and cheerful," Robert Ricci remarked, "reflecting the joy of victory, freedom and happiness found again!"[84]

Perfume and joy were literally in the air during the

spring of the same year when Carven attached thousands of little bottles of its new fragrance, *Ma Griffe,* to tiny green and white parachutes and had them dropped from a small plane flying over Paris. This was a perfume whose name (meaning "my claws" or "my signature" or "my personal stamp") evoked acts of writing, marking, or inscribing. As it sailed on its little parachutes, *Ma Griffe,* one might say, left its imprint, wrote its signature on, in, and through the Paris air! A perfume raining down from the heavens was yet another sign of the celebratory mood taking hold of a country awakening from its dark night and trying to efface, not all that successfully at first, the torments of those desperate years. A similar joy was given sensual expression by Christian Dior in his stunning couture collection of 1947. In reaction to the years of deprivation, when fabrics and textiles were in short supply and luxury was indeed just that, a "luxury" both unaffordable and inaccessible, Dior's "New Look," as it was baptized, inaugurated a new era of full dresses and voluminous skirts constructed from yards and yards of fabric, as if the lavish exuberance of the Second Empire and that of the Empress Eugénie's ball gowns had suddenly reappeared. If fashion, as Dior once said, "comes from a dream," that dream was now one of abundance. Couture was not its only site of expression, as Dior himself made clear when in 1947 he introduced his first perfume, *Miss Dior.* The same aesthetic idea of plentiful, lavish drapery and the same suggestion as in Ricci's *Coeur-Joie* of a youthful, innocent womanhood, as signaled by the title of address ("Miss"), defined the fundamental concept behind *Miss Dior*: "I have created this perfume," Dior explained, "to wrap each woman in exquisite femininity, as if each of my designs, one by one, were emerging from the bottle." Advertisements for *Miss Dior* emphasized this graceful, delicate femininity. One in particular, designed by the artist René Gruau (1909–2004), who would create many advertisements for Dior signed with his distinctive asterisk and "g" logo, especially the ads for *Eau Sauvage* from the sixties and seventies (fig. 115), featured the graceful, delicate image of a pure white swan around whose long, exquisitely arcing neck a cluster of pearls and a long, flowing, black ribbon hang.[85]

Calligrams of Scent

In the last half of the 1940s perfume came to be seen as a spectacle, a performance, a sensational drama. And no more so than in a charming, ingeniously composed book, *L'Opéra de l'odorat* (The Opera of Odors), produced by Lanvin perfumes (and the publisher Aljanvic) in June 1949 with calligrammatic poems by Louise de Vilmorin, watercolors by Guillaume Gillet, and a preface by Colette. The watercolors portray Parisian scenes—a kiosk, a store window filled with large perfume bottles, a cart pulled by a man, a flower girl sitting next to an awning, a man putting up a billboard, sandwich men carrying placards, a woman

Jean Desprez's *Votre Main,* 1939, an elegant white Sèvres bottle, reaches upward gracefully toward the rose porcelain stopper that will release the fragrance within.

holding balloons, and the side of an apartment house—into which the names of five Lanvin perfumes have been cleverly integrated. The kiosk, the perfume containers, the balloons, the man's cart, the flower girl's awning, and the placards feature the words "My Sin," "Scandal," "Prétexte," "Arpège," and "Rumeur," all creations of Lanvin. Following each watercolor is a full-page poem whose letters and words are arranged in the exact shape of the previous illustration: a kiosk, a perfume jar, a cart, an awning, a ladder, a sandwich man, balloons, and the side of a house. The calligrams, composed of words and lines which are quite challenging to decipher, are then followed in their turn by a handwritten, and therefore legible, version of the same poem (figs. 116, 117, 118).

The opening calligram and watercolor of *The Opera of Odors* illustrate the idea of a synaesthetic spectacle of scents. Shaped like a kiosk (those ubiquitous cylindrical billboards posted with announcements of plays, operas, ballets), Vilmorin's poem literally acts as its own kiosk "publicizing" the "spectacle of fragrances" that the following pages of her book will perform: "At the Opera of odors" / What will this evening's program be?" the first calligram asks, before going on to assert that "Perfumes are telegrams. / The song of the prima donna / Mixes jasmine with balsamine. / Her heart given away, the ballerina, / Caressed by perfumes descended from the stars, / Will dance on the end of your nose. / And we kindly inform you / That this perfumed spectacle / Is not for those with colds."[86] Perfumes, according to Vilmorin's metaphors, are performances, dances, songs, messages, and telegrams, a true opera of the senses considering that four of the five senses (taste being excluded) are evoked. Broadcast invisibly through the night air, the spectacle of songs and the telegram of scents wing their way toward a "*destinataire*," as the French call the "addressee," whose ears will "hear" the operatic scents and whose nose will "smell" the aromatic "syllables." A communication has occurred. Like a kiosk, perfume disseminates information; it edifies; and it speaks, albeit synaesthetically.

Several of Vilmorin's poems in *The Opera of Odors* are romantic and sentimental. They refer to the power of perfume to rekindle the amorous past: "This bottle will restore / To our hearts the perfume of chance / And in our arms the longed-for past." They orchestrate playful and lighthearted scenes of courtship as, for example, in the calligram shaped like a ladder where allusions to climbing and the upswelling of an amorous relationship are suggested: "To climb this ladder let us join our hands / Surprise and novelty from rung to rung arise / O steps of scent you take us where? / Breath joined with breath I lead you to the air." Some of the poems play delightfully with rhythmical alliteration: "Ma *rose rousse* s'est enfuie et la pluie m'arrose douce" ("My russet rose is gone, and rain softly sprays me [cries for me]"). Several contain puns and jeux de mots. One, in particular, describes "marigolds" (*soucis*) and "pansies" (*pensées*) growing in a garden now bereft of the secret perfume two lovers once associated with their shared "concerns" (*soucis*) and "thoughts" (*pensées*). Perfume is presented as a magical charm scenting the air with love and with the music of chance. In one of the most charming of Vilmorin's ten calligrams, this one constructed in the form of a building, or more precisely its facade, a lover recounts how the perfumed space of his beloved's top-floor apartment poses a serious dilemma for him. Her room is so saturated with scent that it escapes through the chimney and "sings her virtues everywhere on the wings of chance." Suddenly, unknown men, having been summoned by this remarkable scent, begin to congregate at her doorstep. The lover is beside himself with jealousy because "these men, despite my presence, inhale you." His burning desire is to install himself in her May-scented room and never leave. "Ah," he sighs to his mistress, "lower the jalousies / When comes my jealousy. / I intend henceforth to be alone / In smelling your perfume that embalms / And to chase away the passersby who seek / To inhale the perfume on your palms."

A Tiny Drop of Fragrance

From the hand of Vilmorin also came what is perhaps the most poetic celebration of and homage to perfume written in the 1940s. It was published four months after the German surrender, which took place at the end of the summer of 1945. In December of that year, the couturier and perfumer Marcel Rochas opened an exhibition of perfumes at his Avenue Matignon salon, a show he named "Perfume As Seen Through Fashion, 1765 to 1945" and dedicated to the memory of the couturier, Paul Poiret. The exhibition was accompanied by a catalogue with perfume labels from the eighteenth and nineteenth centuries and illustrations by the artist and designer Georges Lepape who had been creating high-style fashion illustrations and drawings since before World War I. Aside from presenting Rochas's fragrance, *Femme*, which had been launched the previous year, the exhibition sought to display the classic scents of French perfumery by Coty, Guerlain, Lubin, Houbigant, and others in the hope of reintroducing the French public to a perfume tradition that, given the shortage of goods more essential to daily survival than perfume, had gone underground, so to speak, during the war. Vilmorin's preface to Rochas's exhibition catalogue begins with a resounding paean—one of the most lyrical and intense since Baudelaire perhaps—to perfume's resurrectional power and to its historical role as a cultural phenomenon capable of recalling and explaining the past:

> Images, portraits, dead leaves—perfume alone can revive them. A scent and then voices arise; the past instant appears in the present moment; the unknown surges up and reveals itself; the past strikes at our heart; a glove becomes precious, a scarf poignant,

and we are aware of the sighs of an invisible companion. Perfume rescues imagination; it answers questions posed by our tomorrows, and without lying recounts the history of the societies it once crowned with a halo. It explains customs, styles of languor or liveliness, and fashions of the boudoir; [it speaks] of escapes, of refusals. . . . It is the soul of a house, the soul of memory, the soul of nostalgia.[87]

Perfume, Vilmorin continues, is a messenger and guide taking us "to islands of repose or the bedroom of a cherished secret." Perfume, "if it leads us to the future, never forgets to hold open the doors of yesteryear." In the here-and-now of everyday life, perfume looks out at an "invisible color, the color of silence; forgotten moments, forgiven moments, moments one seeks to relive, seasons one glimpses—it is within perfume that the most present hour throbs and the wellspring of the past sings to emotions that are captured once again." The memory of scents past corresponds, Vilmorin suggests, to the remembrance of things past. An entire world can be reborn and spring into being not only from Proust's cup of tea but from a tiny drop of fragrance.

The Eros—
and Thanatos—
of Scents

Chapter 7

"Septième sens" [Seventh Sense]—
the electric sensation of a body
rapturous at being clothed in scents. . . .
"Septième sens," the magic spell of
a perfume that takes hold of souls
thirsting for unknown joys: the perfume
for women who live their passions.
—Advertisement, Sonia Rykiel, 1979

I put my arms around him yes
and drew him down to me so he could
feel my breasts all perfume yes
and his heart was going like mad
and yes I said yes I will Yes.—
—James Joyce

The grave [is] the secret chamber in which
Eros and Sexus settle their ancient quarrel.
—Walter Benjamin

Pheromones of Love

THE EROS OF SCENT—its drive toward life and impulse toward love—is many things. It is biblical. The Shulamite and her lover in the Song of Songs celebrate their passion through aromatic metaphors as ecstatic as they are erotic: "My king lay down beside me / and my fragrance / wakened the night. / All night between my breasts / my love is a cluster of myrrh / . . . / Before day breathes, / before the shadows of night are gone, / I will hurry to the mountain of myrrh, / the hill of frankincense" (1:12–14, 4:6). The eros of scent is also Shakespearean. Cleopatra's barge enters Alexandria floating on the water like the intoxicating vision of a golden cloud of incense: "Purple the sails and so perfumed that / The winds were love-sick with them / . . . / A strange invisible perfume hits the sense / Of the adjacent wharfs" (*Antony and Cleopatra*, II, ii, 198–99, 217–18). And the eros of scent is "Parisian," long before it was even French. When Hera, Pallas Athena, and Aphrodite suddenly appear before a confused Paris, tending sheep on a remote hillside outside of Troy, to demand that he select the fairest among them, Paris decides, under the pressure of their bribes, to award the golden apple not to Hera, who promises to make him lord of Europe and Asia, not to Athena, who promises to help him lead the Trojans to victory over the Greeks, but rather to Aphrodite, who has come to him under the name of Hedone, goddess of "Sensual Pleasure." Smothered in spellbinding perfumes and "all proud of the power of desire," according to Euripides, Hedone succeeds in turning Paris's head with the promise of the hedonistic pleasure that the body and soul of Helen, the fairest woman in the world, will give him.[1]

The eros of scent is ritualistic as well. Maidens destined to sleep with Assyrian kings prepared their bodies for a year in special perfume baths, immersing themselves for six months in myrrh and another six in labdanum or bdellium. Chinese courtesans followed a diet of bland foods mixed with musk. When their bodies were stroked during the act of love, their warm skin, so it was believed, emitted a sweat tinged with muskiness. Cleopatra met Antony in a bedchamber filled with rose petals. Greek women applied particular scents to particular parts of the body; mint was worn on the arms, marjoram in the hair, and rose spirit on the breasts. Ancient women in some cultures fumigated their vulvas with myrrh-smoke.[2] Potential brides in some Middle Eastern cultures were sniffed, and if they did not smell pleasant, they were rejected. Elizabethans, moreover, inherited the ancient custom of "love apples." A peeled apple was placed under a woman's armpit for a full day and then presented to a lover. The heady mixture of apple sweetness and sultry sweatiness (from the apocrine glands) produced a fruit, so it was said, with considerable aphrodisiac powers. Little did the Elizabethans know that their love apples foretold of chemical and physiological discoveries to come concerning the sexually and pheromonally

induced secretions of the apocrine glands, situated not only under the arm, but also around the pubis, the anus, the face, and the scalp. The secrecy with which women of the eighteenth-century court practiced the arts of the toilette, hidden away from public view and calling upon a "science" of adornment unknown to men, contributed to the aura of ritualistic magic surrounding the use of perfume and makeup. As Louis Sebastien Mercier (1740–1814), the chronicler of the late-eighteenth-century court of Louis XVI, observed, women participated in a ritual that was essentially religious:

> Dressed in a white garment, she approaches an altar where several gold and crystal containers are mysteriously arranged. Her head uncovered she addresses vows to the radiant gods of beauty . . . To the side of this altar, where a watchful silence reigns, stands a humble priestess who with lowered eyes prepares the pure essences that will scent her flowing hair. The rites begin . . . From within a thousand small and elegant boxes arise a thousand individual charms . . . The gentle spirit of flowers escapes from golden flasks, and the air is embalmed with perfumes from Arabia.[3]

The eros of scent is finally chemical. For years scientists have known that ovulating female animals use pheromones (chemical signals with the power to modify biology and behavior when exchanged between individuals of the same species) to attract males. A sow in estrus will immediately place herself in a spread-legged mating position when she smells the pheromone contained in the saliva of a male boar. A female moth can spread her odor over a six-and-a-half-mile radius with such intensity that 25 percent of the male moths within that space are attracted to her. In rodents, pheromones can act to enhance or suppress the estrus cycle. Such behavior in the animal world has inspired the still mostly unsuccessful search for a human "love pheromone," which certain researchers believe could possibly be sensed by a second system of olfaction, a "sexual nose," called the vomeronasal organ lying just above the hard palate on the roof of the mouth. Skeptics, however, have vigorously declared this organ to be a fossil, whose functionality, while evident in rats and hamsters, remains yet to be proven in humans.[4]

Yet, two ground-breaking studies, explaining why women living in close social groups tend to be sensitive to each other's menstrual cycles, have offered solid proof for the existence of human pheromones. Conducted in 1971 and 1998 at the University of Chicago these experiments demonstrated that the aromatic steroids, androstenol and androstenone, located in the underarms (the axillary organ) of women (as well as men) and known to act as sexual pheromones in the pig, work to produce menstrual synchrony through smell.[5] Moreover, investigations into the erogenous properties of certain scents and flavors by scientists at the Smell and Taste Treatment and Research Foundation in Chicago have discovered the somewhat extraordinary, if not bizarre, fact that the combined odors of lavender and pumpkin pie increase penile blood flow in human males by an average of 40 percent; the smell of cinnamon buns came in second. Women were most sexually aroused by a combination of licorice and cucumber. While the potential of odors (in the form of pheromones) to excite sexual attraction and provoke mating in animals has been clearly proven, the same cannot be said, at least for now, about humans. "Research into whether human body odors play any part in human sexual behavior," D. Michael Stoddart remarks, "has been largely inconclusive." Yet, "the role of odors in the sexual physiology of non-human primates and other mammals," he continues, "is sufficiently clear for there to be a very strong possibility that they do indeed play some role in our own species." The whisper of hope offered in this observation has been sufficient to inspire two American companies, Erox and the Athena Institute, to market perfumes containing synthetic copies of human pheromones. Erox, founded in the eighties by a University of Utah biochemist ("to delve into the world of human pheromones for the purpose of enhancing fragrance and its sexual power") markets two scents—*Realm Women* and *Realm Men*—under the slogan "Awaken Your Sixth Sense." These fragrances have been marketed as the only ones in the world to use synthesized human pheromones. Whether they do in fact activate a "sixth sense," one associated with the vomeronasal organ and thus potent enough, theoretically speaking, to capture the "subliminal signals" the pheromones emit, still remains open to question. What appears to be a quest for a pheromone-based perfume arises from two facts: first, that women's sense of smell is generally more powerful than that of men and second, that reproductive hormones have been linked scientifically to olfaction. A woman's sense of smell is a thousand times more sensitive to musk than a man's; during ovulation it becomes one hundred thousand times more sensitive. This heightening of response to male odors may have been nature's way of making females in estrus more receptive to mating.[6]

The link between odor and reproduction in animals has been discovered in the sensitivity of mice to those pheromones, primarily communicated and detected through smell, that determine the selection of a sexual partner, as Manfred Milinski and Claus Wedekind have shown. Through odor (that of urine) mice select those members of the opposite sex that are the least similar to them genetically and therefore, from the point of view of evolution, the most advantageous to them as sexual partners. The genes in question belong to the "major histocompatability complex" (MHC), a large chromosomal region charged with protecting the immune system from pathogens and with controlling "immunological self and non-self recognition." Proteins created by the MHC genes function as molecular signals which, when picked up by body cells, convey messages to the immune system about whether help is needed to fight infection. These genes function as indicators of genetic resemblance and probably determine the choice in mice and humans of mates with dissimilar MHC genotypes. Such mixed mating assures a wide immunity for disease-sensitive offspring. An experiment in the mid-1990s using T-shirts impregnated with male sweat revealed that women preferred the odor of the shirts worn by men with the most dissimilar MHC. Thus it was shown that mate selection in humans could be determined by genetics as well as by smell.

In a more recent experiment Milinski and Wedekind asked a test group of 137 men and women to evaluate scent strips impregnated with thirty-six different perfume ingredients (thirty-two natural "fragrants" and four synthetic ingredients). In two different tests over two years, each subject, in addition to smelling the scent strips, was asked to reply to a series of questions about whether the ingredients were pleasant enough to be used by oneself or by one's partner. Results showed that people tend to choose perfumes for their own use that will "amplify in some way body odors that reveal [their] immunogenetics." It is scientifically evident that perfume, even more than revealing our personality as was once believed, enhances our genetically determined body odor.[7] One's perfume "signature" is more than mere writing on the wind. It has evident biological and evolutionary importance, enabling women and men not only to advertise to potential mates the strengths of their genes but to assure that their offspring will be potentially more immune to disease. If eros is the force of life, as Freud believed, then the eros of scent, from a Darwinian point of view, would most definitely contribute to the survival of the fittest.

The Psycho-Pathology of Scent: MANIA, L'INTERDIT, and the Erotics of Bondage

In its represented forms as myth, poetry, song, narrative, advertisement, and, of course, object of desire, scent has been celebrated, extolled, mystified, and eroticized. Such a celebration has often highlighted the paradox, mystery, and instability inherent in the effect of scent on the body and on the projected image of the woman who wears it. From the conflict and then fusion of odors emanating from his mistress's body as she undresses herself—which the seventeenth-century English poet Robert Herrick describes as "This *Camphire, Storax, Spiknard, Glabanum:* / These *Musks*, these *Ambers*, and those other smells" migrating from "silken bodies" to "passive Aire"—to Calvin Klein's slogan for his 1997 oriental perfume *Contradiction*—"She is always and never the same"—the erotic figuration of scent envelops the woman in ambivalence, complexity, and mutability, unduly emphasizing the patriarchal myth of her protean, hybrid, and therefore capricious reality. Such ambiguity is reflected as well in the slogan for *Un Air de Samsara* (Guerlain, 1995)—"neither completely oneself neither completely another"—and for Guerlain's classic fragrance *L'Heure bleue*: "the perfume of the woman who wants everything *and* nothing, yesterday and today." The attraction of the male imagination to images of instability, disorder, and danger associated with the myth of the feminine is confirmed by slogans like "A disturbance in the atmosphere" (*Silver Rain*, La Prairie, 2005), "Inside every woman lies the power of the moon" (*Nokomis*, 1997), and *Trouble* (Boucheron, 2004), a perfume whose name doubles as its slogan and whose ruby-red bottle is capped with a stopper in the form of a coiled serpent.[8]

It is as if femininity were only conceivable when joined with a certain aura of mystery, contradiction, and confusion as in this description of Guerlain's *Mitsouko* (1919), which celebrates the paradox of a self-renewing evanescence: "This 'odor di femina' with its transparent sensuality has no equal in resurrecting the magic of fugitive loves." Not only is fragrant love both ephemeral and lasting, but the perfumed woman is mysterious—"Adopt the mystery of *Mitsouko*," one advertisement counsels—and deeply complex, as Giorgio Armani remarks apropos of his portmanteau-named fragrance *Mania*, of 2000: "Femininity has come into its own again and is finally being seen for what it is—complex, sophisticated, and seductive . . . This scent is about the intangible passions that boil beneath the surface . . . It embodies a woman's moods, desires, and complex sensuality"; it is dedicated to "spontaneous women who live life to its fullest." The CEO of Bulgari, the Italian jewelry company, describes his perfume *BLV* (2000) in similar words: "Women want to be recognized for being multifaceted. They want their fragrance and their clothes to reveal this." As a result, BLV (pronounced "blue") is a complicated scent, composed of high contrasts in which cool and icy notes (ginger, wisteria, and musk) compete with deeper warmer tones (vanilla and sandalwood). All in all, a certain inexplicable complexity intensifies in the male (and female) imagination the myth of the enigmatic woman, "the woman who defies definition," as Fendi's *Theorema* (late 1990s) identifies her. Conversely, an uncomplicated superficiality can sometimes be just as seductive, especially for the woman who, scenting herself with *Imaginez* (1999), projects the "odor of an open book."[9]

Giving Voice to the Body

Whether spiritualizing or mystifying the woman, perfume is notable for giving the female body a voice, a language, an expressive presence. A series of advertisements run by the French Council on Perfume in the 1980s declared that "without perfume, the skin is silent" (see page 305). This voicing of the body through scent is supposed to be, as perfume advertisements are wont to stress, first, empowering (a woman chooses the perfume herself); second, erotic (she selects it to make herself attractive to another, even if that other is herself); and third, expressive (she reveals who she is or wishes to be). Between a woman and her perfume exists yet another kind of eros, what the perfumer Jean-Paul Guerlain identifies (in a press release for his fragrance *Guerlinade*) as a "love affair between a woman and her perfume." This passion for a perfume is also a passion for the perfume's own eros: its power to inspire a love and (equally as important) a narrative of that love. For it is the possibility of eros *and* of narrative that is captivating, according to Guerlain:

> The creation of a perfume owes much to chance encounters, to the power of ideas, to the magic of a glance, to the turmoil of a passionate affair. It is a sensitive, sensual love story. Behind each of our perfumes there is a muse. We have always created a perfume for the woman who is loved, or for a symbol of femininity . . . The role of perfume is to make women even more beautiful and unforgettable. Men remember the woman they love for the perfume she wears, the scent which makes his heart beat faster. Perfume has the absolute power to reveal and display a whole intimate world, present or distant. It is a journey into the realms of imagination, and the most intense form a memory can take.

Again, perfume's power to penetrate the secret, intimate life of human beings, to touch those vulnerable parts of one's being which eros alone can unlock, is made inseparable from the fantasies and romantic associations perfume seeks to create. In purchasing perfume and in applying it to the skin, one envelops oneself above all in a four-fold image: first, the image of a seductive charm, which many stories of love have expressed and for which the perfume becomes yet another narrative version; second, the image of a realization of self, since the scent will complete and perfect the woman, revealing undeveloped regions of her sensuality and femininity; third, the image of a cultural identity or affiliation, for the Frenchness of a perfume offers an aura of luxury, refinement, and distinction available to French and non-French alike; and fourth, the image of desire and desirability—the object we want wants us in return. This is because the love affair between the consumer and the object of her or his desire involves a fetishistic eroticism, as the philosopher Jean Baudrillard has remarked: "By virtue of advertising . . . the product exposes itself to our view and invites us to handle it; it is, in fact, eroticized . . . because the purchase itself, [a] simple appropriation, is transformed into a maneuver, a scenario, a complicated dance which endows a purely practical transaction with all the traits of amorous dalliance: advances, rivalry, obscenity, flirtation, prostitution—even irony." So, a man or woman attracted by advertising is, Baudrillard concludes, "a person who is sexually solicited."[10]

A world, more than a perfume, is being offered to a woman: a universe of pleasure, sensuality, adventure, and intimacy, a world of self-discovery and self-realization. "The perfumer's task," remarks Jean-Paul Guerlain, "is above all to offer a woman a world that will enable her to explore her own intimate secrets, and her own sensuousness. All our perfumes are designed to bring out emotion and sensuality." This sensuality surfaces as an eros inseparable from what is imaginary, for "as you open the bottle, images abound," Guerlain notes. What sails forth on the scent of the fragrance is the constellation of images with which it has been "blended" through naming, advertising, packaging, and design. The vapors of fantasy float on the wings of scent. Perfume is an open sesame for prepackaged worlds of desire, for it tells, Guerlain observes, "a secret story, which is revealed in recurrent detail, a visual leitmotif, or an artistic and emotional universe which unfurls over a few square centimeters; a streaked, stormy sky for *Vol de nuit* or a Tibetan box for *Samsara*" ("Guerlinade," 30–33). Literally, perfume exists as the stuff dreams are made of, for there is no liquid, no scent, other than that fabricated by the image.

And there is no fragrance other than that fabricated by language. An article in Paris *Vogue* announcing Armani's scent *Mania*, not only uncritically accepts as a given the ideology of feminine mystery designed by the perfume house for its advertising campaign, but in overheated language forges a pseudo-psychoanalytic image (and myth) of psychic feminine complexity and depth:

> *Mania*, an introspective perfume, deep and dark, penetrating the heart of a woman's fantasies; a perfume that does not seek to interpret them but to express intuitively and olfactorily their intensity, their sensuality, their mystery, through . . . incense. Mania is a perfume of incense and of essence—deep, troubling, bewitching—an incense freed of its religious meanings and revealed as fiery and smoldering. As much in smelling it as in wearing it each woman will have to find her personality, her strengths, her weaknesses—her manias.

The singularity of *Mania,* despite its anagrammatic resemblance to Armani (it shares almost all the same letters) and its hyperbolic advertisement, is ultimately generic. For what perfume is not in and of itself "introspective"? What perfume does not attempt to reveal the "inner woman" and touch that core of intimacy which is hers alone and which, according to the romantic scenario, she will divulge only to the one she loves? What perfumes (and religions) have not made extensive use of incense? But *Mania* is distinctive in the manner by which it transforms a neurotic and often painful psychological condition (i.e., mania) into a "good," an erotic *good*: a good one can buy. Despite its boast that it penetrates the heart of female fantasy, *Mania* admits with some modesty that it cannot truly know the woman, cannot fully "decode" and interpret her deepest manic wishes; aromas are not psychoanalytic, after all. It merely gives voice to these fantasies, translating their intuitive and unconscious reality into a language of fragrances. Free rein is given to the "intensity, sensuality, and mystery" of mania, redefined by Armani as an experience of benign unpredictability, liberation, self-expression, and bliss. The woman in all her complexity and profundity, both positive and negative—her "character, strengths, weaknesses, and manias"—comes alive maniacally, as it were. Despite scents with names like *Fétiche* (Piver, 1925), *Obsession* (Calvin Klein, 1985), or even Dior's *Addict* (2002), no perfumer has yet named a fragrance *Hysteria*, although there is a historical link between fragrance and the treatment of this disorder. The nineteenth-century French philosopher and physician Cabanis believed that the smell of roses had a therapeutic and restorative effect on the uterus of a woman suffering from hysteria, compelling the wandering organ to return to its fixed and natural position.[11]

Imprisoned by Perfume

Paradoxically, the expression of the body that perfume creates when giving skin its own aromatic signature also does away with the body, transforming it into spirit and therefore into absence, especially at those times when vision is forced to yield to the superior perceptual powers of smell: "One must smell a woman before having even seen her," the perfumer Marcel Rochas remarks, and what, asks Jean-Paul Guerlain, "lingers of a woman at night, if not her perfume?" Fragrance clothes the body in invisible drapery, giving it a different form and contour. But the olfactory layering provided by such abstract, insubstantial "clothing" can also *undress* the body. While perfume for Estée Lauder "is like a new dress . . . it simply makes you marvelous," *Shalimar* is for Guerlain "a dress outrageously décolletée," and *Champs-Elysées* (1996), even more revealingly, "an invisible article of clothing protecting and unveiling the intimacy of a woman, making her uncover her nakedness, her own universe." Encircled by scent, the body is at once present (as emanation, effluvium, aroma, aura, and vapor) and absent (as spirit, trace, memory, and sillage): "To wear a perfume," remarks the couturière Sonia Rykiel, "is to expand, melt away, blend in. To leave behind something strange that causes one to do a double take: once to see and once to ask what one has seen." In the many images she wears, the scented woman exists in a perpetual state of ambiguity, of decorporealized corporeality: at once a body and a soul, a presence and an absence. One is never certain whether one is in contact with the body or the soul, the presence or the absence, because the movement from one state to the other is constant and unpredictable. It is a confusing continuum, as the following description for Givenchy's perfume *Ysatis* (1985) reveals: "Perfume of a thousand women in one, *Ysatis* reflects all facets of a woman: in turn resolute, fragile, sensual, efficient, loving, seductive, perfectly contemporary, and unceasingly captivating."[12] Through the eros of scent a woman becomes a hybrid, a hyphenated being: visible-invisible, proximate-distant, corporeal-spiritual, ephemeral-enduring, earthly-celestial, base-sublime, primitive-civilized, expressive-mute, innocent-seductive. Such an indeterminate, paradoxical reality adheres to the image of the scented woman, at least when fantasized by a male imagination incapable of envisioning her as an empowered physical being and not some ethereal sylph removed from the temporal continuum of life, as the following statements, the first by the designer Oleg Cassini and the second by the turn-of-the century poet Paul Valéry, indicate: "A woman without a fragrance is a woman without a past" and "A woman who wears no perfume has no future."

As if to reinforce the halo of existential and temporal uncertainty which surrounds the woman within the fantasy world that perfume creates, one need only consider the image of erotic "enslavement" evident in a print advertisement for *Jaïpur*, a perfume marketed in 1995 by Boucheron, the Place Vendôme jeweler. Created in the shape of an oversized golden bracelet—or a gigantic golden ring with a simulated sapphire at its center—the *Jaïpur* bottle is shown in one advertisement resting on a large pedestal in a jewelry store window surrounded by other smaller rings and bracelets; "more than a perfume," the text tells us, this is "a jewel." *Jaïpur* is a hybrid, "the perfume-ring," where inside and outside, scent and bottle, are equally precious and expensive. Of course, perfume bottles have, since the beginning of the twentieth century, been created to stand on their own as works of art designed by artisans like Lalique, Baccarat, and Saint-Louis, as discussed in chapter 4. It was René Coty who first appealed to the artistry of these glassmakers for the presentation of his perfume creations, believing that the beauty of the container would only enhance the beauty of the contained.

With its transparent, molded glass, its gold-plated metal, and its large blue sapphire, *Jaïpur*'s "bracelet-bottle" is no exception. What is unique, however, about the *Jaïpur* advertising campaign is the manner in which it makes explicit what has for so long been implicit among the images associated with perfume. It is obvious that scents are commonly presented as rich, artistic, sublime works of art, and that their elegant, delicate, imaginative bottles—luxury objects of longer life than the fragrance—confirm this association. Scent and jewelry both constitute displays of wealth. They both add vibrancy and sparkle to the finger, wrist, neck, and ear—they colonize, so it appears, the same corporeal regions—that show them off. They aestheticize the body, turning anatomy and skin into dazzling, luminous, scintillating flashes of odor and light. They disguise the body's biological and physiological appearance and spiritualize its physical and erotic reality. Perfumed and bejeweled, the woman is no longer a body but a work of art and of artifice. A similarly aesthetic transformation of the female body, whereby the woman is endowed with power (as an image) but in a situation that is fundamentally disempowering, is spelled out in another advertisement for *Jaïpur* (fig. 119). It is almost a cliché of perfume advertising that scent be described as captivating, spellbinding, and enveloping. In the *Jaïpur* advertisement in question these descriptions are divested of any of the subtle associations that they may have had in the past and are turned into a blatant and graphic declaration of captivity, bondage, and envelopment. A woman's naked back is photographed from her shoulder blades to a point just above the back of her knees. Her arms and hands, pulled back to her buttocks, are joined at the wrists by the *Jaïpur* bottle, which now serves not as a bracelet or as a ring, but as a handcuff.[13] The eros of bondage joins the eros of scent (and that of jewelry) to present a woman who has become, through perfume and bottle design, the locus for a scene of erotic fantasy. As a prisoner to perfume, she becomes a passive and obedient slave. Not only does *Jaïpur* envelop her in scent, it incarcerates her in that scent.

As no more than a beautiful objet d'art to be collected, possessed, and displayed the woman has become the prisoner of an image and an image system that present her not as the agent of erotic attraction, but as its object. In the *Jaïpur* advertisement it is not perfume per se, but the female body, so deeply scented that it vaporizes into perfume, that becomes Shakespeare's "prisoner pent in walls of glass." The *Jaïpur* ad projects an image that several perfume advertisements dramatize as well: namely, the mutation of the woman into the perfume she wears so that there is no longer any distinction between body and scent. The body *is* the perfume, and the perfume *is* the body as it exists in another dimension—spiritualized and sublimated—of reality. An even less subtle incarnation of the eros of bondage was incorporated into a series of controversial print and television advertisements produced in 1991 for Chanel's *Coco*. Designed by the artist and impresario Jean-Paul Goude the advertisement represented a woman (the French actress Vanessa Paradis) as a caged bird swinging on a perch in the television commercial and as a scantily clad, delicate bird of paradise, sitting atop a black pedestal and hugging an enormous bottle of *Coco* in the print advertisement. A mass of long, thin black tail feathers (from a Chinese pheasant) fans out from her lower back, while her ankle is delicately tied with a thick red rope meandering down the pedestal and off the picture frame. A bird-woman has literally been imprisoned and leashed; she is all the more captivating for having been made captive.[14]

When Hubert de Givenchy created *L'Interdit* (Forbidden) in 1957, it was not immediately released to the public. For several months prior to its official launch, some say it was a full year, only one woman in the world,

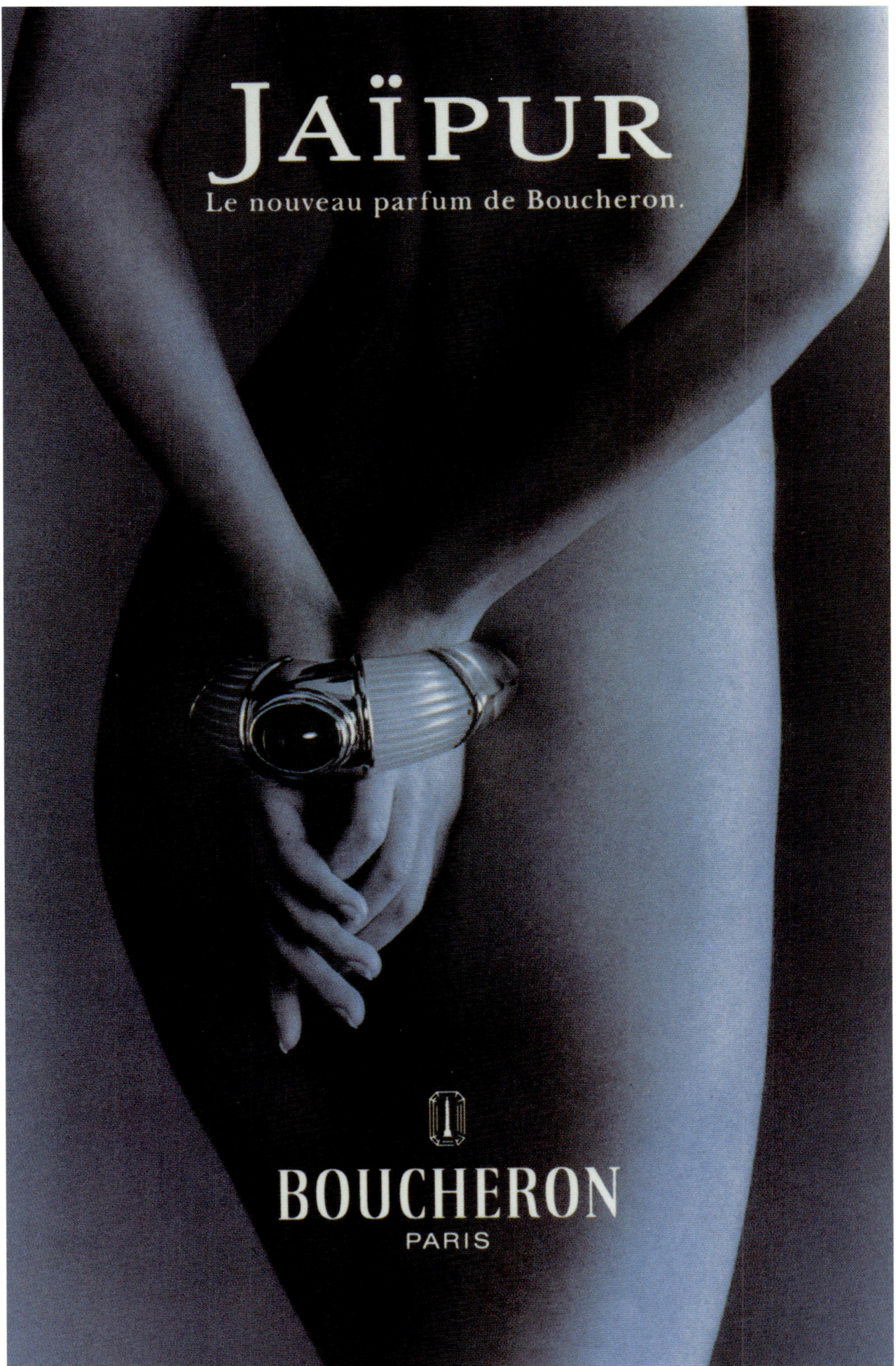

Fig. 119 To be a prisoner of perfume is to be captured and captivated by fragrance as revealed by this bracelet-bottle created by Boucheron, the jewelry company, for *Jaïpur*, 1995.

Previous pages:
Fig. 120 *L'Interdit*
(Forbidden), a
Givenchy perfume
inspired by Audrey
Hepburn in the 1950s,
is reinterpreted in a
more erotic yet still
elegant manner in this
Paris *Vogue* advertise-
ment from 1980 by
the innovative, often
surrealist, French
fashion photographer
Guy Bourdin
(1928–1991).

the legend goes, was allowed to perfume herself with it.
That woman was Givenchy's muse, the actress Audrey
Hepburn, who had made his couture famous in movies like
Sabrina (1954) and *Funny Face* (1957). According to one
story, the perfume had no name when Givenchy conceived
it for Hepburn. When he suggested to her, after the many
months she alone had worn it, that the time had come to
give the rest of the world a chance, Hepburn exclaimed,
"But, you can't; it's *forbidden*; it's my perfume." Hepburn's
incarnation of cool, refined elegance, her aura of sophisticated, reserved charm, and her expression of what Roland
Barthes has called the thematics of "woman as child,
woman as kitten" do not in and of themselves coincide
with the image of the forbidden, the "interdit," as associated, for example, with Eve in the Garden of Eden. Yet, an
advertising photograph for Givenchy (couture and perfume) published in the December 1980 issue of French
Vogue forces transgression and elegance into a cohabitation at once subtle and provocative (fig. 120).[15] Created by
Guy Bourdin, a fashion photographer whose eye for beauty
was never insensitive to a surrealist vision of sex, pain,
death—and humor—pulsing within that beauty, the photograph shows the fingers of a woman at once delicately
and forcefully pressing a bottle of *L'Interdit* into the hollowed lap of her leathery black dress beneath which her
legs are clearly parted. The placement and weight of the
bottle imprint onto the fabric of the dress an intriguing
pattern of palpable creases and folds, leaving little doubt
about the significance of the physical conjunction of lap,
hollow, fold, and bottle. Indeed, the image in and of itself
would, arguably, be unremarkable were it not for the label
on the bottle, whose simple letters spell out two words:
"L'Interdit" and "Givenchy." Clearly, the bottle serves as
a signifier pointing to the realm of the "forbidden." For
Bourdin a bottle of perfume is not just a bottle of perfume.
Despite the dressing up it receives through the elegant representation of fabric, color, couture, nail polish, perfume,
and calligraphy and the geometrical symmetry of line and
triangle, the eroticism of scent remains clearly literal.

The Seduction of Slogans

Different images, stories, and names have over the centuries
tapped into the reservoir of erotic associations that scent
possesses. A list of some of the names of perfumes from the
early 1900s to the present evokes, with different degrees of
subtle and not-so-subtle innuendo, the link between scent
and love and scent and seduction, confirming, as the perfumer Robert Ricci has succinctly declared, that "a perfume
is an act of love." Each name constitutes the embryonic
beginning of an amorous narrative, literally a *pre*-text,
which fantasy (usually, but not necessarily, male) is called
on to enhance and complete. From the years before World
War II come fragrances with decidedly suggestive names:

• *Eros* (Richard Hudnut, c. 1910)
• *Séduction* (Gellé Frères, c. 1913)
• *Fruit défendu* (Forbidden Fruit, Maison Rosine, 1914)
• *Premier Oui* (The First Yes, Arys, 1919)
• *Jouir* (To Enjoy, Fioret, 1920)
• *Ouvrez-moi* (Open Me, Lubin, 1920s)
• *My Sin* (Lanvin, 1925)
• *Moment suprême* (Patou, 1929)
• *Scandal* (Lanvin, 1932)
• *Tabu* (Dana, 1931)
• *Ardente Nuit* (Burning Night, Corday, 1931)
• *Audace* (Boldness / Impudence, Rochas, 1936)
• *Aphrodisia* (Fabergé, 1938).

Since the 1950s, erotic and sexual realities are conjured in
names no less suggestive or concise than those of earlier
decades, although such names are somewhat more evoca-
tive of the "artificial paradises" that perfumes can create:
• *Intimate* (Revlon, 1955)
• *L'Interdit* (Forbidden, Givenchy, 1957)
• *J'ai Osé* (I Dared, Guy Laroche, 1977)
• *Poison* (Dior, 1985)
• *Boudoir* (Vivienne Westwood, 1998)
• *Ce soir ou jamais* (Tonight or Never, Offenthal, 1927, and
   Anick Goutal, 1999)
• *Libertine* (Vivienne Westwood, 1990s)
• *Organza Indécence* (Organza Immodesty, Givenchy, 2000)
• *Volupté* (Delight, Oscar de la Renta, 1992)
• *Le Secret de Vénus* (Weil, 1996)
• *Rush* (Gucci, 1999)
• *Secret Signals* (Victoria's Secret, 1999)
• *Séxüal Pour Homme* (Michel Germain, 2002)
• *Sex One, Sex Two, Sex Three* (scented candles from Sonia
   Rykiel, 2000)
• *Crave* (Calvin Klein, 2002)
• *Sexy Graffiti* (Escada, 2002)
• *Basic Instinct* (Victoria's Secret, 2004).

Any modicum of romantic discretion or erotic subtlety
suggested by these names has been eliminated, however, by
a line of American perfumes named *Candies* (1999) whose
bold slogan "Anywhere you dare" has been matched by a
series of images leaving little to the imagination. In one ad
a woman opens a medicine cabinet overflowing with packets of condoms (and two bottles of *Candies* fragrance). In
another, a woman wearing black underwear and holding a
bottle of *Candies* sits astride a computer monitor while on
the screen a rocket (carrying the space shuttle) vertically
blasts off in a cloud of smoke. A third ad shows a man
pulling down the T-shirt of woman and spraying *Candies*
on to her revealed cleavage.[16]

In addition to these suggestive, evocative, and perhaps unsubtle names, each a narrative node unto itself for
an as yet unwritten story, certain perfumes carry appellations that already encapsulate narratives which are, so to
speak, ready-to-wear as well as ready-to-carry-away. When
a perfume is called *Chamade* (Guerlain, 1969), it evokes
surrender, and when it displays the word *Guet-Apens*

The woman opening her purse in this ad for Lubin's *Ouvrez-moi* (Open Me), 1936, could also be releasing into the air, as the ad declares, "memories of captivating summer fragrances and of the accord of violins and brasses." *Votre Beauté. Revue de la beauté féminine*, Paris, November 1, 1936.

This purse-shaped bottle for Lubin's *Ouvrez-moi* (Open Me), 1936, testifies to a desire to create a clever and humorous flacon as is seen as well in Lubin's earlier scent *Fumée* (Smoking), 1934, a perfume bottle disguised as a pack of cigarettes.

(Ambush, Guerlain, 1999) on its blue lantern-shaped bottle, it provokes images of entrapment. Or when it is known as *Ophélie* (Ophelia, Cardin, 1995), *Amazone* (Hermès, 1974), *Shéhérazade* (Jean Desprez, 1983), *Tristan & Yseult* (Cardin, 2000), *Le Styx* (Coty, 1911), or *Venezia* (Venice, Laura Biagiotti, 1992), it appropriates the mythic and poetic resonance—the ideological and cultural associations—such literary, historical, and geographical figures and realities possess in Western and Eastern societies. A scent with the name *Panthère* (Cartier, 1987) may call to mind the powerfully graceful, sleek, and stealthy movements of a stalking cat, but it evokes as well strategies of entrapment, for the panther was the only animal, so the ancients believed, to emit a perfumed odor attracting victims to its hiding place and thus to their deaths.[17]

Moreover, beyond the succinct, compact, poetically and erotically charged name of the perfume—a sexual phonetics whereby the two or three syllables of the name explode like a cry (*Fracas, Poison, Obsession, X-S, Fétiche, Balafre, Fever*), or caress like a whisper (*Senso, Sensi, Câline, Pleasures, Chant d'arômes, Promesse*), or soothe the spirit with a dream of ideal bliss (*L'Idéal, Truth, Joy, Happy, Eden, Eternity, Timeless, Euphoria*), or promise the passionate and fatal intensity of mad love (*Turbulences, Farouche, Volcan d'Amour, Chaos, Vertige, Yvresse, Pour Troubler, Excited, Tumulte, Addict*)—there exists another register of poetic and erotic evocativeness: namely, the laconic, haikulike slogan accompanying the perfume.[18]

Slogans: The Poetry of Scent and Story ❧

The eros of scent is intensified and concentrated—even before the fragrance has been smelled, since most consumers read an advertisement in a magazine or see one on television before they even get to a store and open the bottle—by slogans expressive of very different messages. They may predict, somewhat pretentiously perhaps, a better life for humankind—"One day tenderness will cover the earth" (*Anaïs, Anaïs*, Cacharel)—or declare the poetic power of silence and smell over that of language and visibility: "Sometimes words are not enough" (*Poême*, Lancôme). They may give personal advice—"Every woman deserves being first" (*First*, Cartier), "There is no life without excess" (*XS*, Paco Rabanne)—or offer a lesson in self-affirmation and confidence: "Alone, you know what is truly important" (*Knowing*, Estée Lauder); "She gets her way" (*Cabochard*, Grès); "The new perfume for insolent women" (*L'Insolent*, Charles Jourdan); "Because you are unique" (*Allure*, Chanel); "Today let's fall in love with the woman in the mirror . . . let's first love who we are" (*Today*, Avon). Perfume slogans may, moreover, promise women a new sexuality, independence, and autonomy—"The perfume

and let him react" (*Le Baiser*, Lalique); "For the seductress within" (*Pure Poison*, Dior). Finally, a slogan can call up fantasies of bliss, joy, and even transgression, as we have seen: "The perfume that goes far beyond" (*Aromatics Elixir*, Estée Lauder); "The forbidden perfume" (*Eden*, Cacharel); "A celebration of laughter . . . love . . . and intense happiness" (*Amarige*, an anagram for the French word "mariage" [marriage] by Givenchy).[19]

Some slogans present perfume as if it were a philosophy of life, "The perfume that makes you question the value of civilization" (*Coriandre*, Jean Couturier); or an existential teaching, "Life is more beautiful when one writes it oneself" (*Champs-Elysées*, Guerlain); or advice for personal renewal, "One must relearn everything" (*Premier jour*, Nina Ricci); or an acceptance of self so evident that only tautology can express it, "I am as I am" (*Cabotine*, Grès); or an irrefutable and anti-idealist truth of being, "The senses don't lie" (*Truth*, Calvin Klein); or, finally, an existential credo, "I sense, therefore I am" (*Sensi*, Armani). Moreover, perfume names can have a syntax of their own, coming together to form not only a sentence or a slogan, but a fable. Jacques Worth (grandson of Charles Frederick Worth, the "father" of modern couture) who, with the

A perfume or a series of fragrances can compose a story as Worth did over a ten-year span with five scents, the name of each one designating a new episode in an ongoing, although segmented, drama, which reads "Dans la Nuit" (bottle on left), "Vers le Jour," "Sans Adieu," "Je Reviens" (bottle on right), "Vers Toi" (In the Night / Just Before Dawn / Without Good-byes / I Come Back / To You).

for a new woman" (*Jaïpur Saphir*, Boucheron), "Boldness has its own number" (*Chanel No. 19*), "The secret world where every woman is a sun" (*24 Faubourg*, Hermès), "In you lies a fascinating power" (*Hypnôse*, Lancôme)—or offer them lessons in erotic comportment: "What is seduction, if not a man, a woman, and a perfume by Caron"; "Put it where you want to be kissed" (*Ici*, Coty); "Prick his heart

perfumer Maurice Blanchet, founded Parfums Worth in the 1920s, designed five perfumes over ten years, each name of which served as a fragment in a short, romantic, one-line poem evoking an irrepressible love: *Dans la Nuit* (1924), *Vers le Jour* (1925), *Sans Adieu* (1929), *Je Reviens* (1932), *Vers Toi* (1934) ("In the night . . . just before dawn . . . because I can't bear to say good-bye . . . I come back . . .

to you"). In a similar vein, Jean Patou launched three scents simultaneously in 1925 with names, considered provocative at the time, that narrate a highly charged, condensed story of love, one that moved fatally from infatuation to folly: *Amour Amour* (Love, Love), *Que sais-je? (*What do I know?*)*, *Adieu Sagesse* (Good-bye reason).[20]

Perfume names and perfume slogans are infused with dynamic narrative power. The fantasies and scenarios they evoke come ready-to-wear and ready-to-believe. "Every woman has a story," claims a Revlon advertisement for lipstick; "it's not how you tell it, it's how you live it" (V-NY, Sept. 2004). To use a cosmetic or a perfume is to enact, to live, the fantasy of the product which word, image, and a certain poetry have created. The new technology of microencapsulation, by which odor molecules are chemically bonded with paper or fabric to produce magazine scent strips or scented clothing, is, figuratively speaking, an old process, because perfumes have always encapsulated narrative "molecules," as it were. Like suits made from fabrics impregnated with microcapsules of lavender, pine, or peppermint, or pantyhose saturated with odor molecules of jasmine, lilac, and white musk—rubbed or touched they emit a fragrance soothing to the wearer—perfume names, whether those of brands like *Poison, After the Rain*, or *Paris*, or those of aromatic ingredients like ylang-ylang, bergamot, neroli, vetiver, galbanum, orris, opoponax, patchouli, olibanum, and labdanum, constitute an exotic language whose words compose an evocative poetry of scent and story, which desire alone can understand and enliven.[21]

Guerlain's Tales of Passion and Love: MITSOUKO, SHALIMAR, and SAMSARA

Perfume advertisements surround not just the name, the slogan, the bottle, the packaging, and the all-over image of a fragrance, but its very ingredients with an aura of provocative, lyrical, and erotic language. To the sometimes strange-sounding, Latinate, oriental, savory, and scientific names of fragrance ingredients, a precise dose of romanticism is almost always added. Enveloped in a halo of heightened lyricism and eroticism, the name of an ingredient loses its strangeness. It becomes a microencapsulated word, provoking amorous associations, recalling exotic places, suggesting rich combinations of freshness and effervescence, releasing a luminous radiance (like that of the sun), and evoking lazy warmth (in its jasmine notes), moderation (in its rose tones), purity (in the whiteness of its neroli and orange blossoms), and sensuality (in its tuberose), all of which are subject to continual change as the floral ingredients and their vapors interact. This is not a stable world, but one in constant metamorphosis. Perfume is much more than a liquid or an aroma; it is an *action*, more choreographic than symphonic, as the advertising copy for Guerlain's *Jardins de bagatelle* (1983) emphasizes:

> Alive and impulsive, [*Jardins de bagatelle*] casts a spell by means of the sensuality of the white flowers it is made from: the languid warmth of jasmine, the calculated charm of tuberose, the discreet presence of rose, the joyous freshness of airborne neroli. Its round, vanilla, and sugary *sillage* is stimulated by wood notes and benzoin, leaving in its wake the signature of a sparkling and sensual solar scent.[22]

The sheer number of adjectives in the description is impressive, as if they and other descriptive elements, like the allusion to the sun, were needed to lend lyrical meaning to names like jasmine, tuberose, rose, neroli, vanilla, and benzoin, which have, for the general consumer, only limited referential power. Surrounded by a host of associations, the name of each ingredient is both poeticized and eroticized. It is drawn into the symphony and the dance that the language—the advertising language—of the perfume creates. The action of *Jardins de Bagatelle* is carefully plotted; first, the perfume is described as casting a spell, then as joining feelings of languor, enchantment, discretion, freshness, and joy to the blend of floral components responsible for these sentiments. Finally, the action of the fragrance is imagined structurally, in terms of its several metamorphoses: its airborne flight, its change from liquid to vapor ("sillage"), its attainment of roundness, which gives it a perfect balance and a smooth, rich mellowness, and its lasting imprint ("signature"), a writing on the wind whereby perfume vaporizes into sunlight.

Another perfume, *Champs-Elysées* (1998), the first fragrance, as Guerlain boasts, to "master" the recalcitrant scent of mimosa, also sentimentalizes and anthropomorphizes its ingredients; that is, it highlights the emotional aura of mimosa, cassis, rose, lilac, and hibiscus, among others, and signals their sensual interplay with the human body and spirit. When the "icy transparence of rose" calms the heated "flight of tender, crushed mimosa leaves," *Champs-Elysées* explodes in "laughter." When cassis "harmonizes" with almond blossoms, "a touch of humor" appears. And when the "silky quivering" of mimosa flowers, each like a "miniature sun," "communicates an unheard-of sensuality to the skin," the perfume becomes a "long caress." Once the "carnal accents" of hibiscus mix with the soft aroma of almond wood, this caress becomes "pure pleasure."

Clearly, these floral components are described in a way that gives them not only a poetic and erotic suggestiveness but an emotional intensity. Ingredients in perfumes are described in terms of their emotional effects, which is to say their "actions," on a potential audience of consumers.

Certain fragrances have their own signature sensuality. Musk, civet, and ambergris are known aphrodisiac stimulants. Incense is believed to provoke a state of ecstasy as ancient Hindus, Egyptians, Hebrews, and Greeks recognized when they incorporated it into solemn rituals where it announced the odorous presence of the divine. For the Egyptians, who had borrowed it from the Hindus around 3600 B.C., incense was the sweat of the gods fallen to earth. Individual flowers as well have been associated—although quite often in subjective, idiosyncratic, and contradictory ways—with particular sensual and sensorial experiences: the rose with "trembling," the iris with "sensual expansiveness," the lily with "seductiveness," and jasmine with "giddiness." There is a long tradition, going back to the Persians and the Ottoman Empire, of sending coded messages to one's beloved through a choice of flowers known to hide symbolic meanings. Brought to Europe in the early eighteenth century, "the language of flowers," as it was called, was a symbolic syntax of love. The first book about this floral language appeared in France in 1818. During the Victorian period ladies used code books and flower dictionaries to decipher the symbolism of the floral messages sent by their beaus. Purple lilacs meant "my heart is yours," tulips "you are irresistible," poppies "my passion is delicate," sweet William "I am your slave," forget-me-nots "don't forget me," and so on.[23]

Of Marie Antoinette and Scheherazade

In print, on television, and almost everywhere one turns, the image with which perfume clothes itself seems to be that of contradiction. Even the historical event that *Jardins de Bagatelle* recalls is layered with ironic and poignant paradox. The "Bagatelle" is a small château in the Bois de Boulogne on the outskirts of Paris. Its construction in 1777 was due to a bet between Marie Antoinette and the comte d'Artois, brother of Louis XVI and himself destined for the throne (as Charles X in 1824). Walking in the Bois—before the Revolution it was already a celebrated spot for amorous rendezvous—with Marie Antoinette, the sister-in-law with whom he may or may not have been having an affair, the count wagered that on the site of a ruined hut he could construct a small château in less than ten weeks. Marie Antoinette accepted the bet, which she would shortly lose, for the château took only sixty-four days to build. Guerlain's advertising copy for *Jardins de Bagatelle* contrasts the grandness of the bet—the impetuousness, insanity, and arrogance it represents, a folly at once grand and petty—with the insignificance of the construction: a mere nothing, a "bagatelle." It goes on to suggest that such excessive signs of passionate love can arise from such mere "nothings"—a simple walk in the park, a momentary whim, an infatuation with one's sister-in-law—and, conversely, that an object as insignificant as a perfume can give continued life to such historical fact. The château of

the Bagatelle, while itself a mere footnote (a "bagatelle") to pre-revolutionary French history, especially considering that the ancien régime had only twelve more years of life before the advent of the Revolution and the Terror, is nevertheless, as the *Jardins de Bagatelle* press release declares,

> One of those sweet and dizzying follies History abounds in. Follies that are not spoken of but can be read, inscribed in a landscape, engraved in a garden, immortalized in a perfume; one of those follies only great men can accomplish, only great passions can inspire, born from a nothing, from an improbable desire, from a *bagatelle* . . . Symbol of a wildly romantic excess (Guerlain, "Le Romantisme est un bouquet . . .").

The encapsulated, ready-to-wear narratives of perfume advertising are often linked to exotic, legendary names like *Mitsouko, Shalimar, Nahéma, Samsara,* and *Mahora,* which all happen to be fragrances created by the house of Guerlain in 1919, 1925, 1979, 1989, and 2001 respectively.[24] Advertising copy for *Mitsouko,* a word meaning mystery (and, incidentally, the preferred perfume of Serge Diaghilev, the director of the Ballets Russes), tells the story of the wife of Admiral Togo, the commander of the Japanese fleet during the Russian-Japanese War—the story is taken from the novel, *La Bataille,* by Claude Farrère published in 1921—who falls so much in love with an English naval officer that she does not hesitate a moment to "follow her desires to their very end" and to enter that "voluptuous universe where the desire to be possessed is more intense than possession itself." As for *Nahéma,* it was designed by Jean-Paul Guerlain to offer women the grace and softness of "an enveloping femininity." It is a fragrance for the "woman's woman," whose refinement and sensuality have made her expert in "this game of seduction whereby one surrenders oneself without ever giving the feeling that one has surrendered entirely." Once again, paradox is the sine qua non of feminine mystery, an ambivalence reflected, as is often the case, in the perfume's name. *Nahéma* is, according to Guerlain's advertising, inspired by the fundamental "duality of the woman," as recounted by Scheherazade in the *Arabian Nights.* The princess Nahéma, a woman possessed of enigmatic intensity and of unplumbed depths of passion, stands in contrast to her twin, princess Mahané, a woman of equal beauty, but whose soft, warm, compassionate, and tender personality offers an opposite, less sensually aggressive, image of femininity.[25]

Samsara, Nirvana, and the Shalimar Gardens

While *Mitsouko,* a chypre-based fragrance heavily scented with wood moss and peach, alludes to the story of an

"Cabochard" means stubborn, strong willed, like its creator, Madame Grès, who after the war began a career as a fashion designer. Following a trip to India, she initiated a line of perfumes, but never did she forget her couture past as the bow surrounding this bottle of her chypre-based fragrance, *Cabochard*, 1959, reveals.

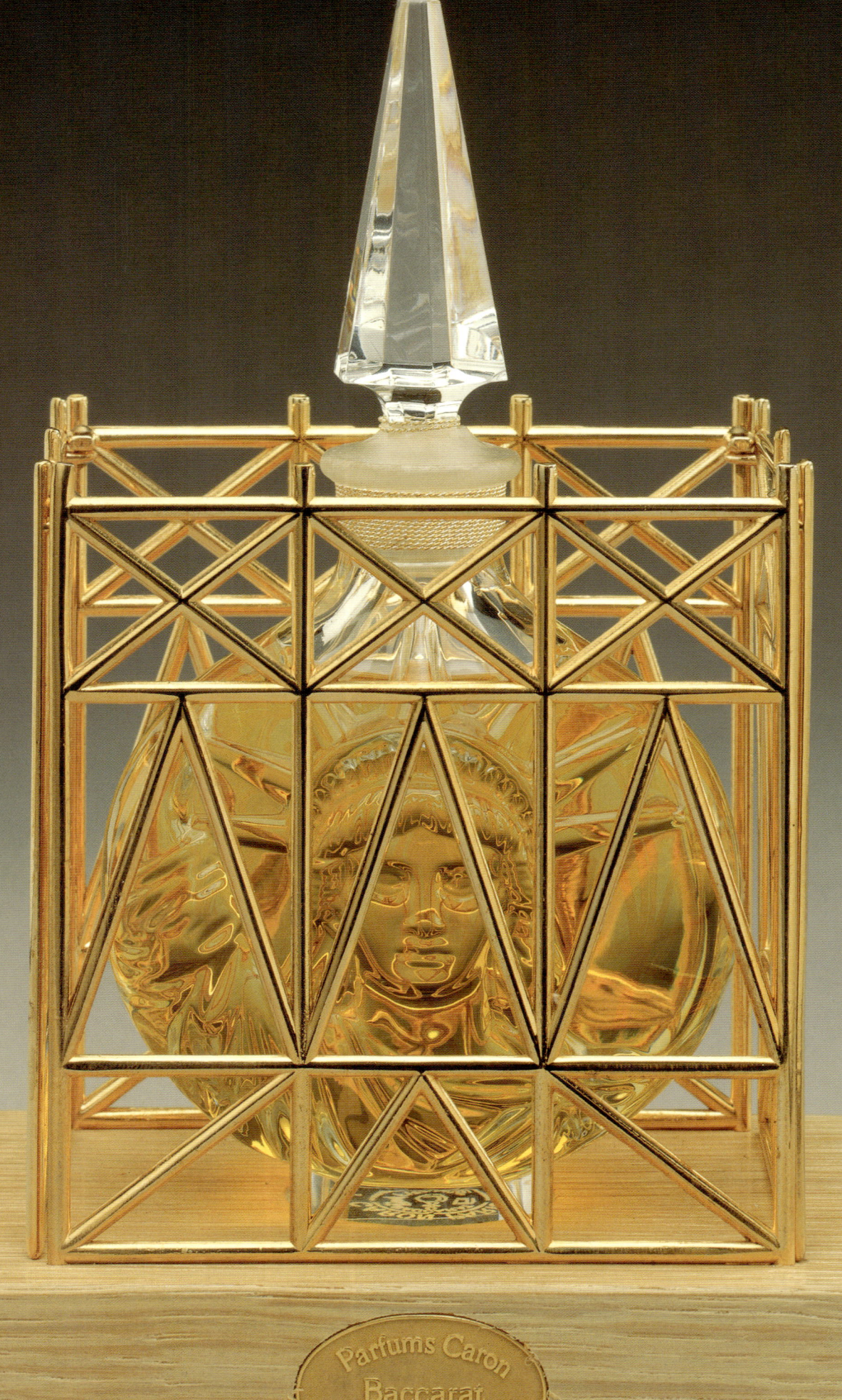

impossible love between an Englishman and a faithful Japanese wife; and while *Shalimar* evokes the sad tale of a dead wife who once walked with her husband, a shah, through the Indian gardens near the Taj Mahal; and while *Nahéma* (meaning "daughter of fire"), a woody, fruity perfume with aggressive notes, alludes to the legend of a willful princess with an enigmatic and passionate temperament; it is the name *Samsara*—from a Sanskrit word evoking spiritual renewal, eternal rebirth, and the endlessly turning wheel of life—that is expressive more of an idea than of a story. *Samsara* invokes a philosophical way of being in the world: the notion, according to Guerlain's publicity, of "an imaginary, sacred, mysterious place at the juncture of East and West . . . the symbol of harmony and of the absolute interaction [*osmosis*] between a woman and her perfume . . . a spiritual journey leading to serenity and inward contemplation." Dominated by the scents of sandalwood and jasmine *Samsara* is associated, from Guerlain's reconception of the idea, with the experience of the absolute, of nirvana (a word with which it shares a final syllable), and of perfection as its slogan suggests: "A few drops of *Samsara*, a few drops of eternity." The red-glass bottle, modeled after the silhouette of a Khmer dancer from the Musée Guimet in Paris, whose hands are clasped in a gesture of offering, invokes the fullness of being and the flowering of femininity. The stopper, in accord with the overarching imagistic associations of serenity, harmony, elegance, mysticism, and exoticism that the constellation of name (*Samsara* with its weighty consonants followed by airy vowels), bottle, and scent (an "oriental amber") seeks to establish, has been fashioned to represent the eye of the Buddha, symbol of the meditation, in this instance more odorous than visual, that will lead to detachment and reawakening. It is not clear how the sensuality of the perfume—and *Samsara* is a fragrance that leaves a remarkably heavy and long-lasting sillage—will in fact lead to a transcending of the senses, something that Buddhism does indeed seek to accomplish, or how the renunciation of worldly pleasures leading to Buddhist enlightenment squares with the approximately $70 million Guerlain spent to launch *Samsara* in 1989.[26]

In fact, the Tibetan Buddhist concept of *samsara* seems to contradict the positive, blissful, life-enhancing values Guerlain's interpretation of the term works to establish. The needs of advertising trump historical and philosophical truths, for the notion of "Samsara" in Mahayana Buddhism is, in reality, nearly the opposite of Guerlain's reading. The Buddhist worldview posits a universe in constant flux and suffering, a cosmic reality from which no being can escape and in which one experiences unrelenting and wrenching rebirth through "beginning and endless time." This is the state of "samsara," "the churning sea of cyclic existence in which beings are ceaselessly thrown about like tide-wrack," a condition of endless and painful rebirth and death. One is "born and born again endlessly into *samsara*," a late-fourteenth-century lama writes, "to suffer without breakthrough its three sorrows," which are desire, aversion, and ignorance, in particular the ignorance of the illusory nature of the self. *Samsara*, or ordinary life, is a "dreary round of perpetual rebirth in one or another of several different states" characterized by six forms of existence: hell-beings, hungry ghosts, animals, human beings, demi-gods, and gods. Karma means rebirth within *samsara*, and those who accumulate good karma are reborn

into a higher, more pleasant state within the samsaric world, while those with bad karma fall into one of the lower, more painful states of existence. Buddhist philosophy encourages escape from this cycle of karma and rebirth through entry into nirvana, the state of enlightenment devoid of all division and separation, which offers the only way out of the unending repetition of suffering and chaos that is *samsara*. Nirvana, Geoffrey Samuel writes, is the "cessation of every passion, of every thought," especially as they conflict within *samsara*.[27] Considering the limited knowledge a majority of European and American consumers might have of the philosophical and religious subtleties of Tibetan Buddhism, Guerlain takes liberties with the concept of "samsara," preferring to substitute for its allusions to torment, chaos, abyss, ignorance, illusion, and unending, repetitive change images of love, serenity, harmony, contemplation, and spiritual renewal—experiences perhaps more relevant to the blissful state of nirvana. Why did Guerlain decide to change the traditional definition of *samsara* in its marketing for *Samsara*, the perfume? Guesswork is required. Perhaps, there was the need, as seems likely, for an unknown, exotic word with strong poetic resonance. "Samsara" is perfect for the role. Its one long vowel ("a"), repeated three times in conjunction with "s," "m," and "r" consonants, gives the word a gentle and airy sound like the drawn-out sonority of a hum or a chant. Perhaps, "Nirvana," a term closer to the experience that Guerlain wished to suggest, may have seemed too trite and too well known to serve as a synonym for bliss. Finally, the existence of *Nirvana*, a perfume created by Bichara around 1913 and described by a woman's magazine of the time as "this heavenly spell so deserving of its name" (Delbourg-Delphis, 72), may have worked against the reappearance of the word on a perfume label.

In all these names, but especially that of *Shalimar* (1925), a myth, a philosophical idea, or a narrative, hardly known to the general public at the time of the perfume's debut, becomes part of the very image that the fragrance attempts to embody and, of course, to offer for consumption. Not only is the myth or story used to sell the scent; it becomes the narrative armature upon which the advertising, the slogan, the bottle, and the packaging are hung. Image and design depend on a story that needs to be taught to the consuming public at the same time the product, i.e., the perfume, is introduced. Publicity and pedagogy coincide. Eventually, as has happened most successfully with *Shalimar,* whose image, reputation, and mythic status as a "classic" fragrance—one of the five great perfumes of the twentieth century—have made it popular among at least four generations of women, the scent and the myth become one. As the product becomes a classic, the myth associated with it sinks its roots into the culture. "Say Shalimar" as an ad from the 1980s declares, and there will come to mind not only the unique bottle with its "batwing" form, its sapphire-blue, fan-shaped stopper, and its singular blend of bergamot, jasmine, iris, and vanilla

wrapped in balsamic notes, which impart to *Shalimar* its distinctively exotic, smoldering, and sensual fragrance, but a full-fledged narrative, hovering over bottle and perfume alike.[28]

Shalimar makes reference in name and aroma to the gardens of Shalimar (a Sanskrit word meaning "the Abode or Hall of Love") located in Agra, India and constructed in 1619 by the Mogul emperor Shah Jahangir. *Shalimar* also alludes to a love story and the myth it expresses. Eight years after the laying out of the Shalimar gardens, Shah Jahan, having succeeded his father to the imperial throne, devotes many blissful, quiet hours walking in these gardens with the favorite of his several wives, Mumtaz Mahal. Tragically, she dies in childbirth three years later. Grief-stricken, the Shah puts thousands of laborers to work for fourteen years constructing a tomb (the Taj Mahal) for his beloved wife, a monument Rabindranath Tagore once described as rising "like a solitary tear suspended on the cheek of time." History and myth join in the image that *Shalimar*, the perfume, puts forth. Here, eternal love and eternal death are commemorated; unending memory and permanent loss coexist. Even the bottle itself, with its upwardly arcing lines evocative of the surge of water in the many fountains of the Shalimar gardens and with its exquisite fan-shaped stopper of the deepest blue, "the color of sky at dusk when the sun disappears behind the horizon," has an "architecture," fusing events that reappear with those that disappear: the memory of a love, reasserting itself and climbing heavenward like a fountain, a *jet d'eau*, and the mourning of a loss which, in tandem with the dying sun, sinks again into oblivion. Like perfume, which is after all a liquid immediately changed into vapor, a body or a skin transformed into evanescent air, and a sign effaced and replaced by a trace, *Shalimar* embodies the myth and reality of presence and absence, the fiction and truth of possession and loss. It joins together the scent of Eros and the aroma of Thantos.[29]

Orgasm, Fetidness, and Death

The popularity of perfumes with enduring sillages, like *L'Origan* (Coty, 1905)—its "fauvist sensibility" made it the first "violent" scent of the century—*Shalimar* (1925), *Opium* (1977), and *Samsara* (1989), has over the twentieth century waxed and waned. A cycle of heavy, captivating scents has, in reaction to the styles of the time, yielded to lighter, more discreet versions of established fragrances, as happened in the 1990s and into the first decade of the twenty-first century, for example, with Guerlain's launching of *Un Air de Samsara* (1995) as a lighter, less aggressive version of *Samsara* and Dior's creating *Tendre Poison* (1994), *Hypnotic Poison* (1998), and *Pure Poison* (2004) as alternatives to its spicier, more opulent *Poison* (1985). One journalist noted that women had become "worried about being provocative, so the majority of fragrances were sporty, light or bright—completely antithetical to traditional perfume." Similarly in the nineteenth century, light, simple, single-floral scents replaced the headier, aggressive, more erotic fragrances popular with Josephine and her entourage during the first decade or so of the century. During the Restoration (1815–1830) and into the years of the July Monarchy (1830–1848), when manuals of savoir-faire and handbooks on the art of living insisted on the importance of cleanliness and purity, only floral-scented waters and oils or simple eaux de cologne were tolerated. Strong animalic scents, like musk, ambergris, and civet, were strictly banned, and if they were worn it was only by women of questionable morals. An issue of the newspaper *Le Messager des modes et de l'industrie* from 1853 identifies ambergris and musk as "the primary perfume ingredients for women of easy virtue (*cocottes*)." The practice of wearing musk-scented gloves, an article in the *Encyclopédie* of 1765 noted, had suffered a decline because of their violent odor. Mercier, the chronicler of social customs in the decade preceding the Revolution, noted this olfactory turnaround as well; the elegant man, he wrote, "does not reek of ambergris." And rarely put off by the presence of a woman, Casanova came close to fainting before the appearance of the elderly Marquise Ursé "whose musk was perceivable from twenty paces away."[30]

Nineteenth-century style dictated light, innocent fragrances, as Madame Celnart, author of a small manual on perfume (1833), indicated in precise and assertive detail: "Strong odors like musk, ambergris, orange blossom, tuberose, and other similar scents should be completely avoided." Those who apply an exaggerated amount of perfume, she warned, will suffer from "pallor, thinness, shadows under the eyes, dejection, and nervous tremors." In her treatise *The Arts of Beauty*, written in mid-century to criticize the use of cosmetics and to advocate a natural look, the actress Lola Montez made unreservedly clear her opposition to a face artificially "encrusted [with] mould" and "as expressionless as that of a painted mummy ... There is no man who does not shrink back with disgust from the idea of kissing a pair of painted lips." The Comtesse de Bradi, in her handbook on the art of living published in 1838 and much consulted during the Second Empire, offered similar advice. While the use of prepared perfumes was out of the question, she counseled, the application of scents that "are spread by natural flowers seem to me very permissible, when they are in no way disturbing." Yet, other voices did not express even this much understanding. "Misuse of perfumes gives birth to all neuroses ... Hysteria, hypochondria, and melancholia are its most usual effects," wrote a Dr. Rostan in 1826. Continual use of these base and penetrating scents could lead to nervous irritability, immorality, debauchery, and, worst of all, feminism. Even as late as the early years of the twentieth century, Octave Uzanne imagines a fictional conversation between Florise, a highly sensitive "olfactophile" who calls herself a "suffragette in the politics of delicate odors," with her uncle, a perfume expert, in which the young woman firmly rejects heavy perfumes; the aroma of patchouli she finds particularly "nauseating." "An odor must not attack," she observes; "it must stroll along at a slow pace."[31]

Obviously, perfume had to be kept at a respectful distance from the body (a remoteness that the scented handkerchief adroitly negotiated) in keeping with the protocols of social interaction and the unstated if not unconscious attitudes toward the status of the senses among the nineteenth-century bourgeoisie. Sensory hierarchy was mimetically reflective of social hierarchy. In fact, in matters of love, strategies of seduction depended, as Corbin notes, on distance: namely, on "a visual caress, a trail of perfume, in sum, an assumed delicacy in the use of the senses." Moreover, the difference between the prestigious, "social" senses (sight and hearing), which presumed a certain separation between perceiver and object of perception, on the one hand, and the more "animal" senses (touch, taste, and smell), which depended on a more direct, immediate, and sensual contact with the perceiver, on the other, followed strict class lines. Workers came to know their worlds of poverty, filth, and toil directly through taste, touch and smell, while the bourgeoisie depended to a greater extent on sight and hearing in order to move through their more refined and delicate social milieus.[32]

Musk as Opiate

This particular change in aromatic taste and perfume fashion was but one of many moments of oscillation between light and dark, floral and animalic, and innocent and sensual fragrances that have characterized perfume history. It may be the case, even today, that every fifty years, as Corbin observed of the eighteenth and nineteenth centuries, "musk and ambergris unleash ... short counteroffensives" against their floral rivals. Despite the nineteenth century's general hostility toward animal-derived fragrances and despite its moralistic attempt to convert the eros of scent into an agape of scent, there were, as described in chapters 2, 3, and 4, several avant-garde writers, like Baudelaire and Huysmans, who along with the perfumer Rimmel, despised their society's "deep aversion to perfume." Edmond de Goncourt was such a writer. Fervently of the opinion that "certain odors seem to have been composed to deepen the enchantment of amorous embraces," he published an ironic, sometimes misogynistic novel, *Chérie*, in 1883 to demonstrate the orgasmic potency of perfume.[33]

The heroine of *Chérie*, Marie Chérie Haudancourt, is obsessed with perfumes, as are other upper-class Parisian women of her acquaintance, all avidly scenting their clothes, hair, and skin with "the strongest and most *nauseating* odors that the perfume industry can distill from animal and vegetal matter," Goncourt observes. Chérie lives continuously in a cloud of scent composed of an "elusive blend of spirits of tuberose, orange blossoms, jasmine, vetiver, opoponax, violet, tonka bean, ambergris, sandalwood, bergamot, neroli, rosemary, benzoin, verbena, and patchouli." From this cocktail of scents she derives a sublime sensation of felicity, well-being, and from time to time "something resembling a nearly imperceptible spasm," not unlike the physical hunger and narcotic stupor of the opium-eater: "Chérie lifted herself up, deeply and passionately inhaling once again the scent, in a movement that pushed her chest—and tilted her head ever so slightly—backwards, her eyes closing with pleasure" (223–24). Like a knight searching for the Grail, Chérie ardently longs to have in her possession a grain of musk; in this desire she resembles Josephine, whose overuse of musk made her rooms at Malmaison nearly uninhabitable to Napoleon. When Chérie purchases this tiny, precious substance, she keeps it in a small gold-lacquered box with her jewelry. Chérie's "addiction" to perfumes finds its erotic apotheosis, however, in a scene of sensual bliss and vertiginous unconsciousness akin to orgasm, where body and soul, touched and penetrated by scent, undergo a distillation into vapor and air. Goncourt literally transforms the woman into perfume, for scent, as the novelist Tom Robbins would write exactly a century later, is "the medium by which the lady magically usurps the sexual powers of the blossom." For Chérie these moments of floral appropriation occur almost every morning. Upon awakening she takes a vaporizer and sprays the scent of white heliotrope under the covers of her bed. She then buries her head under the sheets, taking particular care not to let any of the scent escape from the now hermetically sealed bed:

> She took inexpressible pleasure [*jouissance*] in feeling herself penetrated, caressed, refreshed by the fragrant moistness of the evaporation into which it seemed to her that, although still not fully awake, she half fainted, taking leave of the world, as if her being had been volatilized into perfume, into a fine odor. Finally, she drowsed off again, finding in sleep a sensual pleasure where mental rapture and a feeling of suffocation converged (225–26).[34]

Unconscious of time and world, rendered comatose through bliss, and enraptured by an almost narcotic scent, Chérie lies in a kind of fugue state, which has a certain resemblance to what Des Esseintes, the poet-perfumer of Huysmans's *Against the Grain,* also experiences, although Chérie's scent-provoked orgasm is considerably more pleasurable than what Des Esseintes's body ultimately feels. Besieged by headaches, dizziness, and hallucinations from a neurotic disorder occasioned by a mysterious and imaginary odor of frangipani, which only he, among the inhabitants of his château, can smell, Des Esseintes works feverishly to invent a fragrance that, by means of a kind of

"nasal homeopathy" which only art, imagination, and genius could possibly create, will mask if not neutralize the offending odor. Yet, despite the new syntax of scents Des Esseintes assembles—the harmonious refrains, the melodious aromatic stanzas, the sonorous scented phrasings, the recurring motifs, the balanced accords and notes, the "fragrant orchestration" inspiring him to blend styrax, jonquil, coal tar, linden, and "new mown hay" with allspice, sandalwood, jasmine, hawthorn, and verbena in the hope of giving musical, lyrical form to his "poem" of fragrance—the obsessive odor of frangipani returns. It invades the countryside around his castle, saturates his rooms, and brings him to the brink of unconsciousness, similar to Chérie's in its intensity, but ever so different in the painful misery it causes. Paralysis, unconsciousness, and death are no strangers to perfume, for suddenly "assaulting his overtaxed nostrils, discomposing afresh his ruined nerves, and throwing him into such a state of prostration . . . [Des Esseintes] collapsed in a faint, close to death, on to the wooden sill of the window" (101–02).

The Fragrance of Slippers

The infiltration of one's being by perfume, the dizzying, sometimes deathlike, loss of consciousness, and the vaporization of the self as the body loses the sense of its physical limits characterize the eros of scent. The great nineteenth-century novelist, Gustave Flaubert, felt it, as these lines from a letter written to his mistress Louise Colet on the night of August 6–7, 1846 indicate: "I look at your slippers, handkerchief, your hair, your portrait; I reread your letters; I smell their musky odor. If you only knew what I'm feeling right now! . . . In the night, my heart expands and a rose of love pierces it. A thousand kisses, a thousand, everywhere, *everywhere.*" And two nights later, caressing Louise's slippers, he writes her that "I smell them; they give off the scent of verbena, and your odor expands my soul." It is not only the odor of her slippers that evokes Louise's imaginary presence. Flaubert surrenders to fantasies provoked by memories of her other scents, to which he admits in a long letter of August 11: "I see as if in a dream into the folds of your dress, into the airy curls of your hair . . . Oh, do they smell good! If you knew how I think of . . . your shoulders; I love to inhale their scent!" Louise's fragrant invasion of his soul is repeated a month later when he tells her that the aroma of the perfumed writing paper of her most recent letters "arises to my nose, and the scent of your caressing phrases pierces my heart." Yet, there are times when Flaubert cannot decide whether he prefers Louise perfumed or unperfumed: "Tell me," he writes the night of August 14–15, "when you do use verbena, do you put some on your handkerchiefs, on your nightgown? But no, don't perfume yourself; the finest scent is you, the exhaling of your very being." Clearly, Flaubert, like Baudelaire and like Chérie, is a lover of smells, (*un olfactif*). So it is not surprising that the princess Salammbô, given her exotic lineage (in Flaubert's novel of 1862 of the same name), and Mâtho, the enemy warrior enamored of her, would be as well. Salammbô's apartments are filled with incense burners (*cassolettes*) from which emanate the odors of nard, incense, cinnamon, and myrrh. When she steals into Mâtho's tent to retrieve the sacred veil he has stolen, she wears earrings made of hollow pearls filled with a perfume that slowly drips onto her shoulders, fascinating Mâtho, who is as spellbound by her fragrance as Flaubert was bewitched by Louise's:

> A heaving of his total being pushed him towards her. He would have sought to envelop her, to absorb her, to drink her . . . His nostrils flared to better inhale the perfume flowing from her person. It was an indefinable, cool emanation and yet one that made his head swim like perfumed vapor rising from a *cassolette*. It smelled of honey, pepper, incense, roses, and another odor still.[35]

The body of the woman is sublimated into liquid and air; it is prepared to be absorbed, drunk, and inhaled by the bewitched male, a ritual of penetration and invasion that affects both women (Chérie) and men (Mâtho). "The use of perfumes, by man as well as woman," writes Shaykh Umar ibn Muhammad al-Nefzawi, the sixteenth-century writer of *The Perfumed Garden*, an erotic manual, "excites to copulation," reiterating a belief, acknowledged as far back as the ancient Egyptians, in the sexual potency of perfume.[36] But under the Eros of scent lies the hidden, yet enveloping note of Thanatos. The loss of consciousness, the swooning, the invasion by material substances, now airborne, into the recesses of self and spirit, the effacement of physical and bodily boundaries, the suspension of time and space, and the feeling of a vaporized self flowing into a formless, abstract world—elements characteristic of the poetic and narrative representation of perfume—point as well to the symbiotic co-presence of sexuality and death in the mise-en-scène of scent.

The Perversion of Perfume

In the wake of Sade and Freud, the French philosopher Georges Bataille was sensitive to the fetid odor of mortality, decomposition, and sexuality hidden within all representations of beauty. In this respect, he follows in the footsteps of Baudelaire, who had perceived in the rotting, worm-infested carcass ("Une Charogne") of an animal lying in the road the future image of his beloved (I:31–32). Since perfume compositions combine scents extracted from ephemeral flowers and plants with those removed from animals, in particular from glands or sacs found near the animals' sexual organs, and since these animalic scents serve as "fixatives," holding in place within the

architecture of a fragrance the top and middle notes and giving to the base note its singular tenacity, many contradictory forces, it may be suggested, coexist in a scent: humanity and animality, spirituality and materiality, beauty and corruption. Bataille would agree, although with his usual tendency toward hyperbole, he would see in this conjunction of the sublime and the "base" the very nature of human eroticism. "In the union of bodies, human beauty reveals the opposition between humanity at its most pure and the repulsive animality of organs," he writes.[37] Love and whatever inspires love—be it beauty, art, poetry, even perfume—are sublimations beneath which lie pain, obscenity, depletion, bestiality, baseness, and death: "At the opposite pole of spirituality lies an exuberant sexuality that signifies the tenacity of animal life in us" (*L'Erotisme*, 159). Beauty, which awakens the longing for what is sublime and otherworldly, suddenly tears the veil away from its face revealing the reality of the ugliness and materiality it hides (*L'Erotisme*, 158). Simultaneous with the spasms of orgasm are loss, loneliness, expenditure, and the paroxysm of what he calls "the little death" (i.e., ejaculation): "The spasms of death and those of pleasure are alike"; "the most tender kisses have the aftertaste of a rat." Wherever eroticism is evoked and wherever it is stimulated, even by the sensual, seductive air of an erogenous perfume, death follows; this is because "the movement of love, at its utmost, is the movement of death" (*L'Erotisme*, 47).

In his essay on "The Language of Flowers" Bataille demystifies a predilection in Western culture for the representation of human endeavor as an ideal and sublime experience, one that silences the death rattle and masks the death's head. "If one says that flowers are beautiful," he writes, "it is because they seem to *conform to what must be*; in other words they represent, as flowers, the human ideal."[38] Yet flowers (as was seen in Chapter 3) can be hideous and perverse in appearance, since "even the most beautiful flowers are spoiled in their centers by hairy sexual organs." The apparent elegance of a flower only masks its inner sordidness, covers over "the filth of its organs," and disguises the fragility of its corolla, so

Flaubert's association of slippers and scent finds a twentieth-century reinterpretation in this porcelain cornucopia arising from a gold slipper or shoe and ending in a floral bouquet stopper as designed for Jean Desprez's *Grande Dame*, 1939.

299

easily and indecently touched by rot and a "garish withering." Emerging from dirt, from "the stench of the manure pile," and giving, as it climbs vertically and heavenward in a "flight of angelic and lyrical purity," the illusion of having escaped the base matter of its origin, the flower becomes the symbol of a failure, of an "Icarian" fall. Ashes to ashes and dust to dust, what is most ideal is "rapidly reduced to a wisp of aerial manure." While the flower's visible parts are nobly elevated, the ignoble and sticky roots wallow in the ground, loving rottenness just as leaves love light" ("Language," 12–13).

The Stink of Perfume

If the language of flowers is that of death and eroticism, then the language of scents—given the aura of sweetness, purity, romance, and beauty enveloping them and the technical processes of sublimation, distillation, and vaporization producing them (they are called "essences" and "spirits" after all) is a language of both Eros and Thanatos. Many perfumes have carried and still carry the names of flowers or plants:

• *Fougère Royal* (Royal Fern, Houbigant, 1882)
• *Fleur d'Italie* (Guerlain, 1884)
• *Vera Violetta* (Roger & Gallet, 1892)
• *Jasmin de Corse* (Corsican Jasmin, Coty, 1906)
• *Muguet* (Lily of the Valley, Guerlain, 1908)
• *Narcisse noir* (Black Narcissus, Caron, 1911)
• *Héliotrope* (Coty, 1913)
• *La Violette Ambrée* (Amber Violet, Coty, 1914)
• *Mimosa* (Caron, 1917)
• *Géranium d'Espagne* (Spanish Geranium, 1925)
• *La Fête des Roses* (The Feast of Roses, Caron, 1936)
• *Gardénia Passion* (Annick Goutal, 1989)
• *Tubéreuse Criminelle* (Guilty Tuberose, Serge Lutens, 1999).
• *Pavot d'argent* (Silver Poppy, Roger & Gallet, 2005).

To apply Bataille's demystifying logic to these floral-based fragrances is to see perfume as not only a substance that establishes presence but as one that in the same act of creation initiates decomposition, dissipation, and loss. "As the most sublime sound borders on noise," the philosopher Michel Serres writes, "so the most intense perfume touches the dead and their putrefaction." We have already seen in the example of Goncourt's Chérie, and to a lesser extent in that of Flaubert's Mâtho, how the druglike dominance of a perfume causes human power, energy, and lucidity to surrender to stupor, passivity, and befuddlement. If flowers are inherently eaten away by mortality and if the perfect homage to a rose is the Marquis de Sade tossing petals into a ditch filled with liquid manure (Bataille, "Language," 14), then perfume must not hide the death it inaugurates behind such absolute names as *L'Idéal* (Houbigant, 1900), *Eternity* (Calvin Klein, 1988), *Eden* (Cacharel, 1994), *L'Infini* (Caron, 1970), *Sublime* (Patou, 1992), *Présence*

(Houbigant, 1933), and *Je Reviens* (I Return, Worth, 1932).[39] Although many perfumes are named after love, like *Amour Amour* (Patou, 1925), *Amor Amor* (Cacharel, 2004), and *Rosamor* (Oscar de la Renta, 2004), it will be a long while before the word "absence" or "loss" or even "death" appears on any one of them.

As further confirmation of the coexistence of purity and fetidness, of perfume and stench, and of love and disgust, as Bataille conceived of this relationship, one need only look to the chemistry of perfume creation. Some of the best perfumes are "erogenic" (i.e., they provoke erotic attraction) because they contain, as Stoddart observes, "urinous, fecal or animal notes but at a concentration which does not intrude upon the higher notes." Musk, for example, gives off a slight odor of ammonia mixed with urine, while civet has both urinous and fecal overtones, which undiluted are unbearable but once diluted create a feeling of warmth. Flowers as well have disagreeable—even fecal—odors; nevertheless, they can be sexually arousing. Jasmine contains a high proportion of indole, also found in the feces of carnivores; it forms the basis for skatole, which is the substance that makes human excrement stink. At low concentrations indole has a pleasant jasmine aroma. Moreover, a perfume's top notes, most often floral in nature, are nevertheless formed, as Stoddart, in agreement with Bataille, points out, "from the sexual secretions of flowers, produced to attract animals for the purposes of cross-pollination and often formulated as mimics of the animals' own sex pheromones." Similarly, a perfume's middle notes, usually derived from flowers and from gum or balsamic resins like styrax, benzoin, nard, incense, and opoponax, are composed of "materials which have odors not unlike those of sex steroids." The base notes, composed often of such animalic scents as ambergris, musk, civet, and castoreum, are "mammalian sex attractants with a distinctly urinous or fecal odor."[40]

The scent of Eros moves throughout the space of a perfume and is found at every level of its structure. It is the ghost in the machine, a kind of "phantom of the opera" hiding behind the decor, lying in the underground caverns of the theater, awaiting the propitious moment to appear, uncalled, on stage. Every perfume is a performance of sorts, a theatricalized space in which different emotions and sensations enact a drama of flirtation, seduction, resistance, and domination. Although perfumes, with the assistance of their floral top notes, mask unpleasant odors, in particular the odors of human flesh, they cannot hide everything. "In offering to the perceiver a cocktail of sex attractant odors at low concentration in the base notes," Stoddart observes, perfumes "subconsciously reveal what consciously the strident top notes seek to hide." One's attention is necessarily "drawn to the more volatile and active floral notes much as one is drawn to a newspaper by its headlines; [yet] the real message is carried in the small print" (163).

300

With the launch of Yves Saint Laurent's *Opium* in 1977 perfumes with an "oriental" theme moved in a new direction. Influenced by the mellis accord found in Estée Lauder's *Youth Dew* (originally created as a bath oil in 1952) and the ambreine accord found in Guerlain's *Shalimar* (1925), *Opium*, despite the controversy generated by its name, represented a significant moment in postwar perfume creation.

Perfume as OPIUM

The presence of Eros, death, and perfume, so powerfully united in Goncourt's and Flaubert's nineteenth-century imagination and in the post–World War II writing of Italo Calvino and Patrick Süskind, has a final, recent incarnation in advertising. Taking over the reins of Yves Saint Laurent in May 2000 and deciding to change the house's couture and accessories image, the designer Tom Ford instituted a major transformation in the advertising for *Opium*, the Saint Laurent perfume first launched to great success in October 1977. *Opium* was the first French prestige fragrance to raise the levels of concentrate to 30 percent (for the perfume) and 19 percent (for the eau de toilette) from the 4 to 6 percent which had been used traditionally in the manufacture of toilet water, for example. Despite its obvious name and its classification as an oriental scent, *Opium* represented, according to Yves Saint Laurent, "a lush, heavy, indolent fragrance ... which evokes all the things I love— the refined Orient, imperial China, exoticism." It was created, according to the marketing director for Yves Saint Laurent, "to let people escape from their ordinary lives." *Opium* is an "addictive product, but not a drug, so we put the emphasis on richness, opulence and innovation." However, the political overtones of a perfume called "Opium" met with opposition from the People's Republic of China, which failed to see the fragrance as a tribute to or a celebration of the Chinese national heritage. The perfume's allusion to the opium trade, maintained illicitly by Britain

OPIUM
the fragrance from
YvesSaintLaurent

during the nineteenth century, and to China's defeat in the Opium War, led in January 2000 to the revoking of *Opium*'s registered trademark, making the selling of the perfume illegal in China.[41]

Photographed in the tiny Chinese study of Saint Laurent's Paris apartment, the first French advertisement for *Opium* showed a reclining woman, the model Jerry Hall, in a black dress decorated with thin silver arabesques, her head and arm thrown back and her eyes closed as if she were drifting off into sleep and dream. Other print advertisements over the years have presented women in different poses of lassitude and reverie. In one (a French advertisement from 1986) a woman in a low-cut black dress, her eyes closed, her lips slightly parted, her head and red hair thrown back over the edge of a dark blue sofa as if she were lost in dream reclines under the slogan "Opium . . . Never has perfume provoked such emotion." In a second advertisement (1995), a smiling woman (the model Linda Evangelista) in a flowing red dress designed to match the color of the large red bottle of *Opium* hovering near her, lies seductively on a bed of purple cloth. The shape of the *Opium* bottle was inspired by a Japanese *inro*, the small wooden ornate box with drawers holding spices, medicinal herbs, salt, and opium which samurai warriors at one time wore on their belts.[42] (Obviously, the cultural differences between China and Japan are not primary concerns when designing a perfume.) In these and other advertisements an air of dreamy opulence, rich lushness, and smoldering sensuality prevail. The colors, primarily the reds, browns, and blacks, enhance the smoky red of the *Opium* bottle.

X-Rated Perfume Ads

In autumn 2000, however, Tom Ford, newly appointed as the creative designer for Yves Saint Laurent, abandoned these dusky, dark colors for a sepulchral, chalky whiteness. A nude, milky-white, recumbent model (Sophie Dahl), attired only in one gold stiletto heel and a bracelet and necklace of diamonds and gold (fig. 121), lies on a dark blue-black satin fabric, her knees bent and her legs parted in a sexually receptive position. With her head thrown back, lips slightly parted, and her one visible eye haloed in green eye shadow, she is clearly lost in an experience of ecstasy, or "at the gates of pleasure" as French *Vogue* described it, a turn of phrase Chérie's creator would have admired. While one breast is covered by a hand, the areola and nipple of the other are ever so slightly revealed, although in American magazines they have been airbrushed into invisibility. The red *Opium* bottle, however, is nowhere to be seen. The blue-black satin backdrop strikingly places the model's body in relief, exaggerating her cadaverous skin and intensifying the smooth, marble whiteness of her body. As captured by the fashion photographer Steven Meisel, Dahl is presented as having passively

surrendered herself to a state of objectification in which love and addiction, eros and opium, sexuality and a death-like stupor are synonymous. In a much more graphic and explicit manner the advertisement presents an image of total surrender, one that had merely been implied by the French slogan, "*Opium*: for women who give themselves to Yves Saint Laurent" in the print ads for the fragrance appearing in the 1970s through the 1990s.[43]

Ford's new image, according to French *Vogue*, showed "once more that sex is alive and well." In this day and age, "luxury sex sells luxury," another observer noted. Ford was clearly committed to creating the image of a more candidly sexual, perhaps slightly neurotic, S&M woman. The Saint Laurent woman, he told an interviewer, "is about excess. She eats too much, she drinks too much, she smokes, she has sex . . . She's going to torture you a little bit. You might have sex, but she will drip a little hot wax on you first. This . . . is a more decadent world. It's refined, but very rough." And to a French interviewer, he admitted that "a good perfume must above all have the full power of a drug; it must provoke an addiction," a sentiment that would be fulfilled less than two years later when Dior launched its fragrance, *Addict*, described as "a homage to dazzling, inventive, and incendiary freedom." While in the past it had been *Opium*'s name alone that had provoked scandal, now it was its (and *Addict*'s) advertising image: a woman desperate for a fix, for her "hit" of fragrance. Perfume as drug and as opiate participates with sex and death in a Bataillean ménage à trois. Yet, this mortuary eroticism proved too offensive for England's national advertising board, which, after receiving 1,000 complaints—it was the most protested ad in five years—banned the advertisement's distribution throughout the country. Even the French government felt the need to criticize Saint Laurent's representation of women.[44]

Of course, the furor over the advertisement predated Ford's launching in 2001 of *Nu* (Naked), his own first scent as the head of Saint Laurent, a perfume that would push the outside of the envelope of taste even further. The launch party for the fragrance, held in the Palais Brongniart, the former Paris Stock Exchange, was a stylized, choreographed orgy with naked men and women, nude except for tiny flesh-toned thongs, writhing and gyrating on top of each other inside a thirty-foot Plexiglas container bathed in cobalt-blue light, the color of the disc-shaped *Nu* bottle. Again, Ford's concept involved a Bataillean mix of sex and animality: "We are," he told a French *Vogue* interviewer,

animals and our relationships play out accordingly. Perfume is intimate, close to the skin, truly perceptible in situations of closeness. Who, at such moments, wants to smell pine or plants? It is a question of awakening the senses, of making the other want to bite you. We're talking here about the idea of food, so colossally successful in Mugler's *Angel* with its dominant chocolate notes (Lalanne, 382–83).

Opposite page:
Fig. 121 "What's in a name?" Juliet asks of Romeo. "That which we call a rose / By any other name would smell as sweet"—or as narcotic. So it is that names of perfumes evoke states of blissful intoxication, convulsive sensuality, or agitated ecstasy, like "Poison," "Addict," "Mania," "Fetish," "Obsession," "Chaos," "Trouble," "X-S," "Fever," "Vertigo," and Yves Saint Laurent's *Opium* in this image of the model Sophie Dahl as photographed by Steven Meisel in 2000.

The Postmodern Scents of Loss

There are perfumes, the *New York Times* reported in 1998, called "techno fragrances," with names referring to real-life experiences, names like *Popcorn, Dirt, Funeral Parlor, Rubber, Vinyl, Woodsmoke, Mildew,* and other "scents of the everyday": for example, *Snow, Mahogany, Waffles, Leather, Lobster, Carrot, Tomato, Sushi, Paperback, Christmas Tree, Gasoline,* and even a "peachy pipe-tobacco fragrance . . . called *This Is Not a Pipe*" (in homage to the surrealist painter René Magritte's celebrated representation of a gigantic pipe). According to Demeter, the company producing and marketing these scents, the fragrance *Dirt* has "the smell of the air after a sudden summer thunderstorm, while *Earthworm,* developed in response to customer complaints that *Dirt* didn't smell "dirty" enough, has a richer loamy smell." Demeter is seeking to build, the *Times* reported, a "library of scents from which people can compose their own little evocative moments." The goal is not to perfume the body or a room, not to create an aura or an ambience, but rather to compose "epiphanies of personal reflection." There are scents, Proustian in conception, like *Graham Cracker* and *Orange Juice,* which seek to evoke images of a childhood past, as if they were miniature "photographs" of smells. According to Demeter's founder, the aim of these single-note fragrances is to create "the olfactory equivalent of Imagist poetry." Some of the conceptual scents Demeter seeks to invent "sound like lines from haiku: for example, 'warm pavement after rain in July' or 'cat napping in the sun.'" Since the beginning of the new millennium, however, Demeter's imagination has taken an edgier turn, with *Gin & Tonic, Fuzzy Navel,* and *Sex on the Beach.*[45]

As the fashion houses like Comme des Garçons and Viktor & Rolf have shown, even the experience of absence in the everyday can be reduced to a pocket-sized bottle. Which leads to the suggestion that the one scent that would leave the most powerful postmodern aroma in its wake— the one scent that would stand as *the* invisible fragrance behind all fragrance, as the one great unnamed scent lying behind all past, present, and future perfume names, from Guerlain's *Jicky* of 1889 to Viktor & Rolf's *Flowerbomb* of 2005, and as the one distinctive perfume expressive of uncertainty, evocative of indeterminacy, and heady with the aroma of absence would be named *Loss,* the postmodern fragrance par excellence. The surrealist poet Aragon was thinking in these terms (although before the advent of postmodernism) when he posed the question: "In all the countries of the world, tell me what is the scent of sadness, what is the odor of forgetfulness?" (Delbourg-Delphis, 9). Italo Calvino, the Italian novelist, would in all probability have had an answer, because his short story "The Name, The Nose," written in 1972, asserts first, that in the realm of olfactory experience there is no reality that truly lasts other than the realities of loss and death; second, that perfume leaves in its wake nothing other than absence and uncertainty; and third, that the sillage of a fragrance signals by its evanescence the total impossibility of knowledge. Perfume represents for Calvino, as it did for Baudelaire, a state of the utmost contingency: an experience where scent and savor negate *savoir* (knowledge).

"The Name, The Nose"

Calvino's compelling and complex narrative involves three intertwined stories, which float and dissolve into each other's spaces, intrude into each other's atmospheres, and coil around and lap over each other like three similar, yet slightly different, scents. Three protagonists—a nobleman in nineteenth-century Paris, a quadruped pre-human (on the threshold of erect posture) roaming the savannas during a prehistoric time, and a drummer with a London rock band in the sixties—begin a passionate search for a particular odor and the particular female who once embodied it, only in the end to find her at the moment she dies. The first story concerns Monsieur de Saint-Caliste (68), a French nobleman, who rushes agitatedly into his favorite perfumery and desperately implores the proprietress to help him identify a scent he had smelled at a masked ball the previous night. It is the captivating fragrance worn by an elegant woman about whom the nobleman knows absolutely nothing, not even what she looks like. The Frenchman seeks "to give a name to an olfactory sensation I could neither forget nor hold in my memory without its slowly fading. I had to expect as much: even the perfumes of memory evaporate" (71). But the perfumes that the proprietress suggests he compare to the mystery woman's enigmatic scent cause confusion and mounting oblivion:

> Each new scent I was made to sniff, as it imposed its diversity, its own powerful presence, made still vaguer the recollection of that absent perfume, reduced it to a shadow . . . In this seesawing of the scale of odors, I was lost, I could no longer discern the direction of the memory I should follow: I knew only that at one point of the spectrum, there was a gap, a secret fold where there lurked that perfume which, for me, was a complete woman (71).

Perfume is, as this passage indicates, a presence destined to disappear but whose vanishing into absence has its own power of seduction. The "shadow" of the woman's scent, even as it grows more and more imprecise, strengthens the nobleman's obsession with reversing the loss he is undergoing and his passionate resolve to locate that timeless "gap" or "fold," as he calls it, in which the fascinating fragrance still remains alive. Perfume's bewitching magic is nourished by a power for life made all the more intense by the reality of perfume's evanescence. In the

Sans parfum,
la peau est muette.

"Sans parfum la peau est muette" (Without perfume the skin is silent), advertisement for the Comité français du parfum, 1980s.

wake of the masked woman's scent, which now has taken over the nobleman's existence, comes a memory whose feverish presence approaches that not only of illusion but of hallucination.

The second of Calvino's three stories takes us back to a prehistoric period in the development of Homo sapiens, to that moment in "the savannah, the forest, the swamp," when pre-human types moved on all fours,

> heads down, never losing contact with the ground, using hands and noses to help us find the trail. We understand whatever there was to understand through our noses rather than through our eyes . . . The odor tells you immediately and certainly what you need to know. There are no words, there is no information more precise than what the nose receives (71–72).

In the herd of creatures, as animal as they are subhuman, there is one individual, a male, who is suddenly struck by a powerfully erotic female smell and begins furiously to hunt for the carrier of this odor, sniffing all the females until he identifies her distinctive odor: "I breathed through my nose all of her and her love-summons," he says (72). But like the French aristocrat, the hominid takes from the female only a fleeting whiff. The herd moves on, and the female and her odor are lost in a collective, homogeneous scent.

Calvino's third and final story takes us from the savannah and the immemorial past to a seamy, dirty apartment near the London docks at the end of the 1960s. In a room of drugged, drunken, and sexually exhausted bodies, the drummer of a rock band, whose group has just spent the night with a "herd" of groupies, gets up to put more coins in the gas stove and give the room some much needed heat. Making his way through the tangle of bodies lying all over the floor and fighting off the choking, nauseating stench of beer, tobacco, and vomit, he is suddenly possessed—it is love at first sight, or rather, at first smell—by the complicated odor of "a girl's white skin, a white smell with that special force white has, a slightly mottled skin smell probably dotted with faint or even invisible freckles, a skin that breathes the way a leaf's pores breathe the meadows, and all the stink in the room keeps its distance from this skin" (75). Once again in an everyday world without distinction—the pretentious world of mid-nineteenth-century Parisian salons, the savage world of the Paleolithic savannah, and the bohemian world of a London apartment—an odor creates an epiphany. The sublime arises on the fragrant wings of desire. The drummer, like the hominid on the savannah, hunts for and then finds the source of his stimulation; in the dark, he makes love to her, although he cannot see her face. But the room is still cold, and the drummer again gets up and wends his way toward the gas stove. He gets it started, but when he tries to find his way through the labyrinth of bodies back to the woman of his dreams, whom he knows only by her smell, he becomes disoriented in the darkness and cannot locate her. The "island of her smell," the oasis of her fragrant flesh, is lost forever: "What I want to smell I can't smell, I'm roaming around like a jerk and I can't find her. Have mercy, have

305

mercy on me, I go from one skin to another hunting for that lost skin that isn't like any other skin" (76).

Each of these three parallel stories ends with the death of the anonymous and faceless woman, who in three different yet similar instances succeeds in becoming known only through the sense of smell. "For each woman a perfume exists which enhances the perfume of her own skin, the note in the scale which is at once color and flavor and aroma and tenderness," observes the French nobleman, for whom smell is a multisensual experience, a synthesis of all the five senses coming together to create an extraordinary amalgam of note, color, flavor, aroma, and touch (in the form of "tenderness") (76). From beginning to end, smell progressively dominates the perceptions of the three protagonists as vision gradually reveals itself of little use. In each episode, after the narrators—nobleman, subhuman, and rocker alike—led by their noses as it were, have mounted fruitless searches for the lost other, the woman, her face still invisible, is at last discovered and "known," but only, alas, at the moment she departs from the world. Death succeeds in making the beloved present, where smell, vision, and the other sensorial faculties, having failed, could only reveal absence. And this so-called "knowledge" of the other, which each narrator felt he came to possess after having inhaled the odor of the beloved—a limited knowledge to be sure since it was based solely on smell—turns out to be a knowledge of nothing. In his desperation to locate the female and in order to gain speed, the hominid walks on his hind legs, a gesture causing him to lose the female's scent in the upper reaches of the air, where odors are lighter and less intense. Similarly, the rock musician goes outside the apartment to get a breath of fresh air and knocks his head against a "wall of fog" coming from the Thames. The scent of beauty and of the sublime is obliterated, overwhelmed, and blocked by a myriad of confusing odors emanating from nearby garbage cans and the rotting detritus of life—"fish scales, cans, nylon stockings"—they hold (80).[46] Having experienced the fullness of scent, the three narrators are left with the null and void, with nothingness, death, and loss: in other words, the emptiness which all knowledge represents for Calvino. The other, the world, and even reality itself in all its permutations are unknowable either through language, memory, or smell, as the aristocrat remarks: "I knew nothing of her, but I felt I knew all in that perfume; and I would have desired a world without names, where that perfume alone would have sufficed as name and as all the words she could speak to me: that perfume I knew was lost now" (77).

In each narrative the female object of desire possesses neither face, nor identity, nor personality, and the male pursuer has been seduced by a scent, which, because of the poverty and nominative insufficiency of language and the loss of olfactory sensitivity among humans, can only be discovered at the moment it blends with the odor of death. The mysteriously masked French woman is discovered lying in her coffin, the female hominid thrown in a heap of rotting, lacerated bodies, and the groupie asphyxiated by the smoke of a fire in the apartment. Perfume and death are synonymous, and language, faced with the Eros of scent and with loss, is powerless to offer any possession or knowledge of what is real—be it a name, a person, or a love. The Frenchman enters the masked woman's home and is immediately struck by "a heavy smell, as of rotting vegetation" circulating among the wreaths, garlands, and funereal flowers surrounding the veiled and faceless corpse (81). And yet, he recognizes "the base, the echo of that perfume that resembles no other, merged with the odor of death now as if they had always been inseparable" (81). The hominid as well senses in the stench of death the flower of life and love: "The odor I was following was lost down there . . . and it rises with the stink of the clawed cadavers, the breath of the jackals that tear them apart" (82). As for the drummer, his attempt to isolate the seductive, life-enhancing, and therefore truly erotic scent of the faceless woman (now reduced to a "thing") from the mass of confusing, undifferentiated, yet clearly funerary odors—his description constitutes the story's concluding sentence—strikingly confirms Bataille's mélange of eroticism, death, horror, and baseness, all of which gravitate, according to Calvino, around the word-denying experience of odor, which yields no knowledge other than that of indeterminacy, loss, and mortality:

> On the floor the thing I see before I writhe in a fit of vomiting is the long, white, outstretched form, face hidden by the hair, and as I pull her out by her stiffened legs I smell her odor within the asphyxiating odor, her odor that I try to follow and distinguish in the ambulance, in the first-aid room, among the odors of disinfectant and slime that drips from the marble slabs in the morgue, and the air is impregnated with it, especially when outside the weather is damp. (83)

A truth rises into the air of Calvino's story: namely, that perfume and death are always already inseparable and have been from the start. The search for the other is doomed to failure, because human beings can have no power of memory, of knowledge, and of naming over such experiences of loss and evanescence like perfume: experiences in which death is the hidden and latent seed biding its time until it bursts forth into the dark flower and dark scent of nothingness. Perfume is unnamable, precisely because it contains and sustains death, because it is fundamentally an experience of death, and because its true sillage, its true trace, is death itself.

In each of the three narrative strands of the story the other is unfindable and inexpressible without language. The nose needs a name in Calvino's "The Name, The Nose," if it is to capture, preserve, and possess the nameless and faceless woman. But names fail because odor prevents them from being known. The degradation of human smell through evolutionary selection and the primacy of vision as a strategy for survival have turned smell, odor, and perfume into what the first sentence of Calvino's story calls "Epigraphs in an indecipherable language, half their letters rubbed away by the sand-laden wind" (67). Perfume enacts its own literal meaning: it is smoke (*fumum*, in Latin) passing through (*per* in Latin) the air where it is "left speechless, inarticulate, illegible" (68). The experience of scent guarantees no knowledge, no linguistic confidence, no verbal certainty, no assurance of memory, no mastery of reality, and finally no possession of the world. In the universe of odors, it is ultimately only the smell of death which triumphs. In the wake of perfume only the odor of irreversible loss persists, for, as the twentieth-century poet Henri Michaux once suggested, he or she "who leaves a trace also leaves a wound."[47]

The Perfume of Evil

Where Calvino presents death as the ultimate defeat of knowledge, love, language, and memory, the German novelist Patrick Süskind, in *Perfume: The Story of a Murderer*, reveals it as the ultimate preserver of life, as a counter to loss, and as a fixative (like those stabilizing ingredients used in perfumery) that, reversing the erosions of time, gives permanence to all that is ephemeral. Paradoxically, it is through the medium and agency of death that odors are preserved, because Jean-Baptiste Grenouille, Süskind's eighteenth-century master-perfumer, is a gifted artist of exquisite sensitivity and at the same time an evil creature of misanthropy and horror, more animal than human. In his pursuit of the perfect scent, the odor that will give him power over all of humankind and make him the greatest perfumer of all time, Grenouille consistently sacrifices humanity on the altar of Art. The pursuit of power through artistic genius and an aestheticism inseparable from death turns the delicate perfumer into a brutal fascist. The end—in particular, the search for an enchanting, magical, hypnotizing scent—justifies the means, and Grenouille's means are manipulative, animalistic, and murderous. For Grenouille the sublime comes into being, as Bataille would be happy to agree, through the horror of bestial murder. Baseness and animality are the means to an aesthetic and erotic epiphany. In the pursuit of his ideal, namely a fragrance that would be nothing less than a fusion of absolute beauty and divine creation, Grenouille demonically takes on God. It is murder, not gentleness, evil, not goodness, that become his instruments; they alone create beauty, a satanic beauty: the very perfume of evil. Even Grenouille's own death embodies an Eros and a Thanatos synonymous with the rapture of love and the divine seductiveness of fragrance. Here, love at its most extreme turns into death. The conclusion of Süskind's novel reveals how Eros, impelled by the need for possession, turns into hysterical cannibalism, the bestial appropriation of the other. With lustful madness a crowd devours Grenouille; they consume his odor. But is this cannibalism any different from love in general, from an Eros that seeks to capture, possess, and ingest the being of the beloved? Is it, for that matter, any different from the sense of smell, which longs to take in, to fill the lungs, with the scent of the other?

In the voluptuous desire to become one with the beloved, love and smell (Eros and perfume) seek the death of the other. Under the powerful influence of the Eros and Thanatos of scent we cannot help, even if it only be in our unconscious dreams and fantasies, to love the other to death. The perfumed woman is, Kristeva writes, "a lover so intimately and guiltily involved with carnage and death that she can perfume, disguise, and forget them" (Pillivuyt, *Histoire*, 7). It would seem that the Eros of scent charms death itself. It keeps Thanatos in thrall. But only for a moment. For death breaks the spell. The real dismisses the imaginary. And perfume and poetry confront that death which is the most permanent, immobilizing, and truly base of the three notes that compose perfume's song of love and its threnody of loss.

Fragrant Narratives: The Stories Perfumes Tell (1950–2006)

COMITE FRANÇAIS DU PAR

Chapter 8

*He who ruled scent
ruled the hearts of men.
—Patrick Süskind*

*Fragrance is a conduit for
our earliest memories on the
one hand; on the other, it may
accompany us as we enter
the next life . . .
Prehistory, history, and
the afterworld,
all are its domain.
— Tom Robbins*

The Detection of Scent

IN AN ELABORATE and ultimately successful scheme to catch her cheating husband in flagrante delicto and, more important still, to win herself a divorce, the Marquise de Rennedon, as the novelist Guy de Maupassant imagines the imbroglio in "Saved," his tale of 1885, engages a lady's maid, aptly named Rose, whose physical attributes closely resemble those of her wayward husband's mistress. Unwilling to trust physical resemblance as the only means to lure the husband into a compromising liaison and wishing to see the seduction occur as quickly and efficiently as possible, the marquise instructs Rose to wear verbena, a scent the marquis cannot resist. And so, his nose leading him astray, the marquis is caught by his wife who gets her divorce.[1]

In another country and at a slightly later time, as C. W. Leadbeater's "The Perfume of Egypt" from early in the twentieth century informs us, an English traveler puttering around Cairo enters the room of a sheikh. Immediately, he is struck by a "most peculiar odor . . . indescribably rich and sweet—almost oppressively so," its effect "stimulating and exhilarating." The scent, it turns out, is a sacred perfume used in magical rituals, the formula of which has been handed down for generations by a secret group of mystics. Back in his hotel room, the traveler is greeted with horror by his servant who smells the scent on his master's garments. "Where have you been? How comes this devil-scent upon your clothes?" he asks with choking fear, for the perfume, it seems, belongs to the "old magic of Egypt." The scent is the creation of devils, says the servant. Called "virgin's blood" it is applied to bodies as they are made ready for sacrifice.

One night, fifteen months later, writing in his rooms back in London, the traveler has the sudden and unpleasant impression that he is not alone, a feeling made more frightening by a "soft breath or puff of wind" blowing on his neck and the faint sound of a sigh. Even more surprising is the smell of "that strange subtle perfume of ancient eastern magic" which fills the room.[2] Other astounding and inexplicable events, each and every one accompanied by the magical scent, follow in sequence: the apparition of the ghostly figure of a man writing at a table; a slip of parchment covered with strange writing torn from a book and left behind by the specter; the visit to a dilapidated, haunted country mansion recently inherited by an old Oxford friend, who recounts the family legend of a wicked, mysteriously vanished ancestor, named Sir Ralph; a dream in which the ghost appears before the traveler and points to the last page of a small book he carries in his hand; the discovery in one of the mansion's rooms of an old portrait whose likeness is not only that of the ghost but of Sir Ralph as well; and finally, the decoding of the parchment fragment and the subsequent discovery of a hidden chamber filled with treasures and guarded by the skeleton of Sir Ralph, beside whose remains lies a small parchment memo book from which part of a page has been torn. A wide-mouthed bottle lying on the floor contains the residue of a scented poison, which Sir Ralph, knowing that he could not escape from the secret room whose door had inadvertently closed upon him, swallowed to hasten his death.

Wherever scent appears in "The Perfume of Egypt" the trace of a ghostly past hovers mysteriously and indistinctly in the air. The fragrant signs do not, until the mystery is solved at the end of the tale, yield a clear image of their significance; the traveler has no idea to what the perfumed apparitions refer. Yet, memory and scent can have a more precise and interdependent relationship, to which the postwar Italian writer Primo Levi testifies in his story "The Mnemogogues." A young doctor arrives in a small Italian village and introduces himself to the old physician who has dedicated his professional life to caring for the town's sick. They engage in a philosophical discussion concerning the tenuousness of smells. Saddened by the fading away of memories as he has aged, the old man has been keeping, as it were, a diary of odors, using his training as a pharmacologist to reconstruct "with exactitude and in preservable form, a number of sensations that mean something to me." He takes the young doctor to a cupboard filled with fifty small, numbered bottles, all tightly sealed. These are what he calls "mnemogogues, 'arousers of memories,'" each a kind of unique olfactory photograph of the past. Since "memories, in order to be suggestive, must have an antique flavor," each bottle possesses a particularly personal and autobiographical scent. One bottle contains the odor of elementary schoolrooms. Inhaling it makes the doctor's innards tighten just the way they did when at seven he was called upon to answer a question. From a second bottle comes the breath of a diabetic, that of his father who eventually succumbed to the disease. Yet another bottle contains the scent of hospital wards, immediately provoking "a complex picture" of his life and loves as a young man. A fourth bottle, which he considers his finest preparation, exudes a smell only found high in the mountains, "the odor of peace achieved." However, the doctor has little to say about a fifth bottle, from which emanates "a light airy smell of clean skin, powder, and summer." "This is neither a place nor a time, it is a person," he tells his younger colleague without further explanation, putting the bottle back on its shelf and closing the cupboard—and the past.[3] All these bottles contain scents and consequently stories; the last bottle's story is, undoubtedly, too personal and perhaps too sad to be shared with a stranger. Thus, "Saved," "The Perfume of Egypt," and "The Mnemogogues" are all narratives dependent on the sometimes telltale, sometimes enigmatic signs that scent writes on the air. Narrative threads of all kinds—stories, histories, chronicles, sagas, legends, romances, fairy and folk tales, anecdotes—spiral outward on the wings of fragrance. Each story, in order to be suggestive, must, to paraphrase what Levi's old doctor says about memories, "have an antique flavor." That old and unique flavor is often a tale. "Rare are the perfumes that traverse the ages," observes the perfumer-narrator in René Laruelle's postwar novel *Le Parfum perdu*, the story of a search for an ancient, lost incense. However, when these classic scents do indeed survive "they have something in common: they all tell a story"; they begin with the words "once upon a time."[4] And these fragrant tales, like all stories, provoke acts of detection, decoding, and, of course, interpretation.

Scent is, thus, inseparable from what biblical scholars call hermeneutics—the science of interpreting scripture—and from what linguists call semiology—the science of interpreting signs. When odors appear and when they trigger memories, strategies of detection and interpretation are called into action; a postmortem inquiry into the past is initiated. "He tried to guess," observes the painter-hero of Maupassant's novel *Strong as Death* (1889), the reasons for this rising up of his former life,

> which several times already, though never so insistently as today, he had felt and remarked. A cause always existed for these sudden evocations—a natural and simple cause, an odor, perhaps, often a perfume. How many times a woman's gown had thrown to him in passing, with the evaporating breath of some essence, a host of forgotten events. At the bottom of old perfume-bottles he had often found bits of his former existence; and all wandering odors—of streets, fields, houses, furniture, sweet or unsavory, the warm odors of summer evenings, the cold breath of winter nights—revived within him far-off reminiscences, as if odors kept embalmed within him these dead-and-gone memories, as aromatics preserve mummies.[5]

Along with the gathering clouds of perfume rising into the air and the constellation of lost memories reappearing in the hero's consciousness comes the emergence of a narrative: the sequence of associations, thoughts, sensations, feelings, images, and events "rising up [from a] former life" and organizing themselves into a narrative chain, a spiderweb of stories. The very air itself seems on the verge of spinning tales.

To a savant nose, like that of Jean-Baptiste Grenouille, the hero-perfumer of Patrick Süskind's *Perfume: The Story of a Murderer,* the air is redolent of stories, many imperceptible or incomprehensible, unless one knows, literally, how to read them. In the market district of eighteenth-century Paris, the quarter known as Les Halles, "thousands upon thousands of odors formed an invisible gruel that filled the street ravines, only seldom evaporating above the rooftops and never from the ground below" (39). Most denizens of the *quartier,* accustomed to the smell of the place, are unaware of its stench. Not Grenouille, however, who inhales the miasmas of Les Halles as a reader would avidly decipher the words and phrases of a rare, esoteric, and recently unearthed text:

> Grenouille . . . smelled it all as if for the first time. And he did not merely smell the mixture of odors in the aggregate, but he dissected it analytically into its smallest and most remote parts and pieces. His discerning nose unraveled the knot of vapor and stench into single strands of unitary odors that could not be unthreaded further. Unwinding and spinning out these threads gave him unspeakable joy. (40)

Every ounce of air, endowed with its own particular past and its own specific story, finds in Grenouille the keenest of listeners and the most astute of readers. Once subjected to the perfumer's interpretative examination, a square foot of pavement, a fragment of cobblestone gutter, and the threshold of a building give up their odorous and narrative secrets. The smell of rotting meat detected by Grenouille's nose in the mere drop of blood on a stone could conceivably set in motion a journey of discovery into the labyrinthine layers of time and space which had become enfolded in that odor. Although Süskind does not go this far in his description of Grenouille's powers of detection, he suggests, nevertheless, that for the perfumer every odor is a universe of infinite proportions. It would be quite possible, therefore, for Grenouille to detect in the odor of the beef blood the species to which the animal belonged, the region of France in which it was raised, the kind of grass on which it grazed, the smell of the farmers whose stable it occupied, and that of the butchers who cut its flesh to pieces. Strands of a history—that of landscape, event, time, space, weather, the passage of the seasons— unwind in tandem with the uncoiling, spiraling curls of scent. Air, although invisible, speaks. It recounts and narrates. But only a nose endowed with predatory perception can "hear," "read," "see," "touch," or "consume" what it has to say. So Grenouille would often

> just stand here, leaning against a wall or crouching in a dark corner, his eyes closed, his mouth half open and nostrils flaring wide, quiet as a feeding pike in a great, dark, slowly moving current. And when at last a puff of air would toss a delicate thread of scent his way, he would lunge at it and not let go. Then he would smell at only this one odor, holding it tight, pulling it into himself and preserving it for all time (40).

In this preserved and internalized scent, Grenouille captures the story of a past, the history of a place, even the everydayness of a culture: a chronicle or diary of odors (167). Revisiting the empty market of Les Halles one evening after all the merchants have left for the day, Grenouille first senses and then resurrects the hustle and bustle of the day's activities, including the shouts of the vendors and the smells of the potatoes, spices, vinegar, vegetables, wines, shoes, and other articles which had been for sale:

Grenouille *saw* the whole market *smelling*, if it can be put that way. And he *smelled* it more precisely than many people could *see* it, for his perception was after the fact and thus of a higher order: an essence, a spirit of what had been, something undisturbed by the everyday accidents of the moment, like noise, glare, or the nauseating press of living human beings (41) (italics mine).

Jean-Baptiste Grenouille, this odorophile-collector of aromas, this predator of scents, whose body ironically gives off no scent, is a walking encyclopedia of odors. Later in the story, during a seven-year hibernation in a mountain cave far from the smells of humanity, Grenouille plunges into a dream world of his own invention. He imagines himself in a "great library of odors," surrounded by the millions of volumes of smells he has collected during his lifetime. From vast shelves imaginary servants take down "books" for him to "read." These are the fragrant chronicles of the odors of childhood, of the smells of Paris streets, and of the blissful scent he steals in a most horrible manner from a young redhead one September night in 1753 on the rue des Marais. As he "reads" the odors of the past and recalls the tales they express and, as he sips from bottles of the finest scents he has ever created, stored, and aged in the vast cellars of his hallucinatory castle, symbol of his narcissism and of his megalomaniacal desires, he becomes drunk on his own genius (155–57). It is true that Grenouille is a poetic dreamer, a gifted perfumer, and a cunning murderer as well. But he is also a talented archivist and historian of sorts, who searches for the aroma of the past that will survive the effacement of that past, who seeks the perfume that will outlive its moment, who looks for the story that will remain after its event, and, finally, who yearns to discover the tyrannical ideal that, once wedded to his own barbaric misanthropy, will nearly exterminate humankind.

Perfume and Barbarity: The Holocaust

To link Wilhelm Mülhens's famous eau de cologne of 1792, *Echt Kölnisch Wasser No. 4711* ("Original Eau de Cologne No. 4711"), the oldest of all scented waters still for sale today, to the hunger, the squalid barracks, the roll calls in the numbing cold, the electric fences, the brutal work details, the beatings, and the crematoria of the Auschwitz-Birkenau concentration camp complex put into operation by the Nazis in 1940, is as absurd and grotesque a juxtaposition as one could imagine. What can a fragrance, a refreshing, tangy, chypre scent composed of orange, lemon, rose, musk, and above all bergamot (from an inedible citrus fruit, it is the primary ingredient in Earl Grey tea) possibly have in common with the infernal stench of the concentration camp world? This was a universe where prisoners became so accustomed to "the odor of corpses and raw sewage," as the French writer and survivor Charlotte Delbo observes, that repulsive smells were completely unremarkable?[6] Beyond the all-too-obvious German origin of *No. 4711* and the interesting but somewhat trivial fact that the composer Richard Wagner adored the scent, can one discover a convincing explanation for the possible connection between the aesthetic, elegant, and civilized reality of fragrance and the brutal, barbarous, and horrific void of the Holocaust? Yet, the association of perfume—symbol of beauty, individuality, self-concern, and the freedoms of civilized life—with the nightmare of deprivation, depersonalization, and depravity of the camps does indeed find expression in the imagination and experience of some postwar writers and artists, for whom perfume calls into being a narrative of resistance, one in which human dignity and pride rise up briefly to revolt against an inescapable system of genocide.

Tattoo versus Scent

During the four years she spent at Ravensbrück, a German concentration camp for women fifty miles north of Berlin, where she eventually died in 1944, Milena Jesenská, the twenty-four-year-old Czech translator of Kafka's early short prose and the woman with whom the writer shared a passionate love affair near the end of his life, was a model of indomitable strength and will. She possessed a fervor for living that impressed the nearly forty-year-old Kafka: "You who live your life so intensely down to such depths," he had written to her in one of his passionate letters from 1920 to 1922. Milena's fellow inmates marveled at and took courage from this lust for life. As Margarete Buber-Neumann, who befriended and cared for her at Ravensbrück, observed, "there was something positively provocative in Milena's manner. Her way of speaking, of moving, of holding her head; with every gesture, she said, 'I am a free woman.'"[7] In the extreme conditions of this nightmare world, Milena made a concerted effort to express her freedom and to reveal her fervent commitment to life; "she loved beauty and couldn't live without it," Buber-Neumann writes. She had a passion for pretty things which revealed itself in unremarkable yet meaningful ways: the flower she kept in a container on her desk in the camp infirmary where she worked and the photograph of Prague she pinned to her office wall (29, 153). Her love of fine clothes and the articles she wrote on fashion for a Prague newspaper, where she had been the editor of the women's page before the war, gave her an expertise that, as it turned out, was of use to a fellow inmate, who created a series of comic sketches of camp "dress," entitled the "Ravensbrück Fashions Magazine" (30, 79, 161). In addition, Milena's remarkable gift for empathy was yet another aspect of what Kafka called her "life-giving power." In the days following the

German invasion of Czechoslovakia in 1939 she, a non-Jew from an aristocratic Prague family, sewed the yellow Star of David on her clothes to show solidarity with her Jewish friends. Moreover, she saved many hospitalized inmates in Ravensbrück from certain death by falsifying their medical tests and arranging clandestine treatment for them (10, 145, 166).

Milena's effort to maintain her femininity, dignity, and vitality earned her respectful and flattering nicknames from fellow prisoners; one such name was in its own way quite extraordinary. "4714" was the tattooed serial number Milena wore on her forearm. But her companions, all of whom were well acquainted with the famous German eau de cologne, called her "4711" (150). The seemingly trivial, three-number discrepancy was in its own way expressive of an act of resistance. It subverted the Nazi's attempt to turn human beings into nameless numbers, to reduce their identities, nationalities, and individual styles of being to the anonymity of non-distinctive ciphers, to the impersonality of non-persons. In calling Milena "4711," and thus undermining, symbolically at least, a totalitarian system bent on homogeneous identification, the prisoners succeeded in giving her the kind of unique personality which before the war had been the unquestioned hallmark and defining characteristic of a distinctive human being, one possessed of a name, a self, and a subjectivity. They enveloped Milena not so much in a scent as in the idea or name of a scent, a German one no less and one composed of numbers, which for the short time she had to live gave her once again the uniqueness—of beauty, femininity, spirit, and independence—which she had fully enjoyed as a young and energetic woman living in Vienna and Prague, and which she struggled valiantly to preserve at Ravensbrück.[8]

La Jupe de Milena (Milena's Skirt) and *Les Larmes de Milena* (Milena's Tears) are two large mixed-media sculptures by the contemporary French artist Françoise Quardon, which use the number 4711 to pay homage to Milena Jesenská. Mounted in the Grand Gallery of the Centre Pompidou Musée National d'Art Moderne in Paris during a 1995–1996 exhibition devoted to *Feminine-Masculine: Sex in Art*, Quardon's two large pieces appropriate *Echt Kölnisch Wasser No. 4711* in two different yet fascinating ways: one visual, the other olfactory. *Milena's Skirt* (figs. 123, 125), a large, pillow-soft sculpture made

from satin and shaped like an oblong bottle lying on its side—its support, according to Quardon, comes from metal hoops sewn inside like those found in a crinoline skirt (conversation with the author, November 22, 2004)—reproduces the turquoise-blue background and gold-tooled scrolls, arabesques, and numbers which have adorned the celebrated *Echt Kölnisch Wasser* label since its inception in 1792 (fig. 122). In Quardon's sculpture the number 4711 is repeated several times over the surface of the satin-covered "bottle," each time encircled by the same thick gold braid that gives form to the numbers themselves. Gold appears as well in the swag of knotted braids and hanging tassels encircling the base of the piece. It is the artist's schematic and simplified interpretation of the intertwined volutes and whorls framing the central panel of the original cologne label. Two significant design elements, however, have been added by Quardon to give her "bottle" a larger symbolic meaning. Running down the center of the satin flacon from top to bottom between columns of repeated "4711's" are five words in German: "Stimulans / für / Geist / & / Körper" (Stimulant / for / Mind / & / Body). This sentence is an early slogan for *4711*, once displayed on the label but no longer used, which Quardon had discovered in the documentation that the fragrance's manufacturer had sent to her (Marcel Cohen, personal communication with the author, June 1, 2003). Each of the carefully constructed letters of the slogan has been calligraphically shaped from the same thick gold braid which forms the work's other decorative motifs; a few letters even show frayed and tasseled ends. The second new element in Quardon's reinterpretation of *Echt Kölnisch Wasser No. 4711* involves a symbolic appendage added to the bottle's stopper. Several thick strands of entwined synthetic hair, extending horizontally several feet across the floor from the top of the bottle, form a large black tassel or net of tresses which call to mind, as Marcel Cohen has observed, "the ominous piles of feminine hair discovered at the time the camps were liberated" (letter to the author, February 22, 1996).

Fig. 122 With a top note primarily of bergamot blended with lemon and orange, a middle note of rosemary and rose, and a base note of musk, *Echt Kölnisch Wasser Nc. 4711,* created in 1792 by Mülhens & Kropff, is one of the oldest colognes, if not the oldest, for sale today. Its number refers to the eighteenth-century street address (No. 4711 Glockengasse) of the Mülhens factory in Cologne.

313

Fig. 123 Milena Jesenská, Kafka's translator and his last great love, was imprisoned in the German concentration camp for women at Ravensbrück. Despite the severe punishments meted out for petty offences against the camp's dress code, prisoners like Milena were still concerned with their appearance; "women were still women even in [a] concentration camp," writes Margarete Buber-Neumann, a survivor. To this passionate commitment to life the contemporary French artist Françoise Quardon pays tribute here, in *La Jupe de Milena* (Milena's Skirt), detail, part of her mixed media sculpture, *Hommage à Milena*, 1995.

While the *4711* cologne bottle of "Milena's Skirt" uses a decorative vocabulary of primarily visual and tactile images—turquoise satin, gold-braided letters and numbers, festoons, tassels, ropes, and an overall softness (a wrap-around "skirt" of sorts enveloping, so to speak, the memory of Milena)—to evoke the hair and scent of Milena the woman and Milena the prisoner, *Milena's Tears* (fig. 124) uses similarly visual and tactile phenomena but infuses them with a new, this time odoriferous reality. As *Milena's Skirt* substitutes a pillowlike bottle for the feminine garment suggested by its title, so *Milena's Tears* swerves away from its name to highlight a full set of oversized teeth. Standing upright on double- and single-pointed bases—depending on the type of tooth (molars, incisors, canines)—and arranged in an immense half circle, sixteen enormous white teeth (nearly four and a half feet high), each enveloped by a thick band of brushed red velvet "gum tissue," face the spectator. The shape of the teeth is rendered realistically—the canines are sharp-edged and pointed, the crowns of the molars wide and flat—as is their color; here and there the white enamel has been yellowed or discolored by the appearance of plaque. The most unusual aspect of the work, however, lies on the flat surface of nearly every crown. Here Quardon has

hollowed a shallow depression to hold small amounts of *Echt Kölnisch Wasser No. 4711*, whose fragrant emanations permeated the Pompidou gallery. Mülhens & Kropff, the cologne's manufacturer, donated the fragrance, a wise idea as it turned out. Evaporating quickly under the hot lights shining on the work, the "perfumed tears" as Quardon calls them (conversation with the author, November 22, 2004), had to be replaced every three to four days.

The image of hair in *Milena's Skirt* and that of teeth in *Milena's Tears* leave little doubt about the meaning of these anatomical allusions. Prisoners newly arrived at German concentration camps had their heads shaved within a short time of their having stepped off the transport trains. The mouths of those who had been gassed in the death chambers were scrupulously examined for any gold fillings; when found, their teeth were extracted. In her homage to Milena, Quardon contrasts the atrocities and indignities visited upon the human body in the camps to the care and grooming of the body so common during normal times. The overlapping of seemingly contradictory images of corporal pain and physical beauty, the intertwining of tears and perfume, and the association of death and fashion (a scent, a skirt, a hairstyle) do not merely highlight in some black-or-white, either-or manner, the baseness of inhuman death as opposed to the refined sublimity of art and sophisticated style. Rather, they blur and complicate any clear-cut distinction one may wish to make between good and evil, humanity and bestiality, aestheticism and barbarism, and delight and suffering. The coexistence of both a sensualized and a traumatized body reveals the extent to which an effort was made by Milena and her fellow prisoners to try to recapture the normalcy of the past and insert it into the barbaric living conditions of the camps. They struggled to humanize the mind-numbing, depersonalizing horror of everyday life by rediscovering the consoling habits of an ordinary routine, one that had determined their former lives, and by maintaining a sense of care and caring, for oneself and for others. Thus, Milena's tattoo, consciously misread by her fellow inmates as "4711," brings the idea of scent into the air of Ravensbrück: a truly surrealistic event where the banality of the ordinary, the recalled whiff of a pleasurable fragrance, exists in a tornado of nightmarish nothingness.

To her fellow inmates Milena was a heroic model and incarnation of fortitude and femininity. In every respect, she was a "stimulant for the mind and body," as the *4711* slogan appropriated by Quadron asserts. The artist wants us to remember how Milena Jesenská brought the beauty of scent, or at least the idea of this beauty, into the inhuman, depraved world of the Holocaust. Yet, she also wants to remind us that perfume, along with other forms of human creativity and other artifacts of human civilization (art, music, literature), can never remain completely free of the shadow cast by that dark side of the human mind which conceived and then realized the concentration camp world. It is Quardon's hope that some day the German

314

Fig. 124 Françoise Quardon, *Les Larmes de Milena* (*Milena's Tears*), *Hommage à Milena*, mixed media sculpture, 1995.

manufacturer of *Echt Kölnisch Wasser No. 4711* might decide to add the name "Milena" to its famous blue-gold label (Marcel Cohen, letter to the author, February 22, 1996). Thus would be remembered both the pleasure and the pain, the delight and the horror, associated with this scent and with the German imagination which brought it into existence.[9]

Quardon complicates further the juxtaposition of refinement and horror by constructing her work around a scent that is profoundly German. It may be uncanny to re-imagine a situation where perfume could exist in such depraved and inhuman conditions as were found in Ravensbrück. But to emphasize the iconic Germanness of the scent and to turn its slogan, once destined for a certain bourgeois class of burghers, away from its original con-sumerist function and toward the representation of a revolt, albeit subtle, against the very German ideology and mindset which gave birth to *4711* in the eighteenth century and Ravensbrück in the twentieth, is to replace the uncanny with the surreal. The objects and images ani-mated by Quardon's constructions—the soft bottle of fra-grance with its exquisite blue-satin fabric, the tresses of plaited hair, the row of white teeth embraced by rich red velvet—have been sharpened to an ironic edge, which reveals the strange, almost unimaginable cohabitation of civilization and barbarism: what George Steiner once described as the paradoxical reality in which "a man can read Goethe or Rilke in the evening, . . . play Bach and Schubert, and go to his day's work at Auschwitz in the morning."[10] Quardon's fascination with Milena and with *Echt Kölnisch Wasser No. 4711* teaches us that fragrance and the Holocaust are not, as we may have thought, mutu-ally exclusive. Do viewers of the homage to Milena not

inhale a delightful fragrance while at the same moment casting their eyes upon a row of "extracted" teeth whose name evokes suffering and tears? The artistic gold scrolls and delicate spirals of the lettering on the *4711* label, the beautiful enlaced tresses of a woman's long hair, the sen-sual image of a skirt, and the symmetry of teeth kept healthy by daily care—all examples of civilized, fashion-able, and self-preserving as well as self-gratifying acts of cleanliness and sophistication—are in Quardon's two homages to Milena ultimately negated by the life-denying reality of the concentration camp. For in this universe a long, striped, filthy dress is the only "skirt" a woman can wear. Bald, shaved heads replace strands of hair; white teeth are taken from open mouths paralyzed in screams of death. Tears run down the skin of a face once scented with fragrance, and a tattoo, even when replaced by another more hedonistically evocative number, is still in the end a tattoo, the only sign of identity one can possess.

No. 4711 tells another tale of memory and loss. A forty-year-old man, recounts Marcel Cohen in one of his short stories, enters a perfume store for the first time in his life. Up until this moment he has been content to wear the colognes given to him as Christmas presents by girlfriends. With the help of the saleswoman, the man reduces the field of possible scents to three or four brands and then takes less than thirty seconds to choose the one he finds the most pleasurable. When he returns home and tries the scent again, any lingering doubts he might have had about the fragrance disappear; he knows for certain that this is the absolutely right scent for him: "The bottle's shape, the label's color, now that he looks at them more attentively, add to his certainty." Several weeks later an older friend of the family, seeing the bottle in the bathroom,

tells him that his father, who died in a concentration camp in 1943 and whom he only vaguely remembers, had used *4711* before the war. Subtle are the workings of a memory triggered by smell. Despite the man's never having remembered seeing a bottle of *4711* in his childhood home and despite the few memories of his parents he has retained from this faraway past, some unspoken and unconscious recognition played a significant role in his choice of the scent. "Olfactory memory," Cohen concludes, "is indelible. Beyond the call of language and thus preserved from its unpredictable drifts, memory makes no room for approximation or doubt."[11]

Potent are the memories animated by scent, as Proust knew all too well. Fragrance is linked to a past which ascends into the present as a narrative. Many are the tales and the tales-within-tales that perfumes tell, and the greater the contrast between the beauty of the scent and the foulness of the time and place of its appearance the more poignant the story. The *4711* inspired by Milena's tattoo and the *4711* which the invisible hand of memory pushes the man to purchase in Cohen's story reveal different narrative layers having to do with historical event, private memory, human dignity, and the artist's or writer's own subjective experience of and meditation on history, memory, and ethics. The first day of her arrival at Birkenau (part of the Auschwitz cluster of camps) on January 27, 1943, one of a group of 230 women who had left Compiègne, France, three days earlier, Charlotte Delbo takes what would be her last shower in sixty-seven days. She and her female companions have their heads shaved and are then ordered to undress. All clothing along with everything they have brought with them—nothing can be kept—must be left in their valises which are to be confiscated. Delbo has

brought a small bottle of perfume a friend had given her before the departure from Compiègne. Until now she has used this perfume sparingly. At night, before falling asleep, she has opened the bottle and merely inhaled the scent. Forbidden to take the perfume with her into the shower Delbo slowly empties all its contents between her breasts, taking care under the water not to soap away this perfumed patch of skin. Suddenly, the water stops running, and Delbo enters

> the drying room where Viva, Yvonne, and the others, half-rinsed, were sitting. It made them laugh. It was the last bit of laughter ringing out among us. "How good you smell!" said one of them. "Let me sit down next to you for a moment. We won't inhale delicate smells again." She must have been from the Tours region, so elegantly did she express herself. "Inhale," the word stuck in my memory together with the voice of the one who had spoken it, but I no longer know who she was, nor am I able to recapture her face.

Yet, what Delbo does remember is the name of the scent: *Orgueil* (Pride) by Lelong. "What a fine name for that day," she writes. Indeed, pride in oneself and in one's femininity is expressed by Delbo's act just as it was revealed in Milena's tattoo. In truth, however, Delbo's memory of the scent she used that day may not be completely accurate. Lucien Lelong's *Orgueil* was introduced in Europe in 1946 and presented in a reflective gold glass bottle whose form makes one think of a chess rook without its characteristic crenellated tower.[12] Yet, the name of Delbo's perfume is not in the least important; the mere act of using scent, whatever it might be called, and of asserting one's femininity at a moment of terror and in the antechamber to what would be hell on earth is what is most meaningful.

The Odor of Misanthropy: Perfume and Murder

Perfume and genocide are not mutually exclusive phenomena. Even as far back as 1649 an Italian doctor offered the Venetian Republic an "essence of plague," which by being infused into textiles destined to be sold in enemy territory could be spread among the Turks. The Republic turned down the idea and had the doctor summarily arrested to keep him from offering the "scent" (a weapon of mass destruction before its time) to another nation. This schizophrenic, though not surprising, coexistence of the monstrous and the sublime, of the foul and the fragrant which narratives about perfume and genocide recount receives a greater and more sustained expression in Patrick Süskind's novel *Perfume: The Story of a Murderer*. A detective and historical novel rolled into one, *Perfume: The Story of a Murderer* enjoyed an immense success from the moment it appeared in Germany in 1985; it had sold over three million copies by the summer of 1988 and had been translated into twenty-five languages.[13] The novel, which uses the language of perfume to articulate an allegory of cruelty and misanthropy and to satirize one man's megalomaniacal charismatic power over masses of human beings, opens with a succinct and moral statement regarding the link between the sublime and the bestial, the heroic and the criminal:

> In eighteenth-century France there lived a man who was one of the most gifted and abominable personages in an era that knew no lack of gifted and abominable personages . . . His name is Jean-Baptiste Grenouille, and if his name—in contrast to the names of other gifted abominations, de Sade's, for instance, or Saint-Just's, Fouché's, Bonaparte's, etc.—has been forgotten today, it is certainly not because Grenouille fell short of those more famous blackguards when it came to arrogance, misanthropy, immorality, or, more succinctly, to wickedness, but because his gifts and his sole ambition were restricted to a domain that leaves no traces in history: to the fleeting realm of scent. (3)

Grenouille, who will become the greatest, most sublime perfumer to have ever lived, is placed by Süskind in a pantheon of brutal and megalomaniacal politicians of the French Revolution. Saint-Just's denunciations of Louis XVI, Danton, and other fellow revolutionaries were so effective that he earned the name "The Angel of Death." Fouché, whose repressive policies during the Revolution ultimately got him appointed Napoleon's minister of police in 1799, had a moniker, "The Butcher of Lyon," as chilling as that of Saint-Just. Napoleon's obsessive, often tyrannical pursuit of power and Sade's immoral, revolutionary fantasies of sexual liberation are credentials enough to allow them entry into the same pantheon. Yet, a more modern butcher, megalomaniac, and angel of death is missing from Süskind's list, only for the reason that the novelist has limited his rogues' gallery of political and intellectual figures to eighteenth-century French "blackguards," as he calls them. But Süskind is a postwar German writer, and so the missing personage in question is very much present, albeit as a kind of ghost in the text: a terrible yet fascinating phantom of misanthropy, cruelty, and Aryan superiority lying within Grenouille's unconscious.

Although Grenouille will become one of an august group of powerful and "gifted abominations," he, the future master of refined fragrances, who is French right down to his sarcastic name, has a birth as bestial and inhuman as could be imagined. Born under a fish stall among garbage, gutted fish, and buzzing flies and enveloped in the putrefying stench of a Parisian market on one of the hottest days of 1738, Grenouille, an unwanted love child, is the fifth of his young mother's brood, not one of whom has ever survived his or her day of birth. The repulsive coming-into-being of this perfumer-to-be, whose mother squats down under her gutting table to give birth to a "bloody meat" not all that different from "the fish guts that lay there already" (5), is notable for the fusion of foulness and sublimity, the overlapping of repulsion and joy, and the association of pleasure and pain that will characterize Süskind's schizophrenic depiction of different historical, social, moral, and aesthetic realities in the novel: first, human nature, which is presented as either weak or depraved since nearly all of Süskind's characters are base, rapacious, selfish, and egocentric; second, society, in which collective groups are easily whipped into lascivious and murderous frenzies of mob hysteria; third, art, which grounds the creation of the sublime in violent, sadistic impulses; and finally, perfumery, whereby the purest, most blissful of essences emerge from processes of maceration and distillation that reduce fine, delicate blossoms to a wet, slimy, decomposing mass: a "cooked muck, . . . as flabby and pale as soggy straw, like the bleached bones of little birds, like vegetables that had been boiled too long, insipid and stringy, pulpy, hardly still recognizable for what it was, disgustingly cadaverous, and almost totally robbed of its odor" (115).

The act of scent-theft, the stealing, that is, of the unique spirit and essence of an individual human being and the destruction of a thing of beauty—floral, human, or divine—to create a thing of even greater beauty, hover over Süskind's narrative. In a spiritually aesthetic universe, the end—the creation of sublime art—justifies the means, whether these involve the destruction of a petal or that of a beautiful young maiden; there is little difference in Grenouille's mind. The alchemical magic of human artistry and technology—the use of "fire, water, steam, and a cunning apparatus [an alembic] to snatch the scented soul from matter" (114)—gives Grenouille a Promethean aura. His is a black magic which declares war against matter and nature. It signals man's frenzied need to master the earth, to cast it in his own image, and ultimately to rival God's creation of the universe, which Grenouille hopes to realize through a new genesis:

> That scented soul, that ethereal oil, was in fact the best thing about matter, the only reason for his interest in it. The rest of the stupid stuff—the blossoms, leaves, rind, fruit, color, beauty, vitality, and all those other useless qualities—were of no concern to him. They were mere husk and ballast, to be disposed of (114).

Out of the art of perfumery, Süskind distills a negative ethics founded on the belief that the ends (the creation of a "scented soul") justify the means (the "stupid stuff" to be gotten rid of). The migration of scent from flower to alembic, from ravaged petal to expansive aroma, provides him with the allegorical metaphor for Grenouille's and humanity's desire to make death the precondition of art, destruction the raison d'être of creation, and extermination the sine qua non of purification: a spiritual mission of fascist proportions. The only thing that is important is that spirit be removed from matter, essence spirited away from things, eternity derived from contingency, art and artifice distilled from imperfection, and the immutable Thousand-Year Reich summoned forth out of the flux of time.

Although the novel carries the title *Perfume*, its opening pages—one paragraph, for example, repeats "stench" and "stank" a total of eighteen times (3–4)—are obsessed by putridness: namely, that of eighteenth-century Paris, that of humankind in general, and that of Grenouille in particular. It is as if Süskind wanted the reader to wallow in the malodor of original sin and depravity into which Grenouille has been born. Les Halles, the marketplace of the perfumer's birth (and from the twelfth century until a few years before the Revolution the site of a huge necropolis called Le Cimetière des Innocents where corpses were laid out in long ditches) is nothing less than "the most putrid spot in the whole kingdom" (5). The stench was everywhere inescapable. Manure, urine, mold, rat droppings, spoiled cabbage, stale dust, and greasy sheets gave off noxious odors. Chimneys spewed into the air the smell of sulfur, tanneries that of lye, abattoirs that of blood, rivers that of stale water, and human beings that of sweat, dirty clothes, decaying teeth, rancid cheese, and sickness. Democratic in its embrace of humanity, fetidness favored no one particular class; young and old, male and female, religious and atheist, peasant and aristocrat, commoner and king, they all reeked.[14]

Out of this foul, villainous cesspool of urban humanity arises Grenouille, more beast than man, more animal than human, more devil than angel, as the crescendo of descriptive epithets Süskind invents to give him life intensifies through the novel. In Süskind's bestiary Grenouille is compared more often to a tick than to any other creature, because of his parasitical power to suck the fragrant blood, the scented soul, from his victims. This perfumer is a vampire of odors, who nourishes himself on the scent of the other human beings he comes to possess. Despite Grenouille's sublime appreciation of smell and his phenomenally sensitive nose, his physical reaction to the pure beauty of a scent is, at least when he is young, animalistic. After he commits his first murder, that of a young red-headed girl whose exquisite odor has lead him through the streets of Paris to the courtyard of her home on the rue des Marais, Grenouille sniffs her outstretched body like a predatory beast sizing up its kill:

> He thrust his face to her skin and swept his flared nostrils across her, from belly to breast, to neck, over her face and hair, and back to her belly, down to her genitals, to her thighs and white legs . . . He gathered up the last fragments of her scent under her chin, in her navel, and in the wrinkles inside her elbow . . . He was brimful with her (50).

Like a sponge he absorbs every "drop of her scent," sealing it hermetically in different compartments of his olfactory memory from which he will later, tranquilly, recollect its enticing aroma. He is an insane, yet systematic, collector who, powerless to resist the smells of the world, ingests them at a dizzying pace, feeding on them later in memory (231), even making love to them, until he risks exploding like the blood-gorged tick he resembles. In addition to this girl and the twenty-five other women he murders in cold blood, every one of the people who comes into contact with him for long periods of time—his mother, his wet nurse, the tanner he works for, the perfumer he is apprenticed to, the crackpot-scientist marquis he is adopted by, and a few others—all die unexpectedly.

Although Grenouille is an artist, a genius in fact, whose nose seeks out delicate scents in the upper reaches of the fragrant air, he is also a base creature who carries death with him. No wonder then that he is called "reptilian," "mole-like," and "half decayed" (85, 173, 174); he is a "black toad," a "vermin," "a hermit crab," "a forest creature," and "a soft-fleshed animal" (88, 97, 159, 169). With his "devouring nose," which sometimes "flared its nostrils surreptitiously," he is a savage predator lying in wait like a "feeding pike," a "black spider," even a "bear" (19–20, 40, 90, 169, 177). His humanity is suspect because he is a "gnome," a "little man," a "pre-human creature," a beast disguised as a man, more dead than alive (89, 95, 96, 173, 175). His pockmarked face disfigured by anthrax, his hunchback, and the clubfoot which makes him limp like a wounded animal are captured in allusions to his being "a lump of humankind," a "lump of misery," a "wild Indian," and a "caveman" (86, 169, 180, 192). His nonhuman bearing, his inability to perceive his own odor, his crafty ingenuity in disappearing in the midst of a crowd by covering his body in a scent of invisibility of his own devious concoction, and his profound hatred for humankind transform him into a "cipher," a "miserable nonentity," an "abomination," and "an entirely new specimen of the race . . . that could arise only in exhausted, dissipated times like these," leading ultimately to epithets that leave little doubt about his resemblance to Adolph Hitler. For Grenouille is "a little homicidal man," the devil incarnate, an egotistical maniac, the "Monster" who, paradoxically, is an ideal, if not supernatural, being to the people he deludes with his technically perfect, odorous creations and who respond to him with idolatrous rapture and hysterical love. More precisely, he is a Prometheus, an angel, a savior, a self-generated god of infinite narcissism and egotism (24, 97, 107, 230, 272, 277, 288, 291): "He owed it to no one—not to a father, nor a mother, and least of all to a gracious God—but to *himself* alone. He was in very truth his own God, and a more splendid God than the God that stank of incense and was quartered in churches" (291–92).

If God, the Father, reeks, so also do His daughters and sons. The baseness of humanity is enveloped in a mocking, misanthropic sarcasm in the scene where Grenouille, bent on giving himself the smell of an ordinary person, invents the ordinary odor of humanness. And what are the ingredients blended into this fragrance of everyday mediocrity which he calls "the human-being odor" with its overarching "sweaty-oily, sour-cheesy, quite richly repulsive basic theme" (181–82)? To make its base note Grenouille combines cat excrement, vinegar, salt, rancid cheese, rotten eggs, castoreum, ammonia, civet, alcohol, and a few other putrid substances, which produce a cadaverous odor evocative of the Paris sewers. A covering layer, the middle note, tempers the nauseating power of these primary ingredients by adding peppermint, eucalyptus, lime, lavender, and turpentine to the blend. Capping the concoction and disguising its all-too-human primal odor of death and decomposition is a top note of floral scents: geranium, rose, orange blossom, and jasmine (182–84). When he applies the fragrance to his body, Grenouille acquires the vile, natural, and therefore unremarkable odor of a human being; in itself, however, that is insufficient. To smell even more like an ordinary person, he will have to use a common perfume to hide the naturally disgusting, fundamentally "human" odor he has just invented for himself. So Grenouille creates a second scent, very much like the first except that he makes sure to omit the cadaverous base note. The misanthropic irony is corrosive. First, Grenouille creates a scent of humanness (synonymous with a fetid vileness) and then a perfume to disguise this vile humanness. Obviously, it is not, as the proverb says, the clothes that make the man, but the perfume. Promenading down the streets of Montpellier, Grenouille is greeted by passersby as if he were just another inhabitant. He marvels at his duplicity and at the self-deceptiveness of humans. He, a great hater of mankind and a monster, has adopted the air (in more ways than one) of human normalcy, thus duping the good bourgeois citizens of the city, who politely raise their hats to him as he passes by (187–88).[15]

Grenouille's megalomania is boundless, his defiance of Creation satanic, and his desire to invert the great chain of being only matched by his contempt for all living things. He is the self-acclaimed "Grenouille the Great," "the Supreme Emperor," even "God come to earth" (306), whose most perfect fragrance, created from a collective *odor di femina*—the sublime "diadem of scent" (234) extracted from the hair, clothes, and skin of twenty-five virgins—will, he fervently hopes, enslave the entire universe. The power of creation and domination he has come to possess through an ingenuity gone wild is sustained by a superhuman belief in his own technical artistry; he is as much a super-perfumer as a super-man. Grenouille's genius is more potent than that of money, terror, or even death, because it is "the invincible power to command the love of mankind." This is a power, alas, that perverts love because it belongs to a man preternaturally incapable of loving humankind and for that reason immune to the magic of eros and agape, which his own perfume does, nonetheless, bring into being. The final irony of Süskind's narrative of misanthropy is that love is a cannibalistic act. Having turned the art of perfumery to perverted ends, Grenouille then offers a "moral lesson" of anti-Christian proportions: namely, that love for one's neighbor and selfless concern for the Other are rooted in murder. Through the rapturous, blissful effect of a heavenly scent, Grenouille achieves a monstrous and perverse reinterpretation of Being. While, he, the most bestial of men, becomes an angel and a savior, human beings, God's children, are changed into beasts by the devouring eros his sublimely horrid perfume provokes.

Having committed serial murder to produce a divine scent, having used the hair, skin, and odor (the "matter," in other words "the stupid stuff") of humans in an instrumental way to create an inhuman, unthinkable scent, Grenouille commits suicide by scent, forcing others into an unthinkable, inhuman act of collective murder. Like any powerful and terrifying dictator, Grenouille pushes the limits of the possible to include the morally impossible; and he forces other beings to follow him in doing the same. Not only is perfume perverted by the novel's final act of cannibalism; so, too, are the humanistic ideals of civilized existence: charity, altruism, goodness, justice, and, above all, love. Dousing his body with the full contents of his miraculous and barbaric perfume Grenouille suddenly seems "bathed in beauty like blazing fire" to the crowd of Parisian riffraff (thieves, murderers, cutthroats, whores) camped out in the marketplace square where twenty-eight years earlier he had been born. In this final apotheosis, an aura of scent (namely, the spiritualized essence of twenty-five destroyed young lives) is sublimated into a halo of light. The bloody, homicidal origin of the perfume has been obliterated, masked by a heavenly fragrance as spiritual and pure as light itself. Enveloped in the cocoon of art, murder takes on a fragrant and alluring beauty. This is a truth Grenouille himself has come to know firsthand, when he commits his most sublime and outrageous act of fragrance theft, covering the dead body of his final victim, Laure Richis, with an oil-soaked shroud and employing a centuries-old form of absorption and extraction, *enfleurage à froid* (cold enfleurage), to preserve for all time the quintessential aroma of her skin. This act of appropriation he coldly refers to as a harvesting (262), because the odor of a young woman at the threshold of puberty like Laure is

Here, again, art and imagination join forces, but this time their collaboration has a revisionist effect. They collude to hide and thus revise the reality of the past, transforming history and event (the acts of a beastly, loathsome, obsessive dreamer) into idolatry (the obsessive public fascination with a charismatic figure capable of moving masses of ordinary people to collective action) and into myth (that of the great Founder, the great Demiurge who outperforms God Himself). Radiant with fragrance and light, Grenouille appears like a celestial visitation before the criminal demimonde of wide-eyed onlookers assembled at Les Halles. Awe and amazement cover their faces. But the epiphany

The tradition of disguising perfume bottles to resemble leather-bound books extends back hundreds of years as in this carrying case from the eighteenth century. A special gift edition of Jean-Paul Gaultier's *Le Mâle* was presented in a similar manner for the Christmas season, 1999.

particularly precarious and must be seized at the very moment it explodes into ripeness, not unlike the harvesting of jasmine when the petals' fragrance is at its peak. Having reduced and confined the life and beauty of a maiden to the space of a small perfume bottle, a symbolic deflowering—"he wanted truly to possess the scent of this girl . . . to peel it from her like skin, and to make her scent his own . . . Only now was she really dead for him, withered away, pale and limp as a fallen petal" (208, 268)—Grenouille holds in his hand what death itself cannot possess: the scented soul, disembodied and fixed for all time, of another human being.

Grenouille's final self-glorification in an explosion of light, fire, scent, and beauty, an egotistical act of self-willed martyrdom, endows him with a divine and mythic stature.

quickly turns dark, as emotions of perfumed wondrousness turn to feelings of desire, lust, and rapture:

They felt themselves drawn to this angel of a man. A frenzied, alluring force came from him, a riptide no human could have resisted, all the less because no human would have wanted to resist it, for what that tide was pulling under and dragging away was the human will itself: straight to him. . . . They *lunged* at the angel, *pounced* on him, *threw him* to the ground. Each of them wanted to touch him, wanted to have a piece of him, a feather, a bit of plumage, a spark from that wonderful fire. They *tore away* his clothes, his hair, his skin from his body, they *plucked* him, they drove their *claws* and *teeth* into his flesh, they attacked him like *hyenas* . . . In very short order, the angel was divided into thirty pieces, and every *animal* in the *pack* snatched a piece for *itself,* and then, driven by voluptuous lust, dropped back to *devour* it (308–09; emphasis mine).

Grenouille has succeeded in being loved, loved to death, as it were. Yet, the savagery of the desire he has inspired leads humans away from the fundamental humanness of love. Grenouille has organized a charivari, a carnivalesque ritual commonly practiced in the later Middle Ages and the sixteenth century in which social hierarchies and moral val-

lowing their mob orgy refuse to discuss their shameful collaboration, banishing the event from memory and history through a collective amnesia, the bewitched cannibals, once they have totally consumed and digested Grenouille, glance at each other with only mild and short-lived embarrassment:

> They had all, whether man or woman, committed a murder or some other despicable crime at one time or another. But to eat a human being? They would never, so they thought, have been capable of anything that horrible. And they were amazed that it had been

Admiral Nelson's perfume flask, made in Germany, c. 1760.

ues were turned topsy-turvy—the fool becomes king and the king fool—if only for a day. Grenouille's carnival of misrule, the second such event his sublime fragrance has provoked—the first, at his highly theatrical and ultimately unsuccessful public execution, pushed the good citizens of Grasse into an infernal orgy of 10,000 copulating beings— is neither ceremonial nor symbolic, but catastrophic and ontological: it subverts the very foundations of human existence. It changes the hierarchical order of the great chain of being, because a murderous, bloodthirsty tick with a Hitlerian ego turns into an angel, while humans change into animals. Süskind gives this inversion of high and low, this reversal of good and evil, and this substitution of chaos for order an allegorical spin.

Unlike the guilty citizens of Grasse, who the day fol-

so very easy for them and that, embarrassed as they were, they did not feel the tiniest bite of conscience. On the contrary! Though the meal lay rather heavy on their stomachs, their hearts were definitely light. All of a sudden there were delightful, bright flutterings in their dark souls. And on their faces was a delicate, virginal glow of happiness. . . . They had to smile. They were uncommonly proud. For the first time they had done something out of love (309–10).

Like Freud, but with a more panoramic view of twentieth-century history, Süskind represents the consequences of a civilization established upon the repression of human instinct. (And like Bataille, he reveals the intensity with which love at its most extreme—its most repressed—

321

turns into death.) The cannibalistic massacre of Grenouille, impelled by a collective human desire to devour and internalize the soul or will of a powerfully gifted, evil genius and characterized by the awareness that a line between the thinkable and the unthinkable, the civilized and the uncivilized, has been irreversibly crossed, cannot fail to call to mind the frenzied enthusiasm for and the hysterical obedience to Nazi ideology which took hold of Germany under National Socialism. Süskind appears to allude to the Final Solution when the narrator of *Perfume* observes that Grenouille "would have loved right now to have exterminated these people from the earth, every stupid, stinking, eroticized one of them, just as he had once exterminated alien odors from the world of his raven-black soul."(293).[16]

From the opening paragraph of *Perfume* Süskind makes it clear that if the name Jean-Baptiste Grenouille has not been as famous or notorious as that of Napoleon Bonaparte and others, it was not for lack of genius in the practice of arrogance, injustice, and cruelty. Grenouille was as brutal and powerfully devious as these other political rogues, but his domain of supremacy, the evanescent world of perfumery, is one that leaves "no traces in history" (3). Through this coincidence of anosmia and amnesia Süskind sounds a cautionary note. The traces of an abominable past, he suggests, can easily be overwritten, revised, and forgotten by the ideological aura or odor that later generations choose to give to that past. The fragrance of history and the sillage, or scented wake, of a past event either disappear on the winds of passing time or are layered over with fresher, more contemporary, and sometimes more confusing, if not more agreeable or acceptable scents. Perfume, Süskind's novel suggests, is a fitting allegory for the workings of revisionism. This revisionism, moreover, is not only historical or political; it is also cosmic. Grenouille seeks to re-create the universe, to "turn the world into a fragrant Garden of Eden" (116), a new Holy Land of scent, allowing him to replace God and do a better job at Creation. He envisions himself as "a giant alembic, flooding the whole world with a distillate of his own making" (116). He sees his destiny as "nothing less than to revolutionize the odoriferous world" (51). To this end, he desires to write a new Grenouillian Book of Genesis whose first words, as one might imagine them, would announce: "In the beginning was the Scent, and the Scent was with God, and the Scent was God."

Grenouille's act of genesis through smell (what might be called "osmogenesis") reveals a defiant, spiritual revolt against God and against all creatures which have descended from Him or been created in His image. In this revisionist Garden of Eden, Grenouille is the satanic gardener and the demonic perfumer who uses perfect beauty to exile God from His own paradise and to contaminate Heaven by importing the aroma of hell. Yet, the history of Eden and its odors has been retold in a very different narrative of fragrance by another contemporary writer of fiction. One day, seeing Adam sniffing his own body and realizing that this

man has no odors to smell, God, as the French novelist Michel Tournier imagines the ancient biblical past in his delightful fairy tale, "La Légende des Parfums," decides that the inodorous desert world in which He has placed the first human needs drastic change.[17] And so He creates a perfumed garden, a paradise, and gives Adam another companion, Eve, to share it with. Only the fruit of the "tree of scents" is forbidden to the couple. Were they to partake of this tree's knowledge, their unconscious and spontaneous understanding of the purely natural fragrances of Eden would disappear, replaced forever by the knowledge of perfumery, an art and science in which nature no longer enjoys pride of place. Encouraged by the serpent, Adam and Eve taste the fruit. All at once, the fragrances of paradise turn into trivial if not repulsive scents, signs of the fetidness which coincides with the beginning of mankind's existential misery. For the first time ever, Adam and Eve recoil from each other's smell, now redolent of human sweat (sign of the hard life of labor to come). They realize that they will, henceforth, have to deodorize themselves. If "In Adam's fall / We sinned all," as the seventeenth-century *New England Primer* declared, that universal sin involved, it could be said, the loss of a *perfumed* state of grace.

The history of mankind from Eden to the present has been, according to Tournier, the story of the search for these lost scents from before the Fall: "the fragrances of prehistory" as Tom Robbins calls them, which Adam and Eve once innocently, naturally, and unselfconsciously enjoyed (*Jitterbug Perfume,* 77). Strenuous attempts through the ages, Tournier writes, have been made to rediscover these "great perfumes of Paradise": first, in the recipe for mankind's first scent which God whispered to Moses on Sinai after giving him the Ten Commandments; second, in the incense and myrrh brought by the three Kings to the infant Jesus; third, in the valuable perfume Mary Magdalene poured over Christ's head; and finally, in the great classic French scents of modern perfumery created between 1912 and 1986. For Tournier, these "edenic" fragrances are Guerlain's *L'Heure Bleue,* a scent that "carries one back to the dawn of the world"; Chanel's *No. 5,* recalling the fifth day of Creation; Lanvin's *Arpège*; Balmain's *Jolie Madame*; Hermès's *Bel Ami*; and finally Dior's *Poison,* evocative of "the serpent's potent and seductive odor" of sin and transgression. In Tournier's rewriting of the Garden of Eden story, perfume offers an imaginary route back to the lost mythic past of human prehistory. It is the "open-sesame" magically pushing back the portals to reveal "our paradisiacal past." Perfume, with its "giant's wings," returns us, Tournier concludes, "to the magical garden where the first couple loved innocently under the protective eye of the Great Divine Perfumer." What a beatific, creative demiurge is this truly angelic perfumer and how different He is from Grenouille, a fallen angel who appropriates divine knowledge only for satanic ends, confusing the exaltation of scent with the sublimity of evil. For Grenouille is a dark, primitive perfumer of nothingness

Opposite page: Nina Ricci's *L'Air du Temps,* 1948, in its celebrated "double dove" crystal bottle (created in 1951), has been praised for its "extraordinary simplicity," and its dependence on natural products like jasmine and rose absolutes, which add complexity and richness to its floral bouquet (Calkin and Jellinek).

and death, who, in Süskind's allegorical narrative, may be no more than what the poet Sylvia Plath (in *Ariel*) called "a man in black with a Meinkampf look." [18]

Death by Perfume

Passion, romance, betrayal, transgression, mystery, magic, crime, vengeance, and genocide—all the significant story-lines and emotions of narrative (and life) have been modulated through the medium and metaphor of perfume. In fact, rarely is scent free of a story of some kind. A fragrance's very name triggers the release of a yet-to-be articulated tale. *L'Heure Bleue, My Sin, Tabu, Poison, Trouble, Obsession,* and *Opium* are words in which embryonic narratives, seed-tales, gestate, waiting for fantasy and imagination to midwife them into being. Like the scents they designate, waiting behind glass walls for that liberation into the air heralded by the uncorking of the bottle, the stories these names laconically evoke eventually bloom, and the images they trigger eventually unwind, on waves of fragrance and in tales of desire. Luxury, observes James B. Twitchell, an historian of advertising, "is a story we tell about things." [19] Such a story is always one of desire. The luxury items we purchase are, by the very acts of appropriation and possession we have initiated, immediately enveloped in the ongoing, unfinished tale of who we are and who we want to be.

Considering perfume's potential for narrative expansion, opening a bottle of scent can be like opening a book. Indeed, sometimes it literally involves opening a book. For the Christmas season 1999, Jean-Paul Gaultier's men's fragrance, *Le Mâle,* was sold in a box resembling a rare tome expensively bound in (faux) red leather. Inside could be found a bottle of eau de toilette, a deodorant stick, and, to avoid disappointing any bibliophilic consumer, the small hardbound text of a Christmas fairy tale entitled "The Couturier and the Two Angels," recounting the "story" of Gaultier's perfumes. No air of the fairy tale, however, hovers over the somber story recounted by Percy Kemp in his novel *Musc* from 2000. A healthy, elegant, and vain sixty-nine-year-old former member of the French counter-espionage service, a man appropriately named M. Eme, is discomfited one morning upon opening a new bottle of his favorite eau de toilette, which he has worn faithfully for over forty years; he notices that the scent has been altered, along with the design of the bottle. Because this musk-based cologne, produced in Grasse since 1915, has always served as an extension of his being and his presence in the world—he calls it a kind of super-garment ("survête-ment")—not to mention the powerful role its fragrant aura has played in his successful relationships with women, M. Eme's life goes into decline. First, he develops the obsession to buy and horde all the bottles of the original *Musk,* "his Grail," which he can still find in the world; by his estimate he will need 260 bottles to last him for another twenty years. When he fails to stockpile the needed bottles, he decides to ration his daily consumption. The effect is devastating; he begins to notice signs of aging all over his body. Depressed, disheveled, and in withdrawal from the world inside the "cocoon" of his apartment, the only place the original odor of *Musk* still reigns, M. Eme decides to coordinate the end of his life with the end of his private reserve of the cologne. Thus, he arranges for an embalmer to come to his apartment the morning of his suicide and to massage his corpse with what remains of *Musk.* [20]

The Pillow Boy of the Lady Onogoro

Another tale of perfumed death, occasioned this time by the desire not for cosmic reintegration but for revenge, seems on the surface to be of older and more mythic provenance than the novel *Musc.* The late-tenth- to early-eleventh-century manuscript of *The Pillow Boy of the Lady Onogoro,* composed of stories recounted by the Japanese concubine-poet Onogoro, who engages a blind servant boy to hide behind the screen of her bed and whisper erotically exciting stories into her ear so that, as her lover caresses her, she will experience the orgasms that have been eluding her, tells a tale, as it turns out, neither ancient nor oriental. A literary pastiche written in the mid-1990s by the Scottish novelist and poet, Alison Fell, *The Pillow Boy of Lady Onogoro* is an erotic and narrative tour de force. Of particular interest is one scene in which the novelist's scented imagination testifies to a clever and crafty exuberance. Joining the other concubines and ladies-in-waiting of the Imperial Court who wile away long, insomniac hours in delightful conversation and games, Lady Onogoro participates in a leisurely and amusing competition. The women are invited to imagine the "most suitable death for a faithless lover"; she who tells the best story will win the contest.

Of the three tales recounted, the most interesting, although not the winning story, concerns a "death by perfume." To punish her lover's faithlessness a woman invites him into her "perfume-mixing chamber" so that, as she deviously tells him, he can help her to create a new scent embodying their love for each other. Fancying himself a connoisseur of fragrances, the lover enthusiastically accepts. He enters a realm of overpoweringly beautiful aromas: violet, honeysuckle, lemon balm, hyacinth, cloves, nutmeg, camphor, and other heavenly odors. Removing his clothes and lying down on the robe his mistress has placed on the floor, the lover willingly allows his beloved to apply different kinds of fragrance to different parts of his body. The lady is well acquainted with the homeopathic and magical powers of flowers and scents. She knows, for example, "that, just as an excess of yin transforms itself into the opposite yang principle, so, in certain dosages, the otherwise healing and stimulating flower essences can be induced to take on a negative aspect." Cunningly, she

Paris je t'aime

YVES SAINT LAURENT

A perfume, a city, a horizon—to love one is to love all three and to abandon reason, as the photographer and filmmaker Jean-Paul Goude suggests in a series of ads (1997–1998), featuring a panoramic, bird's-eye view of the City of Light, for Yves Saint Laurent's *Paris* (1983).

applies iris to the lover's temple, yarrow and gentian to his armpits, marigold to the hollow at the base of the throat, and other fragrances to other pulse and pressure points on the man's quickly enraptured body. Yet, in addition to ecstasy, each newly added scent produces a negative psychological effect. Mustard brings on inexplicable gloominess, mimulus the fear of sickness, larch the possibility of failure, honeysuckle a tearful nostalgia for home, heather an intense anxiety, wild rose apathy, and chestnut a searing guilt over past mistakes. Physiological reactions accompany the lover's growing feelings of self-loathing and worthlessness. He sweats, trembles, weeps, and cries out, finally begging his mistress "to deal him a fatal dose, so that he might pay the price for all his crimes against her." Out of pity for his suffering, the lady drops a tiny amount of the poisonous flower aconite on his tongue. As it had for

325

M. Eme and for Grenouille, death again transforms body and flesh into a heavenly effluence of scent: "And so died the faithless lover, all naked and relieved, and not since the death of the Shining Prince himself was there ever a corpse so fragrant at its funeral."[21]

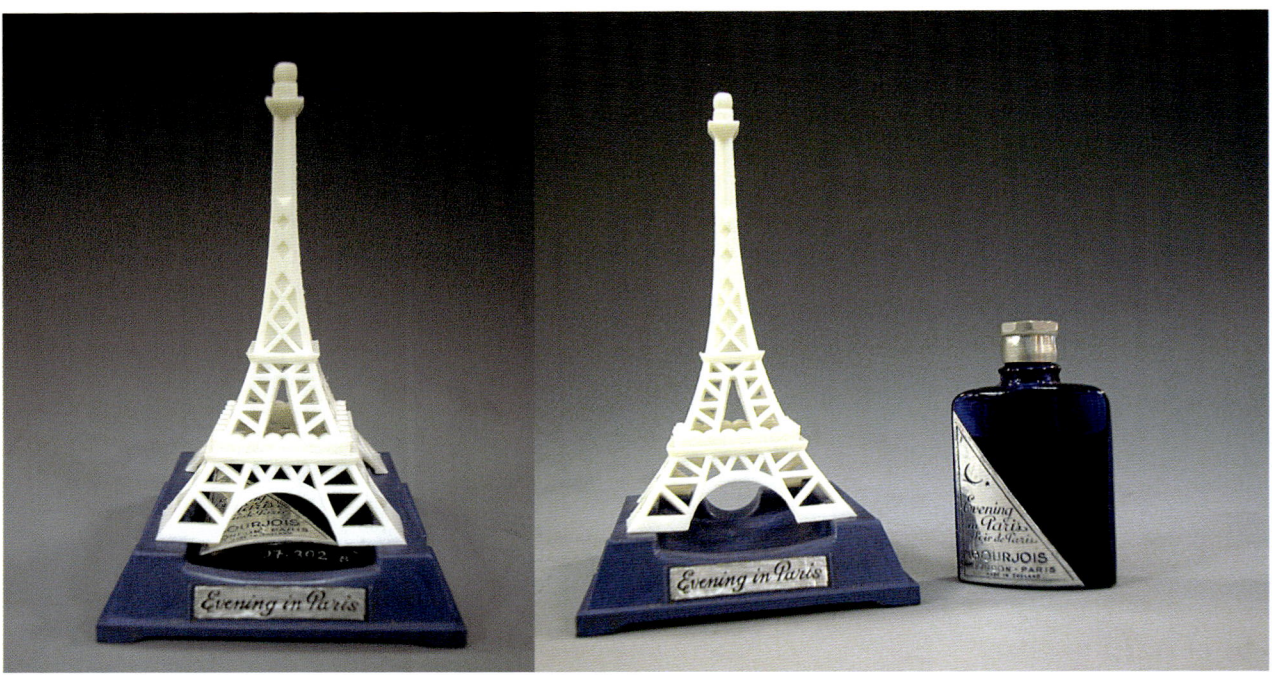

For the American or British woman longing from a distance to visit the City of Light Bourjois offered a midnight blue bottle, a silver label, a crescent moon, and stars to create an image of "Parisness." Its exceedingly popular *Soir de Paris / Evening in Paris,* first created in 1927–1928, is shown here in a plastic Eiffel Tower box created for the U.K. market in 1949; the bottle is seen both nested below and standing to the side of the Tower.

Narrative Visions of Scent: The Advertising, Televising, and Filming of Perfume

Between March and April 1985 Galeries Lafayette, the Parisian department store, offered its customers a high-tech, computerized solution to the daunting problem of finding the "right" perfume. Aptly named "Cleopatra," this computerized "nose" was programmed to analyze the personality of women who sought its advice and then to suggest the two or three perfumes most suited to their particular psychological profile. Cleopatra's memory bank contained over two hundred different scents. To use the computer's resources, women customers were requested to answer precise questions concerning their likes, dislikes, habits, eccentricities, and styles of living, such as: "Does the unpredictable frighten you?" "Do you keep your photo album out in your living room?" "Do you eat in secret?" "Do you talk about your work with the man in your life?" and so on. A total of 15,525 responses were fed into the computer's database and organized according to the prevalence of certain common character traits. This process of reduction produced five general (and highly subjective if not questionable) "types" of women, identified as "narcissistic," "realistic," "conventional," "conflictual," and "imaginative"; to each category was assigned a specific class of perfume. For the woman with a tendency toward "narcissism"—in other words, with "a curiosity, autonomy and individualism bordering on the egocentric and a preoccupation with

Opposite page: Fig. 126 From Guerlain's *Rococo à la Parisienne* and *Paris Nouveau* from the 1880s to Nina Ricci's *Love in Paris* of 2004 the image of Paris has had its own romantic, seductive "fragrance" evoked by a limited set of iconic and stereotypical elements as in this print advertisement for Yves Saint Laurent's *Paris* from the November 1987 issue of *Harper's Bazaar.*

her beauty and her body"—a sharp green scent like Balmain's *Vent vert,* Laroche's *Fidji,* or *First* by Van Cleef et Arpels was recommended. The "realistic" woman, described as an ambitious personality with "a taste for adventure, a certain practicality, and a business acumen touching on the Machiavellian," was encouraged to wear floral aldehyde scents, known for their tenacious sillage and their strong personalities: in particular, Ungaro's *Diva,* Patou's *Joy,* or Chanel's *No. 5.* As for the "conventional" woman, defined as a person of "high principles, charitable sentiments, a sense of family, a willingness to sacrifice, and a need for harmony and tranquility," she was advised to use a conventional floral scent like Estée Lauder's *White Linen* or Nina Ricci's *L'Air du Temps.* The "conflictual" feminine personality, with her penchant for "impulsiveness, fickleness, a taste for change and introspection, and a compelling need to call certain realities into question," was advised to favor mercurial, assertive, and spicy-floral fragrances like Yves Saint Laurent's *Opium,* Guerlain's *Vol de nuit,* or Laroche's *J'ai osé* [I Dared]. Finally, the personality of the "imaginative" woman, with her "taste for fantasy and dream, her nostalgia for the past, . . . her moodiness and lack of practicality, and her artistic sensibility," demanded an exotic, suggestive, and poetic scent: a vanilla, amber oriental, like Guerlain's *Shalimar* or Dana's *Tabu* (Girard, 167–68).

Whatever advice or knowledge—scientific, pseudo-scientific, sociological, commercial, or cultural—Cleopatra, the computer, offered, it was short-lived (Galeries Lafayette ran the service for only one month) and of considerably greater value as advertising than as psychology. What is most revealing about Cleopatra's computerized advice is the fiction it presented: the notion that a person can be reduced to a certain "type" of woman or man and that this psychological category can then be further classified according to the "type" of scent with which it coordinates.

YVESSAINTLAURENT

SAKS FIFTH AVENUE

To accept that one is a "conflictual" woman and therefore in need of an impulsive, changing fragrance or that one is an "imaginative" woman to whom only poetic, dreamy scents would appeal signals a need not just to belong to a fictional type of human being but a desire to make oneself the protagonist in a fictional story: the as-yet-to-be completed scenario which dream and fantasy nourish. The imagined narrative of the woman who is persuaded to think of herself as "conflictual" or "imaginative" will involve the kinds of psychological fictions associated with that personality "type"—scenarios of impulsive, independent, devil-be-damned behavior or sensitive, artistic, bold creativity—and at the same time the kinds of fantasy fictions (the "imaginaries") inspired by the mystery, audacity, and transgression which names like *Opium, J'ai Osé,* and *Tabu* evoke.

Perfume's Narratives of Desire

For consumers overcome with a desire for them, commodities are stories. Through the goods we purchase and consume we write the continuous, never-completed narratives of who we are and who we want to be. These stories may be imitative insofar as we seek to present the look or adopt the identity of a cultural hero whose image we want to acquire; wearing *Glow* by Jennifer Lopez or *White Diamonds* by Elizabeth Taylor will give, we hope, an imaginary spark of their radiance. Or these stories may be revisionist because they enable us to forge a new self-image, to be reborn as a new person in a new guise. The commodity one buys, whether a little black dress, lingerie, lipstick, or perfume, comes with a prepackaged accessory, a "freebie," which is the dream narrative it inspires. "If a perfume does not make you dream," Jean Kerléo, the former chief perfumer for Jean Patou remarks, then "it is not a great perfume." "If love is a sin," observes Jean-Paul Guerlain, a transgression with all the narrative intricacy and power a sinful act can suggest to the imagination, then "a fine perfume is what must compel you to commit it." Advertising tells us that goods—appropriately named considering the "good" we want them to do for us—are there to provide the finishing touches to fantasies of wish fulfillment. Perfume, as Guerlain indicates, "possesses the absolute power to generate and dramatize an entire universe of intimacy, proximate or distant: a journey into the limbo of the imaginary."[22]

Through consumption we live, for a brief moment at least, the conclusion to the story—of desire, identity, existence, fantasy, love—that we never stop "writing." Fashion rhetoric, Barthes remarks, "tends increasingly to the novelistic." With a particular purchase we not only complete an outfit or a look, we complete a story; we give it a happy ending. What we put into action through the objects we consume is a narrative of desire, an unfolding tale in a state of perpetual evolution and revision. Sometimes the story comes to an end, or so we believe: the dress or perfume completes the ensemble. But consumption can only end with the death of the consumer. As long as we live, we consume. And as long as we consume, the story of our desires is without end, although there are moments of illusion and delusion when the object of consumption is so overwhelmingly satisfying as to give a semblance of fulfillment and closure. But advertising never involves the complete closing off of desire. The story must continue. New objects must become the source of new desires; new images must replace the ones already consumed. The fictions of desire are thus without end. With so many tales remaining to be told the narrative power of advertising is a constant source of energy. Since human beings expect that their desires, as Baudrillard remarks, will be "attended to, that they [will] be formulated and expressed in the form of images for [one's] own contemplation," advertising has the power necessary for the proliferation of images, the amplification of stories, and the intensifying of the beliefs that underwrite consumerist culture.[23]

Advertising is a discourse perpetually engaged in speaking to the consumer, in showing her or him new things, in taking an interest in her or his concerns, and in bathing objects in the warm light of comfort. Things appeal to us because they offer imaginary visions that could indeed become ours, the outline of stories in which we could indeed figure as the central character. Objects for sale, Baudrillard writes, "submit themselves to us, they seek us out, surround us, and prove their existence to us . . . We are taken as the object's aims, and the object loves us. And because we are loved, we feel that we exist." The object of desire is eroticized; we love it, but it also loves us in return. It winks at us, flirts with us. Its come-hither glance invites us to take it in hand, caress it, and make it our own. The act of purchase is not only an act of possession but the enactment of a story, "a scenario," according to Baudrillard. It is "a complicated dance" in which the choreography is borrowed from the moves and gestures of "amorous dalliance" and the drama enacts the "advances, rivalry, obscenity, flirtation, [and] prostitution" common to fiction and romance. In this manner, advertising "defines and redirects an imaginary potentiality," weaving "the most colorful of narratives from the most impoverished of raw materials."

Since advertising signs refer to absent objects and to an illusory, imaginary world that has yet to be realized, the signifying elements in an advertisement are no more than promises or, as Baudrillard prefers to call them, "legends" or captions, laconic visual texts present only "for the purpose of being read." They do not refer to the real world but only to a world of fantasy which is activated by "a specific kind of reading" and imagining. By calling attention to the actual absence of what it designates an advertisement refers to an imaginary system of shared beliefs. Because the advertised object of desire is precisely that—the locus for a dream fueled by desire—it can never be fully possessed as a thing separate from its representation, as a reality free of and unmediated by its image and the imaginary system in which it participates. Advertisements are organized, Baudrillard notes, "in terms of a specific system of *satisfaction* which is, however, perpetually determined by the absence of reality, that is to say, by *frustration*": in other words, the disappointment of a broken promise, of a faded hope. Thus, the narrative of desire activated by the advertisement may not after all have the happy ending one expected; and even it if does, this happy ending is, unfortunately, not the end one really desired. So a new narrative, expressive of a new longing, is created by yet another new image.

Paris in a Bottle

Perfume advertisements depend on the rich mental associations an advertisement triggers among coded visual signs (a couple embracing, a dramatically illuminated flacon, the poetry of a name, the romanticism of a landscape, an icon like the Eiffel Tower), smell-memories (the scent of a former lover, of one's mother, of childhood, of intoxicating flowers), and a cultural system founded on the primacy of the image. Arising from clues embedded and inscribed in the visual signs mobilized by the advertisement, the olfactory experience of an individual connects with the collective experience of her or his social and cultural milieu. This correspondence is determined by the perceiver's mental imagination and the encyclopedia of stored knowledge derived from her or his personal experience of scent and from the cultural and social attitudes toward scent (symbolic, ideological, mythic) through which a visual and olfactory sensibility has been formed and in which it continues to be sustained collectively. On the basis of visual stimuli alone the perfume advertisement forces the reader-perceiver to imagine the odor conceptually, to feel it mentally, as it were.[24]

In this mental imagining of scent, narrative plays an important role in generating the sequence of images that give concrete form to what may be, paradoxically speaking, the *optics* of smell: the way odors are first experienced through vision. Narrative in advertising contributes in part to creating the imaginary associations and longings that perfume seeks to evoke. Many print perfume advertisements, for example, offer mini-narratives, embryonic stories—there is a limit after all to how much a one- or two-page display can relate—where the symbolism, the iconography, and the imagery of a culture, for example, are manipulated to stimulate the socially determined fantasies and myths associated with a place (like the cities of Paris or New York, for example). In other words, symbols, icons, and stereotypes activate the imagining and the telling of fantasy stories, which may be based on a firsthand, personal experience of a place, or taken from movies, or inspired by novels, or provoked by the myths of a culture, which are stockpiled among the stereotypic images of the "other" preserved in that culture.

The constellation of images projected by the city of Paris, for example, has indeed been prolific in inspiring many perfumes that offer the consumer the vicarious experience of what is, after all, "Paris-in-a-bottle." The images (at once iconic, mythic, and stereotypic) of the "City of Light" can be purchased thousands of miles from the Seine. With a dab or two of "Parisness" on the skin, one can indulge the imagination, surrendering to a personal fantasy or a barely fleshed-out story of romance. No wonder then that the list of Paris-named perfumes is as old as the origins of modern perfumery at the close of the nineteenth-century and as contemporary as fragrances from the early years of the twenty-first. There have been, for example, scents evoking different seasons, climates, and times of day: *Soir de Paris / Evening in Paris* (Bourjois, 1927–1928), *Mists of Paris* (Coty, 1954), *Un Air de Paris* (Dorin, 1921), *Effluve de Paris,* in an Eiffel Tower flacon (Maison Muriel, 1950). There have been scents recalling Paris streets and neighborhoods: *Parfum des Champs-Elysées* (Guerlain, 1904 and its re-edition as *Champs Elysées* in 1995), *Rue de la Paix* (Guerlain 1908), *Avénue Matignon* (Rochas, 1936), *Rue Royale* (Molyneux, 1927), *Coeur de Paris* (Lenthéric, 1912), *Rive Gauche* (Yves Saint Laurent, 1972), *Quartier Latin* (Brisson, late 1940s), and *Maxim's* (Cardin, 1985), named for the ultrachic right bank restaurant. Scents alluding to the stylishness of Parisian life have been common like *Rococo à la Parisienne* (Guerlain 1887), *Paris Nouveau* (Guerlain 1883–89), *Gloire de Paris* (Roger et Gallet, 1907), *Prestige de Paris* (Sauzé, 1946), *Pearls of Paris* (Coty, 1954), *Gai Paris* (T. Jones, 1912), *French Cancan* (Caron, 1936), *Mademoiselle de Paris* (Lancaster, 1960) in an Eiffel Tower bottle as well, and *Bal à Versailles* (Desprez, 1962), close enough to Paris as a once-royal suburb to qualify. Finally, there are scents that need only mention the city's name to be evocative—Coty's and Saint Laurent's *Paris* (created in 1922 and 1983, respectively) or Nina Ricci's *Love in Paris* (2004)—and fragrances with oblique Parisian references as in Balmain's *ELY 64-83* (1947), the perfume company's telephone exchange (ELY standing for "Elysée") and number. Prior to the 1960s, when Americans were much less mobile than they are today and when the very wealthy alone could journey by luxury liner, the only means of travel to the Continent, Paris was known primarily through its representations (artistic, photographic, literary, cinematic, and so on). In an advertising campaign for its fragrance, *Paris,* specifically aimed at the American market during the late 1930s, Coty assured women that they would discover "the soul of Paris [in] this lasting yet refined fragrance," a promise as difficult to verify as any other secondhand or self-interested statement about the nature of the French spirit. Another advertisement for Bourjois's wildly successful *Soir de Paris* affirmed that it was "the very perfume of Paris, so fascinating, full of dreams and love."[25]

"Nothing is more beautiful than Paris," the filmmaker Chris Marker once remarked, "except the memory of Paris," a sentiment that could just as easily be read as "Nothing is more beautiful than Paris, except the image of Paris." Exported to the United States in the years before and following the war, a bottle of scent displaying the "Made in France" designation—by 1946, 85 percent of all perfume sold in America was so labeled—carried with it an image of luxurious elegance and sophisticated refinement as potent and magical as the fragrance itself (Barillé / Laroze, 95). From the 1980s, when Yves Saint Laurent first launched his new perfume *Paris,* to the present time most print advertisements for *Paris* have presented a constellation of iconic Parisian images from which the Eiffel Tower has never been distant; in one ad, for example, a woman clutches a bouquet of roses in front of a misty Eiffel Tower; in another, a helicopter carries a man hanging upside down from a landing skid to the very edge of the tower's topmost observation deck where he kisses a woman, while below all of Paris spreads for miles and above the French tricolor floats proudly in the wind. In most of these advertisements an immense crystal perfume bottle with a diamond-shaped stopper stands upright, like the iconic Eiffel Tower itself, and the handwritten words "Paris je t'aime" are conspicuously displayed. One of the most interesting of these advertisements, created around 1987, combines four simple elements—a bottle, a few birds, the Eiffel Tower, and a sunset—to construct a visual poem lyrically evocative of Paris's legendary romantic beauty.

A large round bottle of *Paris,* its amber liquid turned honey gold by the rays of the setting sun and a facet of its diamond stopper turned into a dazzling star by a spark of reflected light glancing off its surface, sits on the stone ledge of a balcony; it is photographed in extreme close-up (fig. 126). Trapped within the bottle the light of the sun has liquefied; it has become a node of scented radiance. On the glass the letters "Y-S-L," the couturier's logo as designed in 1960 by Cassandre, are vertically inscribed and then overlaid with the perfume's name, "Paris." Compared to the rest of the scene, the bottle is the only object in precise focus, although the warm, golden light streaming through the glass gives the interior of the flacon a vague and amorphous glow, like the sensation of buttery yellowness one gets when looking at the sun. Caught in blurred flight above the bottle are three dark birds, the motion of their beating wings frozen. Beyond them stands the dark, looming silhouette of the Eiffel Tower, blurred as well by the foreshortening and soft-focus effect of the camera lens; the tower's lower observation deck and supporting arc frame a soft, pinkish blue sky.

One side of the perfume bottle is brilliantly illuminated with diamond facets of light, for it has become the temporary resting place for the disappearing sun. Not only is Paris *in* the bottle, so to speak, but so are the warmth, glow, softness, and romance of "l'heure bleue," that time of early evening when the city is enveloped in satin and silky light, when thoughts (if one yields to the romantic scenario, the "imaginary," of Paris) turn to love, and when

Paris itself becomes the blurred, yet vibrant, backdrop to passion, metaphorically figured in the sublime light emanating from the now "solar" bottle. By its position on the balcony ledge the bottle intimates a connection between the misty, airy, out-of-focus beauty of the exterior city and the comforting, warm order of an off-camera interior space: a living room or bedroom into which the balcony leads. This mediation between outside and inside, between the Paris landscape and a tranquil apartment, is described by Baudelaire in one of his most beautiful and intimate love poems, "The Balcony," which has an uncanny resemblance to the image in Saint Laurent's *Paris* advertisement, if for no other reason than that the sun setting over Paris in Baudelaire's time had the same delicate, romantic, and poetic air that it does today. Standing between the "sweetness of the hearth" warming the room inside and "the spell of evening" softening the air outside, Baudelaire remembers the physical closeness he once enjoyed with a beloved woman (his mistress, Jeanne Duval) with whom he has parted company. Hovering over the scene is the light of erotic passion, both explosive and fading: "Evenings lighted by the burning of the coals, / And evenings on the balcony, veiled with rosy vapors. / . . . / How beautiful the sun is in the warm evening! / How deep is space! How powerful the heart! / As I bent over you, queen of worshipped women, / I believed I could smell the perfume of your blood" ("Le Balcon," I: 37; Fowlie, 51). Baudelaire's evocation of the Paris sunset and the encroaching night expresses a story of romance and lost love of such intensity and intimacy that the woman's inner life, the coursing of her blood, gives off an aroma the poet inhales. In a similar manner, although without Baudelaire's literally sanguine scent, Saint Laurent's *Paris* creates the romantic and lyrical image of a Parisian evening, where the softness of pink light and dewy air and the slowing down of time and movement—the motion of the birds' wings has been stopped—create a decor against which a story of passion and love, suggested by the golden bottle occupying the foreground of the cityscape, can be imagined to unfold.

The Cinema of Scent

With its images of desire, sensuality, femininity, and ecstasy and with its coded objects, poses, colors, shapes, decor, and landscapes, the reality of scent, as perfume advertisements visualize and narrate it, has more resources at its disposal when the story it seeks to tell is not limited to the printed page of a magazine or held in check by the frozen image of a photograph. In other words, in a more sequential, complicated, and even operatic manner, the cinema of scent—namely, the thirty-second advertising film—has a greater potential for telling the story and developing the imaginary associations of a perfume. The commercial not only unites visual images and colors but also orchestrates sounds, music, voice-overs, dance, gestures, theater, suspense, action, and montage (long shots, tracking shots, close-ups, and jump cuts). Several films have been created by well-known directors and photographers since the first sixty-second commercial (entitled "Tomorrow's Women") appeared on American television in the mid-1960s, made by the photographer Richard Avedon for *Chanel No. 5* and starring the actress Catherine Deneuve. Ridley Scott, the director of *Blade Runner, Thelma and Louise,* and *Black Hawk Down,* Roman Polanski, creator of *A Knife in the Water* and *Repulsion,* Luc Besson, director of films like *The Fifth Element* and *La Femme Nikita,* Baz Luhrmann, known for his *Moulin Rouge* (the point of departure for a two-minute commercial called "No. 5, le film" with Nicole Kidman, televised in 2004), and others like Jean-Paul Goude, Patrice Leconte, Bettina Rheims, David Bailey, Lester Bookbinder, and Tony Scott have all created cinematic works of perfume advertising. Many films require complicated and expensive sets and remote locations. The storylines can be dramatic, clever, humorous, and intricate. The editing requires considerable technical expertise, since the entire story must be compressed into twenty or thirty seconds, and in that short time different media must be scrupulously coordinated to communicate and reiterate a cogent, easily perceived message. Perfume and luxury companies spend millions of dollars on these productions, although the cost is only a fraction of what these firms invest to advertise the full line of their products. Estée Lauder, for example, spent $1.1 billion in 2000 (27 percent of its sales), while the luxury conglomerate LVMH spent a bit less (i.e., $900 million). All in all, prestige fragrances (like Calvin Klein's *Eternity,* Chanel's *No. 5,* Lancôme's *Trésor,* Clinique's *Happy*) amount to a $1.6 billion-a-year business.[26]

Created for television in the United States and France and routinely screened in French movie theaters, these advertising mini-dramas all too often follow the same, unimaginative, paradigmatic scenario, humorously described by one French television reviewer as "Je t'ai senti, je te saute dessus" ("I've smelled you, now I jump your bones").[27] To advertise its 1985 fragrance *Clin d'oeil* (Wink) Bourjois created a film clip in which a young man, having inadvertently made the same date for the same place with two different women (one blonde, the other brunette), persuades both of them to drop their rivalry and live with him in a ménage à trois. A similar imbroglio with a similarly "happy ending" characterizes the film created in 1985 for Yves Saint Laurent's *Opium.* A man and a woman who do not know each other walk down a hotel corridor to their neighboring rooms; but the hotel clerk has mixed up their keys. When her key for room 301 and his key for room 303 fail to work—the close-up shots of keys entering and exiting locks lack subtlety, to say the least—the gentleman gives the woman the right key. A while later, a basket of flowers, signed "room 303," is delivered to the woman's room. Another, more dramatic clip, a mini-film noir of sorts, begins with the sound of a gunshot and then the image of a woman hurriedly ascending a staircase. Entering her apartment she puts a tiny revolver on a table and then to calm her nerves, as a police siren sounds in the distance, dabs herself with a few drops of Caron's *Nocturnes.* Her troubles may only be beginning or, as seems more likely, she may have no worries whatsoever, thanks to the perfume.

Chanel's Mini-Films

In the 1970s, 1980s, and 1990s Chanel produced a number of sophisticated, clever, and artistic films for several of its fragrances. The advertising campaign for its *No. 19* stressed the boldness and vitality of the fragrance and the woman who wore it. *No. 19*'s slogan was simply "the impulsive perfume"; it was designed for the determined, spirited, assertive woman full of life and verve. In fact, one publicity brochure proudly announced that "boldness has a number" and that, of course, is "19." Created in 1970 by Henri Robert (and revised eighteen years later in an eau de parfum edition by Jacques Polge), the perfume was envisioned, in one of Chanel's advertising texts, as "imposing a new style, . . . embodying an epoch, the 1970s, when women had taken their lives in hand." This is a perfume for the modern woman whose enthusiasm, optimism, and appetite for life "are the key to [her] seductiveness." For such a woman, *No. 19* is not a fashion accessory but "an ally, an accomplice," making her "seductive but not a seductress." The *No. 19* woman loves to play the game and use chance to her advantage; she is her own person, who "follows her impulses, but also knows how to control them."[28]

A series of short, filmed advertisements from the 1970s and 1980s (directed by David Bailey, Oliviero Toscani, and others) humorously dramatizes the bold impulsiveness of the *No. 19* woman who is seen in different locales and situations. She is at a horse race, Longchamp perhaps, standing next to her male companion and excitedly cheering for a winning horse; or she ambles along a dock of pleasure boats with a man by her side; or she is inside a sports car with a man who reaches out to touch her knee but whose hand she demurely stops in midcourse and places back on the ignition key; or finally, she is walking in a sculpture garden studying works of art and holding a bottle of *No. 19* behind her back, her fingers crossed for good luck while she throws surreptitious glances at a handsome man also looking at the sculptures, and at her. One final action, however, links these different scenes and scenarios, for each film ends with a kiss so impulsive and unexpected that the male protagonist is completely taken by surprise. At Longchamp, the woman grabs the man's tie and with candor, spirit, and determination brusquely pulls his mouth toward hers. Similarly, the connoisseur of sculpture, the man on the dock, and the driver of the sports car are all suddenly "assaulted" by a full-mouth kiss, one that clearly indicates that the *No. 19* woman in all her audacity is very much in charge of the situation.

One particularly delightful, almost giddy, publicity film entitled "L'Orchestre," was created for *Chanel No. 5* in 1996 by the director Gérard Corbiau. As in no small number of such films, a certain magical realism, if not token surrealism, adds humor and spice. In this film a couple walks along the beach, the man in white, the woman in red. The woman turns and looks over her shoulder out to the ocean where suddenly a solo violinist rises from the water. Soon, he is followed by an entire string orchestra playing with gusto the third movement from Beethoven's Violin Concerto in D (Op. 61). It is an epiphany of vision, music, and florid bowing which makes the woman laugh heartily. Music is important in another publicity film for *No. 5* entitled "Monuments," shot in 1986 by Ridley Scott, whose first film

for Chanel in 1979, entitled "L'Invitation au rêve" (Invitation to a Dream), had juxtaposed shots of a blue swimming pool, a sunbathing woman, a tanned male swimmer, and the shadow of an airplane passing overhead to celebrate, somewhat abstractly, *No. 5*'s power of enchantment. In "Monuments," however, the haunting jazz rhythms of Nina Simone's rendition of "My Baby Just Cares for Me" accompanies a sequence of discontinuous images featuring the French actress Carole Bouquet. As Simone's voice announces that "My baby don't care for shows / My baby don't care for clothes / . . . / My baby don't care for cars and races / My baby just cares for me," a series of shots unfolds in which Bouquet, attired in a red Chanel suit, is presented in different places: first, standing against the floor-to-ceiling

V-shaped incisions, calling attention to the third letter of the perfume's name, are etched across the surface of this crystal bottle for Ungaro's *Diva*, 1983, a fragrance composed by Jacques Polge.

windows of a skyscraper office; second, driving away from the building in a sports car, its windshield reflecting the clouds passing overhead; third, moving along a dusty desert road in Arizona, surrounded by the buttes and rock formations of Monument Valley; fourth, at a lonely gas station talking on a pay phone; fifth, standing against the vast background of a sagebrush desert looking skyward as the immense shadow of a plane passes over her; sixth, walking confidently on a dusty road as the camera, closing in on her angular features, frames her face against the stark mountain crest behind her; and seventh, smiling at a handsome man (no cowboy is he!) who waits for her on the road and whom she embraces, as Simone's "My baby don't care for …" trails off, the screen goes black, and the blackness turns into the circular outline of the "o" in "No. 5."

A third promotional film Ridley Scott created (in 1982 for *No. 5*)—he would create a fourth with Carole Bouquet in 1991 called "La Star" and then "Thunder Perfect Mind," a four-and-half-minute commercial for a Prada perfume in 2005—exhibits the most ingenious and complex montage of images in all of Chanel's cinematic advertising. Entitled "Le Jardin" (The Garden) the film begins with a long plunging shot of a formal, classic seventeenth-century garden and reflecting pool, as found at Versailles, for example. The geometric lines of this garden landscape change into immense almost surreal, black-and-white piano keys, which move up and down in harmony with a female voice, accompanied by a piano, singing "I don't want to set the world on fire." The thin lines of the piano keys change then into a nocturnal landscape of parallel train tracks extending from the bottom to the top of the screen. The sky is filled with stars and a crescent moon. A train moves quickly down the tracks, leaving sparks in its wake, just as the singer's voice reaches the word "fire." By the time she finishes pronouncing the word in a long drawn-out final syllable ("fi-rrrre"), the screen is filled with the close-up of the stark glass facade of a skyscraper, photographed from below in a reverse plunging shot; this has the effect of flattening the perspective and exaggerating the vertical lines of the facade's window frames. Moving up and across the building's face passes (yet again) the reflection of a jet plane.

The song's next line—"I just want to start / A flame in your heart"—unfolds in harmony with a sequence of four stylized, geometrically arranged shots: first, a stark, modernist office with V-shaped windows against which a man in silhouette looks out toward the blinking light atop the pyramidal tower of San Francisco's Transamerica building; second, the man's face, seen in close-up turning slowly out of darkness into light; third, a stuffy, baroque, overly decorated room with vases of flowers across which a smiling blonde model in a red Chanel suit approaches the camera, her shadow moving across the back wall; and fourth, the same stark modernist office with the same man against the window, in the same silhouetted pose, toward whom the woman in red, seen from behind, slowly walks,

until he suddenly vanishes. The singer then takes up the song's final line—"In my heart I have but one desire." The mere eight words of this line accompany a series of jump cuts as the film focuses once again on the face of the woman, now back in the baroque room, then moves to a long shot of the Transamerica building, its facade crossed by the shadow of the plane, before returning finally to fix on the woman's face. This time, however, she closes her eyes, raises her head, slightly parts her lips, and waits for a kiss, which does not come. Or does indeed come in the form a large bottle of *No. 5*, which replaces the close-up image of the woman's expectant face. At this point, the singer has reached the final word ("desire") of her line ("In my heart I have but one *desire*"). As with the end words of all the previous lines ("fire," "start," "heart," "desire"), the sound of the final "r" consonant is drawn out for several seconds. With perfectly timed pauses the bass voice of an announcer, synchronizing his words with the singer's elongated "r," speaks the film's final words: "Beyond fashion and years … today and tomorrow … an invitation to dream … *No. 5* from Chanel." Since he reads his sentence in unison with the song's final line, the film makes certain that the name of Chanel's perfume coincides and overlaps with the word "desire."

The juxtaposition of old and new, the coincidence of Versailles and the Transamerica building, the overlapping of a fussy room and a sleek office, the presence of trains and planes, the geometrical relationship between the classical (the garden) and the modern (the skyscraper), the sudden appearance, disappearance, and reappearance of the same protagonists, and the rapid, dreamlike dislocation of seemingly strange and unrelated scenes give the film a surreal atmosphere. Yet, with its profusion of so many images compressed into a short span of time—this is made all the more remarkable by the four short lyrics accompanying the images—Scott's evocative film suggests a tale of dream, fantasy, and desire. With *Chanel No. 5* a woman does not have to change the world or set it afire—in this respect, the film does not follow the revolutionary goals of surrealism—but needs, rather, only to seduce a man and enflame his heart. Wear *No. 5*, the commercial suggests, and romance will come, since what responds to the closed eyes and parted lips of the woman's expectant face are the bottle of perfume and the seductive masculine voice guaranteeing the timelessness of Chanel's "invitation to dream." Responding to the desire for love, *No. 5* sends the message that women need, as Chanel's slogan declares, to "share the fantasy": the fantasy, that is, of a kiss to come.

Other advertising films made by Chanel tap into the dream fantasies and the cultural tastes of Western or westernized consumers; there is a complex network of interrelated and overlapping images and ideologies at play here: chords of desire ready to be orchestrated and performed. One commercial from 1994 shows Carole Bouquet sitting in a cinema, a box of popcorn in her lap, watching a Marilyn Monroe film. When Monroe told the world in the

1950s that all she slept in were "five drops of Number 5," she unwittingly became a spokeswoman for Chanel (Edwards, 47); her future appearance in a Chanel film was just a matter of time. It may have taken nearly forty years, but Chanel did eventually tap the energy of Monroe's mythic status as a sex goddess and apply it cleverly to *No. 5*. In the commercial, Bouquet watches Monroe on the screen, listening to her rendition of "I want to be loved by you, just you, nobody else but you," a song Monroe performed in the 1959 film *Some Like It Hot*. Suddenly, a series of rapid changes occur. Bouquet's short brown coiffure morphs into Monroe's familiar bouffant blonde hairdo. The film turns from black-and-white to color, and the box of popcorn in Bouquet's lap becomes a giant bottle of *No. 5*. Turning toward the camera and in her celebrated slow, sultry, high-pitched, girlish voice, this new Marilyn completes the words of the song the other Marilyn has been belting out on the screen; "boo-boop-bee-do," she sings, followed by the spoken words: "You know what I mean? Number 5." Repeated by the other women in the audience Monroe's final words become a chant of sorts—"number 5, number 5, number 5"—as Bouquet, changed back to her old look and clasping the bottle of perfume to her breast, adds "by Chanel."

Other commercials favor these kinds of visual metamorphoses. The film made in 1994 for Chanel's *Antaeus Pour Homme* (a scent created by Jacques Polge in 1981) pairs the slow-motion shot of a sleek, shiny black sports car exiting a garage, its red door ever so slowly rising, with a similar slow-motion image of a jet-black bottle of *Antaeus* being lowered into a red box. Without warning the car changes into an amorphous, black, plastic, contoured material which then hardens into the muscular back of a male model. In another *Antaeus* advertisement (this time from 1986), the shape-shifting follows a similar trajectory: from hard matter to muscular flesh. Facing each other, two craggy, oblong rocks bathed in the foam of the ocean's crashing waves suddenly morph into the bent knee and thigh of a man and a woman. The stories intimated here involve the metamorphosis of the inanimate (stone, car) into the animate (man himself); they suggest the power of scent to soften, even feminize masculinity. Or at least to civilize it, as Roman Polanski sought to do in a similar advertisement for *Antaeus,* made four years earlier. Entitled "Myth," the film shows a primitive man carrying a rock with the shape of the *Antaeus* bottle.

The metamorphosis of stone into flesh and the fusion of the beastly and the human, a phenomenon common to many myths, fairy tales, and stories (*Pygmalion and Galateus, Sleeping Beauty, The Frog-Prince,* the Gorgon, *The Winter's Tale,* to name a few) have found expression in other film advertisements for Chanel perfumes. One commercial for *Coco,* designed by Jacques Helleu, artistic director of Parfums Chanel, who has supervised and coordinated the production of most of the company's advertising campaigns and publicity films for nearly five decades, was directed by Jean-Paul Goude. Entitled "Coco, L'Esprit de Chanel" (Coco, The Spirit of Chanel), it transforms a woman (the French singer and actress Vanessa Paradis) into a caged bird of paradise. A large airplane hangar on a French military base was commandeered for the set of the film, and a gigantic gilded metal bird cage and trapeze were constructed on the premises. The film, according to Goude, tells a fairy tale. It is a story that is quite banal—who has not seen a large cat eyeing a small bird inside a cage—and yet at the same time mythic and cultural—one thinks of Beauty and the Beast—because it taps into a collective unconscious, which, as Goude observes, is essential to the creation of any successful advertisement.[29]

Dressed in black fishnet stockings, a black trapeze artist's maillot, and thin black tail feathers trailing from her hips, Paradis is seen, as the film begins, crouched on the trapeze bar inside the cage. Swinging back and forth, making chirping bird sounds, she looks warily from side to side and then becomes more fearful as claps of thunder are heard and flashes of lightning seen. Her chirpings segue seamlessly at this point into a whistled rendition of "Stormy Weather." The wind increases, disheveling Paradis's long hair, and "Stormy Weather," now interpreted by a full orchestra, grows in volume. Paradis now swings upside down, holding in her outstretched hand a large bottle of *Coco,* its contents falling out in a graceful, arcing stream of scent. The image fades to the face of a cat, looking larger than life because of the close-up angle of the shot, and staring directly into the bird cage. We are now inside an elegant and stylishly decorated apartment overlooking the Place Vendôme. The birdcage sits on a table and within it a miniature woman and trapeze can be seen swinging to and fro like a metronome. A cat is curled on the table. Also on the table is a bottle of *Coco* toward which an arm clothed in the distinctive cuff of a Chanel suit moves. The camera pulls back to reveal a woman, closely resembling Coco Chanel in body and style—her suit and flat, wide-brimmed hat are replicas of Chanel designs from the 1950s—who looks out an open French door to the lightning flashes illuminating the square below. In the instant it takes for a final thunder clap to resound, the woman disappears and a male voice whispers, "*Coco,* the spirit of Chanel." The emphasis on the word "spirit" is deliberate because the film wishes to invoke the ghostly presence of Coco Chanel.

The bird-woman in this film is a fragile, disempowered, and dehumanized creature. At best, the only positive thing one could say about the scenario is that she is not eaten alive by the feline eyeing her. However, another publicity film, where a more empowered woman masters a savage, wild, and predatory animal, updates a classic fairy tale. Called "Le Loup" (Wolf) and directed by Luc Besson in 1999 as a Christmas television commercial for *No. 5,* the film, which was shot on a sound stage in Rome, stars the American model-actress Estella Warren, who was the incarnation of the *No. 5* woman before that role was taken

ÉGOÏSTE
"PLATINUM"

CHANEL

over by Nicole Kidman in late 2004.[30] Wearing red high-heel shoes laced up around her ankles and a girlish red tutu over a white petticoat, she walks, as if in a dream, down a narrow art deco silver corridor, between high walls of grey granite blocks, toward a large vault door inscribed with a gigantic black "5." Christmas bells, violins, and a chorus of voices are heard on the soundtrack. Warren pushes the "5" on a keypad, and the vault door automatically opens revealing a small room awash in soft yellow light, its walls, floor, and ceiling composed of bricks of gold. Yet, the room's principal source of illumination comes from a wall constructed entirely of bottles of *No. 5*. Red Riding Hood, for that is whom Warren plays with graceful, balletic movements, takes one bottle from the wall and, placing it inside a straw basket lined in red-checked gingham, swings a large red cape over her shoulders and exits the vault. While she has been inside the golden chamber, a sinister black wolf, red tongue hanging from his mouth, has been prowling outside. Red Riding Hood then moves toward a set of immense gold doors. These open to reveal a festive scene of azure light, falling snow, and in the distance the exquisitely illuminated Eiffel Tower. The juxtaposition of colors is breathtaking: the gold of the doors, the red of Warren's cape, the white of the snow, the silver-gold of the Eiffel Tower, and the blue backdrop of the set. But the wolf is suddenly seen loping down the corridor toward Red Riding Hood, who is now standing at the door's outer threshold. Turning toward the wolf and looking him squarely in the eye, she points her finger in his direction as if to say "stop!" This implicit command becomes real when, raising her finger to her lips and fixing the wolf with a charming stare, she tells it to "shhhhh." Obediently, the wolf sits back on its haunches. Smiling, Red Riding Hood covers her head with the hood, turns her back on the pacified animal, and joyously bounds out into the wintry Paris landscape. As the doors close, the abandoned and imprisoned wolf, a large black "5" printed on the floor beneath him, raises his head to the ceiling and longingly begins to howl.

Red Riding Hood and *Chanel No. 5* both possess (to paraphrase the eighteenth-century English dramatist William Congreve) "charms to soothe the savage breast" as well as the savage beast. The woman outfoxes the wolf, if such a mixed animal metaphor can be forgiven. *Chanel No. 5* is a treasure—why else would it be kept in a vault—which women, the advertisement suggests, know how to use. Even Red Riding Hood's Parisian grandmother will soon have her own bottle carried to her in her granddaughter's basket. Perfume offers women mastery and control, the commercial suggests. A few drops of *No. 5*, and relations between the sexes will no longer be determined by the man's taming of the shrew but by the woman's shrewd taming of the man. The ideology of empowerment presented by Besson's film, which revises not only the image of a perfume created in the early 1920s but that of a fairy tale going back a lot farther in time, reflects the feminism of the next-to-the-last year of the twentieth century, an image of power that earlier perfume advertisements never embraced and that even contemporary commercials are still wary of articulating.[31]

Perfume and Sin

More traditional, however, in its sexual stereotyping of women is a commercial produced in 1989 by the English photographer David Bailey for Jean Patou's *1000*, a perfume which had been launched seventeen years earlier. The print advertisement for the scent leaves little doubt about what the number means. Below the black-and-white photograph of a woman's face, obviously on the threshold of orgasm, a question is written: "How many times?" The label of Patou's perfume bottle set below the question provides the answer: "1000." Bailey's promotional film pushed the outside of the erotic and religious envelope even further than the print advertisement, causing the commercial to be banned in some countries, which, of course, only enhanced the perfume's popularity. Susan Irvine gives a frame-by-frame description of Bailey's daring commercial:

> A rich, elegant Parisian woman watches her husband drive off to the office from her window. No sooner is he gone than she is running out in her couture suit. Cut to . . . our heroine ascending in the lift of a seedy building on the wrong side of town. She flings open the door to reveal a young rough diamond lounging on a bed. They fall on the bed, ripping off each other's clothes. Cut to . . . many exhausting hours later she leaves the building, sees a church, goes in. She walks to the confessional and leans towards the screen. "Father, I have sinned." "How many times, my child?" The answer, of course, is "Mille," "A Thousand." Cut to . . . a shot of the bottle round which a rosary wraps itself (143).

Of course, the woman's lack of shame in confessing her sins might be seen as an endorsement of the self-confidence *1000* has given her; yet the film combines the excitement of transgression with guilt and the desire for religious forgiveness. Perfume here encourages self-indulgent pleasure, sexual adventure, even adultery, but it also leads to contrition, as the collaboration, the embrace so to speak, of *1000* and a rosary implies.

Perfume and Narcissism: *Égoïste*

The ambivalence in Bailey's film, which affirms a woman's sexual freedom but also criticizes her sinful passion by displaying her need for religious absolution, is reiterated in the mixed message communicated in another commercial film, made in 1990 by Jean-Paul Goude to launch *Égoïste*, Chanel's new scent for men created by Jacques Polge. The power of a woman's rage against the self-indulgent, insensitive pride

TAKE IT!

CHANCE
CHANEL

THE UNEXPECTED NEW CHANEL FRAGRANCE

Fig. 128 The bottle as superstar. Chanel, *Chance*, 2002, print advertisement, photo Jean-Paul Goude, model Anna Vyalitsyna, *Vanity Fair*, November 2002.

and egotism of a man, who may have abandoned her and others, is portrayed as classic, noble, even theatrical. But this passionate feminine outrage is also seen as a tribute to the power of a masculine scent like *Égoïste*. If a fragrance can have this powerful effect on women, the film seems to argue, then men should definitely buy it. One would have thought that the vociferous expression of anger by thirty-one women, directed at one guilty man hiding from their collective wrath, would hardly qualify as a positive endorsement either for the male ego or the masculine fragrance designed for that ego. But Goude's imaginative, sophisticated, and baroquely theatrical commercial, with its cultural and literary allusions, reveals the impressive effect *Égoïste* (and a man's egoism) can have on women, even when the passion aroused is a passion for revenge.[32]

To make his prize-winning publicity film Goude had the well-known facade of Cannes's luxury Hotel Carlton—it first opened its doors on La Croisette directly facing the Mediterranean in 1912—completely reconstructed (to a slightly smaller scale) on a lot in a suburb of Rio de Janeiro. This is a Potemkin village of sorts, since the stucco facade is supported by scaffolding alone. Thirty-two balconies, symmetrically arranged eight to a floor on four floors, with iron railings and white shuttered French windows, compose the front of the hotel. On all but one of the balconies, furious women, photographed in black and white, hair blowing in the wind, move from side to side, lean over the railings, gesticulate violently, shake their arms, flash wild, overwrought, tearful looks, and grimace in anger—an effect heightened by the tilted angle of the close-ups. In turn, the women take up the attack, aiming their rage at an unseen enemy: "Egoist / Where are you / Come out you scoundrel / Beware my wrath / I will be merciless." The theatrically classical language of accusation becomes even more dramatically charged as four women take turns speaking the first lines (slightly modified) of a famous soliloquy borrowed from Corneille's seventeenth-century play *Le Cid* (I, iv), verses most French men and women would remember from their school days: "O fury! O despair! / O my love betrayed! / Have I only lived so long for this infamy?"[33] The women then all point in the direction of the only window still shuttered, and joining their voices they shout in chorus: "Come out, Egoist!" The closed shutter opens a crack and a man's hand places a bottle of the scent on the balcony's railing. But the film has not ended; there now begins a second part, in color. The women continue to shout, but this time it is simply one furious word: "*Égoïste*." This they pronounce together in incrementally larger groups of three, eight, fifteen, twenty-three, and thirty-one voices within the short span of time it takes them to appear and disappear behind shutters they rapidly open and close. Of course, one window shutter, the site of *Égoïste* (the man and the perfume) never opens. Finally, thirty-one women, standing at every balcony (but one) of the hotel's facade, their voices synchronized with the opening and closing of the shutters, yell in chorus: "*Égoïste*."

The masculine boldness, the positive self-confidence, even the sensitivity to self suggested by the word "egoist"—for Chanel seeks to contest any of the term's negative connotations ("to assume he's uncaring or aloof is to misread him," one ad declares)—are more clearly represented in another publicity film, created by Goude a few years later for a second version of the scent, called *Égoïste* "Platinum," created by Polge and launched in 1993 (fig. 127). This film clip is more macho and surrealistic than its predecessor. No women figure in it, other than an off-screen chorus of female voices chanting "*Égoïste*" five times in succession at the end. The only protagonists are a man and his shadow engaged in a strange boxing match, which has a fairy-tale quality, reinforced by a segment from Prokofiev's opera, *The Love of the Three Oranges,* on the soundtrack. The man, who has just stepped out of his bath or shower—he wears only a towel around his waist—and who has just rubbed *Égoïste* "Platinum" on his face, begins playfully to shadow box with his own image reflected in a mirror.

But the sparring turns more serious when the man's gigantic shadow enters the fray. Pitted against his own reflection and his own shadow, the man fights himself. This is a struggle pictured not only as mano a mano but as ego against ego. *Égoïste* is a fragrance that requires commitment, the commercial suggests. A man must not only stand up *for* himself but also stand up *to* himself, if he is going to wear *Égoïste* successfully; there can be no doubts, no hesitation. A man must feel comfortable enough with his masculinity to use the fragrance. Scent has an antagonistic character here. To smell like *Égoïste*, to project the image of an egoist, to act even like an egoist, one must struggle with one's ghosts; one must put one's manhood to the test and take chances. Moreover, a man must, as an advertisement for the earlier *Égoïste* emphasized, walk "on the positive side of that fine line separating arrogance from an awareness of self-worth" (*New York Times Magazine*, March 17, 1990). So, when the looming shadow first knocks the man to the floor with a right to the jaw, mocking him at the same time—"Egoist, you are nothing but an egoist . . . I follow you like a dog. Beware, one day soon that I don't steal your fragrance and finally take your place, egoist. Ha! Ha!"—and then grabs the bottle of *Égoïste*, the man, his adrenaline stirred, rises to the occasion. Jumping to his feet he delivers two quick punches to the stomach of his overconfident, ghostly alter ego, thus dominating his double. The bottle drops from the shadow's hand, and somersaulting in slow motion through the air, leaves a trail of liquid fragrance.

A Journey into the Limbo of the Imaginary

The fragrant tales perfumes tell can be, as we have seen, barbarous, cruel, violent, misanthropic, misogynist, murderous, mortal, and vindictive—not unlike the societies, cultures, and civilizations in which perfumes have existed since the time of the pharaohs. The narratives of perfume can also recount, as we have seen as well, stories of luxury, elegance, beauty, eroticism, empowerment, and nostalgia. These stories occur at different times and places: in living rooms, offices, hotels, skyscrapers, theaters, sculpture gardens, cars, at horse races, near the ocean, on a beach, in bizarre settings (a birdcage, a vault), and around recognizable sites like the Eiffel Tower, Versailles, or the Arizona desert. The scenarios of scent unwind according to the tempos of ordinary, everyday life—chance encounters, walks in the park, meetings, flirtations, conversations, seductions, dreams, imbroglios, embarrassments, confusions—and to the unsettling, disorienting rhythms of fantasy or surreal life: an orchestra rising out of the ocean, a shadow attacking its own body, a face transformed into that of a celebrated actress, small figures walking on piano keys, and men and women evaporating into thin air. Perfume narratives highlight metamorphoses of all kinds in which ordinary reality (a woman's body or a cast shadow) is suddenly miniaturized or magnified; where inexplicable forces of shape-shifting and hybridism transform a woman into a bird, a car into a man, a rock into a knee, a savage wolf into a whimpering animal; where shadows talk; where fury explodes; where human behavior, once redefined, turns impulsiveness into spiritedness and egoism into natural self-confidence. What, one may ask, has preceded and will follow in the thirty-second narrative where a suspected murderess perfumes her body as the police arrive? Does the femme fatale derive her seductive power of mystery from the inability to forget her femininity even when she is at her most "fatale"? Linking perfumes with ready-made stereotypes, which are narratives in their own right, grounded in the preconceptions and misconceptions of a culture—the myth of the femme fatale, the black-widow spider, and the avenging bella donna—the perfume commercial creates in a half-minute or less a story made from a highly charged and dense syntax which is governed by a carefully conceived and controlled sequence of colors, music, words, and gestures. Only a thirty-second "opera" like this, packed with the compressed juxtapositions and complex layerings of image, sound, and meaning (a density of association characteristic of poetry) gives body and soul to the one sensory experience this visual narrative of fragrance can never directly express: namely, smell.

The Bottle as Idol

Yet, it is not the smell of the scent, of course, which the advertising film seeks to sell. Rather, it is the constellation of images—the idea of femininity perfume embodies, the aura of power it imparts, the promise of love, happiness, and self-renewal it offers, and the confidence it gives—that is presented visually and narratively. This may perhaps explain why the most potent dimension of these commercials is the reverential sanctification of the perfume bottle, usually reserved for the final frame. Here is the true "star" of the commercial: larger than life, at the center of a stage radiant with light, and perfectly symmetrical, compact, and beautiful. This is the one true image that the viewer can take away from the commercial and make real. The other imaginary scenarios and dream images may indeed be absorbed into the viewer's unconscious or linked to her or his own self-image; but the bottle is real. As icon, idol, talisman, and fetish, it is the stuff dreams are made from, "the hope in a jar" Charles Revson knew he was selling along with his Revlon products. The female viewer may not find herself kissing a man in the rugged landscape of Monument Valley and the male viewer may not be pursued by the furious women his egoism has attracted and then rejected. But the bottle—of No. 5 or of Égoïste—can be taken out of the film, out of the fiction, out of the dream, and brought into one's own life where it generates a new narrative: that real, somewhat banal, everyday story of romance and desire which the scenarios of our daydreams play out. The images of spirited and independent, yet sometimes submissive, girlish, even infantilized, women and the portraits of self-assertive, egocentric, muscular men morphing into sports cars and rocks are not in fact the main object of attention, affection, and adoration presented in these commercials. They are mediums of expression: metaphors and images, albeit powerfully evocative ones. In these films the object of idealization, idolatry, and love is, in fact, not a woman or a man, but an object: the perfume bottle and the scent contained within it. If one is to "share the fantasy," as Chanel No. 5 commands, then one need only buy the bottle. And so in these promotional films, models caress the bottles they hold, speak to them as to a lover, embrace them as they swing upside down, worship their very reality, and men fight, even with their shadows, to protect the flacons they possess.[34] In fact, one of the more possessive relationships between woman and bottle is portrayed in the print advertisement for the fragrance Chance—its name echoing the Chanel name—created by Polge in 2002. Chance is a light, fresh, floral scent, specifically targeting a younger woman between the ages of eighteen and twenty-nine. With a launch budget estimated at twelve million dollars, Chanel called once again on the expertise of Jean-Paul Goude, who photographed the print advertisement and produced the television commercial, called "Le Baiser" (The Kiss) in 2003. The film's story involves the chance encounter, set to the song "Taking a Chance on Love," between a young woman and man in Venice, and taps the potent images of mystery, dream, love, water, stone, and light associated with that watery city, "a labyrinth of art and emotion," as the publicity brochure for Chance describes it. Venice is "the mysterious city, where love at first sight and strange occurrences come together in an upwelling of colors and memories, the city of dreams and lovers, the city of chance."[35]

Yet, it is not the film but the print advertisement for *Chance* that shows the woman in the "arms," so to speak, of her great love (fig. 128). In this instance, the woman is the Russian model Anna Vyalitsyna and her great "love" is a gigantic round perfume bottle, noticeably different from the rectangular bottle that has, since the 1920s, invariably held all Chanel scents; this is just one of the reasons Chanel calls *Chance* "the most *unexpected*" of its perfumes. Hanging contentedly from the crystal stopper, her lace-gloved hands possessively enveloping the cap, her eyes closed in a blissful smile, and her slender body in a gossamer gown fused to the rounded surface of the glass, Vyalitsyna embraces the bottle as completely as the bottle appears to contain her. Even her extended legs retain the forward momentum of the jump which has enabled her to grab hold of the bottle, a leap so spontaneous and sudden that it has broken one of her shoulder straps, which flies out behind her. Vyalitsyna has followed almost to the letter a comment Coco Chanel once made about her own life: "A world was ending another was about to be born; . . . Chance presented itself, I took it."[36]

In Goude's "iconic photo" woman and bottle are made one. The advertisement presents an image of fusion and absorption evocative of the intimate embrace of scent and skin, which all perfume creates, as well as of the chance encounter and coincidence of reality and fantasy: an embracing of life, captured in *Chance*'s American slogan: "It's your chance . . . Take it!" This is the precise image of youthful impetuosity and playfulness Chanel has sought to create, as the publicity statement for the fragrance makes clear: "Anna [Vyalitsyna], resolute and devil-may-care, leaps toward the giant flacon. She seizes her chance, an unexpected chance, recognizes it, embraces it, and makes it her own . . . *Chance* is a fragrance of optimism and independence."[37]

In its presentation of Venice, Goude's publicity film for *Chance* attempts to represent this youthful explosion of mad love provoked magically, as the surrealists knew, through the mysterious workings of objective chance. But the blue water of the Grand Canal, the sunlit Gothic facade of the Doge's Palace, the two young lovers embracing on the curved bow of a gondola, and a voice whispering "it's your chance . . . come on, take it!"—these visual, auditory, and romantic images cannot compete with the film's final frame. Against a green-blue underwater background appears, as if in an epiphany, a glass bottle of *Chance*, born from the waves like Venice and Venus alike.

Endnotes

Chapter 1: The Scented Imagination: Perfume in Everyday Life

[1] Anne Goffart mentions the title *Eau de Cologne* in her *Musée d'Art Moderne. Oeuvres choisies* (Brussels: MRBAB, 2001, 116–17). See also Sarah Whitfield and John Elderfeld, *Bonnard* (New York: MoMA, 1998).

[2] Marylène Delbourg-Delphis, "Une Histoire de parfums," *Elle*, 18 Apr. 1983, 95; Camille Labro, "L'Essence de peau de belle femme," *Vogue*, Dec. 1999–Jan. 2000, 207; Charles Baudelaire, *The Painter of Modern Life, and Other Essays*, ed. and trans. Jonathan Mayne (London: Phaidon, 1964), 32.

[3] For a discussion of the poor treatment the sense of smell has received (as far back as ancient Greece) from what Alain Corbin calls "oculo-centrist" philosophers [*Historien du sensible. Entretiens avec Gilles Heuré* (Paris: La Découverte, 2000), 61], see Le Guérer, 227–92 and Michel Onfray, *L'Art de jouir* (Paris: Grasset, 1991), 109–55.

[4] Perfume specialists whose knowledge of fragrances comes from their extensive olfactory memory often look beyond the world of odors for the vocabulary they need to describe fragrances; their descriptive adjectives are often taken from the language of other arts or media. See Maurice Thiboud, "Empirical Classification of Odors," in *Perfumes: Art, Science and Technology*, ed. P. M. Müller and D. Lamparsky (London and New York: Elsevier Science Publishers, 1991), 255, 259.

[5] Le Guérer, 207; Diane Ackerman, *A Natural History of the Senses* (New York: Vintage Books, 1990), 59. See also, Susan Walker and Peter Higgs, eds., *Cleopatra of Egypt: From History to Myth* (Princeton: Princeton UP, 2001), 137, 294.

[6] Faure, 11–15. There have been several attempts to reconstruct ancient scents. Two French researchers partially succeeded in recreating the aroma of "kyphi," the type of incense favored by Egyptian priests for their religious rites (incense was seen as the sweat of the gods) and valued by Egyptian apothecaries as a calming remedy for the relief of insomnia and tension. Relying in part on tomb paintings, hieroglyphs on temple walls, and papyrus documents (as well as Plutarch's writings), in which different steps in the creation of perfume are visually recorded or, in the case of the papyri, described in detail, the researchers composed a facsimile of "kyphi," while acknowledging that there was indeed no credible way to verify its authenticity. The problems of recreation were immense. Which, for example, of several dozen forms of incense did they need to start with; what kind of myrrh (there are fifteen species) should they add; which part of the cinnamon tree—the leaf or the bark—need they choose? [Jean-François Augereau, "Le Kyphi, l'encens mythique des Égyptiens, à nouveau créé," *Le Monde*, 4 Apr 2002, 28 and Annick Le Guérer, *Sur les routes de l'encens* (Paris: Editions du Garde-Temps, 2001), 20–23].

[7] Dominique Paquet, "Le Parfum, chiffre de la forme?" in *Parfums de Sculptures, Sculptures de Parfums*, exhibition catalogue, 2 June–30 July, 1999, Jardin des Plantes de Paris (Paris: Materia Prima, 1999), 13. On the nature of loss and the poetics of absence and presence, see my *Lost Beyond Telling: Representations of Death and Absence in Modern French Poetry*, (Ithaca: Cornell UP, 1990).

[8] The awakening of the soul through the fragrance of the skin, the release of essence through heat and friction, and the unleashing of the body's sensuality through the vaporization of its scent were phenomena well known to early science and to "profound connoisseur[s] in love affairs," as Shaykh Umar ibn Muhammad al-Nefzawi observed in *The Perfumed Garden*, a sixteenth-century manual of love: "Woman is like a fruit, which will not yield its sweetness until you rub it between your hands. Look at the basil plant; if you do not rub it warm with your fingers, it will not emit any scent. Do you not know that the amber, unless it be handled and warmed, keeps hidden within its pores the aroma contained in it. It is the same with woman." (*The Perfumed Garden of the Shaykh Nefzawi* [1886], trans. Sir Richard F. Burton [New York: G. P. Putnam's Sons, 1963], 124).

[9] Louise de Vilmorin, "Le Choix d'un parfum" (1960) in her *Articles de mode* (Paris: Gallimard, 2000), 86, 88. Vilmorin even conceives of perfumes as marks of punctuation ("parfums-ponctuation"), wordlessly accenting particular feelings in a mute language of love; for her, exclamation points, question marks, commas, periods, dashes, semi-colons, parentheses, *accents graves* and *aigus*, and circonflexes create an invisible typography of scented signs.

[10] *New Yorker*, 14 & 21 Oct. 2002, 182; 20 May 1996, 87; 21 Jan. 2002, cover, respectively.

[11] Of course, exceptions for political, comedic, or sarcastic ends have been imagined. "Depression," in a dagger-shaped bottle and with the slogan "more than just a state of mind," was the name given to a scent in the film *The Real Blonde* (1998), directed by Tom DiCillo. In the February 2003 issue of British *Elle*, a public interest advertisement sponsored by Womankind Worldwide made use of stereotypical images of perfume presentation—a bikini-clad woman, a muscular male, a moment of intimacy, an elegant bottle of perfume—to call attention to the abuse of women; the scent was called "Domestic Violence."

[12] Roland Barthes, *A Lover's Discourse*, trans. Richard Howard (New York: Hill and Wang, 1978), 109.

[13] Walter Benjamin, *The Arcades Project*, trans. Howard Eiland and Kevin McLaughlin (Cambridge: Harvard UP, 1999), 393.

[14] James Barron, "Canada Sniffs and Dislikes the Smell," NYT, 15 Aug 1999, sec. 4, 2. The interior of one Halifax church was divided into two separate seating sections, one for its perfumed and the other for its perfume-free parishioners (Pat Seremet, "Beware Second-Hand Scent," *Valley News* [White River Junction, VT], 7 June 2003, C 1); Marianne Rohrlich, "Aromatherapy at the Dishpan," NYT, 6 Mar 2002, Dining In section, C 1, 6; Steven Barrie-Anthony, "On Scent, We've Barely Scratched the Surface," *Los Angeles Times*, 4 Nov. 2004, F 1; "Scent of a Program: Web Technology May Put Some Perfume in Your Printer," *Wall Street Journal*, 1 May 2000, C 25A; Ernest Beck, "Under Your Nose, the Next Big Thing?" NYT, 5 Aug 2004, D 8; "What the Nose Knows," *The Economist*, 11 March 2006, 18–20.

[15] Shahrzad Elghanayan, "Les Musts by Métro," NYT, 14 Mar. 1999, Sunday Styles section, 3; Jocelyne Bonnet, "L'Homme et le parfum," in *Les Coordonnées de l'homme et la culture matérielle*, vol. 1 of *Histoire des moeurs*, Encyclopédie de la Pléiade (Paris: Gallimard, 1990), 717.

[16] Jane Larkworthy, "On the Verge: Taking Manhattan," *W*, April 2003, 144; "Finally making scents of New York!," advertisement, V-P, Mar 2004, 391. "Paris is flowery, pretty," observes Laurice Rahmé, the French-Lebanese founder of Bond No. 9; but "New York has energy, force" (Mary Tannen, "A Slithery Slope," NYT *Magazine*, 18 April 2004, 74.). See also V-NY, no. 529, Sept 2004 and HB, Sept 2005, 169.

[17] Danny Hakim, "New Luxury-Car Specifications: Styling. Performance. Aroma." NYT, 25 October 2003, A 1, B 2; David Wallis, "To Drive It, or to Smell Like It?" NYT, 25 July 1999, sec. 12, 1; *Sephora Catalogue*, Holiday 2004, 21; Phil Patton, "Love the Hummer? Wear the Fragrance," NYT, 7 November 2005, D9; *Cosmopolitan* (Portugal), Dec 1995. The Harley logo is featured on another scent, *Fire Extreme*, packaged in a cigarette lighter-shaped bottle ("Zoombeauté. Le Parfum des hommes," *Elle*, 1 Nov 2004, 70).

[18] Advertisements for Clive Christian perfumes can be found in NYT *Magazine*, 16 Dec. 2001 and *Bergdorf Goodman Magazine*, Fall Collection, 2003; see also "Ultimate Fragrance Luxuries," HB, November 2005, 137; Mary Tannen, "Selling Indulgences," NYT *Magazine*, 23 Dec. 2001, 51; "Nouveautés: Ocean Spray", *France 61* (Spring 2002): 6; the Adidas ad is in HB, May 2003.

[19]Eva Chen, "Elite Models," *Elle*, May 2003, 164; Emma Calder, "Beauty News," British *Vogue*, May 2003, 146; Irvine, 133.

[20]The Pavarotti scent comes with its own promotional CD (*Cosmopolitan* 44 [Dec. 1995], Portuguese edition). *Jordan* was advertised in *Elle*, Dec. 1999, *Glow* in *Elle*, 206 (Oct. 2002), *Manifesto* in French *Elle* 16 Oct. 2000, HB Oct. 2001, *Misha* in V-NY, Nov. 1996, *Pavlova* in HB, Dec. 1987; *Donald Trump* was reported in *W*, Dec. 2004, 52. Other successful celebrity scents have been marketed by Elizabeth Taylor (*Passion*, *White Diamonds*), Paloma Picasso (*Mon Parfum*), and most recently (in 2004-2005) by Céline Dion (*Belong*), Antonio Banderas (*Spirit*: "looks are nothing without spirit"), and the popular novelist Danielle Steel. One tongue-in-cheek review of the Michael Jordan scent appeared under two humorous headlines: "A Fragrant Foul" and "Smell Like Mike? Eau No" (Tony Kornheiser, "A Fragrant Foul," *Washington Post*, 10 Nov. 1996, sec. 3, F 1, 5). See also Irvine, 132-33; Cathy Horyn, "The Sweet Smell of Celebrity," NYT, 30 June 2005, Thursday Styles, E 1, 5; "Bottling a Best-Seller," V-NY, Oct. 2005, 290.

[21]These scents were advertised or described in the following: *360°* in *Vanity Fair*, Nov. 1999, 167; *M7* in Sophie Schulte-Hillen, "Full-Frontal Fragrance," *Nylon*, Dec 2002–Jan. 2003; *First* in *Air France Madame* 64 (June–July 1998); *CK One* in *W*, April 1995; *212* in *Vanity Fair*, Sept. 1999; and "*L*" in Stuart Elliott, "Like the Show? Buy the Book. And the Earrings. And the . . .," NYT 1 Dec. 2005, C, 7. Other "numbers" associated with perfume, which may draw our attention as well, are: the numbers of dollars earned by the U.S. fragrance industry—2.8 billion in 2003—the world retail market in perfume and cosmetics—$201 billion in the same year—the number of bottles of perfume sold daily in France—166,000 in 2005—and the number of new perfumes launched each year. While in 1987, 34 new scents (luxury and non-luxury alike) appeared, twelve years later that figure had more than quadrupled to 150 and by 2003 had reached 492 launches per year (Jane Larkworthy, "Majoring in Classics," *W*, Sept 2004, 354; Gilles Lipovetsky and Elyette Roux, *Le Luxe éternel. De l'âge du sacré au temps des marques* [Paris: Gallimard, 2003], 112; and Annick Le Guérer, *Le Parfum. Des Origines à nos jours* [Paris: Odile Jacob, 2005], 274–75, 277.) See also Jennifer Weil, "Scratch and Sniff," *W*, Sept. 2000, 264; Patrick Cabasset, "Repère snob: Parfumez votre chat," *L'Officiel* 858 (Sept. 2001): 52. It is doubtful these fragrances would win a "Fifi," the trade "Oscars" awarded annually for innovative perfumery by the Fragrance Foundation of New York.

[22]David G. Williams, *Perfumes of Yesterday* (Port Washington, NY: Micelle Press, 2004), 294; Jan Benzel, "When You Need a Dash of Frogness," 7 Jan. 1996, NYT, sec. 1, 31. One American fragrance manufacturer, Nature Labs, has gone a step further, creating pet perfumes with names designed to recall and poke fun at more established couture fragrances. It offers for sale *Timmy Holedigger* (after the designer Tommy Hilfiger), *CK-9* (for Calvin Klein's *CK One*), *Miss Claybone* (after Liz Claiborne), and *White Dalmations*, in homage to Elizabeth Taylor's perfume *White Diamonds*. ("The Month in Fashion: Crying Woof," *W*, Nov. 2002, 86).

[23]The Talk of the Town, "L'Esprit du bébé," *New Yorker*, 6 Feb. 1995, 28; "When Good Babies Smell Bad," *Time*, 3 Sept. 2001, 26; "Bébé Trendy," *L'Officiel* 864 (Apr. 2002): 88; "Baby Formulas," *France* 61 (Spring 2002): 7; Nolwenn Du Laz, "Beauté / Tentation: 0-16 Ans," *Marie-Claire*, Dec. 2002, 326. There is even a scent for the new mother, *Eau d'Amour pour Maman* (from Tartine et Chocolat), simultaneously offering an "intimate and emotional fragrance as well as a maternal presence" (Paule Cornille, "Empire d'essences," *L'Officiel* 874 [April 2003]: 198).

[24]Fabienne Antoniewski, "Parfums et belles manières," *Elle* 3066 (4 Oct 2004): 199–203; Nolwenn Du Laz, "Ces parfums nommés désir," *Marie-Claire* 604 (Dec. 2002): 310; Jane Larkworthy, "Spring Fling," *W*, April 2003, 132; "W Beauty Flash: Full Flavor," *W*, Aug. 2003, 76; Antigone Schilling, "Jeux de rôles," *L'Officiel* 887 (Aug 2004): 142; Lili Barbery, "Beauté: Désir régressif," V-F, May 2005, 145; advertisement for DKNY *Be Delicious*, *Vanity Fair*, Dec. 2004; William L. Hamilton, "I Dreamed I Wore My Martini," NYT, 18 Jan. 2004, sec. 9, Sunday Styles, 6; "Belly Up to the Beauty Bar," NYT, 1 Aug 2004, sec. 9, Sunday Styles, 3; Jane Wardell, "Barbour: The Coat That Says 'Britain,'" *Valley News* (White River Junction, VT), 26 Jan. 2003, C 2; "Be Prepared. Introducing a New Fragrance from Swiss Army," advertisement, NYT *Magazine*, 1 June 1997, 19.

[25]James Bennet, "Peres Waits for Chance To Resume Peace Quest," NYT, 24 Jan. 2003, A 6; Joyce Mansour, *Histoires nocives* (1973), *Prose et Poésie. Oeuvre complète* (Arles: Actes Sud, 1991), 275. "A Tangled Web," *The Economist*, 27 Nov. 1999, 59 and Warren Hoge, "Writer, Actor, M.P. (and a Reliable Source of Spice)," NYT, 2 July 2001, A 4; John. F. Burns, "When Seeing Osama Is Not Enough," NYT, 6 Jan. 2002, Week in Review, 16; Craig S. Smith, "Paris Journal: A Fragrance That by Any Other Name May Sell as Sweet," NYT, 5 Nov 2004, A, 4.

[26]See Michael Bar-Zohar, *Bitter Scent: The Case of L'Oréal, Nazis, and the Arab Boycott* (New York: Dutton, 1996); on the Revelations's suit against Calvin Klein, see Tracie Rozhon, "2 Perfume Companies at Odds Over Territory," NYT, 1 Oct. 2002, 24; on Saint Laurent's *Champagne/Yvresse*, see Irvine, 144–45; and on the Detroit case, see David Shepardson, "Radio DJ Wins $10.6 Million in Stink Over Perfume," *The Detroit News*, 24 May 2005. See also Stéphane Marchand, *Les Guerres du luxe* (Paris: Fayard, 2001), 167–79 for an interesting history of the suit brought in 1999 by Thierry Mugler Parfums against the Grasse perfume company Molinard.

[27]Bonnet, "L'Homme et le parfum," 717; Lynn Snowden, "Scent Trek," HB, Feb. 1996, 80–82; "The Sweet Smell of Success," *The Economist*, 5 September 1998, 75–76, 78; Marlise Simons, "Eau de Rain Forest," NYT *Magazine*, 2 May 1999, 56–61; Lucian Kim, "On the Trail of an Elusive Scent," *Boston Sunday Globe*, 19 Jan. 2003, A 6.

[28]Montaigne, "Of smells," *The Complete Essays of Montaigne*, trans. Donald M. Frame (Stanford: Stanford UP, 1957), 228. The original film, *Profumo di Donna*, based on a novel of the same name by Giovanni Arpino, and starring Vittorio Gassman was released in 1974; a Hollywood remake with Al Pacino, called "Scent of a Woman," appeared in 1992; Labro, 207–08.

[29]Le Guérer, 149-51, 296 and *Le Grand Robert de la Langue Française*, 2nd ed., vol. VII (Paris: Le Robert, 1989). On the techniques of fumigation or aspersion, see Alain Corbin, *The Foul and the Fragrant: Odor and the French Social Imagination* (Cambridge: Harvard UP, 1986), 62–66.

[30]Alain Corbin, "A History and Anthropology of the Senses," in his *Time, Desire and Horror: Towards a History of the Senses*, trans. Jean Birrell (Cambridge: Polity Press, 1995), 185; Michel Serres, Les *Cinq sens. Philosophie des corps mêlés* (Paris: Grasset, 1985), 254. Marx made a similar point when he wrote that "the culture of the five senses is the work of all history." (Quoted in Alain Corbin, "Senses," *Encyclopedia of Social History* [New York: Garland, 1994], 667).

[31]Rimmel, quoted in Bonnet, "L'Homme et le parfum," 718; Corbin, "A History," 189, 190; Guy Thuillier, *L'Imaginaire quotidien au XIXe siècle* (Paris: Economica, 1985), 3.

[32]Corbin, "A History," 191; Thuillier, *L'Imaginaire quotidien*, 3; Yves Pelicier, "De l'historicité du quotidien à l'histoire préventive," preface to Thuillier, *L'Imaginaire quotidien*, xii-xiv; Guy Thuillier, *Pour une histoire du quotidien au XIXe siècle en Nivernais* (Paris and The Hague: Mouton, 1977), 2, 448–49; Corbin "Senses," 667.

[33]Corbin, "Senses," 667, *The Foul*, 68–69, 8, resp. In 1770 the English Parliament passed an act condemning as a sorcerer "any woman who shall entice into marriage any of His Majesty's subjects by means of perfume, false hair, or false hips" (Roy Bedichek, *The Sense of Smell* [Garden City: Doubleday, 1960], 145–46).

[34]Gaston Bachelard, *Air and Dreams: An Essay on the Imagination of Movement* [1943], trans. Edith R. and C. Frederick Farrell (Dallas: The Dallas Institute Publications, 1988), 1,137.

[35]This "shapist-theory" of olfactory recognition—namely, that the scent molecule's shape and that of the cavity into which it settles make a perfect fit—was challenged in 1996 by a controversial "vibrationist theory" put forth by the biophysicist Luca Turin. Turin proposed that the consistent pattern of vibrations coming from atoms held together by the electron bonds in a scent molecule emits a frequency, an unchanging "wave number," like a musical chord, to which the olfactory receptors in the cilia are attuned and which they then recognize as a specific odor. For a fascinating study of the development of Turin's hypothesis and the virulently hostile reaction it received from the scientific establishment, see Chandler Burr, *The Emperor of Scent: A Story of Perfume, Obsession, and the Last Mystery of the Senses* (New York: Random House, 2002).

[36]Bedichek, 42–44; Boyd Gibbons, "The Intimate Sense of Smell," *National Geographic* 170, no. 3 (Sept. 1986): 332–37; *H & R*, 49–54; "Making Sense of Scents," *The Economist*, 13 Mar. 1999, 97; Bettina Malnic, Junzo Hirono, Takaaki Sato, and Linda B. Buck, "Combinatorial Receptor Codes for Odors," *Cell* 96 (5 March 1999): 713–723; Edwin T. Morris, *Fragrance: The Story of Perfume from Cleopatra to Chanel* (Greenwich, CT: E. T. Morris & Co., 1984), 37; Piet Vroon, *Smell: The Secret Seducer,* trans. Paul Vincent (New York: Farrar, Straus and Giroux, 1997), 26–44, 90; Cathryn Delude, "On the Trail of an Odor Map," *The Scientist*, 25 Oct. 2004, 22–24; Onfray, *L'Art de jouir*, 113.

[37]Michel Maffesoli, *Aux creux des apparences: Pour une éthique de l'esthétique* (Paris: Plon, 1990), 78, 101.

[38]Honoré de Balzac, *Traité de la vie élégante*, suivi de *Théorie de la démarche* (Paris: Arléa, 1998), 75; Octave Uzanne, *L'Art et les artifices de la beauté* (Paris: Felix Juven, 1902), 163; Colette quoted in Girard, 56; Corbin, *The Foul*, 8, 195; Constantin Weriguine, *Souvenirs et Parfums: Mémoires d'un parfumeur* (Paris: Plon, 1965), 189–90.

[39]Corbin, *Historien du sensible*, 46, 78; José Saramago, *The History of the Siege of Lisbon*, trans. Giovanni Pontiero (San Diego: Harcourt Brace & Company, 1996,) 8; Eugen Weber, *France, Fin de siècle* (Cambridge: Harvard UP, 1986), 80.

[40]Thuillier, *L'Imaginaire quotidien*, 1–3, 21.

[41]Thuillier, *L'Imaginaire quotidien*, 7–10, 21, 69–80.

[42]Jacques Polge, in conversation with the author, 9 May 2003; Julia Floransac, "Entretien: Jacques Polge," *Senso* 4 (May–June 2002): 115; Laurence Benaïm, "Interview Nez à Nez: Polge Connection, *Stilleto* 6 (spring–summer 2005): 73.

[43]Floransac, 116; Le Guérer, *Le Parfum*, 205-06.

[44]Jean-Paul Guerlain, *Les Routes de mes parfums* (Paris: Le Cherche Midi, 2002), 53.

[45]Floransac, 115.

[46]Fabienne Antoniewski, "Ce que sentent les fleurs," *Elle* (20 May 2002), 206; Jan Moran, *Fabulous Fragrances: How to Select Your Perfume Wardrobe; The Women's Guide to Prestige Perfumes* (Beverly Hills, CA: Crescent House Publishing, 1994), 127–28; Delbourg-Delphis, 196.

[47]Antoniewski, "Ce que sentent," 206.

[48]Annick Le Guérer, "Jean-Claude Ellena: Le retour au naturel," *Parfums & Senteurs* 8 (July 2001): 32. When the perfumer starts out, Ellena observes, "it's more about your passions. At the end, it's intellectual" (Chandler Burr, "Annals of Innovation. The Scent of the Nile," *New Yorker*, 14 March 2005, 88). On Viktor & Rolf's perfume, see Richard Martin, "A Note: Art & Fashion, Viktor & Rolf," *Fashion Theory* 3:1 (1999): 111.

[49]Antoniewski, "Ce que sentent," 206; Jean-Yves Gaborit, *Perfumes: The Essences and Their Bottles* (New York: Rizzoli, 1985), 47.

[50]Charles Baudelaire, *Selected Poems from Les Fleurs du mal*, trans. Norman R. Shapiro (Chicago: U. of Chicago P., 1998) 13, 79. The postwar singer and songwriter Leo Ferré goes further than Rimbaud, suggesting that what the nineteenth-century poet really had in mind was the invention of an alphabet perceptible to all five senses; consonants would have a material consistency ("B," for example, would be greasy), while vowels would emit their own particular smells: "A" varnish, "E," mint, "I," coal, "O," hay, and "U," ether. Leo Ferré, "Technique de l'exil" (1970), *Cahiers d'études Leo Ferré*, 1 (June 1998), 20; John Donne, "The Perfume," *The Elegies and The Songs and Sonnets*, ed. Helen Gardner (Oxford: The Clarendon Press, 1965), 8.

[51]See Giuseppe Donato and Monique Seefried, *The Fragrant Past: Perfumes of Cleopatra and Julius Caesar*, exhibition catalogue (Atlanta: Emory University Museum of Art and Archaeology, 1989), 54. The oldest perfumery yet discovered, with scents more ancient than those found in Egyptian predynastic graves, dates back 4,000 years (to 2000 B.C.). Fourteen different perfumes composed of ten essences (cinnamon, laurel, bergamot, etc.) were recently uncovered at an archeological site in Cyprus (Michael Theodoulou,

"Archeological Dig Sniffs Out World's Oldest Perfumery," *The Scotsman*, 25 Feb 2005).

[52]On Willoughby's art and illustration, see William Connelly, "Of Singular Originality. The Life and Work of Vera Willoughby (1872–1939)," *IBIS* 2 (2002):119–44, esp. 126–27; and Lisa Lodeski, "The Harem as a Site for Sexual Fantasy in the Work of Vera Willoughby," *(detail)* 5, no. 1 (1997):2–3.

[53]Paul Gardner, *Louise Bourgeois* (New York: Universe, 1994), 43–44.

[54]I do not wish to suggest that Pollock consciously set out to imitate the way scent moves. It was, rather, the way art moves as it is being made that interested him in *Untitled (Scent)* and in other drip or poured paintings of the late forties and early fifties. Pollock's work is at its most powerful, Kirk Varnedoe writes, when it reveals him "finding fresh poetries innate to materials.... He showed how a personal art could emerge from giving up the search for 'meaningful' forms and giving in to 'mindless' motions that released an intuitive feel for the medium." Kirk Varnedoe, "Comet: Jackson Pollock's Life and Work," in Kirk Varnedoe with Pepe Karmel, *Jackson Pollock* (New York: MoMA, 1998), 54, 64.

[55]Ian McEwan, *Amsterdam* (New York: Random House, 1998), 172.

[56]*Duke Ellington and His Orchestra 1944–1945*, "The Classics Chronological Series," no. 881, Classics Records, 1996 (compact disc); Duke Ellington, brochure notes, "Jazz Tribune," no. 69 from *The Indispensable Duke Ellington*, vol. 11–12 (1944–1946), RCA 07863 /66679-2 (2 compact discs). Another *sound* medium for perfume, of admittedly lesser artistic quality and sophistication than *Perfume Suite*, was *Boston Blackie: The Perfume Murders*, a radio drama broadcast on March 16, 1951. As a high-priced luxury item that can be easily counterfeited and used in a financial scam, perfume in this drama possesses no olfactory properties whatsoever. The salesman of *Ma Vie* Perfume Company is murdered by a man who then impersonates him (down to his French accent). The murderer attempts to sell two hundred ounces of counterfeit *Ma Vie* to Jackson's Department Store at half its price so long as Mr. Jackson will give him $5,000 in cash for the discounted merchandise. Working in tandem with Inspector Farraday of the Boston police department, Boston Blackie solves the crime (*Boston Blackie: The Perfume Murders*, Golden Age Radio, March 1951; audiocassette).

[57]Holly Brubach, "Beneath the Surface," *NYT Magazine*, Part 2, "Men's Fashions of the Times," 20 Sept. 1998, 66; Serge Gleizes, "Richard Meier, la fibre minimaliste," *L'Officiel* 812 (Feb. 1997):186, 190. See also Anna Barbara and Anthony Perliss's forth-

coming study *The Scent of Architecture* (Skira, 2006).

58The *calligramme* is reproduced in Stefan Themerson, *Apollinaire's Lyrical Ideograms* (London: Gaberbocchus Press, 1968), 16.

59Richard Wilbur, "The Lilacs," *New and Collected Poems* (San Diego: Harcourt Brace Jovanovich, 1988), 118–19.

60William Carlos Williams, *Paterson* III (New York: New Directions, 1963), 96; Elizabeth Bishop, "In the Village," *The Collected Prose*, ed. Robert Giroux (New York: Farrar, Straus Giroux, 1984), 255, 257. "The art of losing's not too hard to master / though it may look like (*Write* it!) like disaster," Bishop writes in her poem "One Art" (*The Complete Poems 1927–1979* [New York: Farrar, Straus and Giroux, 1980], 178).

Chapter 2: The Empire of Perfume: Scent in Nineteenth-Century French Culture

1Regarding an elegant nineteenth-century bourgeois woman's use of her day, see Anne Martin-Fugier, *La Bourgeoise. Femme au temps de Paul Bourget* (Paris: Grasset & Fasquelle, 1983), 225–26.

2Thuillier, *Pour une histoire*, 2. For a theoretical discussion of the notion of the everyday, see Michael Sheringham, *Everyday Life: Theories and Practices from Surrealism to the Present* (Oxford: Oxford UP, 2006).

3Delbourg-Delphis, 100; "Origine de l'eau de Cologne," *La Boutique du Bonheur* (Paris: Roger & Gallet, 1960), n. pag.; Pillivuyt, *Histoire*, 203, 207; *3000 ans*, 79; Jean Hadorn, "Le Jardin des Hespérides," in René Laruelle, ed., *L'Art du parfum.* (Paris: Le Temps apprivoisé, 1993), 95–96; Jean Robiquet "Les Parfums de nos grand'mères, in *La Parfumerie française*, 31; Girard, 43. Some historical reports say that the pastilles had been manufactured by Houbigant, another supplier of fragrances to the Emperor before his exile (Pillivuyt, *Histoire*, 207).

4Jean-Paul Kauffmann, *The Black Room at Longwood: Napoleon's Exile on Saint Helena*, trans. Patricia Clancy (New York: Four Walls Eight Windows, 1997): 57, 268–69 and Cathy Newman, *Perfume: The Art and Science of Scent* (Washington DC: National Geographic Society, 1998): 39. In 1992, Napoleon's Saint Helena cologne was recreated from a formula found hidden in a chest of drawers once belonging to Ali. Jean Kerléo, the perfumer for Jean Patou and the director of the Osmothèque, an archive of scents in Versailles, remade the fragrance. It was given the name *Eau de Cologne de Napoléon Ier à Sainte-Hélène*; the label on the bottle carried the Emperor's coat of arms.

5Annette Green and Linda Dyett, *Secrets of Aromatic Jewelry* (Paris / New York: Flammarion, 1998): 77; Morris, 164; Annick Le Guérer, "Petite Histoire de l'Eau de Cologne," *Parfums & Senteurs* 8 (July 2001): 54. See also the nineteenth-century prospectus for *Aqua Mirabilis*, entitled "Vertus et effets de l'excellente Eau Admirable ou Eau de Cologne," detailing the manner of its use and the cures it would effect against poisons of all kinds, apoplexy, paralysis, stiffness of the neck, heart palpitations, jaundice, catarrh, and other maladies, in Hadorn, 94, 96–98.

6Pillivuyt, *Flacons*, 34. The allusion to Ninon refers in all likelihood to Ninon de Lenclos, born in Paris in 1616 who lived to be almost ninety. Libertine, free of spirit, witty, and cultivated, she took some of the most powerful men of the seventeenth century as lovers. *Le Petit Robert des Noms Propres*, rev. ed. (Paris: Dictionnaires Le Robert, 1994). Morris, 172; Pillivuyt, *Histoire*, 220; Hadorn, 95–96; Girard, 43.

7Barillé / Laroze, 56-58; Le Guérer, "Petite Histoire," 56; Hadorn, 94; Jan Moran, 124–25; see chapter 8, pp. 312ff.

8Kauffmann, xvi, 54–56, 198; Alan R. Hirsch, *Scentsational Sex: The Secret to Using Aroma for Arousal* (Boston: Element, 1998), 74; Pillivuyt, *Histoire*, 201, 207; Georges Vigarello, *Le Propre et le sale. L'Hygiène du corps depuis le Moyen Age* (Paris: Seuil, 1985), 172–73; Corbin, *The Foul*, 179.

9Pillivuyt, *Histoire*, 203, 207; Corbin, *The Foul*, 196. Barillé / Laroze, 68–70; Bonnet, "L'Homme et le parfum," 711; Girard, 42; Octave Uzanne, *Les Parfums et les fards à travers les âges* (Geneva: Charles Blanc, 1927), 35. See also Aileen Ribeiro, *The Art of Dress: Fashion in England and France 1750–1820* (New Haven: Yale UP, 1995), 84, 94–95 and, on Marie-Antoinette's love of scent, Elisabeth de Feydeau, *Jean-Louis Fargeon, parfumeur de Marie-Antoinette* (Versailles: Perrin, 2004).

10Barillé / Laroze, 70–72; Corbin, *The Foul*, 196.

11Girard, 42; F. Ghozland, *Perfume Fantasies* (Toulouse: Milan, 1987), 30, 62; Morris, 171–72, 174; Ribeiro, 94, 120ff.; Pillivuyt, *Histoire*, 201.

12Philippe Perrot, *Le Luxe. Une Richesse entre faste et confort XVIIIe–XIXe siècle* (Paris: Seuil, 1995), 92, 163-64; Octave Uzanne, *La Femme et la mode. Métamorphoses de la Parisienne de 1792 à 1892* (Paris: Librairies-Imprimeries Réunies, 1892), 84.

13Benjamin, *The Arcades Project*, 879; Perrot, *Le Luxe*, 177, 184; Martin-Fugier, *La Bourgeoise*, 198-99, 206–07.

14"*Autour du parfum*" du XVIe au XIXe siècle, exhibition catalogue (Paris: Le Louvre des antiquaires, 1985), 33; "Sachets et cartes parfumées," in *Parfumerie française*, 152–53; Monique Cabré, Marina Sebbag, Vincent Vidal, *Femmes de papier. Une Histoire du geste parfumé / Perfumed Cards . . . A Scented Gesture* (Toulouse: Milan, 1998), 64; "Parfumeur," *Encyclopédie ou Dictionnaire raisonnée des sciences, des arts et des métiers par une société de gens de lettres* (1765); G. Champtoce, "La Marque: Son histoire, sa création, son lancement, sa protection," in *Parfumerie française*, 215; Morris, 170–71; Barillé / Laroze, 55; Eugène Rimmel, *Le Livre des parfums* (Paris: E. Dentu, 1870), 294, 322; Irvine 23; Pillivuyt, *Flacons*, 27; Georges Bourdon, "La Parfumerie française à l'Exposition Internationale des Arts Décoratifs et Industriels Modernes," in *Parfumerie française*, 462.

15Kauffmann, xviii, 55, xvi, 226, resp.

16Bernard Marchand, *Paris. Histoire d'une ville XIXe-XXe siècle* (Paris: Seuil, 1993), 22, 25; Weber, *France* 57–58, 25–26, 37–38, resp.; Gabrielle Cadier-Rey, *Les Français de 1900* (Paris: Circonflexe, 1999), 101.

17Marchand, 27–29, 38.

18Vigarello, *Le Propre et le sale*, 182, 11–12, 94, 97–100, resp.

19Vigarello, 100–102; "Sachets et cartes parfumées," 152. One admirer of sachets, no aficionado of the slender, boyish *garçonne* look of the twenties, wrote in 1925 that the fashion styles of the time were unfortunately rendering the sachet obsolete: "Even the thinnest of sachets could find no place in the few clothes a woman still wears, without at once revealing its presence, for women are no longer even able to find a place for their nipples" ("Sachets et cartes parfumées," 156); Uzanne, *Les Parfums et les fards*, 32.

20Vigarello, 144–46, 169–76, 182–88; Pillivuyt, *Histoire*, 208.

21Weber, *France*, 58; Vigarello, 217, 230–34, 246.

22Pillivuyt, *Flacons*, 27–29; Girard, 40; Corbin, *The Foul*, 68, 74; Pillivuyt, *Histoire*, 207.

23Girard, 43; Barillé / Laroze, 74; Pillivuyt, *Histoire*, 207-08; *3000 ans*, 154.

24Robiquet, 32; Irvine, frontispiece; Michèle Atlas and Alain Monniot, *Guerlain. Les flacons à parfum depuis 1828* (Toulouse: Milan, 1997), 71, 136.

25Pillivuyt, *Histoire*, 216, 124, resp.; Anne Martin-Fugier, *La Vie élégante ou la formation du Tout-Paris, 1815–1848* (Paris: Fayard, 1990), 325; Morris, 170; Algirdas Julien

Greimas, *La Mode en 1830. Langage et société: Ecrits de jeunesse* (Paris: PUF, 2000), 123–24; Delbourg-Delphis, 34.

26 Pillivuyt, *Histoire,* 220-21; Atlas and Monniot, 9–17, 312ff.

27 Delbourg-Delphis, 17, 44; Barillé / Laroze, 74.

28 Balzac, *Traité de la vie élégante,* 47, 75, 82, 44, 45, 33, 54, resp.; Elisabeth Barillé, *Guerlain,* Coll. Mémoires de la beauté (Paris: Assouline, 1999), 7; Vigarello, 181.

29 Honoré de Balzac, *César Birotteau,* trans. Robin Buss (London: Penguin, 1994), 7; hereafter, all page numbers are indicated in the text.

30 Honoré de Balzac, *César Birotteau,* Coll. Folio (Paris: Gallimard, 1975), 192. The illustration in the French edition is not included in the English translation.

31 "L'Humour et la parfumerie," in *Parfumerie française,* 230; Marc Martin, *Trois Siècles de publicité en France* (Paris: Odile Jacob, 1992), 13–15, 21, 401, hereafter cited in the text; for a discussion of the political role of *affiches* during Louis-Napoleon's coup d'état of December 1851, see Maurice Agulhon, *1848, ou l'apprentissage de la République 1848-1852,* rev. ed. (Paris: Seuil, 1992), 184–85; Vicomte G. D'Avenel, "La Publicité," in his *Le Mécanisme de la vie moderne,* 3rd ed., 5 vols. (Paris: Armand Colin, 1921), IV: 149–50.

32 Raymond Gaudriault, *La Gravure de mode féminine en France* (Paris: Les Editions de l'amateur, 1983), 78; Martin, *Trois siècles,* 97–98, 113; D'Avenel, 166.

33 Martin, *Trois siècles,* 104–07; Weber, *France,* 155; Vanessa R. Schwartz, *Spectacular Realities: Early Mass Culture in Fin-de-Siècle Paris* (Berkeley: U of California P., 1998), 34; Monique Cabré and Marina Sebbag, *Les Cartes parfumées* (Paris: Editions Alternatives, 1996), 25.

34 Martin, *Trois siècles,* 109-12; D'Avenel, 173, 176; Ghislaine Wood, "The Age of Paper," *Art Nouveau 1890–1914,* ed. Paul Greenhalgh (London: Victoria and Albert Museum, 2000), 149; Weber, *France,* 155; Barillé / Laroze, 191.

35 Martin, *Trois Siècles,* 117–18; "L'Affiche et la parfumerie," *Parfumerie française,* 188-89.

36 Martin *Trois siècles,* 405–07 and Marc Martin, "La Publicité," in *La France d'un siècle à l'autre, 1914-2000. Dictionnaire Critique,* ed. Jean-Pierre Rioux and Jean-François Sirinelli. (Paris: Hachette, 2000), 402–04.

37 Richard Cobb, *Paris and Elsewhere: Selected Writings,* ed. David Gilmour (London: John Murray, 1998), 152.

38 Benjamin, *The Arcades Project,* 171, 173–74.

39 Louis Aragon, *Paris Peasant* [1926], trans. Simon Watson Taylor (Boston: Exact Change, 1994), 11; Delbourg-Delphis, 73.

40 Charles Diehl, *La République de Venise* (Paris: Flammarion, 1985), 54–56; Jacob Burckhardt, *The Civilization of the Renaissance in Italy,* trans. S. G. C. Middlemore (New York: New American Library, 1960), 266; Green and Dyett, 62, 70, 73–74; and Gianfranco Toso, *Murano: A History of Glass* (San Giovanni Lupatoto: Arsenale, 2000), 25–33.

41 Irvine, 73; Green and Dyett, 78–84, 107, 109, 111–12; Carla Cerutti, *Flacons* (Paris: Celiv, 1994), 50.

42 Morris, 190; Irvine, 75; Green and Dyett, 88; Delbourg-Delphis 45, 43, resp.; *Bourjois: Catalogue Commercial,* 1897, plate 11, Bourjois / Chanel archives, # B-4-13-3-C; Leach, *Perfume Presentation,* 221.

43 Green and Dyett, 92, 96–98, 117; Irvine, 74; Delbourg-Delphis 44; Barillé / Laroze, 191.

44 "Etiquettes et impressions anciennes," *Parfumerie française,* 97; *Les Parfums à travers la mode. Rétrospective de 1765 à nos jours* (Paris: Editions du Chêne, 1945), n. pag.

45 "Etiquettes et impressions anciennes," 99, 101, 103, 130, 121, 156, resp.; *3000 ans,* 146; Perrot, *Le Luxe,* 216.

46 *Les Parfums à travers la Mode.* For illustrations of labels for Dissey et Piver or L. T. Piver perfumes from 1830 through the Second Empire, see Barillé / Laroze, 71; Laurence Mouillefarine, *Objets de la beauté à collectionner* (Boulogne: Editions MDM, 1999), 34.

47 Cabré and Sebbag, *Cartes parfumées,* 30–34, 13, 17, resp.

48 Ibid., 42, 34-35, resp.; see also Cabré, et al, *Femmes de papier,* 44.

49 Eugène Rimmel, *Le Livre des parfums* (Paris: E. Dentu, 1870); Cabré and Sebbag, *Cartes parfumées,* 34–36, 38–39; "Le Temps retrouvé: Archives et vieux papiers," *Parfums & Senteurs* 5 (December 2000):94–97; Green and Dyett, 179, n. 4.

50 *Almanac Rimmel 1880,* Bourjois / Chanel Archives, #B-4-7-1404.

51 Cabré and Sebbag, *Cartes parfumées,* 50–55.

52 Ibid., 29; for images of Rigaud and Poiret scented fans, see Mouillefarine, 42–43, and Cabré, et al, *Femmes de papier,* 97–100; for a discussion of Poiret's Parfums de Rosine, see Yvonne Deslandres, *Poiret* (Paris; Editions du Regard, 1986), 103–05, 231–34, and Pillivuyt, *Histoire,* 226.

53 Alain Plessis, *De la fête impériale au mur des fédérés, 1852-1871,* rev. ed. (Paris: Seuil, 1979), 74, 79; hereafter cited as Plessis in the text; Perrot, *Le Luxe,* 141, 155, n. 36, 148–49, 157, resp.

54 T. J. Clark, *The Painting of Modern Life: Paris in the Art of Manet and His Followers* (New York: Alfred A. Knopf, 1985), 69.

55 Joanna Richardson, *La Vie Parisienne 1852–1870* (New York: Viking Press, 1971), 278; Pierre Guiral, *La Vie quotidienne en France à l'âge d'or du capitalisme 1852–1879* (Paris: Hachette, 1976), 110.

56 On Worth's designs and the Empress's new clothes, see Richardson, 239 and James Laver, *Costume and Fashion: A Concise History,* rev. expanded, updated edition (London: Thames and Hudson, 1982, 1995) 186; Pillivuyt, *Histoire,* 209–10.

57 Perrot, *Le Luxe,* 238, 166–167, 241–42, resp. Marie Simon, *Fashion in Art: The Second Empire and Impressionism* (London: Zwemmer, 1995), 129; Richardson, 235, 237.

58 Guiral, *La Vie quotidienne,* 61, 63, 79, 177; Weber, *France,* 97, 102–03.

59 Richardson, 235, 237, 241; Laver, 184–85.

60 Alain Corbin, "Lumière et romantisme," *Histoire en parfums,* ed. Arielle Picaud, (Paris: Editions du Garde-Temps, 1999), 62; Le Guérer, "Petite histoire," 57; Girard, 45; Pillivuyt, *Histoire,* 208; Georges Bourdon, "Le Mémorial de la parfumerie française," in *Parfumerie française,* 19; *3000 ans,* 152, 155.

61 Girard, 45; Greimas, 221, n. 16; Atlas and Monniot, 62; Morris 175–76, 188; Pillivuyt, *Histoire,* 208; Bourdon, "Le Mémorial, 19.

62 Morris, 180; Girard, 46. On manuals of beauty, see Delbourg-Delphis, 61; Colette Fellous, *Guerlain* (Paris: Denoël, 1987), 22, 35; Corbin, *The Foul,* 183; Lola Montez, *The Arts of Beauty, or Secrets of a Lady's Toilet. With Hints to Gentlemen on the Art of Fascinating* (New York: Ecco Press, 1978), 30, 41. Regarding the erotic power of perfume, see chapter 7.

63 Jean Robiquet, in *Parfumerie française,* 32.

64 Morris, 180; Pillivuyt, *Histoire,* 208, 216–17; Marie-Christine Grasse, *Le Jasmin. Fleur de Grasse* (Bournemouth/Grasse: Editions Parkstone / Musée international de la parfumerie, 1996), 61; Lucienne A. Roubin, *Le Monde des odeurs. Dynamique et fonctions du champ odorant* (Paris: Meridiens Klincksieck, 1989), 80–81, 115.

[65]Pillivuyt, *Histoire*, 225; Morris, 188-89; Roubin, 159; Delbourg-Delphis, 29, 33; Michael Edwards, *Perfume Legends: French Feminine Fragrances* (Levallois: HM Editions, 1996), 16.

[66]Information about the creation of synthetic fragrances comes from the following sources, although not all are agreed on the dates of the discoveries: Girard, 104; Morris, 186-89, 192; Barillé, *Guerlain*, 8; Delbourg-Delphis, 31-32; Greene and Dyett, 88; *H & R*, 79; Hadorn, 129, 136; Le Guérer, *Le Parfum*, 182-84. Regarding the changes in the perfume industry, see also Elisabeth de Feydeau, "De l'hygiène au rêve: l'industrie française des parfums de 1830 à 1939," Ph.D diss, University of Paris IV, Sorbonne, 1997.

[67]Pillivuyt, *Histoire*, 229, n. 31; Delbourg-Delphis, 35-37, 38, 58.

[68]Baudelaire, *The Painter of Modern Life*, 32-33. The relationship between the natural and the synthetic in perfume creation has been from the first appearance of synthetic ingredients a delicate if not problematic one. The contemporary perfumer (and former "nose" of Jean Patou), Jean Kerléo, has remarked that it is the impurities inherent to the natural product that give perfume "'a different odor, an odor that better expresses nature.'" Synthetic jasmine does not, he argues (and not all perfumers would agree), give that full sensation of "'richness and greenness" arising from a field of jasmine (quoted by Le Guérer, *Le Parfum*, 253).

[69]Pillivuyt, *Histoire*, 196; "*Autour du parfum*," 60; Baudelaire, *The Painter of Modern Life*, 32-33; Fellous, *Guerlain*, 39-40; Barillé, *Guerlain*, 8; Edwards, 16.

[70]Edwards, 15, 40; Le Guérer, "Petite Histoire," 57; Fellous, *Guerlain*, 47, 40, resp.; Barillé, *Guerlain*, 8-9.

[71]Huysmans's detailed knowledge of perfume was most likely acquired from reading Septimus Piesse's *Des Odeurs, des parfums, et des cosmétiques* in its second French edition of 1877 (Marc Fumaroli, "Préface," *A Rebours*, coll. Folio [Paris: Gallimard, 1977], 420, n. 136); Joris-Karl Huysmans, *Against Nature (A rebours)*, trans. Margaret Mauldon (Oxford: Oxford UP, 1998), 99: hereafter cited in the text.

Chapter 3: Charles Baudelaire and the Music of Perfume

[1]Charles Baudelaire, *Journaux intimes* in *Oeuvres complètes*, ed. Claude Pichois, 2 vols., Bibliothèque de la Pléiade, (Paris: Gallimard, 1975-76), I: 677, 694, 698, 693, 689, resp.; all future allusions to Baudelaire's work will refer to this edition and hereafter appear in the text. All translations of Baudelaire are mine unless otherwise noted in the text.

Translations by others from which I quote are: *Flowers of Evil and Other Works: A Bantam Dual-Language Book*, ed. and trans. Wallace Fowlie (New York: Bantam, 1964); *Selected Poems from Les Fleurs du mal*, trans. Norman R. Shapiro (Chicago: U of Chicago P., 1998); and *The Flowers of Evil*, ed. Marthiel and Jackson Mathews (New York: New Directions, 1955, 1989); in a few instances I have slightly modified these translations.

[2]Georges Bataille, "The Language of Flowers" (1929), in *Visions of Excess: Selected Writings, 1927-1939*, ed. Allan Stoekl, trans. Allan Stoekl et al., Theory and History of Literature, 14 (Minneapolis: U. of Minn. P. 1985), 12-13.

[3]Baudelaire, *The Painter of Modern Life*, 32; hereafter cited in the text; Corbin, *The Foul*, 198.

[4]Other interesting interpretations of "Parfum exotique" are to be found in Jeanne Theis Whitaker, "Parfum Exotique," in *Understanding Les Fleurs du mal: Critical Readings*, ed. William J. Thompson (Nashville: Vanderbilt UP., 1997), 49-59 and Eléonore M. Zimmermann, *Poétiques de Baudelaire dans Les Fleurs du mal. Rythme, parfum, lueur* (Paris: Lettres Modernes Minard, 1998), 96-99.

[5]G. W. Septimus Piesse, *The Art of Perfumery and The Methods of Obtaining Odours of Plants*, 4th edition (Philadelphia: Presley Blakiston, 1880), 306-10; Green and Dyett, 78

[6]René Laruelle, "Un Vent de fleurs," in Laruelle, *L'Art du parfum*, 111-12, 116.

[7]Walter Benjamin, "On Some Motifs in Baudelaire," in *Selected Writings*, 4 vols., ed. Michael W. Jennings (Cambridge: Harvard UP, 2003), IV: 335.

[8]Louis Bergeron, *Les Industries du luxe en France* (Paris: Odile Jacob, 1998), 119-20; Sylvie Legrand, et al, "La Vêture," Chap. 1 in *Mille Ans de costume français 950-1950* (Thionville: Gérard Klopp, 1991), 55; Julia V. Emberley, *The Cultural Politics of Fur* (Ithaca: Cornell U P, 1998), 11. By the nineteenth century, at least in Germany, fur had become, as Emberley observes, "a representative figure of the vicissitudes of a European cultural inscription of violent excess, both sexual and material, par excellence" (11).

[9]Charles Baudelaire, *Correspondance*, ed. Claude Pichois, 2 vols., Bibliothèque de la Pléiade (Paris: Gallimard, 1973), II: 30-31. Roman law identified *mundus muliebris* with those instruments useful in assuring a woman's cleanliness: in particular, objects such as metal mirrors, brooches, hairpins, combs, unguents, small glass vases containing makeup, flacons of essences, bracelets,

earrings, toothpicks, and scissors (Rimmel, *Le Livre des parfums*, 149).

[10]J.-P. Vernant, "Introduction" in Marcel Detienne, *The Gardens of Adonis: Spices in Greek Mythology*, trans. Janet Lloyd (Atlantic Highlands, NJ: Humanities Press, 1977), viii, vi, xxix, resp.; Faure, 18, 28, 11, resp.; D. Michael Stoddart, *The Scented Ape: The Biology and Culture of Human Odor* (Cambridge: Cambridge UP, 1990), 176; Donato,10; for fragrances in the Bible, see Rimmel, 61-90. Concerning the perfumes of antiquity in general, see Michal Dayagi-Mendels, *Perfumes and Cosmetics in the Ancient World* (Jerusalem: The Israel Museum, 1993); Jean Winand et Michel Malaise, "Les Parfums en Egypte," in Laruelle, *L'Art du parfum*, 13-43; Charles Fontinoy, "Les Parfums dans la Bible," in Laruelle, *L'Art du parfum*, 44-64; Le Guérer, *Sur les routes de l'encens*; and Rimmel, 27-176.

[11]*Classification des parfums et terminologie / Fragrance Catalogue and Terminology* (Paris: Société Française des parfumeurs, 1998), 2, 5-9; Barillé / Laroze, 212-17; Irvine, 57-60; *H&R*, 8, 10.

[12]Stoddart, 155; Le Guérer, *Le Parfum*, 266; Guerlain, *La Route de mes parfums*, 38; Girard, 84, 159. The erotic power of ambergris is also celebrated by one of the characters in the surrealist poet Robert Desnos's novel *Liberty or Love!* (1927). Upon inhaling the "most intimate odors" coming from his mistress's "cambric knickers," this character is immediately struck by their resemblance to the smell of ambergris: "What fabulous whale, of whatever color, could distil a more fragrant ambergris," he exclaims. As a "liquid evoking infinities," ambergris represents freedom for Desnos, the freedom to create new universes of sensation. When the hero of the story in question pours a bottle of liquid ambergris over his lover's body and she begins to "writhe with voluptuousness," he becomes "drunk on dreams." Robert Desnos, *Liberty or Love!*, trans. Terry Hale (London: Atlas Press, 1993), 4.

[13]Pillivuyt, *Flacons*, 29; Green and Dyett, 47-50; Piesse, 236-40; Morris, 10, 164, 226.

[14]Stoddart, 153; Irvine, 18, 24, 51-52; Girard, 84.

[15]Piesse, 247, 258; Morris, 226; Green and Dyett, 44, 46; Pillivuyt, *Histoire*, 207.

[16]Morris, 10; Piesse, 246-50, 257-61, 265; Le chevalier De Jaucourt, "Musc, animal du," in Diderot and d'Alembert, *Encyclopédie, ou Dictionnaire raisonné des sciences, des arts et des métiers par une société de gens de lettres* (Neuchâtel: Samuel Faulche et Cie, 1765), 10: 878-81.

[17]Barillé / Laroze, 68-70; Girard, 41-42; Cerutti, 44; Morris, 176; Claudine Chevrel

and Béatrice Cornet, *Grain de beauté. Un siècle de beauté par la publicité* (Paris: Somogy Editions d'Art / Bibliothèque Forney, 1993), 171; Balzac, *Traité de la vie élégante*, 26.

[18] Atlas and Monniot, 64; Girard, 104; Morris, 187–88; Delbourg-Delphis, 31–32, 35–38; J. Stephan Jellinek, "The Psychological Basis of Perfumery: A Re-Evaluation," in Paul Jellinek, *The Psychological Basis of Perfumery, Translation of the Expanded Fourth German Edition*, ed. and trans. by J. Stephan Jellinek (London: Chapman & Hall, 1997), 51. Today, the price of 2.2 pounds of natural musk is $50,000 (Le Guérer, *Le Parfum*, 268).

[19] Girard, 84; Irvine, 52; Jellinek, 254; Nick Ravo, "Barry Shipp, 62, the Developer of the Jovan Musk Fragrance," NYT, 8 September 1999, Obituary, C 28; Corbin, 73–74.

[20] Donato, 32; Faure, 59; Piesse, 53, 97–100, Williams, 167, 207.

[21] Detienne, 10; Williams, 208; Lise Manniche, *Sacred Luxuries: Fragrance, Aromatherapy, and Cosmetics in Ancient Egypt* (Ithaca: Cornell UP, 1999), 26; John Noble Wilford, "Ruins in Yemeni Desert Mark Route of Frankincense Trade," NYT, 28 January 1997, Science section, C: 1, 4; Fontinoy, in *L'Art du parfum*, 47–48.

[22] Rimmel, 80–81, 146, 153; Wilford, 4; Irvine, 72; Piesse, 52, 122, 167–68, 318; Faure, 32–33; Fontinoy, 50–51.

[23] The following discussion is taken from Piesse, 33–36, 45–49, 50–51, 55. Piesse's ideas seem to accord with the "vibrationist" theory recently put forth by Luca Turin; see above, chapter 1, n. 35.

[24] These fusions are not as bizarre as they may at first seem, since sounds and smells both move in waves through the air, since voice and breath both emanate from the mouth, carrying what is interior out into the external world, and since audition and olfaction both depend on stimuli entering and touching receptor organs (i.e., the tympanum of the ear and the olfactory bulbs of the nose).

[25] See Cerutti, *Flacons*, 45–60.

[26] Corbin, *The Foul* 180. In the first half of the nineteenth century, rubbing dry powder into the hair was the most common way to keep it clean (Vigarello, 188).

[27] Charles Baudelaire, *The Parisian Prowler: Le Spleen de Paris; Petits Poèmes en prose*, trans. Edward K. Kaplan (Athens: U of Georgia P., 1989), 35.

Chapter 4: Traces, Vapors, and Arabesques: Woman as Scent in the Fin de Siècle (1880–1914)

[1] Antoine Bertrand, *Les Curiosités esthétiques de Robert de Montesquiou*, 2 vols. Histoire des idées et critique littéraire 344 (Geneva: Droz, 1996), I: 114; hereafter cited in the text. Philippe Jullian, *Robert de Montesquiou. Un Prince 1900* (Paris: Librairie Académique Perrin, 1965), 85-86; hereafter cited in the text. In his memoirs, Montesquiou observes that he viewed his artistic and decorative arrangements as a "'writing at once literary and musical'" (quoted in Philippe Tiébaut, "Ego imago," in *Robert Montesquiou, ou L'art de paraître* [Paris: Editions de la réunion des musées nationaux, 1999], 11). For a discussion of the "resemblance" between the Count and Des Esseintes, see Marc Fumaroli, "Note sur le personnage de Des Esseintes," in J-K. Huysmans, *A Rebours*, 2nd ed., ed. Marc Fumaroli, coll. Folio (Paris: Gallimard, 1977), 363–71.

[2] Atlas and Monniot, 190.

[3] Philippe Garnier, *Emile Gallé*, rev. ed. (New York: Rizzoli, 1976, 1990), 158; Robert de Montesquiou, *Le Chef des odeurs suaves* (Paris: Georges Richard, 1907), 106–11; hereafter cited in the text. My thanks to Patrick Doucet, Curator of the Chanel and Bourjois Perfume Archives, Neuilly sur Seine, France, for his assistance in obtaining a copy of this extremely rare collection of poems; Robert de Montesquiou, *Roseaux Pensants* [1897] quoted in Garnier, 134-35.

[4] Garnier, 121-22, 109, resp.

[5] For reproductions of these bottles, see Garnier, 16, 18, 106 and Cerutti, 57, 202; Tirza True Latimer, *The Perfume Atomizer: An Object with Atmosphere* (West Chester PA: Schiffer Publishing, 1991), 38-39; Bertrand, I: 212.

[6] Louis de Fourcaud, *Emile Gallé* (Paris, 1903), 61, quoted in Garnier, 98; Roselyne Bouvier, and others, *Album. Musée de l'Ecole de Nancy* (Paris: Editions de la réunion des musées nationaux, 2001), 32-33.

[7] Victor Champier, "The Decorative Arts," in Victor Champier, et al, *Exposition Universelle, 1900: The Chefs-D'Oeuvre*, 10 vols. (Philadelphia: George Barrie & Son, 1902), IX: 107; Latimer, 39; Debora L. Silverman, *Art Nouveau in Fin-de-Siècle France: Politics, Psychology, and Style* (Berkeley: U of California P., 1989), 300, 232, resp.

[8] Lisa Tiersten, *Marianne in the Market: Envisioning Consumer Society in Fin-de-Siècle France* (Berkeley: U of California P., 2001), 178-79; Rhonda K. Garelick, *Rising Star: Dandyism, Gender, and Performance in the Fin de Siècle* (Princeton UP: 1998), 119; hereafter cited in the text.

[9] Stéphane Mallarmé, *Oeuvres complètes*, ed. Bertrand Marchal, 2 vols., Bibliothèque de la Pléiade (Paris: Gallimard, 1998, 2003), II:163; hereafter cited in the text.

[10] Quoted by Arlene Croce, "Degas's Mystery Painting," *New Yorker*, 2 Dec. 2002, 89.

[11] Philippe Jullian, *The Triumph of Art Nouveau: Paris Exhibition 1900*, trans. Stephen Hardman (London: Phaidon Press, 1974), 82; hereafter cited in the text.

[12] Jullian, *The Triumph*, 90 and Paul Morand *1900* (Paris: Editions de France, 1931), 78. Champier, "The Decorative Arts," IX: vi, 46–47.

[13] Rosalind H. Williams, *Dream Worlds: Mass Consumption in Late Nineteenth-Century France* (Berkeley: U. of California P., 1982), 203, 205.

[14] Albert Samain, *Au Jardin de l'Infante* [1893] in *Oeuvres d'Albert Samain* (Paris: Mercure de France, 1913), 66; page numbers are hereafter indicated in the text.

[15] Jean-Pierre Richard, *L'Univers imaginaire de Mallarmé* (Paris, Seuil, 1961), 376; hereafter cited in the text.

[16] Miss Satin [Stéphane Mallarmé], "Gazette de la Fashion." *La Dernière Mode*, 1 Nov. 1874, in *Oeuvres complètes*, II: 582; Marguerite de Ponty [Stéphane Mallarmé], "La Mode." *La Dernière Mode*, 15 Nov. 1874, in *Oeuvres complètes*, II: 599.

[17] Morand, *1900*, 232-33; Proust, *Contre Sainte-Beuve*, Bibliothèque de la Pléiade (Paris: Gallimard, 1971), 506.

[18] Philippe Jullian, *Prince of Aesthetes: Count Robert de Montesquiou, 1855-1921*, trans. John Haylock and Francis King (New York: Viking, 1967), 205. A copy of Montesquiou's original *Rapport* (published in 1900 by Belin Frères of Saint-Cloud) is in the Bibliothèque Forney in Paris; I have taken material from pp. 15, 19-20, 23–24, 40. *Pays des Aromates*, the republished version of the *Rapport*, carried a longwinded subtitle—*Commentaire descriptif d'une collection d'objets relatifs aux parfums, suivi d'une nomenclature des pièces qui la composent, ainsi que du catalogue d'une bibliothèque attenante et orné d'un portrait*—and was nearly sixty pages longer than the original report. From the panoramic history of perfume recounted in the book Montesquiou created a two-page poem also entitled "Pays des Aromates" (*Le Chef*, 218–19). Proust's review of the book, entitled "'Pays des aromates par le Comte Robert de Montesquiou," appeared in the 5 February 1901 issue of the *Chronique des arts et de la curiosité*; it was republished in his *Contre Sainte-Beuve*, 444-45.

[19] Hubert Juin, "Préface" in Montesquiou, *Diptyque de Flandre*, xvii-xviii. Interestingly,

Montesquiou inscribed the words the "sovereign of fleeting things" across a photo of himself which he sent to Proust in 1893 (Patrick Chaleyssin, *Robert de Montesquiou. Mécène et dandy* [Paris: Somogy, 1992]).

[20]"Pays des aromates" in Robert de Montesquiou and Marcel Proust, *Professeur de beauté*, (Paris: Editions La Bibliothèque, 1999), 110.

[21]The "bee of rhyme" was indeed active in Montesquiou's poetry. To show off his rhyming skills he invented puns, anagrams, and erudite allusions as the poem "Santés" (*Le Chef*, 105) shows. Here "folies" (madness) and "fioles" (phials) rhyme, and the words, "voilés," "voix," and "violes," blend alliteratively to create the poem's final line: "Des parfums plus voilés que des voix de violes" ("Perfumes more veiled than the voices of viols").

[22]Morand, *1900*, 231-32.

[23]Paul Poiret, *En habillant l'époque* (Paris: Grasset, 1930), 137-43; Jullian, *La Belle Epoque*, 39; Marcel Rochas, *1925–1950: 25 ans d'élégance* (Paris: Tisné, 1950).

[24]Morand, *1900*, 115-17. The idea of perfume as *decor* was given further elaboration in 1985, when in an article entitled "Décors magiques pour senteurs célèbres" (published in *Vogue Décoration*, Nov. 1985) Françoise Mohrt imagined designs for different rooms and interior spaces that would correspond to the sensory effects (and thus the "imaginary") of certain perfumes. The warm scents of Lanvin's *Arpège*, remarks Mohrt, with its notes of blue hyacinth, wild lily-of-the-valley, and honeysuckle, bring to mind a small, somewhat minimalist pied-à-terre decorated basically with no more than "'a Japanese dresser and a black lacquered Steinway grand piano'" (Girard, 60).

[25]Cerruti, *Flacons*, 61; Barillé / Laroze, 191; Renate Ulmer, *Alfons Mucha* (Cologne: Benedikt Taschen Verlag, 1994), 7–11, 22–25, 38–41, and passim; Morris, 183, 193; Delbourg-Delphis, 54. For reproductions of the flacons, see Jean-Marie Martin-Hattemberg, *Caron* (Toulouse: Milan, 2000), 9; *Hymne au parfum. Deux siècles d'histoire dans les arts décoratifs et la mode* (Paris: Musée des arts de la mode, 1991), pl. 10; Jean-Marie Martin-Hattemberg and Freddy Ghozland, *Précieux effluves* (Toulouse: Milan, n. d.), 51; Sylvie Girard-Lagorce, *100 Parfums de légende* (Paris: Solar, 2000), 89. Guimard's *Kantirix* flacon was sold at auction in 2002 for almost $130,000.

[26]Elisabeth Barillé, *Coty: Parfumeur and Visionary*, trans. Mark Howarth (Paris: Assouline, n.d.), 47, 58; Lefkowith, *Art*, 32; *Roger & Gallet, Parfumeurs et créateurs (1806–1989)* (Bernay: Edition de l'Association pour la Promotion de la Culture

à Bernay, 1987), 49, 51; Atlas and Monniot, 21; Georges Vindry, "La Parfumerie moderne," in *Hymne au parfum*, 22. To this day, perfume and cosmetics remain France's fourth greatest export, after beverages, autos, and airplanes (Le Guérer, *Le Parfum*, 275).

[27]Atlas and Monniot, 85; *Les Parfums à travers la Mode*; Montesquiou, *Musée Rétrospectif ... Rapport ...* , 22; www.perso. wanadoo.fr/corine/phyto/html/vinaigne.htm.

[28]Leconte de Lisle, *Poèmes Tragiques*, vol. 3 of *Oeuvres* (Paris: Alphonse Lemerre, 1884), 70–71.

[29]Charles Cros, *Le Coffret de santal*, coll. Poésie (Paris: Gallimard, 1972), 23; hereafter cited in the text.

[30]Émile Zola, *Au Bonheur des dames (The Ladies' Delight)*, trans. Robin Buss (London: Penguin Books, 2001), 407; Émile Zola, *La Faute de l'abbé Mouret*, coll. Folio Classique (Paris: Gallimard, 1991), 185, 77, 167, resp.; page numbers are hereafter given in the text.

[31]Uzanne, *L'Art et les artifices*, 318; D'Avenel, 177–78.

[32]Tiersten, 69–72, 73.

[33]Marie-Christine Grasse, *Femmes de parfum* (Toulouse, Grasse: Milan / Musée International de la parfumerie, 1996), 76; *Parfumerie A. Bourjois & Cie*, catalogue 1897, Chanel Archives #B-4-13-3-C, plates 8–12; Atlas and Monniot, 162; Delbourg-Delphis, 58.

[34]Chevrel, *Grain de beauté*, 171.

[35]Cabré, *Femmes de papier*, 7.

[36]Bourjois, advertising poster, color lithograph, after Charles Verneau, 1890s, Chanel archives, Neuilly sur Seine. See the entry in Etude Bonduelle et Lancry, *Flacons de Parfum*, Paris, 13 Nov. 1999, p. 22, item no. 104: auction catalogue.

[37]See Cabré, *Femmes de papier*, 49; Grasse, *Femmes de parfum*, 40.

[38]Iris Clair, "Parfums oubliés," *Parfums & Senteurs* 4 (Oct. 2002): 45-51; Delbourg-Delphis, 73; *3000 ans*, 138, n. 666.

[39]Fellous, *Guerlain*, 58.

[40]See Barillé / Laroze, 81.

[41]See Latimer, 14.

[42]Bourdon, "Le Mémorial de la parfumerie française," *Parfumerie française*," 20.

[43]Gaston Leroux, *The Perfume of the Lady in Black* (Cambs, England: Dedalus, 1998), 23–24; hereafter page numbers are given in the text.

[44]The perfumer, Edmond Roudnitska, creator of *Femme* (Rochas, 1944) and *Eau Sauvage* (Dior, 1966), echoes the Baudelairean and symbolist idea that art must re-form and improve on nature: "The composition of perfumes is the abstract art par excellence. Indeed, when a perfume appears to have been inspired by the odors of nature, it does so only by means of a stylization that reduces the odor in question to the status of a pretext" (*Le Parfum*, coll. Que sais-je? [Paris: PUF, 1980], 69).

[45]Delbourg-Delphis, 21, 66; Fellous, *Guerlain*, 57; Silverman, 75, 77.

[46]Roudnitska, *Le Parfum*, 69; Lefkowith, *Art*, 44; Barillé, *Coty*, 93, 96; Leach, *Perfume Presentation*, 19.

[47]Barillé, *Coty*, 122, 101, 6, 40, 22, 76, 119, 160, resp.; Edwards, 21.

[48]Lefkowith, *Art*, 64, 44–45, 50, resp.; Mary Lou and Glenn Utt with Patricia Bayer, *Lalique: Perfume Bottles* (New York: Crown, 1990), 23-24; *Hymne au parfum*, pl. 11; Atlas and Monniot, 156.

[49]Barillé, *Coty*, 126; Utt, 23–24, 63; Lefkowith, *Art*, 66, 89, pl. 79. The theme of Poiret's *Le Fruit défendu*, was even appropriated for interior design; this was one of the cross-over, marketing strategies Poiret developed, through his decorative design firm, Atelier Marine, to advertise his fragrances. (Nancy J. Troy, *Couture Culture: A Study in Modern Art and Fashion* [Cambridge: MIT P, 2003], 84-86).

[50]Barillé, *Coty*, 93, 110–11, 119; Lefkowith, *Art*, 44, 46, pl. 29; Utt, 23; Cabré, *La Légende du chevalier d'Orsay*, 107.

[51]Lefkowith, *Art*, 67; Utt, 62, 25, resp.

[52]Edmond Roudnitska, *Une Vie au service du parfum* (Paris: Thérèse Vian, 1991), 56; Fellous, *Guerlain*, 48–51.

[53]Fellous, *Guerlain*, 39–40, 52; Edwards, 15–19; Atlas and Monniot, 168.

[54]"Autoportraits de femmes, October 1912 / October 1998" publicity brochure, *L'Heure bleue* (Paris: Guerlain, 1998), n. pag; hereafter cited in the text; Edwards, 29–31.

[55]Fellous, *Guerlain*, 64; Atlas and Monniot, 21, 182; Edwards, 30–31.

[56]Atlas and Monniot, 184. In a poem by Geneviève Dormann, one of many commissioned by Guerlain to evoke and advertise its perfumes, *L'Heure bleue* is made lyrical by means of a sequence of idiomatic and cultural allusions to the notion of "blueness": "Blue like winter / Blue of Paris / At the blue hour / When my eyes leave you blue [i.e., flabbergasted] / In the blue train leaving / At

the blue hour / when all over Paris / hovers the odor of Bulgarian roses / I hear the blues / Nineteen hundred and twelve" / Horizon blue / A "petit bleu" [a telegram]/ tells you adieu / Look how my eyes are blue / They light up / Only at the blue hour / Guerlain's *Blue Hour*'" (Ibid.,184).

[57]Edwards, 21, 24; Barillé, *Coty*, 75, 82.

[58]Edwards, 21, 24; Barillé, *Coty*, 75, 82.

[59]Barillé, *Coty*, 71, 74, 86, 93; see also Edwards, 159–61.

[60]Barillé, *Coty*, 172, 96, resp.

Chapter 5: The Scents of Surrealism

[1]Guillaume Apollinaire, "Vendémiaire," *Alcools*, trans. Anne Hyde Greet (Berkeley: U. of California P., 1965), 209; page numbers hereafter given in the text.

[2]*The Selected Poems of Robert Desnos*, trans. Carolyn Forché and William Kulik (New York: The Ecco Press, 1991), 167–68 (translation modified).

[3]Julia Kristeva, "Paradis parfumé," in Pillivuyt, *Histoire,* 6. On the philosophical and social consequences of a world where the deodorizing and effacing of smells risk alienating humankind from its "capacity for what is imaginary" and thus from its very humanity, see Hélène Faivre, *Odorat et humanité en crise à l'heure du déodorant parfumé. Pour une reconnaissance de l'intelligence du sentir* (Paris: L'Harmattan, 2001). Breton, *Oeuvres complètes*, II: 50.

[4]Bedichek, 20; D. C. Richardson, "Scents and Sensibility," NYT *Magazine, Men's Fashions of the Times,* 20 Sept. 1998, 40, 44. See also, Faure, 11–18.

[5]Breton, *Oeuvres complètes*, I: 1237; Guillaume Apollinaire, *Calligrammes*, trans. Anne Hyde Greet (Berkeley: U of California P, 1980), 73; Breton, "Carnet, fin 1920–juillet 1921," *Oeuvres complètes*, I: 618 and *Manifestoes of Surrealism*, trans. Richard Seaver and Helen R. Lane (Ann Arbor: U. of Michigan P, 1969), 20. See Etienne-Alain Hubert, "'Rivalise donc poète avec les étiquettes des parfumeurs,'" *La Revue des lettres modernes*, série *Guillaume Apollinaire* 16 (1983): 179–81.

[6]Desnos archive, Bibliothèque littéraire Jacques Doucet, Paris, DSN 418. See also Katharine Conley, *Robert Desnos: Surrealism, and the Marvelous in Everyday Life* (Lincoln: U. of Nebraska P., 2003): 113; Blaise Cendrars, A*ujourd'hui* (Paris: Grasset, 1931), 209–12.

[7]Founded in 1990 by Jean Kerléo, the resident perfumer for Jean Patou, and col-leagues from other perfume houses, the Osmothèque, located in Versailles, contains 1,300 original fragrances, the earliest going back to the fourteenth century.

[8]Louis Aragon, *Le Mouvement perpétuel,* coll. Poésie (Paris: Gallimard, 1970), 67.

[9]Delbourg-Delphis,, 238, 42, resp.; Lefkowith, *Art,* 68, 202; Martin-Hattemberg, *Précieux effluves,* 86–87; Jacquelyne Y. Jones-North, *Commercial Perfume Bottles* (Atglen, PA: Schiffer Publishing, 1996), 33. For a detailed discussion of Viard's bottle designs, see Christie Mayer Lefkowith, *Masterpieces of the Perfume Industry* (New York: Editions Stylissimo, 2000), 101–17, 130–53.

[10]Delbourg-Delphis, 42; for reproductions of the perfumed cards, see Cabré and Sebbag, *Les Cartes parfumées,* 90; Geneviève Fontan, *Côte Générale des cartes parfumées* (Toulouse: Arfon, 1997, 1998), I: 63 (#A 748-G), II: 61 (# A391-J); "Pour un R de Rigaud," *Parfums & Senteurs* 4 (Oct. 2000): 27–32. Another expensive brochure designed to advertise the full line of fragrances offered by a perfume house was created a few years later by Paul Poiret for his line of Parfums de Rosine. Entitled the *Almanach des lettres et des arts* and containing poetic excerpts, testimonials by famous actresses, and woodcuts by Raoul Dufy, it appeared in 1916, published by the designer's Atelier Martine (Troy, *Couture Culture,* 54–57).

[11]Jones-North, *Commercial Perfume Bottles,* 184. Etienne-Alain Hubert indicates that advertisements for *Un Air embaumé* were common in the weekly and monthly journals published between 1917 and 1922. One, in particular, printed in *L'Artiste contemporain* at the end of 1920, offered the scene of "an ancient style terrace, the ground and columns of which were decorated with roses"; a woman is seen "raising toward the starry night sky an urn from which vapors float" ("Rivalise donc poète," 179–80).

[12]Concerning the influence of fashion on Duchamp's cross-dressing, see Nancy Ring, *New York Dada and the Crisis of Masculinity: Man Ray, Francis Picabia, and Marcel Duchamp in the United States, 1913–1921* (Ann Arbor, MI: UMI Research Press, 1991), 231–41. Regarding the transvestite reality of Rrose Sélavy, see Katharine Conley, *Robert Desnos,* 26–33. Other interesting studies of *La Belle Haleine* can be found in Amelia Jones, *Postmodernism and the En-Gendering of Marcel Duchamp* (Cambridge: Cambridge UP, 1994), 172–75; David Joselit, *Infinite Regress: Marcel Duchamp 1910–1941* (Cambridge: MIT P, 1998), 181–85; and Troy, *Couture Culture,* 298–302. Duchamp may also have wanted to suggest the name of a French dessert (a chocolate-covered pear) called "Poire Belle-Hélène," as Bonnie Jean Garner suggests in her "Duchamp Bottles Belle Greene: Just Desserts For His Canning,"

Tout Fait: The Marcel Duchamp Studies Online, 2 (2000):5: www.toutfait.com/issues/issue_2/News/garner.html.

[13]The cost of iris absolute, as used by Chanel for its *No. 19,* reflects the 1999 market price (Le Guérer, *Le Parfum,* 207), while that of jasmine absolute applies to the 60 pounds harvested in Grasse during the 1996 season (Newman, *Perfume,* 75, Le Guérer, *Le Parfum,* 257). By contrast, a pound of hedione, a jasmine-scented synthetic, costs, according to Le Guérer, a mere $17. See also Guy Robert, *Les Sens du parfum* (Paris: Osman Eyrolles Multimedia, 2000), 198. Another modification Duchamp made to the *Air embaumé* bottle, as Rhonda Roland Shearer has discovered, was to change its original peach color to green (Garner, "Duchamp Bottles," 1).

[14]Another pun expressed by the trans-formed Rigaud bottle, according to Stephen Jay Gould (see Garner, 10), is the exact simi-larity in sound between the perfumer's name (Rigaud) and the French word "rigo" (mean-ing funny or odd) and, less precisely, the verb "rigoler" (to laugh, to joke). Moreover, the final syllable (the "lo") of the adjective "rigolo" (comic) and its noun "un rigolo" (a joker) repeats, so it seems to me, the generic name of Rigaud's and Duchamp's perfumed water: namely, *l'eau* (de toilette). On the pop-ularity in nineteenth-century fashion of the *voilette,* the short, transparent veil attached to a chignon of hair or a hat and descending to the chin, see Uzanne, *L'Art et les artifices de la beauté,* 226–231.

[15]Francis M. Naumann, "Marcel & Maria," *Art in America* 89:4 (April 2001), 110.

[16]Francis M. Naumann, *Marcel Duchamp: The Art of Making Art in the Age of Mechanical Reproduction* (New York: Harry N. Abrams, 1999) 86; Breton, *Oeuvres Complètes*, I: 159; Benjamin, *The Arcades Project,* 173.

[17]Janet Ozzard, "Abstract Expression," *W,* May 1998, 116; Pilar Viladas, "Style: Up From SoHo," NYT *Magazine,* 14 March 1999, 55; Michael Bracewell, "Eau couture," *The Guardian Weekend,* 13 June 1998, 44; Christine Shea, "Beauty Buzz," V-NY, Aug. 1999, 268; "Comme des Garçons au garage," *L'Officiel,* 886, June-July 2004 33; Guy Trebay, "Fashion Diary. Making a Surreal Trip Onto a Nightclub Runway," NYT, 4 March 2004, B 8; Martin, "A Note," 111. For a discussion of Duchamp's readymades, see Naumann, *Marcel Duchamp,* 60–94, and passim.

[18]André Breton, *Poems of André Breton: A Bilingual Anthology,* ed. and trans. Jean-Pierre Cauvin and Mary Ann Caws (Austin: U of Texas P, 1982), 49: translation modified.

[19]Nick Foulkes, *Last of the Dandies: The Scandalous Life and Escapades of Count d'Orsay* (London: Little Brown, 2003), 208.

[20]Cabré, *La Légende,* 9, 14, 16–28, 36–38, 84, 90, 94, 96, 98, 101, 115; Williams, *Dream Worlds,* 121-23; Jones-North, *Commercial Perfume Bottles,* 55–58.

[21]René Char, *Oeuvres complètes,* Bibliothèque de la Pléiade (Paris: Gallimard, 1983), 382.

[22]Brillat-Savarin, the famous gastronomer, invented the very first vaporizer at the end of the eighteenth or the beginning of the nineteenth century. Designed primarily for scenting apartments, it was given the name "irroateur," according to Uzanne (*Les Parfums et les fards à travers les âges,* 38); Latimer, *The Perfume Atomizer,* 7–8, 26–27; Cerutti, 53–54.

[23]The femininity of the atomizer is emphasized in a description from 1925 that points to the object's diffusing power and its ability to turn liquid into air, perfume into cloud. As perfumes have become more and more subtle, the author observes, "it has become more and more necessary to replace the liquid with a cloud; this is the vaporizer's function. Thanks to it, an airborne perfume insinuates itself everywhere, fixes itself on the skin, alights on the hair, penetrates cloth and fur, and causes women, the goddesses of our modern Olympus, to walk among us enveloped in perfumed mists" ("Le Vaporisateur," *Parfumerie française* 148).

[24]Interestingly, *Alien,* Thierry Mugler's scent from 2005, takes up once again this misogynistic, alienated view of femininity, although Mugler's interpretation of "alien" as "that special something a woman possesses that makes her a unique being," stretches the word's meaning. Packaged in an angular purple bottle resembling a *Star-Wars* robot, *Alien* lives up to its name, especially considering the bottle's wide, slightly hunched shoulders which support a grotesque spray head in the form of a long metallic nose (see *W,* Aug. 2005, 105).

[25]Calvino also emphasizes the sexual aura of the vaporizer in "The Name, The Nose." His nineteenth-century narrator enters a *parfumerie* where he is greeted by a new employee "whom I merely grazed with an absent pinch" who then "aimed an atomizer at me, pressing its bulb, as if inviting me to an amorous skirmish" (69). For illustrations of the mentioned atomizers, see Lefkowith, *Art,* 64–65, 80, 82.

[26]The surrealist notion of "the marvelous" had other olfactory dimensions. During the 1938 Exposition Internationale du Surréalisme, held at the Galerie Beaux-Arts in Paris, the aroma of coffee was always in the air. The poet Benjamin Péret, who had once lived in South America, had decided, according to Man Ray, to install a coffee roasting machine. A follow-up exhibition, entitled "First Papers of Surrealism," was mounted in the fall of 1942 by nine of the artists from the previous 1938 Paris exhibition, now exiled by the War in New York City. Invitations to the exhibition promised that a "cedar odor" would be dispersed through the rooms of the show; but it is not clear that the promise was ever kept (Lewis Kachur, *Displaying the Marvelous: Marcel Duchamp, Salvador Dali and the Surrealist Exhibition Installations* [Cambridge: MIT P, 2001], 83, 166, 195).

[27]Paul Eluard, *Oeuvres Complètes,* ed. Marcelle Dumas and Lucien Scheler, Bibliothèque de la Pléiade, 2 vols. (Paris: Gallimard 1968), I: 1003; hereafter cited in the text.

[28]It has been estimated that the picking of 2.2 pounds (one kilo) of jasmine flowers requires a total of 2,000 hand gestures (Grasse, *Le Jasmin,* 36, 41). The harvesting of jasmine in Grasse is an extraordinarily arduous task, more difficult, for example, than the picking of May roses. While an experienced worker can gather a little over a pound of jasmine in an hour, she or he can pick more than ten times that number in rose petals. There are 8,000 flowers in 2.2 pounds of Grasse jasmine. It takes 770 pounds of flowers to produce 2.2 pounds of jasmine concrete, from which finally about one-half quart of liquid absolute is extracted (Jean-François Vieille, in conversation with the author, Grasse, France, October 20, 2005).The rapidity with which newly picked jasmine loses its fragrance requires that the harvesting be divided into two sessions, one in the morning, the other in the afternoon. After each, the flowers are weighed and then within a half-hour's time placed into extracting vats filled with the liquid solvent, hexane, where they remain overnight This explains why a jasmine-based perfume like Chanel's *No. 5* or an ounce of Patou's *Joy,* created from 10,600 jasmine flowers and 336 individual roses, are so costly (see Le Guérer, *Le Parfum,* 210).

[29]*Hymne au Parfum. L'Expo* (Paris: Comité Français du Parfum, 1993), 59; see illustration, chapter 7, p. 305.

[30]Lefkowith, *Masterpieces,* pl. 114; Delbourg-Delphis, 63-64; Lefkowith, *Art,* pl. 13; Utt, 59.

[31]Jacqueline Demornex and Jean-Claude Hervé, *Lancôme* (Paris: Editions du Regard, 1985), 17, 21; and Jacqueline Demornex, *Lancôme,* coll. Mémoire de la Beauté (Paris: Assouline, 1998), 6, 19.

[32]Girard-Lagorce, *100 Parfums de Légende,* 10; Danièle Bott, "Juliette ou la clé . . . des songes," V-P Sept. 1995; Kristeva, in Pillivuyt, *Histoire,* 7.

[33]Eluard, "Je t'aime," II: 439; anonymous translation, "I Love You," from "Defining Style," *Saks Fifth Avenue Catalogue,* Spring 1996, 91, translation slightly modified.

Lancôme's selection of the Eluard poem and its highlighting of the line, "Tu es le grand soleil qui me monte à la tête," were based on a careful, well-informed, even expert decision, which came about in a serendipitous manner. It was made by one of France's foremost Eluard scholars, Colette Guedj, whose son worked for the advertising agency preparing the publicity campaign for the not as yet launched *Poême.* When asked by her son to recommend a French poem or poetic passage, which would succinctly express the essence of love, Professor Guedj suggested the three final lines of Eluard's "Je t'aime" (Colette Guedj, interview with the author, Cerisy la Salle, France, 13 July 2000); see also Colette Guedj, *Eluard à cent ans. Actes du colloque de Nice* (Paris: L'Harmattan, 1998), 11.

[34]See advertisements in *Vanity Fair,* April 1996; V-P, Dec. 1996-Jan. 1997, June–July 1997, Nov. 1999; and HB, Dec. 1997.The association of perfume and planetary convergences is an old and magical one. Based on a theoretical system of cosmic attraction and repulsion, alchemists in the Middle Ages and Cornelius Agrippa in the sixteenth century offered perfume formulas and recipes with the power to influence favorable planetary conjunctions. Perfumes were intermediaries between individuals and their destinies; they were charmed substances with a prophetic power even greater than today's horoscopes. A "lunar perfume," for example, was composed of a frog's head, a bull's eyes, the seed of a white poppy, camphor, incense, and either menstrual or goose blood. A scent that would attract the favor of Venus could be made by blending musk, ambergris, red roses, sparrows' brains, and pigeon blood. As for obtaining the protection of Mercury, the planet associated with *Poême,* it was recommended that one mix mastic resin, cloves, the brain of a fox or a weasel, and magpie's blood (Le Guérer, *Les Pouvoirs,* 123–24).

[35]Guedj, 10–11. "And how about if you were to dip your pen into perfume to write your most beautiful words of love?" asks the text inviting submissions to the contest. "In the wake of *Poême,* a sensual and carnal perfume expressing tumultuous emotions through the medium of flowers, let the beating of your heart resonate. It's up to you to play, imagine, and compose. Up to you to embrace the poetic side of life and share with us your way of looking at feeling, memory, emotion. . . . In all intimacy and with total freedom, write your most beautiful love poem and send it to us" ("Composez votre plus beau Poème d'Amour," advertising pamphlet for *Poême,* "Jeu-Concours *Elle / Lancôme,*" 1997).

[36]Jean-Marie Martin-Hattemberg, "Elsa Schiaparelli. Senteurs surréalistes, flacons d'extravagance," *Parfums & Senteurs* 4 (Oct. 2000): 73; see also Leach, *Perfume Presentation,* 318; and Dilys E. Blum, *Shocking: The Art and Fashion of Elsa*

Schiapparelli (Philadelphia: Philadelphia Museum of Art, 2003), 102, 114–15, 124, 147; Girard-Lagorce, *100 Parfums de légende*, 124–25; Green and Dyett, *Secrets*, 134; Jones-North, *Commercial Perfume Bottles*, 83, 110; Moran, 139; Emmanuelle de l'Ecotais, and Alain Sayag, *Man Ray. La Photographie à l'envers* (Paris: Centre Georges Pompidou / Seuil, 1998), 12, 175; for advertisements of *"Le Classique de Jean Paul Gaultier"* see French *Elle*, 22 Feb. 1999; *L'Officiel* 835 (May 1999): 30; and V-P, May 2000.

[37]Girard-Lagorce, 125; Martin-Hattemberg, "Elsa Schiaparelli," 69; Edwards, 90; Valerie Mendes, "Art Deco Fashion," chap. 23 in *Art Deco 1910–1939*, ed. Charlotte Benton, Tim Benton, and Ghislaine Wood (London: V&A Publications, 2003), 267; Jones-North, *Commercial Perfume Bottles*, 83, 134, 139, 144, 160; Lefkowith, *Art*, 16–17.

[38]Alyce Mahon, "Staging Desire," in *Surrealism: Desire Unbound*, ed. Jennifer Mundy (Princeton: Princeton UP, 2001), 286–87; also in her *Surrealism and the Politics of Eros, 1938-1968* (London: Thames & Hudson, 2005), 159; Breton, "Second Manifesto of Surrealism" (1930), in *Manifestoes*, 180.

Chapter 6: The Fragrant Garçonne (1920–1950)

[1]Victor Arwas, *Art Deco,* rev. ed. (New York: Harry N. Abrams, 1992), 13; Bevis Hillier and Stephen Escritt. *Art Deco Style* (London: Phaidon Press, 1997), 27.

[2]Patricia Bayer. *Art Deco Interiors: Decoration and Design Classics of the 1920s and 1930s* (London: Thames and Hudson, 1990), 47, 28, resp.; Arwas, 30, 47.

[3]Jean Leymarie, *Chanel* (Geneva: Skira, 1987), 167; *Encyclopédie des arts décoratifs et industriels modernes au XXe siècle,* 12 vols. (Paris: Imprimerie Nationale, Office central d'éditions et de librairie, 1925; New York: Garland Publishing, 1977), I, IX; Suzanne Lussier, *Art Deco Fashion* (London: V&A Publications, 2003), 90; Benton, 158–60.

[4]Bayer, 28; Arwas, 28, 34; Alastair Duncan, *Art Deco* (London: Thames and Hudson, 1988), 175; *Encyclopédie des arts décoratifs,* II: 43, pl. XVI.

[5]Arwas, 62; Nancy J. Troy, *Modernism and the Decorative Arts in France: Art Nouveau to Le Corbusier* (New Haven: Yale UP, 1991), 118–19; Bayer, 65; Jean-Paul Bouillon, *Art Deco 1903–1940*, trans. Michael Heron (Geneva: : Albert Skira; New York: Rizzoli, 1989), 176; Mouillefarine, 18. For an image of the "Le Balcon" bottle, see Leach, pl. 124; for an illustration of the sitting room of the *Amours* barge, see Latimer, 68.

[6]Arwas, 28–30; Fellous, *Guerlain*, 83; Hillier and Escritt, 30; Bouillon, 104; Lefkowith, *Art*, 111, and pl. 154.

[7]Bourdon, "La Parfumerie française," 456.

[8]Bayer, 37; Bourdon, "La Parfumerie française," 456, 458.

[9]From 1920 to 1939 Lalique designed not only perfume-specific bottles for several perfume houses—D'Orsay, Gabilla, Guerlain, Houbigant Lubin, Piver, Roger et Gallet, Worth and others—but also non-commercial bottles which were sold empty and then filled by a customer with her favorite scent. Often, these bottles came in sets, part of an ensemble the French call "les garnitures de toilette," a coordinated series of different-sized vessels and containers: for example, three or four perfume bottles, an atomizer, a powder box or two, a soap holder, and small trays for hair pins, combs, and sponges (Cerutti, 65).

[10]Bourdon, "La Parfumerie française," 457; Hillier and Escrit, 30. Testifying to the popularity of Lalique's glass fountain—it may have served as one of the Exhibition's icons—is the cover created for the June 1925 number of the French magazine, *L'Illustration*, where the fountain occupies the very center of the page (Ibid., 26).

[11]Arwas, 91; Duncan, 57–58; Bouillon, 171; Atlas and Monniot, 192; Lefkowith, *Art*, 106, 145.

[12]Bourdon, "La Parfumerie française," 458–61.

[13]Bourdon, "La Parfumerie française," 461; R. Bienaimé, "La Parfumerie Française à l'Exposition des ArtsDécoratifs," Introduction to *La Parfumerie française.*

[14]"Hollow Years" is Eugen Weber's name for the 1930s in his *The Hollow Years: France in the 1930s* (New York: W.W. Norton, 1994).

[15]Duncan, 7–8, 167; Hillier, 24; John Barnicoat, *Posters: A Concise History* (London: Thames and Hudson, 1972), 73.

[16]Lefkowith, *Art*, 113–14; Leach, 18; Mary Louise Roberts, *Disruptive Acts: The New Woman in Fin-de-Siècle France* (Chicago: U. of Chicago P., 2002), 186.

[17]Delbourg-Delphis, 186–89. Even Colette was put out by the unnatural excesses toward thinness—the string-bean look "flat as a cutting board" (*planche à pain*), she called it—of the garçonne style. Alas, she wrote, the year, 1925 "will not see the return to fashion of pleasant curves, proud breasts (*le sein arrogant*), savory hips," (Colette, *Colette et la mode* [Paris: Editions Plume, 1991], 22, 66, 78; hereafter cited in the text).

[18]Girard-Lagorce, *100 Parfums de légende*, 41. For a study of the devirilization experienced by Frenchmen in the aftermath of the war, see Mary Louise Roberts, *Civilization Without Sexes: Reconstructing Gender in Postwar France, 1917–1927* (Chicago: U. of Chicago P., 1994). Girard, *Le Livre du parfum*, 104; Steffen Arctander, *Perfume and Flavor Chemicals (Aroma Chemicals)*, 2 vols. (Montclair NJ, 1969: published by author), 1969: I: monograph nos. 105, 700; II: monograph no. 1788; Laruelle, *L'Art du parfum*, 129; Le Guérer, *Le Parfum*, 217.

[19]Jacqueline Y. Jones North, *Perfume, Cologne, and Scent Bottles* (Atglen, PA: Schiffer Publishing, 1986), 50; Latimer, *The Perfume Atomizer*, 70, 74–75, 109–10. For illustrations of "Le Kid," see *Encyclopédie des arts décoratifs*, II: pl. XXVIII, Sauvat, *Les Objets de beauté*, 106, Girard, *Le Livre du parfum*, 105. See also Henri Mouron, *A. M. Cassandre. Affiches. Arts Graphiques. Théâtre* (Munich: Schirmer; Paris: Mosel, 1991), 12.

[20]Hillier and Escritt, 37; Lefkowith, *Art*, 14, 124, 129, 103, 113, 137, resp.; Atlas and Monniot, 219.

[21]Milton Cross, *Complete Stories of the Great Operas* (Garden City, NY: Doubleday, 1950), 572–580, esp. 579; Atlas and Monniot, 219.

[22]Lefkowith, *Art*, 105, 117, 151, resp.; Leach, 72–73.

[23]Lefkowith, *Art,* 109, 110, 152. A flacon similar to the *Normandie* design is still used for Patou's *Voyageur*, an *eau de toilette* for men (see the ad in Air France's *Atlas Magazine*, June 1996).

[24]*Hymne au parfum*, pl. 15; Martin-Hatteberg, *Précieux effluves*, 78; Lefkowith, *Art*, 118, 33, resp.; Christie Mayer Lefkowith, "Editorial," *Art & Fragrances: Perfume Presentations* 9 Nov 2002, auction catalogue (Geneva, Switzerland: GdB Fine Arts Gallery), 9–10.

[25]Edwards, 62, 63, 64, 66; Janet Wallach, *Chanel: Her Style and Her Life* (New York: Doubleday, 1998), 103–106; *Art et Parfum*, 97.

[26]"Le Parfum, arme de séduction … et luxe nécessaire," *Votre Beauté. Revue de la beauté féminine*, 1 Nov. 1936, n. pag; rpt. Paris: Imprimerie Georges Lang, 1936 in pamphlet form (n. pag.).

[27]Fellous, *Guerlain*, 90; Girard-Lagorce, 41; Chanel, "Parfums d'hier et d'aujourd'hui," press release (Paris, 1993), n. pag.

[28]Delbourg-Delphis, 190–91; Edwards, 62; "Le Parfum, arme de séduction.;" *Votre Beauté*, 1 Nov. 1936.

[29]Chanel, "Cuir de Russie," publicity brochure, Nov. 1936, Chanel archives, Neuilly sur Seine, #C-4-1-560.

[30]The association of perfume with travel is reiterated in the notion of beauty as a journey of discovery, in and of itself. When Guerlain opened its first beauty salon in the spring of 1939 on the second floor of its flagship store at 68, avénue des Champs-Elysées, it installed its clients in small cabins designed to resemble the staterooms of an ocean liner, each cabin named for a different Guerlain perfume. A journalist for *Le Figaro* described the salon as a place where "passengers" came aboard for a "voyage of beauty" (Fellous, *Guerlain*, 96).

[31]"Le Parfum, arme de la séduction; Baudelaire, *The Parisian Prowler,* 56.

[32]Barillé, *Coty,* 99, 152–54.

[33]"Atlas and Monniot, 228; Fellous, *Guerlain,* 90; "Le Parfum, arme de la séduction"; Dominique Borne and Henri Dubief, *La Crise des années 30 (1929–1938),* Nouvelle Histoire de la France contemporaine 13 (Paris: Seuil, 1989): 269. By 1937, flying clubs had over ten thousand members (Weber, *Hollow Years,* 161).

[34]*Hymne au parfum,* 48–49; Barillé / Laroze, 85; Victor Margueritte, *La Garçonne* (Paris: Editions J'ai lu / Flammarion, 1978); hereafter cited in the text. *La Garçonne* sold 20,000 copies in the four days following its publication in July 1922, a phenomenal 300,000 by the end of the year, and a million by the end of the decade (Mary Louise Roberts, *Civilization Without Sexes,* 47–48); Christine Bard, *Les Garçonnes. Modes et fantasmes des années folles* (Paris: Flammarion, 1998), 137; Delbourg-Delphis, 190, 193.

[35]Hall-Duncan, 68–71; "Le Parfum, arme de la séduction."

[36]Borne and Dubief, 269; Valerie Mendes, "Art Deco Fashion," in Benton, 264; Lussier, *Art Deco Fashion,* 52; Lefkowith, *Art,* 97, 191, 198; Weber, *Hollow Years,* 159, 188.

[37]Chanel, "Des maximes signées Chanel," ch. 12 in *Chanel Informations,* typewritten press release and brochure (Paris and Neuilly: Services de presse, Chanel, n.d.), n. pag.

[38]*L'Art du parfum,* 43, 67, 85, 105, 125; *H&R,* 88; North, *Perfume, Cologne and Scent Bottles,* 122; for an image of the "Jack, Junior, and Jill" box, see *Précieux effluves,* 97.

[39]Jim Crow Museum of Racist Memorabilia, "Golliwog Stereotypes," Ferris State University, Big Rapids, MI, http://www.ferris.edu/news/jimcrow/golliwog/homepage.html (accessed 31 Jan. 2003).

[40]Fontan, I: 69, #A824-F; Cabré and Sebbag, *Les Cartes parfumées,* 42, 45. Baker's *Revue*

Nègre started in 1925. The word, "le jazz," according to *Le Petit Robert,* entered the French language in 1918. This was one year after Lieutenant James Reese Europe's Fifteenth New York Regiment army band first performed jazz for the French public at a concert at the Nantes opera house (Geoffrey C. Ward and Ken Burns, *Jazz: A History of America's Music* [New York: Alfred A. Knopf, 2000], 65, 68). Perfume histories that appear to turn a blind eye to the racist image of the *Golli-Wogg* bottle are *Hymne au parfum,* pl. 18, Martin-Hattemberg, *Précieux effluves,* 96, and his "Les Cahiers du collectionneur. La parfumerie européenne du XXe siècle. Africanisme et arts premiers," *Parfums & Senteurs* 10 (Dec. 2001): 86–93. On the Colonial Exhibition of 1931, see Borne and Dubief, 61, Weber, *Hollow Years* 180. In 1995, two French toilet waters carrying the "Un Monde nouveau . . ." label were removed from the shelves of a Washington, D.C. store. As *Vogue* (Sept. 95) reported the event, the perfumes were manifestly racist. The label for one bottle, a scent called *Savage Vanilla,* declared under the heading "Eau Massaï" that "coming from Africa [it contained a] hot & sensuous vanilla for fighting girls"; a crude silhouette of two individuals with spears and the words "Jambo Bwana" decorated the label.

[41]Quoted in Roberts, *Civilization Without Sexes,* 20.

[42]Amy de la Haye and Shelley Tobin, *Chanel: The Couturière at Work* (Woodstock, NY: The Overlook Press, 1994), 40; Bard, 138; Wallach, 59; Duncan, 164; Lussier, 61; Leymarie, 103–04; Chanel, "Chanel. L'Esprit d'une marque vivante," publicity pamphlet, Paris, 1999, 9.

[43]*Clotheslines: A Collection of Poetry and Art,* ed. Stan Tymorek (New York: Harry N. Abrams, 2001), 46; "Chanel. L'Esprit d'une marque," 4, 74–75; Bard, 4; Clément Vautel, *Je suis un affreux bourgeois* (Paris: Albin Michel, 1926), 51–52; hereafter cited in the text.

[44]De la Haye, 42, 53; Duncan, 163, 165, 167–68.

[45]Bard, 38; "Des maximes signées Chanel"; for the *Allure* advertisement, see *Elle* (Paris), 3 June 1996. The search for the perfect equilibrium between the simplicity of appearance and the complexity of design identifies all of Chanel's elegant creations, from her straight-line, unadorned dresses with their complex cut to *No. 5,* the perfume, with its plain bottle, unpoetic name, and yet multifaceted architecture and complex sensuality. It is a "golden liquid in a cube of naked crystal," as Chanel's biographer, Edmonde Charles-Roux, described it (Girard-Lagorce, 45). Edwards, 46–47; Chanel, "Question 19," *Mes Recherches, 1921–1993: No. 5 Chanel* (Neuilly sur Seine: Parfums Chanel, 1993), n. pag.

[46]Chanel, "No. 5" in *Les Parfums Chanel,* press release (Paris: Chanel, 1996), n. pag.; Chanel, *Le Journal de Chanel,* Holiday 1996, 1; Roxana Azimi, "Un Entretien avec Jacques Polge, nez chez Chanel," *Le Journal des arts,* 23–24 Oct. 2002, 6; "Question 13," "Question 30," *Mes Recherches.*

[47]Edwards, 45; Leymarie, 79; Weriguine, 162–63.

[48]See in *Mes Recherches* the texts entitled "Navrant," "Illumination," "Testament."

[49]Wallach, 51, 139; *No. 5* is still, today, the most sold perfume in the world, according to industry statistics; "Question 49," *Mes Recherches; 3000 ans,* 136.

[50]*Mes Recherches,* fig. XXI; Françoise Aveline, *Chanel Parfum* (Paris: Assouline, 2003), 25, 76; Frank DiGiacomo, "The House That Coco Built," *Elle,* 141, May 1997, 180.

[51]Geneviève Fontan, *Générations Bourjois* (Toulouse: Arfon, 2005), 7, 19, 39, 118; Martin-Hattemberg, *Précieux effluves,* 18–19.

[52]Girard-Lagorce, 24. The *Soir de Paris* advertisements referred to are catalogued in the Chanel archives as follows: "Pendant la Valse . . .," *Marie-Claire,* 22 Dec. 1939 (#B-2-2-196c); "Entre'acte à l'Opéra," *Elle,* 17 Dec. 1946 (#B-2-2-197a); "Retour de Première . . ." (1946); *Jardin des modes,* 15 Nov. 1930 (#B-2-2-133a); *Rester Jeune,* Nov. and Dec. 1936 (#B-2-6-155); *L'Illustration,* 29 May 1937 (#B-2-2-162c); *Marie-Claire,* 2 Dec. 1938 (#B-2-2-180); and #B-2-2-536.

[53]Wallach, 135, 138; Chanel archives, #B-2-2-564; *Bourjois Advertising* [catalogue] (New York: Bourjois, 1928), n. pag.

[54]The drawing of Babette's profile appears on the cover of *Les Secrets de Babette,* a bound loose-leaf advertising booklet probably published around 1924 or 1925 (Paris: Bourjois, n.d.), n. pag.; "Babette et le Prince de Galles," typewritten ms., Chanel archives; "Babette Racommode," *Mode Pratique* 15 (12 April 1930), Chanel archives, typewritten text # 244.

[55]"Des maximes signées Chanel"; "Babette et Didi," typewritten manuscript, Chanel archives, text #184; "Babette adore les fleurs," *Eve* 6, no. 228 (8 Feb. 1925): 9.

[56]"Babette au Grand Prix," "Babette à l'Opéra," "Mon Parfum," "Qui est Babette," in *Les Secrets.*

[57]Judith Thurman, *Secrets of the Flesh: A Life of Colette* (New York: Ballantine Books, 1999), 276, 294, hereafter cited in the text; Claude Francis and Fernande Gontier, *Creating Colette,* 2 vols. (South Royalton, VT: Steerforth Press, 1999), II: 34, 38, hereafter cited in the text; see also, Colette, *Lettres à*

Annie de Pène et Germaine de Beaumont, ed. Francine Dugast (Paris: Flammarion, 1995), 5–10.

[58]"C'est la Fatalité," *Mode pratique* 29 (19 July 1930): 576.

[59]"Un Aveu de téléphone," *Mode pratique* 46, (15 Nov. 1930): 905 "Babette rêve d'être poète," *Eve* 7, no. 297 (16 June 1926): 9.

[60]"Babel chez soi," *Mode pratique* 39 (27 Sept. 1930): 763; "Salons d'automne," *Mode Pratique* 45 (8 Nov. 1930): 887; "La Loi sur les assurances sociales," *Mode pratique* 49 (6 Dec. 1930): 968; Roberts, *Civilization Without Sexes,* 86–87.

[61]The descriptions of Babette's personality come from the following "stories": "Babette Déchaînée," *Eve* 7, no. 275 (3 Jan. 1926): 9; "Babette à Deauville," *Les Secrets;* "Babette et les bonbons," *Eve* 7, no. 276 (10 Jan. 1926): 9; "Babette et le saule," *Eve* 7, no. 284 (7 Mar. 1926): 9; "Babette et ses formules magiques," *Eve* 7, no. 322, (28 Nov. 1926): 9; "Le Budget de Babette," *Eve* 5, no. 21 (23 Nov. 1924): 9. Other references are to "Babette rencontre un fou"; "Le Nécessaire de Babette," *Eve* 7, no. 283 (28 Feb. 1926): 9; "Babette Raccommode," typewritten ms., Chanel archives, text #244; "En feuilletant un agenda," *Mode pratique* 52 (27 Dec. 1930): 1026; "Si Babette a une fille," *Eve* 6, no. 258 (6 Sept. 1925): 9; "Babette répond à une enquête," typewritten ms., Chanel archives, text # 200. See also, Roberts, *Civilization Without Sexes,* 25–26.

[62]"Le Coeur de Babette Balance," *Mode Pratique* 2 (11 Jan. 1930): 32; "Babette Séductrice," typewritten ms., Chanel archives.

[63]"Babette Raccommode"; "Le Coeur de Babette Balance," 32; "Babette ne veut pas grandir," *Eve* 6, no. 247 (21 June 1925): 9; "Babette au bois," typewritten ms., Chanel archives, text # 208; "Les Chastes Modes d'Autrefois," *Mode pratique* 37 (13 Sept. 1930): 722; "Refoulement," *Mode pratique* 33 (6 Aug. 1930): 649.

[64]"Quand vient l'automne," *Mode pratique* 47 (22 Nov. 1930): 928; "Babette chez le couturier," *Eve* 6, no. 238 (19 Ap. 1925): 9; "Mon Parfum," *Les Secrets*; "Babette à Deauville"; "Babette au Bal Masqué," advertising poster, Chanel archives; "Le Coeur de Babette Balance."

[65]"Babette et sa photographie," *Eve* 6, no. 229 (15 Feb. 1925): 9.

[66]Claude Pichois and Alain Brunet, *Colette* (Paris: Editions de Fallois, 1999), 324, 327, hereafter cited in the text; Bard, 21; Colette, *Paysages et portraits*, ed. Marie-Françoise Berthu-Courtivron (Paris: Flammarion, 2002) 301, n. 25, hereafter cited in the text;

Colette et la mode, 185; Francis and Gontier II: 177. For an illustration of the Max Fourrures catalogue, see *Colette et la mode*, 181; for scents created by Max Fourrures, see Lefkowith, *Art*, 119, 137; and Martin-Hattemberg, *Précieux effluves*, 70.

[67]Colette, *Oeuvres*, ed. Claude Pichois et al, 4 vols., Bibliothèque de la Pléiade (Paris: Gallimard, 1984–2001), IV: 933; hereafter cited as *O* in the text.

[68]Colette was not afraid, however, to poke fun at women whose faces were covered with a "rouge the color of flame-red hives" or a "blackish sludge." In an essay (it is really a dramatic fable) written in 1924 criticizing the heavy use of cosmetics and perfumes, Colette imagines meeting a male friend at a classy perfume store who has come, not as it turns out to try different colognes—humorously named "Sock of Monsieur" or "Let the Savage Beasts Roam" ("Lâchez les fauves")—but rather to buy makeup: for himself! ("Fards," *O*, II: 1145–48).

[69]"Luxe I," *Prisons et paradis* (Paris: J. Ferenczi et fils, 1932), 250–51; hereafter cited in the text (an English version of part of "Luxe I" translated by Robert Reilly appeared in V-NY, Nov. 1998, 296, 298); "Fragrance" (1929), in *Oeuvres complètes de Colette*, 15 vols., Edition du Centenaire (Paris: Editions du Club de l'Honnête Homme, 1973), 14: 36–37, hereafter cited in the text as *OC*; *Paysages*, 300, nn. 13, 19.

[70]"Fetidité, Fragrance, Nez Fin et Parfums," quoted in *Art et Parfum*, 91; see also "Parfums," *Paysages*, 149; Chevrel, *Grain de beauté*, 165; "Marguerite Moreno," *O*, IV: 1035.

[71]Colette, *La Retraite sentimentale*, coll. Folio (Paris: Mercure de France, 1957), 55, 145, 240 (hereafter cited in the text); "Monologue du gardénia," *O*, IV: 889; *Sido* suivi de *Les Vrilles de la vigne*, coll. Le Livre de poche (Paris: Hachette, 1931), 112, 180, hereafter cited in the text. On Colette's fusion with the scented world and her desire to embrace "the fullness of feeling … through the vibrations of language," see Julia Kristeva, *Colette*, vol. 3 of *Le Génie féminin: La Vie, la folie, les mots* (Paris: Fayard, 2002), 137.

[72]Edmond White, *The Flâneur: A Stroll Through the Paradoxes of Paris* (New York, London: Bloomsbury, 2001), 31.

[73]On Gabilla, see Jones-North, *Commercial Perfumes*, 40; and Lefkowith, *Art*, 63–64, 131.

[74]Jean-Jacques Rousseau, *Emile*, *Oeuvres complètes*, Bibliothèque de la Pléiade (Paris: Gallimard, 1959), IV: 416, cited in *Paysages*, 302, n. 32.

[75]Women's lack of knowledge about the use of fragrances disturbs Colette. During the 1920s there was, she notes, an incongruity

between the simplicity of women's dress and the complexity of their scents. Perhaps this complexity was a necessary corrective to the "extreme simplification" of the garçonne style which had to be counterbalanced by the "vogue of complicated perfumes." A woman might reveal her body but refuse to say a word about her perfume: "The woman, whose body now hides nothing, hems and haws and dissimulates as soon as one wants to discover the secret that perfumes her passage and leaves the air behind her trembling. She refuses to mention the name or evoke the image of even one flower" ("Luxe IV," 260).

[76]Marcel Proust, *Remembrance of Things Past*, 3 vols., trans. C. K. Scott Moncrieff, Terence Kilmartin and Andreas Mayor (New York: Random House, 1981), I: 53–54; hereafter cited in the text. See also Proust's text published in December 1893 in which he describes how the sordid vulgarity of a hotel in Trouville was suddenly transformed for him by the wondrous smell—"an ivory tower of scents"—emanating from twenty broken perfume bottles left behind by English guests in a nearby room (Annie Borrel, ed., *Voyager avec Marcel Proust. Mille et un voyages* [Paris: La Quinzaine littéraire, 1994], 95–96).

[77]Poiret, *En habillant l'époque* (Paris: Grasset, 1930), 113.

[78]Janet Flanner, "Perfumes and Politics," *An American in Paris: Profile of an Interlude Between Two Wars* (New York: Simon and Schuster, 1940), 124–125, hereafter cited in the text; Barillé, *Coty*, 146.

[79]Barillé, *Coty*, 101; Sagan and Hanoteau, 215; Borne and Dubief, 94, 95; Flanner, 129; William Wiser, *The Twilight Years: Paris in the 1930s* (New York: Carroll & Graf, 2000), 123. The data regarding perfumes launched in the 1940s are taken from historical lists of Coty perfumes as reported in Barillé, *Coty*, 177 and Edwards, 290–91.

[80]Roberts, *Civilization Without Sexes*, 37–40; for her comments on Vautel, see 69–70, 131–37, 254, n. 41.

[81]It is not only the novel's final words or the adjective "terrible" attached to the noun "bourgeois" in the title that reflect Vautel's corrosive view of the bourgeoisie. The jacket cover of the original 1924 edition is equally damning. It displays the seated portrait of a massively broad, white-haired gentleman, dressed in black, who projects a sober, stern, even judgmental air. The figure's similarity to Ingres's celebrated portrait of Louis-François Bertin, painted in 1832 and hanging in the Louvre, would not have been missed by a sophisticated Parisian reader. While the addition of spectacles has modernized Bertin's face and while his double-breasted suit and tie have given him a more contemporary look, his hunched-over pose

and his massive, black girth are very much those of Ingres's subject, as is, above all, the clawlike right hand resting on his knee, ready, it would appear, to seize a gold coin or appropriate an asset or two. This is the no-nonsense image of the Ur-bourgeois.

[82]Louise de Vilmorin, "Le Choix d'un parfum" (1960), in *Articles de mode*, 85, 86, hereafter cited in the text; *Chance* ad from V-NY, Sept. 2002; *Eternity Moment* from *Entertainment Weekly*, 9 Oct. 2004; *Organza* from French *Elle*, 23 May 2005, 22; *L'Instant* from V-NY, Aug. 2004; Jean Baudrillard, *De la séduction* (Paris: Galilee, 1979), 107–19.

[83]Anne-Claude Lelieur, *Savignac, affichiste*, new ed. (Paris: Bibliothèque Forney, 2004), 510, 534-35.

[84]Cabré, *Femmes de papier*, 48; Grasse, *Femmes de parfum*, 79; Marie-France Pochna, *Nina Ricci* (Paris: Editions du Regard, 1992), 57; Edwards, 105.

[85]Edwards, 93, 102; Richard Martin and Harold Koda, *Christian Dior* (New York: Metropolitan Museum of Art, 1996), 10–18; *Gruau* (Paris: Herscher, 1989), 92.

[86]Louise de Vilmorin, *L'Opéra de l'odorat* (Paris: Lanvin Parfums, Aljanvic, 1949), n. pag., Chanel archives, # B-4-7-1392; see also André de Vilmorin, *Essai sur Louise de Vilmorin*, coll. Poètes d'aujourd'hui 91 (Paris: Pierre Seghers, 1962), 100–03; and Jean Bothorel, *Louise, ou la vie de Louise de Vilmorin* (Paris: Grasset, 1993), 184–92.

[87]*Les Parfums à travers la Mode.*

Chapter 7: The Eros—and Thanatos—of Scents

[1]*The Song of Songs*, trans. Ariel and Chana Bloch (Berkeley: U. of California P., 1995), 53, 75; Detienne, *The Gardens of Adonis*, 62; Edith Hamilton, *Mythology* (New York: New American Library, 1942), 179.

[2]Uzanne, *Les Parfums et les fards*, 12; Irvine, *Perfume*, 18–19. The sexual scenting of the body practiced by the ancients has had, if the story is true, an influence on modern perfumery, for it is rumored that the perfumer Robert Piguet made the final selection from among the different versions of his perfumes, *Bandit* (1944) and *Fracas* (1948), by having models put the scents on their pubis (Girard, 157, 100; Girard-Lagorce, 116). The aphrodisiac powers of perfume were celebrated by many authors of antiquity. Petrus Castellus advised that "'to make the uterus more greedy for semen . . . civet smeared on the glans penis will increase the woman's pleasure during coitus'" (John Pratt, "Notes on the Unconscious Significance of Perfume," *International Journal of Psychoanalysis* 23 [1942]: 83).

[3]David Howes, "Scent and Sensibility," *Culture, Medicine and Psychiatry* 13 (1989): 95–96; Hirsch, 28–29; Louis Sebastien Mercier, "Toilettes," *Le Tableau de Paris*, 2 vols. (Paris: Mercure de France, 1994): I:1365–66. On the transformative power of scent in ritual, see David Howes, "Olfaction and Transition: An Essay on the Ritual Uses of Smell," *Revue Canadienne de Sociologie et d'Anthropologie* 24 (3) 1987: 398–416.

[4]Stoddart, *The Scented Ape*, 77, 111; Faure, 21; André Holley, *Eloge de l'odorat* (Paris: Odile Jacob, 1999), 194–6, 199. The vomeronasal organ was once known as Jacobson's Organ, after the Danish anatomist who discovered it in 1811; see Lyall Watson, *Jacobson's Organ and the Remarkable Nature of Smell* (New York: W. W. Norton, 2000), 8–10, 25–33.

[5]Stoddart, *The Scented Ape*, 105–08; Holley, 192–93, 199; Natalie Angier, "Study Finds Signs of Elusive Pheromones in Humans," NYT, 12 March 1998, National section, A 22; Vroon, 138–45; Catherine Dulac, and others, "Loss of Sex Discrimination and Male-Male Aggression in Mice Deficient for TRP 2," *Science* 295 (22 Feb. 2002):1493-1500. The musky smell of the human axilla (armpits) is caused by the presence of androstenol. As the same pheromone that is contained in the saliva of boars it is responsible for provoking the mating posture of the female pig (Stoddart, 65, 77, 205).

[6]Hirsch, 83, 100, 24, 30, 38, resp.; see also Marisa Fox, "Sex Chemicals," HB, February 1996, 92, 94; Stoddart, 118, 119; Ehsan Masood, "Erox contre Athena, ou la guerre des fragrances synthétiques," *Le Monde*, 28 Feb. 1997, 22; Christine Lennon, "Sex in a Bottle," *W*, September 1995, 116; Watson, 169–73; see as well Theresa L. Crenshaw, *The Alchemy of Love and Lust* (New York: G. P. Putnam's Sons, 1996), 63–83. Ads for these pheromone-based scents are found in Fontan, *Côte Générale des cartes parfumées* II, 143; *Vogue Man*, supplement to V-NY, Oct. 2001; and a mail-order advertisement, headlined "Let Athena Add Romance to Your Life through Pheromone Power," for *Athena Pheromone 10:13* (a woman's fragrance) and *Athena Pheromone 10X* (an aftershave for men) in *Ambassador Magazine* (American Airlines) January 1996, 45 and (under the headline "Biologist's Pheromone Gets You More Romance") in *Southwest Airlines Spirit* March 2006, 201. Taking another tact, *L'Eau de Kasaneka* (Menard Institute, Paris) advertises an ingredient in its composition that is designed to accelerate the production of a female hormone (Supplement to *L'Officiel*, 891 Dec. 2004-Jan. 2005).

[7]Manfred Milinski and Claus Wedekind, "Evidence for MHC-Correlated Perfume Preferences in Humans," *Behavioral Ecology*, 12, no. 2 (2001): 140–44, 146–48. See as well David Berreby, "Studies Explore Love and the

Sweaty T-Shirt, NYT, 9 June 1998, C 2; Thomas Hayden, "The Scent of a Human," *U.S. News & World Report* 130, no. 12 (26 March 2001), 55; Harriet Coles, "Les Scientifiques sur la piste du site sexuel de l'odorat," *Le Monde*, 28 Feb. 1997, 22. Of a more frivolous nature concerning the link between perfume and the genetic code is the fragrance, *DNA*, sold by Bijan, whose perfume bottle took the shape of a double helix (Amy Harmon, "Twist and Shout! The Double Helix Replicates Itself in Popular Culture," NYT, 25 Feb. 2003, D 10).

[8]Robert Herrick, "Upon *Julia's* unlacing her self," *Hesperides*, in *The Poetical Works of Robert Herrick*, ed. F. W. Moorman (Oxford: Oxford UP, 1921, rpt. 1957), 156; see also his poems "Upon *Julia's* sweat," "The Frankincense," "To his Mistresses," "To *Julia* in the Temple," "His embalming to *Julia*," "On a perfum'd Lady," and "The Perfume." The ads mentioned appeared in French *Elle*, no. 3099, 23 May 2005; V-NY, April 1997; American *Elle*, May 2004.

[9]Guerlain, "Mitsouko," press release (Paris: Guerlain, 1997), n. pag.; Atlas and Monniot, 277; Cara Kagan, "Scent of a Woman," *Elle*, August 2000, 129. *Armani Mania*, V-NY, Sept. 2004; *Theorema*, *W*, Sept. 1998.

[10]Ghozland, *Perfume Fantasies*, 86; Jean-Paul Guerlain, "Guerlinade," press release (Paris: Guerlain, 1998), 3, 28-29, hereafter cited in the text; Jean Baudrillard, *The System of Objects*, trans. James Benedict (London: Verso, 1996), 170–73.

[11]Catherine Jazdzewski, "La Nouvelle cuisine des parfums," V-P, 806 (April 2000): 222; Onfray, *L'Art de jouir*, 130–31. Alain Corbin points out that in the nineteenth century a highly developed olfactory sensibility was seen as a "symptom of hysterical hyperaesthesia" ("A History and Anthropology," 188).

[12]Barillé / Laroze, 86, 120, 95, 124, resp.; Fellous, *Guerlain*, 104; Jean-Paul Guerlain, "Champs-Elysées. L'Eau de parfum. Portrait d'un parfum parisien," press release (Paris: Guerlain, n. d.), n. pag.; Girard, *Le Livre du parfum*, 70.

[13]HB, May 1996; *Mirabella*, Sept.–Oct. 1998; see Nicole and Mick Duprat, *Bijoux Promotionnels de parfumeurs* (Toulouse: Arfon, 2000), 22–23; *Cosmopolitan* (Portugal) 44, Dec. 1995; *W*, May 1995.

[14]Goude's bird of paradise commercial is entitled "Coco, L'Esprit de Chanel," 1991; see also, Chanel, "The Making of Coco 91," a documentary film directed by J. C. Wouters, 1991, Chanel archives, Neuilly sur Seine. For the print ad, see Chevrel, *Grain de beauté*, 196. See chapter 8, p. 336.

[15]Girard-Lagorce, *100 Parfums de légende*, 65; Roland Barthes, *Mythologies*, trans.

Annette Lavers (New York: Hill and Wang, 1972), 57; Guy Bourdin, *Exhibit A*, ed. Fernando Delgado and Samuel Bourdin (Boston: Bullfinch Press, 2001), pl. 29. Eve's transgression is indeed remembered in perfume: namely, in Cacharel's *D'Eau d'Eden* of 1996 ("a perfume of paradise"), the print ad for which, as conceived by Jean-Paul Goude and entitled "Jeune Fille en fleurs," features the model Estella Warren whose standing body, except for her face and one protruding breast, is completely covered with hundreds of fully bloomed white and pink roses. For the ad, see French *Elle*, 3 June 1996; see also Jean-Paul Goude, *Tout Goude*, with the collaboration of Patrick Mauriès (Paris: Editions de la Martinière, 2005), 291.

[16] Barillé / Laroze, 90; *Elle*, Sept. 1999; *Teen Vogue*, Special Issue, Fall 2000; *Elle*, Oct. 1999.

[17] Fellous, *Guerlain*, 103; Baudrillard, *De la séduction*, 106–07.

[18] The perfumes mentioned by name are the creations, listed respectively, of the following *maisons*: (*first group: the name as cry*) Piguet (1948), Dior (1985), Calvin Klein (1985), Paco Rabanne (1994), L. T. Piver (1986), Lancôme (1967), Celine (2005); (*second group: the name as caress*) Ungaro (1987), Jean Patou (1964), Estée Lauder (1995), Guerlain (1962), Cacharel (2005); (*third group: the name as bliss*) Houbigant (1900), Calvin Klein (2000), Jean Patou (1930), Clinique (1999), Cacharel (1994), Calvin Klein (1988), Avon (1974), Calvin Klein (2005); (*fourth group: the name as mad love*) Réveillon (1981), Nina Ricci (1974), Diane von Furstenberg (1981), Donna Karan (1996), Coty (1938), Yves Saint Laurent (1993), Guerlain (1911), Ted Lapidus (2004), Christian Lacroix (2005), Dior (2002).

[19] Anagrams and word games have few limits in perfume nomenclature. There is "J'adore" (1999), the last syllable of which more or less rhymes with Dior, its creator. *Elle, Elle*, a perfume from the fashion house of Lucien Lelong, popular in the 1940s, played on the pronunciation of Lelong's initials: "LL." See Randall B. Monsen, *Monsen and Baer: Memories of Perfume; The Perfumes of Lucien Lelong and Masterpieces of Today. Perfume Bottle Auction VIII, May 16, 1998* (Vienna, VA: Monsen and Baer, 1998), 23.

[20] Edwards, 81; Barillé / Laroze, 85.

[21] "In Seoul, Dressing To Please the Nose," NYT, 18 April 1999, Money & Business section, 3: 13; Ginia Bellafante, "Enhanced Clothing," NYT *Magazine*, special issue on "The Year in Ideas," 15 December 2002, 86; "The Month in Fashion," *W*, June 2001, 48.

[22] Guerlain, "Le Romantisme est un bouquet d'émotions: Jardins de Bagatelle," advertising

brochure (Paris: Guerlain, 1998), n. pag., hereafter cited in the text.

[23] Guerlain, "Champs-Elysées," press release (Paris: Guerlain, 1988), n. pag.; Stoddart, 169, 176; Girard, 158; Jean-Luc Andrei, "Dites-le avec des aubergines," V-P, Dec. 1999-Jan. 2000, 89–91; Delbourg-Delphis, 51–53; Paul Reboux, "Le Langage des fleurs," *L'Elégance à Paris*, Spring 1935, 57–59; Patricia Winters Lauro, "Advertising: Hallmark Now has Hearts and Flowers," NYT, 10 May 2002, Media Business section, C 6; Marina Heilmeyer, *The Language of Flowers: Symbols and Myths*, trans. Rosie Jackson (Munich: Prestel, 2004), 11.

[24] Guerlain does not by any means own the market on such exotic, oriental names. Shiseido has *Zen* (1965), Laroche *Fidji* (1966), Lancôme *Sikkim* (1971), Yves Saint Laurent *Kouros* (1981), Givenchy *Xeryus* (1987), Yves Rocher *Samarkande* (1988), Piver *Pompéïa* (1907), Kenzo *Kahsaya* (1994), Van Cleef & Arpels *Birmane* (1999), and Révillon *Détchema* (1953), which translates as goddess of joy.

[25] Delphis-Delbourg, 189; Guerlain, "Mitsouko"; Fellous, *Guerlain*, 128–31; Guerlain, "Les Secrets du parfum par Guerlain," advertising brochure (Paris: Guerlain, n.d.), 15.

[26] Fellous, *Guerlain*, 30, 73–74, 128–31, 150; Guerlain, "Les Secrets du parfum," 15, 24; Atlas and Monniot, 282-83; Guerlain "Le Livre de Samsara," advertising brochure (Paris: Guerlain, n. d.), 5, 17, 27; Barillé / Laroze, 199.

[27] John Snelling, *The Buddhist Handbook: A Complete Guide to Buddhist Schools, Teaching, Practice, and History* (Rochester, VT: Inner Traditions, 1991), 40–41; Geoffrey Samuel, *Civilized Shamans: Buddhism in Tibetan Societies* (Washington DC: Smithsonian Institution Press, 1993), 17, 375, 378, 200, 203, resp; Giuseppe Tucci, *The Religions of Tibet*, trans. Geoffrey Samuel (Berkeley: U of California P, 1980), 71.

[28] Chevrel, *Grain de beauté*, 183; Guerlain, "Genèse de Shalimar. Fragments de papiers oubliés, qui auraient pu être écrits par Jacques Guerlain," press release (Paris, Guerlain, 1995), 15.

[29] Edwards, 55–59; Atlas and Monniot, 204–11; Ellen Stern, "Shalimar and the House of Guerlain," *Gourmet*, March 1996, 82-84; Fellous, *Guerlain*, 83-89; "Genèse de Shalimar," 7. Although tradition holds that Shah Jahan built the Taj Mahal as a tomb for his wife, new discoveries have led scholars to the conclusion that he may have built it as tomb for himself (Paula Deitz, "Expeditions: What a Little Moonlight Can Do," NYT, 15 July 1999, D 11).

[30] Barillé, *Coty*, 82; Kagan, 128; Delbourg-Delphis, 61; "Autour du parfum," 38.

[31] Fellous, 22; Girard, 127; Montez, 30, 41; Corbin, *The Foul*, 183, 184; Uzanne, *Les Parfums et les fards*, 58, 60, 69.

[32] Corbin, *The Foul*, 183; Corbin, "A History and Anthropology," 188, 191; Corbin, "Senses," 667.

[33] Corbin, *The Foul*, 195; Rimmel, *Le Livre des parfums*, 25-26; Barillé / Laroze, 68; Edmond de Goncourt, *Chérie* (Paris; Ernest Flammarion et Eugène Fasquelle, 1883), 223, hereafter cited in the text.

[34] Tom Robbins, *Jitterbug Perfume*, (New York: Bantam Books, 1984), 225, hereafter cited in the text. Heliotrope, today an all but forgotten scent note, was an important ingredient in Bourjois's *Soir de Paris* and Guerlain's *Après l'ondée* (Jacques Brunel, "L'Homme au nez d'or," *Gloss*, 4, Summer 2003, 40).

[35] Gustave Flaubert, *Correspondance, I (janvier 1830 à juin 1851)*, ed. Jean Bruneau, Bibliothèque de la Pléiade (Paris: Gallimard, 1973), 280, 284, 292, 337–8, 303; Gustave Flaubert, *Salammbô* [1862], coll. Folio (Paris: Gallimard, 1970), 309–11.

[36] Shaykh Umar ibn Muhammad al-Nefzawi, 79. For a more scientific perspective on the psycho-erotic effects of floral odors, perfumes, and perfume materials, see Jellinek, *The Psychological Basis of Perfumery*, 3–39, 46–82, 121, 114–25, 142–47, and passim.

[37] Georges Bataille, *L'Erotisme*, coll. 10/18 (Paris: Editions de Minuit, 1957), 159; hereafter cited in the text; Georges Bataille, *L'Histoire de l'érotisme*, vol. 8 of *Oeuvres complètes* (Paris: Gallimard, 1976), 537; *L'Impossible*, vol. 3 of *Oeuvres complètes*, 156.

[38] Bataille, "The Language of Flowers," 12.

[39] Serres, 178; see Marquis de Sade, "La Fleur de châtaignier," in *Oeuvres complètes* (Paris: Pauvert, 1986), II.

[40] Stoddart, 161–65; see Vroon, 63–64.

[41] Edwards, 173, 175, 179; David Caplan, "Fashion Crackdown," HB, September 2000, 254.

[42] Chevrel, *Grain de beauté*, 177; Edwards, 171–72; Grasse, *Femmes de parfum*, 49.

[43] "Parfum de plaisir," V-P, 812 (Nov. 2000).

[44] Marchand, *Les Guerres du luxe*, 298; Lynn Hirschberg, "Luxury in Hard Times, NYT *Magazine*, 2 Dec. 2001, 92; Olivier Lalanne, "Tout Nu," V-P, 821 (Oct. 2001), 382, hereafter cited in the text; Paule Cornille, "Vous avez dit sensuels?" *L'Officiel* 870 (Nov. 2002), 108; "X is

for X-Rated," HB, April 2001, 146; Suzanne Kapner, "Advertising: Agencies say British regulators are too quick to ban ads," NYT, 4 Jan. 2002, Media Business section, C 4; Jennifer Weil, "Nu Sensation," W, Oct. 2001, 212.

[45]Phil Patton, "Scents of the Everyday Locked in a Bottle," NYT, 15 October 1998, House and Home section, D 2; Julia Szabo, "The Home Front: A Nose with an Eye," NYT Magazine, 1 April 2001, Part 2, "Home Design," 56; Mary Tannen, "A Scent-imental Journey," NYT Magazine, part 2, Fashion of the Times, 20 Aug. 2000, 138.

[46]A similar image of a decaying urban landscape penetrated by the scent of an exquisite perfume is found in the Irish poet Ciaran Carson's poem "Calvin Klein's Obsession," although the beloved in the poem wears Elizabeth Arden's Blue Grass from 1934. (The New Poetry, ed. Michael Hulse, David Kennedy, David Morley [Newcastle upon Tyne: Bloodaxe Books, 1993], 138–40).

[47]Epigraph to Isabelle Fiemeyer, Coco Chanel. Un Parfum de mystère (Paris: Payot, 1999).

Chapter 8:
Fragrant Narratives: The Stories Perfumes Tell (1950–2006)

[1]Guy de Maupassant, The Complete Short Stories (Garden City, NY: Hanover House, 1955), 367–71.

[2]C. W. Leadbeater, The Perfume of Egypt, and Other Weird Stories [1911] (Adyar, India and Wheaton, Ill.: The Theosophical Publishing House, 1967), 4, 5, 7. For other, more contemporary novels about perfume and foreign lands, see René Laruelle, Le Parfum perdu. Basilissa (Paris: Editions Buchet / Chastel, 1996), the story of a search for the most fragrant and blissful of all forms of sacred incense, called "sonteranti;" Rikki Ducornet's novel Gazelle (New York: Knopf, 2003), a story set in the Cairo of the 1950s about a perfumer gifted in the art of creating aphrodisiacs from flowers and other scents; and Martha Cooley's Thirty-Three Swoons (New York: Little Brown, 2005), in which a daughter's search for her identity and for an understanding of her perfumer-father's past friendship with the celebrated Russian theater director of the 1920s and 1930s, Vsevolod Meyerhold, involves lost sketches of a perfume bottle in the shape of a clown, a Pierrot.

[3]Primo Levi, "The Mnemogogues," The Sixth Day, and Other Tales, trans. Raymond Rosenthal (New York: Summit Books, 1990), 15, 16, 17.

[4]Laruelle, Parfum perdu, 52.

[5]Guy de Maupassant, Strong as Death (Doylestown, PA: Wildside Press, n. d.), 92.

[6]Mülhens's fragrance was, as were so many eaux de Cologne at the time, an appropriated version of Farina's truly "original" scent (Hadorn, 94–95). For the history of the creation of eau de Cologne, see chapter 2, pp. 53–56 and H & R, 266; Moran, Fabulous Fragrances, 124–25; Lefkowith, Art, 200. Charlotte Delbo, Useless Knowledge, vol. 2 of Auschwitz and After, trans. Rosette C. Lamont, (New Haven: Yale UP, 1995), 151.

[7]Franz Kafka, Letters to Milena, ed. Willi Haas, trans. Tania and James Stern (New York: Schocken Books, 1953), 10; Margarete Buber-Neumann, Milena, trans. Ralph Manheim (New York: Seaver Books, 1988), 150; hereafter cited in the text.

[8]Marcel Cohen, "La 4711," Autrement (special number on Prague), May 1990, 127–28 and his Le Grand paon-de nuit (Paris: Gallimard, 1990), 83.

[9]The co-presence of pleasure and pain in Milena's Tears is taken up again by Quardon in a second perfume work she has created. Entitled Écume d'amour (Foam of Love, 2004), the work is composed of a vial of clear glass hidden inside a slightly iridescent white porcelain shell. The scent itself, created by a famous contemporary perfumer, begins with a note of slightly faded roses—what Quardon in homage to the German poet Paul Celan names, after one of his poems, "rose de personne" ("no-one's rose")—which slowly takes on an odor similar to that of incense decaying in a cold church. Having moved from life to death, the scent then returns to life by recapturing the rose fragrance it had had at its départ (conversation with the author, Paris, 22 Nov. 2004).

[10]George Steiner, Language and Silence: Essays on Language, Literature and the Inhuman (New York: Atheneum, 1967), ix.

[11]Marcel Cohen, Faits: Lecture courante à l'usage des grands débutants (Paris: Gallimard, 2002), 166–67, and letter to the author, 22 Feb. 1996.

[12]Delbo, 152; Jones-North, Commercial Perfume Bottles, 160; Leach, 72. Orgueil was produced at the end of World War II "as a celebration of the Liberation of France" (Monsen, 20, fig. 8)

[13]Jan Morris, The World of Venice, rev. ed. (San Diego: Harcourt Brace & Co., 1993), 79; Hans J. Rindisbacher, The Smell of Books: A Cultural-Historical Study of Olfactory Perception in Literature (Ann Arbor: U. of Michigan P., 1992), 290, n. 24 and 283-320. In addition to Rindisbacher's excellent study of Süskind's novel, see Bradley Butterfield, "Enlightenment's Other in Patrick Süskind's Das Parfum: Adorno and the Ineffable Utopia of Modern Art," Comparative Literature Studies 32, 3 (1995): 401–418; Judith Ryan, "The Problem of Pastiche: Patrick Süskind's

Das Parfum, "German Quarterly 63 (1990): 396–403; Richard T. Gray, "The Dialectic of 'Enscentment': Patrick Süskind's Das Parfum as Critical History of Enlightenment Culture," PMLA 108, 3 (1993):489–505.

[14]For a superb history of the smells and stenches of eighteenth-century Paris, see Corbin, The Foul, 27–56, 111–27 and Vigarello, Le Propre et le sale, 155–68.

[15]Another fictional and ironic instance of scent-masking is described by the novelist Tom Robbins in his fast paced, iconoclastic, comic fable of postmodernist magical realism, Jitterbug Perfume, published a year before Süskind's Perfume. Bringing together a mythic personage like the god Pan, a contemporary family of Parisian parfumeurs, a group of American get-rich-quick entrepreneurs, and a magical and ageless couple, who move from century to century, the novel makes them all "jitterbug" around in the search for a perfume purported to be the secret essence of the universe (see, in particular, 188–90, 212).

[16]A note of National Socialism also finds its way into the totalitarian fragrance invented by the protagonist-perfumer of Tom Robbins's Jitterbug Perfume. This scent, a postmodernist, anti-nostalgic creation, designed to push the sweet, oriental fragrances of the sixties and the clean, wholesome, herbal perfumes of the seventies into the dustbin of history, is named New Wave. Endowed with the smell of "control, conformity, [and] domination," New Wave gives off "the sinister vapors of fascism" and invokes "the olfactory silhouette of the Nazi" (76–77). Equally as dominant, in a less ideological, yet more misogynistic vein, is the scent that the narrator in Roald Dahl's short story "Bitch" imagines creating: "What I intend to do," he confesses, "is to produce a perfume which will have the same electrifying effect upon a man as the scent of a bitch in heat has upon a dog!" (Switch Bitch [New York: Alfred A. Knopf, 1974]).

[17]Michel Tournier, "La Légende des parfums," Le Médianoche amoureux (Paris: Gallimard, 1989), 253–58.

[18]Sylvia Plath, "Daddy," Ariel (New York: Harper & Row, 1965), 51.

[19]Patricia Cohen, "In Defense of Our Wicked, Wicked Ways," NYT, 7 July 2002, Sunday Styles, 2; see , James B. Twitchell, Lead Us Into Temptation: The Triumph of American Materialism (New York: Columbia UP, 1999) and Living It Up: Our Love Affair with Luxury (New York: Columbia UP, 2002).

[20]"Rêve de gosse," L'Officiel, 841, Dec. 1999. Miniature perfume cases containing tiny flacons and disguised as books bound in red leather were created as early as the eighteenth century (Pillivuyt, Flacons, 39).

Another (quite different) link between book and scent was the reproduction of the cover of Karen Moline's steamy 1998 novel *Belladonna: A Novel of Revenge* (New York: Warner Books) on the label of a Demeter perfume bottle of the same name; see also Holly Brubach, "Style. Literary Sachet," NYT *Magazine*, 22 Sept. 1996, 91; Percy Kemp, *Musc* (Paris: Albin Michel, 2000), 15–16, 87, 112–13, 146.

[21]Alison Fell, *The Pillow Boy of the Lady Onogoro* (San Diego: Harcourt Brace & Co., 1994), 110–12.

[22]Irvine, 132; Guerlain, "Le Romantisme"; Jean-Paul Guerlain, "Guerlinade," 29.

[23]Roland Barthes, *The Fashion System*, trans. Matthew Ward and Richard Howard (Berkeley: U of California P, 1983), 261; Baudrillard, *The System of Objects*, 171–176.

[24]For semiotic, thematic, and postcolonial analyses of perfume advertising, see Mariette Julien, *L'Image publicitaire des parfums. Communication olfactive* (Paris: L'Harmattan, 1997), esp. 29–30, 51, 85; Henriette Touillier-Feyrabend, "Odeurs de séduction," *Ethnologie française* 19, 2 (1989): 123–29; Veleda J. Boyd and Marilyn M. Robitaille, "Scent and Femininity. Strategies of Contemporary Perfume Ads," in Luigi and Alessandra Manca, eds., *Gender & Utopia in Advertising: A Critical Reader* (Lisle, IL: Procopian Press, 1994), 49–54; and Judith Williamson, "Woman is an Island. Femininity and Colonization," in Tania Modleski, ed., *Studies in Entertainment: Critical Approaches to Mass Culture* (Bloomington: Indiana UP, 1986), 106–07.

[25]Delbourg-Delphis, 194; Bourjois, "Soir de Paris," Chanel archives, Neuilly sur Seine, #B-2-2-536.

[26]Ghozland, *Perfume Fantasies*, 23; "Mythe Movie," V-P, 852 (Nov. 2004):135; Baz Luhrmann, "Take Five," V-NY, Sept. 2004, 717–21, 825–26; Louise Finlay, "Nicole Kidman: Quel numéro?" *Elle*, 3066 (4 Oct.

2004):170–75; Marchand, *Les Guerres du luxe*, 303; Patricia Winters Lauro, "Advertising: A New Calvin Klein Campaign," NYT, 14 Jan. 2002, C, 9.

[27]Marie-Eve Chamard and Gérard Lefort, "Qu'importe le parfum, la pub reste en carafe," *Libération*, n.s. 1433 (27 Dec. 1985): 10.

[28]"Spécial Chanel" [advertising brochure], *Cosmopolitan* (France), May 1998, 6, 8–9.

[29]Chanel, "The Making of Coco 91." See also Jacques Helleu, *Jacques Helleu et Chanel* (Paris: Editions de la Martinière, 2005) and Goude, 269-70. Another possible cultural reference for the *Coco* commercial is to the animated Warner Brothers cartoon series "Tweety Bird and Sylvester Cat," popular from the 1940s through the 1960s. This is because the commercial, the end of which takes place in an apartment resembling Coco Chanel's Place Vendôme residence, shows a large cat hungrily eyeing a bird cage inside which a miniature woman swings on a perch. In fact, Coco Chanel kept a small golden bird cage in her apartment; it was a present from the Duke of Westminster, her love of many years (Goude, 270).

[30]Some of the different "faces" of *No. 5* over the past fifty years have been the models Suzy Parker, Jean Shrimpton, Lauren Hutton, Cheryl Tiegs, Inès de la Fressange, Laetitia Casta, Claudia Schiffer, Kate Moss, Estella Warren and the actresses Ali MacGraw, Candice Bergen, Catherine Deneuve, Maud Adams, Carole Bouquet, Vanessa Paradis, Nicole Kidman, and Anna Mouglalis (see Aveline, 77–79).

[31]One of the images of feminine empowerment that represented a turning point in perfume advertising was the celebrated and infamous (the *New York Times* refused to publish it) "fanny pat" that Revlon created for its fragrance *Charlie* (1973). Below the heading "She's very Charlie," a tall woman confidently lays her hand on the derrière of her shorter male companion. See James B.

Twitchell, *20 Ads That Shook the World: The Century's Most Groundbreaking Advertising and How It Changed Us All* (New York: Crown Publishers, 2000), 162–73.

[32]The "egoist," Goude writes, is a "male who thinks only of himself, of the delights and annoyances of his life. I decided to take the meaning of 'egoist' literally" but at the same time to "reverse things and let the women who are the victims of this problem speak out" (Goude, 267-68).

[33]Pierre Corneille, *The Cid, Cinna, The Theatrical Illusion*, trans. John Cairncross (Penguin Books, 1975), 42. Goude changed Corneille's words "O old age, my enemy!" to "O my love betrayed."

[34]One example of a woman talking to a perfume bottle as if to a lover is seen in the commercial for Ungaro's *Senso* (1993) where the actress Nastassja Kinski addressing her perfume directly, passionately declares: "You excite me, I love it when you caress me; I love your brazenness, I love you because you are free, free like me when I have you *on* my skin, when I have you *in* my skin."

[35]Jane Larkworthy, "Sweet Scent of Youth, *W*, Oct. 2002, 182; Chanel, *Coup de foudre à Venise. Une aventure signée Jean-Paul Goude*, advertising brochure (Paris: Chanel, 2002). n. pag.

[36]Anne-Laure Robert, "Rencontre: Françoise Montenay, dans les pas de Mademoiselle," *Atmosphères* 63 (May 2003): 58.

[37]V-NY, Sept. 2002; Chanel, *Coup de foudre à Venise*. A later print ad for *Chance* (French *Elle*, no. 3120, 17 Oct. 2005) makes the bottle of the earlier advertisement seem small by comparison. Over a two-page spread seventeen inches wide, the bottle, only half of which is shown, takes up about sixteen inches (or 95 percent) of the space. The upper curve of this gargantuan bottle supports the bodies of an embracing couple, their heads romantically nestled under the flacon's enormous stopper.

Selected Bibliography

3000 ans de la parfumerie: Parfums, Savons, Fards et Cosmétiques, de l'Antiquité à nos jours. Grasse: Musée d'Art et d'Histoire, 1980.

"A Tangled Web." *The Economist*, 27 Nov. 1999, 59.

Abram, David. *The Spell of the Sensuous: Perception and Language in a More-Than-Human World.* New York: Pantheon Books, 1996.

Ackerman, Diane. *A Natural History of the Senses.* New York: Vintage Books, 1990.

"L'Affiche et la parfumerie." In *La Parfumerie française et l'art dans la présentation,* 187–89.

Aftel, Mandy. *Essence and Alchemy: A Book of Perfume.* New York: North Point Press / Farrar, Straus and Giroux, 2001.

Agulhon, Maurice. *1848, ou L'apprentissage de la République, 1848-1852.* Rev. ed. Paris: Seuil, 1992.

Alphandery, Benedetta. *Iris: The Perfume of Flowers.* Milan: Idea Books, 1998.

Andrei, Jean-Luc. "Dites-le avec des aubergines." *Vogue* (Paris), Dec. 1999–Jan. 2000, 89–91.

Angier, Natalie. "Study Finds Signs of Elusive Pheromones in Humans." *New York Times,* 12 Mar. 1998, A 22.

Antoniewski, Fabienne. "Ce que sentent les fleurs." *Elle,* 20 May 2002, 206.

_____. "Parfums et belles manières." *Elle,* 4 Oct. 2004, 199–203.

Apollinaire, Guillaume. *Alcools.* Translated by Anne Hyde Greet. Berkeley: U of California P, 1965.

_____. *Calligrammes.* Translated by Anne Hyde Greet. Berkeley: U of California P, 1980.

Aragon, Louis. *Le Mouvement perpétual.* Collection Poésie. Paris: Gallimard, 1970.

_____ *Paris Peasant.* Translated by Simon Watson Taylor. Boston: Exact Change, 1994.

Arctander, Steffen. *Perfume and Flavor Chemicals (Aroma Chemicals).* 2 vols. Montclair NJ: published by author, 1969.

Arwas, Victor. *Art Deco.* Rev. ed. New York: Harry N. Abrams, 1992.

Atlas Michèle, and Alain Monniot. *Guerlain: Les flacons à parfum depuis 1828.* Toulouse: Milan, 1997.

Augereau, Jean-François. "Le Kyphi, l'encens mythique des Egyptiens, à nouveau créé." *Le Monde,* 4 Apr. 2002, 28.

"Autour du parfum" du XVIe au XIXe siècle. Paris: Le Louvre des antiquaires, 1985.

Aveline, Françoise. *Chanel Parfum.* Paris: Assouline, 2003.

Azimi, Roxana. "Un Entretien avec Jacques Polge, nez chez Chanel." *Le Journal des arts,* 23–24 Oct. 2002, 6.

"Baby Formulas." *France* 61 (Spring 2002): 7.

Bachelard, Gaston. *Air and Dreams: An Essay on the Imagination of Movement.* Translated by Edith R. and C. Frederick Farrell. Dallas: The Dallas Institute Publications, 1988.

Bagot, Jean-Didier, Christine Ehm, and others. *L'ABCdaire des cinq sens.* Paris: Flammarion, 1998.

Balzac, Honoré de. *César Birotteau.* Translated by Robin Buss. London: Penguin, 1994.

_____. *Traité de la vie élégante,* suivi de *Théorie de la démarche.* Paris: Arléa, 1998.

Banes, Sally. "Olfactory Performances." *The Drama Review* 45, no. 1 (Spring 2001): 68–76.

Barbe, Simon. *Le Parfumeur Royal, ou L'art de parfumer.* 1699. A facsimile of the first edition with an introduction by Jean Kerléo. Paris: Klincksieck, 1992.

Barbery Lili. "Beauté: Désir régressif." *Vogue* (Paris), May 2005, 145.

Bard, Christine. *Les Garçonnes: Modes et fantasmes des années folles.* Paris: Flammarion, 1998.

Barillé, Elisabeth. *Coty: Parfumeur and Visionary.* Translated by Mark Howarth. Paris: Assouline, n.d.

_____. *Guerlain.* Collection Mémoires de la beauté. Paris: Assouline, 1999.

_____, and Catherine Laroze. *Le Livre du parfum.* Paris: Flammarion, 1995.

Barnicoat, John. *Posters: A Concise History.* London: Thames and Hudson, 1972.

Barrie-Anthony, Steven. "On Scent, We've Barely Scratched the Surface." *Los Angeles Times,* 4 Nov. 2004, F1.

Barry, Nicolas de, Maïté Turonnet, and Georges Vindry. *L'ABCdaire du parfum*. Paris: Flammarion, 1998.

Barthes, Roland. *A Lover's Discourse*. Translated by Richard Howard. New York: Hill and Wang, 1978.

_____. *Mythologies*. Translated by Annette Lavers. New York: Hill and Wang, 1972.

_____. *The Fashion System*. Translated by Matthew Ward and Richard Howard. Berkeley: U of California P, 1983.

Bar-Zohar, Michael. *Bitter Scent: The Case of L'Oréal, Nazis, and the Arab Boycott*. New York: Dutton, 1996.

Bataille, Georges. *L'Erotisme*. Collection 10/18. Paris: Editions de Minuit, 1957.

_____. *L'Histoire de l'érotisme*. Vol. 8 of *Oeuvres complètes*. Paris: Gallimard, 1976.

_____. *L'Impossible*. Vol. 3 of *Oeuvres complètes*. Paris: Gallimard, 1976.

_____. *Visions of Excess: Selected Writings, 1927–1939*. Edited and translated by Allan Stoekl, et al. Theory and History of Literature, 14. Minneapolis: U of Minnesota P, 1985.

Baudelaire, Charles. *Correspondance*. Edited by Claude Pichois. 2 vols. Bibliothèque de la Pléiade. Paris: Gallimard, 1973.

_____. *Les Fleurs du mal*. In *Oeuvres complètes*, 1:3–178.

_____. *The Flowers of Evil*. Edited by Marthiel and Jackson Mathews. New York: New Directions, 1955, 1989.

_____. *Flowers of Evil, and Other Works: A Bantam Dual-Language Book*. Edited and translated by Wallace Fowlie. New York: Bantam, 1964.

_____. *Journaux intimes*. In *Oeuvres complètes*, 1:647–708.

_____. *Oeuvres complètes*. Edited by Claude Pichois. 2 vols. Bibliothèque de la Pléiade. Paris: Gallimard, 1975–1976.

_____. *The Painter of Modern Life, and Other Essays*. Edited and translated by Jonathan Mayne. London: Phaidon, 1964.

_____. *The Parisian Prowler: Le Spleen de Paris; Petits Poèmes en prose*. Translated by Edward K. Kaplan. Athens: U of Georgia P, 1989.

_____. *Selected Poems from Les Fleurs du mal*. Translated by Norman R. Shapiro. Chicago: U of Chicago P, 1998.

_____. *Le Spleen de Paris. Petits Poèmes en prose*. In *Oeuvres complètes*, 1:273–374.

Baudrillard, Jean. *De la séduction*. Paris: Galilée, 1979.

_____. *The System of Objects*. Translated by James Benedict. London: Verso, 1996.

Bayer, Patricia. *Art Deco Interiors: Decoration and Design Classics of the 1920s and 1930s*. London: Thames and Hudson, 1990.

"Bébé Trendy." *L'Officiel*, Apr. 2002, 88.

Beck, Ernest. "Under Your Nose, the Next Big Thing?" *New York Times*, 5 Aug 2004, D 8.

Bedichek, Roy. *The Sense of Smell*. Garden City, NY: Doubleday, 1960.

Bellafante, Ginia. "Enhanced Clothing." *New York Times Magazine*, 15 Dec. 2002, 86.

"Belly Up to the Beauty Bar." *New York Times*, 1 Aug 2004, sec. 9, 3.

Benaïm, Laurence. "Interview Nez à Nez: Polge Connection." *Stilleto*, Spring-Summer 2005, 72–74.

Benjamin, Walter. *The Arcades Project*. Translated by Howard Eiland and Kevin McLaughlin. Cambridge: Harvard UP, 1999.

_____. "On Some Motifs in Baudelaire." Vol. 4, *Selected Writings, 1938–1940*. Edited by Michael W. Jennings. Cambridge: Harvard UP, 2003.

Bennet, James. "Peres Waits for Chance To Resume Peace Quest." *New York Times*, 24 Jan. 2003, A 6.

Benzel, Jan. "When You Need a Dash of Frogness." *New York Times*, 7 Jan. 1996, sec. 1, 31.

Berger, Claude and Danielle. *Tous les parfums du monde*. Toulouse: Milan, 1995.

Bergeron, Louis. *Les Industries du luxe en France*. Paris: Odile Jacob, 1998.

Berreby, David. "Studies Explore Love and the Sweaty T-Shirt." *New York Times*, 9 June 1998, C 2.

Bertrand, Antoine. *Les Curiosités esthétiques de Robert de Montesquiou*. 2 vols. Histoire des idées et critique littéraire 344. Geneva: Droz, 1996.

Bienaimé, R. "La Parfumerie française à l'Exposition des Arts Décoratifs." Introduction to *La Parfumerie française et l'art dans la présentation,* n. pag.

Bishop, Elizabeth. *The Collected Prose.* Edited by Robert Giroux. New York: Farrar, Straus Giroux, 1984.

_____. *The Complete Poems 1927–1979.* New York: Farrar, Straus Giroux, 1980.

Blamont, Véronique. *Souvenirs de parfums: Histoires et secrets de senteurs.* N.p.: Mille et une nuits, 1998.

Blanc-Mouchet, Jacqueline, ed. *Odeurs: L'essence d'un sens.* With the collaboration of Martyne Perrot. *Autrement,* no. 92 (Sept. 1987).

Blum, Dilys E. *Shocking: The Art and Fashion of Elsa Schiaparelli.* Philadelphia: Philadelphia Museum of Art, 2003.

Boillot, Francine, Marie-Christine Grasse, and André Holley, eds. *Olfaction et patrimoine: Quelle transmission?* Aix-en-Provence: Edisud, 2004.

Bonnefis, Philippe. *Parfums: Son nom de Bel-Ami.* Paris: Galilée, 1995.

Bonnet, Jocelyne. "L'Homme et le parfum." In *Les Coordonnées de l'homme et la culture matérielle.* Vol. 1 of *Histoire des moeurs.* Edited by Jean Poirier. Encyclopédie de la Pléiade. Paris: Gallimard, 1990, 679–722.

Bordignon, Carla. *Perfume Bottles / Profumi Mignon.* San Francisco: Chronicle Books, 1986, 1995.

Borillo, Mario, and Anne Sauvageot. *Les Cinq sens de la création: Art, technologie, sensorialité.* Seyssel: Champ Vallon, 1996.

Borne, Dominique, and Henri Dubief. *La Crise des années 30 (1929–1938).* Nouvelle Histoire de la France contemporaine 13. Paris: Seuil, 1989.

Borrel, Annie, ed. *Voyager avec Marcel Proust: Mille et un voyages.* Paris: La Quinzaine littéraire, 1994.

Boston Blackie: The Perfume Murders. Golden Age Radio, March 1951. Audiocassette.

Bothorel, Jean. *Louise, ou La vie de Louise de Vilmorin.* Paris: Grasset, 1993.

Bott, Danièle. *Chanel.* Paris: Ramsay, 2005.

_____. "Juliette ou la clé... des songes." *Vogue* (Paris), Sept. 1995.

Boudonnat, Louise, and Harumi Kushizaki. *La Voie de l'encens.* Arles: Editions Philippe Picquier, 2000.

Bouillon, Jean-Paul. *Art Deco 1903–1940.* Translated by Michael Heron. Geneva: Albert Skira; New York: Rizzoli, 1989.

Bourdin, Guy. *Exhibit A.* Edited by Fernando Delgado and Samuel Bourdin. Boston: Bulfinch Press, 2001.

Bourdon, Georges. "Le Mémorial de la parfumerie française." In *La Parfumerie française et l'art dans la présentation,* 5–21.

_____. "La Parfumerie française à l'Exposition Internationale des Arts Décoratifs et Industriels Modernes." In *La Parfumerie française et l'art dans la présentation,* 455–62.

Bourjois. *Bourjois Advertising.* Catalogue. New York, 1928.

_____. *Bourjois: Catalogue Commercial,* 1897. Chanel archives, Neuilly sur Seine, # B-4-13-3-C.

_____. *Parfumerie A. Bourjois & Cie.* Catalogue, 1897. Chanel archives, Neuilly sur Seine, #B-4-13-3-C.

_____. *Les Secrets de Babette.* Paris, c. 1924-1925. Chanel archives, Neuilly sur Seine.

_____. "Soir de Paris." Chanel archives, Neuilly sur Seine, #B-2-2-536.

Bourny-Romagné, Brigitte. *Secrets de plantes à parfum.* Toulouse: Milan, 2003.

Bouvier, Roselyne, Valérie Thomas, François Parmantier, and Jérôme Perrin. *Album: Musée de l'Ecole de Nancy.* Paris: Editions de la réunion des musées nationaux, 2001.

Boyd, Veleda J., and Marilyn M. Robitaille. "Scent and Femininity: Strategies of Contemporary Perfume Ads." In Luigi and Alessandra Manca, eds. *Gender & Utopia in Advertising: A Critical Reader.* Lisle, IL: Procopian Press, 1994, 49-54.

Bracewell, Michael. "Eau couture." *The Guardian Weekend,* 13 June 1998, 44.

Breton, André. *Manifestoes of Surrealism.* Edited and translated by Richard Seaver and Helen R. Lane. Ann Arbor: U of Michigan P, 1969.

_____. *Poems of André Breton: A Bilingual Anthology.* Translated and edited by Jean-Pierre Cauvin and Mary Ann Caws. Austin: U of Texas P, 1982.

Browne, Alix. "Scent of A Movie. *New York Times Magazine,* 20 Feb. 2005, 47.

Brubach, Holly. "Beneath the Surface." *New York Times Magazine*, part 2, "Men's Fashions of the Times," 20 Sept. 1998, 66.

Brunel, Jacques. "L'Homme au nez d'or." *Gloss*, Summer 2003, 40.

Buber-Neumann, Margarete. *Milena*. Translated by Ralph Manheim. New York: Seaver Books, 1988.

Burckhardt, Jacob. *The Civilization of the Renaissance in Italy*. Translated by S. G. C. Middlemore. New York: New American Library, 1960.

Burns, John. F. "When Seeing Osama Is Not Enough." *New York Times*, 6 Jan. 2002, Week in Review, 16.

Burr, Chandler. "Annals of Innovation: The Scent of the Nile." *New Yorker*, 14 March 2005, 78–88.

_____. *The Emperor of Scent: A Story of Perfume, Obsession, and the Last Mystery of the Senses*. New York: Random House, 2002.

Butterfield, Bradley. "Enlightenment's Other in Patrick Süskind's *Das Parfum*: Adorno and the Ineffable Utopia of Modern Art." *Comparative Literature Studies* 32, no. 3 (1995): 401–418.

Cabasset, Patrick. "Repère snob: Parfumez votre chat." *L'Officiel*, Sept. 2001, 52.

Cabré, Monique. *La Légende du chevalier d'Orsay: Parfums de dandy*. Toulouse: Milan, 1997.

_____, and Marina Sebbag. *Les Cartes parfumées*. Paris: Editions Alternatives, 1996.

_____, Marina Sebbag, and Vincent Vidal. *Femmes de papier: Une Histoire du geste parfumé / Perfumed Cards... A Scented Gesture*. Toulouse: Milan, 1998.

Cadier-Rey, Gabrielle. *Les Français de 1900*. Paris: Circon-flexe, 1999.

Calder, Emma. "Beauty News." *Vogue* (London), May 2003, 146.

Calkin, Robert R, and J. Stephan Jellinek, eds. *Perfumery: Practice and Principles*. New York: John Wiley & Sons, 1994.

Calvino, Italo. "The Name, The Nose." In *Under the Jaguar Sun*. Translated by William Weaver. San Diego: Harcourt Brace Jovanovich, 1988.

Candau, Joël. *Mémoire et expériences olfactives: Anthropologie d'un savoir-faire sensoriel*. Paris: PUF, 2000.

_____, Marie-Christine Grasse, and André Holley, eds. *Fragrances: Du désir au plaisir*. Marseille: Editions Jeanne Laffitte, 2002.

Cannell, David. "Fragrance as an Art Form." *Beauty Fashion,* Jan. 1979, 70–77; Oct. 1981, 40–48; Nov. 1981, 72–78; Dec. 1981; Jan. 1982, 46–49.

Caplan, David. "Fashion Crackdown." *Harper's Bazaar,* September 2000, 254.

Carrière-Chardon, Sarah. *L'Art dans la pub*. Paris: Musée de la Publicité / Union centrale des arts décoratifs, 2000.

Carson, Ciaran. "Calvin Klein's *Obsession.*" In *The New Poetry*. Edited by Michael Hulse, David Kennedy, and David Morley. Newcastle upon Tyne: Bloodaxe Books, 1993.

Cendrars, Blaise. *Aujourd'hui*. Paris: Grasset, 1931.

Cerutti, Carla. *Flacons*. Paris: Celiv, 1994.

Chaleyssin, Patrick. *Robert de Montesquiou: Mécène et dandy*. Paris: Somogy, 1992.

Chamard, Marie-Eve, and Gérard Lefort. "Qu'importe le parfum, la pub reste en carafe." *Libération*, n.s., 1433 (27 Dec. 1985): 10.

Champier, Victor. "The Decorative Arts." Vol. 9 of Victor Champier, et al. *Exposition Universelle, 1900: The Chefs-D'Oeuvre*. 10 vols. Philadelphia: George Barrie & Son, 1902.

Champtoce, G. "La Marque: Son histoire, sa création, son lancement, sa protection." In La *Parfumerie française et l'art dans la présentation*, 213–22.

Chanel. "Chanel: L'Esprit d'une marque vivante." Publicity pamphlet. Paris, 1999.

_____. *Coup de foudre à Venise: Une aventure signée Jean-Paul Goude*. Advertising brochure. Paris, 2002.

_____. . "Cuir de Russie." Publicity brochure. Paris, Nov. 1936. Chanel archives, Neuilly sur Seine, #C-4-1-560.

_____. "Des maximes signées Chanel." In *Chanel Informations*. Typewritten press release and brochure. Paris and Neuilly, Services de presse, n.d.

_____. *Le Journal de Chanel*, Holiday 1996.

_____. *Mes Recherches 1921-1993: No. 5 Chanel*. Advertising brochure. Neuilly sur Seine, 1993.

_____. "No. 5." In *Les Parfums Chanel*. Press release. Paris, 1996.

_____. "Parfums d'hier et d'aujourd'hui." Press release. Paris, 1993.

_____. "The Making of Coco 91." A documentary film directed by J. C. Wouters, 1991. Chanel archives, Neuilly sur Seine.

Char, René. *Oeuvres complètes*. Bibliothèque de la Pléiade. Paris: Gallimard, 1983.

Chastrette, Maurice. *L'Art des parfums*. Collection Questions de science. Paris: Hachette, 1995.

Chauvière, André. *Parfums et senteurs du Grand Siècle*. Lausanne: Favre, 1999.

Chen, Eva. "Elite Models," *Elle*, May 2003, 164.

Chevrel, Claudine, and Béatrice Cornet. *Grain de beauté: Un siècle de beauté par la publicité*. Paris: Somogy Editions d'Art / Bibliothèque Forney, 1993.

Clair, Iris. "Parfums oubliés." *Parfums & Senteurs* 4 (Oct. 2002): 45–51.

Clark, T. J. *The Painting of Modern Life: Paris in the Art of Manet and His Followers*. New York: Alfred A. Knopf, 1985.

Classen, Constance, David Howes, and Anthony Synnott. *Aroma: The Cultural History of Smell*. London and New York: Routledge, 1994.

Classification des parfums et terminologie / Fragrance Catalogue and Terminology. Paris: Société Française des parfumeurs, 1998.

Clotheslines: A Collection of Poetry and Art. Edited by Stan Tymorek. New York: Harry N. Abrams, 2001.

Cobb, Richard. *Paris and Elsewhere: Selected Writings*. Edited by David Gilmour. London: John Murray, 1998.

Cochet, Vincent. "Odeurs intérieures, atmosphères parfumées aux XVIIe et XVIIIe siècles." *Histoire de l'art* 48 (June 2001): 39–52.

Cohen, Marcel. *Faits: Lecture courante à l'usage des grands débutants*. Paris: Gallimard, 2002.

_____. "La 4711." *Autrement*, May 1990, 124–28.

_____. *Le Grand paon-de nuit*. Paris: Gallimard, 1990.

Cohen, Patricia. "In Defense of Our Wicked, Wicked Ways." *New York Times*, 7 July 2002, sec. 9, 2.

Coles, Harriet. "Les Scientifiques sur la piste du site sexuel de l'odorat." *Le Monde*, 28 Feb. 1997, 22.

Colette. *Colette et la mode*. Paris: Editions Plume, 1991.

_____. *Lettres à Annie de Pène et Germaine de Beaumont*. Edited by Francine Dugast. Paris: Flammarion, 1995.

_____. *Oeuvres*. Edited by Claude Pichois, Alain Brunet, and others. 4 vols. Bibliothèque de la Pléiade. Paris: Gallimard, 1984-2001.

_____. *Oeuvres complètes de Colette*. 15 vols. Edition du Centenaire. Paris: Editions du Club de l'Honnête Homme, 1973.

_____. *Paysages et portraits*. Edited by Marie-Françoise Berthu-Courtivron. Paris: Flammarion, 2002.

_____. *Prisons et paradis*. Paris: J. Ferenczi et fils, 1932.

_____. *La Retraite sentimentale*. Collection Folio. Paris: Mercure de France, 1957.

_____. *Sido*, suivi de *Les Vrilles de la vigne*. Collection Le Livre de poche. Paris: Hachette, 1931.

"Comme des Garçons au garage." *L'Officiel*, June–July 2004, 33.

"Composez votre plus beau Poème d'Amour." Advertising pamphlet for *Poême*. "Jeu-Concours *Elle* / Lancôme," 1997.

Conley, Katharine. *Robert Desnos: Surrealism, and the Marvelous in Everyday Life*. Lincoln: U of Nebraska P, 2003.

Connelly, William. "'Of Singular Originality.' The Life and Work of Vera Willoughby (1872–1939)," *IBIS* 2 (2002):119–44.

Cooley, Martha. *Thirty-Three Swoons*. New York: Little Brown, 2005.

Corbin, Alain. "A History and Anthropology of the Senses" In *Time, Desire and Horror: Towards a History of the Senses*. Translated by Jean Birrell. Cambridge: Polity Press, 1995.

_____. *The Foul and the Fragrant: Odor and the French Social Imagination*. Cambridge: Harvard UP, 1986.

_____. *Historien du sensible: Entretiens avec Gilles Heuré*. Paris: La Découverte, 2000.

_____."Lumière et romantisme." In *Histoire en parfums*. Edited by Arielle Picaud. Paris: Editions du Garde-Temps, 1999.

_____. "Senses." In *Encyclopedia of Social History*. New York: Garland, 1994.

Corneille, Pierre. *The Cid, Cinna, The Theatrical Illusion*. Translated by John Cairncross. Harmondsworth, UK: Penguin Books, 1975.

Cornille, Paule. "Empire d'essences." *L'Officiel*, April 2003, 198.

_____."Vous avez dit sensuels?" *L'Officiel*, Nov. 2002, 108.

Courset, Jean-Michel, and Philippe Dekindt. *6000 miniatures de parfum: Le Marché international de l'échantillon contemporain, récent et ancien*. Toulouse: Milan, 1998.

Crenshaw, Theresa L. *The Alchemy of Love and Lust*. New York: G. P. Putnam's Sons, 1996.

Cros, Charles. *Le Coffret de santal*. Collection Poésie. Paris: Gallimard, 1972.

Cross, Milton. *Complete Stories of the Great Operas*. Garden City, NY: Doubleday, 1950.

D'Avenel, Vicomte G. "La Publicité." In *Le Mécanisme de la vie moderne*. 3rd ed. 5 vols. Paris: Armand Colin, 1921.

Dahl, Roald. "Bitch." In *Switch Bitch*. New York: Alfred A. Knopf, 1974.

Dayagi-Mendels, Michal. *Perfumes and Cosmetics in the Ancient World*. Jerusalem: The Israel Museum, 1993.

Deitz, Paula. "Expeditions: What a Little Moonlight Can Do." *New York Times*, 15 July 1999, D 11.

Delbo, Charlotte. *Useless Knowledge*. Vol. 2 of *Auschwitz and After*. Translated by Rosette C. Lamont. New Haven: Yale UP, 1995.

Delbourg-Delphis, Marylène ."Une Histoire de parfums." *Elle*, 18 Apr. 1983, 95.

_____. *Le Sillage des élégantes: Un siècle d'histoire des parfums*. Paris: Jean-Claude Lattès, 1983.

Delude, Cathryn. "On the Trail of an Odor Map." *The Scientist*, 25 Oct. 2004, 22–24.

Demornex, Jacqueline. *Lancôme*. Collection Mémoire de la beauté. Paris: Assouline, 1998.

_____, and Jean-Claude Hervé. *Lancôme*. Paris: Editions du Regard, 1985.

Déon, Michel. "Un parfum de jasmin." In *Un parfum de jasmin*. Collection Folio. Paris: Gallimard, 1967.

Deslandres, Yvonne. *Poiret*. Paris: Editions du Regard, 1986.

Desnos, Robert. *Liberty or Love!*. Translated by Terry Hale. London: Atlas Press, 1993.

_____. *The Selected Poems of Robert Desnos*. Translated by Carolyn Forché and William Kulik. New York: The Ecco Press, 1991.

Detienne, Marcel. *The Gardens of Adonis: Spices in Greek Mythology*. Translated by Janet Lloyd. Atlantic Highlands, NJ: Humanities Press, 1977.

Dictionnaire des parfums / Dictionary of Perfumes. 11th ed. Edited by Patrick Sermadiras. Paris: Editions Sermadiras, 1996.

Diderot, [Denis], and [Jean Le Rond] D'Alembert. *Encyclopédie, ou Dictionnaire raisonné des sciences, des arts et des métiers par une société de gens de lettres*. Neuchâtel: Samuel Faulche et Cie, 1765.

Diehl, Charles. *La République de Venise*. Paris: Flammarion, 1985.

DiGiacomo, Frank. "The House That Coco Built." *Elle* 141 (May 1997): 180.

Donato, Giuseppe, and Monique Seefried. *The Fragrant Past: Perfumes of Cleopatra and Julius Caesar*. Atlanta: Emory University Museum of Art and Archaeology, 1989.

Donne, John. *The Elegies and The Songs and Sonnets*. Edited by Helen Gardner. Oxford: The Clarendon Press, 1965.

Donzel, Catherine. *Le Parfum*. Collection Les Carnets de la mode. Paris: Editions du Chêne, 2000.

Döring, Jürgen. *Parfum: Ästhetik und Verführung*. Munich: Prestel, 2005.

Drobnick, James, ed. *The Smell Culture Reader*. Oxford: Berg, 2006.

Ducornet, Rikki. *Gazelle*. New York: Knopf, 2003.

Dulac, Catherine, and others. "Loss of Sex Discrimination and Male-Male Aggression in Mice Deficient for TRP 2." *Science* 295 (22 Feb. 2002): 1493–1500.

Dulau, Robert, and Jean-Robert Pitte, eds. *Géographie des odeurs*. Collection Géographie et Cultures. Paris: L'Harmattan, 1998.

Du Laz, Nolwenn. "Beauté / Tentation: 0–16 Ans." *Marie-Claire*, Dec. 2002, 326.

_____. "Ces parfums nommés désir." *Marie-Claire*, Dec. 2002, 310.

Duncan, Alastair. *Art Deco*. London: Thames and Hudson, 1988.

Duperey, Anny, ed. *Essences et parfums: Textes choisis*. Paris: Ramsay, 2004.

Duprat, Nicole, and Mick Duprat. *Bijoux Promotionnels de parfumeurs*. Toulouse: Arfon, 2000.

L'Ecotais, Emmanuelle de, and Alain Sayag. *Man Ray: La Photographie à l'envers*. Paris: Centre Georges Pompidou / Seuil, 1998.

Edwards, Michael. *Perfume Legends: French Feminine Fragrances*. Levallois: HM Editions, 1996.

Elghanayan, Shahrzad. "Les Musts by Métro." *New York Times*, 14 Mar. 1999, sec. 9, 3.

Ellington, Duke. *The Indispensable Duke Ellington*. Vol. 11–12 (1944–1946). "Jazz Tribune," no. 69. RCA 07863 /66679-2 (2 compact discs).

_____. *Duke Ellington and His Orchestra 1944–1945*. "The Classics Chronological Series," no. 881, Classics Records, 1996 (compact disc).

Eluard, Paul. *Oeuvres complètes*. Edited by Marcelle Dumas and Lucien Scheler. 2 vols. Bibliothèque de la Pléiade. Paris: Gallimard 1968.

Emberley, Julia V. *The Cultural Politics of Fur*. Ithaca: Cornell U P, 1998.

Encyclopédie des arts décoratifs et industriels modernes au XXe siècle. 12 vols. Paris: Imprimerie Nationale, Office central d'éditions et de librairie, 1925; New York: Garland Publishing, 1977.

Enes, Bill, and Peggy Enes. *Silent Salesmen Too: The Encyclopedia of Collectible Vending Machines*. Lenexa, KS: Enes Publishing, 1995.

"Etiquettes et impressions anciennes." In *La Parfumerie française et l'art dans la présentation*, 97–103.

Faivre, Hélène. *Odorat et humanité en crise à l'heure du déodorant parfumé: Pour une reconnaissance de l'intelligence du sentir*. Paris: L'Harmattan, 2001.

Farrère, Claude. *La Bataille*. Paris: Calmann-Lévy, 1921.

Faure, Paul. *Parfums et aromates de l'Antiquité*. Paris: Fayard, 1987.

Fell, Alison. *The Pillow Boy of the Lady Onogoro*. San Diego: Harcourt Brace, 1994.

Fellous, Colette. *Guerlain*. Paris: Denoël, 1987.

Ferré, Leo. "Technique de l'exil." *Cahiers d'études Leo Ferré* 1 (June 1998): 20.

Feydeau, Elisabeth de. "De l'hygiène au rêve: l'industrie française des parfums de 1830 à 1939." Ph.D diss., University of Paris IV, Sorbonne, 1997.

_____. *Jean-Louis Fargeon, parfumeur de Marie-Antoinette*. Versailles: Perrin, 2004.

_____, Freddy Ghozland, and Marie-Christine Grasse. *L'Un des sens: Le Parfum au XXe siècle*. Toulouse: Milan, 2001.

Fiemeyer, Isabelle. *Coco Chanel: Un Parfum de mystère*. Paris: Payot, 1999.

Finlay, Louise. "Nicole Kidman: Quel numéro?" *Elle*, 4 Oct. 2004, 170–75

Flanner, Janet. *An American in Paris: Profile of an Interlude Between Two Wars*. New York: Simon and Schuster, 1940.

Flaubert, Gustave. *Correspondance, I (janvier 1830 à juin 1851)*. Edited by Jean Bruneau. Bibliothèque de la Pléiade. Paris: Gallimard, 1973).

_____. *Salammbô*. Collection Folio. Paris: Gallimard, 1970.

Floransac, Julia. "Entretien: Jacques Polge," *Senso*, May-June 2002, 114–16.

Fontan, Geneviève. *Côte Générale des cartes parfumées*. 4 vols. Toulouse: Arfon, 1997–2002.

_____. *Générations Bourjois*. Toulouse: Arfon, 2005.

_____. *Générations Guerlain*. Toulouse: Arfon, 2006.

_____. *Parfums de Gloire: Résultats d'enchères des flacons de parfums anciens*. Toulouse: Arfon, 1999.

Fontinoy, Charles. "Les Parfums dans la Bible." In Laruelle, *L'Art du parfum*, 44–67.

Foulkes, Nick. *Last of the Dandies: The Scandalous Life and Escapades of Count d'Orsay.* London: Little Brown, 2003.

Fox, Marisa. "Sex Chemicals." *Harper's Bazaar,* February 1996, 92.

Francis, Claude, and Fernande Gontier. *Creating Colette.* 2 vols. South Royalton, VT: Steerforth Press, 1999.

Fumaroli, Marc. "Note sur le personnage de Des Esseintes." In Huysmans, *A Rebours*, 363–71.

_____. "Préface." Huysmans, *A Rebours,* 7–52.

Gaborit, Jean-Yves. *Perfumes: The Essences and Their Bottles.* Translated by Clark Candy. New York: Rizzoli, 1985.

Gardner, Paul. *Louise Bourgeois.* New York: Universe, 1994.

Garelick, Rhonda K. *Rising Star: Dandyism, Gender, and Performance in the Fin de Siècle.* Princeton: Princeton UP, 1998.

Garner, Bonnie Jean. "Duchamp Bottles Belle Greene: Just Desserts For His Canning." *Tout Fait: The Marcel Duchamp Studies Online* 2 (2000): 5. http://www.toutfait.com.issues.issue_2/News /garner.html.

Garnier, Philippe. *Emile Gallé.* Rev. ed. New York: Rizzoli, 1976, 1990.

Gaudriault, Raymond. *La Gravure de mode féminine en France.* Paris: Les Editions de l'amateur, 1983.

Ghozland, F. *Perfume Fantasies.* Toulouse: Milan, 1987.

Gibbons, Boyd. "The Intimate Sense of Smell." *National Geographic* 170, no. 3 (Sept. 1986): 324–60.

Girard, Sylvie. *Le Livre du parfum.* Paris: Messidor, 1986.

Girard-Lagorce, Sylvie. *100 Parfums de légende.* Paris: Solar, 2000.

Gleizes, Serge. "Richard Meier, la fibre minimaliste." *L'Officiel,* Feb. 1997, 186–190.

Goncourt, Edmond de. *Chérie.* Paris; Ernest Flammarion et Eugène Fasquelle, 1883.

Gontier, Josette, and Jean-Claude Ellena. *Mémoires du parfum.* Collection L'Imagier. Barbentane: Equinoxe, 2003.

Goude, Jean-Paul. *Tout Goude.* With the collaboration of Patrick Mauriès. Paris: Editions de la Martinière, 2005.

Grasse, Marie-Christine. *Femmes de parfum.* Toulouse: Milan; Grasse: Musée International de la Parfumerie, 1996.

_____. *Le Jasmin: Fleur de Grasse.* Bournemouth: Editions Parkstone; Grasse: Musée international de la Parfumerie, 1996.

_____, ed. *L'Egypte: Parfums d'histoire.* Paris: Somogy; Grasse: Musée international de la Parfumerie, 2003.

_____, and Pascal Lardellier, eds. *Evanescenses: Parfums et odeurs, de l'anthropolgie à la communication: Actes du colloque organisé par la Ville de Grasse.* Grasse: Musée international de la Parfumerie, 2000.

Gray, Richard T. "The Dialectic of 'Enscentment': Patrick Süskind's *Das Parfum* as Critical History of Enlightenment Culture." *PMLA* 108, no. 3 (1993): 489–505.

Green, Annette, and Linda Dyett. *Secrets of Aromatic Jewelry.* Paris and New York: Flammarion, 1998.

Groom, Nigel. *Perfume: The Ultimate Guide to the World's Finest Fragrances.* Philadelphia and London: Running Press / Quintet Publishing, 1999.

Gruau. Paris: Herscher, 1989.

Guerlain. "Autoportraits de femmes, October 1912 / October 1998." Publicity brochure for *L'Heure bleue.* Paris, 1998.

_____. "Champs-Elysées." Press release. Paris, 1988.

_____. "Genèse de Shalimar: Fragments de papiers oubliés, qui auraient pu être écrits par Jacques Guerlain." Press release. Paris, 1995.

_____. "Le Livre de Samsara." Advertising brochure. Paris, n. d.

_____. "Mitsouko." Press release. Paris, 1997.

_____. "Le Romantisme est un bouquet d'émotions: Jardins de Bagatelle." Advertising brochure. Paris, 1998.

_____. "Les Secrets du parfum par Guerlain." Advertising brochure. Paris, n. d.

Guerlain, Jean-Paul. "Champs-Elysées: L'Eau de parfum; Portrait d'un parfum parisien." Press release. Paris: Guerlain, n. d.

_____. "Guerlinade." Press release. Paris: Guerlain, 1998.

_____. *Les Routes de mes parfums.* Paris: Le Cherche Midi, 2002.

Guiral, Pierre. *La Vie quotidienne en France à l'âge d'or du capitalisme 1852–1879*. Paris: Hachette, 1976.

Gullino, Alain. *Odeurs et saveurs*. Collection Dominos. Paris: Flammarion, 1997.

H & R Fragrance Guide / Duftatlas / Atlas Olfactif: Fragrances on the International Market. 3rd rev. and updated edition. Hamburg: Glöss, 1995.

Hadorn, Jean. "Le Jardin des Hespérides." In Laruelle, *L'Art du parfum*, 85–105.

Hakim, Danny. "New Luxury-Car Specifications: Styling. Performance. Aroma." *New York Times*, 25 Oct. 2003, A 1.

Hamilton, William L. "I Dreamed I Wore My Martini." *New York Times*, 18 Jan. 2004, sec. 9, 6.

Harmon, Amy. "Twist and Shout! The Double Helix Replicates Itself in Popular Culture." *New York Times*, 25 Feb. 2003, D 10.

Hayden, Thomas. "The Scent of a Human." *U.S. News & World Report*, 26 March 2001, 55.

La Haye, Amy de, and Shelley Tobin. *Chanel: The Couturière at Work*. Woodstock, NY: The Overlook Press, 1994.

Healy, Orla. *Coty: The Brand of Visionary*. New York: Assouline, n.d.

Heilmeyer, Marina. *The Language of Flowers: Symbols and Myths*. Translated by Rosie Jackson. Munich: Prestel, 2004.

Helleu, Jacques. *Jacques Helleu et Chanel*. Paris: Editions de la Martinière, 2005.

Herrick, Robert. *Hesperides*. In *The Poetical Works of Robert Herrick*. Edited by F. W. Moorman. Oxford: Oxford UP, 1921, rpt. 1957.

Hillier, Bevis, and Stephen Escritt. *Art Deco Style*. London: Phaidon Press, 1997.

Hirsch, Alan R. *Scentsational Sex: The Secret to Using Aroma for Arousal*. Boston: Element, 1998.

Hirschberg, Lynn. "Luxury in Hard Times." *New York Times Magazine*, 2 Dec. 2001, 92.

Hoge, Warren. "Writer, Actor, M.P. (and a Reliable Source of Spice)." *New York Times*, 2 July 2001, A 4.

Holley, André. *Eloge de l'odorat*. Paris: Odile Jacob, 1999.

Horyn, Cathy. "The Sweet Smell of Celebrity." *New York Times*, 30 June 2005, E 1.

Howes, David. "Olfaction and Transition: An Essay on the Ritual Uses of Smell." *Revue Canadienne de Sociologie et d'Anthropologie* 24, no. 3 (1987): 398–416.

———. "Scent and Sensibility." *Culture, Medicine and Psychiatry* 13 (1989): 88–97.

———. "Le Sens sans parole: Vers une anthropologie de l'odorat." *Anthropologie et société* 10, no. 3 (1986): 29–45.

Hubert, Etienne-Alain. "'Rivalise donc poète avec les étiquettes des parfumeurs.'" *La Revue des lettres modernes*, série *Guillaume Apollinaire* 16 (1983): 179–81.

"L'Humour et la parfumerie." In *La Parfumerie française et l'art dans la présentation*, 227–230.

Huysmans, Joris-Karl. *Against Nature (A rebours)*. Translated by Margaret Mauldon. Oxford: Oxford UP, 1998.

———. *A Rebours*. 2nd expanded ed. Edited by Marc Fumaroli. Collection Folio. Paris: Gallimard, 1977.

Hymne au parfum: Deux siècles d'histoire dans les arts décoratifs et la mode. Paris: Musée des arts de la mode, 1991.

Hymne au Parfum: L'Expo. Paris: Comité français du parfum, 1993.

"In Seoul, Dressing To Please the Nose," *New York Times*, 18 April 1999, Money & Business sec., 13.

Irvine, Susan. *Perfume: The Creation and Allure of Classic Fragrances*. London: Aurum, 1995.

Jaucourt, le Chevalier de. "Musc, animal du." In Diderot and D'Alembert, 10: 878–81.

Jazdzewski, Catherine. "La Nouvelle cuisine des parfums." *Vogue* (Paris), April 2000, 222.

Jellinek, J. Stephan. *L'âme du parfum: Nature et effets, choix et utilisation; Parfums classiques et modernes*. Translated by Dominique de Saint-Ours and J. Stephan Jellinek. Paris: Editions Philippe Auzou, 1997.

———. "The Psychological Basis of Perfumery: A Re-Evaluation." In Paul Jellinek, *The Psychological Basis of Perfumery. Translation of the Expanded Fourth German Edition*. Edited and translated by J. Stephan Jellinek. London: Chapman & Hall, 1997.

Jellinek, Paul. *The Practice of Modern Perfumery*. Translated and revised by A. J. Krajkeman. London: Leonard Hill Limited, 1954.

Jim Crow Museum of Racist Memorabilia. "Golliwog Stereotypes." Ferris State University. http://www.ferris.edu/news/ jimcrow/golliwog/home-page.html (accessed 31 Jan. 2003).

Jones, Amelia. *Postmodernism and the En-Gendering of Marcel Duchamp.* Cambridge: Cambridge UP, 1994.

Jones-North, Jacqueline Y. *Perfume, Cologne, and Scent Bottles.* Atglen, PA: Schiffer Publishing, 1986.

Jones-North, Jacquelyne Y. *Commercial Perfume Bottles.* Atglen, PA: Schiffer Publishing, 1996.

Joselit, David. *Infinite Regress: Marcel Duchamp 1910–1941.* Cambridge: MIT P, 1998.

Julien, Mariette. *L'Image publicitaire des parfums: Communication olfactive.* Paris: L'Harmattan, 1997.

Jullian, Philippe. *Prince of Aesthetes: Count Robert de Montesquiou, 1855–1921.* Translated by John Haylock and Francis King. New York: Viking, 1967.

Jullian, Philippe. *Robert de Montesquiou: Un Prince 1900.* Paris: Librairie Académique Perrin, 1965.

———. *The Triumph of Art Nouveau: Paris Exhibition 1900.* Translated by Stephen Hardman. London: Phaidon Press, 1974.

Kachur, Lewis. *Displaying the Marvelous: Marcel Duchamp, Salvador Dali and the Surrealist Exhibition Installations.* Cambridge: MIT P, 2001.

Kafka, Franz. *Letters to Milena.* Edited by Willi Haas. Translated by Tania and James Stern. New York: Schocken Books, 1953.

Kagan, Cara. "Scent of a Woman." *Elle,* August 2000, 129.

Kapner, Suzanne. "Advertising: Agencies Say British Regulators are Too Quick to Ban Ads." *New York Times,* 4 Jan. 2002, C 4.

Kaufman, William I. *Perfume.* New York: E. P. Dutton, 1974.

Kauffmann, Jean-Paul. *The Black Room at Longwood: Napoleon's Exile on Saint Helena.* Translated by Patricia Clancy. New York: Four Walls Eight Windows, 1997.

Kemp, Percy. *Musc.* Paris: Albin Michel, 2000.

Keyser, Samuel Jay. "There is Method in Their Adness: The Formal Structure of Advertisement." *New Literary History* 14, no. 2 (Winter 1983): 305–34.

Kim, Lucian. "On the Trail of an Elusive Scent." *Boston Sunday Globe,* 19 Jan. 2003, A 6.

Kleiner, Diana E. E. *Cleopatra and Rome.* Cambridge: Belknap Press, Harvard UP, 2005.

Kohl, James Vaughn, and Robert T. Francoeur. *The Scent of Eros: Mysteries of Odor in Human Sexuality.* New York: Continuum, 1995.

Kornheiser, Tony. "A Fragrant Foul." *Washington Post,* 10 Nov. 1996, sec. 3, F 1, 5.

Kristeva, Julia. "Paradis parfumé." In Pillivuyt, *Histoire du parfum.* 6–7.

———. *Colette.* Vol. 3 of *Le Génie féminin: La Vie, la folie, les mots.* Paris: Fayard, 2002.

Labro, Camille. "L'Essence de peau de belle femme." *Vogue* (Paris), Dec. 1999–Jan. 2000, 207.

Lalanne, Olivier. "Tout Nu." *Vogue* (Paris), Oct. 2001, 382.

Larkworthy, Jane.. "Majoring in Classics," *W,* Sept 2004, 354.

———. "On the Verge: Taking Manhattan." *W,* April 2003, 144.

———. "Spring Fling." *W,* April 2003, 132.

———. "Sweet Scent of Youth, *W,* Oct. 2002, 182.

Laruelle, René, ed. *L'Art du parfum.* Paris: Le Temps apprivoisé, 1993.

———. *Le Parfum perdu: Basilissa.* Paris: Editions Buchet / Chastel, 1996

Laszlo, Pierre, and Sylvie Rivière. *Les Sciences du parfum.* Collection Que sais-je? Paris: PUF, 1997.

Latimer, Tirza True *The Perfume Atomizer: An Object with Atmosphere.* West Chester PA: Schiffer Publishing, 1991.

Lauro, Patricia Winters. "Advertising: A New Calvin Klein Campaign." *New York Times,* 14 Jan. 2002, C 9.

———. "Advertising: Hallmark Now Has Hearts and Flowers…" *New York Times,* 10 May 2002, C 6.

Laver, James. *Costume and Fashion: A Concise History.* Rev. expanded, updated edition. London: Thames and Hudson, 1995.

Leach, Ken. *Perfume Presentation: 100 Years of Artistry.* Toronto: Kres Publishing, 1997.

Leadbeater, C. W. *The Perfume of Egypt, and Other Weird Stories*. Adyar, India and Wheaton, Ill.: The Theosophical Publishing House, 1967.

Le Breton, David. *Anthropologie du corps et modernité*. Paris: PUF, 2000.

Lefkowith, Christie Mayer. *The Art of Perfume: Discovering and Collecting Perfume Bottles*. London: Thames and Hudson, 1994.

———. "Editorial." In *Art & Fragrances: Perfume Presentations*. Geneva: GdB Fine Arts Gallery, 9 Nov 2002. An auction catalogue.

———. *Masterpieces of the Perfume Industry*. New York: Editions Stylissimo, 2000.

Legrand, Sylvie, Perrine Mane, and Françoise Piponnier. "La Vêture." Chap. 1 in *Mille Ans de costume français 950–1950*. Thionville: Gérard Klopp, 1991.

Le Guérer, Annick. "Jean-Claude Ellena: Le retour au naturel." *Parfums & Senteurs* 8 (July 2001): 32.

———. *Le Parfum: Des Origines à nos jours*. Paris: Odile Jacob, 2005.

———. "Petite Histoire de l'Eau de Cologne." *Parfums & Senteurs* 8 (July 2001): 54.

———. *Les Pouvoirs de l'odeur*. Paris: Editions François Bourin, 1988.

———. *Sur les routes de l'encens*. Paris: Editions du Garde-Temps, 2001.

Lelieur, Anne-Claude. *Savignac, affichiste*. New ed. Paris: Bibliothèque Forney, 2004.

Le Maquet, Jocelyne, Jean-Paul Le Maquet, Marie-Christine Grasse, and Jean-Claude Ellena. *Sous le signe du parfum: Edmond Roudnitska, compositeur-parfumeur*. Thonon-les-Bains: Editions de l'Albaron, 1991.

Lennon, Christine. "Sex in a Bottle." *W*, September 1995, 116.

Leroux, Gaston. *The Perfume of the Lady in Black*. Cambs, UK: Dedalus, 1998.

Levi, Primo. "The Mnemogogues." In *The Sixth Day, and Other Tales*. Translated by Raymond Rosenthal. New York: Summit Books, 1990.

Leymarie, Jean. *Chanel*. Geneva: Skira, 1987.

Lipovetsky, Gilles, and Elyette Roux. *Le Luxe éternel: De l'âge du sacré au temps des marques*. Paris: Gallimard, 2003.

Lisle, Leconte de. *Poèmes Tragiques*. Vol. 3 of *Oeuvres*. Paris: Alphonse Lemerre, 1884.

Lodeski, Lisa. "The Harem as a Site for Sexual Fantasy in the Work of Vera Willoughby." *(detail)* 5, no. 1 (1997): 2–3.

Lovenou-Melki, Nathalie. *L'Univers du parfum: L'Histoire des odeurs*. N. p.: Editions Ouest-France, 2005.

Luhrmann, Baz. "Take Five." *Vogue* (New York), Sept. 2004, 717–21, 825–26.

Lussier, Suzanne. *Art Deco Fashion*. London: V&A Publications, 2003.

Maffesoli, Michel. *Aux creux des apparences: Pour une éthique de l'esthétique*. Paris: Plon, 1990.

Mahon, Alyce. "Staging Desire." Chap. 11 in *Surrealism: Desire Unbound*. Edited by Jennifer Mundy. Princeton: Princeton UP, 2001.

———. *Surrealism and the Politics of Eros, 1938–1968*. London: Thames & Hudson, 2005.

"Making Sense of Scents." *The Economist*, 13 Mar. 1999, 97.

Mallarmé, Stéphane. *Oeuvres complètes*. Edited by Bertrand Marchal. 2 vols. Bibliothèque de la Pléiade. Paris: Gallimard, 1998, 2003.

———. *Selected Poems*. Translated by C. F. MacIntyre. Berkeley: U of California P, 1971.

———. *See* Miss Satin, Ponty, Marguerite de.

Malnic, Bettina, Junzo Hirono, Takaaki Sato, and Linda B. Buck. "Combinatorial Receptor Codes for Odors." *Cell* 96 (5 March 1999): 713–723.

Manniche, Lise. *Sacred Luxuries: Fragrance, Aromatherapy, and Cosmetics in Ancient Egypt*. Ithaca: Cornell UP, 1999.

Mansour, Joyce. *Histoires nocives: Prose et Poésie; Oeuvre complète*. Arles: Actes Sud, 1991.

Marchand, Bernard. *Paris: Histoire d'une ville; XIXe-XXe siècle*. Paris: Seuil, 1993.

Marchand, Stéphane. *Les Guerres du luxe*. Paris: Fayard, 2001.

Margueritte, Victor. *La Garçonne*. Paris: Editions J'ai lu / Flammarion, 1978.

Martin, Bronwen, and Felizitas Ringham, eds. *Sense and Scent: An Exploration of Olfactory Meaning*. Dublin: Philomel, 2003.

Martin, Marc. "La Publicité." In *La France d'un siècle à l'autre, 1914-2000: Dictionnaire Critique*. Edited by Jean-Pierre Rioux and Jean-François Sirinelli. Paris: Hachette, 2000, 402–06.

_____. *Trois Siècles de publicité en France*. Paris: Odile Jacob, 1992.

Martin, Richard. "A Note: Art & Fashion; Viktor & Rolf." *Fashion Theory* 3, no. 1 (1999): 109–20.

_____, and Harold Koda. *Christian Dior*. New York: Metropolitan Museum of Art, 1996.

Martin-Fugier, Anne. *La Bourgeoise: Femme au temps de Paul Bourget*. Paris: Grasset & Fasquelle, 1983.

_____. *La Vie élégante, ou La formation du Tout-Paris, 1815–1848*. Paris: Fayard, 1990.

Martin-Hattemberg, Jean-Marie. "Les Cahiers du collectionneur: La parfumerie européenne du XXe siècle; Africanisme et arts premiers." *Parfums & Senteurs* 10 (Dec. 2001): 86–93.

_____. *Caron*. Toulouse: Milan, 2000.

_____. "Elsa Schiaparelli: Senteurs surréalistes, flacons d'extravagance." *Parfums & Senteurs* 4 (Oct. 2000): 69–73.

_____, and Freddy Ghozland. *Précieux effluves*. Toulouse: Milan, n. d.

Masood, Ehsan. "Erox contre Athena, ou La guerre des fragrances synthétiques." *Le Monde*, 28 Feb. 1997, 22.

Maupassant, Guy de. *The Complete Short Stories*. Garden City, NY: Hanover House, 1955.

_____. *Strong as Death*. Doylestown, PA: Wildside Press, n. d.

Mayle, Peter. "How to Be a Nose." In *Encore Provence: New Adventures in the South of France*. New York: Knopf, 1999, 100–15.

McEwan, Ian. *Amsterdam*. New York: Random House, 1998.

Meininghaus, Heiner, Christa Habrich, and Tanja Volz. *Düfte und edle Flakons aus fünf Jahrhunderten / Five Centuries of Scent and Elegant Flacons*. Stuttgart: Arnoldsche, 1998.

Mendes, Valerie. "Art Deco Fashion." Chap. 23 in *Art Deco 1910-1939*. Edited by Charlotte Benton, Tim Benton, and Ghislaine Wood. London: V&A Publications, 2003.

Mercier, Louis Sebastien. "Toilettes." In *Le Tableau de Paris*. 2 vols. Paris: Mercure de France, 1994.

Meskell, Lynn. "Embodied Knowledge." Chap. 6 in *Private Life in New Kingdom Egypt*. Princeton: Princeton UP, 2002.

Milinski, Manfred, and Claus Wedekind. "Evidence for MHC-Correlated Perfume Preferences in Humans." *Behavioral Ecology* 12, no. 2 (2001): 140–49.

Miller, Judith. *Perfume Bottles*. New York: DK Publishing, 2006.

Miss Satin [Stéphane Mallarmé]. "Gazette de la Fashion." *La Dernière Mode*, 1 Nov. 1874. In Mallarmé, *Oeuvres complètes*, 2: 582–83.

Mohrt, Françoise. "Décors magiques pour senteurs célèbres." *Vogue Décoration*, Nov. 1985.

Moline, Karen. *Belladonna*. New York: Warner Books, 1998.

Monsen, Randall B. *Monsen and Baer: Memories of Perfume; The Perfumes of Lucien Lelong and Masterpieces of Today; Perfume Bottle Auction VIII, May 16, 1998*. Vienna, VA: Monsen and Baer, 1998.

Montaigne, Michel de. "Of Smells." In *The Complete Essays of Montaigne*. Translated by Donald M. Frame. Stanford: Stanford UP, 1957.

Montesquiou, Robert de. *Le Chef des odeurs suaves*. Paris: Georges Richard, 1907.

_____. *Musée Rétrospectif de la classe 90: Parfumerie (matières premières, matériel, procédés et produits) à l'Exposition Universelle Internationale de 1900 à Paris; Rapport de M. le comte Robert de Montesquiou*. Saint-Cloud: Belin Frères, 1900.

_____. "Pays des aromates." In Robert de Montesquiou and Marcel Proust. *Professeur de beauté*. Paris: Editions La Bibliothèque, 1999.

Montez, Lola. *The Arts of Beauty, or Secrets of a Lady's Toilet. With Hints to Gentlemen on the Art of Fascinating*. New York: Ecco Press, 1978.

Moran, Jan. *Fabulous Fragrances: How to Select Your Perfume Wardrobe; The Women's Guide to Prestige Perfumes*. Beverly Hills, CA: Crescent House Publishing, 1994.

Morand, Paul. *1900*. Paris: Editions de France, 1931.

Morris, Edwin T. *Fragrance: The Story of Perfume from Cleopatra to Chanel*. Greenwich, CT and New York: E. T. Morris & Co., 1984.

_____. *Scents of Time: Perfume from Ancient Egypt to the 21st Century.* New York: Metropolitan Museum of Art; Boston: Bulfinch Press, 1999.

Morris, Jan. *The World of Venice.* Rev. ed. San Diego: Harcourt Brace, 1993.

Mouillefarine, Laurence. *Objets de la beauté à collectionner.* Boulogne: Editions MDM, 1999.

Mouron, Henri. *A. M. Cassandre: Affiches; Arts Graphiques; Théâtre.* Munich: Schirmer; Paris: Mosel, 1991.

Müller, P. M., and D. Lamparsky. *Perfumes: Art, Science and Technology.* London and New York: Elsevier Applied Science, 1991.

Munier, Brigitte. *Le Parfum à travers les siècles: Des dieux de l'Olympe au cyber-parfum.* Paris: Editions du Félin, 2003.

Musée international de la Parfumerie, Grasse. *Vanilles & Orchidées.* Aix-en-Provence: Edisud, 1993.

Musset, Danielle, and Claudine Fabre-Vassas, eds. *Odeurs et parfums.* Paris: Comité des travaux historiques et scientifiques, 1999.

"Mythe Movie." *Vogue* (Paris), Nov. 2004, 135.

Naumann, Francis M. "Marcel & Maria." *Art in America* 89, no. 4 (April 2001): 99–110, 157.

_____. *Marcel Duchamp: The Art of Making Art in the Age of Mechanical Reproduction.* New York: Harry N. Abrams, 1999.

Newman, Cathy. *Perfume: The Art and Science of Scent.* Washington: National Geographic Society, 1998.

Nikly, Michelle. *The Perfume of Memory.* New York: Arthur A. Levine Books, 1999.

"Nouveautés: Ocean Spray." *France*, Spring 2002, 6.

Oakes, John. *The Book of Perfumes.* Sydney: HarperCollins, 1996.

Onfray, Michel. *L'Art de jouir.* Paris: Grasset, 1991.

"Origine de l'eau de Cologne." In *La Boutique du bonheur.* Paris: Roger & Gallet, 1960.

Ozzard, Janet. "Abstract Expression." *W*, May 1998, 116.

Paquet, Dominique. "Le Parfum, chiffre de la forme?" in *Parfums de Sculptures, Sculptures de Parfums.* Paris: Materia Prima, 1999, 9–16.

"Le Parfum, arme de séduction...... et luxe nécessaire." *Votre Beauté: Revue de la beauté féminine*, 1 Nov. 1936. Rpt. Paris: Imprimerie Georges Lang, 1936.

"Parfum de plaisir." *Vogue* (Paris), Nov. 2000.

La Parfumerie française et l'art dans la présentation. Paris: La Revue des marques de la Parfumerie et de la Savonnerie, April 1925.

"Parfumeur." In Diderot and D'Alembert, 11: 941–42.

Les Parfums à travers la Mode: Retrospective de 1765 à nos jours; Chez Marcel Rochas. Paris: Editions du Chêne, 1945.

Patton, Phil. "Love the Hummer? Wear the Fragrance," *New York Times*, 7 November 2005, D9.

_____. "Scents of the Everyday Locked in a Bottle." *New York Times*, 15 October 1998, D 2.

Pavia, Fabienne. *L'Univers des parfums.* Paris: Solar, 1995, 2003.

Pelicier, Yves. "De l'historicité du quotidien à l'histoire préventive." Preface to Thuillier, *L'Imaginaire quotidien*, v-xvi.

Perrin, Eliane. *L'Age d'or de la parfumerie à Grasse, d'après les archives Chiris (1768-1967).* In collaboration with Olivier Buttner. 2nd edition. Aix-en-Provence: Edisud, 1996.

Perrot, Philippe. *Le Luxe: Une Richesse entre faste et confort XVIIIe –XIXe siècle.* Paris: Seuil, 1995.

_____. *Le Travail des apparences: Le corps féminin, XVIIIe-XIXe siècle.* Collection Points-Histoire. Paris: Seuil, 1984.

_____. *Les Dessus et les dessous de la bourgeoisie: Une histoire du vêtement au XIXe siècle.* Paris: Fayard, 1981.

Picaud, Arielle, ed. *Histoire en parfums.* Paris: Editions du Garde-Temps, 1999.

Pichois, Claude, and Alain Brunet. *Colette.* Paris: Editions de Fallois, 1999.

Piesse, G. W. Septimus. *The Art of Perfumery and The Methods of Obtaining Odours of Plants.* 4th edition. Philadelphia: Presley Blakiston, 1880.

Piesse, S[eptimus]. *Histoire des parfums et hygiène de la toilette: Poudres, Vinaigres, Dentifrices, Fards, Teintures, Cosmétiques, etc.* French edition. Paris: J.-B. Baillière et fils, 1905.

Pillivuyt, Ghislaine. *Les Flacons de la séduction: L'Art du parfum au XVIIIe siècle.* Lausanne: La Bibliothèque des Arts, 1985.

_____. *Histoire du parfum: De l'Egypte au XIXe siècle; Collection de la parfumerie Fragonard.* Paris: Denoël, 1988.

Plessis, Alain. *De la fête impériale au mur des fédérés, 1852–1871.* Rev. ed. Paris: Seuil, 1979.

Pochna, Marie-France. *Nina Ricci.* Paris: Editions du Regard, 1992.

Poiret, Paul. *En habillant l'époque.* Paris: Grasset, 1930.

Ponty, Marguerite de [Stéphane Mallarmé]. "La Mode." *La Dernière Mode,* 15 Nov. 1874. In *Oeuvres complètes,* 2: 599–602.

"Pour un R de Rigaud." *Parfums & Senteurs* 4 (Oct. 2000): 27-32.

Pratt, John. "Notes on the Unconscious Significance of Perfume." *International Journal of Psychoanalysis* 23 (1942): 80–83.

Proust, Marcel. *Contre Sainte-Beuve.* Bibliothèque de la Pléiade. Paris: Gallimard, 1971.

_____. *Remembrance of Things Past.* 3 vols. Translated by C. K. Scott Moncrieff, Terence Kilmartin and Andreas Mayor. New York: Random House, 1981.

Ravo, Nick. "Barry Shipp, 62, the Developer of the Jovan Musk Fragrance." *New York Times,* 8 September 1999, Obituary, C 28.

Reboux, Paul. "Le Langage des fleurs." *L'Elégance à Paris,* Spring 1935, 57–59.

Remaury, Bruno. *Marques et récits: La Marque face à l'imaginaire culturel contemporain.* Paris: Editions de l'Institut français de la mode / Editions du Regard, 2004.

"Rêve de gosse," *L'Officiel,* 841, Dec. 1999.

Ribeiro, Aileen. *The Art of Dress: Fashion in England and France 1750–1820.* New Haven: Yale UP, 1995.

Richard, Jean-Pierre. *L'Univers imaginaire de Mallarmé.* Paris: Seuil, 1961.

Richardson, D. C. "Scents and Sensibility." *New York Times Magazine,* part 2, "Men's Fashions of the Times," 20 Sept. 1998, 40, 44.

Richardson, Joanna. *La Vie Parisienne 1852–1870.* New York: Viking Press, 1971.

Rimmel, Eugène. *Le Livre des parfums.* Paris: E. Dentu, 1870.

_____. *The Book of Perfumes.* London: Chapman and Hall, 1867.

Rindisbacher, Hans J. *The Smell of Books: A Cultural-Historical Study of Olfactory Perception in Literature.* Ann Arbor: U of Michigan P, 1992.

Ring, Nancy. *New York Dada and the Crisis of Masculinity: Man Ray, Francis Picabia, and Marcel Duchamp in the United States, 1913–1921.* Ann Arbor, MI: UMI Research Press, 1991.

Rival, Pierre, and François Baudot. "Fragrance." In *Savoir Faire: Great Traditons in French Elegance.* Paris: Flammarion, 1995, 60–87.

Robbins, Tom. *Jitterbug Perfume.* New York: Bantam Books, 1984.

Robert, Anne-Laure. "Rencontre: Françoise Montenay, dans les pas de Mademoiselle." *Atmosphères,* May 2003, 58.

Robert, Guy. *Les Sens du parfum.* Paris: Osman Eyrolles Multimedia, 2000.

Roberts, Mary Louise. *Civilization Without Sexes: Reconstructing Gender in Postwar France, 1917–1927.* Chicago: U of Chicago P, 1994.

_____. *Disruptive Acts: The New Woman in Fin-de-Siècle France.* Chicago: U of Chicago P, 2002.

Robiquet, Jean. "Les Parfums de nos grand'mères." In *La Parfumerie française et l'art dans la présentation,* 23–31.

Rochas, Marcel. *1925–1950: 25 ans d'élégance.* Paris: Tisné, 1950.

Roche, Daniel. *Histoire des choses banales: Naissance de la consommation dans les sociétés traditionnelles (XVIIe–XIXe siècle).* Paris: Fayard, 1997.

Roger & Gallet, Parfumeurs et créateurs (1806–1989). Bernay: Edition de l'Association pour la Promotion de la Culture à Bernay, 1987.

Rohrlich, Marianne. "Aromatherapy at the Dishpan." *New York Times,* 6 Mar 2002, C 1.

Roubin, Lucienne A. *Le Monde des odeurs: Dynamique et fonctions du champ odorant.* Paris: Meridiens Klincksieck, 1989.

Roudnitska, Edmond. *L'Esthétique en question: Introduction à une esthétique de l'odorat.* Paris: PUF, 1977.

_____. *Le Parfum*. Collection Que sais-je? Paris: PUF, 1980.

_____. *Une vie au service du parfum*. Paris: Thérèse Vian, 1991.

_____, René Bourdon, and Odile Moreno, eds. *L'Intimité du parfum*. Paris: Olivier Perrin, 1974.

Rousseau, Jean-Jacques. *Emile*. In *Oeuvres complètes*, Bibliothèque de la Pléiade. Paris: Gallimard, 1959.

Rozhon, Tracie. "2 Perfume Companies at Odds Over Territory. *New York Times*, 1 Oct. 2002, C 24.

Ryan, Judith. "The Problem of Pastiche: Patrick Süskind's *Das Parfum*." *German Quarterly* 63 (1990): 396–403.

"Sachets et cartes parfumées." In *La Parfumerie française et l'art dans la présentation*, 151–56.

Samain, Albert. *Au Jardin de l'Infante*. In *Oeuvres d'Albert Samain*. Paris: Mercure de France, 1913.

Samuel, Geoffrey. *Civilized Shamans: Buddhism in Tibetan Societies*. Washington: Smithsonian Institution Press, 1993.

Sandrel, Carole, and Lia Gurgand. *Le Guide du parfum*. N.p.: Garancière, 1987.

Saramago, José. *The History of the Siege of Lisbon*. Translated by Giovanni Pontiero. San Diego: Harcourt Brace, 1996.

Sauvat, Catherine. *Les Objets de beauté*. Collection Les Carnets du chineur. Paris: Editions du Chêne, 2003.

"Scent of a Program: Web Technology May Put Some Perfume in Your Printer." *Wall Street Journal*, 1 May 2000, C 25A.

Schilling, Antigone. "Jeux de rôles." *L'Officiel*, Aug. 2004, 142.

Schulte-Hillen, Sophie. "Full-Frontal Fragrance." *Nylon*, Dec. 2002–Jan. 2003.

Schwartz, Vanessa R. *Spectacular Realities: Early Mass Culture in Fin-de-Siècle Paris*. Berkeley: U of California P, 1998.

Seremet, Pat. "Beware Second-Hand Scent." *Valley News* [White River Junction, VT], 7 June 2003, C 1.

Serres, Michel. *Les Cinq sens: Philosophie des corps mêlés*. Paris: Grasset, 1985.

Shaykh Umar ibn Muhammad al-Nefzawi. *The Perfumed Garden of the Shaykh Nefzawi*. Translated by Sir Richard F. Burton. New York: G. P. Putnam's Sons, 1963.

Shea, Christine. "Beauty Buzz." *Vogue* (New York), Aug. 1999, 268.

Shepardson, David. "Radio DJ Wins $10.6 Million in Stink Over Perfume." *The Detroit News*, 24 May 2005, 1.

Sheringham, Michael. *Everyday Life: Theories and Practices from Surrealism to the Present*. Oxford: Oxford UP, 2006.

Silverman, Debora L. *Art Nouveau in Fin-de-Siècle France: Politics, Psychology, and Style*. Berkeley: U of California P., 1989.

Simon, Marie. *Fashion in Art: The Second Empire and Impressionism*. London: Zwemmer, 1995.

Simons, Marlise. "Eau de Rain Forest." *New York Times Magazine*, 2 May 1999, 56–61.

Smith, Craig S. "Paris Journal: A Fragrance That By Any Other Name May Sell as Sweet." *New York Times*, 5 Nov 2004, A 4.

Snelling, John. *The Buddhist Handbook: A Complete Guide to Buddhist Schools, Teaching, Practice, and History*. Rochester, VT: Inner Traditions, 1991.

Snowden, Lynn. "Scent Trek." *Harper's Bazaar*, Feb. 1996, 80–82.

The Song of Songs. Translated by Ariel and Chana Bloch. Berkeley: U. of California P., 1995.

Stamelman, Richard. "La Culture du parfum." *Pleine Marge* 36 (December 2002): 27–54.

_____. "The Eros—and Thanatos—of Scents." *Sites: The Journal of 20th-Century Contemporary French Studies* 6, no. 1 (2002): 79–102.

_____. *Lost beyond Telling: Representations of Death and Absence in Modern French Poetry*. Ithaca: Cornell UP, 1990.

Steiner, George. *Language and Silence: Essays on Language, Literature and the Inhuman*. New York: Atheneum, 1967.

Stern, Ellen. "Shalimar and the House of Guerlain." *Gourmet*, March 1996, 82–84.

Stoddart, D. Michael. *The Scented Ape: The Biology and Culture of Human Odor*. Cambridge: Cambridge UP, 1990.

Süskind, Patrick. *Perfume: The Story of a Murderer.* Translated by John E. Woods. New York: Alfred A. Knopf / Washington Square Press, 1986.

"The Sweet Smell of Success." *The Economist,* 5 September 1998, 75–76, 78.

Szabo, Julia. "The Home Front: A Nose With an Eye." *New York Times Magazine,* part 2, "Home Design," 1 April 2001, 56.

The Talk of the Town, "L'Esprit du bébé," *New Yorker,* 6 Feb. 1995, 28.

Tannen, Mary. "A Scent-imental Journey." *New York Times Magazine,* part 2, "Fashions of the Times," 20 Aug. 2000, 138.

_____. "A Slithery Slope." *New York Times Magazine,* 18 April 2004, 74.

_____. "Selling Indulgences." *New York Times Magazine,* 23 Dec. 2001, 51.

"Le Temps retrouvé: Archives et vieux papiers." *Parfums & Senteurs* 5 (December 2000): 94–97.

Themerson, Stefan. *Apollinaire's Lyrical Ideograms.* London: Gaberbocchus Press, 1968.

Theodoulou, Michael. "Archeological Dig Sniffs Out World's Oldest Perfumery." *The Scotsman,* 25 Feb 2005.

Thiboud, Maurice. "Empirical Classification of Odors." Chap. 8 in Müller and Lamparsky, *Perfumes: Art, Science and Technology,* 253–86.

Thuillier, Guy. *L'Imaginaire quotidien au XIXe siècle.* Paris: Economica, 1985.

_____. *Pour une histoire du quotidien au XIXe siècle en Nivernais.* Paris and The Hague: Mouton, 1977.

Thurman, Judith. *Secrets of the Flesh: A Life of Colette.* New York: Ballantine Books, 1999.

Tiébaut, Philippe. "Ego imago." In *Robert Montesquiou, ou L'art de paraître.* Paris: Editions de la réunion des musées nationaux, 1999.

Tiersten, Lisa. *Marianne in the Market: Envisioning Consumer Society in Fin-de-Siècle France.* Berkeley: U of California P., 2001.

Tosa, Gianfranco. *Murano: A History of Glass.* San Giovanni Lapatoto, Italy: Arsenale, 2000.

Touillier-Feyrabend, Henriette. "Odeurs de séduction." *Ethnologie française* 19, no. 2 (1989): 123–29.

Tournier, Michel. "La Légende des parfums." In *Le Médianoche amoureux.* Paris: Gallimard, 1989.

Trebay, Guy. "Fashion Diary: Making a Surreal Trip Onto a Nightclub Runway." *New York Times,* 4 March 2004, B 8.

Troy, Nancy J. *Couture Culture: A Study in Modern Art and Fashion.* Cambridge: MIT P, 2003.

_____. *Modernism and the Decorative Arts in France: Art Nouveau to Le Corbusier.* New Haven: Yale UP, 1991.

Tucci, Giuseppe. *The Religions of Tibet.* Translated by Geoffrey Samuel. Berkeley: U of California P, 1980.

Turin. Luca. *Parfums: Le Guide.* Paris: Editions Hermé, 1994.

Turonnet, Maïté. *Parlons Parfum.* Vevey: Editions Mondo, 1993.

Twitchell, James B. *Lead Us Into Temptation: The Triumph of American Materialism.* New York: Columbia UP, 1999.

_____. *Living It Up: Our Love Affair with Luxury.* New York: Columbia UP, 2002.

_____. *20 Ads That Shook the World: The Century's Most Groundbreaking Advertising and How It Changed Us All.* New York: Crown Publishers, 2000.

Ulmer, Renate. *Alfons Mucha.* Cologne: Benedikt Taschen Verlag, 1994.

Utt, Mary Lou, and Glenn Utt. *Lalique: Perfume Bottles.* With Patricia Bayer. New York: Crown, 1990.

Uzanne, Octave. *L'Art et les artifices de la beauté.* Paris: Felix Juven, 1902.

_____. *La Femme et la mode: Métamorphoses de la Parisienne de 1792 à 1892.* Paris: Librairies-Imprimeries Réunies, 1892.

_____. *Les Parfums et les fards à travers les âges.* Geneva: Charles Blanc, 1927.

Van Toller, Steve, and George H. Dodd, eds. *Perfumery: The Psychology and Biology of Fragrances.* London and New York: Chapman and Hall, 1988.

_____, and G. H. Dodd, eds. *Fragrance: The Psychology and Biology of Perfume.* London and New York. Elsevier Applied Science, 1992.

Varnedoe, Kirk. *Jackson Pollock.* With Pepe Karmel. New York: MoMA, 1998.

Vautel, Clément. *Je suis un affreux bourgeois*. Paris: Albin Michel, 1926.

Verhoeven, Isabelle, ed. *Art & Parfum: Histoire des flacons*. Liège: Pierre Mardaga, 1989.

Vernant, J.-P. "Introduction." In Detienne, *The Gardens of Adonis*: *Spices in Greek Mythology*, i-xxv.

Veuillet-Gallot, D. *Le Guide du parfum*. N. p.: Editions Hors Collection, 1995.

Vigarello, Georges. *Histoire de la beauté: Le Corps et l'art d'embellir de la Renaissance à nos jours*. Paris: Seuil, 2004.

_____. *Le Propre et le sale: L'Hygiène du corps depuis le Moyen Age*. Paris: Seuil, 1985.

Viladas, Pilar. "Style: Up From SoHo." *New York Times Magazine*, 14 March 1999, 55.

Vilmorin, André de. *Essai sur Louise de Vilmorin*, Collection Poètes d'aujourd'hui 91. Paris: Pierre Seghers, 1962.

Vilmorin, Louise de. *Articles de mode*. Paris: Gallimard, 2000.

_____. *L'Opéra de l'odorat* . Paris: Lanvin Parfums, Aljanvic, 1949.

Vindry, Georges. *Aimer Grasse et le parfum.* Rennes: Editions Ouest-France, 1992.

_____."La Parfumerie moderne." In *Hymne au parfum*, 7-25.

Visionaire 42. Scent. New York: Visionaire Publishing, 2003.

Vroon, Piet. *Smell: The Secret Seducer*. Translated by Paul Vincent. New York: Farrar, Straus and Giroux, 1997.

Wallach, Janet. *Chanel: Her Style and Her Life*. New York: Doubleday, 1998.

Wallis, David. "To Drive It, or To Smell Like It?" *New York Times*, 25 July 1999, sec. 12, 1.

Walter, Frédéric, ed. *Extraits de parfums: Une anthologie de Platon à Colette*. Paris: Editions de l'Institut français de la mode / Editions du Regard, 2003.

Ward, Geoffrey C., and Ken Burns. *Jazz: A History of America's Music*. New York: Alfred A. Knopf, 2000.

Wardell, Jane. "Barbour: The Coat That Says 'Britain.'" *Valley News* [White River Junction, VT], 26 Jan. 2003, C 2.

Watson, Lyall. *Jacobson's Organ and the Remarkable Nature of Smell*. New York: W. W. Norton, 2000.

Weber, Eugen. *France, Fin de siècle*. Cambridge: Harvard UP, 1986.

_____. *The Hollow Years: France in the 1930s*. New York: W.W. Norton, 1994.

Weil, Jennifer. "Nu Sensation." *W*, Oct. 2001, 212.

_____."Scratch and Sniff." *W*, Sept. 2000, 264.

Weriguine, Constantin. *Souvenirs et Parfums: Mémoires d'un parfumeur*. Paris: Plon, 1965.

"When Good Babies Smell Bad." *Time*, 3 Sept. 2001, 26.

Whitaker, Jeanne Theis. "Parfum Exotique." In *Understanding Les Fleurs du mal. Critical Readings*. Edited by William J. Thompson. Nashville: Vanderbilt UP, 1997, 49–59.

White, Edmond. *The Flâneur: A Stroll Through the Paradoxes of Paris*. New York, London: Bloomsbury, 2001.

Wilbur, Richard. *New and Collected Poems*. San Diego: Harcourt Brace Jovanovich, 1988.

Wilford, John Noble. "Ruins in Yemeni Desert Mark Route of Frankincense Trade." *New York Times*, 28 January 1997, C 1, 4.

Williams, David G. *Perfumes of Yesterday*. Port Washington, NY: Micelle Press, 2004.

Williams, Rosalind H. *Dream Worlds: Mass Consumption in Late Nineteenth-Century France*. Berkeley: U of California P, 1982.

Williams, William Carlos. *Paterson* III. New York: New Directions, 1963.

Williamson, Judith. *Decoding Advertisements: Ideology and Meaning in Advertising*. London: Marion Boyars, 1978.

_____. "Woman is an Island: Femininity and Colonization." Chap. 6 in Tania Modleski, ed. *Studies in Entertainment: Critical Approaches to Mass Culture*. Bloomington: Indiana UP, 1986.

Winand, Jean, and Michel Malaise. "Les Parfums en Egypte." In Laruelle, *L'Art du parfum*, 13–43.

Winter, Ruth. *The Smell Book: Scents, Sex, and Society*. Philadelphia and New York: J. B. Lippincott, 1976.

Wiser, William. *The Twilight Years: Paris in the 1930s.* New York: Carroll & Graf, 2000.

Wood, Ghislaine. "The Age of Paper." Chap. 9 in *Art Nouveau 1890–1914.* Edited by Paul Greenhalgh. London: Victoria and Albert Museum / National Gallery of Art, 2000.

"X is for X-Rated." *Harper's Bazaar,* April 2001, 146.

Zimmermann, Eléonore M. *Poétiques de Baudelaire dans Les Fleurs du mal: Rythme, parfum, lueur.* Paris: Lettres Modernes Minard, 1998.

Zola, Emile. *Au Bonheur des dames (The Ladies' Delight).* Translated by Robin Buss. London: Penguin Books, 2001.

———. *La Faute de l'abbé Mouret,* Collection Folio Classique. Paris: Gallimard, 1991.

"Zoombeauté: Le Parfum des hommes." *Elle,* 1 Nov 2004, 70.

Photo Credits

la parfumerie, Art Deco Exhibition, Paris, 1925 © 2005 Artists Rights Society (ARS), New York / ADAGP, Paris; Fig. 93: Published in *Parfumerie française*, 1925. Fig. 109: © 2005 Artists Rights Society (ARS), New York / ADAGP, Paris

Fig. 104: Advertisement courtesy of Chanel, Paris; all rights reserved; pages 332–333: Photo Richard Avedon, courtesy of Chanel, Paris

Figs. 111–112: Image courtesy of Bourjois, Paris. All rights reserved.

Fig. 113: © 2005 Artists Rights Society (ARS), New York / ADAGP, Paris

Fig. 114: © 2005 Artists Rights Society (ARS), New York / ADAGP, Paris. Advertisement courtesy of Nina Ricci (Puig Prestige Beauté), Neuilly sur Seine

Fig. 119: Advertisement from *Cosmopolitan* (Portugal), no. 44, Dec. 1995

Fig. 120: Estate of Guy Bourdin / Art + Commerce Anthology /*Exhibit A* / Dress: Givenchy. Fragrance: *L'Interdit* by Givenchy. *Vogue*, Paris, Dec. 1980

Fig. 121: Advertisement from *Harper's Bazaar*, October 2001

Figs. 123, 124, 125: Photograph courtesy of Françoise Quardon

Figs. 127, 128: Advertisement courtesy of Chanel, Paris

Page 35: Jacques Polge; Photo Sebastian Straessle, courtesy of Chanel, Neuilly sur Seine

Fig. 98; Pages 66, 67, 157, 185 (top, bottom), 187, 295 (left, right, Shalimar): Courtesy of Guerlain

Page 79 (top, "The Whiffs of Fragrance"; bottom, The "Lady" Perfume Sprayer): From Bill Enes and Peggy Enes, *Silent Salesmen Too. The Encyclopedia of Collectible Vending Machines*, revised and expanded edition (Lenexa, KS: Enes Publishing Co., 1995), 169

Page 325: *Air France Madame*, no. 64, June–July 1998.